Artificial Intelligence Paradigms for Smart Cyber-Physical Systems

Ashish Kumar Luhach
The PNG University of Technology, Papua New Guinea

Atilla Elçi
Hasan Kalyoncu University, Turkey

A volume in the Advances in Systems Analysis,
Software Engineering, and High Performance
Computing (ASASEHPC) Book Series

Published in the United States of America by
IGI Global
Engineering Science Reference (an imprint of IGI Global)
701 E. Chocolate Avenue
Hershey PA, USA 17033
Tel: 717-533-8845
Fax: 717-533-8661
E-mail: cust@igi-global.com
Web site: http://www.igi-global.com

Library of Congress Cataloging-in-Publication Data

Names: Luhach, Ashish Kumar, 1985- editor. | Elçi, Atilla, editor.
Title: Artificial intelligence paradigms for smart cyber-physical systems /
  Ashish Kumar Luhach and Atilla Elçi, editors.
Description: Hershey, PA : Engineering Science Reference, [2021] | Includes
  bibliographical references and index. | Summary: "This book focuses upon
  the recent advances in the realization of Artificial Intelligence-based
  approaches towards affecting secure Cyber-Physical Systems. It features
  contributions pertaining to this multidisciplinary paradigm, in
  particular, in its application to building sustainable space by
  investigating state-of-art research issues, applications and
  achievements in the field of Computational Intelligence Paradigms for
  Cyber-Physical Systems"-- Provided by publisher.
Identifiers: LCCN 2020019421 (print) | LCCN 2020019422 (ebook) | ISBN
  9781799851011 (h/c) | ISBN 9781799858461 (s/c) | ISBN 9781799851028
  (ebook)
Subjects: LCSH: Computer networks--Security measures--Data processing. |
  Internet of things--Security measures--Data processing. | Cooperating
  objects (Computer systems) | Artificial intelligence--Industrial
  applications.
Classification: LCC TK5105.59 .A79 2021 (print) | LCC TK5105.59 (ebook) |
  DDC 005.8--dc23
LC record available at https://lccn.loc.gov/2020019421
LC ebook record available at https://lccn.loc.gov/2020019422

This book is published in the IGI Global book series Advances in Systems Analysis, Software Engineering, and High Performance Computing (ASASEHPC) (ISSN: 2327-3453; eISSN: 2327-3461)

British Cataloguing in Publication Data
A Cataloguing in Publication record for this book is available from the British Library.

For electronic access to this publication, please contact: eresources@igi-global.com.

Advances in Systems Analysis, Software Engineering, and High Performance Computing (ASASEHPC) Book Series

Vijayan Sugumaran
Oakland University, USA

ISSN:2327-3453
EISSN:2327-3461

MISSION

The theory and practice of computing applications and distributed systems has emerged as one of the key areas of research driving innovations in business, engineering, and science. The fields of software engineering, systems analysis, and high performance computing offer a wide range of applications and solutions in solving computational problems for any modern organization.

The **Advances in Systems Analysis, Software Engineering, and High Performance Computing (ASASEHPC) Book Series** brings together research in the areas of distributed computing, systems and software engineering, high performance computing, and service science. This collection of publications is useful for academics, researchers, and practitioners seeking the latest practices and knowledge in this field.

COVERAGE

- Enterprise Information Systems
- Distributed Cloud Computing
- Parallel Architectures
- Virtual Data Systems
- Computer System Analysis
- Performance Modelling
- Computer Networking
- Network Management
- Engineering Environments
- Software Engineering

IGI Global is currently accepting manuscripts for publication within this series. To submit a proposal for a volume in this series, please contact our Acquisition Editors at Acquisitions@igi-global.com or visit: http://www.igi-global.com/publish/.

Titles in this Series

For a list of additional titles in this series, please visit:
http://www.igi-global.com/book-series/advances-systems-analysis-software-engineering/73689

Advancements in Model-Driven Architecture in Software Engineering
Yassine Rhazali (Moulay Ismail University of Meknes,Morocco)
Engineering Science Reference • © 2021 • 287pp • H/C (ISBN: 9781799836612) • US $215.00

Cloud-Based Big Data Analytics in Vehicular Ad-Hoc Networks
Ram Shringar Rao (Ambedkar Institute of Advanced Communication Technologies and Research, India) Nanhay Singh (Ambedkar Institute of Advanced Communication Technologies and Research, India) Omprakash Kaiwartya (School of Science and Technology, Nottingham Trent University, UK) and Sanjoy Das (Indira Gandhi National Tribal University, India)
Engineering Science Reference • © 2021 • 312pp • H/C (ISBN: 9781799827641) • US $245.00

Formal and Adaptive Methods for Automation of Parallel Programs Construction Emerging Research and Opportunities
Anatoliy Doroshenko (Institute of Software Systems, Ukraine) and Olena Yatsenko (Institute of Software Systems, Ukraine)
Engineering Science Reference • © 2021 • 279pp • H/C (ISBN: 9781522593843) • US $195.00

Agile Scrum Implementation and Its Long-Term Impact on Organizations
Kenneth R. Walsh (University of New Orleans, USA) Sathiadev Mahesh (University of New Orleans, USA) and Cherie C. Trumbach (University of New Orleans, USA)
Engineering Science Reference • © 2021 • 268pp • H/C (ISBN: 9781799848851) • US $215.00

Balancing Agile and Disciplined Engineering and Management Approaches for IT Services and Software Products
Manuel Mora (Universidad Autónoma de Aguascalientes, Mexico) Jorge Marx Gómez (University of Oldenburg, Germany) Rory V. O'Connor (Dublin City University, Ireland) and Alena Buchalcevová (University of Economics, Prague, Czech Republic)
Engineering Science Reference • © 2021 • 354pp • H/C (ISBN: 9781799841654) • US $225.00

Urban Spatial Data Handling and Computing
Mainak Bandyopadhyay (DIT University-Dehradun, India) and Varun Singh (MNNIT-Allahabad, India)
Engineering Science Reference • © 2020 • 300pp • H/C (ISBN: 9781799801221) • US $245.00

701 East Chocolate Avenue, Hershey, PA 17033, USA
Tel: 717-533-8845 x100 • Fax: 717-533-8661
E-Mail: cust@igi-global.com • www.igi-global.com

Table of Contents

Detailed Table of Contents

Section 1
Artificial Intelligence and Cyber-Physical Systems

Jan Bosch, Chalmers University of Technology, Sweden
Helena Holmström Olsson, Malmö University, Sweden
Ivica Crnkovic, Chalmers University of Technology, Sweden

Artificial intelligence (AI) and machine learning (ML) are increasingly broadly adopted in industry. However, based on well over a dozen case studies, we have learned that deploying industry-strength, production quality ML models in systems proves to be challenging. Companies experience challenges related to data quality, design methods and processes, performance of models as well as deployment and compliance. We learned that a new, structured engineering approach is required to construct and evolve systems that contain ML/DL components. In this chapter, the authors provide a conceptualization of the typical evolution patterns that companies experience when employing ML as well as an overview of the key problems experienced by the companies that they have studied. The main contribution of the chapter is a research agenda for AI engineering that provides an overview of the key engineering challenges surrounding ML solutions and an overview of open items that need to be addressed by the research community at large.

Rania Salih Ahmed, Sudan University of Science and Technology, Sudan
Elmustafa Sayed Ali Ahmed, Red Sea University, Sudan
Rashid A. Saeed, Taif University, Saudi Arabia

Cyber-physical systems (CPS) have emerged with development of most great applications in the modern world due to their ability to integrate computation, networking, and physical process. CPS and ML applications are widely used in Industry 4.0, military, robotics, and physical security. Development of ML techniques in CPS is strongly linked according to the definition of CPS that states CPS is the mechanism of monitoring and controlling processes using computer-based algorithms. Optimizations adopted with ML in CPS include domain adaptation and fine tuning of current systems, boosting, introducing more safety and robustness by detection and reduction of vulnerabilities, and reducing computation time in time-critical systems. Generally, ML helps CPS to learn and adapt using intelligent models that are generated from training of large-scale data after processing and analysis.

Chapter 3

Evren Daglarli, Istanbul Technical University, Turkey

Today, the effects of promising technologies such as explainable artificial intelligence (xAI) and meta-learning (ML) on the internet of things (IoT) and the cyber-physical systems (CPS), which are important components of Industry 4.0, are increasingly intensified. However, there are important shortcomings that current deep learning models are currently inadequate. These artificial neural network based models are black box models that generalize the data transmitted to it and learn from the data. Therefore, the relational link between input and output is not observable. For these reasons, it is necessary to make serious efforts on the explanability and interpretability of black box models. In the near future, the integration of explainable artificial intelligence and meta-learning approaches to cyber-physical systems will have effects on a high level of virtualization and simulation infrastructure, real-time supply chain, cyber factories with smart machines communicating over the internet, maximizing production efficiency, analysis of service quality and competition level.

Chapter 4

Merve Yildirim, Erzurum Technical University, Turkey

Due to its nature, cyber security is one of the fields that can benefit most from the techniques of artificial intelligence (AI). Under normal circumstances, it is difficult to write software to defend against cyber-attacks that are constantly developing and strengthening in network systems. By applying artificial intelligence techniques, software that can detect attacks and take precautions can be developed. In cases where traditional security systems are inadequate and slow, security applications developed with artificial intelligence techniques can provide better security against many complex cyber threats. Apart from being a good solution for cyber security problems, it also brings usage problems, legal risks, and concerns. This study focuses on how AI can help solve cyber security issues while discussing artificial intelligence threats and risks. This study also aims to present several AI-based techniques and to explain what these techniques can provide to solve problems in the field of cyber security.

Chapter 5

Rohit Rastogi, Dayalbagh Educational Institute, India & ABES Engineering College, Ghaziabad, India
Priyanshi Garg, ABES Engineering College, Ghaziabad, India

The world is witnessing an unprecedented growth of cyber-physical systems (CPS), which are foreseen to revolutionize our world via creating new services and applications in a variety of sectors such as environmental monitoring, mobile health systems, and intelligent transportation systems and so on. The information and communication technology (ICT) sector is experiencing significant growth in data traffic, driven by the widespread usage of smart phones, tablets, and video streaming, along with the significant growth of sensors deployments that are anticipated soon. This chapter describes suspicious activity detection using facial analysis. Suspicious activity is the actions of an individual or group that is outside the normally acceptable standards for those people or that particular area. In this chapter, the authors propose a novel and cost-effective framework designed for suspicious activity detection using facial expression analysis or emotion detection analysis in law enforcement. This chapter shows a face detection module that is intended to detect faces from a real-time video.

Section 2
IDS/IPS for Smart Cyber-Physical Systems

Chapter 6

Sara A. Mahboub, Sudan University of Science and Technology, Sudan
Elmustafa Sayed Ali Ahmed, Red Sea University, Sudan
Rashid A. Saeed, Taif University, Saudi Arabia

One of the most important requirements is security and accessibility efforts which are represented as a critical issue that should be considered in many applications for the purpose of system confidentiality and safety. To ensure the security of current and emerging CPSs by taking into consideration the unique challenges present in this environment, development of current security mechanisms should be further studied and deployed in a manner that make it becomes more compatible with CPS environment, introduce a safer environment and maintain the quality of service at the same time. Systems known as intrusion detection systems (IDS) and intrusion prevention systems (IPS) are the most common security mechanisms used in networking and communication applications. These systems are based on artificial intelligence (AI) where computer-based algorithms are used to analyze, diagnose, and recognize that threats pattern according to an expected suspicious pattern.

Chapter 7

Srikanth Yadav M., VFSTR University, India
Kalpana R., Pondicherry Engineering College, India

In the present computing world, network intrusion detection systems are playing a vital part in detecting malicious activities, and enormous attention has been given to deep learning from several years. During the past few years, cyber-physical systems (CPSs) have become ubiquitous in modern critical infrastructure and industrial applications. Safety is therefore a primary concern. Because of the success of deep learning (DL) in several domains, DL-based CPS security applications have been developed in the last few years. However, despite the wide range of efforts to use DL to ensure safety for CPSs. The major challenges in front of the research community are developing an efficient and reliable ID that is capable of handling a large amount of data, in analyzing the changing behavioral patterns of attacks in real-time. The work presented in this manuscript reviews the various deep learning generative methodologies and their performance in detecting anomalies in CPSs. The metrics accuracy, precision, recall, and F1-score are used to measure the performance.

Chapter 8

Recently, with the increase in Internet usage, cybersecurity has been a significant challenge for computer systems. Different malicious URLs emit different malicious software and try to capture user information. Signature-based approaches have often been used to detect such websites and detected malicious URLs have been attempted to restrict access by using various security components. This chapter proposes using host-based and lexical features of the associated URLs to better improve the performance of classifiers for detecting malicious web sites. Random forest models and gradient boosting classifier are applied to create a URL classifier using URL string attributes as features. The highest accuracy was achieved by random forest as 98.6%. The results show that being able to identify malicious websites based on URL alone and classify them as spam URLs without relying on page content will result in significant resource savings as well as safe browsing experience for the user.

Chapter 9

The issue of security is paramount in any organisation. Therefore, the authors intend to aid in the security of such organisations by bringing a video based human authentication system for access control which is a type of cyber physical system (CPS). CPS is an integration of computation and physical processes; here the computation is provided by face detection and recognition algorithm and physical process is the input human face. This system aims to provide a platform that allows any authorized person to enter or leave the premise automatically by using face detection and recognition technology. The system also provides the administrator with the access to the logs, wherein he/she would be able to access the details of the people entering or leaving the organisation along with the live video streaming so that there is no sneaking of any unauthorized person with any other authorized person. The administrator can also do registration on behalf of a new person who requires access to the premises for a restricted amount of time only as specified by the administrator.

Section 3
Engineering Applications in CPS

Chapter 10

Mehmet Akif Cifci, Istanbul Aydin University, Turkey

Progress in wireless systems has enabled the creation of low-cost, ergonomic, multi-functional, miniature sensing devices. These devices come together in large numbers creating wireless sensor networks (WSNs), which serve for sensing, collecting, analyzing, and sending detected data to a base station. Problems arise, however, due to the limitations of sensor nodes (SNs), incorrect aggregation of data, redundant and similar data problems, data security and reliability, and some others related to WSN topology. This chapter proposes a novel method for solving WSNs problems to improve cyber-physical systems (CPS). As WSN is of increasing interest in CPSs, the authors put forward an approach for reconstructing WSNs. For traditional methods are not able to cope with such problems, this study takes up rendering WSNs more functional through artificial intelligence (AI) techniques which are considered to develop smart SNs through "intelligent computing," "deep learning," "self-learning," and "swarm learning" ability on the network to improve functionality, utility, and survivability of WSNs.

Chapter 11

Abhishek Kumar, Lovely Professional University, India

A cyber-physical system over field-programmable gate array with optimized artificial intelligence algorithm is beneficial for society. Multiply and accumulate (MAC) unit is an integral part of a DSP processor. This chapter is focused on improving its performance parameters MAC based on column bypass multiplier. It highlights DSP's design for intelligent applications and the architectural setup of the broadly useful neuro-PC, based on the economically available DSP artificial intelligence engine (AI-engine). Adaptive hold logic in the multipliers section determines whether another clock cycle is required to finish multiplication. Adjustment in algorithm reduced the aging impact over cell result in the processor last longer and has increased its life cycle.

Chapter 12

Rohit Rastogi, Dayalbagh Educational Institute, India & ABES Engineering College,
Ghaziabad, India
Rishabh Jain, ABES Engineering College, Ghaziabad, India
Puru Jain, ABES Engineering College, Ghaziabad, India

Robotization has changed into a fundamental piece of our lives. Everybody is completely subject to mechanization whether it is an extraordinary bundling or home robotization. So as to bring home automation into thought, everybody now needs a heterogeneous state security, and in our task on residential robotization, such high security highlights are completely on the best possible consumption. Piezoelectric sensors are compelling for sharpening appropriated wellbeing checking and structures. An intrusion detection system (IDS) is a structure that screens for suspicious movement and issues alarms when such advancement is found. Some obstruction divulgence structures are fit to take practice when poisonous improvement or peculiar action is perceived.

Most of the decisions taken in and around the world are based on data and information. Therefore, the chapter aims to develop a method of data transmission based on discrete event concepts, being such methodology named CBEDE, and using the MATLAB software, where the memory consumption of the proposal was evaluated, presenting great potential to intermediate users and computer systems, within an environment and scenario with cyber-physical systems ensuring more speed, transmission fluency, in the same way as low memory consumption, resulting in reliability. With the differential of this research, the results show better computational performance related to memory utilization with respect to the compression of the information, showing an improvement reaching 95.86%.

Chapter 14

A smart grid is an advanced utility, stations, meters, and energy systems that comprises a diversity of power processes of smart meters, and various power resources. The cyber-physical systems (CPSs) can play a vital role boosting the realization of the smart power grid. Applied CPS techniques that comprise soft computing methods, communication network, management, and control into a smart physical power grid can greatly boost to realize this industry. The cyber-physical smart power systems (CPSPS) are an effective model system architecture for smart grids. Topics as control policies, resiliency methods for secure utility meters, system stability, and secure end-to-end communications between various sensors/ controllers would be quite interested in CPSPS. One of the essential categories in CPSPS applications is the energy management system (EMS). The chapter will spotlight the model and design the relationship between the grid and EMS networks with standardization. The chapter also highlights some necessary standards in the context of CPSPS for the grid infrastructure.

Cyber-physical systems, also known as CPS, have come to stay. There is no doubt, CPS would one day outnumber humans in industries. How do we evaluate the adaptation progress of these systems considering changing environmental conditions? A failed implementation of a CPS can result to a loss. Since CPSs are designed to automate industrial activities, which are centred on the use of several technologies, collaboration with humans may sometimes be inevitable. CPSs are needed to automate several processes and thus help firms compete favourably within an industry. This chapter focuses on the adaptation of CPS in diverse work environment. Considering the ecosystem of the CPS, the authors present a Bayesian model evaluating the progress of adaptation of a CPS given some known conditions.

Preface

Due to recent advancement in technology and their adaptability across various industries, the evolution of the Cyber-Physical Systems (CPSs) increased exponentially. The CPS became ubiquitous, complex, sophisticated, and somewhat intelligent. The CPS and their associated applications are widely used in various industries, for example CPS smart grid widely used in the energy sector, smart factory and industry 4.0, intelligent transportation systems, healthcare and medical systems, and robotic systems. The most difficult task carried out by CPS is to decide on the behavior as normal or faulty by analyzing the disturbances caused by unintentional and intentional events. That is, the modern CPS is expected to maintain the complex interaction between heterogeneous cyber and physical subsystems composed of a myriad of components, some archaic some recently introduced high-technology pieces. Additionally, the security issues have increased for CPS due to the intensifying number of cyber-attacks. Intrusion Detection and Prevention Systems (IDS/IPS) are traditional methods to ensure the security of systems from attacks but they fail to combat modern-day cyber-attacks, as every day new types are created by hackers. Such new cyber-attacks are not defined in the security system database due to their unknown behavior.

Recently, a new age of cybersecurity mechanisms based on Artificial Intelligent (AI) is under development to protect the CPSs from these evolved cyber-attacks. For instance, machine learning technologies are used to analyze the huge and heterogeneous data that are coming from various IoT resources embedded in CPS. By analyzing this huge and heterogenous data, machine learning models and technologies predict likely new attack patterns or process structures. On the other hand, game-theoretic approaches are used for improved decision making, i.e., whether the objected/suspected device is a genuine attacker or not. In preventing the modern-day cyber-attacks it is now advisable, indeed it may be essential, for security experts to integrate different AI approaches including machine learning and game theory with their traditional security scenarios. Involving human intervention in decision-making leads to improved attack detection since the purpose of human-machine interaction is to reduce the number of false positives. Likewise, the infusion of AI towards resolving, at least aiding, the existing challenges of CPSs is expected to alleviate realizing the expected advantages of CPSs sooner and better.

The main aim of this book is to focus upon the status and recent advances in the realization of Artificial Intelligence-based approaches towards affecting Smart Cyber-Physical Systems. This book attracted contributions in important aspects of this multidisciplinary paradigm, in particular, in its application to building sustainable smart computational cyberspaces.

We are highly thankful to our valuable authors for their contribution and for enduring us editors' repeated requests for updates. We are grateful to the select members of our technical program committee for their immense support and motivation for making the first edition of this book a success. We cannot omit to mention them by name: Prateek Agrawal, Mahmoud Al-Rawy, Kiavash Bahreini, Mehmet

Akif Çifçi, Sujata Dash, Evren Dağlarlı, Rajiv Kumar, Suresh Kumar, San Murugesan, Ashish Luhach, Ronald Poet, Rashid Saeed, Kshira Sagar Sahoo, Arif Sarı, Sathiyamoorthi V, Rajveer Shekhawat, Sajjan Singh, Vimal S, Anil Yadav, Srikant Yadav, and Merve Yıldırım. We express our sincere gratitude to our publisher, IGI Global, for standing by us during the prevailing uncertain work atmosphere due to Covid-19 Pandemic.

ORGANIZATION OF THE BOOK

This book is organized into three sections encompassing 15 chapters. A brief description of each follows.

Section 1: Artificial Intelligence and Cyber-Physical System

Chapter 1: Engineering AI Systems – A Research Agenda

This chapter provides a conceptualization of the typical evolution patterns that companies experience when employing ML as well as an overview of the key problems experienced by the companies. It presents the unique research topics for three application domains in which ML/DL technologies are being deployed, i.e. cyber-physical systems, safety-critical systems and autonomously improving systems. The main contribution of the chapter is a research agenda for AI engineering that provides an overview of the key engineering challenges surrounding ML solutions and an overview of open items that need to be addressed by the research community at large.

Chapter 2: Machine Learning in Cyber-Physical Systems in Industry 4.0

This chapter gives details about machine learning (ML) in CPS for industry 4.0 applications. It provides a brief description of ML/CPS architecture, security, and attack issues related to industry 4.0 in addition to Cyber-Physical Production Systems and AI future directions. It discusses the model architecture and other considerations related to self-aware machines, embedded low latency applications, and fog computing.

Chapter 3: Explainable Artificial Intelligence (xAI) Approaches and Deep Meta-Learning Models for Cyber-Physical Systems

The integration of explainable artificial intelligence and meta-learning approaches to cyber-physical systems is likely to be an answer to defeat limitations in old-style deep learning techniques. This chapter takes up deep learning, cyber-physical systems, explainable artificial intelligence, and meta-learning; then on it deals with explainable meta-reinforcement learning (XMRL) integrated cyber-physical systems.

Chapter 4: Artificial Intelligence-Based Solutions for Cyber Security Problems

This study focuses on how AI can help solve cybersecurity issues while discussing artificial intelligence threats and risks. This study also presents several AI-based techniques and explains what they can provide to solve problems in the field of cybersecurity.

Chapter 5: *Social Perspective of Suspicious Activity Detection in Facial Analysis – An ML-Based Approach for Indian Perspective*

In this chapter, the authors propose a novel and cost-effective framework designed for suspicious activity detection using facial expression analysis or emotion detection analysis in law enforcement.

Section 2: IDS/IPS for Smart Cyber-Physical Systems

Chapter 6: *Smart IDS and IPS for Cyber-Physical System*

This chapter provides an understanding of Intrusion Detection Systems (IDS) and Intrusion Prevention Systems (IPS). These are the most common security mechanisms used in networking and communication applications. These systems are based on Artificial Intelligence (AI) where computer-based algorithms are used to analyze, diagnose, and recognize threats patterns according to an expected suspicious pattern.

Chapter 7: *A Survey on Network Intrusion Detection Using Deep Generative Networks for Cyber-Physical Systems*

Network intrusion detection systems using deep learning approaches are playing a vital part in detecting malicious activity in Cyber-Physical Systems (CPSs) which have become ubiquitous in modern critical infrastructure and industrial applications. The work presented in this chapter reviews the various deep learning generative methodologies and their performance in detecting anomalies in CPSs. The metrics of Accuracy, Precision, Recall, and F1-score are used to measure their performance.

Chapter 8: *Malicious URL Detection Using Machine Learning*

Malicious URLs emit malicious software and try to capture user information. This chapter proposes using host-based and lexical features of the associated URLs to better improve the performance of classifiers for detecting malicious web sites. The results show significant resource savings as well as a safe browsing experience for the user.

Chapter 9: *Video-Based Human Authentication System for Access Control*

This chapter brings a video-based human authentication system for access control, which is a type of Cyber-Physical System (CPS). This system aims to provide a platform allowing an authorized person to enter or leave the premise by using face detection and recognition technology. The system also provides the administrator with access to the logs, live video streaming, and privileged user management.

Section 3: Engineering Applications in CPS

Chapter 10: *Optimizing WSNs for CPS Using Machine Learning Techniques*

This chapter proposes a novel method for solving WSN problems to improve cyber-physical systems (CPS). As WSN is of increasing interest in CPSs, the authors put forward an approach for reconstructing WSNs. This study takes up rendering WSNs more functional through Artificial Intelligence (AI) techniques which are considered to develop smart SNs through "intelligent computing," "deep learning," "self-learning" and "swarm learning" ability on the network to improve functionality, utility, and survivability of WSNs.

Chapter 11: Multiplier for DSP Application in the CPS System

This chapter is focused on improving the performance of CPS by using parameters such as MAC-based on column bypass multiplier. It highlights DSP's design for intelligent applications and the architectural setup of the broadly useful neuro-PC, based on the economically available DSP artificial intelligence engine (AI-engine).

Chapter 12: IoT Applications in Smart Home Security – Addressing Safety and Security Threats

The manuscript presents a detailed study of a home security system through its design, parts, implementation, and verification. The security framework involves the use of RFID, Piezo sensors, LCD, Zero PCB associations, Arduino, and their programming in building IDS. The Advantage of this Cyber-Physical System is that it requires low or almost negligible external supply, forming a Clean System of Intrusion Detection.

Chapter 13: Applying a Methodology in Data Transmission of Discrete Events From the Perspective of Cyber-Physical Systems Environments

The present study develops the CBEDE method of data transmission based on discrete event concepts. The memory consumption of the proposal, evaluated using the MATLAB software, presents great potential to intermediate users and computer systems, within an environment and scenario with cyber-physical systems ensuring more speed, transmission fluency, and reliability. Thus the CBEDE methodology can be used in conjunction with CPS and IoT systems, aiming for a faster connection, accurate and secure data in real-time.

Chapter 14: Cyber-Physical System for Smart Grid

Cyber-physical systems (CPSs) can play a vital role to boost the realization of the smart power grid. Applied CPS techniques that comprise soft computing methods, network and communication mediums, and management and control into a smart physical power grid can greatly boost to realize this industry. One of the important categories in CPSPS applications is the energy management system (EMS), the chapter will spot a light on the model and design the relationship between the grid and EMS networks and standardization.

Chapter 15: Bayesian Model for Evaluating Real-World Adaptation Progress of a Cyber-Physical System

For CPSs are designed to automate industrial activities using several technologies, collaboration with humans may sometimes be inevitable. CPSs are needed to automate several processes and thus help firms compete favorably within an industry. This chapter focuses on the adaptation of CPS in a diverse work environment. Considering the ecosystem of the CPS, we present a Bayesian model evaluating the progress of adaptation of a CPS given some known conditions.

Editors,

Ashish Kumar Luhach
The PNG University of Technology, Papua New Guinea

Atilla Elçi
Hasan Kalyoncu University, Turkey

Section 1
Artificial Intelligence and Cyber-Physical Systems

Chapter 1
Engineering AI Systems:
A Research Agenda

Jan Bosch
https://orcid.org/0000-0003-2854-722X
Chalmers University of Technology, Sweden

Helena Holmström Olsson
Malmö University, Sweden

Ivica Crnkovic
Chalmers University of Technology, Sweden

ABSTRACT

Artificial intelligence (AI) and machine learning (ML) are increasingly broadly adopted in industry. However, based on well over a dozen case studies, we have learned that deploying industry-strength, production quality ML models in systems proves to be challenging. Companies experience challenges related to data quality, design methods and processes, performance of models as well as deployment and compliance. We learned that a new, structured engineering approach is required to construct and evolve systems that contain ML/DL components. In this chapter, the authors provide a conceptualization of the typical evolution patterns that companies experience when employing ML as well as an overview of the key problems experienced by the companies that they have studied. The main contribution of the chapter is a research agenda for AI engineering that provides an overview of the key engineering challenges surrounding ML solutions and an overview of open items that need to be addressed by the research community at large.

INTRODUCTION

The prominence of artificial intelligence (AI) and specifically machine- and deep-learning (ML/DL) solutions has grown exponentially, see Amershi et al. (2019), and Bernardi et al. (2019). Because of the Big Data era, more data is available than ever before, and this data can be used for training ML/DL

DOI: 10.4018/978-1-7998-5101-1.ch001

solutions. In parallel, progress in high-performance parallel hardware such as GPUs and FPGAs allows for training solutions of scales unfathomable even a decade ago. These two concurrent technology developments are at the heart of the rapid adoption of ML/DL solutions.

Virtually every company has an AI initiative ongoing and the number of experiments and prototypes in the industry is phenomenal. Although earlier the province of large Software-as-a-Service (SaaS) companies, our research shows democratization of AI and broad adoption across the entire industry, ranging from startups to large cyber-physical systems companies. ML solutions are deployed in telecommunications, healthcare, automotive, internet-of-things (IoT) as well as numerous other industries and we expect exponential growth in the number of deployments across society. As examples, ML solutions are used in the automotive industry to explore autonomous driving and as a means to increase efficiency and productivity. In domains such as e.g. mining, autonomous vehicles are currently being used in under-ground operations where human safety is a concern and in situations where there is a risk of accidents. Similarly, self-driving trucks can operate largely automatically within e.g. harbor or airport areas which helps to increase both productivity and safety. In the defense domain, AI segmentation is used to identify buildings, roads, or any type of land at pixel level from a great height. Besides, AI technologies provide a range of opportunities in a fast-moving emergency where there is conflicting information and where there is a need to rapidly establish an understanding of the current situation, as well as for prediction of future events.

Across industries, image recognition capabilities are key and as an example from the packaging domain, ML is used for checking the inner sides of packages to detect any flaws or deviations in sealings and for analyzing temperature, anomalies, and edges to ensure quality.

Unfortunately, our research, see Arpteg et al. (2018), Lwaktare et al. (2019), and Munappy et al. (2019), shows that the transition from prototype to the production-quality deployment of ML models proves to be challenging for many companies. Though not recognized by many, the engineering challenges surrounding ML prove to be significant. In our research, we have studied well over a dozen cases and identified the problems that these companies experience as they adopt ML. These problems are concerned with a range of topics including data quality, design methods, and processes, the performance of models as well as deployment and compliance.

To the best of our knowledge, no research exists that provide a systematic overview of the research challenges associated with the emerging field of AI engineering, which we define as follows:

AI Engineering is an engineering discipline that is concerned with all aspects of the development and evolution of AI systems, i.e. systems that include AI components. AI engineering is primarily an extension of Software Engineering, but it also includes methods and technologies from data science and AI in general.

In this chapter, we provide a research agenda that has been derived from the research that we have conducted to date. The goal of this research agenda is to inspire for the software engineering research community to start addressing the AI engineering challenges.

The purpose and contribution of this chapter are threefold. First, we provide a conceptualization of the typical evolution patterns concerned with the adoption of AI that companies experience. Second, we provide an overview of the engineering challenges surrounding ML solutions. Third, we provide a research agenda and overview of open items that need to be addressed by the research community at large.

The remainder of this chapter is organized as follows. The Introduction section is followed by the Background section. In Research Methods Background section we present the method underlying the research in this paper. In the section The Challenge of AI Engineering, we present an overview of the problems that we identified in our earlier research as well as a model capturing the evolution pattern of companies adopting AI solutions. Subsequently, we present our research agenda in section AI Engineering: A Research Agenda. Finally, we conclude the paper in sections Future Research Directions In AI Engineering, and Conclusion.

Background

For decades, software engineering (SE) research has been concerned with the processes and methods that are used in designing, developing, and maintaining software. Typically, SE research seeks to create tool-supported methods and techniques to ensure the robust and reliable design of software and with major efforts spent on supporting and advancing requirements-driven development approaches in which specification, testing, and traceability of requirements is key, see Lwakatare et al. (2019). For companies in the software-intensive industry, the applicability and adoption of novel software engineering practices are critical as a means to stay competitive and to continuously improve product performance.

However, today's software-intensive business is in the midst of profound changes concerning the development of software systems. With a rapid pace, and across industry domains, sophisticated technologies for data collection and analysis are implemented to provide developers with real-time input on how the systems they develop perform in the field. Fueled by the increasing availability and access to data, artificial intelligence (AI) and technologies such as machine learning (ML) and deep learning (DL) are rapidly adopted in a variety of domains. Recent years show increasing use of these technologies in the industry with companies such as e.g. Google, Apple, and Facebook leading the way but with software-intensive companies in the embedded systems domain as fast adopters. For these companies, ML/DL components are rapidly complementing the traditional software components in the systems they develop, and we can already see how companies across domains have started complementing their requirements-driven development approaches with novel approaches such as outcome-driven and AI-driven development approaches, see Bosch et al. (2018). Machine learning (ML) and Deep Learning, as a rapidly developing branch of AI, provides the companies with key capabilities for improving and accelerating innovation in their offerings based on operational system data. The application areas of ML/DL to real-world problems are vast and range from large use in recommendation systems of social media, see Lin, J., & Kolcz (2012), and e-commerce, services see Liu at al. (2017), to highly regulated products, such as autonomous vehicle prototypes.

For several years, the field of SE has benefited from ML research by having various ML techniques applied to the activities of SE, see Tsai et al. (1988), such as defect prediction, test-case generation, and refinement in software testing, see Briand (1988), and Durelli et al. (2019). Several studies report on improved software quality and decreased development efforts as the primary benefits of applying ML techniques to solve problems in existing software development processes, see Tosun et al. (2009). In our research, and in contrast to research that focuses on how AI technologies help SE, we focus on how the traditional approach to SE is changing as new components, such as AI components, are introduced into software-intensive systems. The practice has shown that building ML/DL-based systems involves challenges that go beyond ML techniques and algorithms, see Sculley et al. (2015), and Dahlmeier (2017) and that include the integration and evolution of these models as part of larger software-intensive systems. As a consequence, and due to the specific characteristics and complexities involved in the development of ML/DL components, the entire software development process requires new methods and new ways-of-working, see Masuda et al. (2018), and Amershi et al. (2019). Going forward, competitive advantage will involve more than mastering the requirements-driven approach to software engineering. As argued in this paper, it will involve the engineering of systems that include software as well as ML/DL components, and that requires novel engineering approaches.

Although there are state-of-the-art surveys in the area of ML covering the general use of ML techniques, see Hatcher and Yu (2018) and its application in domains such as e.g. automotive, see Luckow et al (2016), and telecommunication, see Klaine et al (2017), these studies tend to focus on the technical aspects of ML rather than the role these play in software-intensive embedded systems and how to effectively engineer systems consisting of technologies with very different characteristics. Up to date, there are a few studies that report on the end-to-end development process of ML-based systems in embedded systems industrial contexts, e.g. John et al. (2020), John et al. (2020-1), Munappy et al. (2020), and Munappy et al. (2020-1), However, to the best of our knowledge, there is no study that provides a systematic overview of the research challenges associated with the emerging field of AI engineering (which we define as an extension of Software Engineering with new processes and technologies needed for development and evolution of AI systems). In what follows, and to address this shortcoming, we report on the challenges we identified concerning the transition from prototype to the production-quality deployment of ML models in large-scale software engineering and we provide a research agenda for how to address what we define as AI engineering challenges.

RESEARCH METHOD

In the context of Software Center[1], we work with more than a dozen large international Cyber-physical systems (CPS) and embedded systems (ES) companies, including Ericsson, Tetra Pak, Siemens, Bosch, Volvo Cars, Boeing, and several others around, among other topics, the adoption of ML/DL technologies. Also, we frequently have the opportunity to study and collaborate with companies also outside of the Software Center that operate as SaaS companies in a variety of business domains.

For this chapter, we have selected a set of 16 primary cases as the foundation for the challenges we identify and the research agenda we outline. However, it should be noted that the work reported in this chapter is based also on learning from more than 20 companies from around the world, though with a focus on the software-intensive embedded systems industry in Europe, mostly Nordic countries. With this as our empirical basis, we believe that the challenges we identify, and the research agenda we outline, reflect the key engineering challenges that companies in a variety of domains experience when employing and integrating ML/DL components in their systems. Below, we present the research approach adopted in this work and the cases we selected as the basis for this chapter.

Research Approach and Selected Cases

The goal of this research is to provide an understanding of the typical evolution patterns that companies experience, and the challenges they face, when adopting and integrating ML/DL components in their systems. Based on this understanding, we develop a research agenda in which we identify the open research questions that need to be addressed by the research community.

Figure 1. Roles and cases that were selected as the empirical basis for this study

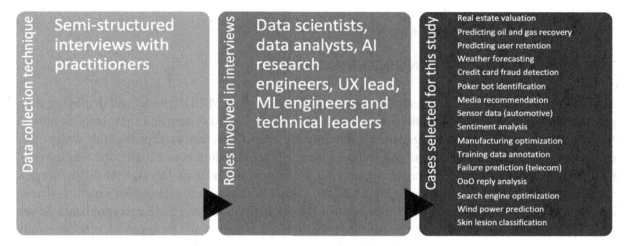

In alignment with this research goal, our research builds on multiple-case study research, see Maxwell (2012), and Flick (2018), with semi-structured interviews and observations as the primary techniques for data collection. The findings we present build on a total number of 16 cases representing startups as well as large multinational companies in domains such as e.g. real estate, weather forecasting, fraud detection, sentiment analysis, and failure prediction. Each case represents a software-intensive system that incorporates ML and DL components and involves challenges ranging from data management and data quality to creation, training, and deployment of ML/DL models. For data collection, we used semi-structured interviews with data scientists, data analysts, AI research engineers, UX lead, ML engineers, and technical leaders. The research approach as well as the roles and cases that were selected as the basis for this study are outlined in Figure 1.

For analysis and coding of the empirical data, we adopted a thematic data analysis approach, see Maguire and Delahunt (2018). Following this approach, all cases were documented and interviews were recorded. During the analysis of our empirical findings, the interview transcripts were read carefully by the researchers to identify recurring elements and concepts, i.e. challenges experienced by the practitioners in the case companies we selected for this study, see Maxwell (2012), and Eisenhardt (1989).

The details of the case studies, as well as several additional cases that were not selected for this particular chapter, can be found in our previously published research Arpteg et al. (2018), Lwakatare et al. (2019), and Munappy et al. (2019). In this research, we identified and categorized challenges, and in particular data management challenges, that practitioners experience when building ML/DL systems and we concluded that there is a significant need for future research on this topic. In this chapter, and to build on and advance our previous research, we map the challenges we identified to a set of strategic focus areas that we recognize in industry. Furthermore, and based on this mapping, we outline a research agenda for AI engineering research to help the research community structure and conceptualize the problem space. As recommended by, see Walsham (1995), the generalizations made based on case study research should be viewed as insights valuable for contexts with similar characteristics. With the opportunity to work closely with more than a dozen large CPS and SaaS companies, we believe that the insights we provide on the challenges these companies experience when building ML/DL systems will be valuable also outside the specific context of these companies. Also, and as the main contribution of this chapter, we believe that the research agenda we present will provide support and structure, as well as inspiration, for the research community at large.

THE CHALLENGE OF AI ENGINEERING

Engineering the AI systems is often portrayed as the creation of an ML/DL model and deploying it. In practice, however, the ML/DL model is only a small part of the overall system and significant additional functionality is required to ensure that the ML/DL model can operate reliably and predictably with proper engineering of data pipelines, monitoring, and logging, etc. see Bernardi et al. (2019), and Sculley et al. (2015). To capture these aspects of AI engineering we defined the Holistic DevOps (HoliDev) model, see Bosch et al. (2018), where we distinguish between requirements-driven development, outcome-driven development (e.g. A/B testing), and AI-driven development. In the model, we outline requirements-driven development as an approach in which software is built to specification and an approach predominantly used when new features or functionality are well understood. Outcome-driven development refers to an approach where development teams receive a quantitative target to realize and are asked to experiment with different solutions to improve the metric. Typically, this development approach is used for new and for innovation efforts. The third approach is AI-driven development where a company has a large data set available and uses ML/DL solutions to create components that act based on input data and that learn from previous actions. We conclude that the selection and combination of development approaches will be key for competitive advantage.

AI Adoption in Practice

The challenge of AI engineering is that the results of each of the aforementioned type of development end up in the same system and are subject to data collection, monitoring of behavior as well as the continuous deployment of new functionality. In industrial deployments that we have studied, also AI models

Figure 2. The AI adoption evolution model

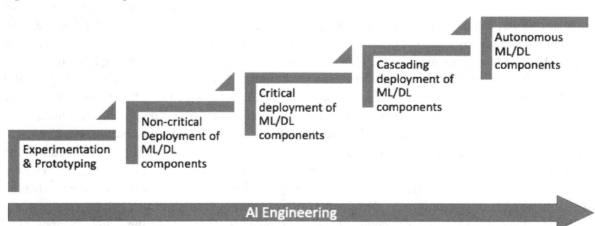

are constantly improved, retrained, and redeployed and consequently follow the same DevOps process as the other software components.

In a transformation to AI-driven development, companies, over time, tend to develop more skills, capabilities, and needs in the ML/DL space, and consequently, they evolve through several stages. In the AI Evolution model in Figure 2, we illustrate how companies, based on our previous research Munappy et al. (2019), and Bosch et al (2019), evolve over time. The maturity of companies concerning AI evolves through five stages:

- **Experimentation and Prototyping**: This stage is purely exploratory and the results are not deployed in a production environment. Consequently, AI engineering challenges are not present at this stage.
- **Non-critical Deployment**: In this stage, an ML/DL model is deployed as part of a product or system in a non-critical capacity, meaning that if the model fails to perform, the overall product or system is still functional and delivers value to customers.
- **Critical Deployment**: Once the confidence in the ML/DL models increases, key decision-makers become sufficiently comfortable with deploying these models in a critical context, meaning that the product or system fails if the ML/DL model does not perform correctly.
- **Cascading Deployment**: With the increasing use of ML/DL models, the next step is to start to use the output of one model as the input for the next model in the chain. In this case, monitoring and ensuring the correct functioning of the system becomes more difficult as the issues may be emergent, rather than directly associated with a specific ML/DL model.
- **Autonomous ML/DL Components**: In the final stage, ML/DL models monitor their behavior, automatically initiate retraining, and can flag when the model observes that, despite retraining using the latest data, it does not provide acceptable accuracy.

Each of the steps above requires increased activities of "AI engineering", i.e. a set of methods and tools that originated from software engineering in a system life cycle, and procedures, technologies, and tools from data science and AI. While the first step, which is today state of the practice, typically covers the end-to-end ML development cycle (data acquisition, feature engineering, training and evaluation, and deployment), the next steps require the existing approaches from software engineering (e.g. system testing) as well as completely new methods that will need to become an integrated part of the software and AI engineering (e.g. continuous training, or version management of code and data).

AI Engineering Strategic Focus

During our research, we worked with a variety of companies and identified over 30 problems that are a concern in multiple cases that we studied. We have presented some of these in detail in earlier publications, specifically Arpteg et al. (2018), Lwakatare et al. (2019), and Munappy et al. (2019), so we will not discuss each identified problem in this chapter. Instead, we provide an overview in Figure 3 and we present a categorization of the identified problems. The categories represent four strategic focus areas that relate to the typical phases of an ML project. These four areas are the following:

- **Data Quality Management**: One of the key challenges in successful AI projects is to establish data sets and streams that are of sufficient quality for training and inference. Specifically, data sets

Figure 3. Overview of cases and identified problems

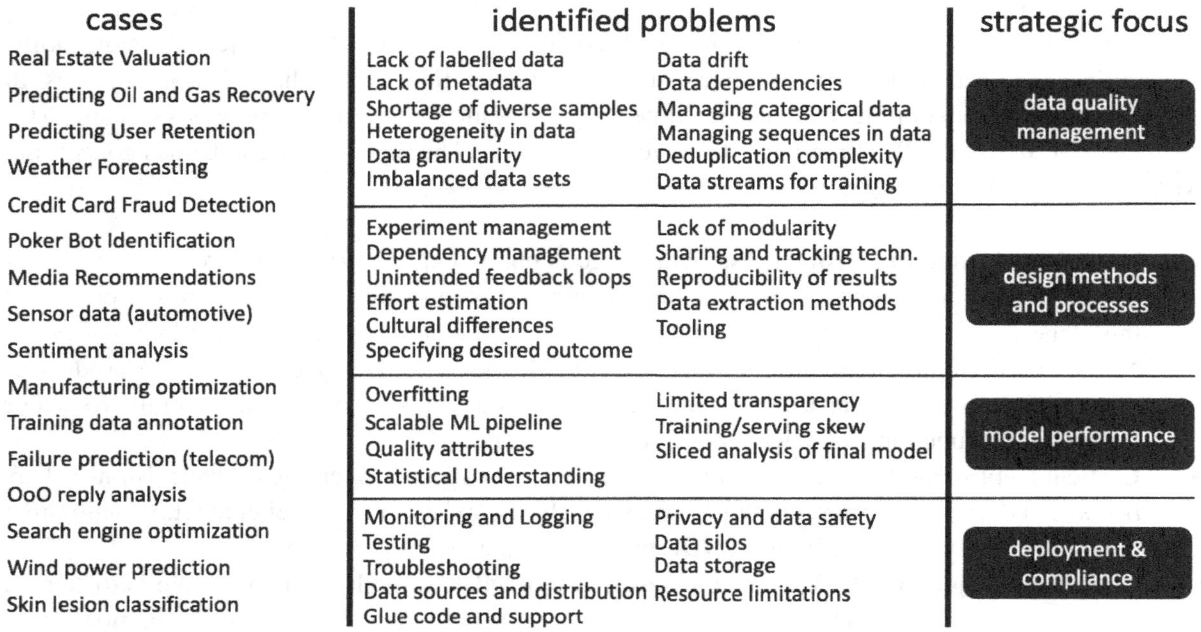

cases	identified problems		strategic focus
Real Estate Valuation	Lack of labelled data	Data drift	
Predicting Oil and Gas Recovery	Lack of metadata	Data dependencies	**data quality management**
Predicting User Retention	Shortage of diverse samples	Managing categorical data	
Weather Forecasting	Heterogeneity in data	Managing sequences in data	
Credit Card Fraud Detection	Data granularity	Deduplication complexity	
Poker Bot Identification	Imbalanced data sets	Data streams for training	
Media Recommendations	Experiment management	Lack of modularity	
Sensor data (automotive)	Dependency management	Sharing and tracking techn.	**design methods and processes**
Sentiment analysis	Unintended feedback loops	Reproducibility of results	
Manufacturing optimization	Effort estimation	Data extraction methods	
Training data annotation	Cultural differences	Tooling	
Failure prediction (telecom)	Specifying desired outcome		
OoO reply analysis	Overfitting	Limited transparency	
Search engine optimization	Scalable ML pipeline	Training/serving skew	**model performance**
Wind power prediction	Quality attributes	Sliced analysis of final model	
Skin lesion classification	Statistical Understanding		
	Monitoring and Logging	Privacy and data safety	
	Testing	Data silos	**deployment & compliance**
	Troubleshooting	Data storage	
	Data sources and distribution	Resource limitations	
	Glue code and support		

tend to be unbalanced, have a high degree of heterogeneity, lack labels, tend to drift over time, contain implicit dependencies, and generally require vast amounts of pre-processing effort before they are usable.

- **Design Methods and Processes**: Although creating an ML model is relatively easy, doing so at scale and in a repeatable fashion proves to be challenging. Specifically, managing a multitude of experiments, detecting and resolving implicit dependencies and feedback loops, the inability of tracing data dependency, estimating effort, cultural differences between developer roles, specifying desired outcome and tooling prove to be difficult to accomplish efficiently and effectively.
- **Model Performance**: The performance of ML/DL models depends on various factors, both for accuracy and general quality attributes. Some of the specific problems that we have identified include a skew between training data and the data served during operation, lack of support for quality attributes, over-fitting of models, and scalable data pipelines for training and serving.
- **Deployment & Compliance**: Finally, one area that is highly underestimated is the deployment of models. Here, companies struggle with a multitude of problems, including monitoring and logging of models, testing of models, troubleshooting, resource limitations, and significant amounts of glue code to get the system up and running.

AI ENGINEERING: A RESEARCH AGENDA

The subject of AI and the notion of engineering practices for building AI systems is a multi-faceted and complex problem. Consequently, few, if any, models exist that seek to create a structure and conceptualization of the problem space. In this section, we provide a structured view on the challenge of AI engineering and we provide a research agenda (Figure 4). In the research agenda, we organize the challenges into two main categories, i.e. generic AI engineering and domain-specific AI engineering. Within generic AI Engineering (AI Eng.), we categorize the challenges into three main areas, i.e. architecture, development, and process. For domain-specific AI Engineering (D AI Eng.), we have identified one set of challenges for each domain that we have studied in the case study companies.

As a second dimension, we follow the strategic focus areas that are related directly to the four main phases of a typical ML/DL project, i.e. data quality management (related to assembling data sets), design methods and processes (related to creating and evolving ML/DL models), model performance (related to training and evaluating) and finally deployment and conformance, related to the deploy phase. In figure 4, the model is presented graphically. In the remainder of the section, we discuss the key research challenges in more detail.

As the data science activities shown in Figure 4 are the regular AI/data science activities, we will discuss these only briefly:

- **Assemble Data Sets**: The first activity in virtually any ML/DL project is to assemble the data sets that can be used for training and evaluation and to evaluate these to understand the relevant features in the data.
- **Create & Evolve ML/DL Model**: After analyzing the data sets, the next step is to experiment with different ML algorithms or DL models and to select the most promising one for further development.
- **Train & Evaluate**: Once the model has been developed, the next step is to train and validate the model using the data.
- **Deploy**: Once the model has been trained and is shown to have sufficient accuracy, recall, and/or other relevant metrics, the model is deployed in a system where it typically is connected to one or more data streams for inference.

The data science process above has many additional aspects and is typically conducted iteratively. In Figure 4, we show two of these iterations, i.e. between training and modeling and between deployment and the assembling of new data sets. However, as this paper is concerned with AI engineering and not with the specific data science aspects, we do not discuss these aspects in more detail.

AI Engineering: Architecture

In the context of AI engineering, architecture is concerned with structuring the overall system and decomposing it into its main components. Constructing systems including ML/DL components require components and solutions not found in traditional systems and that need to address novel concerns. Below we describe the primary research challenges that we have identified in our research.

- **Data Versioning & Dependency Management**: The quality of the data used for training is central to achieving high performance of models. Especially in a DevOps environment, data generated by one version of the software is not necessarily compatible with the software generated by the subsequent version. Consequently, the versioning of data needs to be carefully managed. Also, systems typically generate multiple streams of data that have dependencies on each other. As data pipelines tend to be less robust than software pipelines Munappy et al. (2019), it is important to provide solutions for the management of data quality. This can be concerned with simple checks for data being in range or even being present or more advanced checks to ensure that the average for a window of data stays constant over time or that the statistical distribution of the data remains similar. As ML/DL models are heavily data-dependent, the data pipelines needed for feeding the models as well as the data generated by the models need to be set up. This can be particularly challenging when different types of data and different sources of data are used; in addition to questions of availability, accuracy, synchronization, and normalization, significant problems related to security and privacy appear.

- **Federated Learning Infrastructure**: Most of the cases that we studied concern systems where ML models are deployed in each instance of the system. Several approaches exist for managing training, evaluation, and deployment in such contexts, but one central infrastructure component is the support for federated learning. As it often is infeasible to move all data to a central location for training a global model, solutions are needed for federated learning and the sharing of model parameters such as neural network weights as well as selected data sets that, for instance, represent cases not well handled by the central model. Federated learning requires an infrastructure to achieve the required quality attributes and to efficiently and securely share models and data.

- **Storage and Computing Infrastructure**: Although many assume that all ML/DL deployments operate in the cloud, our interaction with industry shows that many companies build up internal storage and computing infrastructure because of legal constraints, cost, or quality attributes. Developing these infrastructures, for example for the development of autonomous driving solutions, is a major engineering and research challenge. Typically, collection and storing of data are organized centrally on the enterprise level, while the development of AI solutions is distributed over several development teams.

- **Deployment Infrastructure**: Independent of the use of centralized or federated learning approaches, models still need to be deployed in systems in the field. As most case study companies have adopted or plan to soon adopt DevOps, it is important for a deployment infrastructure to reliably deploy subsequent versions of models, measure their performance, raise warnings and initiate rollbacks in the case of anomalous behavior. This infrastructure is by the necessity of a distributed nature as it requires functionality both centrally as well as in each system that is part of the DevOps approach. Deployment of MD/DL models may require a substantial change in the overall architecture of the system.

AI Engineering: Development

Building and deploying successful ML/DL components and systems requires more than data science alone. In this section, we focus on the development of systems including ML/DL components. This is important because also ML/DL models, in most cases that we have studied, are subject to the same DevOps activities as the other software in systems, meaning that models evolve, are retrained, and deployed continuously. Based on our case study research, we present the four primary research challenges concerning development in AI engineering below.

- **DataOps**: Although considered a buzzword by some, DataOps raises the concern of managing everything data with the same structured and systematic approach as that we manage software within a traditional DevOps context. As typical companies ask their data scientists to spend north of 95% of their time cleaning, pre-processing, and managing data, there is a significant opportunity to reduce this overhead by generating, distributing, and storing data smarter in the development process. DataOps requires high levels of automation, which requires alignment and standardization to achieve continuous value delivery.

- **Reuse of Pre-Developed Models**: Most companies prefer to employ models developed by others or that have been developed earlier inside the company. However, the reuse of existing ML/DL models is not trivial as the separation between the generic and specific parts of the model are not always easy to separate, in particular when the run-time context is different from that used in the training phase.

- **Quality Attributes**: In data science, the key challenge is to achieve high accuracy, recall, or other metrics directly related to the ML performance of the machine learning model. In an AI engineering context, however, several other quality attributes become relevant including the computation performance, in terms of the number of inferences per time unit the system can manage, the real-time properties, robustness of the system in case of data outside the scope of the training set, etc. Ensuring satisfactory adherence to the quality requirements on the ML components in the system is a research challenge that is far from resolved.

- **Integration of Models & Components**: As we discussed earlier in the paper, ML/DL models need to be integrated with the remainder of the system containing regular software components. However, it is not always trivial to connect the data-driven ML/DL models with the computation-driven software components. Also, traditional testing and evaluation of the models must be integrated in such a way that software methods and data-science evaluation methods are combined seamlessly. Depending on the criticality of the ML/DL model for the overall performance of the system, the validation activities need to be more elaborate.

Figure 4. Research agenda for AI engineering

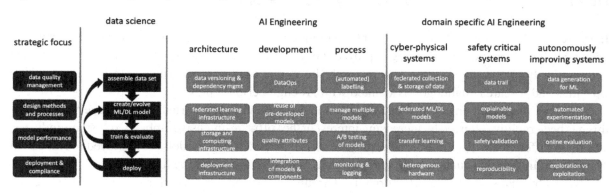

AI Engineering: Process

Although the notion of the process has gone out of vogue with the emergence of agile, it is hard to argue that no process is required to align the efforts of large groups of people without prohibitively high coordination costs. The context of AI engineering is no different, but there are surprisingly few design methods, processes, and approaches available for the development and evolution of ML/DL models. Experienced data scientists do not need these, but with the rapidly growing need for AI engineers, many less experienced data scientists and software engineers are asked to build these models. These professionals would very much benefit from more methodological and process support. We have identified four main process-related challenges that require significant research efforts to resolve constructively and efficiently. Below we describe each of these in more detail.

- **Automated Labeling**: As the data sets that a company starts with are limited sources for training and validation, ideally, we want to collect the data sets for training evolving models during operation in deployment. Although it is easy to collect the input data, the labels used in supervised learning are often much harder to add. Consequently, we need solutions for, preferably, automated labeling of data so that we have a constant stream of recent data for training and validation purposes during evolution.
- **Manage Multiple Models**: The first concern that often surfaces in teams working on ML/DL models is that it is difficult to keep track of all the models that are being considered during the development phase. We discussed parts of this challenge in, see Bernardi et al. (2019).
- **A/B Testing of Models**: During evolution, the improved model is deployed for the operation. However, experience shows that models that perform better in training do not necessarily perform better in operations. Consequently, we need solutions, often variants of A/B testing, to ensure that the new model also performs better in deployment.
- **Monitoring & Logging**: Once the model is deployed and used in operation, it is important to monitor its performance and to log events specific to the performance of the model. As ML/DL models tend to lack the explainability front, the monitoring and logging are required to build confidence in the accuracy of the models and to detect situations where the performance of a model starts to deteriorate or is insufficient from the start.

Domain-Specific AI Eng.: Cyber-Physical Systems

In the remainder of this section, we present the unique research topics for three application domains in which ML/DL technologies are being deployed, i.e. cyber-physical systems, safety-critical systems and autonomously improving systems. Our research shows that each domain brings with it a set of unique activities and research challenges associated with AI engineering topics.

Although the recent emergence of ML/DL models in the industry started in the online SaaS world, this has been rapidly followed by increasing interest in the software-intensive embedded systems industry. The main difference with cloud-based deployments is that the ML/DL models are deployed in embedded systems out in the field such as base stations, cars, radars, sensors, and the like.

Cyber-physical systems are often organized around three computing platforms, i.e. the edge device where the data for ML/DL is collected, an on-premise server of some kind, and the infrastructure in the cloud. Each of these platforms has its characteristics in terms of real-time performance, security and privacy, computational and storage resources, communications cost, etc.

The consequence is that data management, training, validation, and inference associated with ML/DL models tend to become federated as it requires these three computing platforms as most capabilities that customers care about will cross-cut all three platforms. This leads to a set of unique research challenges for this domain that we discuss below.

- **Federated/Distributed Storage of Data**: Parallel to the model, the data used for training and inference needs to be managed in a distributed and federated fashion. Local storage on device instances minimizes communication costs but tends to increase the bill-of-materials for each device and these architectural drivers need to be managed.

- **Federated/Distributed Model Creation**: Due to the presence of multiple computing platforms, the architect or data scientist needs to distribute the ML/DL model over these computing platforms, resulting in a federated model. This is an open research area related to the system and data lifecycles, performance, availability, security, computation, etc.

- **Transfer Learning**: Especially for companies that have thousands or millions of devices deployed in the field, the challenge is the balancing between centralized and decentralized learning. The most promising approach is to distribute centrally trained models and to allow each device to apply its local learnings to the centrally trained model using transfer learning approaches. However, more research is needed.

- **Deploy on Heterogeneous Hardware**: Finally, because of both cost and computational efficiency, embedded systems often use dedicated hardware solutions such as ASICs and FPGAs. Additionally, MD/DL models require huge amounts of parallel computation, both during training and implementation, realized in e.g. GPUs. These execution platforms use different development environments, programming languages, and execution paradigms. Embedded systems tend to have constraints on computational and storage resources as well as power consumption. Deploying ML/DL models on these types of hardware frequently require engineering effort from the team as there are no generic solutions available.

One challenge that is not yet one of the primary ones but that has appeared on the horizon is the mass-customization of ML/DL models. As some CPS companies have many instances of their products in the field, the ML/DL models deployed in these instances should, ideally, adjust their behavior to the specifics of the users using the instance, i.e. mass-customization. However, there are few solutions available for combining both continuous deployments of centrally trained models with the customization of each product instance.

Domain-Specific AI Eng.: Safety-Critical Systems

A special class of cyber-physical systems is safety-critical systems, i.e. those systems whose failure or malfunction may result in significant bodily, environmental, or financial harm. The community struggles with balancing two forces. On the one hand, we seek to avoid harm by taking conservative approaches and introducing new technologies only after careful evaluation. On the other hand, the slow introduction of new technologies may easily cause harm in that the new technologies can help avoid safety issues that were not possible to avoid with conventional technologies only.

One of these new technologies is, of course, ML/DL. In the automotive industry, among others, the use of ML/DL allows for advanced driver support functions as well as fully autonomous driving. The open challenge is establishing the safety of these systems. In our research, we have defined the four primary research challenges specific to safety-critical AI-based systems.

- **Data Trail**: One of the key challenges in safety-critical systems is that the collection of safety-related evidence before the deployment of systems and the creation of a data trail during operations to ensure the safe operation of the system. In the context of ML/DL models, this requires maintaining a clear trail of the data that was used for training as well as the inferences that the model provided during operation. Little research exists that addresses this challenge for AI components and consequently this is a significant research challenge.

- **Explainable Models**: As it is virtually impossible to test a system to safety, the community often uses various approaches to certify systems. This is performed by assessors who need to understand the functionality of the system. This requires that ML/DL models are explainable, which today is unsolvable or at least a non-trivial problem for most models.

- **Validation of Safety-Critical Systems**: The basic enabler for the deployment of ML/DL models in safety-critical systems is the validation of these systems. Validation concerns both the correct behavior in situations where an application should act, but we also need to show that the system will not engage in situations where it is not necessary or even dangerous to do so. Validation of safety-critical systems starts from requirements of justifiable prediction and of deterministic system behavior, while ML/DL solutions are based on statistical models, so in principle non-deterministic behavior. In practice, the ML/DL models can be more accurate and reliable, but the justification of these models requires new approaches, methods, and standards in the validation process.

- **Reproducibility**: For a variety of factors, an ML/DL model may end up looking different when it is given a different seed, order of training data, infrastructure it is deployed on, etc. Especially for safety-critical systems, it is critical that we can predictably reproduce the model, independent of the aforementioned factors.

Domain-Specific AI Eng.: Autonomously Improving Systems

There is an emerging category of systems that uses ML/DL models with the intent of continuously improving the performance of the system autonomously. In practice, there are humans involved in the improvement of the system, but the system employs mechanisms for experimentation and improvement that do not require human involvement.

The primary way for systems to achieve this is through the use of ML/DL models that analyze the data, train using it, and then provide interference. This requires forms of automated experimentation where the system itself generates alternatives and, for example, deploys these alternatives in A/B testing or similar contexts and measures the impact of these changes. Four research challenges need to be addressed for autonomously improving systems:

- **Data Generation for Machine Learning**: Traditional ML/DL model development requires data scientists to spend significant amounts of time to convert available data sets that often are intended for human consumption into data sets that are usable for machine learning. In autonomously improving systems, the data that is generated by the system needs to be machine-interpretable without any human help. How to accomplish this, though, is an open research question.

- **Automated Experimentation**: Although the notion of automated experimentation is conceptually easy to understand, actually realizing systems that can operate in this fashion is largely an open research challenge where little work is available.

- **Online Evaluation**: As autonomously improving systems generate alternatives for evaluation at run-time, these alternatives need to be deployed and evaluated during the regular operation of the system. This requires solutions for dynamically adjusting the behavior of the system to select, for a small percentage of the cases, the new alternative for evaluation as well as to keep track of statistical validity of the test results associated with each alternative.

- **Exploration vs Exploitation**: In autonomously improving systems, the system autonomously experiments with different responses to the environment in which it operates with the intent of improving its performance. The challenge is that some or even many of these experiments will result in worse performance than the current default response. This is referred to as regret in optimization theory. The challenge is that it is impossible to find better ways of doing things without trying out these new ways, but especially in embedded systems, there is a limit to how poor the alternative can be. This means that we need research to help assess the worst-case outcomes for each experiment with the intent of balancing the cost of exploration with the cost too much exploitation.

Other Domain-Specific Systems

We described the domain-specific research challenges for building ML/DL systems for specific types of systems. There of course are other domains that likely have specific research challenges as well. These challenges might be the same as for non-AI-based systems, but new methods must be developed to meet these challenges (for example develop new methods to ensure system reliability, availability, security, reusability, or other non-functional properties). However, in many cases introducing ML/DL solutions cause new challenges such as quality of data, real-time data access, and increase in efforts in the development life cycle as well as challenges in a combination of security, functionality, and privacy, etc.

FUTURE RESEARCH DIRECTIONS IN AI ENGINEERING

In the previous section, we have provided a research agenda with an exhaustive list of topics relevant to research in AI Engineering. The identified problems (Figure 3) indicate the currently important research directions. The topics related to a) data quality management, b) design methods and processing, c) model performance and d) deployment & compliance are recognized by the industry as big challenges and even possible showstoppers of AI-based development in large. AI Engineering, forming as a new discipline, includes several research challenges related to system and software architecture, development methods and theologies, and processes, as shown in Figure 4. Many of these challenges are new, not previously present in software engineering (for example, data versioning and dependencies, managing multiple models, A/B testing of AI-based components), while others are related to known challenges (for example safety, reliability, real-time requirements) that require new methods and processes to obtain the solutions.

In addition to these research directions that originate from the concrete problems the industry faces today, several meta-level challenges originate from the AI/ML nature – dependence of data and algorithm and generality. While the domain-specific problems related to the algorithms and procedures can be generalized, it is significantly more difficult with data-related problems, as it is more difficult to generalize and abstract data on which the ML models depend. Examples of these challenges are related to the following questions: a) How to manage data and algorithms versions? b) How to relate changes in data to changes in ML models? c) How to measure when changes of data require new ML-models? How to synchronize run-time context changes with re-training frequency?

While AI is not a new research discipline, its application in different domains, and the operational aspects are new, which leads to many unpredictable results. A typical example is that an ML model works perfectly in a training/evaluation environment, while in operation the system becomes unreliable, and its development unpredictable. One of the sources of this challenge is the inability of data science to manage the problem. In the development process, domain knowledge is inevitable for providing the proper semantics of the results provided by data-related and statistical methods. The other challenge is related to the complexity and ineffectiveness of software that is used as a glue code and additional logic required to connect results from ML-based models. That requires interdisciplinary research, and by that research about roles and impact on different stakeholders in the development and operational process.

During at least a decade the topics from the present research agenda will be highly prioritized in the research community and the industry.

CONCLUSION

Artificial intelligence, and specifically machine- and deep-learning, has, over the last decade, proven to have the potential to deliver enormous value to industry and society. This has resulted in most companies experimenting and prototyping with a host of AI initiatives. Unfortunately, our research Arpteg et al. (2018), Lwakatare et al. (2019), and Munappy et al. (2019) show that the transition from prototype to industry-strength, production-quality deployment of ML models proves to be very challenging for many companies. The engineering challenges surrounding this prove to be significant Briand (1988), even if many researchers and companies fail to recognize this.

To the best of our knowledge, no papers exist that provide a systematic overview of the research challenges associated with the emerging field of AI engineering. In this chapter we provide a conceptualization of the typical evolution patterns that companies experience when adopting ML, we present an overview of the problems that companies experience based on well over a dozen cases that we studied and we provide a research agenda that was derived from the research that we conducted to date and that needs to be addressed by the research community at large. The goal of this research agenda is to inspire for the software engineering research community to start addressing the AI engineering challenges.

AI and ML have the potential to greatly benefit the industry and society at large. For us to capture the value, however, we need to be able to engineer solutions that deliver production-quality deployments. This requires research to address the AI engineering challenges that we present in this paper. In future work, we aim to address several of these research challenges in our research and our collaboration with industry. In particular collaboration with industry in real industrial settings is crucial since ML methods build upon empirical methods and directly depend on the amount and types of data. For this reason, we frequently organize events in the Nordics and at international conferences to create awareness for the identified challenges and to encourage other researchers to join us in addressing these.

ACKNOWLEDGMENT

The research in this paper has been supported by the Software Center, the Chalmers Artificial Intelligence Research Center (CHAIR), and Vinnova.

REFERENCES

Amershi, S., Begel, A., Bird, C., DeLine, R., Gall, H., Kamar, E., . . . Zimmermann, T. (2019). Software engineering for machine learning: A case study. In *Proceedings IEEE/ACM 41st International Conference on Software Engineering: Software Engineering in Practice -ICSE-SEIP* (pp. 291–300). IEEE.

Arpteg, A., Brinne, B., Crnkovic-Friis, L., & Bosch, J. (2018). Software engineering challenges of deep learning. In *Proceedings 44th Euromicro Conference on Software Engineering and Advanced Applications -SEAA* (pp. 50–59). IEEE.

Bernardi, L., Mavridis, T., & Estevez, P. (2019), 150 successful machine learning models: 6 lessons learned at booking. Com. In *Proceedings of the 25th ACM SIGKDD International Conference on Knowledge Discovery & Data Mining* (pp. 1743–1751). ACM.

Bosch, J., Olsson, H. H., & Crnkovic, I. (2018). It takes three to tango: Requirement, outcome/data, and ai driven development. In *Proceedings SiBW* (pp. 177–192). Academic Press.

Briand, L. C. (2008). Novel applications of machine learning in software testing. In *Proceedings 8th International Conference on Quality Software* (pp. 3–10). IEEE. 10.1109/QSIC.2008.29

Dahlmeier, D. (2017) On the challenges of translating NLP research into commercial products. In *Proceedings of the 55th Annual Meeting of the Association for Computational Linguistics* (vol. 2, pp. 92–96). 10.18653/v1/P17-2015

Durelli, V. H. S., Durelli, R. S., Borges, S. S., Endo, A. T., Eler, M. M., Dias, D. R. C., & Guimares, M. P. (2019). Machine learning applied to software testing: A systematic mapping study. *IEEE Transactions on Reliability*, *68*(3), 1189–1212. doi:10.1109/TR.2019.2892517

Eisenhardt, K. M. (1989). Building theories from case study research. *Academy of Management Review*, *14*(4), 532–550.

Flick, U. (2018). Designing qualitative research. *Sage (Atlanta, Ga.)*.

Hatcher, W. G., & Yu, W. (2018). A survey of deep learning: Platforms, applications and emerging research trends. *IEEE Access: Practical Innovations, Open Solutions*, *6*, 24411–24432. doi:10.1109/ACCESS.2018.2830661

John, M. M., Olsson, H. H., & Bosch, J. (2020). Developing ML/DL models: A design framework. *Proceedings of the International Conference on Software and Systems Process (ICSSP)*. 10.1145/3379177.3388892

John, M. M., Olsson, H. H., & Bosch, J. (2020-1). AI on the Edge: Architectural Alternatives. *Proceedings of the Euromicro Conference on Software Engineering and Advanced Applications (SEAA)*.

Klaine, P. V., Imran, M. A., Onireti, O., & Souza, R. D. (2017). A survey of machine learning techniques applied to self organizing cellular networks. *IEEE Communications Surveys and Tutorials*, *19*, 2392–2431.

Lin, J., & Kolcz, A. (2012) Large-scale machine learning at Twitter. In *Proceedings SIGMOD International Conference on Management of Data* (pp. 793–804). ACM.

Liu, S., Xiao, F., Ou, W., & Si, L. (2017). Cascade ranking for operational e-commerce search. In *Proceedings International Conference on Knowledge Discovery and Data Mining* (pp. 1557–1565). ACM.

Luckow, A., Cook, M., Ashcraft, N., Weill, E., Djerekarov, E., & Vorster, B. (2016). Deep learning in the automotive industry: Applications and tools. In *Proceedings International Conference on Big Data* (pp. 3759–3768). 10.1109/BigData.2016.7841045

Lwakatare, L. E., Raj, A., Bosch, J., Olsson, H. H., & Crnkovic, I. (2019). A taxonomy of software engineering challenges for machine learning systems: An empirical investigation. In *Proceedings International Conference on Agile Software Development* (pp. 227–243). Springer. 10.1007/978-3-030-19034-7_14

Maguire M., & Delahunt, B. (2017). Doing a thematic analysis: A practical, step-by-step guide for learning and teaching scholars. *AISHE-J: The All Ireland Journal of Teaching and Learning in Higher Education, 9*(3).

Masuda, S., Ono, K., Yasue, T., & Hosokawa, N. (2018). A survey of software quality for machine learning applications. In *Proceedings International Conference on Software Testing, Verification and Validation Workshops – ICSTW* (pp. 279–284). IEEE.

Maxwell, J. A. (2012). *Qualitative research design: An interactive approach* (Vol. 41). Sage publications.

Munappy, A., Bosch, J., Olsson, H. H., Arpteg, A., & Brinne, B. (2019). Data management challenges for deep learning. In *Proceedings 45th Euromicro Conference on Software Engineering and Advanced Applications - SEAA* (pp. 140–147). IEEE.

Munappy, R. A., Bosch, J., Olsson, H. H., & Wang, T. J. (2020). Modeling Data Pipelines. *Proceedings of the Euromicro Conference on Software Engineering and Advanced Applications (SEAA).*

Munappy, R.A., & Mattos, D.I., & Bosch, J. (2020). From Ad-hoc Data Analytics to DataOps. *Proceedings of the International Conference on Software and Systems Process (ICSSP).*

Sculley, D., Holt, D., Golovin, G., Davydov, E., Phillips, T., Ebner, D., . . . Dennison, D. (2015) Hidden technical debt in machine learning systems. In Proceedings Advances in neural information processing systems (NIPS) 28 (pp. 2503–2511). Curran Associates, Inc.

Tosun, A., Turhan, B., & Bener, A. (2009) Practical considerations in deploying ai for defect prediction: A case study within the Turkish telecommunication industry. In *Proceedings of the 5th International Conference on Predictor Models in Software Engineering* (pp. 11:1–11:9). ACM. 10.1145/1540438.1540453

Tsai, W. T., Heisler, K. G., Volovik, D., & Zualkernan, I. A. (1988). A critical look at the relationship between AI and software engineering. In *Proceedings Workshop on Languages for Automation Symbiotic and Intelligent Robotics* (pp. 2–18). IEEE. 10.1109/LFA.1988.24945

Walsham, G. (1995). Interpretive case studies in IS research: Nature and method. *European Journal of Information Systems, 4*(2), 74–81. doi:10.1057/ejis.1995.9

ADDITIONAL READING

Amershi, S., Begel, A., Bird, C., DeLine, R., Gall, H., Kamar, E., . . . Zimmermann, T. (2019). Software engineering for machine learning: A case study. *In Proceedings IEEE/ACM 41st International Conference on Software Engineering: Software Engineering in Practice -ICSE-SEIP* (pp. 291–300). IEEE.

Arpteg, A., Brinne, B., Crnkovic-Friis, L., & Bosch, J. (2018). Software engineering challenges of deep learning. *In Proceedings 44th Euromicro Conference on Software Engineering and Advanced Applications -SEAA* (pp. 50–59). IEEE

Russell, S., & Norvig, P. (2018). *Artificial Intelligence: A Modern Approach.* Pearson Education Limited.

Sculley, D., Holt, D., Golovin, G., Davydov, E., Phillips, T., Ebner, D., . . . Dennison, D. (2015) Hidden technical debt in machine learning systems. In Proceedings Advances in neural information processing systems (NIPS) 28 (pp. 2503–2511). Curran Associates, Inc.

KEY TERMS AND DEFINITIONS

AI Engineering: Is an engineering discipline that is concerned with all aspects of the development and evolution of AI systems, i.e. systems that include AI components. AI engineering is primarily an extension of Software Engineering, but it also includes methods and technologies from data science and AI in general.

Artificial Intelligence: The theory and development of computer systems able to perform tasks normally requiring human intelligence, such as visual perception, speech recognition, decision-making, and translation between languages.

Deep Learning: One part of the broader family of machine learning methods based on artificial neural networks with representation learning. Learning can be supervised, semi-supervised or unsupervised.

Machine Learning: The study of computer algorithms that improve automatically through experience. It is seen as a subset of artificial intelligence. Machine learning algorithms build a mathematical model based on sample data, known as "training data", to make predictions or decisions without being explicitly programmed to do so.

Software Engineering: The systematic application of engineering approaches to the development of software.

ENDNOTE

[1]   https://www.software-center.se/

Chapter 2
Machine Learning in Cyber–Physical Systems in Industry 4.0

Rania Salih Ahmed
Sudan University of Science and Technology, Sudan

Elmustafa Sayed Ali Ahmed
Red Sea University, Sudan

Rashid A. Saeed
https://orcid.org/0000-0002-9872-081X
Taif University, Saudi Arabia

ABSTRACT

Cyber-physical systems (CPS) have emerged with development of most great applications in the modern world due to their ability to integrate computation, networking, and physical process. CPS and ML applications are widely used in Industry 4.0, military, robotics, and physical security. Development of ML techniques in CPS is strongly linked according to the definition of CPS that states CPS is the mechanism of monitoring and controlling processes using computer-based algorithms. Optimizations adopted with ML in CPS include domain adaptation and fine tuning of current systems, boosting, introducing more safety and robustness by detection and reduction of vulnerabilities, and reducing computation time in time-critical systems. Generally, ML helps CPS to learn and adapt using intelligent models that are generated from training of large-scale data after processing and analysis.

INTRODUCTION

The term Industry 4.0 refers to the fourth industrial revolution that been developed by Germany from 2011. The basic principle of Industry 4.0 is the adoption of the internet or the interconnectivity between all industry components from product manufacturing to user experience. This technology integration involves the Cyber-Physical System CPS field in the development of Industry 4.0. Internet of Things (IoT) is an important element in Industry 4.0 which enables the connectivity between various manu-

DOI: 10.4018/978-1-7998-5101-1.ch002

facturing components in the industrial environment and outside at consumer's experience environment. The development of Industry 4.0 is not only concerned by connectivity solutions but also should offer a self-optimized manufacturing feature that enables using data acquired from consumers while experiencing the products. This self-optimization feature should address the potential problems and issues in both manufacturing and consumer environments. Users satisfaction is considered as one of the whole process, which is dependent on the predictive solutions given by analyzing system data by using Machine Learning algorithms (Jia et al., 2016). For the importance of ML use with CPS in industry 4.0 applications, this chapter provides detail about the concepts of using ML integration to CPS for optimizing industry 4.0 monitoring processes and control.

This chapter is organized as follows. The chapter background is presented and followed by the concept of ML in CPS applications. The chapter provides detail about ML in CPS for industry 4.0, discussing the model architecture and other considerations related to self-aware machines, embedded low latency applications, and fog computing. Also, it provides a brief idea about the classifications of ML for attack detection in CPS 918-920(Košťál and Holubek, 2012). Moreover, the chapter reviews the cyber-physical production system concept, in addition to adaptive and cooperative production systems. The most common use cases of AI in industry 4.0 applications are presented in this chapter, gives a brief review of the possible future research directions related to ML/CPS in industry 4.0.

BACKGROUND

Cyber-physical Systems and industry 4.0 are bonded concepts in the industrial revolution. CPS is the infrastructure of industry 4.0 standard, which describes the new industrial environment proposed in industry 4.0. It involved intelligent senses and controls to approximately all manufacturing processes. This development doesn't consider an ordered pattern of innovations, but a package of functionalities and features are introduced in a parallel way (Jiang, 2017). Where while the development of some technology another one is been developed too. Researchers and developers had found the way along to achieve objectives of industry 4.0 by adopting the ML techniques with the industrial process which adds the intelligence feature. The approach of intelligent manufacturing is been developed from the 70th and 80th of the last century, while the official initiation of ML in industrial manufacturing can be tracked lately to the 90th. Instead of industrial manufacturing, ML has various types of techniques for different types of applications. The most common ML methods include statistical methods, rule induction, genetic algorithm, nearest neighbor clustering, decision trees, and neural networks (Lee, 2018).

The impact of ML was obvious in the development of industry 4.0, as can be also obtained by the revolution of CPS architecture that is standardized by ANSI with the introduction of IEC/ISO 62264, ISA-95 Architecture, then 3C, 5C, and 8C architectures are developed. While this rabid development, revolutionary systems are raised such as intelligent manufacturing systems (IMS), holonic- and agent-based systems. From these developments, the usage of ML in different processes is obtained, as resulted in various developing technologies such as self-aware machines, real-time and low latency embedded applications, fog computing, cooperative manufacturing systems, and context-adaptive autonomous systems. Is also obtained the major role of ML is security and privacy application in industry as in intrusion detection and threats mitigation. A highlighted use cases for ML that led into an industrial artificial intelligence are predictive maintenance, quality assurance, and prediction, optimization of manufacturing process and supply chain, automated management and security, smart assistant, intelligent resource exploration, intelligent research & development tools (Maliszewska and Schlueter, 2019).

MACHINE LEARNING IN CPS

ML algorithms are the main factor behind the AI applications and Data Mining science. ML techniques and methods according to its common applications can be either classification or clustering techniques. The most common ML algorithms used in industrial applications are statistical methods, rule algorithms, nearest neighbor and clustering, decision trees, and neural networks (Loskyll and Schlick, 2013).

- **Statistical Methods** are the most common techniques that used in data analysis and different theoretical calculations on statistics to obtain specific patterns from data records, some of these methods are regression, curve fitting, principal component analysis, and factor analysis (Michel et al, 2019).
- **Rule Induction Method** is an unsupervised learning technique for knowledge discovery for a not readily or clarity available. This technique is mainly used to discover all potentially required data patterns in the database with the required rules, while it can be used to make predictions also.
- **A Genetic Algorithm** is a heuristic search technique that is inspired by the theory of natural evolution. This algorithm considers the natural selection process where to produce the seed of the next population, the fittest individuals are selected.
- **Nearest Neighbor and Clustering**, both of these techniques were first used in machine learning and data mining sciences, also they both works by grouping data samples together according to similarity, the similarity here refers to how that data samples are close to each other in term of specific attributes. Nearest Neighbor and clustering are easy and simple in implementation and has a variety of deployments in different data science-based application (Mohammed et al, 2018).
- **Decision Trees** represent the tree for classification predictive model, where its branches are the classification question, and its leaves are the partitions of the training dataset. The training dataset includes predefined features and their responses. Then the prediction is generated by using a series of sequential decisions, by searching at the predictors and values that are selected in each split of the tree (Mona et al, 2020).
- **Neural Networks** are more complex computer implementations that are developed to simulate human brain learning mechanism, where the predictive model represented by the knowledge gained from learning the NN with training it using a dedicated dataset, and when the predictive model is built with large historical dataset high accuracy solutions can be found to solve the problem. Generally, NN is used as a clustering technique in data mining, where datasets are divided into sub-sets according to a predefined set of attributes, NNs are widely used in applications that required prediction, detection, and recognition of specific patterns (Monostori, 2014).

Machine learning algorithms are increasingly influencing the decisions, and interacting with CPS to provide safety and intelligence CPS applications (see Figure 1). Machine learning and artificial intelligence techniques have been applied to several decision making and control problems in cyber-physical. Smart machines and industrial robots' systems are an example of using human-in-the-loop cyber-physical systems. Industrial robots consist of a console remotely operated by a human or by another machine

(Ahmadi et. al., 2018); an embedded system hosting the robot automated control, and the physical robotic actuators and sensors. Machine learning algorithms help to model human skills and decisions, workflow, environment, and integration of this knowledge into the control and automation of industrial robots. Moreover, it will detect and classify the faults of operations and evaluate the industry workflow (Munirathinam, 2020).

Figure 1. ML in CPS applications

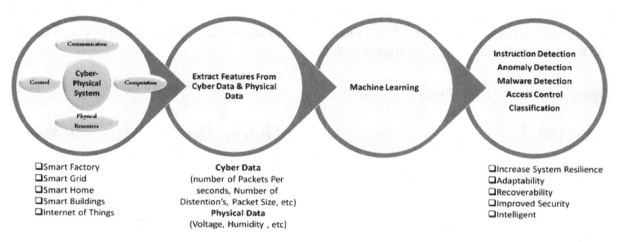

In industry 4.0, especially in sensitive industries, cybersecurity use data science methods to process and analyses a large set of data that can be secret. Machine learning is used for the successful implementation of authentication systems, evaluating the protocol implementation, and assessing the security of human interaction proofs. The use of machine learning in industrial IoT (IIoT) will develop an awareness of what normal network activity looks like and use this as a reference to determine the probability of suspicious activity. By machine learning, the cybersecurity systems can easily analyze the pattern and can attain the knowledge to find countermeasures to avoid similar attacks (O'Donovan et al, 2018).

CPS WITH ML IN INDUSTRY 4.0

Industry 4.0 describes the same technological evolution from the microprocessor embedded manufacturing systems to the emerging CPS, smartly linking the demand of industry manufacture, supply, and services by the internet. The ML with CPS components in industry 4.0 is related to Decentralized Computing, Cloud Computing, and Model-Based Integration. Decentralized Computing which describes computing operations without a central decision-maker enables the self-organizing system, self-adaption, self-management, and self-diagnosis (Nikoloudakis et al, 2017). The private clouds are used in Industry 4.0 to restrict the data to the usage of the industry management section and serve as service linking between the private and public network by data share and access policies and with the interaction of optimized CPS. The integration of the whole-system is related to embedded automation systems which refer to control systems that encompass the control and data domains in addition to modeling the CPS with big data and obtain any profitable secure analysis for prediction (Park and Jeon, 2019).

CPS-ML Architecture

An industry 4.0 based basic architecture represented is the ANSI International Society of Automation ISA-95 architecture that also known as IEC/ISO 62264 standard which is later referred to by 3C (Communication, Computation, and Control) architecture. 3C CPS architecture refers to the integration of the three components of CPS i.e. (human, cyber and physical components), the 3C architecture is considered as the traditional or base architecture where more evolutionary architectures are also introduced i.e. 5C and 8C for smart manufacturing (Ratasich et al, 2019).

Figure 2. Industry 4.0 architecture

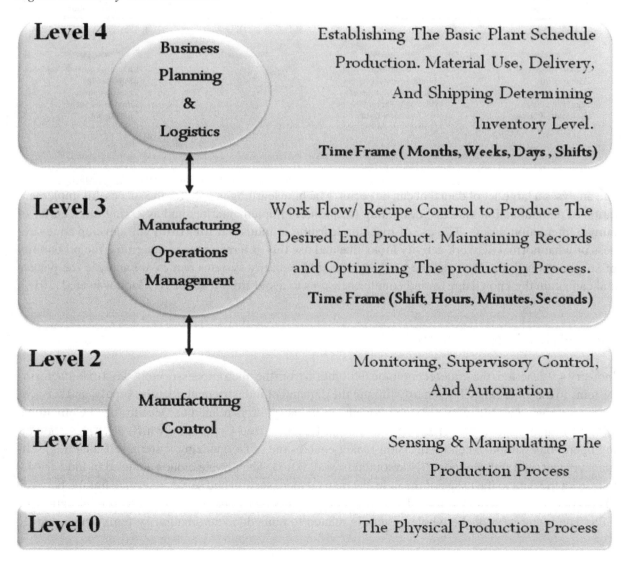

Table 1. Technologies & features in industry 4.0 ISA-95 architecture

Level 2	Supervisory Control and Data Acquisition (SCADA) system, the Distributed Control System (DCS), and the Programmable Logic Controller (PLC).
Level 3	Manufacturing Execution System (MES), Production Information Management System (PIMS), Warehouse Management System (WMS), and Computerized Maintenance Management System (CMMS).
Level 4	Enterprise Resource Planning (ERP), Product Lifecycle Management (PLM), Human Resource Management (HRM), Customer Relationship Management (CRM), and Supply Chain Management (SCM) systems (Ravi, 2017).

In Figure 2, Level 0 and 1 are the basis of manufacturing that is subjected to development at higher levels. The key features and technologies introduced by each evolutionary level in ISA-95 architecture are summarized in Table 1.

An enhancement of 3C CPS architecture is introduced (see Figure 3), by presenting the main interfacing elements i.e. connectors, protocols, sub-elements, human, cyber, and physical parts. Also, the adaptation of sub-interfacing components enhances the standardization level of human, cyber and physical components for Industry 4.0 (Pavic and Dzapo, 2018).

Figure 3. Evolutionary 3C CPS-industry 4.0 architecture

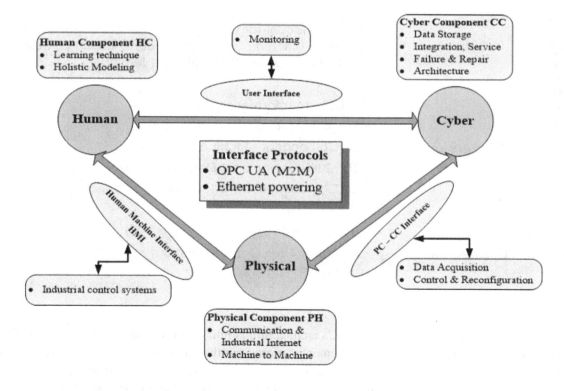

The 5C architecture developed is consisted of 5Cs levels of Connection, Conversion, Cyber, Cognition, and Configuration (Sargolzaei et. al., 2016). This evolutionary architecture adds more functionalities and features and specifies more requirements and capabilities that should be considered as illustrated in Figure 4. A smart connection level is used to accurately acquiring data from machines and system components used in developing CPS applications. The reliable information will be concluded from that acquired data at the conversion level, and the central information hub is represented by the cyber level at the center to maintain all information required by higher levels. At the cognition level, an appropriate display of the obtained knowledge helps superintendents in taking the correct decision. The use of feedback from cyberspace to physical space at the configuration level, achieves self-configuration, self-adjustment, and self-optimization adaptively (Saldaña et, al., 2009).

Figure 4. 5C CPS architecture for self-aware machines in industry 4.0 environment

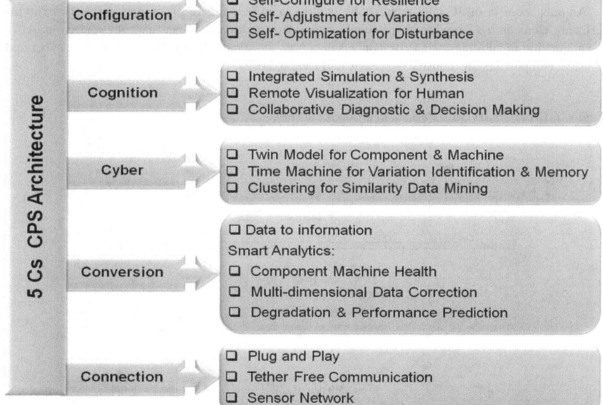

Additionally, an improved version of 5Cs architecture is introduced by adding 3C facets which are Coalition, Customer, and Content. The customer facet concerns the satisfaction of the customer in service order (Settanni et al, 2018), delivery, and quality. Also, in the customer facet, the quantity of demand or order should never affect the quality of service, which will be obtained through direct or indirect feedback. The Content facet concerns of the traceability of all information of the products before and after-sale that can be useful in future inquiries. In Industry 4.0 CPS architectures based ML (see figure 4), the turn of ML becomes obvious, where different types of information and data records will be used from historical production and sale operations to be used either improvement of future production process cycle or avoidance of an issued problem that can affect the quality of product or service. At this point, it comes to mind that the process of manufacturing should pass through four major steps; production, storage, delivery, and rating. Information gathered at the production process will be related to product quality that should be rated by the customer after delivery, this information can be only useful in the production process, but information gathered from the rating process can be related affect the production, storage, and/or delivery processes. This information gathered from different processes should be fed to an appropriate ML technique after performing a proper preprocessing to help in better decision making at that various manufacturing environment processing (Skrop, 2018).

From this literature of Industry 4.0 CPS architectures, the turn of ML becomes obvious, where different types of information and data records will be used from historical production and sale operations to be used either improvement of future production process cycle or avoidance of an issued problem that can affect the quality of product or service (Shu al, 2018). At this point, it comes to mind that the process of manufacturing should pass through four major steps; production, storage, delivery, and rating. Information gathered at the production process will be related to product quality that should be rated by the customer after delivery, this information can be only useful in the production process, but information gathered from the rating process can affect the production, storage, and or delivery processes. This information gathered from different processes should be fed to appropriate ML techniques after performing a proper preprocessing to help in better decision making at that various manufacturing environment processing (Souppaya and Scarfone; 2013).

Self-Aware Machines

There are two dimensions of awareness which are awareness as experience and awareness as self-monitoring. In principle, awareness as experience is obtained when an agent understands the environment and practices it from within in the form of visual content, sensations, thoughts, and so on; as such, consciousness or awareness occurs when a creature can concentrate attention outward toward the environment (Someswararao et al, 2020). Alternatively, self-awareness comes when the agent focuses attention inward and realizes the self in its distinct expressions, like emotions, thoughts, attitudes, sensations, motives, physical attributes, which considerably includes neural fiction of internal experiences. Self-Aware Machines or Machine Self-Awareness is an integration of Artificial Intelligence techniques with machinery or agents to help it to understand its working environment such as in industry and smart applications. Self-Awareness is the ability to distinguish between things by either self-learning or through a pre-defined knowledge. To develop CPS based self-awareness in Industrial Machines, there are five aspects, should be considered, they are (Varshney and Alemzadeh, 2016) (Sravanthi et al, 2019):

- Interaction and perception between machine and environment.
- Actions learning.
- Machine to human interaction.
- Decision making.
- The architecture of cognitive integration of all aspects.

Embedded Low-Latency Applications

The extreme development in electronics applications is highly dependable on embedded systems and scale integration of electronics components as came to Nanotechnology occurrence at these days, this development does only consider the size of equipment but also introduces high computational capabilities that enable the introduction of real-time and low-latency application (Zengen et al, 2019). Technologies behind real-time and low latency applications are complex and developing rabidly, Field Programmable Gate Array (FPGA) is one of those technologies used in real-time applications due to its parallel computation feature upon other beneficial computation features. Virtualization technology with multi-core processors also enables real-time applications as its integration with real-time operating systems (RTOS), (Xia, 2019).

In robotics and industry, an embedded low latency application plays an important role in the integration of modern RTOS high accuracy and computational capabilities are enabled. Computational capabilities are required to perform Digital Signal Processing DSP, memory and storage management, events scheduling, and so on, (Zeinab et al, 2020). Embedded low-latency is deployed in various applications such as smart TVs, GPS navigation systems, smartphones, missile guidance systems, Space exploration (Rovers), automobiles like anti-lock braking system (ABS) and Airbags, industries i.e. assembly robots, road safety systems such as traffic monitoring and collision alert systems) and many other applications (Bagheri et al, 2015).

A Fog Computing

In networking, fog computing is an extension of cloud computing to high enterprise network requirements to enhance frequent services, low latency, and big data analysis. Fog computing occurs with the usage of massive devices of Wireless Sensor Networks WSN and Internet of Things IoT. In Industry 4.0, the use of fog computing is operated in real-time embedded machine learning applications delivery (Xia, 2019). The fog's ability to deliver consistent and reliable cyber-physical interactions for real-time engineering scenarios i.e. industrial control processes is initiated, where cloud computing is found to help challenging technical scenarios that are permissive to accidental failures and uncorrelated by time limitations. However, those factories adopting Industry 4.0 design principles, real-time decision-making, and self-optimizing operations must discover the fog's ingrained advantages more suitable to achieve failure minimization and high-latency communications reduction.

ATTACK DETECTION AND CLASSIFICATION IN CPSs USING ML

ML plays a noticeable role in CPS security and privacy; ML enables classification ability with various types of the classifier which are applied in security to obtain and detect malicious patterns that occur in cyber-attacks. ML application in the security of CPS applies different techniques. Many inclusive surveys of existing cybersecurity solutions for the smart industry system has been introduced. In many studies, authors classify these solutions into four categories; authentication, privacy-preserving, key management systems, and intrusion detection systems. For industry 4.0 applications, intrusion detection systems are important especially with the CPS based on the ML mechanism (Xia, 2019).

Intrusion Detection Systems

According to the machine learning methods used by the intrusion detection system (IDS), IDS solutions are classified into deep learning-based IDS, artificial neural networks-based IDS, support vector machine-based IDS, decision tree-based IDS, rule-based IDS, Bloom filter-based IDS, random forest-based IDS, random subspace learning-based IDS, and deterministic finite automaton-based IDS.

Intrusion/Anomaly Detection and Malware Mitigation

Sometimes, intrusion detection techniques are classified into either anomaly or signature-based. In signature-based intrusion detection, an attack is detected according to a well-known signature within a signature database that predefined for familiar attacks, weakness, and limitation of signature-based detection can be avoided by new attack signatures where an attacker can fabricate new attacks with a new signature. While in anomaly-based intrusion detection an attack is detected by comparing the suspected patterns with the normal network traffic or the baseline in such way any odd or unusual patterns can be detected. Anomaly-based IDSs are better that signature-based ones where new attacks can be detected and even attack tries to manipulate the IDS itself (Xia, 2019).

Malware or malicious software is a piece of codes or small programs or scripts that are written to perform undesired activities in victim machine, solutions for mitigating malware are developed in software and hardware solutions such as firewalls, Anti-viruses, Intrusion Detection System IDS, Intrusion Prevention System IPS, security updates and upgrades of know vulnerabilities, probable security configurations, encryption, content filtering/inspection, application whitelisting, BIOS protection, sandboxing, browser separation, segregation through virtualization, and so on (Alberto Diez-Olivan et al, 2019).

CYBER-PHYSICAL PRODUCTION SYSTEMS (CPPSs)

CPPS is an intelligent manufacturing environment proposed by the German Initiative Industry 4.0 to arrange traditional hierarchical arrangements and cover the demands and necessities for new markets. CPPS is mainly contributed with Smart Factories to efficiently meet the demands of Manufacturing Systems control by including autonomous and collaborative integrated components with the Industrial Internet of Things (IIoT) and other related technologies (Saldivar,2015). An implementation approach of CPRS arises new paradigms based on autonomous intelligent entities called Holon's and Agents, which results in distributed (non-hierarchical) systems where all paradigms include an appropriate communication protocol to connect with other resources in the real-world as a virtual to physical connection. Development of Holon's results in holonic manufacturing system (HMS), and development in agents generates a multi-agent system (MAS), and a hybrid structure with holarchies (multiple Holon's) combined with multiple subagents could make a holonic multi-agent systems (HMAS) scheme (Ceccarelli et al., 2016).

Amplification of CPPSs on integrated process planning and scheduling of industry 4.0 is developed as analyzed the core components of interconnectedness, decentralization, smart machines and products, big data, and cyber-security were identified and afterward their impact on integrated process planning and scheduling. A model for integrating the knowledge management system (KMS) and system integrator(s) in CPPS is also proposed. The developed tacit knowledge management system (TKMS) model includes uniformity of supported operations within the enterprise network by the KMS and by the system integrator of CPSS, Source of Knowledge (SoK) definition from experts within a network, acquiring tacit knowledge acquisition from the defined SoK, tacit knowledge classification, and finally the knowledge base for the network (Mäkitaloet al, 2018).

Intelligent Manufacturing Systems (IMS)

Traditionally, manufacturing systems are the integrated combination of various functions such as design, process planning, production planning, quality assurance, storing and shipment, etc. Several activities are carried out in each of these functions. Intelligent behavior is presented by the machines in all of these functions. This turns the attention of the researcher to "unmanned factories" and there have been quite interesting studies and implementations along this line. IMS is the modern manufacturing technology that enables full functional production process from entries to the outcomes processing with intelligent sensory and control equipment components and with the flexibility to variations in surrounding environment and failure, but of course, with the highest quality and lowest costs constrains. In general, IMS adopts intelligence into all manufacturing system components that include design, process planning, scheduling, control, maintenance, and quality management as illustrated in Figure 5 (Oztemel, 2010).

Roots of CPPS in Manufacturing

Cyber-physical production systems (CPPS), depends on the latest and predictable ongoing developments of computer science (CS), information and communication technologies (ITC), and manufacturing science and technology (MST) may lead to the 4th industrial revolution, frequently noted as Industry 4.0. From the federal ministry of education and research, Germany (BMBF): Industry is on the edges of the fourth industrial revolution. Operated by the Internet, both real and virtual worlds are rising close to each other to take shape of the Internet of Things. The up-next Industrial production will be distinguished by the strong uniqueness and individualization of products under the conditions of highly flexible (large series) production, the extensive integration of customers and business partners in business and value-added processes, and the linking of production and high-quality services leading to so-called hybrid products (Setoya. 2011) H.

Context-Adaptive and Autonomous Systems

A concept of using a context as a tool for adaptive control in autonomous systems is introduced in, by providing a mechanism to represent the context information and apply it to devise a practical methodology to prioritize the operations in an autonomous system. The context-specific information is used as input parameters to the decision support mechanism that controls the operations in an autonomous system. Specification of the context allows it to change dynamically, as the system operations progress. A context that changes dynamically thus provides a modified set of input parameters to the operations control mechanism, so that the forward-looking behavior of the autonomous system can be modulated adaptively. The context-based adaptive control (CBAC) is an additional module, as shown in Figure 6, which uses the context information to provide a more agile control in the behavior of the autonomous system (Alberto Diez-Olivan et al, 2019).

Figure 5. Intelligent manufacturing systems aspects

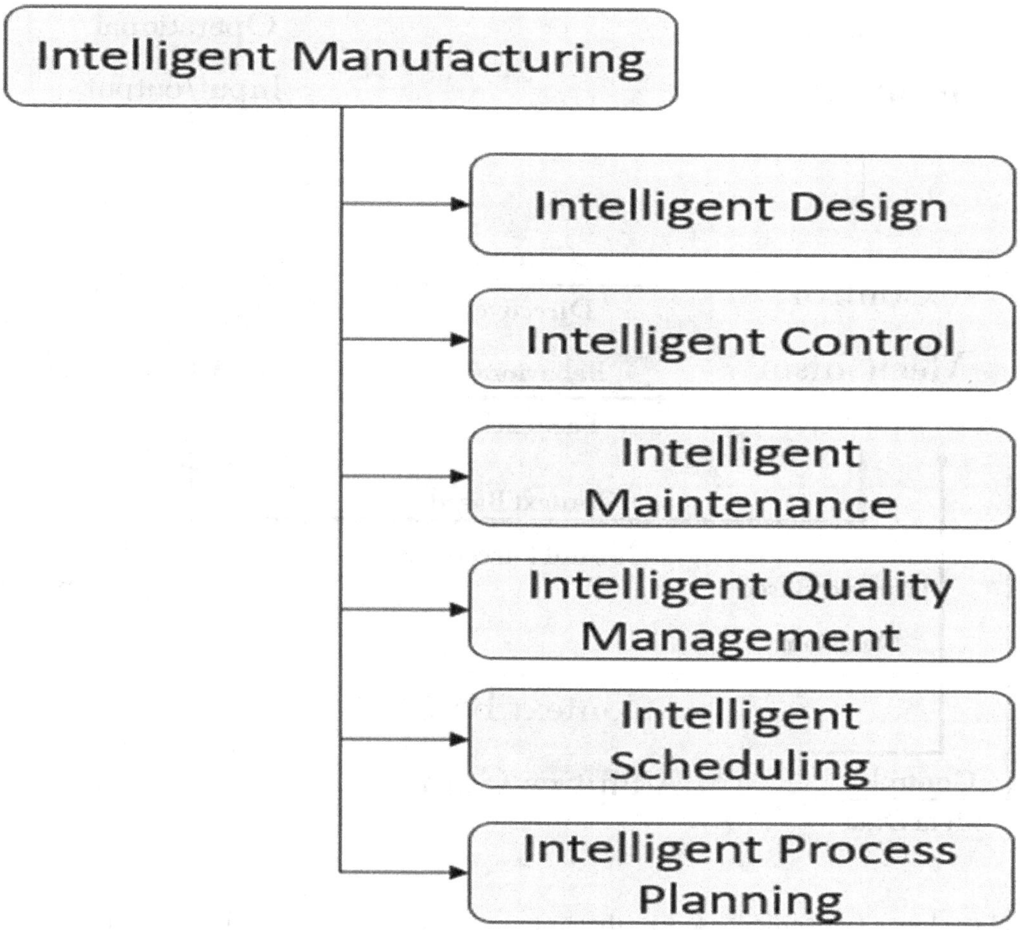

Cooperative Production Systems

A cooperative production system model can be described as a set of producers providing products to their customers and a constrained external customer are also available but they have an agreement states that they only buying products by a lower price only if a desired service quality level is guaranteed. If producers could not provide the external customers required service level and at the presented price on their own, they collaborate in a cooperative network (Meissner & Aurich,2019). Cooperation in a network that uses a dynamic routing policy with the on-line inventory information of the network members brings significant benefits especially when the requested service level is high. Using a dynamic routing policy that utilizes the on-line inventory information in a cooperative network leads to a higher improvement for a network with heterogeneous members compared to a network with homogeneous members, since the dynamic routing policy can react to changes in the inventory levels of heterogeneous producers effectively (Al-Sakib et al., 2014).

CPS and CPPS are expected to make industry 4.0 technology more robustness, autonomy, self-organization, self-maintenance, self-repair, transparency, predictability, efficiency, interoperability,

Figure 6. A context-based adaptive control (CBAC)

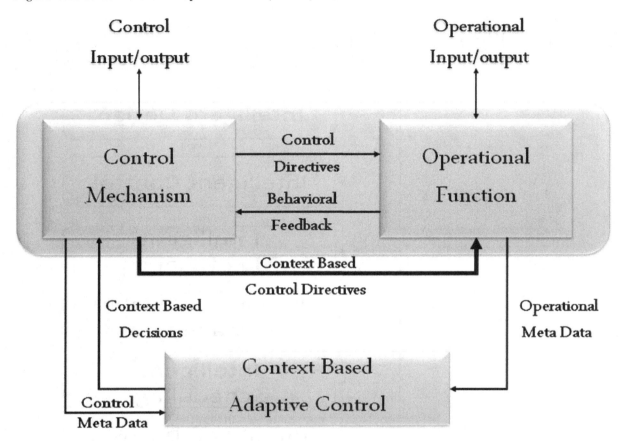

and global tracking. To handle these specifications, cyber-physical production systems must provide a means of intelligence to enable cooperative control, taking the advantages of AI in multi-agent systems (MAS), complex adaptive systems (CAS), emergent systems, sensor networks, and data mining. Co-operative production systems achieve efficient algorithms for consensus-seeking, cooperative learning, and distributed detection.

Fault Detection in Vehicular CPS (VCPSS)

A complex system obtained from the involvement of vehicular ad-hoc network (VANET) and the cooperative form model of Vehicles on the road is referred to by the vehicular CPS (VCPSs), a typical application scenario of a platoon-based VCPS presented in Figure 7. Where the On-Board Units (OBU) and Road Side Units (RSU) are components of the VANET system architecture used for vehicle to vehicle (V2V) communication protocol (Bagheri and Kao, 2015).

Recently, the robustness concept of cyber-physical systems-of-systems (CPSoS) is extended to consider also the security issues in CPS as well. Robustness is the dependability concerning external faults including malicious external actions (Amal et. al., 2015). Types of faults according to the CPS layers architecture are described as follows;

Figure 7. A typical application scenario of a VCPS

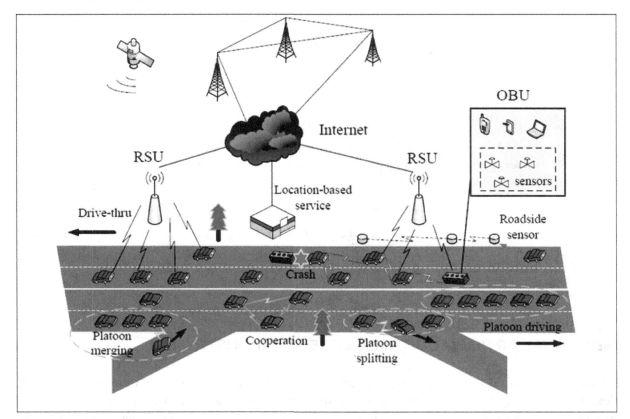

- **Physical Faults**: Broken connector, i.e. due to aging effects, radiation noise, signal interference, power transients, power down or short generated by the attacker, denial of service by jamming
- **Development Faults**: related to hardware production defect or design error, a software bug in program or data for reasons of memory leaks or wrong set of parameters, or any unforeseen circumstances of the system.
- **Interaction Faults**: related to, input mistake, message collision, spoofing, modifying information with viruses, and denial of service by flooding, hacked sensor producing inaccurate data causing incorrect control decisions and actuator actions (Amal et. al., 2016).
- **Permanent Faults**: represents design faults, broken connectors or noise, ground voltage due to short, logic bomb carried by virus or crashing system.
- **Transient Faults**: power transients, input mistake, intrusion attempt via inalienability, heating rams to trigger memory error

Anomaly-based detection refers to an identification method for abnormal patterns or behavior caused by a fault, a random failure, a design error, or an intruder. Figure 8 shows the classification of detection mechanisms depending on the application or type of the mechanism (Avizienis et, al., 2004).

Figure 8. Taxonomy of methods for fault detection

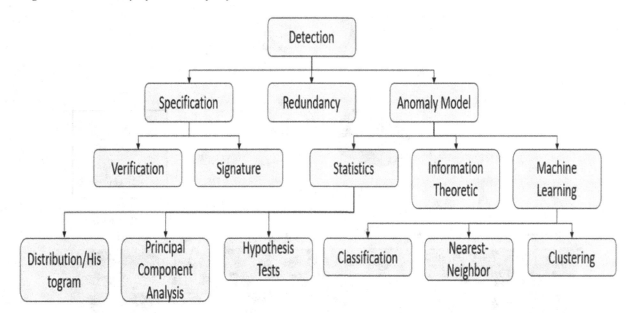

INDUSTRIAL ARTIFICIAL INTELLIGENCE FOR INDUSTRY 4.0

Implementation of AI in industrial environments requires a systematic structure to realize smart and flexible industrial systems and enable them to become self-organizing, on-demand, and fault resolvable. Architecture for Industrial Artificial Intelligence Systems (IAIS) depends on the integration of AI in industry and turns the lights to ML (Awad, 2018). ML application in IAIS opens the opportunity for data science applied strategies and its deployment in industry. The most common use cases for AI in industry 4.0 are as follow:

- **Predictive Maintenance**: Makes use of advanced Machine Learning analytics to define the situation of a single asset or a set of assets i.e. a factory (Balasingham, 2016).
- **Quality Inspection and Assurance**: A quality control system based on a deep learning-enabled system can be fully integrated into the flow of the final assembly process, which can release the testing area needed in a controlled environment.
- **Manufacturing Process Optimization**: Replication of monotonous human tasks by autonomous assets in the manufacturing process, with data mining techniques such as reinforcement learning technique achieves sufficient accuracy (Caiza, 2020).
- **Supply Chain Optimization**: Using AI tools to develop predictive inventory management influences predictive analytics for multiple tasks related to stocking or inventory as to decrease inventory planning time, reduce costs of inventory, repairmen optimization, and identifying optimal reorder points (Chatila et al, 2018).
- **AI-driven Cyber Security & Privacy**: Usage of AI and ML in cybersecurity has a wide range of benefits such as threats and attacks detection and prevention, real-time infrastructure observa-

tion, network traffic analysis, endpoint detection and response, malware sandboxes, etc (Chen et al, 2017).

- **Automated Physical Security**: Real-time monitoring of manufacturing sites or workers is required for observation and automatic physical threat detection and/or potential safety hazards.
- **Automated Data Management**: AI helps industrial companies to employ data management solutions that perform data acquisition, data filtering, data cleaning, and integration tasks in real-time.
- **Smart Assistants:** AI integrates smart assistants in manufacturing settings (e.g. Voice assistant) with real-time industrial surveillance and control systems allows workers to perform actions without coding the distinct commands or printing long technical reports (Chella et. al., 2020).
- **AI-driven Research and Development**: Digital twins and simulations often complement the AI techniques by letting software autonomously develop a lot of various designs in a short time with a given set of predefined constraints, the optimal design can be chosen afterward (Choudhary and Odubiyi, 2004).
- **Autonomous Resource Exploration**: AI can be especially useful in the analysis and processing of a large amount of data to detect the optimal point for resource extraction, especially in mining and discovering in Oil & Gas industries.

Instead of previously pointed use cases of AI in industrial, there is also a package of complementary functions and features that are enabled by AI especially in accessibility and other modern manufacturing luxuries (Elmustafa, Elatif, 2015).

FUTURE RESEARCH DIRECTIONS

Industry 4.0 or the Industrial Internet of Things is recently being determined by disruptive revolutions that potentials to bring the limitless new value of opportunities throughout all major industry sectors that continuous interaction with different and a large number of devices. The Cyber-Physical System (CPS) is vital for the intelligent implementing of Industry 4.0 (Dehaene, et al, 2017). However, present internet protocols are overwhelmed by the intrusion, cybersecurity, and data privacy issues that would cause key challenges and barriers for Industry 4.0 to be adopted and industrialized. Artificial Intelligent and deep learning for a data traffic analysis for early intrusion detection and security threats are problematic challenges and should be one of the hot topics for future works, (Elmustafa and Saeed, 2014).

The web-based design, modeling, and implementation of machine learning in cyber-physical systems in Industry 4.0 are one of the simplicity of industry operation concerns. The web-based design makes simple for the convolutional neural network (CNN), support vector regression (SVR), support vector classification (SVC), and deep neural network (DNN) modeling (Ferrag, et al, 2020). The design can simplify modeling hyperparameters, un-trainable parameters, hyperparameters optimization and reproducibility, and hyper-heuristics. Integration of the industrial production line, logistics, and facilities sections into smart industry 4.0 cyber-physical systems of system (CPSoS) scheme with a cloud-based platform is needed to be discussed to allow adaptive, seamless, and real-time several appliances interaction. The study should address precise direction, key mechanisms, potential issues, and problematic challenges of the future machine learning (ML) and reinforcement learning algorithms (Ferrag et al, 2020).

Integration of digital twin (DT) and deep learning is recently raised in the research arena that due to its vital influences on glue the gap between the physical and cyber systems, where its global market has been expected to scope $26.07 billion by 2025, (Oztemel et al, 2018). The growing adoption of cyber-physical systems (CPS), IoT, big data analytics, and fog computing in industry 4.0 systems have cemented the road for low cost, simplicity, and execution of DT. Successful implementation of DT in industry 4.0 with the support of deep learning would improve transparency, collaboration, elasticity, pliability, time to market, scalability, and production competence (Gilberto et al, 2019). Machine learning in DT for cyber and physical systems in industry 4.0 realizes of intelligent industry and improves cooperative and independent interactions between sensors, network, and fog/cloud computing across appliances properties (Giang Nguyen et al, 2019).

Industry 4.0 embraces IoT, AI, cyber-physical systems, Machine learning, and cognitive computing which enables the startups for smart factories. An experimental and prototype use case for industry 4.0, artificial intelligence (AI), and machine-learning to pave the way for vast rebellion for industrial companies with different future opportunities (Garcíaet al, 2018). The use cases with a list of operations and steps or event-driven are typically defining the flow and procedures between designs, models, and real systems to accomplish an objective. The use case of the smart industry and manufacturing 4.0 can be implemented where a large amount of information can be collected, measured, and analyzed to enhance the manufacturing process (Honegger and Pollefeys, 2014).

In close future machine learning (ML) in cyber-physical systems (CPS) Industry 4.0 rebellion, cybersecurity will be on one of the vital issues. Attackers would be one of the serious and problematic challenges that affect the system performance, which can easily harm physical and cyberspace. For example, an attacker can control nuclear facilities or medical device remotely (Košťál and Holubek,2012), by monitoring and analyzing data traffic. Such serious concerns should be highlighted shortly addressing state-of-the-art for trust, cryptography, integrity algorithms, and machine learning in cybersecurity. ABI research presented by (M. Michel et al, 2019) forecasts that security threats for industry 4.0 big data may cost $96 billion by 2021. The integration of machine learning and cybersecurity in CPS systems should be one of the hot topics for research in the future direction. Modern cybersecurity threats like malware detection, intrusion detection, and data leakage can't be solved by using mathematical models alone.

Intrusion Detection Systems (IDS) and Intrusion Prevention Systems (IPS) are the most common security mechanisms used for CPS in networking and communication applications. Artificial intelligence is considered a vital player in IDS and IPS and is largely considered as the future direction of both technologies in CPS. One of the creative features of AI, that it can be implemented to real-time applications and CPS traffic analysis, especially to network traffic data analysis for financial and banking sectors and services (Alfredo, 2015).

CONCLUSION

Machine Learning Algorithms has a sufficient role in industry 4.0 by deploying classification, clustering, and other ML methods to provide intelligent behavior to manufacturing systems. In this chapter, CPS with ML components in industry 4.0 is discussed and further study is performed to obtain ML correlation within different CPS architectures proposed. Also, relative technologies that are introduced while the development of CPS and Industry 4.0 are discussed, such technologies are Self-Aware Machines, Embedded Low-Latency Applications, and A fog Computing. Nevertheless, it's obtained the role of ML in the security and privacy of CPSs specifically in intrusion and threat detection and mitigation as applied in intrusion detection and prevention systems. The concept of CPS industrial application is referred to by Cyber-Physical Production Systems (CPPSs) is further discussed historically, in addition to various technologies and development contributed with CPPS such as Intelligent Manufacturing Systems (IMS) Context-Adaptive and Autonomous Systems, Cooperative Production Systems, and Fault Detection in vehicular CPS (VCPSs). Finally, Industrial Artificial Intelligence for industry 4.0 is determined with the highlighted use case of AI in industry 4.0.

REFERENCES

Ahmadi, A., Sodhro, A., Cherifi, C., Cheutet, V., & Ouzrout, Y. (2018). Evolution of 3C Cyber-Physical Systems Architecture for Industry 4.0. *Proceedings of SOHOMA*, 448-459.

Ahmed & Elatif. (2015). Network Denial of Service Threat Security on Cloud Computing A Survey. International Journal of Scientific Research in Science, Engineering and Technology, 1(5).

Ahmed & Saeed. (2014). A Survey of Big Data Cloud Computing Security. *International Journal of Computer Science and Software Engineering*, 3(1).

Avizienis, A., Laprie, J., Randell, B., & Landwehr, C. (2004). Basic concepts and taxonomy of dependable and secure computing. EEE Transactions on Dependable and Secure Computing, 1(1), 11–33. doi:10.1109/TDSC.2004.2

Awad, A. I. (2018). Introduction to information security foundations and applications. In *Information Security: Foundations, Technologies and Applications*. IET.

Bagheri, B., Yang, S., Kao, H.-A., & Lee, J. (2015). Cyber-physical Systems Architecture for Self-Aware Machines in Industry 4.0 Environment. IFAC-PapersOnLine, 48(3), 1622–1627. doi:10.1016/j.ifacol.2015.06.318

Balasingham, K. (2016). Industry 4.0: Securing the Future for German Manufacturing Companies. University of Twente. School of Management and Governance Business Administration.

Caiza, G., Saeteros, M., Oñate, W., & Garcia, M. (2020). Fog computing at industrial level, architecture, latency, energy, and security: A review. *Heliyon (London)*, 6(4), e03706. doi:10.1016/j.heliyon.2020.e03706 PubMed

Ceccarelli, A., Bondavalli, A., Froemel, B., Hoeftberger, O., & Kopetz, H. (2016). Basic Concepts on Systems of Systems. In *Cyber-Physical Systems of Systems: Foundations – A Conceptual Model and Some Derivations: The AMADEOS Legacy*. Springer International Publishing.

Chatila, R., Renaudo, E., Andries, M., & Chavez-Garcia, R.-O. (2018). Toward Self-Aware Robots. Frontiers in Robotics and AI, 5.

Chella, A., Pipitone, A., Morin, A., & Racy, F. (2020). Developing Self-Awareness in Robots via Inner Speech. Frontiers in Robotics and AI, 7.

Chen, Y., Sun, E., & Zhang, Y. (2017). Joint optimization of transmission and processing delay in fog computing access networks. *9th International Conference on Advanced Infocomm Technology (ICAIT)*, 155-158.

Choudhary, A., & Odubiyi, J. (2004). Context-based adaptive control in autonomous systems. *Proceedings from the Fifth Annual IEEE SMC Information Assurance Workshop.*

Dehaene, S., Lau, H., & Kouider, S. (2017). What is consciousness, and could machines have it? *Science, 358,* 486–492.

Diez-Olivan, A., Del Ser, J., Galar, D., & Sierra, B. (2019). Data Fusion and Machine Learning for Industrial Prognosis: Trends and Perspectives towards Industry 4.0. *Information Fusion, 50,* 92–111. doi:10.1016/j.inffus.2018.10.005

Eltahir, Saeed, Mukherjee, & Hasan. (2016). Evaluation and Analysis of an Enhanced Hybrid Wireless Mesh Protocol for Vehicular Ad-hoc Network. *EURASIP Journal on Wireless Communications and Networking.*

Eltahir & Saeed. (2015). Performance Evaluation of an Enhanced Hybrid Wireless Mesh Protocol (E-HWMP) Protocol for VANET. *International Conference on Computing, Control, Networking, Electronics and Embedded Systems Engineering (ICCNEEE),* 95 – 100.

Jr, F. (2019). A comprehensive survey on network anomaly detection. In *Telecommunication Systems: Modelling, Analysis, Design and Management.* Springer.

Ferrag, M. A., Babaghayou, M., & Yazici, M. A. (2020). Cyber security for fog-based smart grid SCADA systems: Solutions and challenges. Journal of Information Security and Applications, 52.

Ferrag, M. A., Maglaras, L., Moschoyiannis, S., & Janicke, H. (2020). Deep learning for cyber security intrusion detection: Approaches, datasets, and comparative study. Journal of Information Security and Applications, 50.

García, M. V., Irisarri, E., Pérez, F., Marcos, M., & Estevez, E. (2018). From ISA 88/95 meta-models to an OPC UA-based development tool for CPPS under IEC 61499. 2018 14th IEEE International Workshop on Factory Communication Systems (WFCS), 1-9.

Honegger, D., Oleynikova, H., & Pollefeys, M. (2014). Real-time and low latency embedded computer vision hardware based on a combination of FPGA and mobile CPU. IEEE/RSJ International Conference on Intelligent Robots and Systems, 4930-4935. doi:10.1109/IROS.2014.6943263

Jia, D., Lu, K., Wang, J., Zhang, X., & Shen, X. (2016). A Survey on Platoon-Based Vehicular Cyber-Physical Systems. *IEEE Communications Surveys and Tutorials, 18*(1), 263–284. doi:10.1109/COMST.2015.2410831

Jiang, J. (2017). An improved Cyber-Physical Systems architecture for Industry 4.0 smart factories. International Conference on Applied System Innovation (ICASI), 918-920. doi:10.1109/ICASI.2017.7988589

Nguyen, G., Dlugolinsky, S., Bobák, M., Tran, V., López García, Á., Heredia, I., ... Hluchý, L. (2019). Machine Learning and Deep Learning frameworks and libraries for large-scale data mining: A survey. *Artificial Intelligence Review, 52*(1), 77–124. doi:10.1007/s10462-018-09679-z

Oztemel, E. (2018). Literature review of Industry 4.0 and related technologies. *Journal of Intelligent Manufacturing.*

Saldivar. (2015). Industry 4.0 with Cyber-Physical Integration:A Design and Manufacture Perspective. 21st International Conference on Automation & Computing, 11-12. doi:10.1016/j.jisa.2020.102500

von Zengen. (2019). *A Communication Architecture for Cooperative Networked Cyber-Physical Systems. In 16th IEEE Annual Consumer Communications & Networking Conference.* CCNC.

Košťál, P., & Holubek, R. (2012). The Intelligent Manufacturing Systems. *Advanced Science Letters*, ●●●, 19.

Varshney & Alemzadeh. (2016). On the Safety of Machine Learning:Cyber-Physical Systems, Decision Sciences, and Data Products. arXiv.org

Ahmed, Z. E., Saeed, R. A., Ghopade, S. N., & Mukherjee, A. (2020). Energy Optimization in LPWANs by using Heuristic Techniques. In B. S. Chaudhari & M. Zennaro (Eds.), *LPWAN Technologies for IoT and M2MApplications.* Elsevier., doi:10.1016/B978-0-12-818880-4.00011-9.

Hassan, M. B., Ali, E. S., Mokhtar, R. A., Saeed, R. A., & Chaudhari, B. S. (2020). NB-IoT: Concepts, Applications, and Deployment Challenges. In B. S. Chaudhari & M. Zennaro (Eds.), *LPWAN Technologies for IoT and M2MApplications.* Elsevier., doi:10.1016/B978-0-12-818880-4.00006-5.

Lee, J., Bagheri, B., & Kao, H.-A. (2015). A Cyber-Physical Systems architecture for Industry 4.0-based manufacturing systems. Manufacturing Letters, 3, 18–23. doi:10.1016/j.mfglet.2014.12.001

Lee, J., Davari, H., Singh, J., & Pandhare, V. (2018). Industrial Artificial Intelligence for industry 4.0-based manufacturing systems. Manufacturing Letters, 18, 20–23. doi:10.1016/j.mfglet.2018.09.002

Loskyll, M., & Schlick, J. (2013). Cyber physical production systems. *Automatisierungstechnik*, *61*, 690–699.

Mäkitalo, N., Nocera, F., Mongiello, M., & Bistarelli, S. (2018). Architecting the Web of Things for the fog computing era. *IET Software*, *12*(5), 381–389. doi:10.1049/iet-sen.2017.0350

Meissner, H., & Aurich, J. C. (2019). Implications of Cyber-Physical Production Systems on Integrated Process Planning and Scheduling. Procedia Manufacturing, 28, 167–173. doi:10.1016/j.promfg.2018.12.027

Michel, M., Beck, D., Block, N., Blumenfeld, H., Brown, R., Carmel, D., ... Yoshida, M. (2019). Opportunities and challenges for a maturing science of consciousness. *Nature Human Behaviour*, *3*(2), 104–107. doi:10.1038/s41562-019-0531-8 PubMed

Mohammed, M. (2018). *Requirements of the Smart Factory System: A Survey and Perspective.* MDPI Machines Journal.

Monostori, L. (2014). Cyber-physical Production Systems: Roots, Expectations and R&D Challenges. Procedia CIRP, 17, 9–13. doi:10.1016/j.procir.2014.03.115

Munirathinam, S. (2020). Industry 4.0: Industrial Internet of Things (IIOT). *Advances in Computers*, *117*(1), 129–164.

Nikoloudakis, Y., Panagiotakis, S., Markakis, E., Mastorakis, G., Mavromoustakis, C. X., & Pallis, E. (2017). Towards a FOG-enabled navigation system with advanced cross-layer management features and IoT equipment. In Cloud and Fog Computing in 5G Mobile Networks: Emerging advances and applications. Institution of Engineering and Technology.

O'Donovan, P., Gallagher, C., Bruton, K., & O'Sullivan, D. T. J. (2018). A fog computing industrial cyber-physical system for embedded low-latency machine learning Industry 4.0 applications. Manufacturing Letters, 15, 139–142. doi:10.1016/j.mfglet.2018.01.005

Oztemel, E. (2010). Intelligent Manufacturing Systems. In *Artificial Intelligence Techniques for Networked Manufacturing Enterprises Management*. Springer London.

Park, H. M., & Jeon, J. W. (2019). OPC UA based Universal Edge Gateway for Legacy Equipment. IEEE 17th International Conference on Industrial Informatics (INDIN), 1002-1007. doi:10.1109/INDIN41052.2019.8972187

Patalas Maliszewska, J., & Schlueter, N. (2019). Model of a Knowledge Management for System Integrator(s) of Cyber-Physical Production Systems (CPPS). International Scientific-Technical Conference Manufacturing, 92-103. doi:10.1007/978-3-030-18715-6_8

Pavic, I., & Dzapo, H. (2018). Virtualization in multicore real-time embedded systems for improvement of interrupt latency. 41st International Convention on Information and Communication Technology, Electronics and Microelectronics (MIPRO), 1405-1410. doi:10.23919/MIPRO.2018.8400253

Ratasich, D., Khalid, F., Geißler, F., Grosu, R., Shafique, M., & Bartocci, E. (2019). A Roadmap Toward the Resilient Internet of Things for Cyber-Physical Systems. *IEEE Access : Practical Innovations, Open Solutions*, 7, 13260–13283. doi:10.1109/ACCESS.2019.2891969

Ravi. (2017). Embedded System and Its Real Time Applications. Available: https://www.electronicshub.org/embedded-system-real-time-applications/

Saldaña, A., Vila, C., Rodríguez, C. A., Ahuett, H., & Siller, H. R. (2009). Cooperative Analysis of Production Systems with Simulation Techniques. In Cooperative Design (pp. 27–31). Berlin: Visualization, and Engineering. doi:10.1007/978-3-642-04265-2_4

Sargolzaei, A., Crane, C. D., Abbaspour, A., & Noei, S. (2016). A Machine Learning Approach for Fault Detection in Vehicular Cyber-Physical Systems. 15th IEEE International Conference on Machine Learning and Applications (ICMLA), 636-640. doi:10.1109/ICMLA.2016.0112

Setoya. (2011). History and review of the IMS (Intelligent Manufacturing System). IEEE International Conference on Mechatronics and Automation.

Settanni, G., Skopik, F., Karaj, A., Wurzenberger, M., & Fiedler, R. (2018). Protecting cyber physical production systems using anomaly detection to enable self-adaptation. IEEE Industrial Cyber-Physical Systems (ICPS), 173-180.

Skrop, A. (2018). Industry 4.0 - Challenges in Industrial Artificial Intelligence, International Scientific Conference on Tourism and Security. International Scientific Conference on Tourism and Security.

Someswararao, C., Reddy, S., & Murthy, K. (2020). Cyber-Physical System—An Overview. In Smart Intelligent Computing and Applications (pp. 489–497). Springer. doi:10.1007/978-981-32-9690-9_54

Souppaya, M., & Scarfone, K. (2013). Guide to Malware Incident Prevention and Handling for Desktops and Laptops. NIST Special Publication 800-83 Revision 1.

Sravanthi, K. (2019). Cyber Physical Systems: The Role of Machine Learning and Cyber Security in Present and Future. Computer Reviews Journal, 4.

Tay. (2018). An Overview of Industry 4.0: Definition, Components, and Government Initiatives. Journal of Advanced Research in Dynamical and Control Systems.

Xia, X., Liu, C., Wang, H., & Han, Z. (2019). *A Design of Cyber-Physical System Architecture for Smart City*. Recent Trends in Intelligent Computing, Communication and Devices.

KEY TERMS AND DEFINITIONS

ANSI: Stands for, American National Standards Institute. It is a primary organization for fostering the development of technology standards in the United States works with industry groups and is the U.S. member of the International Organization for Standardization (ISO) and the International Electrotechnical Commission (IEC).

Digital Twin (DT): Meant as the virtual and computerized counterpart of a physical system that can be used to simulate it for various purposes, exploiting a real-time synchronization of the sensed data coming from the field; such synchronization is possible thanks to the enabling technologies of Industry 4.0.

Holonic-Based Systems: Is a manufacturing system (MS) that is distributive controlled according to the holonic system paradigm. Holon's means, manufacturing system components are modeled as autonomous, collaborative entities (agents).

IEC/ISO 62264: Describes the manufacturing operations management domain (Level 3) and its activities, and the interface content and associated transactions within Level 3. It defines transactions in terms of information exchanges between applications performing business and manufacturing activities.

Intelligent Manufacturing Systems: Name of an international organization devoted to developing the next generation of manufacturing and processing technologies. The organization provides support for projects consistent with the protection of intellectual property rights.

ISA-95 Architecture: Is the international standard for the integration of enterprise and control systems. It was developed to be applied in all industries, and all sorts of processes.it provides consistent terminology for supplier and manufacturer communications, consistent information models, and consistent operations models which is a foundation for clarifying application functionality and how information is to be used.

Source of Knowledge (SoK): Is the leading educational content capture and distribution company, for the IT industry, focusing on software, hardware, and firmware user groups, in addition to computer security groups.

Chapter 3
Explainable Artificial Intelligence (xAI) Approaches and Deep Meta-Learning Models for Cyber-Physical Systems

Evren Daglarli

iD https://orcid.org/0000-0002-8754-9527

Istanbul Technical University, Turkey

ABSTRACT

Today, the effects of promising technologies such as explainable artificial intelligence (xAI) and meta-learning (ML) on the internet of things (IoT) and the cyber-physical systems (CPS), which are important components of Industry 4.0, are increasingly intensified. However, there are important shortcomings that current deep learning models are currently inadequate. These artificial neural network based models are black box models that generalize the data transmitted to it and learn from the data. Therefore, the relational link between input and output is not observable. For these reasons, it is necessary to make serious efforts on the explanability and interpretability of black box models. In the near future, the integration of explainable artificial intelligence and meta-learning approaches to cyber-physical systems will have effects on a high level of virtualization and simulation infrastructure, real-time supply chain, cyber factories with smart machines communicating over the internet, maximizing production efficiency, analysis of service quality and competition level.

DOI: 10.4018/978-1-7998-5101-1.ch003

INTRODUCTION

The principle of "interoperability" in Industry 4.0 design is the most important feature that can be provided by all components (Alcaraz & Lopez, 2020). Thanks to the virtual office and remote access facilities, time, and space constraints are eliminated for doing business together. The principles of "virtualization" and "dissemination of responsibility" are realized through Cyber-Physical Systems (CPS) and Smart factories (Waschull, Bokhorst, Molleman, & Wortmann, 2020). The future of the business world, namely organizational development, management styles, and organizational charts, infrastructure changes, employee qualifications and perceptions, labor cost / financial processes, customer profiles, behaviors, and demands will be shaped by Cyber-Physical Systems (CPS) embodied with new generation artificial intelligence approaches (Mittal & Tolk, 2020).

The fourth version of the industrial revolution is quite different from all other stages. While the first industrial revolution was based on the production mechanism working with water and steam power, it was followed by the transition to mass production with the help of the second industrial revolution, electrical energy. Later, the third industrial revolution, the digital revolution, was realized and electronic use was increased. However, version 4.0 is expressed as a project to encourage the existing industry towards computerization and to equip it with high technology. With this project, machines will be able to understand what is happening around them and communicate with each other via internet protocols (Yin, Kaynak, & Karimi, 2020). To save resources in industrial environments, an integrated receiver/ actuator equipment, communication between machines, and active smart product memories will be expanded with new optimization methods (Delicato, 2020). In other words, industry 4.0, together with the Internet of Things (IoT) and cyber-physical systems (CPS), aims to transfer this new technology to business models, product production chains, and industry by combining artificial intelligence, machine learning, and embedded system technology with smart product production processes (Shishvan, Zois and Soyata, 2020).

The explainable artificial intelligence - XAI is one of the examination points that has been captivating as of late (Dağlarli, 2020). Today, regardless of whether we are toward the start of understanding this kind of model, the investigations that show fascinating outcomes about this issue are getting an increasingly serious topic. Sooner rather than later, it is anticipated that there will be years when the interpretability of artificial consciousness and meta-learning models is now and again investigated (Adadi and Berrada, 2018). It is believed to be an answer to defeat limitations in old-style deep learning techniques.

In traditional deep learning methodologies, we much of the time experience deep learning strategies accessible today. At present, in classic deep learning techniques, input information and target (class) data can be prepared with the elite and tried with new information input (Došilović, Brčić, and Hlupić, 2018). These deep learning strategies can yield exceptionally viable outcomes as per the informational index size, informational collection quality, the techniques utilized in include extraction, the hyper boundary set utilized in deep learning models, the enactment capacities, and the improvement calculations (Center et al., 2006). Numerous layers in a profound system permit it to perceive things at various degrees of deliberation. For instance, in a structure intended to perceive hounds, the lower layers perceive basic things, for example, diagrams or shading; the upper layers perceive increasingly complex things like hiding or eyes, and the upper layers characterize them all as a canine. A similar methodology can be applied to different information sources that lead a machine to educate itself. For instance, it tends to be effortlessly applied to the sounds that make up the words in the discourse, the letters, and words that structure the sentences in the content, or the controlling developments required to drive.

In any case, there are significant weaknesses that current deep learning models are presently lacking (Schnack, 2020). For deep learning, immense informational indexes are expected to prepare on, and these informational collections must be comprehensive/fair-minded, and of good quality (Huang et al., 2020). Also, conventional deep learning requires a ton of time to prepare models for fulfilling their motivation with an allowable measure of precision and significance (Malik, 2020). Albeit deep learning is self-sufficient, it is exceptionally vulnerable to mistakes. Expect that a calculation is prepared with informational collections sufficiently little to not be comprehensive (Schnack, 2020). The model prepared by along these lines causes superfluous reactions (one-sided forecasts originating from a one-sided preparing set) being shown to clients (Ahuja R., Chug, Gupta, Ahuja P., and Kohli, 2020). One of the most significant issues in deep learning models is straightforwardness and interpretability (Mill operator, 2019). These artificial neural network-based models are discovery models that sum up the information transmitted to it and gain from the information. Along these lines, the social connection among info and yield isn't perceptible (Samek, Wiegand, and Müller, 2017). At the end of the day, when you get yield information against the info information, the deep learning model can't give the data to which reason the yield is produced. The client can't completely get a handle on the inner elements of these models and can't discover answers to address why and how the models produce the appropriate responses (Fernandez, 2019). This circumstance makes challenges in the application zones of these models from numerous perspectives. For instance, you halted a taxi and jumped on it. The driver is such a driver, that when he takes you to your goal, he turns right, turns left, and attempts to get you on a particular course then you expect, however when you inquire as to why he did as such, he can't offer you a good response. Okay, be apprehensive? On the off chance that there is no issue for you, you can ride a self-sufficient driverless vehicle. As another model, when you go to the specialist, the specialist you send your grumbling requests tests and when you have those tests and send it to the specialist, the specialist mentions to you what your sickness is. Even though he says his treatment, he doesn't give logical data about the reason for your sickness. For this situation, questions stay about what caused the illness and you would not be happy with the specialist. This is a significant unsolved in deep learning algorithms and artificial neural network models.

The explainable artificial intelligence (XAI) approach may be regarded as a zone at the crossing point of a few zones (Dağlarli, 2020). One of these regions is the end client clarification area that incorporates sociologies. This zone gives computerized reasoning to increase psychological capacities. Another territory is the human-machine interface, where it can show the capacity to clarify. Since logical reasoning needs elevated level cooperation with the client. Lastly, deep learning models are a significant piece of a reasonable artificial reasoning methodology.

In this new methodology, it is meant to give the client the capacity to clarify the yield information created just as being prepared at superior with the info information and target (class) data and tried with the new information contribution as in the old-style AI models. This will make another age man-made brainpower approach that can set up circumstances and logical results connection among info and yield (Dağlarli, 2020). It will likewise be the component of observing the dependability of artificial reasoning from the client perspective. While an exemplary deep learning model might answer "what" or "who" questions, learning models in reasonable man-made consciousness paradigms may likewise answer "why", "how", "where" and "when" questions (Fernandez, 2019).

Reasonableness and exactness are two separate areas. As a rule, models that are worthwhile as far as precision and execution are not exceptionally effective as far as logic. In like manner, techniques with high reasonableness are additionally disadvantageous as far as precision. For instance, techniques, for

Figure 1. Explainable artificial intelligence (XAI) (Miller, 2019)

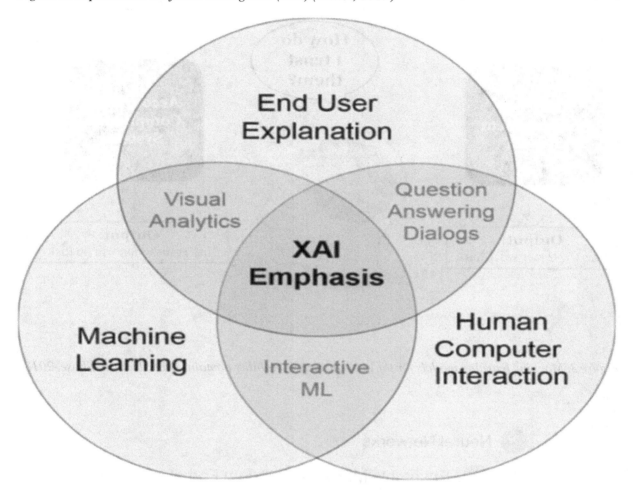

example, old-style deep learning models, artificial neural networks, and support vector machines are bad regarding explanation ability but rather they are very acceptable as far as exactness and execution. Rule-based structures, choice trees, relapse calculations, and graphical techniques are acceptable explainability yet not invaluable as far as execution and precision. Now, explainable artificial intelligence (XAI), which is focused to be at the most elevated level of both explanation ability and exactness and execution, uncovers its significance (Dağlarli, 2020).

The chapter is structured as follows. The next section provides background information about the chapter. The third section is related to the description of cyber-physical systems. The fourth section deals with explainable artificial intelligence (XAI). The fifth section gives information about meta-learning. The sixth section introduces explainable meta-reinforcement learning (XMRL) integrated cyber-physical systems. The seventh section explains the future research directions. The final section presents a discussion of conclusions.

Figure 2. How can explainable artificial intelligence (XAI) be reliable (Kaushik, 2018)

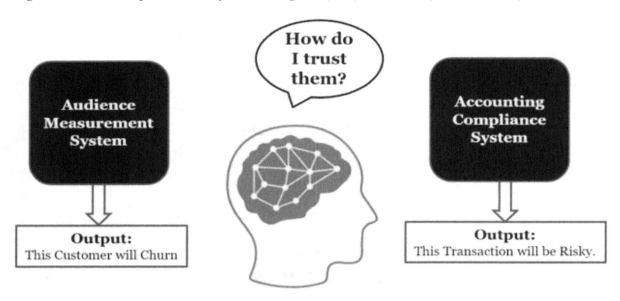

Figure 3. Machine learning models for the accuracy-explainability domain (Dam, Tran, & Ghose, 2018)

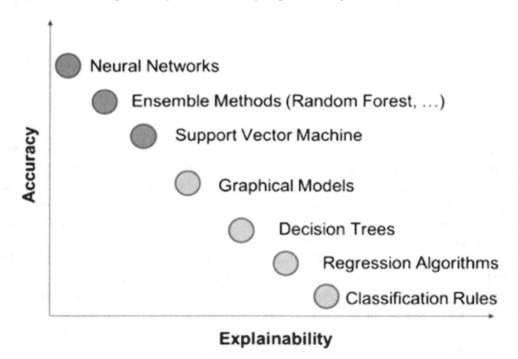

BACKGROUND

There is a change of AI that has been going on since the 1950s, here and there quicker and once in a while slower. The most considered and noteworthy territory in the ongoing past is computational learning, which plans to display the live choice framework, conduct, and reactions. Victories in the field of deep learning prompted the fast increment of computer-based intelligence applications. Further examinations guarantee to be self-governing frameworks fit for self-observation, learning, dynamic, and activity (Ha, Lee, and Kim, 2018).

Particularly after the 1990s, albeit deep learning idea and establishments return to the past, the going with repetitive neural systems, convolutional neural systems, deep reinforcement learning, and adversarial generative systems have accomplished striking victories. Albeit victories are acquired, these frameworks are deficient as far as clarifying the choices and activities to human users and there are limits.

U.S. Division of Defense (DoD) clarifies that it is confronting the difficulties presented via self-ruling and cooperative frameworks, which are getting more intelligent as time passes. Clarifying artificial brainpower or particularly illustrative AI is significant as far as being a review that clients will experience machines with human-like computerized reasoning later on (Gunning, 2017; Gunning and Aha, 2019). Explainable artificial intelligence is one of the Defense Advanced Research Projects Agency (DARPA) programs focused on the improvement of another age of synthetic brainpower frameworks, where they comprehend the specific situation and condition wherein machines work and manufacture spellbinding models that empower them to describe this present reality marvel after some time. For this reason, DARPA as of late gave a call letter for the explainable artificial intelligence (XAI) - Informative Computerized Reasoning Task (Gunning and Aha, 2019). Inside the extent of the undertaking, it is intended to build up an arrangement of AI methods that emphasis on AI and human-machine communication and produce illustrative models that will empower end clients to get, trust and oversee developing artificial intelligence frameworks. As indicated by the analysts from DARPA; the striking achievements in AI have prompted an enormous blast in new computer-based intelligence capacities that empower the creation of self-sufficient frameworks that see, learn, choose and follow up on their own. Although these frameworks give huge advantages, their viability is constrained because of the powerlessness to clarify machine choices and activities to human clients.

The explainable artificial intelligence venture is planned to build up the machine learning and human-computer cooperation apparatuses to guarantee that the end client, who relies upon the choices, suggestions, or activities delivered by the artificial reasoning framework, comprehends the explanation for the framework's choices (Adadi and Berrada, 2018). For instance, a knowledge examiner who gets proposals from enormous information examination calculations may need to comprehend why the calculation encourages them to look at a specific action further. Additionally, the administrator, who tests a recently evolved independent framework, needs to see how he settles on his own choices to decide how the framework will utilize it in future undertakings.

The XAI apparatuses will furnish end clients with clarifications of individual choices, which will empower them to comprehend the qualities and shortcomings of the framework, as a rule, give a thought of how the framework will carry on later on, and maybe instruct how to address the framework's missteps. The XAI venture tends to three innovative work difficulties: how to assemble more models, how to structure a clarification interface, and comprehend mental prerequisites for successful clarifications (Došilović et al., 2018).

For the principal issue, the XAI venture means to create AI strategies to have the option to fabricate informative models. To illuminate the subsequent test, the program imagines incorporating best in class human-machine collaboration methods with new standards, methodologies, and procedures to deliver powerful clarifications. To take care of the third issue, the XAI venture intends, to sum up, scatter and apply existing mental hypothesis clarifications. There are two specialized territories in the program; The first is to build up a logical learning framework with an informative model and a clarification interface, and the second specialized region covers mental hypotheses of clarification (Mill operator, 2019).

In 2016, a self-driving vehicle was propelled on calm streets in Monmouth Region, New Jersey. This exploratory apparatus created by analysts at chip creator Nvidia didn't appear to be unique from different self-ruling vehicles; be that as it may, Google was not quite the same as what Tesla or General Engines presented and demonstrated the rising intensity of computerized reasoning. The vehicle had not adhered to solitary guidance given by an architect or software engineer. Rather, it depended totally on a calculation that permitted him to figure out how to drive by viewing an individual driving (Center et al., 2006). It was a great accomplishment to have a vehicle self-driving along these lines. However, it was likewise to some degree upsetting as it was not so much clear how the vehicle settled on its own choices. The data from the vehicle's sensors went legitimately to an immense neural system that forms the information and afterward conveys the orders expected to work the directing wheel, brakes, and different structures. The outcomes appear to coordinate the responses you can anticipate from a human driver. Yet, consider the possibility that one day something sudden occurs; hits a tree or stops at the green light. As per the current circumstance, it might be hard to track down the reason. The framework is intricate to the point that even the specialists who planned it can think that its hard to pinpoint the reason for any activity. Besides, you can't ask this; There is no undeniable method to plan such a framework, that can generally clarify why it does what it does. The strange psyche of this vehicle focuses on an unclear looking issue of computerized reasoning. Computerized reasoning innovation, which is situated at the base of the vehicle and known as deep learning, has demonstrated to be exceptionally solid in critical thinking as of late and this innovation has been generally applied in works, for example, evaluating picture content, voice acknowledgment, and language interpretation. Presently similar strategies can be utilized to analyze deadly ailments, settle on million-dollar business choices, and so forth to change all enterprises. There are trusts that he can do endless things like.

Presently, the scientific models are utilized to help figure out who will be on parole, who will be affirmed to acquire cash, and who will be employed. If you can get to these numerical models, it is conceivable to comprehend their thinking. Be that as it may, banks, the military, businesses, and others are currently directing their concentration toward progressively complex AI draw near. These methodologies can settle on computerized dynamic unfathomable. The most well-known of these methodologies speaks to deep learning, and in a general sense distinctive method of programming PCs. Regardless of whether it's a speculation choice or a clinical choice, or a military choice, you would prefer not to depend exclusively on a 'discovery' strategy (Adadi and Berrada, 2018). There is as of now a discussion that it is a principal lawful option to scrutinize an arrangement of man-made brainpower about how it comes to its results. Beginning in the late spring of 2018, the European Association may expect organizations to give clients a clarification of the choices made via robotized frameworks. This might be inconceivable in any event, for frameworks that look similarly straightforward on a superficial level, for example, applications and sites that utilization profound figuring out how to offer to promote or tune proposals. PCs playing out these administrations have modified themselves and have done as such in manners we can't comprehend. Indeed, even the architects who assemble these applications can't completely clarify their conduct.

As innovation propels, we can go past certain edges where utilizing artificial intelligence as of late requires an act of pure trust. The humankind is not generally ready to completely clear our points of view; however, we discover an assortment of strategies to instinctively confide in individuals and measure them (Ding, Han, Wang, and Ge, 2020). Will this be feasible for machines that think and settle on choices uniquely in contrast to an individual? We have never fabricated machines that work in manners that their makers don't comprehend. To what extent would we be able to want to convey (and manage) keen machines that can be unusual or endless? These inquiries take an excursion towards innovation research on artificial reasoning mechanisms, from Google to Apple and numerous different spots between them, incorporating a discussion with probably the best scholar within recent memory.

On the other hand, the cyber-physical systems establish communication between mechanical and electronic components through information technologies, ensuring each one's communication and continuity within a network system. The first form of these technologies is RFID technology, which came into use in 1999. It is reported that the development of these systems takes place in three phases. Cyber-physical systems are not just network machines, they create a smart network that encompasses machines, smart products, people — everything that is in the entire value chain and product cycle (Fang, Qi, Cheng, & Zheng, 2020). Such smart networks are the most important infrastructure blocks of smart factories supporting Industry 4.0.

The industry 4.0 environment is surrounded by internet infrastructure and components. Everything is related to everything in a network. All kinds of processes and elements from the building used to production machinery, from logistics activities to information/data security to business environment to social networks are under the influence of intelligent (explainable artificial intelligence (XAI) and deep meta-learning) information technologies. Although big data is very useful, it is also very risky due to the unnecessary wrong and missing data it contains, and considering the cumbersome data in terms of the IT capacity of the circulating data, it can be difficult to reach the desired and necessary data (Shu et al., 2020). In the Industry 4.0 design, it is recommended that firms consider six principles. These six principles are; Interoperability is expressed as Virtualization, Dissemination of Responsibility, Real-Time Competence, Service Orientation, Modularity.

CYBER-PHYSICAL SYSTEMS

For this new version of the industrial revolution, it is known that more software and embedded smart systems are intertwined, and electronic systems with artificial intelligence that produce advanced predictive algorithms are needed. Production of instant communication systems that can manage and decide on their own is included in the scope of this project (Ray, 2020). Cyber-Physical Systems is the name given to the system that combines calculations in production with physical processes. Medical devices that demand high reliability, defense systems, smart cities (traffic control, smart buildings, environmental waste management, demand for electricity supply, critical network control mechanisms such as water resources and communication systems), autonomous factories (robotic systems, advanced automation systems, process control, energy conservation, measuring devices, smart production systems based on rapid prototyping).

Figure 4. Cyber-physical systems (Barreto, Amaral, & Pereira, 2017; Jeschke, Brecher, Song, & Rawat, 2017)

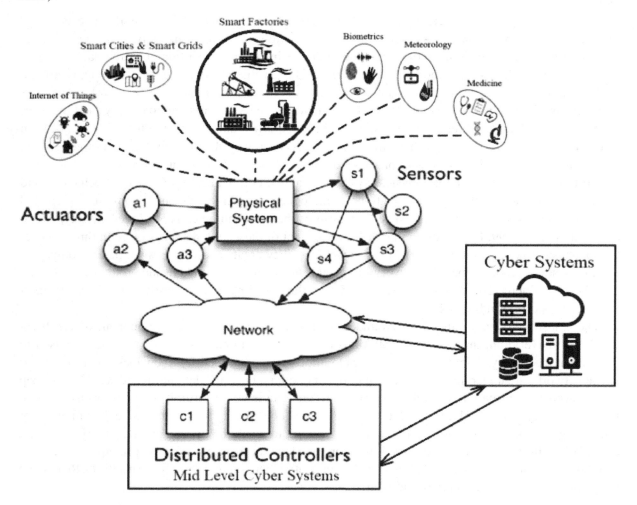

Cyber-Physical Systems (CPS) connect the physical world with the virtual computing world with the help of data collection units (sensors, cameras, etc.) and output units (actuators). CPS, consisting of different founding components, creates global behaviors in cooperation (Kravets, Bolshakov, & Shcherbakov, 2020). These components include software systems, communication technologies, sensors/actuators, usually embedded technologies to interact with the real world. Cyber-Physical Systems, which unite these two worlds, consists of two important elements. A network of objects and systems communicating with each other over the internet and with a designated internet (IP) address; is the virtual environment that emerges by simulating real-world objects and behavior in the computer environment (Cardno, 2020).

Together with the internet of things (IoT) and the internet of industrial things (IIoT), Cyber-Physical Systems which create a vast network of communication to lift the boundary between the real and virtual worlds is one of the key forces underlying Industry 4.0. CPS enabled Industry 4.0 based production processes are based on systems connecting to different networks and communicating with different services through various interfaces.

The most obvious example of this is "Smart Factories". Automation processes in Smart Factories mean that machines not only communicate with each other but also interact with physical systems and determine their production processes within themselves. For instance, if there is a shortage of resources at any stage of production, the necessary resource order is automatically placed, the malfunctions that occur can be detected and corrected immediately and on-site, the system can be operated at full capacity and without any problems (Rao, Murthy, Appaji, & Shankar, 2020). This CPS enabled Industry 4.0 concept also connects cyber systems involving the communication between devices (IoT networks) to physical systems (smart factories, machines). Cyber-Physical Systems play a major role not only in production but also in many places. For example, the research-development process can make significant differences in design and marketing processes, before a factory is physically established, all necessary feasibility studies can be done through simulation.

In today's business world, companies have problems with the rapid transfer of big information between systems to produce advanced products. Since many manufacturing systems do not have smart and analytical thinking systems, they are not yet ready to transfer and manage big data to systems quickly (Zhang, Liu, Deng, & Fan, 2020). The fourth industrial revolution focuses on production and service innovation, including the Cyber-Physical System. In cyber-physical systems, modern information and communication technologies such as Cloud Computing will be integrated into the systems to increase efficiency, quality, and flexibility in the manufacturing industry, and will provide an advantage in a competitive environment by analyzing possible efficiency situations.

Depending on the risk level of the areas in which they are used, Cyber-Physical Systems, which may be likely to harm the objects or people they work within any error, will make it safer to keep them in isolated areas against such dangers. Besides, various protection mechanisms (firewalls) are integrated into network systems for the cybersecurity of these systems (Wolf & Serpanos, 2020).

EXPLAINABLE ARTIFICIAL INTELLIGENCE (XAI)

You can't perceive how the deep neural system functions just by peering inside. The thinking of a system is implanted in the conduct of thousands of nerves, which are stacked and attached to tens or even several layers, combined (Daglarli, 2020). Every one of the nerves in the primary layer gets the info, for example, the voltage of a pixel in a picture, and afterward plays out a figuring before imparting another sign as a yield. These yields are sent to the following layer in an unpredictable system, and this procedure proceeds until a general yield is delivered. There is likewise a procedure known as a back spread that alters the computations of individual nerves with the goal that a system figures out how to deliver an ideal yield. Since deep learning is characteristically a dull black box naturally, artificial learning models structured with a large number of synthetic nerve cells with several layers like conventional deep learning models are not reliable (Adadi and Berrada, 2018). Their dependability is addressed when straightforward pixel changes can be truly misled by causing huge deviations in the weight esteems in all layers of the neural system, particularly in a model, for example, a one-pixel-assault (Su, Vargas, and Sakurai, 2019). So it gets unavoidable to pose the inquiry of how it can succeed or come up short. With the accomplishment of this sort of cutting edge applications, its multifaceted nature additionally increments and its comprehension/lucidity gets troublesome.

It is meant to be able to clarify the reasons for new artificial learning frameworks, distinguish their qualities and shortcomings, and see how they will carry on later on. For a perfect artificial intelligence framework, the best precision and best execution, just as the best reasonableness and the best interpretability are required inside the reason impact relationship. The methodology created to accomplish this objective is to grow new or changed deep learning procedures that will deliver progressively logical models. These models are planned to be joined with cutting edge human-computer intuitive interface procedures that can be converted into justifiable and helpful clarification discoursed for the end client.

Figure 5. Explainable artificial intelligence (XAI) project proposed by DARPA (Gunning, 2017; Gunning & Aha, 2019)

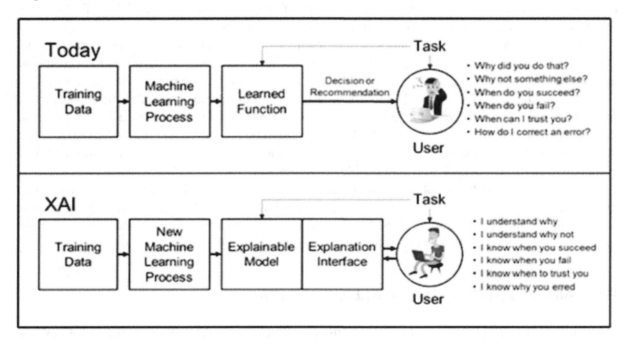

In this structure, not at all like the old style deep learning draws near, two unique components draw consideration just as another AI procedure. One of these is the explanatory model and the other is the clarification interface. The procedure of deep neural system based machine learning is clarified at the center of the artificial intelligence approach. Among the known deep learning models, autoencoder, convolutional, intermittent (LSTM), deep belief network or deep reinforcement learning can be used. In any case, it is additionally conceivable to utilize a crossover structure where a few deep learning approaches are utilized together. Autoencoder type model deep neural systems are multilayered perceptron structure. In Convolution neural system type models, layers comprise of a convolutional layer, reLU enactment capacity, and max pool layer. A regular part of the LSTM is made out of a memory cell including info, yield, and overlook entryways. For preparing, the backpropagation through time calculation can be utilized. Even though the most widely recognized type of deep reinforcement learning model is a deep Q network (DQN), a wide range of varieties of this model can be tended to. A wide range of calculations is utilized as an improvement calculation. Inclination based calculations are the most widely recognized type of these algorithms.

Figure 6. Deep learning models: autoencoder (Prakash & Rao, 2017)

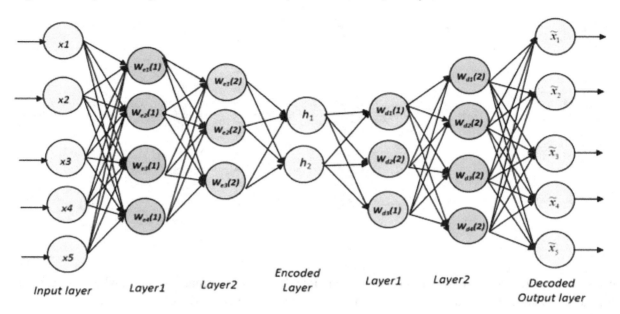

The explainable machine learning model is a versatile rule-based reasoning framework. It is a structure that uncovers the reason impact relations between input information and the outcomes acquired from the AI procedure. This causal structure learns the principles with its own inside deep learning technique. Thusly, the explainable artificial reasoning model permits it to investigate the causes and grow new methodologies against various circumstances (Keneni et al., 2019).

The clarification interface is a piece of the client association. It is like the inquiry answer interface in voice advanced collaborators. This interface, it comprises of a decoder that assesses the requests of the

Figure 7. Deep learning models: the convolutional neural network (Karn, 2016)

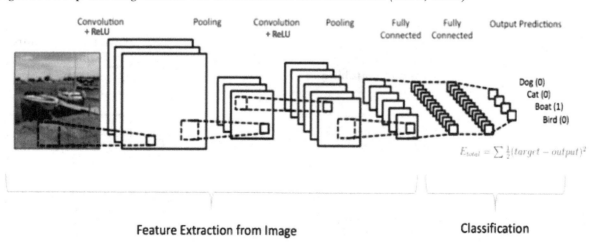

Figure 8. Deep learning models: recurrent (LSTM) neural network (Schmidt, 2019)

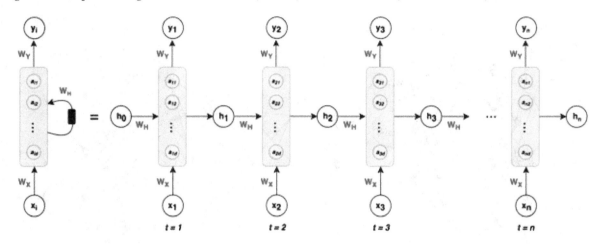

client and an encoder unit that empowers the reactions from the informative model, which establishes the causal system of the explainable artificial intelligence, to the client (Daglarli, 2020).

The enormous systems of semantic advancements (substances) and connections related to Information Charts (KGs) give a valuable answer for the issue of understandability, a few thinking components, extending from consistency checking to causal surmising (Futia and Vetrò, 2020). The ontologies under-

Figure 9. Semantic knowledge matching for explainable artificial intelligence model (Futia & Vetrò, 2020)

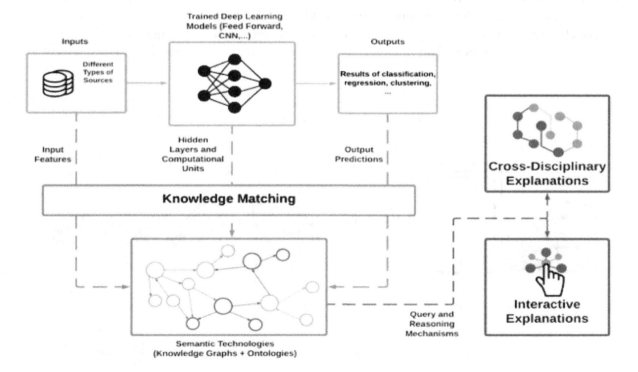

standing these thinking methods give a proper portrayal of semantic elements and connections applicable to a specific circle of information (Futia and Vetrò, 2020). The information, concealed layers, encoded includes and anticipated yield of profound learning models are passed into information diagrams (KGs) or ideas and connections of ontologies (information coordinating) (Futia and Vetrò, 2020). For the most part, the interior working of calculations to be progressively straightforward and intelligible can be acknowledged by information coordinating of deep learning segments, including input highlights, concealed units and layers, and yield expectations with KGs and metaphysics segments (Futia and Vetrò, 2020). Next to that, the conditions for cutting edge clarifications, cross-disciplinary and intuitive clarifications are empowered by the question and thinking components of KGs and ontologies (Futia and Vetrò, 2020).

Though explainable artificial intelligence frameworks are of altogether different structures, all modules, for example, this clarification interface, explanatory model, and deep learning work in a joint effort with one another. For instance, while a deep learning process is obtaining classes, the explainable artificial intelligence model (xAI apparatus) created by IBM, the idea include information acquired from this procedure and another deep learning process utilizing a similar information informational collection delivers a logical yield for the anticipated class mark yield (Melis and Jaakkola, 2018).

Figure 10. Explainable artificial intelligence (XAI) tool developed by IBM (Melis & Jaakkola, 2018)

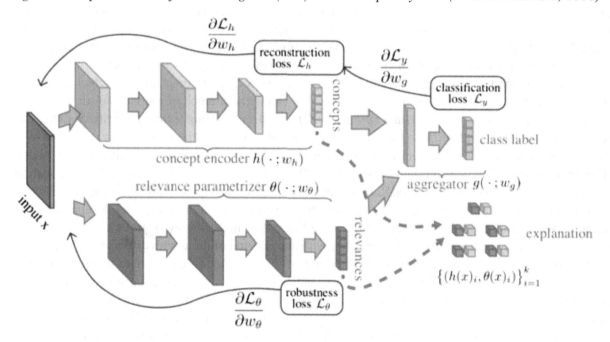

The explainable artificial intelligence (XAI) apparatus created by IBM is alluded to as a self-explainable neural system (SENN) which can be prepared to start to finish with back-propagation if there should arise an occurrence of that *g* relies upon its contentions in a persistent manner (Karn, 2016). The info is changed into a little arrangement of interpretable premise highlights by an idea encoder (Melis and Jaakkola, 2018). The importance scores are delivered by an information subordinate parametrized. A forecast to be produced is converged by an accumulation work. The full model to act locally as a direct capacity on *h(x)* with boundaries $\theta(x)$, creating a translation of the two ideas and pertinent relationships are prompted by the strength misfortune on the parametrizer (Melis and Jaakkola, 2018). $\theta(x)$ displaying limit is significant with the goal that the model extravagance acknowledging higher-limit designs is supported although the ideas are picked to be crude information sources (i.e., h is the identity).

META-LEARNING

As exploration and innovation on AI advances, computerized reasoning operators reliably show noteworthy learning exhibitions that meet and surpass the intellectual abilities of individuals in various fields. Nonetheless, most simulated intelligence programs depend on registering innovation and even reinforcement learning (RL) models that attempt to normally improve their insight to coordinate human execution. Conversely, individuals can rapidly learn new abilities of new aptitudes, basically by having another expertise (Vilalta and Drissi, 2002). The learning of the human mind so productively has surprised neuroscientists for a considerable length of time.

In conventional deep learning methods, the framework builds up an information explicit model that is transmitted to it by gaining from the information. The learning framework will play out a specific errand just for a specific situation. On account of another condition, when different information is transmitted to it, this deep learning model will be lacking to play out the undertaking (Pfahringer, Bensusan, and Giraud-Bearer, 2000). This issue uncovers hard obliges on the using of AI or information mining techniques, since the connection between the learning issue and the viability of various learning calculations isn't yet comprehended. Under perfect conditions, a framework ought to be planned in which the nature of the information given to the framework varies and it can without much of a stretch adjust to changes in various situations (Finn, Abbeel, and Levine, 2017). The deep learning techniques utilized in the current circumstance are not fruitful in these circumstances. Now, meta-realizing, which figures out how to learn, is an incorporated and various leveled learning model more than a few distinctive natural models (Chan and Stolfo, 1993; Schweighofer and Doya, 2003). As a subfield of AI, meta-learning algorithms are applied to metadata about AI tests. Rather than traditional AI moves toward that just get familiar with a particular errand with a single gigantic dataset, meta-learning is a significant level AI approach that learns different undertakings together. Along these lines, this methodology requires a various leveled structure that figures out how to become familiar with another undertaking with dispersed progressively organized metadata. It is commonly applied for hyper boundary modification; late applications have begun to concentrate on a few learning tasks. For instance, if the framework has just taken in a couple of various models or assignments, meta-learning can sum them up and figure out how to learn all the more proficiently. Along these lines, it can learn new assignments proficiently and make a structure that can without much of a stretch adjust to changes in numerous errands in various conditions.

Individuals are acceptable at making sense of the importance of a word in the wake of seeing it utilized distinctly in a couple of sentences. So also, we need our ML calculations to be summed up to new undertakings, without the requirement for a huge informational index each time, and to change conduct after a couple of tests. In ordinary learning (on a solitary dataset), each example test target pair capacities as a preparation point. Nonetheless, in a few learning circumstances, each "new" example territory is another errand in itself. At the end of the day, understanding the way that you utilize one of a kind words in a specific social condition, turns into another errand for your language-getting model,

Figure 11. Meta-learning approach (Amit & Meir, 2017)

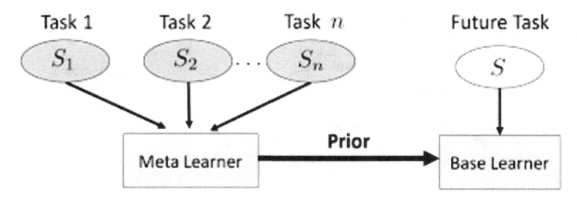

and when you enter an alternate social condition, it implies that the framework can adjust to an alternate language-understanding model than before since it requires to command the words that are explicit to that social condition. To ensure an ML structure can carry on also, we need to prepare it on various assignments all alone, so we make every informational index another case of preparing (Santoro, Bartunov, Botvinick, Wierstra, and Lillicrap, 2016).

Figure 12. Meta-reinforcement Learning (stack of sub-policies representation) (Frans, Ho, Chen, Abbeel, & Schulman, 2017)

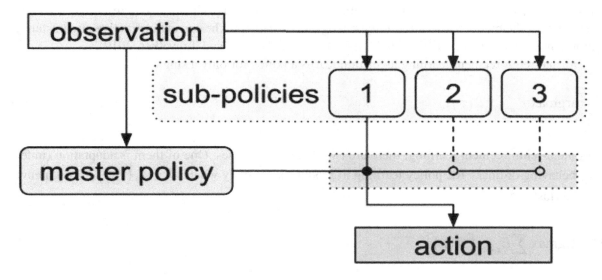

An option is to deal with the undertaking continuously as a successive info exhibit and make a redundant model that can make a portrayal of this cluster for another assignment. Commonly, for this situation, we have a solitary preparing process with a memory or attention repetitive system (Chan and Stolfo, 1993). This methodology additionally gives great outcomes, particularly when the establishments

Figure 13. Meta-reinforcement Learning (inner-outer loop representation) (Botvinick et al., 2019)

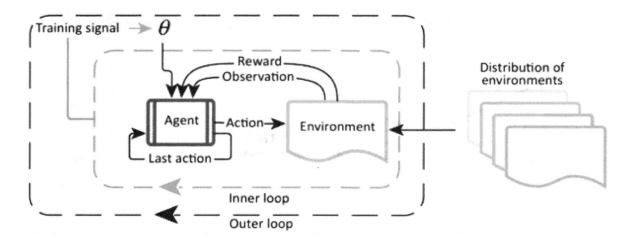

are appropriately intended for the assignment. The count performed by the streamlining agent during the meta-forward training process is fundamentally the same as the figuring of a tedious system (Vanschoren, 2019). It more than once applies similar boundaries over a progression of information sources (continuous loads and inclinations of the model during learning). By and by, this implies we meet a typical issue with a repetitive network. Since the models are not prepared to dispose of preparing blunders, they experience difficulty coming back to a sheltered way when they commit errors, and the models experience issues summing up longer groupings than those utilized in the request in which they were utilized. To beat these issues, if the model learns an activity strategy identified with the current instructive circumstance, reinforcement learning approaches can be liked (Khodak, Balcan, and Talwalkar, 2019).

A formal reinforcement learning algorithm learns a policy for only a single task.

$$\theta^* = \underset{\theta}{\arg\max} \, E_{\pi\theta(\tau)}\big(R(\tau)\big) \tag{1}$$

In meta-reinforcement learning, there are two distinct processes. One of them is adaptation (inner-loop) behaving ordinary RL policy learning to produce sub-policy where $\phi_i = f_\theta(\mathcal{M}_i)$ for each environment (task) $\mathcal{M}_i$.

$$\theta^* = \underset{\theta}{\arg\max} \sum_{i=1}^{n} E_{\pi\phi_i(\tau)}\big[R(\tau)\big] \tag{2}$$

Another process is meta-training (outer-loop) which is described as meta-policy learning from all sub-policies in the adaptation process (inner-loop).

One of the fundamental contrasts between the human cerebrum and artificial reasoning structures, for example, deep neural systems, is that the mind uses various synthetic concoctions known as synapses to perform distinctive psychological capacities. Another examination by DeepMind accepts that one of these synapses assumes a significant job in the mind's capacity to rapidly learn new points. Dopamine goes about as a reward function that fortifies associations between neurons in the mind.

The DeepMind group has utilized distinctive meta-reinforcement learning procedures that mimic the job of Dopamine in the learning procedure. Meta-learning prepared a repetitive neural system (speaking to the prefrontal cortex) utilizing standard deep reinforcement learning methods (speaking to the job of dopamine) and afterward analyzed the movement elements of the repetitive network system with genuine information from past discoveries in neuroscience tests (Schweighofer and Doya, 2003). Repetitive systems are a genuine case of meta-learning since they can disguise past activities and perceptions and afterward utilize these encounters while preparing on different assignments.

The meta-learning model reproduced the Harlow explore by saying a virtual computer screen and randomly chose pictures, and the trial demonstrated that the 'meta-RL expert' was found out along these lines to the creatures found in the Harlow Analysis, in any event, when given the Harlow Trial. Every single new picture never observed. The meta-learning agent immediately adjusted to various undertakings with various principles and structures.

EXPLAINABLE META-REINFORCEMENT LEARNING (XMRL) INTEGRATED CYBER-PHYSICAL SYSTEMS

In this part, we will talk about the advancement of deep reinforcement learning models with a reasonable way to deal with artificial intelligence. Deep reinforcement learning models are AI models that realize what move to make as per status and reward data by augmenting reward (Schweighofer and Doya, 2003). It is broadly favored in autonomous robots, driverless vehicles, unmanned airborne vehicles, and games. Explainable artificial intelligence gives the information on why move ought to be made against the circumstance and award for deep reinforcement learning models. Along these lines, it will be conceivable to pick up the causal dynamic capacity of the model by uncovering the social connections between the info and yield of the created expert (agent).

Figure 14. Forward reinforcement learning (Jangir, 2016)

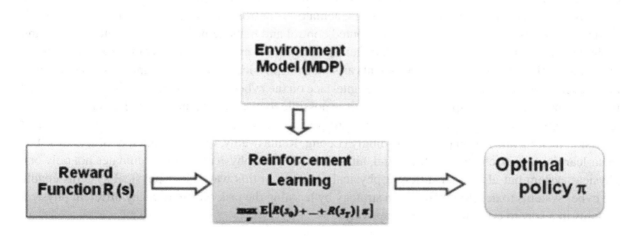

Figure 15. Inverse reinforcement learning (Jangir, 2016)

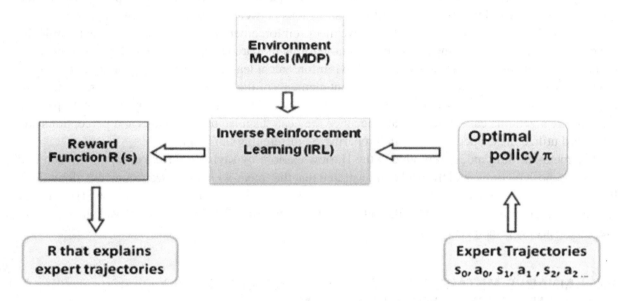

Beside of that, it is conceivable to become familiar with the reward induction instrument by utilizing the inverse reinforcement learning model (Rakelly, Zhou, Quillen, Finn, and Levine, 2019; Sugiyama, Schweighofer, and Izawa, 2020). For this situation, in contrast to the past methodology, a meta-cognitive artificial intelligence model that can adjust to different conditions rather than only one condition is created (Parisotto et al., 2019; Jabri et al., 2019). Taken along with the explainable artificial intelligence methodology, the created operator will be able to build up his technique by setting up a reason impact relationship. For instance, the explainable meta-reinforcement learning agent to be created implies that, as far as meta-learning, it can figure out how to play Go, chess, checkers, and even learn and adjust when it is experiencing another game, as far as reasonable man-made reasoning, it implies that monitoring why it is doing a particular activity against a move made by the rival, and it can clarify this (Daglarli, 2020).

Computers and networks with embedded systems often control and monitor systems where feedback cycles and physical processes significantly affect computations (Karimipour & Leung, 2020). These systems mostly consist of networked receivers, actuators, control, and communication units. Also, the common features of these systems are distributed control and management, no time limit, scalable and self-managing features. Explainability of artificial intelligence in cyber-physical systems means establishing a cause-effect relationship between events arising from physical systems and a more human-specific, high-level cognitive interaction with the user interface on the cyber system side. By using the reinforced learning approach in cyber-physical systems, it is possible to evaluate the input data from physical systems, to learn the system according to the reward function, and to control the physical system learned (decision making and action plan) accordingly (Leong, Ramaswamy, Quevedo, Karl, & Shi, 2020). The meta-learning approach, on the other hand, aims that the cyber-physical system dominates not only one physical system but also other different physical systems. In this way, cyber-physical systems enable the cyber systems to develop their action strategy by learning the task related to many different physical systems in a way to coordinate them adaptively.

FUTURE RESEARCH DIRECTIONS

Following era, artificial intelligence structures are anticipated to have a progressive meta-learning capacity that can adjust to numerous distinctive situations and cyber-physical frameworks, other than being a causal and illustrative control by setting up a cause-effect relationship. For this, genuine exertion is still required to make adaptable and interpretable models that can hold suppositions from numerous distinctive disciplines together and work in concordance.

Within the future, next-generation deep learning and artificial intelligence structures are anticipated to reach the level of intelligence (singularity), which has higher execution and ability than the human level. Within the same way, it can be expressed that artificial intelligence forms will offer assistance to the arrangement of self-awareness and artificial consciousness structures based on substance and causality. As a result, xAI and deep meta-reinforcement learning empowered Cyber-Physical Frameworks, and so Industry 4.0, are promising in terms of creating arrangements that we may not have envisioned nowadays, progressing asset utilization and expanding proficiency.

CONCLUSION

We can't overlook the preferences this will give us. For instance, if we start with a clinical application, after the patient information is inspected, both the doctor must comprehend and disclose to the patient why he/she proposed that the logical choice emotionally supportive network recommended to the related patient that there was a "risk of a heart attack". Simultaneously, as a meta-learning specialist of this framework, it has a similar capacity against every single other illness and it will be conceivable to create fitting treatment systems.

While resulting in these present circumstances stage, what information is assessed first is another significant basis. It is additionally important to clarify what information is required and why, and what is required for legitimate assessment. Artificial intelligence and deep learning structures referenced in this segment are thought to reveal insight into arriving at these levels. Specifically, it tends to be said that meta-learning approaches are fit for supporting the development of structures that figure out how to learn and adjust to various undertakings and are likewise called general artificial intelligence (AGI) (Daglarli, 2020).

Cybersystems driven by XAI and meta-learning can monitor and control physical or business processes. Also, they contain secured user engagement/interaction. It provides adaptation and development to the reactive changes in the environment through real-time configuration, distribution, or assignment in cyber-physical systems. Requiring a high degree of reliability, CPS constantly monitors and optimizes its performance. Besides, these systems require integration of different technical disciplines and different areas of application, as well as highly hierarchical decision systems at local, regional, national, and global levels (Deng, Wang, Wen, Xu, & Lin, 2020).

REFERENCES

Adadi, A., & Berrada, M. (2018). Peeking inside the black-box: A survey on Explainable Artificial Intelligence (XAI). *IEEE Access: Practical Innovations, Open Solutions, 6,* 52138–52160. doi:10.1109/ACCESS.2018.2870052

Ahuja, R., Chug, A., Gupta, S., Ahuja, P., & Kohli, S. (2020). Classification and Clustering Algorithms of Machine Learning with their Applications. In *Nature-Inspired Computation in Data Mining and Machine Learning* (pp. 225–248). Cham: Springer. doi:10.1007/978-3-030-28553-1_11

Alcaraz, C., & Lopez, J. (2020). Secure interoperability in cyber-physical systems. In *Cyber Warfare and Terrorism: Concepts, Methodologies, Tools, and Applications* (pp. 521–542). IGI Global. doi:10.4018/978-1-7998-2466-4.ch032

Amit, R., & Meir, R. (2017). *Meta-learning by adjusting priors based on extended PAC-Bayes theory.* arXiv preprint arXiv:1711.01244

Barreto, L., Amaral, A., & Pereira, T. (2017). Industry 4.0 implications in logistics: An overview. *Procedia Manufacturing, 13,* 1245–1252. doi:10.1016/j.promfg.2017.09.045

Botvinick, M., Ritter, S., Wang, J. X., Kurth-Nelson, Z., Blundell, C., & Hassabis, D. (2019). Reinforcement learning, fast and slow. *Trends in Cognitive Sciences, 23*(5), 408–422. doi:10.1016/j.tics.2019.02.006 PMID:31003893

Cardno, A. (2020). *6 Critical Ideas behind the Smart Factory and Internet of Things.* Retrieved from: https://blog.vizexplorer.com/6-critical-ideas-behindthe-smart-factory-and-internet-of-things-iot/)

Chan, P. K., & Stolfo, S. J. (1993). Experiments on multistrategy learning by meta-learning. In *Proceedings of the second international conference on information and knowledge management* (pp. 314-323). Academic Press.

Chan, P. K., & Stolfo, S. J. (1993). Toward parallel and distributed learning by meta-learning. In AAAI workshop in Knowledge Discovery in Databases (pp. 227-240). Academic Press.

Core, M. G., Lane, H. C., Van Lent, M., Gomboc, D., Solomon, S., & Rosenberg, M. (2006). Building explainable artificial intelligence systems. In AAAI (pp. 1766-1773). Academic Press.

Dağlarli, E. (2020). *Explainable Artificial Intelligence (XAI) Approaches and Deep Meta-Learning Models. In Advances in Deep Learning.* IntechOpen.

Dam, H. K., Tran, T., & Ghose, A. (2018). Explainable software analytics. In *Proceedings of the 40th International Conference on Software Engineering: New Ideas and Emerging Results* (pp. 53-56). Academic Press.

Delicato, F. C., Al-Anbuky, A., Kevin, I., & Wang, K. (2020). *Smart Cyber-Physical Systems: Toward Pervasive Intelligence Systems.* Academic Press.

Deng, C., Wang, Y., Wen, C., Xu, Y., & Lin, P. (2020). Distributed Resilient Control for Energy Storage Systems in Cyber-Physical Microgrids. *IEEE Transactions on Industrial Informatics, 1.* doi:10.1109/TII.2020.2981549

Ding, D., Han, Q. L., Wang, Z., & Ge, X. (2020). Recursive Filtering of Distributed Cyber-Physical Systems With Attack Detection. *IEEE Transactions on Systems, Man, and Cybernetics. Systems*, 1–11. doi:10.1109/TSMC.2019.2960541

Došilović, F. K., Brčić, M., & Hlupić, N. (2018). Explainable artificial intelligence: A survey. In *2018 41st International convention on information and communication technology, electronics and microelectronics (MIPRO)* (pp. 0210-0215). IEEE.

Fang, C., Qi, Y., Cheng, P., & Zheng, W. X. (2020). Optimal periodic watermarking schedule for replay attack detection in cyber-physical systems. *Automatica*, *112*, 108698. doi:10.1016/j.automatica.2019.108698

Fernandez, A., Herrera, F., Cordon, O., del Jesus, M. J., & Marcelloni, F. (2019). Evolutionary fuzzy systems for explainable artificial intelligence: Why, when, what for, and where to? *IEEE Computational Intelligence Magazine*, *14*(1), 69–81. doi:10.1109/MCI.2018.2881645

Finn, C., Abbeel, P., & Levine, S. (2017). Model-agnostic meta-learning for fast adaptation of deep networks. In *Proceedings of the 34th International Conference on Machine Learning-Volume* 70 (pp. 1126-1135). JMLR. org.

Frans, K., Ho, J., Chen, X., Abbeel, P., & Schulman, J. (2017). *Meta-learning shared hierarchies*. arXiv preprint arXiv:1710.09767

Futia, G., & Vetrò, A. (2020). On the Integration of Knowledge Graphs into Deep Learning Models for a More Comprehensible AI—Three Challenges for Future Research. *Information*, *11*(2), 122. doi:10.3390/info11020122

Gunning, D. (2017). *Explainable artificial intelligence (XAI)*. Defense Advanced Research Projects Agency (DARPA).

Gunning, D., & Aha, D. W. (2019). DARPA's Explainable Artificial Intelligence Program. *AI Magazine*, *40*(2), 44–58. doi:10.1609/aimag.v40i2.2850

Ha, T., Lee, S., & Kim, S. (2018). Designing explainability of an artificial intelligence system. In *Proceedings of the Technology, Mind, and Society* (pp. 1-1). Academic Press.

Huang, F., Zhang, J., Zhou, C., Wang, Y., Huang, J., & Zhu, L. (2020). A deep learning algorithm using a fully connected sparse autoencoder neural network for landslide susceptibility prediction. *Landslides*, *17*(1), 217–229. doi:10.100710346-019-01274-9

Jabri, A., Hsu, K., Gupta, A., Eysenbach, B., Levine, S., & Finn, C. (2019). Unsupervised Curricula for Visual Meta-Reinforcement Learning. *Advances in Neural Information Processing Systems*, 10519–10530.

Jangir, R. (2016). *Apprenticeship learning using Inverse Reinforcement Learning*. Retrieved from: https://jangirrishabh.github.io/2016/07/09/virtual-car-IRL/

Jeschke, I. S., Brecher, C., Song, H., & Rawat, D. B. (2017). *Industrial Internet of Things and Cyber Manufacturing Systems*. Springer International Publishing. doi:10.1007/978-3-319-42559-7_1

Karimipour, H., & Leung, H. (2020). Relaxation-based anomaly detection in cyber-physical systems using an ensemble Kalman filter. *IET Cyber-Physical Systems: Theory & Applications*, *5*(1), 49–58.

Karn, U. (2016). *Intuitive explanation convolutional-neural networks,* Retrieved from https://www. kdnuggets.com/2016/11/intuitive-explanation-convolutional-neural-networks.html/3

Kaushik, S. (2018). *Enterprise explainable AI,* Retrieved from https://www.kdnuggets.com/2018/10/ enterprise-explainable-ai.html

Keneni, B. M., Kaur, D., Al Bataineh, A., Devabhaktuni, V. K., Javaid, A. Y., Zaientz, J. D., & Marinier, R. P. (2019). Evolving rule-based explainable artificial intelligence for unmanned aerial vehicles. *IEEE Access: Practical Innovations, Open Solutions, 7,* 17001–17016. doi:10.1109/ACCESS.2019.2893141

Khodak, M., Balcan, M. F. F., & Talwalkar, A. S. (2019). Adaptive gradient-based meta-learning methods. *Advances in Neural Information Processing Systems,* 5915–5926.

Kravets, A., Bolshakov, A. A., & Shcherbakov, M. V. (2020). *Cyber-physical Systems: Industry 4.0 Challenges.* Springer. doi:10.1007/978-3-030-32648-7

Leong, A. S., Ramaswamy, A., Quevedo, D. E., Karl, H., & Shi, L. (2020). Deep reinforcement learning for wireless sensor scheduling in cyber-physical systems. *Automatica, 113,* 108759. doi:10.1016/j. automatica.2019.108759

Malik, M. M. (2020). *A Hierarchy of Limitations in Machine Learning.* arXiv preprint arXiv:2002.05193

Melis, D. A., & Jaakkola, T. (2018). Towards robust interpretability with self-explaining neural networks. *Advances in Neural Information Processing Systems,* 7775–7784.

Miller, T. (2019). Explanation in artificial intelligence: *Insights from the social sciences. Artificial Intelligence, 267,* 1–38. doi:10.1016/j.artint.2018.07.007

Mittal, S., & Tolk, A. (2020). *Complexity Challenges in Cyber-Physical Systems: Using Modeling and Simulation (M&S) to Support Intelligence, Adaptation, and Autonomy.* John Wiley & Sons.

Parisotto, E., Ghosh, S., Yalamanchi, S. B., Chinnaobireddy, V., Wu, Y., & Salakhutdinov, R. (2019). *Concurrent meta reinforcement learning.* arXiv preprint arXiv:1903.02710

Pfahringer, B., Bensusan, H., & Giraud-Carrier, C. G. (2000). Meta-Learning by Landmarking Various Learning Algorithms. In ICML (pp. 743-750). Academic Press.

Prakash, P. K. S., & Rao, A. S. K. (2017). *R deep learning cookbook.* Packt Pub. Ltd.

Rakelly, K., Zhou, A., Quillen, D., Finn, C., & Levine, S. (2019). *Efficient off-policy meta-reinforcement learning via probabilistic context variables.* arXiv preprint arXiv:1903.08254

Rao, C. S., Murthy, K. V. S., Appaji, S. V., & Shankar, R. S. (2020). Cyber-Physical Systems Security: Definitions, Methodologies, Metrics, and Tools. In *Smart Intelligent Computing and Applications* (pp. 477–488). Singapore: Springer.

Ray, L. (2020). Cyber-Physical Systems: An Overview of Design Process, Applications, and Security. In *Cyber Warfare and Terrorism: Concepts, Methodologies, Tools, and Applications* (pp. 128–150). IGI Global. doi:10.4018/978-1-7998-2466-4.ch008

Samek, W., Wiegand, T., & Müller, K. R. (2017). *Explainable artificial intelligence: Understanding, visualizing, and interpreting deep learning models.* arXiv preprint arXiv:1708.08296

Santoro, A., Bartunov, S., Botvinick, M., Wierstra, D., & Lillicrap, T. (2016). Meta-learning with memory-augmented neural networks. In *International conference on machine learning* (pp. 1842-1850). Academic Press.

Schmidt, R. M. (2019). *Recurrent Neural Networks (RNNs): A gentle Introduction and Overview.* arXiv preprint arXiv:1912.05911

Schnack, H. (2020). Bias, noise, and interpretability in machine learning: From measurements to features. *Machine Learning*, 307–328.

Schweighofer, N., & Doya, K. (2003). Meta-learning in reinforcement learning. *Neural Networks*, *16*(1), 5–9. doi:10.1016/S0893-6080(02)00228-9 PMID:12576101

Shishvan, O. R., Zois, D. S., & Soyata, T. (2020). Incorporating Artificial Intelligence into Medical Cyber-Physical Systems: A Survey. In *Connected Health in Smart Cities* (pp. 153–178). Cham: Springer. doi:10.1007/978-3-030-27844-1_8

Shu, H., Qi, P., Huang, Y., Chen, F., Xie, D., & Sun, L. (2020). An Efficient Certificateless Aggregate Signature Scheme for Blockchain-Based Medical Cyber-Physical Systems. *Sensors (Basel)*, *20*(5), 1521. doi:10.339020051521 PMID:32164220

Su, J., Vargas, D. V., & Sakurai, K. (2019). One pixel attack for fooling deep neural networks. *IEEE Transactions on Evolutionary Computation*, *23*(5), 828–841. doi:10.1109/TEVC.2019.2890858

Sugiyama, T., Schweighofer, N., & Izawa, J. (2020). Reinforcement meta-learning optimizes visuomotor learning. *bioRxiv*

Vanschoren, J. (2019). Meta-learning. In *Automated Machine Learning* (pp. 35–61). Cham: Springer. doi:10.1007/978-3-030-05318-5_2

Vilalta, R., & Drissi, Y. (2002). A perspective view and survey of meta-learning. *Artificial Intelligence Review*, *18*(2), 77–95. doi:10.1023/A:1019956318069

Waschull, S., Bokhorst, J. A. C., Molleman, E., & Wortmann, J. C. (2020). Work design in future industrial production: Transforming towards cyber-physical systems. *Computers & Industrial Engineering*, *139*, 105679. doi:10.1016/j.cie.2019.01.053

Wolf, M., & Serpanos, D. (2020). *Safe and Secure Cyber-Physical Systems and Internet-of-Things Systems.* Springer International Publishing. doi:10.1007/978-3-030-25808-5

Yin, S., Kaynak, O., & Karimi, H. R. (2020). IEEE Access Special Section Editorial: Data-Driven Monitoring, Fault Diagnosis, and Control of Cyber-Physical Systems. *IEEE Access: Practical Innovations, Open Solutions*, *8*, 54110–54114. doi:10.1109/ACCESS.2020.2980404

Zhang, Z. H., Liu, D., Deng, C., & Fan, Q. Y. (2020). A dynamic event-triggered resilient control approach to cyber-physical systems under asynchronous DoS attacks. *Information Sciences*, *519*, 260–272. doi:10.1016/j.ins.2020.01.047

ADDITIONAL READING

Abraham, A. (2004). Meta-learning evolutionary artificial neural networks. *Neurocomputing, 56*, 1–38. doi:10.1016/S0925-2312(03)00369-2

Baheti, R., & Gill, H. (2011). Cyber-physical systems. The impact of control technology, 12(1), 161-166.

Doran, D., Schulz, S., & Besold, T. R. (2017). What does explainable AI mean? A new conceptualization of perspectives. arXiv preprint arXiv:1710.00794.

Giraud-Carrier, C., Vilalta, R., & Brazdil, P. (2004). Introduction to the special issue on meta-learning. *Machine Learning, 54*(3), 187–193. doi:10.1023/B:MACH.0000015878.60765.42

Holzinger, A. (2018, August). From machine learning to explainable AI. In *2018 World Symposium on Digital Intelligence for Systems and Machines (DISA)* (pp. 55-66). IEEE. 10.1109/DISA.2018.8490530

Holzinger, A., Biemann, C., Pattichis, C. S., & Kell, D. B. (2017). What do we need to build explainable AI systems for the medical domain? arXiv preprint arXiv:1712.09923.

Lee, E. A. (2008, May). Cyber-physical systems: Design challenges. In 2008 11th IEEE International Symposium on Object and Component-Oriented Real-Time Distributed Computing (ISORC) (pp. 363-369). IEEE.

Lee, J., Bagheri, B., & Kao, H. A. (2015). A cyber-physical systems architecture for industry 4.0-based manufacturing systems. *Manufacturing Letters, 3*, 18–23. doi:10.1016/j.mfglet.2014.12.001

Prodromidis, A., Chan, P., & Stolfo, S. (2000). Meta-learning in distributed data mining systems: Issues and approaches. Advances in distributed and parallel knowledge discovery, 3, 81-114.

KEY TERMS AND DEFINITIONS

Artificial General Intelligence (AGI): This term covers the intelligence of a machine that can successfully perform all mental tasks which an ordinary person can do.

Cyber-Physical Systems (CPS): Cyber-physical systems (CPS) connect the physical world with the virtual computing world with the help of sensors and actuators. CPS, consisting of different founding components, creates global behaviors in cooperation. These components include software systems, communication technologies, sensors/actuators, usually embedded technologies to interact with the real world.

Deep Learning (DL): Deep learning is a sub-branch of machine learning theory. It allows us to train an agent model to predict outputs with a given dataset. Both supervised and unsupervised learning can be used for deep learning models.

Explainable Artificial Intelligence (XAI): This term aims to enable the end-user to understand the reason behind the system's decisions by developing machine learning and computer/human interaction tools, depending on the decisions, recommendations, or actions produced by the artificial intelligence system.

Industry 4.0: It is an industry-technology integration that began its preparations years ago and started to be implemented in developed countries. After significant industrial revolutions in the production sector, countries and companies have had to keep up with these global changes and have developed some strategies to maintain their competitive advantage among the increasingly competitive conditions.

Internet of Things (IoT): Internet of things (IoT) term is the network where physical objects are linked to each other or larger systems. It is envisaged that the objects can work together over the Internet infrastructure by marking them with a unique identifier, thus creating larger values than the sum of the small parts.

Meta-Learning (ML): Meta-learning is a subfield of machine learning, where automatic learning algorithms are applied to metadata related to machine learning experiments to learn (induce) the learning algorithm itself, how automatic learning can become flexible in solving learning problems.

Singularity: Singularity, or technological singularity, is the hypothetical point in the future, where artificial intelligence is believed to go beyond human intelligence and radically change civilization and human nature. It is believed that such intelligence will make the future of humanity unpredictable, as it will be more capable than imagined by humanity.

Chapter 4
Artificial Intelligence-Based Solutions for Cyber Security Problems

Merve Yildirim
Erzurum Technical University, Turkey

ABSTRACT

Due to its nature, cyber security is one of the fields that can benefit most from the techniques of artificial intelligence (AI). Under normal circumstances, it is difficult to write software to defend against cyber-attacks that are constantly developing and strengthening in network systems. By applying artificial intelligence techniques, software that can detect attacks and take precautions can be developed. In cases where traditional security systems are inadequate and slow, security applications developed with artificial intelligence techniques can provide better security against many complex cyber threats. Apart from being a good solution for cyber security problems, it also brings usage problems, legal risks, and concerns. This study focuses on how AI can help solve cyber security issues while discussing artificial intelligence threats and risks. This study also aims to present several AI-based techniques and to explain what these techniques can provide to solve problems in the field of cyber security.

INTRODUCTION

In the beginning, Artificial Intelligence (AI) emerged as a concept that mimics the human brain and tries to bring a human perspective and approach to the problems encountered. AI enables large amounts of data to be stored and intelligently processed with functional tools. AI has been widely used to create smart applications in a variety of fields, such as health, advertising, defense, industry 4.0, intelligent transportation systems, or space exploration. Cybersecurity systems are another critical area that AI mechanisms can be used for them to improve these systems.

AI can be defined as intelligence created to solve complicated and difficult problems in a computer or machine. It uses the combination of soft information technology and concrete human intelligence to solve problems. By recognizing artificial intelligence patterns, adaptive choices can be made, and the

DOI: 10.4018/978-1-7998-5101-1.ch004

ability to think by learning from experience can be provided. AI can briefly make machines behave like humans, but it performs much faster than them. These features of AI provide an important advantage in solving its cybersecurity problems.

Cybersecurity covers all of the technologies used to protect networks, data, computer software, and hardware from attacks and unauthorized access (Kaspersky Lab, 2018). Cybersecurity can also be called information technology security. It is a broad concept that includes many issues, from information security to end-user education. AI has a strong relationship with cybersecurity as cybersecurity is based on people's activities, organizational processes, and information technology (Vähäkainu and Lehto, 2019).

Organizations started using cybersecurity artificial intelligence to provide better information security against attackers who continuously improve their attack methods. Artificial intelligence helps to identify attacks and fight against information security breaches. As more cybersecurity attacks are specifically targeted to the networks every day, to address the challenge of defeating novel complex threats can be possible with using AI techniques. Cybersecurity practices are becoming more effective and comprehensive by using these techniques. Zero-day and multi-step attacks are among the most common attacks in the networks. Besides statistical analysis, machine learning can also be used to track these attacks in the AI field. Machine learning (ML) includes the detection of behavioral anomalies and event sequence tracking. Applications of AI involve online intrusion detection and offline security investigation. A recent study has provided a review of both statistical analysis and ML approaches to track some cyber-attacks which are hard to detect. They proposed a comprehensive framework for the study of detection and investigation of complex attacks. This work primarily facilitates the reduction of new complex threats by using AI-based countermeasures (Parrend et al., 2018).

Using AI for cybersecurity is for monitoring and analyzing the events that occur in a computer network to detect malicious activity that is mostly based on behavioral or signature. Therefore, most of the cybersecurity studies have focused on these fields. However, some traditional security mechanisms such as intrusion detection and prevention systems and Access control are not adequate to detect specific types of attacks, including zero-day threats. Because these types of attacks exhibit unknown misbehavior, which is not defined in the signatures' database of the cybersecurity systems. Recently, new cybersecurity mechanisms based on artificial intelligence (AI) have been developed to protect CPS from these zero-day attacks. Machine learning technologies are used to generate different types of attacks automatically, thereby managing a large amount of complex data from different sources of information to predict the wrong behavior of future attackers accurately. Game theoretical approaches have also been used in the context of cyber defense to solve whether the suspect device is an attacker and predict the attack. This approach is used to examine the interaction between security agents and competitors, such as IDS and IPS, to determine the optimal decision of security agents to classify or not classify the suspect opponent as an intruder.

This study discusses some artificial intelligence techniques which are suitable to be used in the cybersecurity domain. These can be used to predict and prevent information security threats and abnormalities. An overview of cybersecurity solutions using artificial intelligence and their capabilities and effectiveness is presented in this paper.

The aim of this study is mainly to highlight the shortcomings of traditional security measures and to demonstrate the progress made so far by applying AI techniques to cybersecurity. It reviews recent studies related to AI-based cybersecurity solutions applied to cyber-physical systems (CPSs). Most of these studies focus on AI-based cyber defense mechanisms to detect abnormalities in the network and attackers targeting CPS. The other studies investigate the cyber protection based solutions with machine learning for CPS. Besides, this study emphasized the concerns about future advances by investigating the current conditions of AI.

The rest of this chapter is organized as follows: First, a broad background including the cyber threats and the relationship between cybersecurity and artificial intelligence is provided. Followed by the background section, an overview of the related artificial intelligence techniques is presented. Limitations and future studies are presented in the next section and finally, the conclusion of the chapter is given in the last section.

BACKGROUND

Artificial intelligence, in its original name, machine intelligence, has been revealed in the hope of creating a system that is smarter than humans in the future. As an example, a robust system was created that would defeat a human being who played a game of intelligence like chess best. Whereas, in the beginning, it seemed almost impossible to create such a system. Artificial intelligence has typically emerged as a field of science for developing smart machines that can make logical decisions and tries to provide ways to identify and solve complex problems that cannot be solved under normal circumstances. Artificial intelligence can be used as a science for applications that require intelligence and support information, such as making the right choices when facing problems. It is also possible to apply such AI techniques when dealing with cybersecurity problems.

Within the scope of artificial intelligence, a variety of ways have been developed to solve difficult problems that require intelligence based on a human perspective. Some of these ways have found an opportunity to be developed with some algorithms that support them. For example, data processing algorithms emerged from the training sub-field of AI and found some application areas. In this study, various categories such as neural networks, knowledgeable systems, smart agents, search, machine learning, data processing, and finding restrictions are presented. Information on the use of unique ways of cybersecurity is provided through these categories. In this study, some specific applications of artificial intelligence, such as linguistic perception and computer vision are left out. Because specific application areas such as robotic systems and computer vision are useful, but they do not have a connection yet with cybersecurity-related issues.

Cybersecurity requires risk management and security vulnerabilities to be eliminated. It aims to detect abnormalities and malware on the network and ensure information security. In other words, cybersecurity can be defined as measures against cyber-attacks and their consequences. Organizations must conduct a threat analysis to ensure cybersecurity. For an organization to ensure information security, it needs to determine its cybersecurity strategy well and take measures based on predictive threats and risk analysis. For this reason, especially large organizations should prepare targeted cybersecurity strategy and guidance.

Organizations should take the necessary precautions against cyber threats and try to provide adequate protection against the effects of possible attacks. Some of the measures that can be taken against cyber-attacks are increasing the awareness of the employees about information security, improving operational capacity, and protecting security. The main issue in ensuring cybersecurity is to continue working under an attack without interruption, to eliminate the problem quickly, and to restore the organization's working order immediately. Many studies have been conducted in the literature to explain these problems and discuss the precautions that can be taken against cyber-attacks (Anwar and Hassan, 2017).

The concepts of cyber threats, vulnerability, and risk in systems need to be evaluated together. The system to be defended against threats could be a valuable investment, idea, or any intangible right that needs protection. Vulnerability is a natural weakness that increases the likelihood of potential threats occurring. Security vulnerabilities can be identified through risk analysis. Risk analysis requires the calculation of possible losses in the organization. Risk management consists of risk assumption, reduction, avoidance, limitation, planning, and transfer factors. Regulation, organizational, and security technology solutions determine the measures that can be taken (Lehto, 2015).

Artificial intelligence can not only identify cyber threats and risk factors but can also help to prevent these attacks. Artificial intelligence and cognitive data processing are used to detect cyber-attacks, take action against these attacks, and ensure the privacy of the organization. Information security solutions are based on rules created by IT security experts, but the human approach can cause errors and slowness when producing solutions. Machine learning approaches follow a way of identifying abnormalities on network systems, being alert to any attacks that may occur in the system, and investigating possible problems (Dale, 1995).

In a very recent study, a distributed control security architecture for fog radio and optical networks in CPSs is suggested. When security is disabled, the functional assets and interoperability procedure of the security architecture was investigated. In the study, it was proved that malicious CPS nodes were detected with high accuracy, and the possibility of packet loss, latency, and blocking was reduced (Yang et a;., 2020).

In a study of authentication and authorization security research, the authors proposed an approach to providing security based on the artificial intelligence (AI) algorithm to achieve rapid authentication and progressive authorization on large-scale Internet of Things (IoT) networks. In the results of the experiment, they prove that IoT wireless communication is effectively protected against cyber-attacks (Fang et al., 2020). Another exciting study presented an integrated virtual emotion system based on an AI algorithm that treats the virtual emotion barrier, virtual emotion map, and virtual emotion block to protect CPS-enabled smart cities. This study can be a guide for future studies on artificial intelligence supported virtual emotion system (Kim and Ben-Othman, 2020).

In another study, an AI method based on an edge computation system is proposed to protect the CPS from connectivity problems and optimize the use of sensors. Based on a machine learning algorithm and edge computation system, two buffer queues to reduce the degree of connection of the system in parallel are developed. The results of the study show that the AI method based on an edge computation system reduces programming cost, increases resource utilization, and extends the life of the CPS (Wang et al., 2020).

One of the two ML-based studies highlighted the security issues of network slicing, examine the machine learning solution to protect slices against network attacks. The authors analyzed the robustness of their solutions against Denial of Service (DoS) attacks. The experimental result shows that the learning security solution reduces the occurrence of DoS attacks that target network slicing (Liu et al., 2020). In the other study, a machine learning algorithm based on a clustering approach was proposed to provide a faster and more effective leak detection carried out by cyber-attacks in a CPS network. Based on the simulation results, the proposed cluster-based leak detection system shows high accuracy detection against network attacks (Zhang et al., 2020).

In another study, the authors propose an intrusion detection framework based on reinforcement learning algorithms to protect the tool network from internal and external attacks. Experiments in this study have shown results in improving both intrusion detection and prevention decision over time (Xiong et al., 2020).

In another recent study, the authors propose a field monitoring mechanism based on a two-way repetitive neural network to protect the CPS network against GPS identity fraud attacks. The proposed tracking mechanism verifies every power received by analyzing and evaluating the GPS timing error to detect malicious GPS signals and thus detect fraud attacks. Simulation results prove that the proposed mechanism has fast detection time and low timing error prediction accuracy (Bhamidipati et al., 2020).

In the next section, several cyber threats have been listed.

Cyber Threats

Institutions and organizations are required to protect personal data within the scope of the law. For this, the entire IT system needs to be strengthened and protected as all data is protected. If personal data is obtained through cyber-attacks, there is a risk that all information about a particular or identifiable person will be lost. It refers to any process performed on data such as processing personal data, obtaining, storing, making any changes to it, classifying it, transferring it to others and making it accessible to others, or preventing its use and use by others.

In the Turkish constitution, the processing of personal data has been regulated to a certain extent and subject to international standards, as specified by the Law No. 6698 on the Protection of Personal Data. Protection of personal data has been handled by stating that the Constitutional Court has the most fundamental right of individuals as stated in the decision of "the right to protect personal data, as a special form of the right of the person to protect human dignity and to develop his personality freely, during the processing of personal data."

There have been many security breaches over the world, especially in recent years, that show how easily personal data is accessible. Especially in the past few years, it was a period when big companies had difficulties in protecting personal data. Important institutions and structures such as Facebook, Aadhar, and Google have experienced serious data breaches. These events show how accessible personal data is, and IT teams are not able to serve properly.

In 2016, new malware appeared every 4.6 seconds, while in 2017, this dropped to 4.2 seconds. According to the Symantec explanations, 1 of the 13 URLs they analyzed in 2017 reported that it was malicious and that this figure was 1 in 20 in 2016.

Aadhaar is the Indian government identity database managed by the Unique Identification Authority of India (UIDAI). Due to some privileges granted to users who have the Aadhaar number, as high as 1.1 billion of the population of India gave their data to UIDAI. As a result of the violation in the Aadhar database in 2018, critical personal data from the birth date of the individuals to iris scanning information were leaked. This violation was considered the most significant cybersecurity problem of 2017.

In a massive decentralized denial of service (DDoS) attack involving significant companies such as Amazon, Netflix, and Twitter, which appeared in October 2017, thousands of cameras were used to lose the functionality of websites and to overthrow systems by sending billions of baseless requests.

In May 2017, the great attack WannaCry, which affects thousands of computers in over 100 countries, can be given as one of the cybersecurity breaches. This virus had encrypted personal data, making them unavailable and accessible to real users. Users who had not yet backed up their data had to either decode the Bitcoins password or lose their data.

In 2018, Facebook discovered a security issue that could potentially affect 90 million out of service users. The figure was then reduced to 50 million and 30 million afterward, although the exact amount is unknown. The FBI participated in the investigation, and there is limited information about who is behind this highly coordinated attack. Facebook noticed an extraordinary activity in the "View As" feature on September 15, 2018. It was predicted that three different zero-day vulnerabilities were used in the attack. Cyber attackers were able to steal access tokens that will be used to control the accounts of affected users. A wide range of personal data was captured, from the users' age and gender to photos tagged. Also earlier this year, Facebook admitted that it stores passwords for users in plain text. The two security problems that were experienced in a row probably damaged the trust in Facebook to a large extent.

Also, in 2018, the famous hotel Marriott announced a major data breach. But it took them three months to inform their customers that they might be affected. The leaked information included customers' names, phone numbers, payment information, postal addresses, e-mail addresses, and passport numbers. Evidence after the investigation showed that attackers had accessed their systems in early 2014. After the researchers decrypted the files found, they proved to be the customers' personal information, and the full disclosure took place about three months later. This situation caused serious damage to Marriott's reputation.

Wipro Ltd., the outsourcing and consulting giant of Indian IT, announced that the company was attacked by phishing in 2019. The firm confirmed that its IT systems were hacked and stated that it had applied to a forensic firm to address the situation. It was later found that the attackers used the remote access tool ScreenConnect to compromise the security of working machines in Wipro. It was also found that the attackers may have been linked to recent malicious activities in 2017 or even 2015, and reuse most of the previous attacks infrastructure for their current attacks. Many customers were affected by this attack. Naturally, trust in the company decreased.

Dunkin Donuts first said that 2019 was attacked by stuffing towards the end of November. After the attack in January, the company warned its users about more account violations. In this attack, hackers used user credentials leaked to other sites to enter DD Perks reward accounts. A DD Perks reward account includes the user's name and surname, e-mail address (username), and 16-digit DD Perks account number and QR code information types. As a result of this violation, the user's information was taken over by the attackers, and the company lost its reputation and trust.

Toyota's second data breach affected millions of users. On March 29, 2019, the official website of Toyota announced that the violation potentially affected 3.1 million people. The company said hackers do not believe it would have access to private customer or employee data in this case. It is also confirmed that Toyota's IT team is communicating with international cybersecurity experts to get advice on getting to the bottom of the issue.

The FBI claimed that employees from one of Walmart's technology suppliers illegally monitored the e-mail communication of the retailer. The New York Times reported in late 2015 that in early 2016, Compucom employees who were assigned to Walmart's help desk used their access to track certain e-mail accounts at the retailer and allegedly used this information to prevent competitors. According to the FBI report, the plan was discovered by sending a Compucom technician to a Walmart employee with whom he chatted in an instant messaging system after taking a photo of a Walmart discipline e-mail.

On March 6, 2019, the FBI, Stan Black, CISSP, and Citrix's CSIO claimed that international cyber-criminals entered the internal Citrix network unauthorized. While the FBI is continuing its investigations, thehackernews.com reported that the Iranian-backed Iridium hacker group attacked Citrix and stole extensive sensitive data, including e-mails, plans, and other documents. The Iranian hacking group was responsible for cyber-attacks against many government agencies.

UK-based telecommunications provider Virgin Media has announced that it is experiencing a data leak incident that reveals roughly 900,000 customers' personal information. Approximately 900,000 personal information of Virgin Media UK-based customers emerged after one of the marketing databases was not secure on the Internet and made accessible to anyone without any authentication required. The company assured customers that the misconfigured marketing database does not contain affected customers' account passwords or financial information such as credit cards or bank account numbers. The unprotected database was first discovered by researchers at TurgenSec and then reported it responsibly to Virgin Media's security team according to the National Media Cyber Security Centre (NCSC) cybersecurity guidelines. The company said that immediately after the discovery, unauthorized access to the database was shut down, and it launched a fully independent judicial investigation to determine the extent of the violation incident. Affected customers should generally suspect cyber criminals' phishing e-mails, the next step with such data, and should not give users more details, such as their passwords and banking information.

There are many more examples of similar security vulnerabilities that happen to large companies. Cybersecurity Venture predicts that by 2021 cybercrime will cost the world \$ 6 trillion a year. This shows that cyber criminality is more profitable than many illegal activities. It is anticipated that the turnover of the IT sector, which should be evaluated with cybersecurity, will increase more than the previous years.

It may not always be possible for companies to detect data breaches quickly; often, it takes months. The extent of the probable effects of cyber-attacks and the proportion of damage to companies in proportion to this can be vast. For this reason, the funds allocated for the detection of cyber-attacks in companies and the methods to be developed against these attacks should be sufficient. Because soon, the most economically destructive factors for companies are expected to be cyber-attacks.

Cybercriminals can use computer networks or software and hardware components for their interests for various purposes. Often, the target is to attack the company to harm the company, steal money or information, or threaten it. They can utilize all technological components to run malicious code and algorithms. Cyber-attacks can come across in many different ways. The main ones are attacks that threaten data integrity. Attacks such as unauthorized use of personal data and credit card fraud can be given as examples. Attackers may also make violations that serve purposes such as racism, pornography, and terrorism, using their information systems for their destructive purposes. Also, attacks can be made for malicious purposes, where information technologies and communication networks are naturally possible. Examples of these are online fraud and money laundering.

In a few decades, cyber-attacks were generally carried out to tender information privacy. Today, however, the situation has gained a much more complex and dangerous dimension. Even some governments can now support some cybercriminals secretly. Cyber-crimes can now cause much more significant damage to the international cap.

Looking at the security and risk management measures taken in companies in recent years, it is evident that the financial risks caused by cyber threats in the business world have begun to be understood, and security strategies are given more importance. To reduce risks, companies comply with various regulations and organize their security policies to protect their critical data. Also, these security policies help them to come to the fore with their corporate identities. Especially in recent years, companies can make their needs analysis and company planning more effectively and manage their risk processes more effectively by using cloud technology widely. However, cloud systems also provide a favorable ground for cybercrime.

Technological developments such as cloud, IoT, mobile networks, smart devices, and sensors also bring security deficits. If companies using these technologies are not adequately protected, unauthorized access to this data and systems from outside is very likely. In cybercrime, social engineering techniques are applied, and the weaknesses of the system infrastructure and human errors are utilized, making it easier to steal sensitive data.

Cyber threats show great diversity when technical creativity, the number of victims affected, the area of distribution and material resources seized, and the volume of confidential data taken into consideration. In addition to their diversity, cybercrime shows an unexpected rapid change and development.

DDoS attacks and ransomware attacks come first among the most encountered cyber-crimes.

DDoS Attacks

DoS attacks are attacks by hackers to limit or eliminate a particular website, server, or online service. There are multiple ways to make the DoS attacks, but the most popular one is DDoS (distributed denial of service). Connected devices such as multiple computer systems or Internet of Things (IoT) devices are used as a source of attack traffic in DDoS attacks. During the attack, computers or other resources that have probably been exposed to a virus or Trojan target a single system and are forced to drown a data into a server until it becomes unusable. Therefore, both the targeted system and all systems used by the hacker for malicious purposes become victims of the DDoS attacks. While DDoS attacks sometimes cause only minor distress in the target system, sometimes it can cause a long-term collapse in the system. In some cases, wrong encodings, missing updates, unbalanced systems, and even legitimate requests for target systems can cause DDoS-like results.

Attackers who want to carry out DDoS attacks have to take control of an online machine network. The attacker turns his targeted computers or other resources into zombies or bots through malware. Thus, the attacker would have remote control over a group of computers acting in harmony with each other called botnets. After the installation of Botnet is completed, the attacker sends instructions to each boat via a remote control method, and botnets transmit the scheduled requests to the target server. As a result, the target server exposed to data traffic above its regular traffic cannot bear this load and become inoperable. In other words, as a result of the attack, the service provided by the target server is disrupted, and customers' access to the website is blocked. In DDoS attacks, it is quite difficult to distinguish between attack traffic and regular traffic.

DDoS attacks can pose serious business risks with long-term effects. That's why it's essential to understand the threats, vulnerabilities, and risks associated with DDoS attacks for information technology managers and other corporate executives. Although it is almost impossible to prevent being on the receiving side of such an attack, the effects of the attack can be minimized with various basic information security practices. Reviewing the application architecture; analyze stress points and user characteristics; using test tools to imitate attacks and get an idea of weak points; monitoring regular traffic and being prepared for abnormal traffic; examine social media and news about upcoming attacks; prepare a response plan with clear procedures, communication, and customer support plans; using alert tools to inform the team in the event of unexpected traffic patterns and connectivity issues are a few ways to be prepared for a DDoS attack.

Ransomware Attacks

Ransomware is a type of malware that data on a victim's computer is often locked by encryption. Payment is requested before the affected data is decrypted, and the access to the victim is returned. Ransomware attacks are almost always related to money. Unlike other types of attacks, the victim is often notified in the event of an attack and learns the instructions to follow to get rid of the attack. Usually, payments are requested to be made with cryptocurrencies such as bitcoin, so that the identity of the cyber-criminal is unknown.

Ransomware is not a virus. Viruses infect files and software and can replicate. However, ransomware scrambles files and requests payment to make them unusable. Both can be removed with anti-virus software, but if the files are encrypted, retrieval is not possible.

Ransomware damages corporate functioning. The inability to access company files even for a day due to malware causes income to be negatively affected. Ransomware attacks can often leave victims offline for at least a week, sometimes months, and cause serious losses. Systems stay offline for so long, not only because of ransomware locks systems but also because of all the effort required to clean and restore networks. And this business will not only cause financial short-term losses; Also, consumers are afraid to give their data to institutions that they think are not safe and to work with those brands.

Relationship Between Cybersecurity and Artificial Intelligence

Security firms use machine learning, neural networks, advanced analytics, and AI technologies to predict and stop cyber-attacks to prevent data loss in companies. Through AI technology used in cybersecurity, malicious software behaviors can be detected, attack vectors and network abnormalities can be detected, and intrusions can be detected in advance. The problem here is that cybercriminals can also use the same technologies for their attacks.

Cybersecurity will also provide the maximum possible benefit from artificial intelligence for attack detection, as in other methods. Companies cannot rely solely on their knowledge of human intelligence to combat cyber-attacks that are increasing in number, and their damage is exacerbated. Companies must allocate more resources for security strategies and keep up with the developing technology.

Artificial intelligence can help save time and resources, streamline the production process, and help tackle cyber-attacks to help improve their processes. Even though artificial intelligence is undeniably great, human control remains a necessity. AI helps reduce costs and minimize data breaches. It provides more robust security by increasing efficiency. It also supports identification and authentication technologies. Artificial intelligence also helps identify vulnerabilities in the system and saves attack detection time. It is used to provide cyber strategy approaches, to investigate and obtain feasible intelligence, to identify security vulnerabilities in system infrastructures, and to identify distressed and insecure network systems and practices.

Security companies use machine learning to develop security tools for different areas. For example, machine learning helps automate complex processes to detect cyber-attacks and take action. This facilitates concrete and proactive results in processes such as detection, analysis, and prediction of attacks. Detailed information may be required for the detection of attacks. Still, machine learning will be able to learn by recognizing them to identify and combat these attacks and have the ability to develop precautions using technological resources.

In systems that deal with cyber defense, it is necessary to benefit from each of the machine learning, artificial intelligence, and automation techniques to increase human and machine cooperation. For artificial intelligence to be applied to cybersecurity problems, new methods are needed to define the mentioned security deficits, and existing techniques need to be revised. As cybercriminals have already mentioned, artificial intelligence-based security tools must be able to detect and resolve these vulnerabilities, as the system also exploits the weaknesses of the networks and software systems. Also, it should be designed in such a way that it can take action against and prevent attacks when a weakness is detected in the system that is planned to be protected.

MIT's Computer Science and Artificial Intelligence Laboratory (CSAIL) and PatternEx conducted a study on how computers and humans can collaborate to detect cyber threats. In this study, where they consistently included datasets, they developed an artificial intelligence platform aimed at predicting possible cyber-attacks with more reliable results than other systems in use. This platform, called AI2, uses Active Contextual Modeling, a continuous feedback loop between the human resource and the artificial intelligence system. Composed of a combination of machine learning modeling and human expertise, this system works more efficiently than only learning-based solutions. (Conner and Simons, 2016)

OVERVIEW OF ARTIFICIAL INTELLIGENCE TECHNIQUES

Various AI techniques that can be used to prevent cyber-attacks are discussed in this section. As mentioned above, the human approach can lead to delays and mistakes in detecting and preventing cyber threats from time to time. For this reason, as in other areas, machine-based systems are needed in the field of cybersecurity that can make smarter decisions from people. As cyber threats and attacks evolve rapidly with the development of technology, organizations need to include AI techniques in cybersecurity strategies to take precautions against these attacks.

Intelligent Agents

A smart agent (IA) is a self-sustaining computer system that uses observation and communicates with each other through sensors and actuators that regulate their actions to achieve their goals. Intelligent agents, which can be very simple or complex, can learn and use the information to achieve their goals.

Intelligent agent technology is suitable for coping with cyber-attacks, thanks to its mobile structure and adaptability. Intelligent agents are explicitly used to fight Distributed Denial of Service (DDoS) attacks. Defense methods for DDoS attacks sometimes attempt to detect and discard illegitimate traffic, sometimes causing a certain percentage of legitimate packages to be left in the process, which reduces the quality of service. Intelligent agent-based defense methods for DDoS Attacks are fully distributed, providing an early warning when pre-attack activities are detected using trust mechanisms (Duraipandian et al., 2014).

Infrastructure needs to be installed to support cyber agents' movements and communication, but this infrastructure must be inaccessible to enemies. Tools such as neural network-based intrusion detection and hybrid multi-mediated techniques are required for cybersecurity applications (Herrero et al., 2007). An agent-based distributed intrusion detection is shown in (Pedireddy and Vidal, 2003).

Neural Nets

Neural networks gained importance after the perceptron was created in 1957 by Frank Rosenblatt. After this date, artificial neurons were evaluated as essential components of neural networks (Rosenblatt, 1957). Perceptron can learn and solve challenging issues, even though they consist of only a few variations. Neural networks are different because they have numerous artificial neurons. Thus, neural networks can do parallel learning and decision making processes to a greater extent and rapidly. Processing speed is an important feature of neural networks. It successfully performs pattern recognition to detect cyber-attacks (Klein et al., 2010). Neural networks supported by software or hardware components are also used to detect and prevent intruders (Bai et al., 2006, Barika et al., 2009, Bitter et al., 2010, Chang et al., 2007 and DeLooze, 2006). Neural networks can be used in many areas, such as detecting DoS attacks, malware classification, spam detection, zombie detection, and computer worm identification and forensic research (Ahmad et al., 2009, Stopel et al., 2006 and Fei et al., 2005).

Neural networks provide high speed when supported by hardware or graphics processor components and can therefore be used as a cyber defense mechanism. Thanks to the developing technologies in neural networks day by day, developments have been experienced. 3G neural networks are examples of these. Neural networks can better imitate biological neurons in this way and provide various application opportunities. Using Field Programmable Gate Arrays (FPGAs) enabled the rapid development of neural networks. At the same time, significant progress has been made to strengthen its capacity to resist changing threats in line with the advancement of technology.

Expert Systems

Expert systems are the most used AI tools. These systems are software that tries to respond to the questions of consumers, customers, or other software on commercial platforms. Expert systems can be used as a decision support mechanism in the field of finance, type, or cybersecurity. Simple or complex expert system software can also work as a small diagnostic system only or turn into a more sleepy hybrid system. Thanks to this structure, it can be a beneficial and robust system for solving complex and difficult problems.

Within a specialist system, there is a database where expert information related to the application area in which it is used is kept. It also includes an inference engine to get answers to by keeping more information about the situation in question. The expert system shell contains an empty knowledge base and extraction engine when no information is loaded at the beginning. These fill up as information flows. An expert system shell should be used to add new information to the database software. The system can be expanded with different programs that can be used in collaboration with client programs and hybrid expert systems.

Expert systems can work effectively and practically in many applications. For example, it is convenient to be used in simulations and calculations. Expert systems contain many different illustration forms, but the most commonly used are rule-based ones. The associate expert system works by the standard of the information field in the expert system and regardless of the information illustration. This situation leads to problems in the development of applications. Since the cybersecurity expert system is designed for security, it decides which security measures to be chosen and simplifies the selection process. While doing this, it uses limited resources in the most effective way (Anderson et al., 1995 and Lunt et al.,

1988). For example, while intrusion detection is performed, cybersecurity expert systems work in a way that takes precautions.

Specific information about different network attack behaviors is stored in the relevant database and used later when called from that database. These are usually stored as a web application component. To determine and use the suitability of real-time data packets, a series of rules must pass. These rule sets are also kept in the relevant database for the application infrastructure and used as needed.

Search

Search is another kind of artificial intelligence technique that is inherent to problems. Under normal circumstances, the search is applied continuously, without listening. It is necessary to use general search formulas to perform the search process. For this, some solution candidates should be identified, and a procedure should be found to decide whether they meet the requests. Utilizing additional information to direct the search process can significantly increase search power. Search power provides many advantages for programs and is a critical factor in increasing the performance of the program. Based on the program's needs and content, a search method has been developed to evaluate search information to eliminate search problems. Various ways of searching have also been developed in artificial discipline, and they can be widely used in various programs. However, in some cases, these search techniques may not appear as artificial intelligence applications. For example, dynamic programming is used to find optimal security issues; the search is hidden inside the package and does not appear as an AI application. Search packages, trees, $\alpha\beta$-search, minimax search, and random search frame size are widely used and help in deciding for cybersecurity. The $\alpha\beta$-search formula initially developed for pc chess is typically an implementation of useful divide and conquer preparation. This method is used to find problems and mostly to decide after two enemies choose their absolute best action. Uses predictions of minimum safe gain and maximum feasible loss. This typically allows the system to ignore too many options and rush the call (Ojamaa et al., 2008).

Especially in recent years, search algorithms have started to be used with learning the machine and deep learning methods. A better understanding of these algorithms and using them where necessary can significantly improve the performance of search processes of applications. Also, as more powerful computing technologies such as quantum computing begin to be used, the likelihood of using search-based artificial intelligence will increase.

Learning

Machine learning develops computational strategies to gain new knowledge. It includes new capabilities and better approaches to structuring existing information. The learning problem can be encountered in many different ways. The situation is easier in simple parametric learning. However, when the situation progresses to complex symbolic learning styles, sampling, learning concepts, and behavior, and including grammar and functions, the problem of learning becomes complicated. At this stage, both supervised and unsupervised learning can be used.

Unsupervised learning should be used when there is a large amount of data. Cyber defense systems, in which a wide range of records can be collected, are structurally suitable for unattended learning techniques. The use of unattended learning techniques in artificial intelligence discipline has revealed the concept of data mining.

One of the neural networks that use the unattended learning technique is Self-Organizing Maps (SOM) (Bai et al., 2006; Pachghare et al., 2009). SOM is generally used for classification purposes. Since it is unsupervised (it can learn on its own), it is a model whose output can be represented in the desired space. Although its algorithm is simple, in practice, the number of cycles must be determined firmly; otherwise, this method may forget what has been learned.

SOM can also be used to detect security threats in computer networks. A software examines each network packet that generates regular network traffic and a self-organizing map is created on the pack with specific features. This neural network will create a certain pattern. This is the learning process for a self-organizing map. After this learning process has a certain maturity, the examination process can be started. In other words, each package will be examined in network traffic; if the package examined does not comply with the general pattern, it will be perceived as a threat. This package will also be included in the learning process. In other words, as long as the situation, which is defined as a threat at first, is repeated, it can no longer be a threat and be compatible with the pattern.

A recent article using the SOM technique as a data analysis system aims to explain how far this approach can be pushed to analyze network traffic and detect malicious behavior in the wild. For this purpose, three different unsupervised SOM training scenarios are designed, implemented, and evaluated for different data collection conditions. The approach is evaluated in public network traffic and web server access datasets. The results show that the approach has a high potential as a data analysis tool on unknown traffic/web service requests and invisible attack behavior (Le et al., 2019).

Parallel learning algorithms executed in parallel hardware are also a kind of learning method. These learning techniques use genetic algorithms and neural networks. For example, genetic algorithms and fuzzy logic have been used to identify some threat detection systems (Hosseini et al., 2010). In other studies like this, this kind of practice has also been performed (Suroor et al., 2017; Hassan, 2016 and Hassan, 2017).

Constraint Satisfaction

In artificial intelligence, constraint satisfaction is called a process of finding solutions to constraints that try to impose the conditions that the variables must meet (Tsang, 2014). Based on this solution discovery process, it creates a set of values for a field in the applicable region, which corresponds to all constraints for the variables.

The techniques used in constraint satisfaction vary depending on the type of constraints evaluated. Restricted satisfaction problems are used frequently, and they are called restrictions on a limited area since they operate with problems based on restrictions in a finite area. These types of problems are often resolved by the search method, in particular by a trackback or local search format. Constraint spread is one of the other methods used in such problems. This method can solve many problems or say that it cannot be solved effectively, but this is not always possible. Constraint propagation methods can also be used in some cases with search methods to facilitate solving a particular problem. Other types of constraints considered use variable elimination or simplex algorithm to solve problems. All restriction-determining strategies aim to limit the search, taking into account only relevant information. It can also be used with constraint method, scenario analysis, and logic programming.

LIMITATIONS AND FUTURE STUDIES

Short-term and long-term goals should be evaluated separately when analyzing the artificial intelligence techniques used in Cyber Security or when developing and implementing new techniques. In Cyber Security, various artificial intelligence methods can be applied directly to some problems today. There are also urgent Cyber Security issues that require advanced intelligent solutions in the future. This study focuses on artificial intelligence applications. In the future, completely new data processing methods for situation management and decision-making may be introduced to detect and prevent new attacks being encountered, and they may offer more effective solutions to the cybersecurity issue. For this, a standard and hierarchical data design should be used in software systems that can decide and operate accordingly. For the internet-based cyber-attack mechanisms to work properly, an effective data processing system must work. Only automatic data management will ensure those decision-makers make the right choice at any level and make a quick assessment. Intelligent systems are currently used in various applications that are integrated into a software system and come as default and are often hidden in an application such as security measures. However, for complex problems, including cyber-attack problems that are difficult to detect, large data flows are required, so large databases should be developed. Thus, intelligent systems can have a wider application area. For this, it may be necessary to allocate sufficient resources and regularly invest in data collection and development of large-scale databases.

Considering future studies, it is assumed that the development of artificial intelligence will increase significantly, and the expected level will come in a few decades. Developments in artificial intelligence also bring with it the dangers that this progress can pose. As a result of these developments, the concept of "singularity" emerges. Singularity is the creation of synthetic intelligence that can be smarter than humans by utilizing technology. Many technologies can be used for this purpose. Even though artificial neural networks are one of the first things that come to mind, there are also entirely different technologies that will help create a smarter system than human beings.

The creation of technology that includes smarter minds than humans should be designed to overcome the capacity and vision of existing advanced devices. Some researchers believe that by introducing the concept of singularity, effectiveness will change. It is meaningless to perceive the concept of singularity as a threat, but with the rapid development of information technology, some technologies must change to advance software systems to become more intelligent in the coming years. Whether a synthetic intelligence that is different from human intelligence is obtained or the concept of singularity has come, the main issue is the ability to use higher AI in cybersecurity than criminals have.

CONCLUSION

Given the rapid development of the malware and cyber-attack class, the development of smart cybersecurity routes is inevitable. The expertise in DDoS mitigation shows that large-scale attacks are successfully prevented when using smart systems, despite the use of very limited resources. It is seen that most of the studies in the field of cybersecurity are provided by analysis in artificial visual networks; the most commonly applied AI results in focus. Such applications of visual networks can be used in cybersecurity, especially in the detection phase of cyber-attacks. In areas where neural networks cannot be used as the most appropriate technology, implementation of other types of intelligent cybersecurity routes may become imperative. These situations are usually provided with support, scenario awareness, and data management steps. The availability of professional system technology provides advantages at this stage. On the other hand, the rapid progression of general computing is complicated, but there remains a threat that a level of computing can be used, which is caused by the compromise of information processing, and attackers change that. New approaches and insights in machine learning, their simulation, and new developments in design can create opportunities to increase significantly the cybersecurity capability of the systems that will use them.

With the existence of continually developing information technology, it is arising from increasingly complex security problems. Many organizations have set out to investigate how these risks in cybersecurity can be reduced by using artificial intelligence methods. This situation causes an increase in the use of artificial intelligence in cyber-attack systems. In the field of cybersecurity, some organizations have not yet used any artificial intelligence methods, as well as companies that are already in use. These have to provide a set of criteria and determine a suitable security strategy in the application of artificial intelligence techniques to cybersecurity problems. Organizations need to identify a strategy that addresses infrastructure, data systems, implementation areas, governance, and case selection. Making this plan will help organizations avoid losses and even access additional sources of income.

REFERENCES

Ahmad, I., Abdullah, A. B., & Alghamdi, A. S. (2009, October). Application of artificial neural network in detection of DOS attacks. In *Proceedings of the 2nd international conference on Security of information and networks* (pp. 229-234). 10.1145/1626195.1626252

Anderson, D., Frivold, T., & Valdes, A. (1995). Next-generation intrusion detection expert system (NIDES). *The Summary (Indianapolis, Ind.)*.

Anwar, A., & Hassan, S. I. (2017). Applying Artificial Intelligence Techniques to Prevent Cyber Assaults. *International Journal of Computational Intelligence Research*, *13*(5), 883–889.

Bai, J., Wu, Y., Wang, G., Yang, S. X., & Qiu, W. (2006, May). A novel intrusion detection model based on multi-layer self-organizing maps and principal component analysis. In *International Symposium on Neural Networks* (pp. 255-260). Springer. 10.1007/11760191_37

Barika, F., Hadjar, K., & El-Kadhi, N. (2009). Artificial neural network for mobile IDS solution. *Security Management*, 271–277.

Bhamidipati, S., Kim, K. J., Sun, H., & Orlik, P. V. (2020). Artificial-Intelligence-Based Distributed Belief Propagation and Recurrent Neural Network Algorithm for Wide-Area Monitoring Systems. *IEEE Network*, *34*(3), 64–72. doi:10.1109/MNET.011.1900322

Bitter, C., Elizondo, D. A., & Watson, T. (2010, July). Application of artificial neural networks and related techniques to intrusion detection. In *The 2010 International Joint Conference on Neural Networks (IJCNN)* (pp. 1-8). IEEE. 10.1109/IJCNN.2010.5596532

Chang, R. I., Lai, L. B., Su, W. D., Wang, J. C., & Kouh, J. S. (2007). Intrusion detection by backpropagation neural networks with sample-query and attribute-query. *International Journal of Computational Intelligence Research*, *3*(1), 6–10. doi:10.5019/j.ijcir.2007.76

Conner-Simons, A. (2016). *System predicts 85 percent of cyber-attacks using input from human experts.* Massachusetts Institute of Technology.

Dale, R. (1995). An introduction to natural language generation. *European Summer School in Logic, Language and Information, ESSLLI'95.*

DeLooze, L. L. (2006, July). Attack characterization and intrusion detection using an ensemble of self-organizing maps. In *The 2006 IEEE International Joint Conference on Neural Network Proceedings* (pp. 2121-2128). IEEE.

Duraipandian, M., & Palanisamy, C. (2014, February). An intelligent agent based defense architecture for ddos attacks. In *2014 International Conference on Electronics and Communication Systems (ICECS)* (pp. 1-7). IEEE. 10.1109/ECS.2014.6892819

Fang, H., Qi, A., & Wang, X. (2020). Fast Authentication and Progressive Authorization in Large-Scale IoT: How to Leverage AI for Security Enhancement. *IEEE Network, 34*(3), 24–29. doi:10.1109/MNET.011.1900276

Fei, B. K. L., Eloff, J. H. P., Olivier, M. S., Tillwick, H. M., & Venter, H. S. (2005). Using self-organising maps for anomalous behaviour detection in a computer forensic investigation. *Proceedings of the Fifth Annual Information Security South Africa Conference.*

Hassan, S. I. (2016). Extracting the sentiment score of customer review from unstructured big data using Map Reduce algorithm. *International Journal of Database Theory and Application, 9*(12), 289–298. doi:10.14257/ijdta.2016.9.12.26

Hassan, S. I. (2017). Designing a flexible system for automatic detection of categorical student sentiment polarity using machine learning. *International Journal of u-and e-Service. Science and Technology, 10*(3), 25–32.

Herrero, Á., Corchado, E., Pellicer, M. A., & Abraham, A. (2007). Hybrid multi agent-neural network intrusion detection with mobile visualization. In *Innovations in Hybrid Intelligent Systems* (pp. 320–328). Springer. doi:10.1007/978-3-540-74972-1_42

Hosseini, R., Dehmeshki, J., Barman, S., Mazinani, M., & Qanadli, S. (2010, July). A genetic type-2 fuzzy logic system for pattern recognition in computer aided detection systems. In *International Conference on Fuzzy Systems* (pp. 1-7). IEEE. 10.1109/FUZZY.2010.5584773

Kaspersky lab. (2018). *What is Cyber-Security?* AO Kaspersky Lab. Retrieved to 10.01.2020 https://www.kaspersky.com/resource-center/definitions/what-is-cyber-security

Kim, H., & Ben-Othman, J. (2020). Toward Integrated Virtual Emotion System with AI Applicability for Secure CPS-Enabled Smart Cities: AI-Based Research Challenges and Security Issues. *IEEE Network, 34*(3), 30–36. doi:10.1109/MNET.011.1900299

Klein, G., Ojamaa, A., Grigorenko, P., Jahnke, M., & Tyugu, E. (2010, September). Enhancing response selection in impact estimation approaches. In *Military Communications and Information Systems Conference (MCC)*, Wroclaw, Poland.

Le, D. C., Zincir-Heywood, A. N., & Heywood, M. I. (2019). Unsupervised monitoring of network and service behaviour using self organizing maps. *Journal of Cyber Security and Mobility*, *8*(1), 15–52. doi:10.13052/jcsm2245-1439.812

Lehto, M. (2015). Phenomena in the cyber world. In *Cyber Security: Analytics, Technology and Automation* (pp. 3–29). Cham: Springer. doi:10.1007/978-3-319-18302-2_1

Liu, Q., Han, T., & Ansari, N. (2020). Learning-Assisted Secure End-to-End Network Slicing for Cyber-Physical Systems. *IEEE Network*, *34*(3), 37–43. doi:10.1109/MNET.011.1900303

Lord, N. (2017). *What is Cyber Security? Data Insider*. Retrieved to 15.01.2020 https://digitalguardian.com/blog/what-cyber-security

Lunt, T. F., & Jagannathan, R. (1988, April). A prototype real-time intrusion-detection expert system. In *IEEE Symposium on Security and Privacy* (Vol. 59). IEEE.

Ojamaa, A., Tyugu, E., & Kivimaa, J. (2008, November). Pareto-optimal situaton analysis for selection of security measures. In MILCOM 2008-2008 IEEE Military Communications Conference (pp. 1-7). IEEE. doi:10.1109/MILCOM.2008.4753520

Pachghare, V. K., Kulkarni, P., & Nikam, D. M. (2009, July). Intrusion detection system using self organizing maps. In *2009 International Conference on Intelligent Agent & Multi-Agent Systems* (pp. 1-5). IEEE. 10.1109/IAMA.2009.5228074

Parrend, P., Navarro, J., Guigou, F., Deruyver, A., & Collet, P. (2018). Foundations and applications of artificial Intelligence for zero-day and multi-step attack detection. *EURASIP Journal on Information Security*, *2018*(1), 1-21.

Pedireddy, T., & Vidal, J. M. (2003, July). A prototype multiagent network security system. In *Proceedings of the second international joint conference on Autonomous agents and multiagent systems* (pp. 1094-1095). 10.1145/860575.860812

Rosenblatt, F. (1957). *The perceptron, a perceiving and recognizing automaton Project Para*. Cornell Aeronautical Laboratory.

Stopel, D., Boger, Z., Moskovitch, R., Shahar, Y., & Elovici, Y. (2006, July). Application of artificial neural networks techniques to computer worm detection. In *The 2006 IEEE International Joint Conference on Neural Network Proceedings* (pp. 2362-2369). IEEE.

Tsang, E. (2014). *Foundations of constraint satisfaction: the classic text*. BoD–Books on Demand.

Vähäkainu, P., & Lehto, M. (2019, February). Artificial Intelligence in the Cyber Security Environment. In *ICCWS 2019 14th International Conference on Cyber Warfare and Security: ICCWS 2019* (p. 431). Academic Conferences and Publishing Limited.

Wang, T., Liang, Y., Yang, Y., Xu, G., Peng, H., Liu, A., & Jia, W. (2020). An Intelligent Edge-Computing-Based Method to Counter Coupling Problems in Cyber-Physical Systems. *IEEE Network*, *34*(3), 16–22. doi:10.1109/MNET.011.1900251

Xiong, M., Li, Y., Gu, L., Pan, S., Zeng, D., & Li, P. (2020). Reinforcement Learning Empowered IDPS for Vehicular Networks in Edge Computing. *IEEE Network, 34*(3), 57–63. doi:10.1109/MNET.011.1900321

Yang, H., Zhan, K., Kadoch, M., Liang, Y., & Cheriet, M. (2020). *BLCS: Brain-like based distributed control security in cyber physical systems.* arXiv preprint arXiv:2002.06259

Zhang, L., Mu, D., Hu, W., & Tai, Y. (2020). Machine-Learning-Based Side-Channel Leakage Detection in Electronic System-Level Synthesis. *IEEE Network, 34*(3), 44–49. doi:10.1109/MNET.011.1900313

ADDITIONAL READING

Demertzis, K., & Iliadis, L. (2015). A bio-inspired hybrid artificial intelligence framework for cyber security. In *Computation, Cryptography, and Network Security* (pp. 161–193). Cham: Springer. doi:10.1007/978-3-319-18275-9_7

Dilek, S., Çakır, H., & Aydın, M. (2015). Applications of artificial intelligence techniques to combating cyber crimes: A review. *arXiv preprint arXiv:1502.03552.*

Li, J. H. (2018). Cyber security meets artificial intelligence: A survey. *Frontiers of Information Technology & Electronic Engineering, 19*(12), 1462–1474. doi:10.1631/FITEE.1800573

Morel, B. (2011, October). Artificial intelligence and the future of cybersecurity. In *Proceedings of the 4th ACM workshop on Security and artificial intelligence* (pp. 93-98). 10.1145/2046684.2046699

Sedjelmaci, H., Guenab, F., Senouci, S. M., Moustafa, H., Liu, J., & Han, S. (2020). Cyber Security Based on Artificial Intelligence for Cyber-Physical Systems. *IEEE Network, 34*(3), 6–7. doi:10.1109/MNET.2020.9105926

Taddeo, M., McCutcheon, T., & Floridi, L. (2019). Trusting artificial intelligence in cybersecurity is a double-edged sword. *Nature Machine Intelligence*, 1-4.

Talwar, R., & Koury, A. (2017). Artificial intelligence–the next frontier in IT security? *Network Security, 2017*(4), 14–17. doi:10.1016/S1353-4858(17)30039-9

Yampolskiy, R. V., & Spellchecker, M. S. (2016). Artificial intelligence safety and cybersecurity: A timeline of AI failures. *arXiv preprint arXiv:1610.07997.*

KEY TERMS AND DEFINITIONS

Denial of Service (DoS): A DoS (denial of service) attack is a targeted attack, preventing the system from providing service and preventing users from accessing the system. Every system has a volume of network traffic it can handle. When these resources of the system are overloaded by the attackers, the system services slow down, and even the services provided by the system collapse completely as a result of these attacks.

Distributed Denial of Service (DDoS): DDoS (distributed denial of service) occurs by starting the attack from a large number of different sources, not from one source. botnets consisting of devices called zombies are used to carry out DDoS attacks. These zombie devices are electronic devices captured by hackers and used for attackers' purposes. DDoS attacks are more successful than Dos attacks in achieving what is desired. Since it is carried out from multiple sources towards the target, it becomes difficult to identify the main source.

Field-Programmable Gate Array (FPGA): FPGAs are digital integrated circuits consisting of programmable logic blocks and interconnections between these blocks and have wide application areas. It is produced to realize the logic functions needed by the designer.

Internet of Things (IoT): The internet of things is defined as "a worldwide network of uniquely addressable objects created among themselves, and the objects in this network communicating with each other with a specific protocol". Also, this concept can be defined as a system of devices that communicate with each other through various communication protocols and have formed an intelligent network by connecting and sharing information.

Intrusion Detection System (IDS): The intrusion detection system (IDS) is used to detect malicious activity or links in network traffic. monitors all inbound and outbound network activity and identifies suspicious patterns that could indicate a network or system attack from someone trying to break into or hijack a system.

Intrusion Prevention System (IPS): An intrusion prevention system (IPS) is a form of network security that works to detect and prevent identified threats. Intrusion prevention systems constantly monitor your network, look for potential malicious events, and collect information about them. IPS reports these events to system administrators and takes preventative actions such as closing access points and configuring firewalls to prevent future attacks. IPS solutions can also be used to detect issues with corporate security policies and deter employees and network guests from violating the rules contained in these policies.

Self-Organizing Maps (SOM): A self-organizing map (SOM) is a low-dimensional (typically two-dimensional) type of neural network that has been trained using unsupervised learning to represent training instances as a discrete representation of the input field. Self-organizing maps differ from other neural networks in that they implement competitive learning versus error-correction learning (such as backpropagation with reverse descent) and use a neighborhood function to preserve the topological characteristics of the entrance area. SOM can also be used to detect security threats in computer networks. Each network package that creates regular network traffic is analyzed by software and a self-organizing map is created with certain features on the package. This neural network creates a certain pattern and the learning process begins. If a packet examined in network traffic does not match the general pattern, it is detected as a threat and included in the learning process. As long as the situation that was initially defined as a threat is repeated, it may come out of being a threat and be compatible with the pattern.

Chapter 5
Social Perspective of Suspicious Activity Detection in Facial Analysis:
An ML–Based Approach for the Indian Perspective

Rohit Rastogi

(iD) https://orcid.org/0000-0002-6402-7638

Dayalbagh Educational Institute, India & ABES Engineering College, Ghaziabad, India

Priyanshi Garg

ABES Engineering College, Ghaziabad, India

ABSTRACT

The world is witnessing an unprecedented growth of cyber-physical systems (CPS), which are foreseen to revolutionize our world via creating new services and applications in a variety of sectors such as environmental monitoring, mobile health systems, and intelligent transportation systems and so on. The information and communication technology (ICT) sector is experiencing significant growth in data traffic, driven by the widespread usage of smart phones, tablets, and video streaming, along with the significant growth of sensors deployments that are anticipated soon. This chapter describes suspicious activity detection using facial analysis. Suspicious activity is the actions of an individual or group that is outside the normally acceptable standards for those people or that particular area. In this chapter, the authors propose a novel and cost-effective framework designed for suspicious activity detection using facial expression analysis or emotion detection analysis in law enforcement. This chapter shows a face detection module that is intended to detect faces from a real-time video.

DOI: 10.4018/978-1-7998-5101-1.ch005

INTRODUCTION

Suspicious Activity

The chapter describes initially the basics of initial crime status at world, face recognition and its tells and techniques, machine learning and data analytics, and its tool and techniques. For ease of audiences, it also gives a brief review of Data mining, Regression, AI, and CPS. In the next section of the literature review, the famous authors and the gist of their work on the content have been enlisted. Then in the application section, the latest classification techniques of support SVM, Dlib, CNN, and RNN has been introduced and their application on the data set is reflected. In the result section, the different emotions and objects have been recognized and their accuracy has been discussed. Then in the later part the recommendations, novelty, application, limitations have of the research work are explained followed by concluding remarks.

Face Recognition

The world is going through an extraordinary heightening of the CPS also known as cyber-physical systems, which are envisaged to transfigure our world by creating new software applications and services in a large variety of domains such as intelligent transportation systems, systems for monitoring the environment, and intelligent transportation systems and so on. The ICT sector also known as the information and communication technology sector is also going through an impact making growth in data traffic, which is driven by the high usage of tablets, smart cellphones, and video streaming along with the notable growth of deployment of sensors that are forecasted soon [Toygar et al., 2003; Viola et al., 2004].

Machine Learning

If the performance at tasks as measured by the performance measure (known as P) improves, then the agent is said to have to gain knowledge or learning from experience denoted by E for some set of tasks denoted by T. For example, Mailing System [Mitchell, 1997], Playing Checkers game.

There are different categories of machine learning:

1. Supervised machine learning teaches us about learning an input and output map (classification: categorical output, regression: continuous output)
2. Unsupervised machine learning teaches us about discovering patterns in the input dataset (clustering: cohesive grouping, --association: frequent co-occurrence)
3. Reinforcement machine learning – learning control

Data Analysis

This is the technique used for extracting useful, relevant, and meaningful information from the huge amount of data in a structured manner for fulfilling the purpose of Parameter estimation also known as inferring the unknowns, identification and classification of features, testing of Hypothesis, and detection of fault and Development and Prediction of Model also known as Forecasting.

Tools of Data Analysis: Weka, R, Python

Python is a high-level language, which is also object-oriented and is used highly in the problems of semantic dynamic and also used for general-purpose programming. It is interpreted programming language. It is used for: web development (server-side), software development. The way to run a python file is like this on the command line:

helloworld.py
print ("Hello, World!")

Weka and R

It is a freely available s/w package containing a collection of machine learning algorithms under the GNU (General Public License). It is an open-source. The algorithms present in Weka are all coded in java and they can be used by calling them from their java pod. However with also provides a graphical user interface from which the algorithms can directly be applied to data sets.

R software: R is the programming language. It is freely available s/w. It is used for, statistical and analysis, data manipulation, graphic display. Effective data handling and storage of o/p is possible.

> 2 + 2=4 [Tripathi et al., 2014].

DATA MINING AND REFERENTIAL TECHNIQUES

Data Mining (DM)

Data mining refers to taking out the most useful information that is not known previously from a huge amount of input dataset. For example web, images, and text of databases. Likely outcomes prediction, focusing on large datasets and datasets and automatic discovery of patterns are the key properties of Data mining.

Figure 1. Examples of classification [Chowanda et al., 2016]

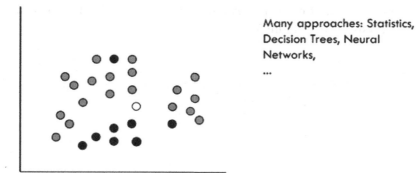

Many approaches: Statistics,
Decision Trees, Neural
Networks,

...

Tracking Patterns

Learning to recognize patterns from the huge input datasets is one of the top techniques in data mining.

Classification

Learning a method to predict the class of frequency with the help of classified (pre-labeled) examples. Input to output is mapped by supervised learning by following two techniques:

1. Classification-categorical output
2. Regression-continuous output

Error is generally measured by the task of classification (as per Figure1).

Association (Dependency Modeling)

Going through the following set of record of data, each of which has a few numbers from the collection are given;

●   The occurrence of an object based on the incidence of other items will be predicted by the production of dependency rules (as per Figure 2.).

Figure 2. Production of dependency rules [Chowanda et al., 2016]

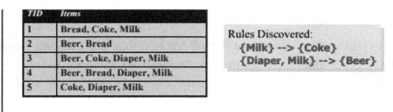

Outlier Detection (Anomaly/ Deviation Detection)

The verification or identification of particular data records that might be the data errors or interesting that requires further analysis (as per Figure 3).

Clustering

An example of cluster can be seen in Figure 3.

Regression

Trying to find a function that represents the data with minimum accuracy. A predictor is constructed that predicts a continuous-value function, or ordered value, as opposed to a categorical label.

Figure 3. Example of clustering [Chowanda et al., 2016]

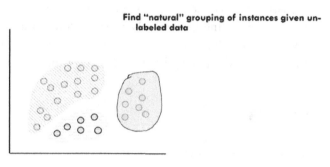

Regression is a static methodology that is most often used for numeric prediction.

Rule-Based Inferences

This is a very important method: There are different ways to handle uncertainty. The different ways of uncertainty: one can be probabilities where specify the likelihood of a conclusion, apply Bayesian reasoning. And the certainty factor is an estimate of confidence in conclusions. It is an estimate provided by the experts. It is not as mathematically precise as is the case of probabilities but it is also very effective. e.g. - MYCIN is a medical expert system for analysis of meningitis infections. MYCIN uses a backward chaining rule-based expert system.

Applications of Data Mining

1. Data Mining in agriculture.
2. Mass surveillance /Surveillance
3. NSA (National security agency)
4. Customer analytic
5. Educational data mining
6. Retail and services
7. Manufacturing
8. Finance and insurance
9. Telecommunication and utilities
10. Transport industry
11. Healthcare and medical industry

ARTIFICIAL INTELLIGENCE

The branch of computer science that deals with the research and formation of computers and exhibits intelligence in some form are called Artificial Intelligence (AI). The exhibiting intelligence of computer systems is very similar to the natural intelligence of human beings. The concept of artificial intelligence is wholly based on the concept of knowledge. So for now, we are discussing some of the pieces of data that can give us the information, and then that information helps in building knowledge from raw data. Knowledge is a piece of information that is used to perform a particular task or concluding some important results. In the context of artificial intelligence, there are different forms of knowledge such as operational or procedural knowledge, which talks about the procedures that will have to be adopted too; the knowledge that we are adopting will come up with a particular problem,

CYBER PHYSICAL SYSTEMS

CPSs or Cyber-Physical Systems also often known as the smart systems consists of the networks of physical and computational components that are co-engineered. Interacting networks of physical components and computational. So, computational is the cyber one-and physical is the physical world in which these systems are operating, physical world. Cyber-Physical Systems are embedded systems. So, these are cyber-physical systems are you can think of the conceptually as a cyber-physical system, conceptually as an embedded system plus the physical system together with you what you get is the cyber-physical system.

CPSs are large-scaled, federated, life-critical, and geographically dispersed systems that comprise control and actuators, components of networking, and sensors. Some examples of cyber-physical systems include smart grids, pervasive health care systems, unmanned aircraft systems, and first responder situational awareness systems. These systems consist of many control loops, tight timing requirements, foreseeable network traffic, legacy components, and possibly wireless network segments. CPSs fuse cyber (comprising network components and commodity servers) and physical (comprising sensors and actuators) domains [Khatoun, 2017].

The modern development of technology is fueled by Data Science and AI, communication, simultaneous advances in software, actuators, materials, sensors, and some of their combinations such as batteries, AR and VR, and 3D printing. Different types of perspectives on these advances in technology have led to the formation of many terms such as Industry 4.0, IoT, CPS, and Swarm that helps us to represent new classes of systems that are technologically enabled. As a general notion, we focus on CPS. The CPSs were introduced in 2006 in the United States to characterize "the integration of physical systems and processes with networked computing" for the systems that "use computations and communication deeply embedded in and interacting with physical processes to add new capabilities to physical systems". In the context of the above discussion, the word cyber can be alternatively referred to as the dictionary definition of "relating to or involving computers or computer networks" or more general systems of feedback as in the cybernetics field pioneered by Wiener. Unless otherwise noted, we consider both interpretations of CPS to be valid and, use the term cyber to refer to the software or computing parts of a CPS.

LITERATURE SURVEY AND PREVIOUS WORK

The third stage includes object detection. Pradhan and Team (2012) mention CNN-based deep learning techniques. He focused on the fact that CNN is trained per line from the raw pixel level to the final object categories. He also told about various challenges, which need to be removed in the form of partial or complete obstruction, separating the state of light, position, scale, etc. The reader also said that when the feature map is generated with pooling layers, the image which is decorated by map activation can be treated from this feature map. The process is repeated until the desired result is produced. He also mentioned about important datasets for object detection such as Microsoft COCO, CIFAR-10, and CI-FAR-100, CUB-200-2011, Caltech-256, ILSVRC, PASCAL VOC Challenge dataset.

Pradhan, A. (2012) has discussed various approaches for object detection in his work. 'You Only Look Once' (YOLO) is one such framework for object detection in real-time. The improved model YOLO9000 can categorize into 9000 object categories. According to him, YOLO9000 combines a distinct dataset using a joint training approach [Sharma and Rameshan, 2017].

They have discovered the need for near-sensor data to detect real-time objects and have uncovered this problem for integrating a centralized and powerful processor to process data from different servers because the large datasets are deep to learn necessary. Pathak concluded that there is a scope of providing "Object Detection as a Service" in a variety of applications. The last stage involves speech recognition. Andy and Allen have suggested an approach to learning the conversation in the Indonesian language using the long-short-term memory and neural network that is recurrent. He used to use words in vocabulary with a vector-based model.

According to Miles, B. (2018), the conversation system is categorized into two groups: retrieval-based which picks the best answer from possible answers, and a generative model in which the answers are loaded previously. Their work exposes deficiencies that are the difficulty in training, errors of grammar, and the challenge of finding the best dataset for a generative model. He explained that by using the statistical method in vector, word formatting can be implemented.

Miles, B. (2018) also discovered a way to deep learn a conversation in which the training model learns from a sequence of words from both the input and output dataset. Initial processing involves finding and filtering. Initially, data (news data over five years from Compass) is collected from two sources. Crawled data is then filtered by removing punctuation and split paragraphs in one sentence per line. Then processed data is used to create vectors via intensification of learning words, which by using the Dual Encoder LSTM can learn a conversation. They simultaneously searched for two pre-trained models: Conversation models and word representation vectors to learn deeper conversations.

Capabilities, success rate, and speed of attacks can be increased and augmented by the malicious use of artificial intelligence. Opportunities to commit a crime and to create a new threat landscape for new criminal tactics can be expanded by the Information and communication technologies also known as ICTs and Artificial Intelligence [Brundage, 2018]. In the report on malicious AI, the authors warned about the changing threat landscape by the malicious uses of AI technologies. The AI field is broadly distinguished between the rule-based techniques and the machine learning (ML)-based techniques, which allow computer systems to learn from a large amount of data.

Attack process is now become automated as Cybercriminals learn to use AI technologies enhanced algorithms and approaches and used them as a weapon. The shift to AI technologies with use cases such as vector machines support, reinforcement learning, deep learning, and genetic algorithms which has some highly unintended consequences such as facilitating the criminal actions more efficiently [Goodfellow et al., 2016].

Therefore, awareness of new trends in cybercrime is becoming significantly more important to drive appropriate defensive actions. Based on the way the crime is committed, we can classify it as a computer crime when it is carried out with the use of a computer and as a cybercrime when it is carried out with the use of a network. Along with cybercrime, artificial intelligence also supports cybercriminal activities without any human intervention for example data-based learning and automating fraud. In the context of CPS, recent works discussed advanced threats against sCPS from a different level of sophistication: an indirect self-learning attack on well-hardened computing infrastructure (CI) by compromising the cyber-physical control systems, whereas another study presented a framework to build cyber-physical botnets attacking a water distribution system but without learning aspects involved in this attack model. Therefore, smart CPS (sCPS) is a potentially fruitful area for committing artificial intelligence crimes (AICs) due to the decision-making and interconnectivity features [Antonioli et al., 2018].

Traditional CPS are systems that seamlessly integrate sensing, control, networking, and computational algorithms into physical components, connecting them to the Internet and each other. sCPS has applications in transportation, building systems, physical security, robotics, military, manufacturing, healthcare, communication, infrastructure, and energy. Integrating networked computational resources with physical systems that control various sensors and actuators impacts the environment. Advances in connectivity enable the evolution of scraps. The term CPS refers to a new generation of embedded systems, which are increasingly interconnected, and their operations are dependent on software, such as industrial IoT. Although the capabilities are increased, the systems become more sophisticated and can collect data from various sources to address the problems of the real-world for example traffic management [King, et al., 2019].

Bures et al. defined sCPS as follows: "Smart Cyber-Physical Systems (sCPS) are modern CPS systems that are engineered to seamlessly integrate a large number of computation and physical components; they need to control entities in their environment smartly and collectively to achieve a high degree of effectiveness and efficiency."

A key to the "smartness" of those systems is their ability to handle complex tasks through the features of self-awareness, self-optimization, and self-adaptation. The feature of smartness becomes apparent from sCPS being highly connected, having cooperative behavior with others, and being able to make effective decisions automatically. Bures et al. said that "most of the smartness is implemented in software, which makes the software one of the most complex and most critical constituents of sCPS." An outcome relates to highly sophisticated capabilities aimed at providing some degree of automation. Emerging technologies can be used to perform increasingly sophisticated functions in various sCPS, including smart healthcare systems, smart grids, smart buildings, autonomous automotive systems, autonomous ships, robots, smart homes, and intelligent transportation systems, with little or no human oversight. They represent the areas of innovation that are integrated into many CPS components to improve the quality of our lives [Khatoun, 2017].

METHODOLOGY- SVM, DLIB, CNN, RNN

The methodology to achieve the aim is that we first have to identify the facial expressions to detect whether there is anything suspicious or not. We will detect faces using Haar Cascade algorithms and LBP

[Vishnupriya et al., 2018] to find facial expressions. Haar Cascade is an approach of machine learning that can train the features of cascade with many negative and positive images. It requires both positive images (face images) and negative images (no faces).

The sum of pixels under the white and black rectangles are needed to find for each feature calculation. To solve this, the concept of an integral image was introduced. This concept makes it quite easy to calculate no. of pixels. 4 pixels is the maximum no. of pixels associated with it. Using Adaboost, the 160000+ features are selected. The algorithm is first trained with the dataset of people's face images in the LBP approach. In greyscale, an 8*3 grid is obtained and a threshold value is decided. If the threshold value is decided is greater than the threshold value then it's assigned 1 else 0. Now, as we have a binary matrix, we have to concatenate them in a clockwise direction and then convert to decimal form and assign it to the central pixel [Eleyan, 2017].

.In the image that we have in the grayscale, each of the histogram will contain only 255 locations (0 to 255), which represent the events of each pixel intensity. Then a new and big histogram is created from the old one and then the face is identified. Each one of the histogram created is used to represent each image from the training dataset. The approach of LBP is faster but it is less accurate than the Haar Cascade approach. Therefore, if in case a face is not detected using the LBP approach, then we have to again perform face detection using the Haar Cascade approach to prevent incorrect results.

RESULT AND DISCUSSION

The result and discussion section elaborate on the product perspective where the author team is presenting the website and snapshots of the app which will be used for suspicious activity detection.

Figure 4. Extracted frames from the video

Module 1: Face detection

Face detection approach in computer science has been used in a large variety of applications that helps us to identify faces of human in digital images. It is also referred to as a psychological process by which humans can locate and attend faces in a visual scene.

1. Video Slicing

    A cut is referred to as removing a section of the video clip. To do a cut, we have to cut in two places and lift out the middle section and then join the leftover video back together. In case if you have a very long video, you can just cut into sections to work with separately, and then splitting your video.

Detecting Faces

As every 6 frames are taken, it resulted in the 52 frames, and from every frame, the face is detected. The module detected faces for 45 frames (didn't detect faces for frame numbers 6, 7, 8, 10, 14, 15, 16). 44 Correct cases and 1 false case (for frame number 17) were produced. This was the best result among all is found when the minimum neighbors parameter and scale factor for LBP were adjusted to 5 and 1.2 respectively. And in the case of the Haar Cascade approach, the minimum neighbors parameter and scale factor for LBP were adjusted to 3 and 1.2 respectively. (as per Figure 4 and Figure 5).

Figure 5. Facial Expressions of Faces detected from the extracted frames

Figure 6. Cohn Kanade Dataset

Module 2: Face Expression Recognition

Biometrics markers are used to detect emotions in human faces in facial expression recognition software. More precisely, it is a sentiment analysis tool. It can automatically detect universal expressions: disgust, fear, sadness, anger, surprise, and happiness.

Raw Dataset

For module 2, the facial expressions can be detected by module Cohn Kanade's CK, and a huge dataset is used to train this model for accurate face expression prediction (as per Figure 6).

There are similar kinds of images for the chon Canada data set in each folder (as per Figure 7).

Figure 7. Similar kind of images in each folder

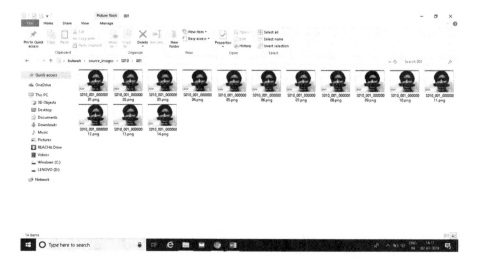

Figure 8. Sorted dataset for 'disgust'

Sorting the Dataset for a Different Emotion

According to corresponding expressions, the dataset is first sorted and then arranges into different folders (as per Figure 8).

Training and Test Data

To make a program understand how to learn and produce sophisticated results and to apply technologies, the training data is the initial data set that is used. It may be complemented by the subsequent sets of data called testing and validation sets.

The test data consists of types that have been specifically identified for use in tests. Some of the data is to be used in a confirmatory way, to verify whether a function is producing the expected result or not.

Figure 9. Dividing the sorted dataset into training and test data

Then this dataset is divided into a ratio of 4:1 for training and testing respectively (as per Figure 9).

Training Support-Vector Machines(SVM) and Calculating Accuracies

In machine learning, there are some models based on supervised learning known as SVM. They have some learning algorithms associated with them that are used to analyze the data used for regression analysis and classification analysis.

Figure 10. The model gives an approximate accuracy of 82%

Figure 11. Dataset- faces94 from the University of Essex, U.K.

The distance calculated from every coordinate of the face (find with the help of Dlib) to the center of gravity is given in the training data set. The parameters probability and kernel are set to true and linear respectively and a support vector classifier is used. The prediction score obtained is approximately 82% (as per Figure 10).

There are some more datasets added to improve the accuracy of this module: Dataset- faces94 from the University of Essex, U.K., Dataset- faces95 from the University of Essex, U.K. (as per Figure 11 and Figure 12).

Figure 12. Dataset- faces95 from the University of Essex, U.K.

For every implemented module, the result and discussion are as follows:

For module 1 which is wholly focused to detect faces from a video clip, the code was tested for a 10-second video which was 30 frames per second. For module 2, we have used Cohn Kanade's CK+ dataset to recognize facial expression from faces detected from module 1. The dataset is used to train the whole model for the prediction of the facial expressions (as per Figure 6). As per the corresponding expression, this raw dataset is first sorted and then managed into different folders (as per Figure 7). Then the whole dataset is divided into the ratio of 1:4 for testing and training respectively. The distance calculated from every coordinate of the face (find with the help of Dlib) (as per Figure 8) to the center of gravity is given in the training data set. The parameters probability and kernel are set to true and linear respectively and a support vector classifier is used. The prediction score obtained is approximately 82% (as per Figure 9).

CHAPTER CONTRIBUTION

We aim to develop a system to detect suspicious activities. This system consists of the following modules:

1. Speech recognition
2. Object Recognition
3. Face detection
4. Face expression recognition

These are the modules that are mostly used in the systems and software developed so far. But here we need to develop an efficient system to detect any kind of suspicious activity in the environment. The face detection modules make our code run faster as it eliminates the background and detects only faces. The facial expression recognition uses these faces to detect their facial expressions and detects a possible combination that would automatically detect suspicious activity.

LIMITATIONS AND POSSIBLE SOLUTIONS

The following are the limitations of our system:

Case 1

In case when there is more than one person, our system is unable to detect activity. As suspicious activity happens in crowded places so our facial expression recognition module will not be able to tell that which facial expressions belong to which one of the person. To implement this, we need object/face recognition which can detect between different – different people and can tell about their facial expressions individually.

Case 2

There are many situations when people may have fake facial expressions and it can lead to wrong results. We need the interference of the third person to solve this problem as he/she can verify the situation. The role of the third person will be played best by the security staff or authority of the police.

Figure 13. Device demo shot to show it as an alternative [Tripathi et al., 2014]

APPLICATIONS

The device finds its applications in various situations: For the safety of solo travelers in a public conveyance in almost all public places (schools, colleges, etc.) (as per Figure 13).

There is an exponential growth in the applications of CPSs and artificial intelligence. However, As SCs also known as correct smart contracts and framing resilient have very high complexity that's why these are quite high challenging tasks. Smart contracts are modernizing the business, industrial and technical processes and it is self verifiable and self-executable also. To save administration as well as service costs, it is embedded into the BC that eliminates the trust for the third party systems.

FUTURE RESEARCH DIRECTIONS

This system has a good future scope that can surely overcome its limitations. Some of them are as follows:

Whenever a module of object recognition is incorporated into the system, its accuracy becomes automatically improved and it starts giving more accurate and reliable results. Through this module, we can detect objects like a gun, knife which can cause potential harm and it would also help us to distinguish between one or more persons and also helps the facial expression recognition module to assign the facial expression to a particular person.

CONCLUSION

The level of intelligence is now increasing day by day and is embedded in things like communication devices, consumer electronics, homes, cars, and other devices. Very soon the following products will interact autonomously with each other and even humans will also interact with such rapidly enhanced smart products.

Industries like energy and utility process plants, smart cities, and factory production lines are dependent on the CPSs as it assists the system to self-monitor and even optimize the complexity and make its infrastructure, transportation, and buildings autonomous. In the future, CPSs will depend more on the AI-enabled core processors and less on the control of the human.

Although all the manufacturers of the industrial sectors are struggling to meet the demand of customer for the "smart product" market, they face really major challenges in manufacturing and developing these complex systems and products which are new and have increased demand. The CPSs require perfect coordination between the computational world or the virtual world and the physical world or continuous world. To meet these integration and complexity requirements, designers od CPSs are using embedded integration of system design, simulation platforms that are used in model-based mechatronic systems, and some other simulation models that can validate system design and product in the physical world.

In metro and semi-urban cities, crimes like robbery, sexual assaults, kidnapping, murders, etc are increasing day by day (Figure 14).

Figure 14. Map showing the comparative rate of violence against women in Indian states and Union Territories, 2012[Tripathi et al., 2014]
(https://commons.wikimedia.org/wiki/File:2012_Crime_Rate_against_Women_per_100000_in_India_by_its_States_and_Union_Territories,_VAW_Map.svg)

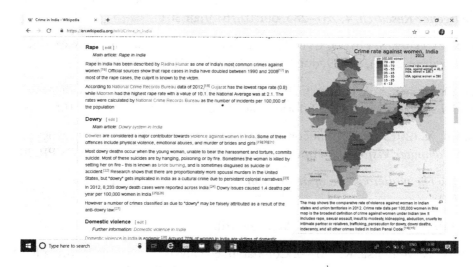

ACKNOWLEDGMENT

Our Sincere thanks to all direct and indirect supporters and well-wishers. Esteem gratitude to the Management of Dev Sanskriti Vishwavidyalaya Hardwar and Shantikunj where the image processing experiments and study were conducted. We Are specially thanked for ABESEC, Ghaziabad management, and staff for their time contribution to be part of this study. We also convey gratitude to officers of the Dayal Bagh Educational Institute for their mentorship and timely valuable suggestions.

REFERENCES

Brunelli, R., & Poggio, T. (1993, October). Face Recognition: Features versus Templates. *IEEE Transactions on Pattern Analysis and Machine Intelligence*, *15*(10), 1042–1052. doi:10.1109/34.254061

Bures, T., Weyns, D., Schmer, B., Tovar, E., Boden, E., Gabor, T., ... Tsigkanos, C. (2017). Software engineering for smart cyber-physical systems: Challenges and promising solutions. *Software Engineering Notes*, *42*(2), 19–24. doi:10.1145/3089649.3089656

Cassell, J., Bickmore, T., Campbell, L., Vilhjalmsson, H., & Yan, H. (2000). Human Conversation As a System Framework: Designing Embodied Conversational Agents. In *Embodied conversational agents* (pp. 29–63). Cambridge, MA: MIT Press. doi:10.7551/mitpress/2697.003.0004

Chowanda, A., Blanchfield, P., Flintham, M., & Valstar, M. (2016). Computational models of emotion, personality, and social relationships for interactions in games. *Proceedings of the 2016 International Conference on Autonomous Agents & Multiagent Systems,* 1343–1344.

Eleyan, A. (2017). Comparative Study on Facial Expression Recognition using Gabor and Dual-Tree Complex Wavelet Transforms. *International Journal of Engineering & Applied Sciences, 9*(1).

Kaelbling, L. P., Littman, M. L., & Moore, A. W. (1996). Reinforcement learning: A survey. *Journal of Artificial Intelligence Research, 4*, 237–285. doi:10.1613/jair.301

Khatoun, R., & Zeadally, S. (2017). Cybersecurity and privacy solutions in smart cities. *IEEE Communications Magazine, 55*(3), 51–59. doi:10.1109/MCOM.2017.1600297CM

Krizhevsky, A., Sutskever, I., & Hinton, G. E. (2012). ImageNet Classification with Deep Convolutional Neural Networks. Advances in Neural Information Processing Systems, 1097–1105.

Liang, M., & Hu, X. (2015). Recurrent convolutional neural network for object recognition. *The IEEE Conference on Computer Vision and Pattern Recognition*, 3367-3375. 10.1109/CVPR.2015.7298958

Miles, B. (2018). *The malicious use of artificial intelligence: Forecasting, prevention, and mitigation.* arXiv: 1802.07228

Mitchel, M. F. (1997). *Machine Learning*. McGraw Hill.

Nugrahaeni, R.A., & Mutijarsa, K. (2017). Comparative analysis of machine learning KNN, SVM, and random forests algorithm for facial expression classification. *IEEE Xplore.*

Pradhan, A. (2012). Support vector machine-A survey. *International Journal of Emerging Technology and Advanced Engineering, 2*(8), 82–85.

Rastogi, Chaturvedi, Arora, Trivedi, & Singh. (2017). Role and efficacy of Positive Thinking on Stress Management and Creative Problem Solving for Adolescents. *International Journal of Computational Intelligence, Biotechnology and Biochemical Engineering, 2*(2).

Rastogi, Chaturvedi, Sharma, Bansal, & Agrawal. (2017). Understanding Human Behaviour and Psycho Somatic Disorders by Audio Visual EMG & GSR Biofeedback Analysis and Spiritual Methods. *International Journal of Computational Intelligence, Biotechnology and Biochemical Engineering, 2*(2).

Rastogi, Chaturvedi, Arora, Trivedi, & Mishra. (2018). Swarm Intelligent Optimized Method of Development of Noble Life in the perspective of Indian Scientific Philosophy and Psychology. *Journal of Image Processing and Artificial Intelligence, 4*(1). http://matjournals.in/index.php/JOIPAI/issue/view/463

Rastogi, Chaturvedi, Arora, Trivedi, & Chauhan. (2019). Framework for Use of Machine Intelligence on Clinical Psychology to Study the effects of Spiritual tools on Human Behavior and Psychic Challenges. *Journal of Image Processing and Artificial Intelligence, 4*(1).

Rastogi, R., Chaturvedi, D., Sharma, S., Bansal, A., & Agrawal, A. (2017). Audio-Visual EMG & GSR Biofeedback Analysis for Effect of Spiritual Techniques on Human Behaviour and Psychic Challenges. *Journal of Applied Information Science, 5*(2), 37-46. Retrieved from http://www.i-scholar.in/index.php/jais/article/view/167372

Rastogi, R., Chaturvedi, D. K., Arora, N., Trivedi, P., & Mishra, V. (2017). Swarm Intelligent Optimized Method of Development of Noble Life in the perspective of Indian Scientific Philosophy and Psychology. *Proceedings of NSC-2017 (National system conference) IEEE Sponsored conf. of Dayalbagh Educational Institute, Agra.*

Rastogi, R., Chaturvedi, D. K., Satya, S., Arora, N., Bansal, I., & Yadav, V. (2018). Intelligent Analysis for Detection of Complex Human Personality by Clinical Reliable Psychological Surveys on Various Indicators. *The National Conference on 3rd Multi-Disciplinary National Conference Pre-Doctoral Research.*

Rastogi, R., Chaturvedi, D. K., Satya, S., Arora, N., Saini, H., Verma, H., . . . Varshney, Y. (2018). Statistical Analysis of EMG and GSR Therapy on Visual Mode and SF-36 Scores for Chronic TTH. *Proceedings of International Conference on 5th IEEE Uttar Pradesh Section International Conference.* 10.1109/UPCON.2018.8596851

Rastogi, R., Chaturvedi, D. K., Satya, S., Arora, N., Singh, P., & Vyas, P. (2018). Statistical Analysis for Effect of Positive Thinking on Stress Management and Creative Problem Solving for Adolescents. *Proceedings of the 12th INDIACom; INDIACom-2018.*

Rastogi, R., Chaturvedi, D. K., Satya, S., Arora, N., Yadav, V., & Chauhan, S. (2018). An Optimized Biofeedback Therapy for Chronic TTH between Electromyography and Galvanic Skin Resistance Biofeedback on Audio, Visual and Audio Visual Modes on Various Medical Symptoms. *The National Conference on 3rd Multi-Disciplinary National Conference Pre-Doctoral Research.*

Ren, S., He, K., Girshick, R., & Sun, J. (2017). Faster R-CNN: Towards Real-Time Object Detection with Region Proposal Networks. *IEEE Transactions on Pattern Analysis and Machine Intelligence, 39*(6), 1137–1149.

Savran, A., & Sankur, B. (2017). Non-rigid registration based model-free 3D facial expression recognition Comput. *Vis. Image Underst., 162*, 146–165. doi:10.1016/j.cviu.2017.07.005

Sharma, K., & Rameshan, R. (2017). Dictionary Based Approach for Facial Expression Recognition from Static Images. *Int. Conf. Comput. Vision, Graph. Image Process, 39*–49. 10.1007/978-3-319-68124-5_4

Singh, S., Kaur, A., & Taqdir, A. (2015). Face Recognition Technique using Local Binary Pattern Method. *International Journal of Advanced Research in Computer and Communication Engineering, 4*(3).

Technology Trends. (2018). https://www.gartner.com/smarterwithgartner/gartner-top-10-strategic-technology-trends-for-2018

Thomas, C. (2019, February 14). Artificial intelligence crime: An interdisciplinary analysis of foreseeable threats and solutions. *Science and Engineering Ethics.* PMID:30767109

Toygar, O., & Acan, A. (2003). Face Recognition Using PCA, LDA, and ICA Approach on Colored Images. *Journal of Electrical and Electronics Engineering (Oradea), 3*(1), 735–743.

Tripathy, R., & Daschoudhary, R. N. (2014). Real-time face detection and Tracking using Haar Classifier on SoC. *International Journal of Electronics and Computer Science Engineering., 3*(2), 175–184.

Turing, A. M. (1950). Computing machinery and intelligence. *Mind, 59*(236), 433–460. doi:10.1093/mind/LIX.236.433

Uřičář, M., Franc, V., & Hlaváč, V. (2012). The detector of facial landmarks learned by the structured output SVM. *VISAPP'12: Proceedings of the 7th International Conference on Computer Vision Theory and Applications*, 1, 547-556.

Viola, P., & Jones, M. (2001). Rapid object detection using a boosted cascade of simple features. *Computer Vision and Pattern Recognition.*, *1*, 511–518.

Viola, P., & Jones, M. (2004, May). Robust Real-Time Face Detection. *International Journal of Computer Vision*, *57*(2), 137–154. doi:10.1023/B:VISI.0000013087.49260.fb

Vishnu Priya, T. S., Sanchez, G. V., & Raajan, N. R. (2018). Facial Recognition System Using Local Binary Patterns (LBP). *International Journal of Pure and Applied Mathematics*, *119*(15), 1895–1899.

Welinder, P., Branson, S., Mita, T., Wah, C., Schroff, F., Belongie, S., & Perona, P. (2010). *Caltech-UCSD Birds 200.* California Institute of Technology. CNS-TR-2010-001.

Zhu, L., Chen, L., Zhao, D., Zhou, J., & Zhang, W. (2017). Emotion Recognition from Chinese Speech for Smart Affective Services Using a Combination of SVM and DBN. *New Advances in Identification Information & Knowledge on the Internet of Things.* https://towardsdatascience.com/face-recognition-how-lbph-works-90ec258c3d6b

ADDITIONAL READING

Babiceanu, R. F., & Seker, R. (2017). 'Trustworthiness requirements for manufacturing cyber-physical systems. *Procedia Manuf.*, *11*, 973–981. doi:10.1016/j.promfg.2017.07.202

Gunsekaran, A., & Ngai, E. W. T. (2014). Expert systems and Artificial Intelligence in the 21st-century logistics and supply chain management. *Expert Systems with Applications*, *41*(1), 1–4. doi:10.1016/j.eswa.2013.09.006

Gupta, R., Tanwar, S., Al-Turjman, F., Italiya, P., Nauman, A., & Kim, S. W. (2020). Smart Contract Privacy Protection Using AI in Cyber-Physical Systems: Tools, Techniques and Challenges. *IEEE Access: Practical Innovations, Open Solutions*, *8*, 24746–24772. doi:10.1109/ACCESS.2020.2970576

Klumpp, M. (2018). Innovation Potentials and Pathways Merging AI, CPS, and IoT. *Applied System Innovation.*, *1*(1), 5. doi:10.3390/asi1010005

Leitão, P., Karnouskos, S., Ribeiro, L., Lee, J., Strasser, T., & Colombo, A. (2016). Smart Agents in Industrial Cyber-Physical Systems. *Proceedings of the IEEE*, *104*(5), 1086–1101. doi:10.1109/JPROC.2016.2521931

Mikusz, M. (2014). Towards an Understanding of Cyber-Physical Systems as Industrial Software-Product-ServiceSystems. *Procedia CIRP*, *16*, 385–389. doi:10.1016/j.procir.2014.02.025

KEY TERMS AND DEFINITIONS

Face Analysis: A facial recognition system is a technology capable of identifying or verifying a person from a digital image or video frame from a video source. There are multiple methods in which facial recognition systems work, but in general, they work by comparing selected facial features from a given image with faces within a database.

Machine Learning: Machine learning (ML) is the scientific study of algorithms and statistical models that computer systems use to perform a specific task without using explicit instructions, relying on patterns and inference instead. It is seen as a subset of artificial intelligence.

Speech Recognition: Speech recognition is an interdisciplinary subfield of computational linguistics that develops methodologies and technologies that enables the recognition and translation of spoken language into text by computers. It is also known as automatic speech recognition (ASR), computer speech recognition, or speech to text (STT). It incorporates knowledge and research in the linguistics, computer science, and electrical engineering fields.

Suspicious: Having or showing a cautious distrust of someone or something or causing one to have the idea or impression that someone or something is questionable, dishonest, or dangerous or having the belief or impression that someone is involved in the illegal or dishonest activity.

Section 2
IDS/IPS for Smart Cyber–Physical Systems

Chapter 6
Smart IDS and IPS for Cyber–Physical Systems

Sara A. Mahboub
Sudan University of Science and Technology, Sudan

Elmustafa Sayed Ali Ahmed
Red Sea University, Sudan

Rashid A. Saeed
iD https://orcid.org/0000-0002-9872-081X
Taif University, Saudi Arabia

ABSTRACT

One of the most important requirements is security and accessibility efforts which are represented as a critical issue that should be considered in many applications for the purpose of system confidentiality and safety. To ensure the security of current and emerging CPSs by taking into consideration the unique challenges present in this environment, development of current security mechanisms should be further studied and deployed in a manner that make it becomes more compatible with CPS environment, introduce a safer environment and maintain the quality of service at the same time. Systems known as intrusion detection systems (IDS) and intrusion prevention systems (IPS) are the most common security mechanisms used in networking and communication applications. These systems are based on artificial intelligence (AI) where computer-based algorithms are used to analyze, diagnose, and recognize that threats pattern according to an expected suspicious pattern.

INTRODUCTION

The extreme development and rapid spread of technology in numerous communication aspects led the requirement to focus efforts on security and privacy, especially when these technologies are deployed with industry and infrastructure applications. These applications have multiple control loops, strict timing requirements, predictable network traffic, legacy components, and possibly wireless network segments.

DOI: 10.4018/978-1-7998-5101-1.ch006

Such as in industry 4.0, which integrates the internet of things (IoT), and machine-to-machine technology (M2M) with Cyber-Physical Systems (CPS). The CPS intrusion detection is more important to addresses the attacks in the physical environment of CPS (Juan et al, 2018). The use of CPS IDS/IPS detection and prevention techniques will help to monitor the misbehavior of a physical component the IDS look for to detect intrusions. For unknown misbehavior threats that are not defined in the signatures database of the security systems, the use of conventional cybersecurity mechanisms, like intrusion detection and prevention systems (IDS/IPS), and access control have not the capability to detect, prevent and block this category of cyber-attacks (Juan et al,2017).

Artificial intelligence (AI), with CPS cybersecurity mechanisms, can protect the CPSs from such attacks. Machine learning can be used to manage a huge amount of heterogeneous data that come from different sources of information to generate automatically different attacks patents and hence predict accurately the future attackers' misbehavior. Due to the importance of security and privacy issues in the industry 4.0 application. The authors present this chapter to contribute and provide a concept about smart IDS and IPS for the cyber-physical system. The rest of the chapter is organized as follows: a background of the chapter is presented, followed by a detailed review of vulnerability analysis and threat modeling in CPS. The chapter reviews the description of CPS security and privacy in industrial control. Besides, it provides a brief concept about IDS and IPS system methodological and effective management. The chapter also reviews the concept of the IDS/IPS protection mechanism for the CPS system and provides a smart IDS and IPS security solutions based on AI. Moreover, the chapter discussed two types of IDS and IPS for CPS applications, gives a brief review of IDS and IPS deployment strategies in CPS with possible future research directions.

BACKGROUND

Cyber-physical system (CPS) enables control and monitoring of the physical systems in many smart communications and networking applications. These applications are requiring improvement in CPS because it exceeds the simple embedded systems in operation concerning capability, adaptability, scalability, and security issues. Information security is a critical mission in cyber systems; it includes the detection of different types of threats and attacks, also, to prevent them from infecting the system (Huang et al, 2009). IDS and IPS provides a secure means to the current and emerging CPSs. Smart intrusion detection and prevention systems involve developed AI and ML techniques to enhance detection techniques which depended on patterns comparison. AI-based security solutions introduce day zero attack detection, which made it more suitable for CPS applications in the industry 4.0 revolution. Vulnerability analysis provides a routine for penetration testing or examining the strength of the configured security procedures. The threat modeling helps for security experts to find system weakness that can introduce a threat and develop the opposite solution to prevent it (Nazarenko & Safdar, 2019). Both of these techniques as essential and basics of security procedures that are used in legacy and modern security solutions considered in CPSs in addition to other developed security mechanisms.

Security aspects for CPS addressed by the CyBOK project (Bristol, 2020) are divided into internal and external threats. Each of these threats has an associated menace. NIST standard sets procedures and methods to improve the security and privacy in such a cyber system and even for the industrial environment (Amin et al, 2019). Attacks and threats in cyber systems are categorized according to their relevant layer. For example, in basic CPS architecture, there are three layers; physical, network, and application layer (Krotofil et al, 2014). In the physical layer, an attacker can physically attack equipment by destroying or causing damages and failure in a machine or at any exposed lines. Networking physical layer attacks may be issued to such as infiltration and intrusion of electromagnetic, service blocking, data interception and manipulation, and others (McLaughlin,2013) (Amin et al,2013). In the network layer, various routing attacks are issued such as sink node and black hole attacks, direction preventing, sinkhole, routing loop, flooding and spoofing, selective forwarding, false routing, and tunnel attack (Jakaria et al,2016) (Hegde et al,2017). While in the application layer various applications' related threats are considered in addition to rigged control commands, loophole, database injection, viruses, malware, and Trojan horses (Gao et al,2013) (Alnakhalny et al,2014) (Singh et al,2010)(Merwe et al,2018)(Suman & Shubhangi, 2016)(Vaid & Kumar, 2013)(Ziegler et al,2019). The history of industrial security has a massive attacks background and threats are widely occur, some of these threats in CPS applications affect the national or organizational infrastructure (Trifan, 2012) (ZHANG et al, 2013) (Ahuja et al, 2016) (Vats & Saha, 2019). Defenses and security solutions for such threats are also dependent on CPS layers (Kornecki & Zalewski, 2010). Control-flow integrity (CFI) or fine-grained code randomization, trusted safety verifier (TSV), C2 architecture, and secure system simplex architecture (S3A) are application-layer solutions which implemented in software and firmware used in CPS (Choudhary et al,2012)(Roemer et al,2012) (McLaughlin et al,2016). In the network layer, intrusion detection systems (IDS), intrusion prevention systems (IPS) are used (Teixeira et al,2013), (Giraldo et al,2017). While in the physical layer false data injection (FDI) detection mechanisms, smart meter protocol, semantic PLC, autoregression behavioral model, and tamper-resistant meters are the commonly proposed solution (Abadi et al, 2009).

Generally, three aspects should be followed in the security and privacy mission of CPS; management of secrets and keys, authentication and access control, and data security (McLaughlin et al, 2014) (Niggemann et al, 2015). For this proposes intrusion detection and prevention systems were founded and developed by adaptation of machine learning and artificial intelligence techniques, IDS/IPS are deployed with various applications of CPS such as healthcare, transportation, and power grids (Zhu & Sastry,2010) (Bobba et al,2014). With an appropriate deployment strategy of IDS/IPS systems, a CPS security can be maintained and further improved.

VULNERABILITY ANALYSIS AND THREAT MODELING

Accessibility is a permanent consideration in any cyber-based system such as CPS, and as the development of that system also vulnerabilities and threats are increasing, this led to finding the appropriate tools and methods to model and analysis all kinds of expectable scenarios that can affect the system performance and stability. And hence that CPS includes both cyber and physical components then security procedures should be considered in both aspects. CPS is the most critical system to vulnerability because it comprises the infrastructure applications of the national to danger strategically, some of these applications are water resource management systems, power grids, food, and transportation system. Any manipulation on one of these CPS based applications can affect national safety and make governmental systems prone to critical situations and danger. The vulnerability analysis in CPS can be performed through either manual or automatic procedures, or by a combination of both (Nazarenko & Safdar,2019). In the manual analysis, the critical operations scenarios should be performed manually with the experimentation of all available options and tuning that can be used without restrictions to figure out which procedure can affect the system with detected usage. In the automatic analysis, dedicated tools and mechanisms are deployed to perform that manual testing automatically with various configurations and usages with different test bench attributes while maintaining the results to keep track if any critical situation occurs.

A helpful study was introduced by (Huang et al, 2009) developing threat models approach for control systems attacks and Denial of Service (DoS) attacks, that models are beneficial for analyzing and evaluating the attacker actions taken to control system assets and on the physical process being controlled after gaining access to the system, the study was very meaningful and concluded by evaluating the physical and economic consequences of the attacks on a chemical reactor system as a case study. A couple of related studies by (Sandberg et al, 2010) and (Teixeira et al, 2013) investigate the hidden or stealthy false-data attacks against state estimators. The first one focused on the attack applications in SCADA systems used in power networks, where a malicious attacker corrupts the measurement data. They introduced two security modeling points for the state estimators. These points quantify the minimum effort required to execute the attack and achieve its goals while bypassing bad-data warnings in the control center of power network known as stealthy attacks (Teixeira et al, 2013). The points introduced relay on the power network physical topology and the obtainable measurements and can assist the operator to detect manipulation patterns of the scattered data, the information about detected patterns can be used to boost the security i.e. positioning of encryption devices. Then a convex optimization framework is used as complementary of the proposed mechanism to help in the evaluation of more complex attacks by taking into account the model variations and varied goals of attack. The security points are tested with an example and results in forcing the attacker to use large magnitudes in the data manipulation pattern by using a large measurement redundancy, but the pattern still can be comparatively scattered. The developing work proposes various control systems cyber-security quantification formulation, considering the typical architecture for the networked control system under attack and under the modeling framework introduced by previous publication. These formulations capture trade-offs in terms of attack impact on the control performance, attack detect-ability, and adversarial resources as studied numerically for a quadruple-tank process as an example.

The aspects of vulnerability analysis and threats modeling from different literature provided by (Giraldo et al,2017) (Nazarenko et al,2019) and from the scope of the CyBOK project denotes that the main security framework of security in CPS can be generally represented by two main areas, inner security area that responsible of infrastructure, systems, software, and platforms security in the center. And the outer security area as in the left and right sides as shown in Figure 1. Whereat the left side is the human, organizational, and regularity aspects. And the right side represents attacks and defense aspects.

In Figure 1, CPS systems infrastructure security is represented by hardware security, network security, cyber-physical systems security, physical layer, and telecommunication security. While System security is represented by operation systems and virtualization security, cryptography, and distributed systems security, authorization authentication, and accessibility (AAA). The software and platform security are represented by Web and Mobile Software lifecycle security. Considering a CPS controlled physical process, where a group of sensors reporting the controller by process state records, that accordingly manage actuators i.e. a valve by control signals to achieve the system to the required state. Usually, the controller shares information with a supervisory device i.e. a SCADA system that can be used for monitoring and/or reconfiguring system settings. This CPS general architecture is illustrated in Figure 2. According to the CPS architecture, an attack can happen at any one of the eight points positions as shown in Figure 3. These attacks are described as follows.

Figure 1. Security aspects in CPS

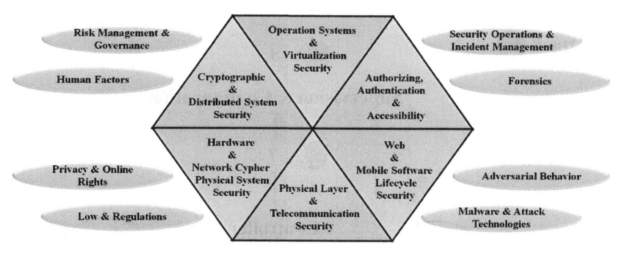

Attack (1): False or fake sensor data can be injected into the system by the attacker, such malicious data may cause undesired activities on the system according to manipulated control logic. This case may occur if the attacker gains an access to sensors key material or sensor data left unauthenticated (Huang et al,2009).

Figure 2. General CPS architecture

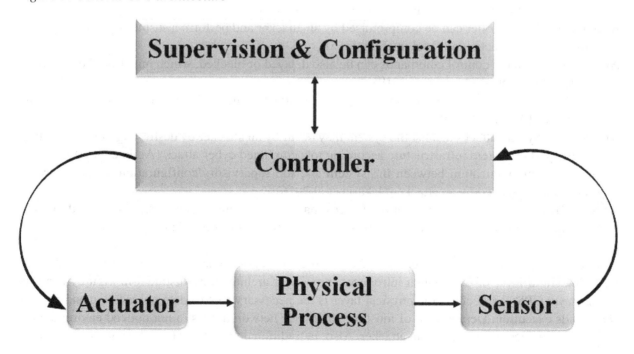

Figure 3. Attack points on CPS architecture

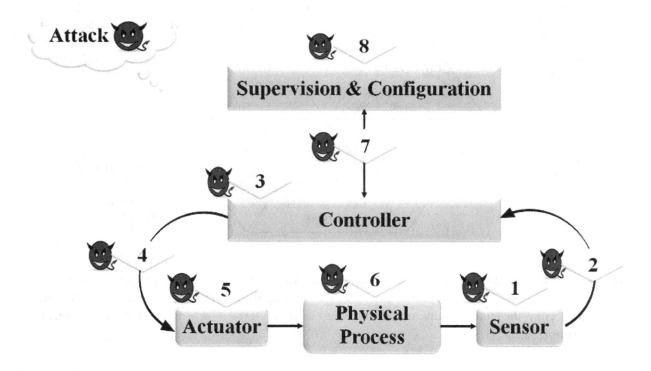

Attack (2): Sensor data may be delayed or blocked from the microcontroller, which may cause the controller with blind information port and cause the system to operate with outdated data and missing actual state action (Amin et al,2019) (Krotofil et al,2014).

Attack (3): The controller can be compromised by an attacker and perform a suspicious action by controlling system actuators (McLaughlin,2013).

Attack (4): Actuators control commands can be also delayed or blocked, which may lead the system to a denial of control (Amin et al,2019).

Attack (5): System actuators can be compromised by an attacker and perform unintended control actions directly (Teixeira et al,2012).

Attack (6): Physical attacks against the system may occur by an attacker by destroying or manipulating some part of system infrastructure according to a combined cyber-attack (Amin et al,2013).

Attack (7): Communication between the system and the supervisory/configuration devices may be delayed or blocked by an attacker (Jakaria et al,2016).

Attack (8): Supervisory or configuration devices may be compromised or impersonated and execute pernicious control or configuration changes to the system controller (Halperin et al,2008).

The study presented by (Gao et al,2013), provides a model security threat of CPS according to an architectural layer of CPS which introduces three-layer architecture illustrated in Figure 4. In this Three-Layer CPS architecture, the physical layer is the necessary root of data observation and control commands execution. Deployment of most physical layer network nodes in not noticed environments, make it easily become targets for an attacker. Also, in traditional systems, where data processing, com-

Figure 4. CPS 3-layer architecture

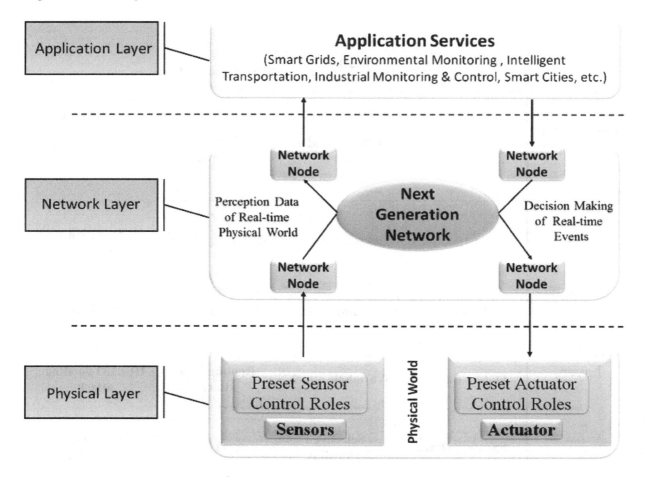

munications, and storage capacities of the nodes are limited, then conventional security techniques cannot be directly applied to the physical layer perception network. Next-generation networks are utilized as the core bearer network for the CPS network layer, where architecture, access methods, and network equipment will introduce a concerning amount of security threats for CPS (Morris and Gao,2013). Also, network congestion may occur due to huge amounts of data and massive nodes using the network layer, where the system will be compromised to DoS or Distributed DoS attacks. Also, new security issues will be reproduced relatively to gateway authentication, Data exchange, and interchange of security policies between diversified networks. In the application layer, privacy data of users collected by some applications such as consumption and transaction information states are critical data, thus the protection of such data must be considered in CPS. Also, various types of CPS applications may require various protection techniques that differ from an application to another. The principal types of threats that should be considered in CPS are modeled according to its relative architecture layer is reviewed in Figure 5. Further brief descriptions of all presented security threats are summarized in table.1. Categorized by CPS architecture layers accordingly.

Figure 5. Principal threats in different CPS layers

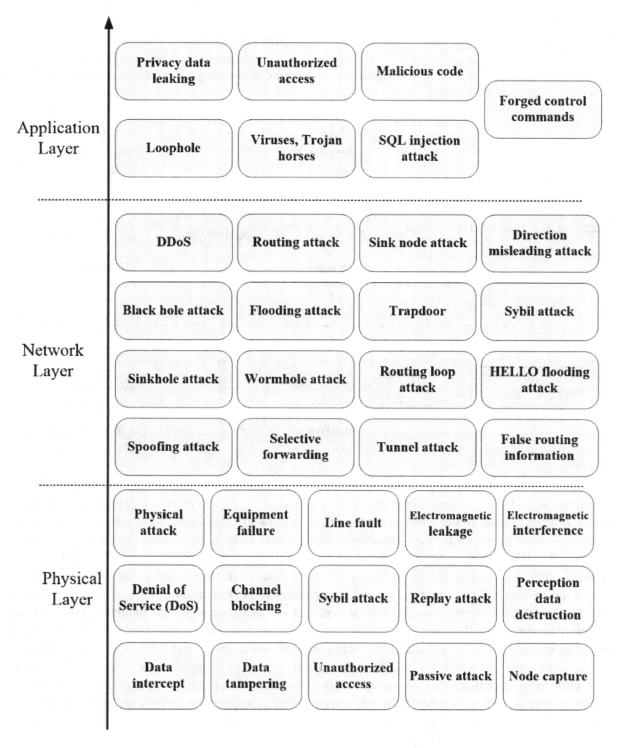

SECURITY AND PRIVACY IN INDUSTRIAL CONTROL

It's clear that any cyber-based system is compromised to security holes that make it prone to different types of attacks, some of the major attacks and threats that may exist with CPS are discussed in the previous section. This leads to establishing deployment and development of security and privacy mechanisms that will be also discussed as literature in this section as a survey of surveys. Figure 7 highlights the most famous cyber-attacks on ICS as a timeline. Security of systems refers to the procedures, restrictions, and permissions that should be followed and executed by any object on the environment that should be secured. While privacy concerns about the information, maybe the user's related information or organizational information of interest. Both security and privacy have different concerns as shown in Figure 6.

In traditional industrial control security and privacy weren't a challenging task because of the closed environment and limitations of technology, where all production and processing operations were driven from classic control to distributed control systems (DCS) passing through PLC, SCADA, and other technologies. The importance of security and privacy rises when remote operability and supervision functions are introduced, such as in the adoption of IoT with industrial control. So, in traditional industrial control, only indoor security and privacy mechanism was needed, but know with the intrusion of cyber components in industrial control security is required from inside and outside of the industrial environment(Hadžiosmanović et al,2014). An exploration of the commonness between safety and security together treated as an integrated view of the same problem, but security can be defined as safeguard a computer-based system from the external environment threats, while safety is an environmental and computer system protection procedures from potential dangers that can occur at any part of the environment of interest (Kornecki & Zalewski,2010). As industrial control systems (ICSs) are transforming from traditional electromechanical based systems to modern information and communication technology (ICT) based systems founding a tide relationship between cyber and physical components. Test-beds that take the interactions between the various layers of an ICS and current trends in ICS attacks and defenses are discussed by (McLaughlin et al,2016). This study has introduced extensive research in ICS based on 5 layered architecture (see Figure 8). The ICS architecture layers are described by hardware, firmware, software, network, and ICS or physical process.

The term security in ICS is defined by a wide range of procedures and methods specified according to the layer of ICS that is vulnerable to an expected threat. Table 2 summarizes these security methods and procedures in ICS according to the layered architecture shown in Figure 8 from the literature.

IDS AND IPS SYSTEM METHODOLOGICAL AND EFFECTIVE MANAGEMENT

The first step in deploying security in any framework is enabling of detection mechanism that can recognize the threat pattern or sense it from other traffic or legal usage data passing in a framework environment. This can be referred to by the intrusion detection system (IDS). Additionally, the prevention function represents the reaction performed after detection of threat which is the responsibility of the intrusion prevention system (IPS). IDS and IPS are the most familiar and basic tools in the security of highly sensitive applications infrastructure. The methodological concept behind IDS and IPS systems represented by artificial intelligence (AI) techniques that use various applications of machine learning (ML) that are applied in classification, detection, recognition, and optimization (Hallenstein,2018)(Nourian et al,2015). In IDS sensors are represented by the scanner that analyzing traffic signal passing through system nodes,

Table 1. Security threats summary

Security threats	Description
Physical Layer Security Threats	
Physical attack	Destroy or damage of a physical node in the system.
Failure of Equipment	Reduce or lose of an equipment's performance that can be forced externally, or due to environment or longevity.
Line failure	Insufficiency of power on one or multiple system nodes.
Electromagnetic infiltration	If the equipment's electromagnetic signal at field spread out, the original data can be restored by an attacker using appropriate signal processing.
Electromagnetic intrusion	Degradation on system performance may occur due to undesirable electromagnetic signals or disorder results in a negative influence on beneficial signals.
Denial of Service (DoS)	By consuming network bandwidth with massive requests, an attacker can force the attacked system to stop supplying services (Jakaria et al,2016) (Dao et al,2016)(Bahashwan et al,2020).
Channel blocking	Communication channels taken for a long time may prevent data transmission until occupied channels are set free.
Sybil attack	One malicious system node with a large number of pseudonymous, can raid the system by taking control over most of the other nodes (John et al,2015).
Replay attack	An attacker can inject valid data acquired before, to become reliant on the system.
Perception of data destruction	An unauthorized extension, cancellation, alteration, and demolition of observation data gathered by sensors or other system nodes.
Data intercept	Through the communication channel interception, illegitimate access to the data in the transaction is possible.
Data manipulate	If data interception successes, an attacker can modify the data and forward tampered data to the destination which may be a controller to process it or to an actuator on the system.
Unauthorized access	Forbidden users' illegal access to data resources using stolen or forged credentials.
Passive attack	Collection of information by sniffing it from open transmission medium or unrestricted access (Singh et al,2013) (Kaur et al,2016).
Node capture	If an attacker could get holds a physical gateway node that is a part of the system, then the node can be reprogrammed and redeployed with tampered configuration and compromise system information to the attacker.
Network Layer Security Threats	
DDoS	Multiple malicious nodes perform DoS attack against the targeted system server simultaneously (A. H. M. Jakaria et al,2016) (Dao et al,2016) (Bahashwan et al,2020).
Routing attack	Interfering routing process with rigged routing information.
Sink node attack	Attacking of sink node (an intermediate node) can cause data interfering transmission between the physical and network layer (Singh et al,2013) (Kaur et al,2016) (Hegde et al,2017).
Direction perverting attack	Type of routing disruption attack happens when a virulent node changes the addresses of source and destination in a data packets, then results in an undelivered packet and wrong reception in a node with a forged destination address.
Blackhole attack	A virulent node deceives other nodes by acting as a router to make other nodes send a packet to it, then packets will be discarded, resulting in high packet loss. Also called the Packet drop attack.
Flooding attack	An attack using Smurf and DDoS on the network layer causing overflowing of the network resources or system servers. The Smurf attack is a type of DDoS attack in which a massive internet control message protocol (ICMP) packets with the intended attacked node mimicked source IP are transmitted to a network node using a broadcast address (Alnakhalny et al,2014).
Trapdoor	An alternative access method that predefined or invented by an attacker to gain an access to the system without using a legal way.
Sybil attack	One malicious system node with a large number of pseudonymous, can raid the system by taking control over most of the other nodes.
Sinkhole attack	Similar to the black hole attack, but here the Malicious node advertises itself as a sink node to only capture traffic passing through it.
Wormhole attack	Multiple Malicious nodes positions themselves in an effective location on the network strategically to represent some type of tunnel, which enables them to record all network information between them.
Routing loop attack	Modification of data path by a Malicious node that causes an unbounded routing loop, by making the router never knows the endpoint of the transmission inside its tunnel.
HELLO flooding attack	Routing information broadcasting with a strong signal by a Malicious node indicating other nodes in the network that it's their direct neighbor with aggressive behavior (Singh et al,2010).
Spoofing attack	Cheating normal nodes by making them sends their data through an invalid or inoperative path or to a node with failure, resulting in data drop or packet loss (Merwe et al,2018).
Selective forwarding	Malicious node intentionally drops some or all of the main data in a transmission that should be forwarded (Suman & Shubhangi,2016).
Tunnel attack	The real link distance between nodes is hidden by a Malicious node to appeal the other nodes to setup routing links through them.
False routing information	Tampered routing information is used in the network layer by Malicious node, resulting in packet loss.
Application Layer Security Threats	
Privacy data leaking	Infiltrate of system user's privacy data due to the lack of security in data submission, warehousing, or transmission (Vaid & Kumar,2013) (Ziegler et al,2019).
Unauthorized access	Permitted access to system nodes, resources, or transmission channels (Vaid & Kumar,2013) (Ziegler et al,2019).
Malicious code	A small program with the unknown reference inside the system running with processes, may not affect the system performance but may cause a security risk.
Rigged control commands	Damaging or performing undesired actions in the system by forging control commands.
Loophole	The vulnerability of an application in the system that may be used to attack the system from the application layer (Trifan,2012).
Viruses, Trojan horses	Most familiar security threats in the application layer (Trifan,2012)(ZHANG et al,2013).
SQL injection attack	A familiar type of attack against databases (Ahuja et al,2016) (Vats & Saha,2019).

then the suspicious pattern is detected or recognized commonly using one of the classification algorithms that are widely deployed in networking and data communication strategies. IPS adds reaction decision made after IDS is triggered, these reactions may perform blocking or notifying management or super-

Figure 6. Security and privacy concerns

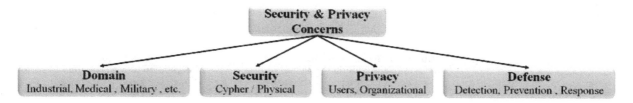

visory by threat or suspected activity which helps management operation sufficiently in early detection and avoidance of problems that would affect the system performance (Nourian et al, 2015).

Machine learning with Intrusion Detection and Prevention System (IDPS) technologies enable to detect attacks by using different classes of detection methodologies, i.e. signature-based, anomaly-based, and stateful protocol analysis. ML provides a means of intelligent learning to compare signatures against observed events to identify possible attacks. In anomaly-based detection, ML enables us to extract and evaluate the definitions of the features of what activity is considered normal against observed events to identify significant deviations (Stouffer et al,2015). It provides an intelligent comparative method to characteristics the current activity to thresholds related to the CPS normal behaviors. ML helps to identify unexpected sequences of commands after IPS authenticated successfully for stateful protocol analysis.

LEGACY CPS SYSTEM FOR IDS AND IPS PROTECTION MECHANISMS

Best practices of security in legacy CPS applications are mainly standardized by the U.S national institute of standards and technology (NIST) who's introduced ICS, power grids, and Industrial IoT security guidelines (Falco et al,2011) (Hallenstein,2018). Several industry-specific organizations have basic security standards for their systems such as the North American Electric Reliability Corporation (NERC) critical infrastructure protection standards for the power grid or the international society of automation (ISA) security standards for process control systems (Nourian et al,2015) (Wan et al,2018).

CPS Key Management

In a cryptosystem, key management refers to cryptographic keys' management (Wan et al,2018). Similarly, key management in a CPS refers to the setup of communication keys with desired integrity between the embedded processors in the computation and networking components that uses data exchange functionality. The main aspects of Key management are key distribution by sharing secret keys between entities, and key invalidation or revocation by securely removing keys that become compromised, expired, or no longer valid (Houbing et al,2017) (Song et al,2017). The main requirement that key management must meet in CPS is illustrated in Figure 9.

Additionally, the design principles of key management for required CPS characteristics are summarized in table 3. These design principles still challenging tasks and open research issues in the deployment and development of modern CPSs, in addition to security integration and support of legacy CPSs which represents a difficult challenge in key management also.

Figure 7. Timeline of highlighted cyber-attack on ICS

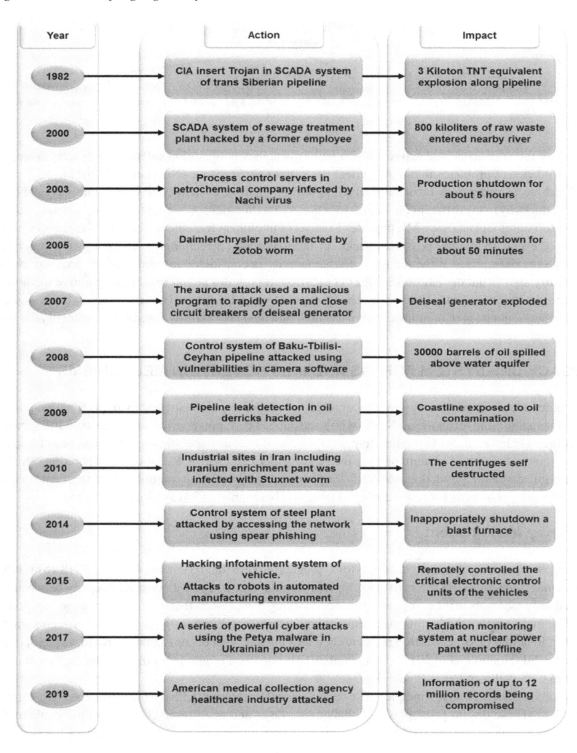

Figure 8. Layered architecture of ICS

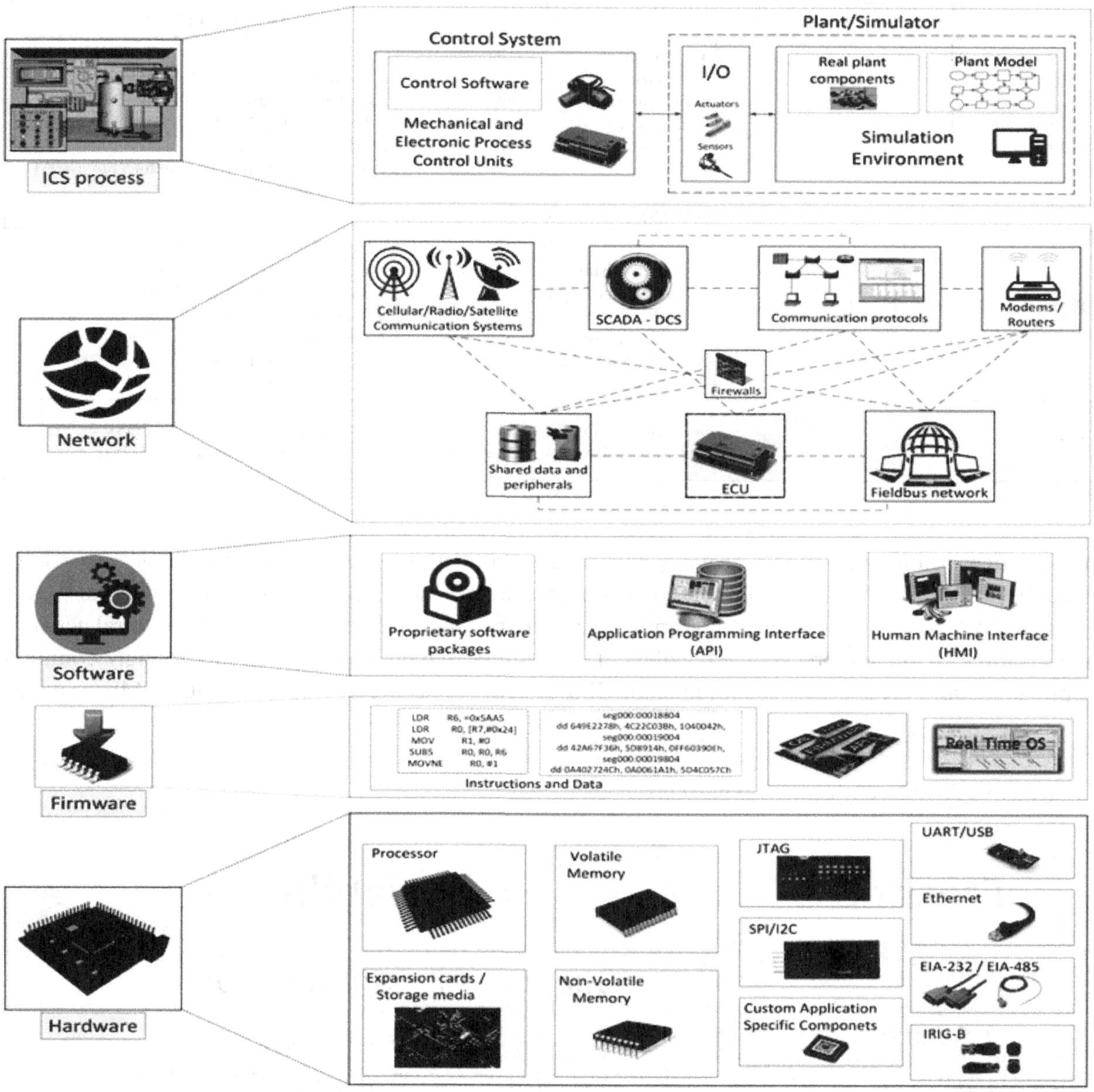

CPS Authentication and Access Control

According to increased demands of flexibility in possible CPSs applications, the integrity of authentication and access control tasks are the most important considerations that should be strictly deployed and followed to introduce higher immunity for CPSs against most types of attacks. user and data origin authentication services, in addition to identity verification for user control commands and sensor measure-

Table 2. Main security threats, impact, and defenses in ICS

Layer	Threat	Impact	Defenses and Secure
Software and Firmware	Memory Buffer Overflow	■ Code injection attack (Choudhary et al, 2012). ■ Return-oriented programming (Roemer et al, 2012). ■ Code-reuse attacks (Shakarian, 2011). ■ allows an attacker to execute arbitrary malicious code	■ Control-Flow Integrity (CFI) or fine-grained code randomization (Abadi et al, 2009). ■ Trusted Safety Verifier (TSV) (Niggemann et al, 2015), C2 Architecture. ■ Secure System Simplex Architecture (S3A) (McLaughlin et al,2014)
Physical or ICS process	Control and Sensor Channels Attacks	■ Compromising Control Signal causes Malicious commands injection. ■ Corrupting sensor readings cause bad decision making	■ False Data Injection (FDI) Detection Mechanisms (Mohan et al,2012). ■ Smart Meter Protocol (Zhu & Sastry,2010) ■ Semantic PLC Auto regression Behavioral Model (Berthier & Sanders,2011) ■ Tamper-Resistant Meters (Liang, 2019) (Bobba et al, 2014).
Network	All Communication and Networking Vulnerabilities and Threats	■ Compromising system to unauthorized control and supervision	■ Intrusion Detection System (IDS) ■ Intrusion Prevention System (IPS).

ment sources, should be issued as security requirements collection as developed in the eco-system (Song et al,2017). While access control refers to guarantee access to the CPS by authorized individuals only.

Recent years have seen significant improvements in machine learning (ML) and deep neural network architectures enabled unprecedented analytical capabilities, which have become increasingly common applications and production technologies in CPS systems to secure access and control. ML provides

Figure 9. CPS key management requirement

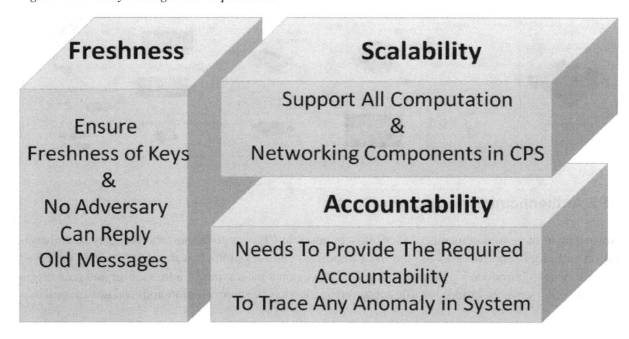

Table 3. Design principles for required CPS Characteristics

Characteristic	Design principle
Heterogeneity	Scalability to meet embedded processors resource qualifications
Real-time availability	Establishment of synchronization routines and real-time availability for events and updates freshness
Flexibility to attacks	Ability to fast restoration after incidents
Interoperability	Compatibility between various in-system components and outside contributed systems
Survivability	The ability of continuation under critical circumstances

secured intrusion detection mechanisms and decision accuracy in CPS. In the accessing process, ML enables an assessment of the possibility of hacking to access the CPS system by enhancing the learning of unreliable access attempts by analyzing the different authorized processes and attack methods (Fan et al, 2019). The use of ML in this way helps extract most of the potential outcomes for unauthorized access and management of the CPS control operations.

Data Security and Privacy

Data security and privacy is a critical task for the responsible authority of data management and security especially in sensitive CPS applications such as in Healthcare (Čaušević et al, 2017), such authority is managed and maintained by IDSs. Major procedures of data security and privacy are implemented in data warehouses or storages that are managed in the application layer but also vulnerabilities in another layer can affect it. Open issues and challenges still rising in legacy data warehouses, but also integrated solutions are introducing as in the development of storage platforms by cloud computing technology (Elmustafa & Rashid 2014).

One of the most promising technologies is using data-based approaches which enables learning to monitor and diagnose knowledge by monitoring and analyzing system behavior. CPSs collect and report large amounts of data via standardized interfaces. Artificial intelligence enables to benefit of the big data by using it for detection and analysis of the nature of data CPSs (Song et al,2017) (Niggemann et al,2015). ML methods provide an intelligent mechanism to monitor the private behavior of data interaction in CPSs, and identify unusual situations during operations, to take appropriate measures for repair and maintenance planning. The use of ML enhances the ability to protect data by analyzing data to derive patterns, strip data, and find out its usability. ML mechanisms can generate models for regular system behavior to detect abnormal patterns in data (Song et al,2017). In addition to that, identify the root causes for noticing problems or anomalies and heterogeneity of the data.

SMART IDS AND IPS FOR CPS

Today, most IDS/IPS techniques are not able to detect and prevent the dynamic and complex nature of cyber-attacks especially in applications related to the internet. Efficient adaptive methods like various techniques based on AI solutions and machine learning can result in higher detection rates, lower false alarm rates, and reasonable computation and communication costs. This section gives brief concepts about smart methods and solutions that can be used to build efficient CPS based on smart IDS/IPS techniques.

AI-Based Security Solutions

Services and applications of AI security solutions are widely used; especially in cybersecurity where analysis and recognition of traffic and data patterns mainly depend on AI techniques. Security solutions driven by AI prove it worth in all fields with high accuracy and precision. Deployments of AI-based security solutions include (Xenonstack,2019):

- Pattern Recognition
- Anomaly, and Intrusion Detection
- Intrusion Response
- Statistical Methodology
- Malware and Spam Detection
- Data Privacy, Risk and Decision Making
- Threat Monitoring

Anomaly, intrusion detection, and pattern recognition are considered important issues related to CPS security access. Pattern recognition enables us to recognizes the patterns in data by the machine learning algorithm. The pattern recognition process categorizes data based on the knowledge already acquired or on the statistical information extracted from the patterns and their representation (Xenonstack,2019). This method enables us to discover the properties arrangements of data that produce information about the CPS system so that it enables predictive analysis in data and pattern recognition to isolate suspicious and potential data traffic for some attacks statistically.

AI is used in anomaly detection to identify abnormal behavior within the data set. AI algorithms provide solutions with anomaly detection algorithms to automatically analyzing data sets and identifying parameters of natural behavior and breaches in patterns that indicate an anomaly in the CPS system during monitoring. ML-based anomaly detection enables to enhance the accuracy, speed, and quality of anomaly detection (Ding, 2015). The intrusion detection system (IDS) detects cyber-attacks or malicious activities and AI plays a vital role in discovering intrusions and is widely seen as the best way to adapt and build IDS. Neural networks help to keep defensive duties on the front lines on intrusion detection systems (Shanker et al, 2016) (Scarfone, & Mell, 2007). IDS rules are subject to all traffic to a set of access strategies before being allowed to pass to the CPS system. Algorithm-based IDs use machine learning to dynamically create new detection-based algorithms.

IDS/IPS Based on Machine Learning

In an IDS and IPS, ML techniques are considered as a virtual analyst, that defends the networking environment from threats by measure and analyze the impact of threat or suspicious activity according to one of the supervised or unsupervised learning techniques or more complicated algorithms such as deep neural networks.

1. Unsupervised learning; K-Means clustering is used to test whether results can be found using clustering algorithms. K-means is a simple clustering algorithm and already indicates whether a problem can be solved using clustering, or whether clustering offers no advantage. However, no method was found to verify whether to clusters that the K-means algorithm made were correct.

One-class support vector machines are used in an attempt to use binary classification. They are quite fast in execution. They were used to find out whether it is a viable technique to preprocess incoming data and check whether a one-class support vector machine finds it to be abnormal behavior before passing it to other algorithms.

2. Supervised learning; Support vector machines have been used in the implementation. It is a popular algorithm and can do both linear and non-linear classification which makes it a promising choice to test in the implementation. K-nearest neighbors were the most promising algorithm. This algorithm is used extensively throughout the implementation and the tests. The fact that the classification happens on basis of the different neighbors instead of trying to make a classifier seemed to fit the feature data better.

Human-Machine Interaction

The deployment of CPSs is not limited to specialized systems managed by tech-savvy people. Many of the applications of CPSs are systems in everyday use operated by non-technical people medical monitoring systems, smart infrastructures, and so on. Therefore, security solutions for CPSs should have a high degree of usability plug&play nature and security transparency a characteristic that today's cyber-only security solutions do not consider (Banerjee et al,2012). In the socio-technical system, human behavior plays a significant role throughout the CPS operation, from a physical environment to a cyber system, control procedure, information process, and final application and management. IDPRS can take the role of regulating and controlling human behavior toward CPSs, particularly identifying potential innocent and malicious operations in the system. As a non-optional role, human behavior should be modeled and integrated into systems in various levels and procedures (Ding,2015). Besides enhanced user experience for human-to-human (H2H) or human-to-machine (H2M) interactions, autonomous machine-to-machine (M2M) interaction has gained significant importance. This mechanism improves and extends CPS application and performance. Autonomic security will be of great benefit to the protection of complex dynamic CPSs.

Agile Cryptography and Security

Cryptography is an irreplaceable operation in security, and as the complexity of cryptography increases, its immunity to cracking increases. But there is always a trade-off and also there are not absolute cryptographic techniques with time. So, the approach of the required solution to meet the demands of current and future data security is the agility, where agile cryptography will provide the basis and the platform for system flexibility and the ability to adapt quickly to newly develop cryptographic algorithms (Mousta & Soukharev, 2018). Many CPS applications have a degree of internal agility through integrated software updates. But this usually requires downloading large update packages and restarting. Also, some of these systems depend on the crypto included in the operating systems and may need to rebuild the system to support these updates. In recent years, there have been some groundbreaking discussions on crypto agility. One of the mechanisms for graceful encryption is the adoption of agile certificates in the context of the cipher key infrastructure so that the crypto keys share some common features such as the name of a potential subject and double-signature (CA) signatures (Nourian et al,2015). The term 'agility' may be included in CPS systems by adopting graceful protection and security methods against any potential attackers and affecting the physical systems by disrupting services. Moreover, ensuring system integrity and preventing cyber threats to CPSs can be provided by agile cyphering with enable to providing practical recommendations to CPS designers for future secure updating.

IDS AND IPS FOR CPS APPLICATIONS

IDS and IPS have found its way in various fields and applications, but in CPS it's still seeking a way to meet the huge integration and different deployments as they are developing every day. In this section some review of IDS/IPS in CPS applications such as smart transportation and power grids.

Smart Transportation System Security

Sometime, companies may consider that security is not a big concern in the transportation industry. But quite the opposite, security threats have a critical impact on transportation and it may be considered as national infrastructure. Application CPS in transportation includes a commonly known intelligent transportation system ITS, vulnerabilities, and threats in IDS can cause a danger that couldn't be recovered easily, especially when it becomes to human lives. Crashes, fatalities, congestion, and public chaos are among the possible outcomes of tampering with transportation network critical infrastructures (Kelarestaghi et al,2018). Further research is needed to assess the risk conferred by threats in ITS and the messages they convey. Also, countermeasures proposed i.e. encryption and IDS need to be studied and prioritized as potential long-term and short-term strategies.

Power Grid

In a power grid application, security threats are founded at three common branches of the power grid; generation, transmission, and distribution. Generation is controlled by both, local (automatic voltage regulator and governor control), and wide-area (automatic generation control) control schemes identify the various parameters associated with the control loops in the generation system. The transmission system normally operates at voltages above 13 kV and the components controlled include switching and reactive power support devices. It is the responsibility of the operator to ensure that the power flowing through the lines is within safe operating margins and the correct voltage is maintained. The distribution system is responsible for delivering power to the customer (Sridhar et al,2012). With the emergence of the smart grid, additional control loops that enable direct control of the load at the end-user level are becoming common.

Industry 4.0

For Industry 4.0, integrating cutting-edge technologies in industrial environments introduces new scenarios and services such as available production lines or predictive maintenance systems. This integration will bring new challenges that must be overcome by developing mechanisms to protect and detect threats. An example of these threats will affect control and management protocols. Besides, it should include the detection of anomalies that affect operations in the control of virtual industrial environments. Bearing in mind, which most elements of Industry 4.0 are interoperable with each other that will need to develop new detection mechanisms, focused on analyzing both the behavior and interactions of these semi-autonomous systems (Rubio et al, 2017). The use of smart IDS/IPS in the CPS industry system such as considers many factors i.e. adaptability, inclusivity, solidarity, and intelligence. For adaptability, IDS/IPS must be able to cover all interactions and potential elements for industry deployment 4.0. Additionally, it should be easily upgradeable with new detection algorithms. IDS/IPS for CPS must able to acts by inclusivity, Where the various parts of the system, conditions, and interactions, potential points of failure, and successive impacts must be taken into account comprehensively. The concept of solidarity is related to the ability of IDS/IPS to interact closely with other protection mechanisms and with other related Industry 4.0 services as well (Rubio et al, 2018). In general, the intelligent method should be considered in detecting more advanced attacks in CPS and including more advanced detection techniques such as behavioral analysis.

IDS AND IPS DEPLOYMENT STRATEGIES

According to the IDS position, intrusion detection mechanisms are categorized into five different categories: Host-based IDS, Network-based IDS, Wireless IDS, Distributed IDS, and Application-based IDS (Singh et al, 2019).

- **Host-Based Intrusion Detection Systems HIDS**: Protect a single host against malicious incidents and attacks by monitoring and collecting the host's information (Shanker et al, 2016). HIDS detects intrusion using analyzing system files, system calls, events, etc. and can be deployed easily on a hypervisor or virtual machine (VM). Special security policies can be enforced to the host by HIDS.
- **Network-Based Intrusion Detection System NIDS**: Detects threats i.e. Dos, port, and scan by monitoring network traffic. This type of IDS collects data from all over the network and it compares it with predefined patterns from known attacks. NIDS detects intrusion by monitoring each packet's IP and transport layer headers (John et al, 2015). This type of IDS employs signature-based and anomaly-based intrusion detection methods which are not very visible to the users of the network. NIDS cannot decrypt encrypted traffic to be able to analyze the contents.
- **Wireless Intrusion Detection System**: NIDS and WIDS are similar with only one major difference. Unlike NIDS, WIDS records the traffic from Ad-Hoc and Wireless sensor networks as well (Teixeira et al, 2012).
- **Distributed intrusion detection system:** A distributed IDS is a cooperation of more than one NIDS, WIDS, and HIDS which communicate with the central server and with each other.
- **Application-Based Intrusion Detection System:** This category of IDSs is considered as a subcategory of HIDS in some of the articles. These types of IDSs focus on a specific assigned application and will analyze that application only, which means their monitoring is limited to that application on the host. Therefore, they are capable of detecting all malicious activities from virtual users that are trying to abuse that specific application.

And according to methodology or detection technique IDS are categorized into three types: anomaly-based, signature-based, and stateful protocol analysis.

- **Anomaly-Based IDS and IDS** that is anomaly based will monitor network behavior and compare it against an established baseline. The baseline will identify what is "normal" for that network, such as what sort of bandwidth is usually used, what protocols are used, and what ports and devices mostly connect, and alert the administrator or user when traffic is detected that is anomalous or significantly different from the baseline.
- **Signature-based IDS** termed a misuse detection system that will monitor network behavior and compare it with a database of signatures or attributes from known malicious threats. Identification engines perform well by monitoring these patterns of known misuse of system resources. This is similar to the way most antivirus software detects malware.
- **Stateful protocol analysis** identifies deviations of protocol states. Once the protocols are fully decoded, the intrusion detection system analysis engine can evaluate different parts of the protocol for anomalous behavior or exploits against predetermined profiles of generally accepted definitions of benign protocol activity for each protocol state.

Figure 10. IDPRS architecture

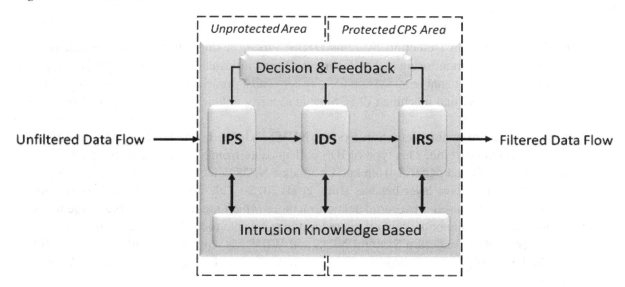

IDS and IPS have an important role in CPS performance specifically with system stability and risk management, even so, more developments are deployed such as intrusion detection, prevention, and response system (IDPRS) (Xenonstack,2019) (Ding,2015). IPS are network security appliances to identify malicious activity, log information for this activity, attempt to block/stop it, and report it. IPS are considered extensions of IDS because they monitor network traffic and system activities for malicious activity. Unlike IDS, IPS are placed in-line and can actively prevent/block intrusions that are detected. More specifically, IPS can take such actions as sending an alarm, dropping the malicious packets, resetting the connection, or blocking the traffic from the offending destinations. An IPS can also correct cyclic redundancy check (CRC) errors, un-fragment packet streams, prevent transmission control protocol (TCP) sequencing issues, and clean up unwanted transport and network layer options (Scarfone; & Mell,2007).

Figure 11. IDS deployment tasks

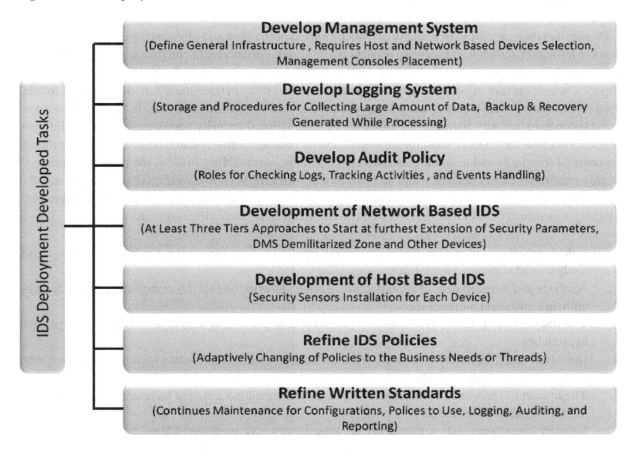

Intrusion Response System (IRS) are systems to produce a corresponding response for system intrusion. A good response must consist of preplanned defensive measures that include an incident response team and ways to collect IDS logs for future use and evidence when needed. The IRS has responsibility for: keeping up to date with the latest threats and incidents; generating notifications whenever an incident occurs; assessing the damage and impact of every incident, to avoid exploitation of the same vulnerability; and making decisions to recover from the incident (Stakhanova et al,2007). IDS, IPS, and IRS do not work independently. They share a common knowledge base and update the knowledge in the common base. Most of the time, they work together or integrated into one security protection system, to maximize the protection functions of the whole IDRPS (see Figure 10). As in other networking applications and technology infrastructures, IDS, and IPS with appropriate consideration and design may introduce the desired security in the deployed environment. The industry standard states an ordered procedure for IDS deployment project tasks that may lead to a maintainable security degree as explained in Figure 11. And technically IDS deployment draws in two dimensions; detection strategy and an audit platform.

FUTURE RESEARCH DIRECTIONS

CPS requires more attention in security considerations in both cyber and physical aspects, even more efforts in human-based physical security aspects are required. Enhancements on data security and privacy are strongly recommended especially for legacy CPS, that operated with limited resource embedded devices, where current efforts are focused due to leak of security in traditional functions and protocols. Both cyber and physical based security aspects of CPS should be considered in early in the design process, by standardized security recommendations set by international security societies such as the internet engineering task force (IETF) and information security management standards (ISMS), and the national institute of standards and technologies (NIST). To achieve survivability in CPS, the real-time feature is highly required for early detection and activation of security triggers. In cooperative manufacturing, the coordinated change in a business partner requires more security in activities and privileges management. Highlighted security challenges in CPS that can draw future research directions are:

1. Enhancement of cyber situational awareness by digital twin utilization for higher sensitivity of analysis and scanning capabilities.
2. Analysis and development of Manufacturer Usage Description (MUD) standard for better devices authentication and authorization.
3. The impact of real-time performance with active data collection techniques compared to passive approaches.
4. Detection and prevention of security-related changes in industrial control system application with a coordinated change management technique.
5. The impact of ignorance or misestimating of insider threat in CPS, and techniques used for securing CPS against such threats.
6. Security integration and compatibility between legacy and developed CPSs.
7. The impact of IoT and two-way communication devices vulnerabilities, and security techniques experienced.
8. Meeting privacy concerns and key management in CPS using cryptography techniques.
9. Impact of underestimated leaked information in CPS security, such as links and identifiers printed in payment or transaction invoices.
10. The flexibility of security mechanisms against agility and scalability of CPSs such as in transportation and healthcare systems

IDS and IPS in the CPS area are quite new and the direction in the future is quite open and rich. One of the vital issues is the definition of the parameters of CPS IDS and IPS performance metrics (ZHANG et al, 2013). Second, High detection rates for IPS and IDS are always required however the excessive time and detection latency are considered critical metrics in the literature, which needs extensive research in the future. Third, the cooperative multi-trust approach is also an open issue in IPS and IDS for CPS. Multi-trust merits additional devotion, this due to that IDS and IPS should use the dataset in their procedures. Multi-trust can be a key design metric in building future amalgamated CPS IDSs, IPS, and IRS. Fourth, IDS and IPS CPS network-based research is also needing more attention. However, it deserves attention because traffic profiles are one of the important metrics that IPSs should leverage (Stouffer et al, 2015).

Industry 4.0 or Industrial Internet of Things is recently being determined by disruptive revolutions that potentials to bring the limitless new value of opportunities throughout all major industry sectors.

However, present internet protocols are overwhelmed by the intrusion, cybersecurity, and data privacy issues that would cause key challenges and barriers for Industry 4.0 to be adopted and industrialized. If IDs, IRS, and IPS challenges are not well studied, the dream of Industry 4.0 would never come through (J. Ding,2015). Artificial intelligence was considered a vital player in IDS and IPS and was largely considered as the future direction of both technologies in CPS. One of the creative features of AI, that it can be implemented to real-time applications and CPS traffic analysis, especially to network traffic data analysis for financial and banking sectors and services (Kelarestaghi et al,2018).

IDS and IPS are long time being dominant with capabilities of the cybersecurity stack. Though, functioning complication and cost have limited their use to many network applications, at the enterprise networks level or the borders of supervisory obedience zones. Researches are needed for a new network structure that breakdowns this conventional trade-off between the extensiveness of cybersecurity coverage and operational complexity. The solution that encirclements a smart and intelligent distributed approach, that tackles traffic analysis and inspection out to every station and removing the need to sniff traffic to distinct appliances (N. Stakhanova et al,2007). This should be implemented so that to ensure operational simplicity, comprehensive coverage, and handling IDS and IPS functionality at each processor.

CONCLUSION

Revolution in the industry is an attractive field that brings the attention of attackers and competitors. In CPS security a lot of famous criminals and threats are recorded, and national infrastructures are under threat with it. Development of security mechanism is also growing by researchers and developers by the deployment of threat modeling and vulnerabilities analysis for established threats and develops procedures to defend the system and prevents the attacks. IDS and IPS are the core frameworks in securing developed systems, by using AI techniques as in ML to improve scanning and detection process with speed and accuracy. Various types of IDS are introduced to meet different types of requirements, while in CPS deployment of IDS/IPS requires a combination and distributed security systems as a CPS branched. Finally, security procedures in the industry follow a scheduled task and constrained that should be carefully followed and reviewed periodically to maintain security demands.

REFERENCES

Abadi, M., Budiu, M., Erlingsson, Ú., & Ligatti, J. (2009). Control-flow integrity principles, implementations, and applications. ACM Trans. Inf. Syst. Secur., 13. doi:10.1145/1609956.1609960

Ahuja, Jana, Swarnkar, & Halder. (2016). On Preventing SQL Injection Attacks. *IIT Panta Journal, 395*, 49-64.

Ali, E. S., & Saeed, R. A. (2014). A Survey of Big Data Cloud Computing Security. *International Journal of Computer Science and Software Engineering, 3*(1), 78–85.

Alnakhalny, Almomani, Taha, Gupta, & Manickam. (2014). ICMPv6 flood attack detection using DENFIS algorithms. *Indian Journal of Science and Technology, 7*, 168-173.

Amin, S., Cárdenas, A. A., & Sastry, S. S. (2019). Safe and Secure Networked Control Systems under Denial-of-Service Attacks. Hybrid Systems: Computation and Control, 31-45.

Amin, S., Litrico, X., Sastry, S., & Bayen, A. (2013). Cyber Security of Water SCADA Systems—Part I: Analysis and Experimentation of Stealthy Deception Attacks. *IEEE Transactions on Control Systems Technology, 21*(5), 1963–1970. doi:10.1109/TCST.2012.2211873

Arash. (2015). A System Theoretic Approach to the Security Threats in Cyber Physical Systems Applied to Stuxnet. *IEEE Transactions on Dependable and Secure Computing.*

Bahashwan, A., Anbar, M., & Hanshi, S. M. (2020). Overview of IPv6 Based DDoS and DoS Attacks Detection Mechanisms. *International Conference on Advances in Cyber Security.* 10.1007/978-981-15-2693-0_11

Banerjee, A., Venkatasubramanian, K. K., Mukherjee, T., & Gupta, S. K. S. (2012). Ensuring Safety, Security, and Sustainability of Mission-Critical Cyber–Physical Systems. *Proceedings of the IEEE, 100*(1), 283–299. doi:10.1109/JPROC.2011.2165689

Berthier, R., & Sanders, W. (2011). Specification-Based Intrusion Detection for Advanced Metering Infrastructures. *IEEE 17th Pacific Rim International Symposium on Dependable Computing.* 10.1109/PRDC.2011.30

Bobba, R., Davis, K., Wang, Q., Khurana, H., Nahrstedt, K., & Overbye, T. (2014). *Detecting False Data Injection Attacks on DC State Estimation.* Retrieved from https://www.researchgate.net/publication/228373879

Bristol, U. o. (2020). *the Cyber Security Body of Knowledge.* Retrieved from https://www.cybok.org/

Cardenas, A. (2019). *Cyber-Physical Systems Security Knowledge area.* University of California.

Čaušević. Hossein, & Lundqvist. (2017). Data Security and Privacy in Cyber-Physical Systems for Healthcare. Wiley Online Library.

Choudhary. (2012). CIDT: Detection of Malicious Code Injection Attacks on Web Application. International Journal of Computer Applications, 52(2), 19-26.

Dao, N.-N., Kim, J., Park, M., & Cho, S. (2016). Adaptive Suspicious Prevention for Defending DoS Attacks in SDN-Based Convergent Networks. *PLoS One, 11*(8), e0160375. doi:10.1371/journal.pone.0160375 PMID:27494411

Ding, J. (2015). *Intrusion Detection, Prevention, and Response System (IDPRS) for Cyber-Physical Systems (CPSs).* In A.-S. K. Pathan (Ed.), *Securing Cyber-Physical Systems* (pp. 371–392). CRC Press.

Gao, Y., Peng, Y., Xie, F., Zhao, W., Wang, D., & Han, X. (2013). Analysis of security threats and vulnerability for cyber-physical systems. *Proceedings of 3rd International Conference on Computer Science and Network Technology, ICCSNT*, 50-55. 10.1109/ICCSNT.2013.6967062

Giraldo, J., Sarkar, E., Cardenas, A. A., Maniatakos, M., & Kantarcioglu, M. (2017). Security and Privacy in Cyber-Physical Systems: A Survey of Surveys. *IEEE Design & Test, 34*(4), 7–17. doi:10.1109/MDAT.2017.2709310

Hadžiosmanović., Sommer, Zambon, & Hartel. (2014). Through the eye of the PLC: semantic security monitoring for industrial processes. *Proceedings of the 30th Annual Computer Security Applications Conference.*

Hallenstein. (2018). *Review of Cyber and Physical Security Protection of Utility Substations and Control Centers.* Retrieved from http://www.psc.state.fl.us/Files/PDF/Publications/Reports/General/Electricgas/Cyber_Physical_Security.pdf

Halperin, D., Heydt-Benjamin, T. S., Ransford, B., Clark, S. S., Defend, B., & Morgan, W. (2008). Pacemakers and Implantable Cardiac Defibrillators: Software Radio Attacks and Zero-Power Defenses. *2008 IEEE Symposium on Security and Privacy*, 129-142. 10.1109/SP.2008.31

Hegde, Sridhar, & Shashank. (2017). Preservation of Sink-Node Location in WSN for SDN Paradigm. The National Institute of Engineering.

Houbing, S., Glenn, A. F., & Sabina, J. (2017). Key Management in CPSs. In *Security and Privacy in Cyber-Physical Systems: Foundations, Principles, and Applications* (pp. 117–136). IEEE.

Houbing, Fink, & Jeschke. (2017). *Security and Privacy in Cyber-Physical Systems: Foundations, Principles and Applications.* Wiley-IEEE Press.

Huang, Y.-L., Cárdenas, A. A., Amin, S., Lin, Z.-S., Tsai, H.-Y., & Sastry, S. (2009). Understanding the physical and economic consequences of attacks on control systems. *International Journal of Critical Infrastructure Protection*, 2(3), 73–83. doi:10.1016/j.ijcip.2009.06.001

Jakaria, A. H. M., Yang, W., Rashidi, B., Fung, C., & Rahman, M. (2016). VFence: A Defense against Distributed Denial of Service Attacks Using Network Function Virtualization. *IEEE 40th Annual Computer Software and Applications Conference (COMPSAC).* 10.1109/COMPSAC.2016.219

John, R., Cherian, J. P., & Kizhakkethottam, J. J. (2015). A survey of techniques to prevent sybil attacks. *2015 International Conference on Soft-Computing and Networks Security (ICSNS)*, 1-6. 10.1109/ICSNS.2015.7292385

Kaur, Deepali, & Kalra. (2016). Improvement and analyst security of WSN from passive attack. *2016 5th International Conference on Reliability, Infocom Technologies and Optimization (Trends and Future Directions) (ICRITO)*, 420-425.

Kelarestaghi, Heaslip, Fessmann, Khalilikhah, & Fuentes. (2018). Intelligent Transportation System Security: Hacked Message Signs. *SAE International Journal of Transportation Cybersecurity and Privacy, 1.*

Kelarestaghi, Foruhandeh, Heaslip, & Gerdes. (2018). *Vehicle Security: Risk Assessment in Transportation.* arXiv.org

Kornecki, A., & Zalewski, J. (2010). Safety and security in industrial control. *ACM International Conference Proceeding Series.*

Krotofil, Cardenas, Larsen, & Gollmann. (2014). Vulnerabilities of cyber-physical systems to stale data determining the optimal time to launch attacks. *International Journal of Critical Infrastructure Protection.*

Li. (2013). Security threats and measures for the cyber-physical systems. *Journal of China Universities of Posts and Telecommunications, 20*, 25–29. doi:10.1016/S1005-8885(13)60023-0

Liang, C., Wen, F., & Wang, Z. (2019). *Trust-Based Distributed Kalman Filtering for Target Tracking under Malicious Cyber Attacks*. Chalmers University of Technology.

Liang, F. (2019). *Machine Learning for Security and the Internet of Things: the Good, the Bad, and the Ugly. IEEE Access. Security and Privacy in Emerging Decentralized Communication Environments*.

McLaughlin, S. (2013). CPS: stateful policy enforcement for control system device usage. *Proceedings of the 29th Annual Computer Security Applications Conference*.

McLaughlin, S., Konstantinou, C., Wang, X., Davi, L., Sadeghi, A.-R., Maniatakos, M., & Karri, R. (2016). The Cybersecurity Landscape in Industrial Control Systems. *Proceedings of the IEEE, 104*(5), 1–19. doi:10.1109/JPROC.2015.2512235

McLaughlin, S., Zonouz, S., Pohly, D., & McDaniel, P. (2014). *A Trusted Safety Verifier for Process Controller Code*. San Diego, CA: NDSS. doi:10.14722/ndss.2014.23043

Merwe, Zubizarreta, Lukcin, Rügamer, & Felber. (2018). Classification of Spoofing Attack Types. *Conference: European Navigation Conference (ENC)*. doi:10.1145/2523649.2523673

Mohan, Bak, Betti, Yun, Sha, & Caccamo. (2012). *S3A: Secure System Simplex Architecture for Enhanced Security of Cyber-Physical Systems*. arXiv.org

Morris & Gao. (2013). *Classifications of Industrial Control System Cyber Attacks*. First International Symposium for ICS & SCADA Cyber Security Research.

Mousta, N., & Soukharev, F. (2018). *Crypto Agility is a Must -Have for Data Encryption Standards*. Retrieved from https://www.cigionline.org/articles/crypto-agility-must-have-data-encryption-standards

Nazarenko, A., & Safdar, G. (2019). Survey on security and privacy issues in cyber physical systems. *AIMS Electronics and Electrical Engineering, 3*, 111–143. doi:10.3934/ElectrEng.2019.2.111

Niggemann. (2015). Data-Driven Monitoring of Cyber-Physical Systems Leveraging on Big Data and the Internet-of-Things for Diagnosis and Control. *Proceedings of the 26th International Workshop on Principles of Diagnosis*.

Roemer, R., Buchanan, E., Shacham, H., & Savage, S. (2012). Return-Oriented Programming: Systems, Languages, and Applications. ACM Trans. Inf. Syst. Secur., 15. doi:10.1145/2133375.2133377

Rubio, J. E. (2017). Analysis of Intrusion Detection Systems in Industrial Ecosystems. *14th International Conference on Security and Cryptography*. 10.5220/0006426301160128

Rubio. (2018). Analysis of cyber security threats in Industry 4.0: the case of intrusion detection. *Lecture Notes in Computer Science, 10707*, 119-130.

Sandberg, H., Teixeira, A., & Johansson, K. (2010). *On Security Indices for State Estimators in Power Networks. First Workshop on Secure Control Systems (SCS)*, Stockholm, Sweden.

Scarfone, K., & Mell, P. (2007). Guide to Intrusion Detection and Prevention Systems (IDPS). NIST IR-7628 - SP 800-94.

Shanker, R., Luhach, A. K., & Sardar, A. (2016). To enhance the security in wireless nodes using centralized and synchronized IDS technique. *Indian Journal of Science and Technology*, *9*(32), 1–5.

Singh, Sweta, & Jyoti. (2010). Hello Flood Attack and its Countermeasures in Wireless Sensor Networks. *International Journal of Computer Science Issues, 7*.

Singh, D. P., Goudar, R. H., & Wazid, M. (2013). Hiding the Sink Location from the Passive Attack in WSN. *Procedia Engineering*, *64*, 16–25. doi:10.1016/j.proeng.2013.09.072

Singh, P., Krishnamoorthy, S., Nayyar, A., Luhach, A. K., & Kaur, A. (2019). Soft-computing-based false alarm reduction for hierarchical data of intrusion detection system. *International Journal of Distributed Sensor Networks*, *15*(10), 1550147719883132. doi:10.1177/1550147719883132

Sridhar, S., Hahn, A., & Govindarasu, M. (2012). Cyber-Physical System Security for the Electric Power Grid. *Proceedings of the IEEE*, *100*(1), 210–224. doi:10.1109/JPROC.2011.2165269

Stakhanova, N., Basu, S., & Wong, J. (2007). A taxonomy of intrusion response system. *International Journal of Information and Computer Security*, *1*(1/2), 169. doi:10.1504/IJICS.2007.012248

Stouffer. (2015). *Guide to Industrial Control Systems (ICS) Security*. NIST Special Publication 800-82.

Suman & Shubhangi. (2016). A Survey on Comparison of Secure Routing Protocols in Wireless Sensor Networks. *International Journal of Wireless Communications and Networking Technologies*, *5*, 16–20.

Teixeira, A., Shames, I., Sandberg, H., & Johansson, K. (2012). Revealing Stealthy Attacks in Control Systems. *50th Annual Allerton Conference on Communication, Control, and Computing (Allerton)*. 10.1109/Allerton.2012.6483441

Teixeira, A., Sou, K. C., Sandberg, H., & Johansson, K. H. (2013). Quantifying Cyber-Security for Networked Control Systems in Control of Cyber-Physical Systems. In Workshop held at Johns Hopkins University. Springer International Publishing.

Trifan, M. (2012). Cyber-Attacks (Viruses, Trojan Horses and Computer Worms) Analysis. *International Journal of Information Security and Cybercrime, 1*, 46-54.

Vaid, R., & Kumar, V. (2013). Security Issues and Remidies in Wireless Sensor Networks- A Survey. *International Journal of Computers and Applications*, *79*(4), 31–39. doi:10.5120/13731-1528

Vats, P., & Saha, A. (2019). *An Overview of SQL Injection Attacks*. SSRN Electronic Journal.

Wan. (2018). Physical Layer Key Generation: Securing Wireless Communication in Automotive Cyber-Physical Systems. *ACM Transactions on Cyber-Physical Systems*.

Xenonstack. (2019). *The Impact of Artificial Intelligence on Cyber Security*. Retrieved from https://www.xenonstack.com/artificial-intelligence-solutions/cyber-security/

Zhu & Sastry. (2010). *SCADA-specific Intrusion Detection/Prevention Systems: A Survey and Taxonomy*. University of California at Berkeley.

Ziegler, S., Crettaz, C., Kim, E., Skarmeta, A., Bernal Bernabe, J., & Trapero, R. (2019). *Privacy and Security Threats on the Internet of Things. In Internet of Things Security and Data Protection* (pp. 9–43). Springer. doi:10.1007/978-3-030-04984-3_2

KEY TERMS AND DEFINITIONS

Autoregression Behavioral: It's a model that predicts future behavior based on past behavior. It's used for forecasting when there is some correlation between values in a time series and the values that precede and succeed them.

C2 Architecture: Architectural software style developed by the Institute for Software Research at the University of California. It focuses on the construction of a flexible and extensible software system using a component and message-based architecture.

Control-Flow Integrity (CFI): Is a term given to computer security techniques that prevent a wide variety of malware attacks from redirecting the flow of execution of a program.

CyBOK Project: Stands for Cyber Security Body of Knowledge project is a collaborative initiative mobilized in 2017 with an aspiration to codify the foundational and generally recognized knowledge on Cyber Security. The project, funded by the National Cyber Security Program, is led by the University of Bristol's.

False Data Injection Detection: It's a mechanism to detects the False data injection attacks. These kinds of attacks aim to compromise the readings of multiple smart sensors and phasor measurement units in smart applications to mislead the operation and control centers.

K-Means Clustering: Is a method of vector quantization, originally from signal processing, that aims to partition n observations into k clusters in which each observation belongs to the cluster with the nearest mean serving as a prototype of the cluster.

Manufacturer Usage Description: Is an embedded software standard defined by the IETF that allows IoT Device makers to advertise device specifications, including the intended communication patterns for their device when it connects to the network.

NIST Standard: Represents the National Institute of Standards and Technology. It is known as a physical sciences laboratory and a non-regulatory agency of the United States Department of Commerce. Its mission is to promote innovation and industrial competitiveness.

Secure System Simplex Architecture (S3A): Is a term given to the integrated security framework that prevents damage from malicious intrusions in safety-critical systems as well as aids in rapid detection through side-channel monitoring.

Trusted Safety Verifier (TSV): The term defines how to enable demonstrative test cases to system operators. It's a minimal TCB for the verification of safety-critical code executed on programmable controllers.

Chapter 7
A Survey on Network Intrusion Detection Using Deep Generative Networks for Cyber–Physical Systems

Srikanth Yadav M.

ⓘ https://orcid.org/0000-0003-2796-7978

VFSTR University, India

Kalpana R.

Pondicherry Engineering College, India

ABSTRACT

In the present computing world, network intrusion detection systems are playing a vital part in detecting malicious activities, and enormous attention has been given to deep learning from several years. During the past few years, cyber-physical systems (CPSs) have become ubiquitous in modern critical infrastructure and industrial applications. Safety is therefore a primary concern. Because of the success of deep learning (DL) in several domains, DL-based CPS security applications have been developed in the last few years. However, despite the wide range of efforts to use DL to ensure safety for CPSs. The major challenges in front of the research community are developing an efficient and reliable ID that is capable of handling a large amount of data, in analyzing the changing behavioral patterns of attacks in real-time. The work presented in this manuscript reviews the various deep learning generative methodologies and their performance in detecting anomalies in CPSs. The metrics accuracy, precision, recall, and F1-score are used to measure the performance.

DOI: 10.4018/978-1-7998-5101-1.ch007

INTRODUCTION

In the present computing world, the volume of the data or information is increased rapidly, and the role of computers in managing and maintaining the integrity of the networks is quickly expanded in domains such as social networks, e-commerce, and health care. More human activities are also grown in these domains; this leads to the occurrence of more internal intrusion within the network. The role of the Intrusion Detection System (IDS) is to protect networks from vulnerable attacks from both external and internal intruders. An IDS (P Anderson, 1980) is either a software or hardware used to monitor the activities of computer networks. The IDS protects the network from the threats by analyzing patterns of captured data packets. These threats can be overwhelming; for example, Denial of service (DoS) attacks prevent genuine user's resources by generating unwanted traffic (Mitchell & Chen, 2014). In contrast, Malware or Trojans are the hidden programs installed by the attackers to interrupt network systems (Kettani & Cannistra, 2018). Many IDS exist in the contemporary digital era, but most of the IDS services have experienced the difficulty of a high false alarm rate. This is also one of the challenges to be handled in designing efficient IDS. One more significant issue to be resolved is to reduce the load on the administrator and useful classification of assigning class labels to the unlabelled records. Another difficulty of some existing IDS is their incapability to recognize unknown attacks. These IDS depends on the signatures of acknowledged attacks.

An active IDS can be designed by using various machine learning techniques. The machine learning classification schemes are used to separate regular traffic from abnormal traffic. The machine learning model is developed by training on an NSL-KDD (Farahnakian & Heikkonen, 2018) dataset to forecast an attack using classification schemes. Many machine learning approaches have been productively implemented as classifiers on IDS. But these approaches have several flaws such as high false alarm rate (FAR) and low throughput.

Cyber-physical systems (CPS) can be referred to as modern systems with assimilated computational and physical capabilities that can communicate with humans in new ways. Such technologies have an immense effect on several sectors, such as environmental management, smart transport, manufacturing, smart grid, smart house, smart infrastructure, and smart healthcare. Both of these domains are network-dependent because they involve remote data transmission to transmit data from sensors to actuators through the control center. Contact in a large network renders the device fragile and creates a humongous space for adversaries to attack.

The Internet of Things (IoT), one of the core sub-domains of CPS, has introduced major technical developments to a whole new stage where data is the driving power. In tandem with actuators, motors, cameras, applications, and networking, IoT has opened up a new layer to facilitate communication, processing, and data sharing. While generally acknowledged, almost 85 percent of IoT systems remain susceptible to a large variety of cyberattacks. These are vulnerable to different forms of threats, such as man-in-the-center, data and identity stealing, distributed denial of service (DDoS), computer hijacking, etc. To secure protection vital structures from intruders, rigorous monitoring procedures to identify all types of intruders must be taken into consideration.

The IDS is responsible for monitoring network activity and device data for unauthorized behaviors and for providing warnings, which are the first and foremost component of the security policy in the CPS environment. Getting clear awareness of the precise place and period at which particular anomalies produce hazards in the environment tends to minimize impacts by taking suitable measures, and therefore, intrusion management mechanisms step into the frame. The intrusion avoidance program operates at the same time as the intrusion detection device to avoid the intruder from doing further harm to the network.

Machine learning-based IDS can find anomalies in the System with considerable accuracy. Even though the emerging IT CPS trends such as Industry 4.0, IoT, Big Data, and Cloud Computing adds more momentum, it introduces Many bugs, too. Also, the architectural novel The compositions bring sophistication to the pattern due to Unknown emerging behavior. There needs to be an individual IDS Built to observe their relationship with this complex System, but insufficient data is limiting model training. Besides, most of these datasets are unbalanced. Where different types of attack data are not available on a large scale Scaling compared to the normal data.

Types of Intrusion Detection Systems

Generally, IDS is broadly classified into two major categories. They are network intrusion detection system (NIDS) and host-based intrusion detection system (HIDS)

Network Intrusion Detection System (NIDS)

NIDS is an independent intrusion detection system that recognizes an intrusion by investigating network traffic, as well as it monitors multiple numbers of hosts. The NIDS gains admittance by linking to a network switch or a network hub. The detecting sensors are placed at various choke points to monitor the entire network. The individual network data packets are captured and analyzed by the sensors for identifying malicious packets. The NIDS provides a secure prevention mechanism for external intruders. Generally, the NIDS has high response time against external intruders.

Host-Based Intrusion Detection System (HIDS)

In HIDS, a software agent is inbuilt in sensors that recognize intrusions by analyzing system calls, log files, access controls, and other host system activities. The HIDS provides a secure prevention mechanism for internal intruders. Usually, the HIDS has low responsiveness for real-time attacks. The researchers have designed system specific IDS such as honeypots with customized tools. Most of the IDS use one of the two detection methodologies, either an anomaly-based intrusion detection system or a signature-based intrusion detection system.

Anomaly-Based IDS

The Anomaly-based IDS identifies intrusions using standard traffic estimation, and it uses regular traffic as a baseline parameter. Anomaly-based IDS is used to detect whether the network data traffic is within the measured lines or not. If any packet is observed maliciously, it triggers an alarm to the administrator.

Signature-Based IDS

The Signature-based IDS examines network traffic with predefined patterns called signatures. Nowadays, many attacks have a unique signature. The signature database is updated periodically to diminish active threats.

Figure 1. Classification of deep generative networks

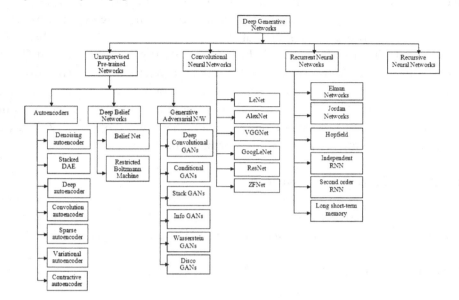

Role of Deep Learning

An immense awareness about deep learning has been increased over several years in the research community for many diversified applications, such as computer vision, natural language processing, and image processing, and so on. In this survey paper, the authors have focused on various existing methodologies of deep learning. The authors have surveyed the latest studies on deep learning and evaluated the performances of learning methods for anomaly-based intrusion detections.

This survey paper is structured as follows. The "Deep Learning Classification Of Intrusion Detection System" section describes an overview of the classification of deep learning schemes. The "Literature Review" section portrays a literature review of existing methodologies proposed by various eminent authors. The "Experimental Study" section focuses on measuring the performance of deep learning frameworks as an initial experiment. The authors concluded the presentation with a summary of the survey in "Future Research Directions" and "Conclusion" sections.

DEEP LEARNING CLASSIFICATION OF INTRUSION DETECTION SYSTEM

Many researchers have developed efficient IDS by incorporating deep learning methodologies. Deep networks play an essential role in the detection of intrusions by increasing the size of big data. This manuscript mainly focuses on the role of deep networks in the designing of efficient IDS. The intrusion detection majorly depends on the source of data and techniques used. The broader classification of deep generative architectures is shown in Figure 1. The Deep generative networks are broadly classified into four major categories, namely, unsupervised pre-trained networks, convolution neural networks, recurrent neural networks, and recursive neural networks.

Figure 2. Architecture of stacked denoising auto encoders

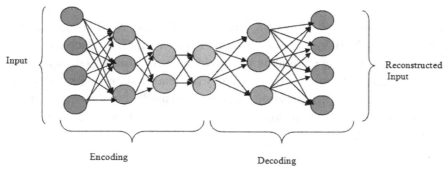

Unsupervised Pre-Trained Networks

Unsupervised pre-training is a discriminative natured neural network, and it uses an unsupervised learning approach to train the model. Unsupervised pre-training networks help deal with issues like optimization and overfitting. The detailed evolution of unsupervised pre-training networks is explained comprehensively.

Autoencoders

An autoencoder (Bourlard & Kamp, 1988; LeCun, 1987) is a neural network approach that is trained to endeavor to copy its input to its output. The internal structure of the autoencoder consists of input nodes, hidden nodes, and output nodes. Let $\mathbf{d}$ be the input dataset, $\mathbf{r}$ is the output dataset, and $\mathbf{h}$ is the mapping function of the hidden layer. The autoencoder network consists of two technical functions encoder and decoder. An encoder function can be expressed as $\mathbf{h} = \mathbf{f}\,(\mathbf{d})$, and a decoder function which produces a reconstruction is represented as $\mathbf{r} = \mathbf{g}\,(\mathbf{h})$. The autoencoder network can be expressed as $\mathbf{g}\,(\mathbf{f}\,(\mathbf{d})) = \mathbf{d}$.

Mostly, the autoencoders are used for dimensionality reduction to obtain a reduced feature set. If the number of extracted dimensions is less than the input dimensions of the dataset $\mathbf{d}$, then it is called under complete autoencoder. Learning an under complete illustration captures the most prominent features of the training dataset. The learning process is portrayed simply as a minimized loss function,

$$L\,(d, g\,(f\,(d)))$$

where $\mathbf{L}$ is a loss function penalizing $\mathbf{g}\,(\mathbf{f}\,(\mathbf{d}))$ for being similar from $\mathbf{d}$, such as the mean squared error

Denoising autoencoder (DAE)

The autoencoders are commonly used for feature selection and extraction. However, if the number of nodes in the hidden layer is more than the nodes in the input layer, then this leads to an identity or null function mismatching. This problem can be resolved by introducing denoising autoencoders (Soulié, Gallinari, Le Cun, & Thiria, 1987), by setting a default value zero to the randomly selected input nodes. The percentage of a random selection of input nodes is varied from 30 to 50 percent.

Stacked Denoising Autoencoders (SDA)

The stacked denoising autoencoders (Vincent, Larochelle, Bengio, & Manzagol, 2008) are a kind of stacked autoencoders SAE (Y. Bengio, P. Lamblin, D. Popovici, 2007), which can be implemented by applying unsupervised pre-training method on their hidden layers. During the initial stage, each layer is undergone with functional pre-training activity to carry out feature subset selection and extraction from the other layers; on the other hand, supervised fine-tuning is applied in the second stage. The multiple denoising autoencoders are combined to form Stacked denoising autoencoders. The representation of the SDA is shown in Figure 2.

Convolution autoencoders (CAE)

Another variant of autoencoders is convolutional autoencoders (Krizhevsky, Sutskever, & Hinton, n.d.), which uses the convolution operator to develop the observation. The learning activity is carried out

Figure 3. Graphical representation of CAE

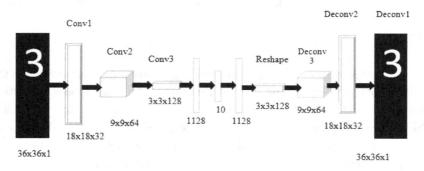

using simple signals, and later these autoencoders are used to reconstruct the input data. The primary application areas of CAE are medical image reconstruction, colorization of the image, and clustering of latent space. The graphical representation of the CAE is depicted in Figure 3.

Deep Autoencoders

The deep autoencoder network is an unsupervised learning scheme, and it comprises of three-layered architecture. The DAE consists of an input layer, a hidden layer(s), and an output layer. An autoencoder becomes deep networks when it has several multiple hidden layers. The architecture of DAE can also convert as a stacked autoencoder or denoising autoencoders. The learning scheme in DAE can be implemented with an essential operation such as encoding and decoding. The encoding process maps the data in the input layer with the functions of the hidden layer. The other activity called decoding, which maps extracted information of hidden layers is mapped with output layers. The sample representation of DAE is shown in Figure 4. Unfortunately, the deep autoencoders are failed to achieve better accuracy for backpropagation training schemes. The pre-training of DAE using the greedy layer is the suggestible

Figure 4. Architecture of simple deep autoencoder

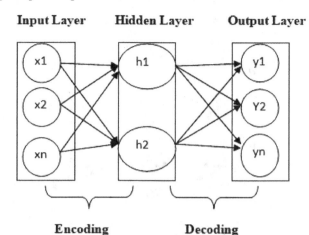

solution to solve the backpropagation learning scheme. Throughout cyber-physical systems, it is used to identify malicious code, identify malware variants, and detect abnormalities.

Sparse Autoencoder (SAE)

Sparse autoencoders(Liu et al., 2014) provides an alternative approach for dealing with an information bottleneck problem without reducing the nodes of hidden layers. The sparse autoencoders are used to construct a loss function such that penalizes activations within a hidden layer. The sparse autoencoder contains a single hidden layer, which is linked to the input layer by a weight matrix forming the encoding step. The hidden layer then outputs to the reconstruction vector, using the bound weight matrix to form the decoder. Simple single-layer, sparse auto-encoder with an equal number of inputs (n), outputs (n'), and hidden nodes (z). The darker yellow nodes are in an active state. Usually, the autoencoder will have a bottleneck, which means that the hidden layer/layer has fewer nodes than the input and output. However, this is not a requirement if there is an additional constraint on the network. The particular constraint that we are considering is the sparseness that we are imposing on the hidden units. By constraining the

Figure 5. Architecture of a sample SAE

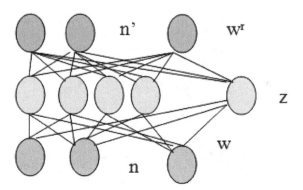

Figure 6. DBN with three hidden-layers and one visible layer

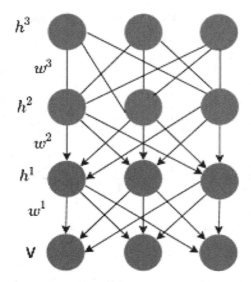

activation of hidden nodes, we are effectively reducing the number of firing neurons. Thus, despite an equal or greater number of hidden nodes than input/output nodes, we will have the data compression needed to learn the latent features. The pictorial representation of SAE is shown in Figure 5.

Variational Autoencoder (VAE)

Variational autoencoders (VAE) (Chen, Kingma, et al., 2016)are capable of dealing with complex and large datasets. The VAE can produce high-resolution digital images.

Contractive Autoencoder (CAE)

A contractive autoencoder (Rifai, Vincent, Muller, Glorot, & Bengio, 2011) is one of the unsupervised deep learning schemes which helps a neural network encoder unlabeled training records. This is achieved

Figure 7. Pictographic representation of belief networks

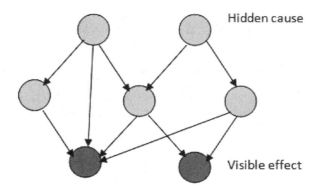

Figure 8. The graphical representation of RBM

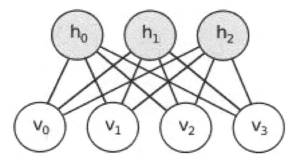

by constructing a loss term that penalizes massive derivatives of our hidden layer activations concerning the input training examples, essentially penalizing instances where a small change in the input leads to a substantial difference in the encoding space.

Figure 9. A sample Boltzmann machine

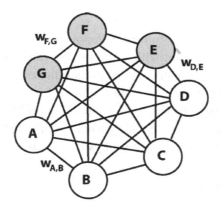

Deep Belief Networks (DBN)

Deep belief networks (DBN) (Hinton, Osindero, & Teh, 2006) are also a generative graphical model, and it is the stacked representation of Restricted Boltzmann machines (RBM). RBM is capable of generating a learning model with additional hidden layers for discrimination tasks. Generally, DBN is a probabilistic model that uses joint probability distributions in the learning phase. The graphical representation of the DBN is shown in Figure 6. During the learning phase, the hidden layers act as feature detectors, and later the trained network can be used to perform classification. DBN uses both supervised fine-tuning and unsupervised pre-training methods to develop the models. Figure 6 portrays a DBN consisting of a Restricted Boltzmann Machine Stack (RBM) and one or more additional discriminating layers. The training aims to learn the weights between the layers once the structure of a DBN is determined. Each node is autonomous of other nodes in the same layer given all nodes, which give it the property to train RBM generative weights. It then passes through a gullible layer by a layer learning algorithm that learns

Figure 10. A sample deep Boltzmann machine

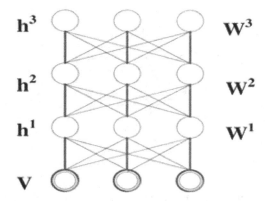

every stack of the layer of RBM. In Figure 6 left, the lower layers in the blue form directed the sigmoid belief network, and the top layers in the red form an RBM.

Belief Network

Generally, belief networks (Y. Bengio, P. Lamblin, D. Popovici, 2007) are composed of stochastic binary-valued layers, and each node is associated with some weight value. The state of the belief network is either 0 or 1. The bias value is used to determine the probability of having a binary state of 1. Directed acyclic graphs are used for a pictorial representation of belief networks. Utilizing the belief network, the authors have solved the inference problem and the learning problem. The pictographic depiction of belief networks is shown in Figure 7. BNs are widely used in multiple fields including intrusion prevention and malware identification functions in cyber-physical networks.

Restricted Boltzmann Machine

Generally, the Boltzmann machine is a stochastic neural network with recurrent nature with stochastic binary units and undirected edges between units. It is not practical and has scalability issues, to resolve these issues, Restricted Boltzmann Machine (RBM) was introduced. Restricted Boltzmann Machine (Shone, Ngoc, Phai, & Shi, 2018) has only one layer of hidden units, and it restricts connections between hidden units. This allows for a more efficient algorithm. The pictorial interpretation of RBM is shown in Figure 8. They are used in many applications including speech and picture recognition, grouping, reduction in size, collection of functionality, and cyber-physical systems. It was used for activities like intrusion prevention, anomaly prevention, and malicious code detection in cyber-physical systems.

Deep Boltzmann Machine (DBM)

A deep Boltzmann machine (DBM) (Naseer et al., 2018) is a type of binary pairwise undirected probabilistic graphical model (Markov random field) with multiple layers of hidden random variables. DBM is a network of symmetrically coupled stochastic binary units. A graphical representation of the Boltzmann machine [14] is shown in Figure 9. The dependency is represented using an undirected edge along with

Figure 11. A sample RBM

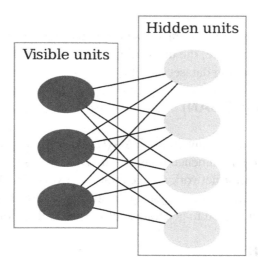

its weight. In this sample diagram, there are three hidden nodes and four visible nodes. The unidirectional graphical representation of DBM [15] is shown in Figure 10.

The efficient, practical learning scheme of DBM is a restricted Boltzmann machine (RBM). Intralayer connections are not allowed between hidden nodes. After training one RBM network, the hidden unit's data can be used for higher-level RBM training. The primary application areas of RBM are handwritten reorganization and speech reorganization tools. The graphical representation of RBM is shown in Figure 11.

GENERATIVE ADVERSARIAL NETWORKS (GAN)

Generating adversarial networks (GANs) are algorithmic structures that use two neural networks, trying to pit against the other to generate new, computational data instances that can be passed through for actual data. They are commonly included in the production of pictures, video, and audio. GANs was introduced in a paper by Ian Goodfellow, in 2014. GANs are neural networks that produce synthesized data based on certain input data. For example, GANs can be trained on how to produce images from the textual content. Generative Adversarial Networks consists of two models, generative and discriminatory. The discriminatory model seeks to predict certain classes, given certain characteristics. The generative model attempts to predict the characteristics of the classes. This includes calculating the likelihood of a given class function.

The GAN has two main components: the generator and the discriminator. The generator creates new instances of an entity while the discriminator decides if the new instance is part of the existing dataset.

Working of GAN

One neural network, called the generator, generates new data instances, while the other, the discriminator, evaluates them for authenticity; i.e. the discriminator decides whether each instance of data that it reviews belongs to the actual training dataset or not.

Deep Convolution GAN (DCGAN)

The improved version of GAN is deep convolution GAN (Radford, Metz, & Chintala, 2015). The DCGAN can produce more stable and high eminence images. The DCGAN is composed of two basic network modules; they are the discriminator network and generator network. The batch normalization function is executed in both networks. One of the major application areas of DCGAN is pattern transfer. For example, a dress design pattern is used to generate shoe design in the same pattern.

Conditional GAN (CGAN)

Conditional GAN (Isola, Zhu, Zhou, & Efros, 2017)are used to produce enhanced quality images using additional labeled information. The CGAN is trained to provide better images by feeding information to the model. These networks are much capable of dealing with high complex images.

Stack GAN (SGAN)

The problem of the image synthesizing from the text description is resolved by proposing Stack GAN. The authors have intended SGAN (Huang, Li, Poursaeed, Hopcroft, & Belongie, 2017) to produce 256x256 realistic images from text descriptions. The authors have decomposed the large image into smaller subsets

Table 1. Comparison results of ILSVRC competitions

CNN Type	Year of winner	Proposed by	No. of Layers	Convolution Size	No. of parameters	The error rate of top-5	Applications
Lenet-5	1998	(LeCun, 1987)	7	3x3	60 thousand	N.A	to read digits in images
AlexNet	2012-winner	(Krizhevsky et al., n.d.)	7 with more filters per layer	11x11, 5x5, 3x3	60 million	15.3%	computer vision
ZFNet	2013- winner	(Zeiler & Fergus, 2014)	8	3x3	51 million	14.8%	computer vision
GoogLeNet	2014- winner	Google	27	3x3	4 million	6.67%	computer vision
VGG Net	2014- 1ˢᵗ runner	(Simonyan, Andrew Zisserman, & Zisserman, 2014)	16	3x3	138million	7.3%	computer vision
ResNet	2015-winner	(He, Zhang, Ren, & Sun, 2016)	152	3x3	122 million	3.6%	computer vision

Figure 12. Elman RNN

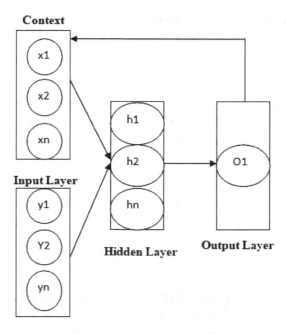

by using a sketch refinement procedure. The proposed network is composed of two stages. The primary role of stage-I is to generate low-resolution images from text descriptions. In stage-II, high-resolution images are produced with realistic image details.

Figure 13. Jordan RNN

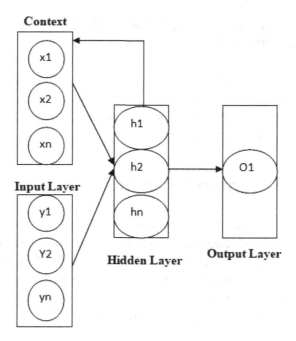

Figure 14. A Single auto-encoder

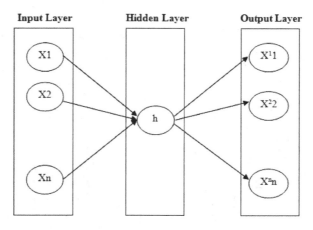

Info GAN (IGAN)

The informative extension to GAN is infoGAN (Chen, Duan, et al., 2016), and this proposed scheme can deal with the complex dataset. These networks can extract the essential features of images. The extraction of image features is done with the help of an unlabelled dataset of CGAN.

Wasserstein GAN (WGAN)

WGAN (Arjovsky, Chintala, & Bottou, 2017) are proposed to produce lossless images using Wasserstein distance. These loss functions are used to correlate the image quality. Reconstruction of corrupted images is done effectively using WGAN.

Discover Cross-Domain Relations with Generative Adversarial Networks (Disco GAN)

The authors have suggested a method to discover relations between different domains using Disco GAN (Kim, Cha, Kim, Lee, & Kim, 2017). The Disco GAN is used to find out the relations and found relations used to transfers patterns or styles from one domain to another. The disco GAN preserves the critical attributes of palm identity and facial identity.

CONVOLUTION NEURAL NETWORKS (CNN)

Convolution neural networks (Simonyan & Zisserman, 2014) are a different category of multi-layered neural networks, which are intended to identify visual image patterns directly from input images using minimal pre-processing process. The evolution of CNN is described as follows. The performance results of ILSVRC ImageNet Large Scale Visual Recognition Competitions conducted during the period 1998 to 2018 are compared based on the parameters, namely, number of layers, size of convolution, several parameters, and top-5 error rate which are portrayed in Table 1.

Figure 15. A Sample NDAE

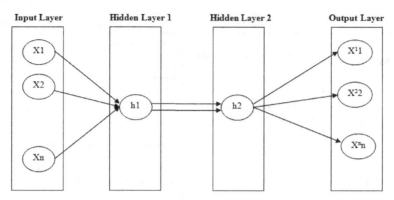

RECURRENT NEURAL NETWORKS (RNN)

The RNN is one of the deep networks that can be implemented using either supervised or unsupervised learning schemes. The RNN network model is having a feedback loop linking layer by layer, and it can store information of preceding input nodes. In general, there are two types of architecture for RNN, namely Elman RNN (Elman, 1990) and Jordan RNN (Zeliadt, 2013). Elman model is having a feature of simple feedback looping layer by layer. The Jordan RNN deep network model has feedback looping of neurons within a layer to the next layer. Both Elman RNN and Jordan RNN are depicted in Figure 12 and Figure 13, respectively.

Elman Networks

The Elman network is composed of a 3-layered network with an input layer, hidden layer, and output layers with an additional set of context units. The hidden layers are connected with context units. Each context unit is assigned with a fixed distance value one. The input is feed-forwarded for each iteration, and an imperative learning rule is applied. The previous values of the hidden values are stored in the back connections.

Jordan Networks

Conceptually, Jordan networks and Elman networks are similar to each other. The context unit values are taken from the output layer rather than from the hidden layer. The context layers are also termed as state layer.

Hopfield

Hopfield networks(Hopfield, 1982) is a recurrent neural network with symmetric connections. The Hopfield network requires stationary inputs as it is unable to process sequences of patterns. Using the Hebbian learning training approach, they can design networks capable of robust content addressable memory, and connection alterations are not permitted.

Table 2. Comparison of performances of various deep learning schemes

Author(s)	Dataset Used	Limitations	Problem identified
Non-symmetric deep autoencoder (NDAE) and Stacked NDAE (Shone et al., 2018)	KDD Cup '99 and NSL-KDD datasets	5-class and 13- class classification is used on both KDD 99 and NSL-KDD datasets	21-Class classification can be done on both KDD 99 and NSL-KDD datasets
convolution auto-encoder (CAE) based anomaly detection method for HTTP messages (Park et al., 2018)	Modified National Institute of Standards and Technology (MNIST) dataset	One-class SVM classification	There scope to classify multi-class labeled data.
self-taught learning (STL) IDS framework (Al-Qatf et al., 2018)	NSL-KDD	Used only the NSL-KDD dataset More training and testing time	There is a possibility to enhance STL into multi-stage STL
Stacked Sparse Auto-encoder (SSAE) (Yan & Han, 2018)	NSL-KDD, KDD and Kyoto	Effectively detected DoS and Probe attacks	There is scope to enhance the proposed scheme able to detect R2L and U2R attacks
Developed Convolution Neural Networks, Autoencoders and Recurrent Neural Networks models (Naseer et al., 2018)	NSLKDD	Tested and detected only anomaly attacks	The proposed scheme can be extended to detect signature-based attacks.
Stacked sparse auto-encoders and binary tree ensemble (Baoan Zhang, Yanhua Yu and Jie Li, 2016)	NSL-KDD	Due to sparse architecture, more trained time is required	Scope to reduce the size of the architecture by using symmetric sparse architecture
Sequential LSTM auto-encoders (Ali H. Mirza and Selon Cosan)	ISCX IDS 2012	Less number of training instances	Scope to test on a large volume of the dataset

Independent RNN

The Independently recurrent neural network (IndRNN) (Li, Li, Cook, Zhu, & Gao, 2018) handles problems like the gradient vanishing and exploding. Each neuron is associated with context units, which receive past state information. The neurons are independent without storing other neuron's history.

Second-Order RNNs

To deal with higher-order weights rather than standard weights, second-order RNNs are proposed.

This feature allows mapping directly between the state with finite data in training and representation. One of the example networks is long short term memory (LSTM) with no formal mappings between the states.

Long Short-Term Memory

The vanishing gradient descendent problem can be solved using a deep learning approach called long short-term memory (LSTM). LSTM is composed of recurrent units called forget gates. Using LSTM Backpropagation errors are prevented from vanishing. The LSTM is capable of recognizing context-sensitive languages based on hidden memory modules.

RECURSIVE NEURAL NETWORKS

Recursive neural networks and recurrent neural networks are much alike and capable of handling variable-length input data. The primary dissimilarity is that recurrent neural networks are capable of modeling the hierarchical structures in the training dataset. Generally, the recursive neural network is composed of a binary tree structure that allows the recursive network to learn varying sequences of words or parts of an image and a shared-weight matrix. The primary application areas are image decomposition and generating textual transcription from audio.

LITERATURE REVIEW

Non-symmetric Deep Auto-Encoder (NDAE) methodology is proposed by (Shone et al., 2018), which is an unsupervised approach. A novel deep learning classification model is constructed using stacked NDAEs. They focused on challenges like accuracy, low-frequency attacks, and diversity. An unsupervised neural networks algorithm called *auto-encoder is* used in feature extraction or dimensionality reduction activity. An auto-encoder is more capable of providing non-linear generalization than standard principal component analysis (PCA). An auto-encoder consists of an input layer, a hidden layer, and an output layer. The single sample auto-encoder is shown in Figure 14. By reducing the feature set using dimensionality reduction, the auto-encoder can extract the essential attributes. NDAE is comprised of more than one hidden layer, termed as stacked auto-encoders. The sample NDAE is shown in Figure 15.

(Park, Kim, & Lee, 2018), proposed anomaly detection for Hypertext Transfer Protocol (HTTP) messages using convolution autoencoder (CAE). The CAE is composed of an encoder and a decoder that follows convolution neural networks (CNN) structures symmetrically. The proposed character level image transformation scheme is capable of detecting intrusions embedded in HTTP request packets. The primary objective is to transform an HTTP message into a binary image. The encoded information consists of 68 characters, including lower case alphabets, numerals, and special symbols, which are acceptable to be transformed. If any unusual HTTP request is detected, the binary cross-entropy (BCE) of the message is calculated. BCE is used as a decision variable. If the BCE value of the abnormal packet is higher than the threshold value, the message is transformed using a character embedding approach. They adopted the unsupervised one-class Support Vector Machines (SVM) machine learning scheme for classification.

(Al-Qatf, Lasheng, Al-Habib, & Al-Sabahi, 2018) have proposed a self-taught learning Intrusion detection system (STL-IDS). They used the prescribed approach for dimensionality reduction and features learning. They offered an unsupervised deep learning model STL by combining sparse au-

Table 3. NSL-KDD training and testing data files

File	Description	# records	normal %	Anomaly (%)
KDDTRAIN+	Complete NSL-KDD training set	117,864	59.456	49.56
KDDTRAIN 20	20% of NSL-KDD training set	24,793	12.872	48.08
KDDTEST +	Complete NSL-KDD testing set	23,412	96.41	58.82
KDDTEST20	20% of NSL-KDD testing set	12,150	22.43	81.54

toencoder (SAE) and SVM. The proposed method consists of two major activities. In the first stage, the unsupervised feature learning (UFL) approached is used to label the unlabeled records. During the second stage, labeled data is used for classification using SVM. They adopted SAE, which applies the backpropagation algorithm to obtain optimal values and also to minimize the cost function. The Gaussian radial basis function (RBF) is applied for classification. The proposed methodology has been tested using NSL-KDD training and testing datasets.

(Yan & Han, 2018) have suggested an unsupervised deep learning approach using Stacked Sparse Auto-encoder (SSAE) to achieve a prominent feature subset by applying dimensionality reduction. The proposed SSAE is compared with the existing dimensionality reductions procedures. The auto-encoder scheme has converted definite feature vectors into an abstract feature set. The nonlinear transformation of high dimensional vector data space into low dimensional vector data space is used to obtain an abstract vector subset. The suggested system has been testing on KDD99, NSL-KDD, and Kyoto2006 datasets. The proposed scheme effectively detected DoS and probe attacks; on the other hand, the proposed system has recorded low accuracy while detecting R2L and U2R attacks.

(Naseer et al., 2018) have tested NSL-KDD datasets using popular deep learning approaches like convolution neural networks, autoencoders, and recurrent neural networks. The proposed scheme is tested on the NSL-KDD dataset, and the authors adopted popular classification learning schemes like Random forest (RF), naïve Bayes, decision tree, and SVM. Both deep convolution neural networks (DCNN) and long short term memory (LSTM) models are used to measure the performance of deep networks. The comparisons among the existing schemes are displayed in Table 2.

EXPERIMENTAL STUDY

Dataset for Experimental Study

The most popular datasets in the research community, such as KDDCUP99 and NSL-KDD datasets, have been used for initial experimental purposes. Both datasets have been used as training and testing datasets. The brief description of this dataset is provided as follows.

KDDCUP99

KDD CUP 1999 dataset has been extensively used for intrusion detection methods. The training dataset is composed of 487,000 records with 41 attributes, which are used to classify and to label the data packet as either normal or an attack. The attacks are broadly classified into four major categories as follows

- **Denial of Service Attack (DoS):** This attack intended to make the computational resources and memory resources too busy or overloaded.
- **User to Root Attack (U2R):** This attack tries to get root-level access and spreads susceptibility activities over the network
- Remote to Local Attack (R2L): This attack happens by sending packets onto the network without any authentication or privileges to log into the system.
- Probe attack: These type of attacks tries to acquire secured information about the network to violate security breaches.

NSL-KDD Dataset

The NSL-KDD dataset is developed by overcoming the drawbacks of the KDDCCUP99 dataset. KDD-CUP99 dataset contains a vast number of redundant or duplicate records. Nearly 70 to 80% of duplicate records are available in both training and testing datasets. The NSL-KDD is an enhanced version of KDDCUP99 data, and it is extensively adopted for intrusion detection activities. The authors have used the four files labeled as KDDTRAIN+, KDDTRAIN20, for the training dataset, and on the other hand, the labels KDDTEST+, KDDTEST20 are used to represent the testing dataset. Table 3 presents a summary of the four files in the dataset.

During our initial experimental process, the authors tested the dataset on a deep learning framework using autoencoders using Tensor flow in the Amazon web services platform. The process is initiated with necessary data preparation and preprocessing activity. NSL-KDD dataset is composed of both numerical and nominal data values, to classify the data, the NSL-KDD dataset has to undergo a data transformation process. To normalize the values, min-max normalization is used. The preprocessed and normalized data is passed to the framework. Table 4 represents the experimental results with necessary measures such as accuracy, precision, recall, and F1-Score.

Table 4. Experimental outcome with the NSL-KDD dataset using autoencoders

Composition	Accuracy (%)	Precision (%)	Recall (%)	F1-score (%)
KDDTRAIN+ / KDDTEST+	88.5	89.8	93.7	92.0
KDDTRAIN20 / KDDTEST+	91.5	89.3	94.7	92.1
KDDTRAIN+/ KDDTEST−	84.0	86.5	93.8	91.0
KDDTRAIN20 / KDDTEST−	83.1	88.8	94.6	91.1

FUTURE RESEARCH DIRECTIONS

Given the generalization of DL models, Deep Learning lacks a theoretical foundation for trials and errors without a consistent direction towards enhancing the model's efficiency. It is an incredible concern when utilizing DL in sensitive structures like CPS. The gathering of further data at present appears to be one of the positive solutions to ensuring that model generalization is strengthened. It is a big downside about using CPS DL templates as it can be expensive or often impractical to obtain data because of logistical limitations or health concerns. To address the above problems, enhancing understandability utilizing the explainable AI is a crucial move for the CPS implementation of A DL models. For new DL methods, the key issue being that they are not clear to the customer and that consumer trust in the program. Design A explainable AI can further improve the simplicity of ML models and ultimately increase the widespread usage of ML models and increase human trust in DL methods. Adverse machine learning has shown a powerful insight into ML models ' weaknesses. This may be used to detect bugs and weaknesses in machine learning systems, such that it can be used to improve the system's adaptability to emerging cyber-physical data or new threats. Explanatory AI and competitor ML offer resources to explain whether a specific model does not function. It is an interesting method for DL software analysis and debugging that offers the patient information into how to strengthen the concept's generalization. Ultimately, a stronger theoretical context is necessary to improve comprehension of DL models and to have consistent guidance for adapting sound methodologies of regularization to sensitive structures such as CPS.

CONCLUSION

With the advancement in real-time data sizes, designing an effective and reliable intrusion detection system is a challenging task. The solution is deep networks; in the present computing world, deep networks have gained a significant curiosity among the research community. This paper mainly focuses on an overview of the evaluation of deep networks and the effective use of deep learning methodologies in the designing of NIDS. The existing methods used for developing IDS are discussed. The scope of this manuscript is to classify the various existing deep learning generative models used in the designing of an effective intrusion system for cyber-physical systems. The major findings of this chapter are, the proposed autoencoder methods have produced an accuracy of 88.5% for Kddtrain+ / Kddtest+, and an accuracy of 91.5% for Kddtrain20 / Kddtest+ of NSL-KDD dataset. Another major finding is that various existing deep learning classifications techniques are discussed in detail with outcomes.

REFERENCES

Al-Qatf, M., Lasheng, Y., Al-Habib, M., & Al-Sabahi, K. (2018). Deep Learning Approach Combining Sparse Autoencoder with SVM for Network Intrusion Detection. *IEEE Access: Practical Innovations, Open Solutions*, 6(c), 52843–52856. doi:10.1109/ACCESS.2018.2869577

Arjovsky, M., Chintala, S., & Bottou, L. (2017). *Wasserstein GAN*. Retrieved from http://arxiv.org/abs/1701.07875

Bengio, Y., Lamblin, P., & Popovici, D. (2007). Greedy Layer-Wise Training of Deep Networks. *Proceedings of the Advances in Neural Information Processing Systems*. 10.7551/mitpress/7503.003.0024

Bourlard, H., & Kamp, Y. (1988). Auto-association by multilayer perceptrons and singular value decomposition. *Biological Cybernetics*, 59(4-5), 291–294. doi:10.1007/BF00332918 PMID:3196773

Chen, X., Duan, Y., Houthooft, R., Schulman, J., Sutskever, I., & Abbeel, P. (2016). *InfoGAN: Interpretable Representation Learning by Information Maximizing Generative Adversarial Nets*. Retrieved from http://arxiv.org/abs/1606.03657

Chen, X., Kingma, D. P., Salimans, T., Duan, Y., Dhariwal, P., Schulman, J., ... Abbeel, P. (2016). *Variational Lossy Autoencoder*. Retrieved from http://arxiv.org/abs/1611.02731

Elman, J. L. (1990). Finding structure in time. *Cognitive Science*, 14(2), 179–211. doi:10.120715516709cog1402_1

Farahnakian, F., & Heikkonen, J. (2018). A deep auto-encoder based approach for the intrusion detection system. *International Conference on Advanced Communication Technology, ICACT, 2018-February*, 178–183. 10.23919/ICACT.2018.8323688

He, K., Zhang, X., Ren, S., & Sun, J. (2016). *Identity Mappings in Deep Residual Networks Importance of Identity Skip Connections Usage of Activation Function Analysis of Pre-activation Structure.* doi:10.1007/978-3-319-46493-0_38

Hinton, G. E., Osindero, S., & Teh, Y.-W. (2006). A fast learning algorithm for deep belief nets. *Neural Computation, 18*(7), 1527–1554. doi:10.1162/neco.2006.18.7.1527 PMID:16764513

Hopfield, J. J. (1982). Neural networks and physical systems with emergent collective computational abilities (associative memory/parallel processing/categorization/content-addressable memory/fail-soft devices). *Proc. NatL Acad. Sci. USA.*

Huang, X., Li, Y., Poursaeed, O., Hopcroft, J., & Belongie, S. (2017). Stacked generative adversarial networks. In *Proceedings - 30th IEEE Conference on Computer Vision and Pattern Recognition, CVPR 2017* (pp. 1866–1875). Institute of Electrical and Electronics Engineers Inc. 10.1109/CVPR.2017.202

Isola, P., Zhu, J. Y., Zhou, T., & Efros, A. A. (2017). Image-to-image translation with conditional adversarial networks. In *Proceedings - 30th IEEE Conference on Computer Vision and Pattern Recognition, CVPR 2017* (pp. 5967–5976). Institute of Electrical and Electronics Engineers Inc. 10.1109/CVPR.2017.632

Kettani, H., & Cannistra, R. M. (2018). Cyber Threats to Smart Digital Environments. In Icsde 18 (pp. 183–188). doi:10.1145/3289100.3289130

Kim, T., Cha, M., Kim, H., Lee, J. K., & Kim, J. (2017). *Learning to Discover Cross-Domain Relations with Generative Adversarial Networks.* Retrieved from http://arxiv.org/abs/1703.05192

Krizhevsky, A., Sutskever, I., & Hinton, G. E. (n.d.). *ImageNet Classification with Deep Convolutional Neural Networks.* Retrieved from http://code.google.com/p/cuda-convnet/

LeCun, Y., & Fogelman-Soulié, F. (1987). Modèles connexionnistes de l'apprentissage. *Intellectica, 2*(1), 114–143. doi:10.3406/intel.1987.1804

Li, S., Li, W., Cook, C., Zhu, C., & Gao, Y. (2018). *Independently Recurrent Neural Network (IndRNN): Building {A} Longer and Deeper {RNN}.* Retrieved from http://arxiv.org/abs/1803.04831

Liu, Y., Hou, X., Chen, J., Yang, C., Su, G., & Dou, W. (2014). *Facial expression recognition and generation using sparse autoencoder.* doi:10.1109/SMARTCOMP.2014.7043849

Mitchell, R., & Chen, I.-R. (2014). A Survey of Intrusion Detection Techniques for Cyber-Physical Systems. *ACM Computing Surveys, 46*(4), 1–29. doi:10.1145/2542049

Naseer, S., Saleem, Y., Khalid, S., Bashir, M. K., Han, J., Iqbal, M. M., & Han, K. (2018). Enhanced network anomaly detection based on deep neural networks. *IEEE Access: Practical Innovations, Open Solutions, 6*(8), 48231–48246. doi:10.1109/ACCESS.2018.2863036

Park, S., Kim, M., & Lee, S. (2018). Anomaly Detection for HTTP Using Convolutional Autoencoders. *IEEE Access, 1.* doi:10.1109/ACCESS.2018.2881003

Radford, A., Metz, L., & Chintala, S. (2015). *Unsupervised Representation Learning with Deep Convolutional Generative Adversarial Networks.* Retrieved from http://arxiv.org/abs/1511.06434

Rifai, S., Vincent, P., Muller, X., Glorot, X., & Bengio, Y. (2011). *Contractive Auto-Encoders: Explicit Invariance During Feature Extraction*. Academic Press.

Shone, N., Ngoc, T. N., Phai, V. D., & Shi, Q. (2018). A Deep Learning Approach to Network Intrusion Detection. *IEEE Transactions on Emerging Topics in Computational Intelligence*, 2(1), 41–50. doi:10.1109/TETCI.2017.2772792

Simonyan, K., & Zisserman, A. (2014). VGGNet. *ICLR*. doi:10.1016/j.infsof.2008.09.005

Simonyan, K., & Zisserman, A. (2014). *Very Deep Convolutional Networks for Large-Scale Image Recognition*. ArXiv 1409.1556

Soulié, F. F., Gallinari, P., Le Cun, Y., & Thiria, S. (1987). Automata Networks and Artificial Intelligence. In *Centre National De Recherche Scientifique on Automata Networks in Computer Science: Theory and Applications* (pp. 133–186). Princeton, NJ: Princeton University Press.

Vincent, P., Larochelle, H., Bengio, Y., & Manzagol, P.-A. (2008). Extracting and composing robust features with denoising autoencoders. *Proceedings of the 25th international conference on Machine learning - ICML '08*. 10.1145/1390156.1390294

Yan, B., & Han, G. (2018). Effective Feature Extraction via Stacked Sparse Autoencoder to Improve Intrusion Detection System. *IEEE Access: Practical Innovations, Open Solutions*, 6(c), 41238–41248. doi:10.1109/ACCESS.2018.2858277

Zeiler, M. D., & Fergus, R. (2014). *LNCS 8689 - Visualizing and Understanding Convolutional Networks*. Academic Press.

Zeliadt, N. (2013). QnAs with Ann M. Graybiel. *Proceedings of the National Academy of Sciences*. 10.1073/pnas.1315012110

ADDITIONAL READING

Mitchell, R., & Chen, I.-R. (2014). A Survey of Intrusion Detection Techniques for Cyber-Physical Systems. *ACM Computing Surveys*, 46(4), 1–29. doi:10.1145/2542049

Park, K.-J., Zheng, R., & Liu, X. (2012). Cyber-physical systems: Milestones and research challenges. *Computer Communications*, 36(1), 1–7. doi:10.1016/j.comcom.2012.09.006

Ramakrishnan, Anandkumar & Ramanujam, Kalpana. (2019). A-Survey-on-Chaos-Based-Encryption-Technique (1). . doi:10.4018/978-1-5225-6023-4.ch007

Reddy, Y. (2014). Cyber-Physical Systems. *Survey (London, England)*.

Sadiku, M., Wang, Y., Cui, S., & Musa, S. (2017). Cyber-Physical Systems: A Literature Review. *European Scientific Journal*, 13(36), 52. doi:10.19044/esj.2017.v13n36p52

Sanislav, T., & Miclea, L. (2012). Cyber-physical systems - Concept, challenges and research areas. *Control Engineering and Applied Informatics.*, 14, 28–33.

Wan, J., Yan, H., Suo, H., & Li, F. (2011). Advances in Cyber-Physical Systems Research. *TIIS*, *5*(11), 1891–1908. doi:10.3837/tiis.2011.11.001

KEY TERMS AND DEFINITIONS

Auto-Encoder: An autoencoder is a particular type of unsupervised ANN that provides compression and other functionality in the field of machine learning.

Convolution Neural Networks: A convolution neural network is a kind of ANN used in image recognition and processing of image data.

Deep Generative Networks: Deep generative modeling is the use of artificial intelligence, statistics, and probability in applications to produce a representation or abstraction of observed phenomena or target variables that can be calculated from observations.

Deep Learning: Deep learning is a compilation of algorithms used in machine learning, and used to model high-level abstractions in data through the use of model architectures.

Intrusion Detection: An intrusion detection system is a system that monitors network traffic for suspicious activity, and issues alert when such action is discovered. While anomaly detection and reporting is the primary function.

NIDS: A network-based intrusion detection system is used to examine and investigate network traffic to defend a system from network-based intrusions.

Recurrent Neural Networks: A recurrent neural network is a type of ANN commonly used in speech recognition and natural language processing.

Chapter 8
Malicious URL Detection Using Machine Learning

Ferhat Ozgur Catak
(iD) https://orcid.org/0000-0002-2434-9966
Simula Research Laboratory, Oslo, Norway

Kevser Sahinbas
Istanbul Medipol University, Turkey

Volkan Dörtkardeş
Şahıs Adına, Turkey

ABSTRACT

Recently, with the increase in Internet usage, cybersecurity has been a significant challenge for computer systems. Different malicious URLs emit different malicious software and try to capture user information. Signature-based approaches have often been used to detect such websites and detected malicious URLs have been attempted to restrict access by using various security components. This chapter proposes using host-based and lexical features of the associated URLs to better improve the performance of classifiers for detecting malicious web sites. Random forest models and gradient boosting classifier are applied to create a URL classifier using URL string attributes as features. The highest accuracy was achieved by random forest as 98.6%. The results show that being able to identify malicious websites based on URL alone and classify them as spam URLs without relying on page content will result in significant resource savings as well as safe browsing experience for the user.

INTRODUCTION

The significance of the World Wide Web (WWW) has attracted increasing attention because of the growth and promotion of social networking, online banking, and e-commerce. While new development in communication technologies promote new e-commerce opportunities, it causes new opportunities for attackers as well. Nowadays, on the Internet, millions of such websites are commonly referred to as mali-

DOI: 10.4018/978-1-7998-5101-1.ch008

cious web sites. It was noted that the technological advancements caused some techniques to attack and scam users such as spam SMS in social networks, online gambling, phishing, financial fraud, fraudulent prize-winning, and fake TV shopping (Jeong, Lee, Park, & Kim, 2017). In recent years, most attacking methods are applied by spreading compromised URLs and fishing, and malicious Uniform Resource Locators (URLs) addresses are the leading methods used by hackers to perform malicious activities. Common types of attacks using malicious URLs can be categorized into Spam, Drive-by Download, Social Engineering, and Phishing (Kim, Jeong, Kim, & So, 2011). Spam is called to be sent to unsolicited messages by force for advertising or phishing, which we do not request and do not want to receive. These attacks have caused a tremendous amount of damage (Verma, Crane, & Gnawali, 2018). The download of malware while visiting a URL is called as Drive-by download (Cova, Kruegel, & Vigna, 2010). Lastly, Social Engineering and Phishing attacks guide users to reveal sensitive and private information by acting as genuine web pages (Heartfield & Loukas, 2015). The attackers create copies of the popular web pages used by users such as Facebook and Google and compromise victim computers by placing various pieces of malicious code in the manipulated web site's HTML code. Besides, the ubiquitous use of smartphones encourages the increase of mobile and Quick Response (QR) code phishing activities, especially to deceive the elderly that encode fake URLs in QR codes. The dark side of the Internet has attracted increasing attention and bedeviled the world (Patil & Patil, 2015). Internet security software cannot always detect malware from malicious websites and drive-by downloads. It can, however, prevent you from getting them in the first place (Symantec, 2020). Malicious URLs detection is not adequately addressed yet and causes enormous losses each year. In the fourth quarter of 2019, more than 162,000 unique phishing URLs were detected globally (Statista, 2020).

Even though the security components used today are trying to detect such malicious sites and web addresses, these components are evading by using different methods implemented by the attackers. Researchers have studied to gather effective solutions for Malicious URL Detection. One of the most popular ways is the blacklist method that uses records of known malicious URLs to filter the incoming URLs. However, blacklists have some limitations, and this approach useless for new malicious sites that are created continuously. Security components have started to use innovative applications of machine learning and artificial intelligence-based prediction models to cope with this problem, during the last decades (Garera, Provos, Chew, & Rubin, 2007) (Kuyama & Kakizaki, 2016) (Ma, Saul, Savage, & Voelker, Beyond blacklists: learning to detect malicious web sites from suspicious URLs, 2009) (Ma, Saul, Savage, & Voelker., Learning to Detect Malicious URLs, 2011). They have started to prefer machine learning and artificial intelligence prediction instead of being signature-based for Malicious URL Detection. Machine Learning approaches apply a set of URLs as training data and learn a prediction function to classify whether a URL is malicious or benign. This approach allows them to generalize to new URLs, unlike blacklisting methods. Soon, these solutions will need to be used in Cyber-Physical Systems (CPS), and the other area will be to identify harmful sites and URL addresses. As a result, it can be noted that Artificial Intelligence-based antimalware tools will aid to detect recent malware attacks and develop scanning engines.

This chapter aims to present the basics of machine learning-based malicious URL detection. The rest of the chapter is organized as follows. In the Background section, a review of the existing approach and a summary of the literature in the field of URL classification is presented, In Dataset and Analysis section, the publicly available dataset is discussed. In Method Section, the fundamentals of machine-learning models are explained. In the Experiment section, the detection performance comparisons of different algorithms are evaluated. Lastly, conclusion and future directions remarks are given.

Background

This section presents a review of the existing approach and a summary of the literature in the field of URL classification. Previous work on this topic has involved content analysis of the page itself (Ntoulas, Najork, Manasse, & Fetterly, 2006). These typically include creating features from the HTML structure of the page, links, and anchor text, such as the number of words on a page, average word-length, and the number of words in the title. Other methods involve looking at the amount and percentage of hidden content (not visible to a user) on a page.

Another approach is first to determine what are important features in terms of ranking in a search engine and then find which features are likely to be used by spammers (Egele, Kolbitsch, & Platzer, 2009). The downside to this approach is that it is infeasible to enumerate every ranking element, and thus important features may be missed.

Another work attempt to classify web spam into buckets, such as link spam, redirection, cloaking, and keyword stuffing (Gyongyi & Garcia-Molina, 2005). While splitting spam into more specific buckets will likely lead to improvements in classifier ability, this paper will focus on building a general classifier for all types of spam.

While relying on the page content and links increase the amount of data available for spam classification, there are strong motivations for being able to classify spam before crawling a page. This paper explores using the URL string as the primary feature in spam classification.

Shabtai et al. present a classification model for malware detection mainly by focusing on machine learning algorithms such as Bayesian Networks, K-Nearest Neighbor, Artificial Neural Networks, Naive Bayes, and feature selection techniques. Gupta and Singhal examine that the RF tree achieves an excellent result to detect Phishing URLs in minimum execution time. Firdausi et al. analyzed malware and benign files by collecting 250 unique benign and 220 individual malware software samples to train Support Vector Machine (SVM), Multilayer Perceptron (MLP) neural network, k-Nearest Neighbor, Naive Bayes and J48 decision tree on their dataset. They gained the highest accuracy of 96.8% by the J48 decision tree. Bazrafshan et al. categorize detecting malicious software into behavior-based methods, signature-based methods, and heuristic-based methods. Santos et al. collected 1, 000 for benign files and 1, 000 malicious files to apply SVMs, Decision Trees, and KNNs to detect malicious URLs. Souri et al. provide two methods for malware detection approaches as signature-based methods and behavior-based methods. Parekh et al. propose a model that applied Random Forest and gained a 95% accuracy rate as the highest to detect phishing websites. Rieck et al. gathered 10, 072 unique samples and divided them into 14 malware families to train Support Vector Machine and achieved 88% accuracy in testing correct malware. Ucci et al. present a model that applied machine learning algorithms to feature types extracted from Portable Executable files. Ye et al. analyze feature selection, feature extraction, and classification by applying machine learning techniques for malware detection. Alshboul et al. applied Support Vector Machine (SVM) classifiers and Decision Trees for Malicious URL/web detection and claimed that SVM classifier is one of the most widely used for Malicious URL Detection. In the literature, Logistic Regression has attracted increasing attention for Malicious URL Detection . Canali et al. proposed a model that applied Naive Bayes for Malicious URL Detection. The extreme Learning Machines (ELM) approach is used for classifying the phishing web sites . Singh et al. propose a method for malware detection by applying the Support Vector Machine. Kazemian et al. have used machine learning techniques such as K-Nearest Neighbor, Support Vector Machines, Naive Bayes Classifier, and K Means rather than traditional methods of detecting whether they exist in a predetermined blacklist for detecting harmful web pages. Hou et al. identify dynamic HTML codes that made it difficult to detect harmful web pages by easily hiding and changing with the method they proposed in a study they conducted.

For the tests, a data set consisting of 176 harmful samples and 965 harmless samples collected from StopBadware site were used. In tests performed using the Decision Tree, Naive Bayes, Support Vector Machines, and AdaBoost Decision Tree classifiers, it was determined that the best result belonged to the AdaBoost Decision Tree classifier with a rate of 96.14%. Komiya et al. aim to detect SQL Injection and XSS attacks in a study they conducted. In tests performed using the Nearest Neighbor and Support Vector Machine, a success rate of 99.16% for SQL Injection and 98.95% for XSS was obtained in the classification process using SVM and Gauss cores. In a study by Liu et al., they aimed to classify suspicious URLs using machine learning techniques. For this purpose, regardless of the content of a web page, using URL features directly, harmless (secure web pages), harmful (web pages that disrupt computer operations, collect sensitive information or private access systems) and phishing (username, passwords, credit card information, etc.) labeling has been carried out in three classes: web pages that appear to be reliable, designed to capture data. Using only URL features has eliminated runtime latency and the possibility of users exposed to browser-based vulnerabilities. Manek et al. aim to detect harmful web pages by using the features of the web page based on URL-based properties, server information, and the content of the web page. Support vector machines and Naive Bayes classifiers and web pages created for phishing and malware distribution were determined with high accuracy.

DATASET AND ANALYSIS

Overview

While there are a variety of features that one can use to classify if a web page is spam, this project aims to use only the URL and limited metadata information to classify if web pages are spam/not spam. This choice was made for performance reasons, as scraping HTML from web pages is resource-intensive and not useful since the page must have already been crawled. In the context of a search engine, it is often advantageous to be able to detect if a given URL is malicious before a page being crawled. This way, URL's that are likely to be malicious can be deprioritized during crawling, and those resources can be used to crawl more useful pages that are less likely to be malicious.

Data

In this work, we used an open public original dataset of UCI Machine Learning Repository and seen in this address: https://archive.ics.uci.edu/ml/datasets/URL+Reputation. It is an Anonymized 120-day subset of the ICML-09 URL data containing 2.4 million examples and 3.2 million features. Each day's data is stored in separate files in SVM-light format. A label of +1 corresponds to a malicious URL, and -1 corresponds to a benign URL (Ma, Lawrence, Saul, Stefan, & Geoffrey, 2009).

Features

The features used in this research are anonymized. On the other hand, the features match the lexical and host-based features obtained for each URL. *Table 1* shows the types of lexical and host-based features

Table 1. Feature breakdown on Day 100 of the experiments

Lexical		Host-Based	
Feature type	**Count**	**Feature type**	**Count**
Hostname	835,764	WHOIS info	917,776
Primary domain	738,201	IP prefix	131,930
Path tokens	124,401	AS number	39,843
Last path token	92,367	Geographic	28,263
TLD	522	Conn. Misc.	37
Lexical	1,791,261	Host-Based	1,117,901

and the numbers of each class contribution. Word types make up 62% of the features, and host-based types make up 38%. Feature types and reasons for including them for classification will be explained.

Lexical features allow us to understand the difference between malicious URLs that lead to "look different" than benign URLs. For example, the appearance of the '.com' token at the URL 'www.google.com' is usual. On the other hand, the presence of '.com' in 'www.google.com.phishy.biz' or 'phish.biz/www.google.com/index.aspx' may show an attempt to emulate the domain name of a valid business web site. Furthermore, there are explicitly indicating keywords that tend to appear in malicious URLs — e.g., 'googleisapi' would frequently appear in the context of URLs trying to spoof a Google page.

To fulfill these features, we use a bag-of-words description of tokens in the URL, where '/', '?', '.', '=', '-', and" are delimiters. We discover tokens that appear in the hostname, path, the top-level domain (TLD), the primary domain name, and the last token of the path. Consequently, 'com' in the TLD position of a URL would be a different token from 'com' in other parts of the URL. We also use additional features; the lengths of the hostname and the URL as features.

Host-based features explain characteristics of the Web site host as recognized by the hostname portion of the URL. This feature allows us to approximate "where" malicious sites are hosted, "who" own them, and "how" they are managed. We examine the following sets of properties to construct host-based features:

The location feature refers to the host's geography, IP address prefix, and the autonomous system (AS) number. If a specific IP prefix of an Internet service provider (ISP) hosts malicious URLs, then this ISP is considered as malicious.

Connection speed feature: If a malicious URL tends to live on compromised residential machines, then host connection speed is recorded.

Membership in blacklists features: If the URLs were present in blacklists.

Other DNS-related properties feature: These include time-to-live (TTL), spam-related domain name heuristics, and whether the DNS records share the same ISP.

Feature Engineering

In real-world problems, the data volume is huge; the correlations among features and patterns are changing over time are complicated in malicious URLs detection. To cope with these problems, feature engineering has a significant role in addressing these problems. The main idea behind feature engineering is to provide features to machine learning algorithms to apply better. Feature engineering studies are used at the stage of obtaining very critical and processable data for data science. In many cases, there are many different advantages, such as the solution of missing data, the ability to solve many various problems, such as text processing, image processing, which are typically difficult to process, and that the data can be used as a time-dependent series.

In most cases, it is also possible to say that the feature extraction consists of steps connected in the form of a pipeline. It is possible to see attribute engineering as a process that increases the success of the system in general. However, this approach has the possibility of misleading. In general, the results achieved are a result of the selected models and attributes, and excellent results do not always indicate a competent data mining process. For example, correct attributes obtained as a result of good attribute engineering enable simpler models to work more successfully. Simple models, on the other hand, are significant for building systems that operate faster, are understood, and can be maintained simply. In this respect, it can be said that attribute engineering contributes to the flexibility of the system.

Feature engineering is used in many different fields. For example, extracting attributes on time-dependent values and time series, mining data on text, and even using some metrics obtained on social networks as attributes pose some common problems in the literature.

In some studies, it is seen that these features are extracted from different areas and used in cross areas.

Feature extraction consists of five necessary steps, and these steps can be listed as follows (Zhang, Ren, & Jiang, Application of feature engineering for phishing detection, 2016):

- Indicator Variables
- Interaction Features
- Feature Representation
- External Data
- Error Analysis

METHODS

This section presents the theoretical review of Random Forest and Gradient Boosting algorithms.

Random Forest

Random Forest (RF) is the ensemble classifier, which collects the results of many decision trees by majority vote . In ensemble learning, the results of multiple classifiers are brought together, and a single decision is made on behalf of the community. Each decision tree in the forest is created by selecting different samples from the original data set using the bootstrap technique . Then, the decisions made by many different individual trees are subject to voting and present the class with the highest number of votes as the class estimate of the committee. In the RF method, trees are created by CART (Classification and Regression Trees) algorithms and boot bagging combination method. The data set is divided into training and test data. From the training data set, samples are selected as Bootstrap (resampled and sampled) technique, which will form trees (in a bag) and data that will not build trees (out of the bag). 1/3 of the training set is divided into data that will not form trees, and 2/3 of them will be data that will build trees. m variables are selected in each node among all variables, and the best separations are provided by using the Gini index. In the formula below, the mathematical calculation of the Gini index is indicated:

$$Gini(p) = \sum_{k=1}^{K} P_k (1 - P_k) \qquad (1)$$

P_k is the frequency of instances of class k in the node, and k is the total number of classes. Estimations are made, and estimation errors are calculated in the model established thanks to the data that does not create trees. By combining the out of bag estimates made by each tree, the error of the decision tree is estimated. Each tree is given a weight based on the out of bag error rate, and the tree with the lowest error rate receives the highest weight, while the tree with the highest error rate receives the lowest weight (Han, Kamber, & Pei, 2012). Each decision tree that classifies gets individual votes, and at the end of the transaction, the classification made by the decision tree with the highest vote is used. Since each decision tree cannot show the same performance when it encounters a different data group than the data group it is trained in, the method combines a large number of decision trees, thereby increasing the classification performance and correct classification rate. In the RF method, the tree starts with a single node. If all the samples belong to the same class, the node ends as a leaf, and a class label is given. If the examples are not included in the same class, the feature that will best divide the samples into classes is selected. One of the advantages of the RF method is that it determines the degree of importance among the features. While deciding the feature importance, the following steps are carried out:

- After the decision tree is created, the classes predicted according to out of the bag are placed from top to bottom, and the correct classification number is recorded.
- m in out of the bag. The values of the variable are relocated and now become the changed out of the bag.
- The modified out of bag values are placed from top to bottom on the previously created decision tree, and the correct classification number is calculated.
- The out of bag correct classification number is changed from the out of bag exact classification number and the d_i is calculated.

$$Feature\ Importance\ Score = \frac{\bar{d}}{SH_{d_i}} \qquad (2)$$

The steps described are applied individually for each variable. Thus, the severity scores of each variable are calculated. Another method for varying severity levels was calculated with the help of Gini values. The difference between the Gini index values before the branching from the variable takes place, and the Gini values after the branching are taken. This value is calculated for all trees, and the values obtained are summed. This value is calculated for all variables, and their significance is calculated from here. Random forest is a well-known ensemble method using different decision trees using independent and identically distributed random samples from the input dataset. Each decision tree classifier (c_i) selects a sample X_i from training dataset X. Then the algorithm builds an independent decision tree algorithm using this sub dataset. Algorithm 1 shows the pseudo-code of the Random Forest algorithm.

Algorithm 1: *Random Forest*

Input:Number of classifier c, Training dataset X
for i to c do
Random sampling $\mathbf{X}_i$ with replacement from X
Build full decision tree classifier using $\mathbf{X}_i$
Return all classifiers

Gradient Boosting

In general, augmentation algorithms try to find a robust prediction model by combining weak prediction models in a recurring manner according to specific rules. Gradient Boosting, which is a boosting algorithm, was first proposed for use in classification problems, and over time it has become a preferred method both for classification and regression problems (Friedman, 2002). Gradient Boosting creates a f_1 function that generates predictions during the first iteration. Calculates the difference between estimates and target value and creates f_2 function for these differences. In the second refresh, f_1 and f_2 combine functions and the difference between re-estimates and calculated targets are combined. In this way, it tries to add the success of the f_1 function continuously and reduce the difference between predictions and goals to zero (Bengio, Simard, & Frasconi, 1994).

Although the gradient boosting method is generally similar to the random forest method, it contains some structural differences. The trees created in this method are interdependent. When adding a new tree, some correction is provided in error generated by the tree, which was created and trained before. **Figure 1** indicates the general overview of the Gradient Boosting Algorithm.

Experiments

Dataset

In this section, we will present detailed information about the dataset. In this study, we used the publicly available URL reputation dataset. We will show the details of the dataset using the data visualization techniques applying the exploratory data analysis methods. Since the number of features of the data set is 3231961, we have transformed the data set into nine features using the PCA method. *Figure 2* shows the scatter plots of 9 features. As shown in the figure, the scatter plot graphics of the features are separable from each other. Thus, the data set resulting from the applied PCA model, the decision boundaries are clear and linearly separable.

The highly correlated features in a data set have adverse effects on the classification performance of the model. Besides, the high number of features causes an increase in the execution time of the classification algorithms. For this reason, the correlation matrix of the dataset should be used and examined, and if there are highly correlated features, they should be converted. *Figure 3* shows the correlation matrix of the URL reputation dataset. As shown in the figure, the correlation values between the features are very close to 0. For this reason, the new dataset will have a positive effect on both execution time and classification performance.

Unfortunately, there is not enough data in the cybersecurity field. Currently, There are more publicly available datasets such as malware and Apache Http logs [44,45]. The URL reputation data set used in this study was created in 2009.

Figure 1. Training and testing the dataset using a gradient boosting algorithm

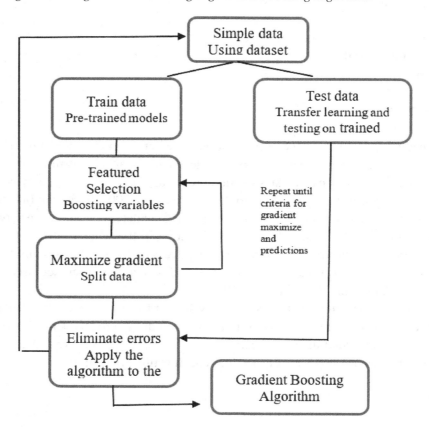

Data Pre-Processing

Raw data is available in the SVM light data format. *load_svmlight_file* function is used to read the data from operating system files into a sparse matrix.

The data to be used for learning has over 3 million features, and it is far more than samples of data available for training. To be used for training, feature reduction is to be done using the appropriate dimensionality reduction technique. The two methods that are available for dimensionality reduction are Principal Component Analysis (PCA) and Truncated SVD. PCA uses the covariance matrix for factorization, and it requires operating on the entire matrix, and therefore it cannot be here. TruncatedSVD is used here for dimensionality reduction as it can perform on sparse matrices.

TruncatedSVD's kernel is failing for n_components greater than 32, so we will continue further analysis based on these 32 features. Figure 2 indicates the explanation of variance by all 32 features.

Figure 4 presents that 32 dimensions can capture about 46% of the overall variation. Labels are encoded into 0 and 1 using the LabelEncoder.

Figure 2. Pairplots of the 9 PCA features

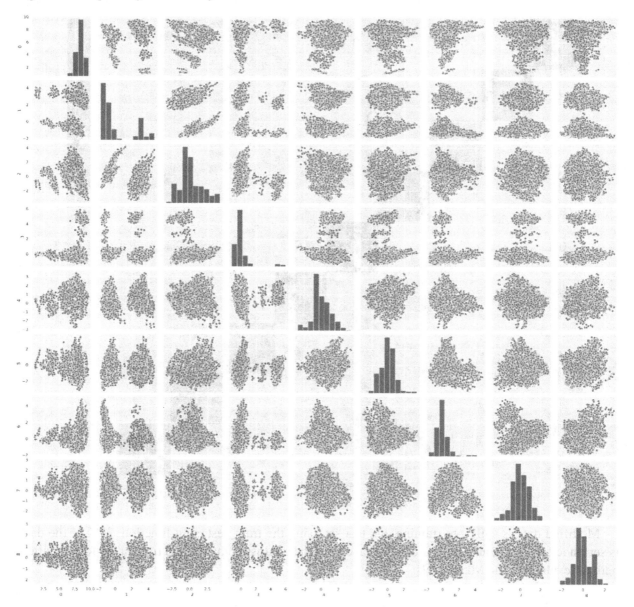

Dataset Split Strategy

While measuring the performance of a model to be used, it should not only be looked at the learning algorithm used but also the size of the training and test sets, incorrect classification or class distribution play an important role. The data set is divided into two as education and test data sets. Here, the training data set is used for the training of the selected classifier model. The most appropriate parameter values and performance measures for the model creation phase are determined at this stage. The test data set is also used to measure the overall performance of the model.

Figure 3. Correlation matrix of the URL reputation dataset

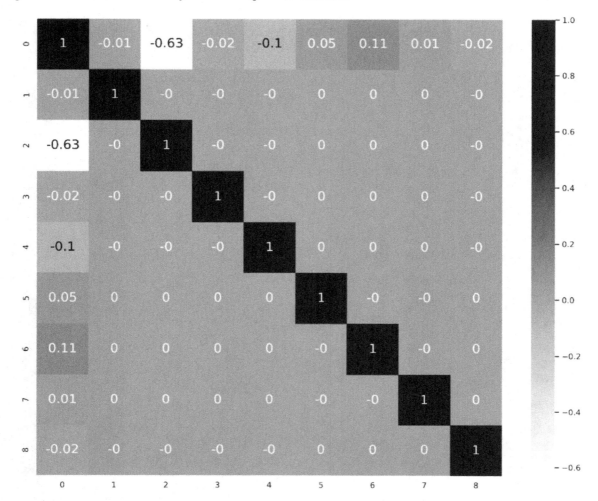

Modified data is split into training and test set using the train_test_split function. 30% of the data is set aside for testing and evaluation. We have used the confusion matrix and time taken for execution here for evaluating the ML models.

Evaluation

Based on the TP, TN, FP, and FN metrics, we compute the accuracy, sensitivity, and specificity of our proposed model. The equations introducing the metrics are equations 3, 4, 5, and 6 (Makhoul, Kubala, Schwartz, & Weischedel, 1999).

Accuracy is one of the most widely used criteria for classification performance, showing the overall correct classification success of the model created. With the correctly classified samples, the ratio to the total number of samples is calculated as in Equation 2.

Figure 4. Explanation of variance by these 32 features

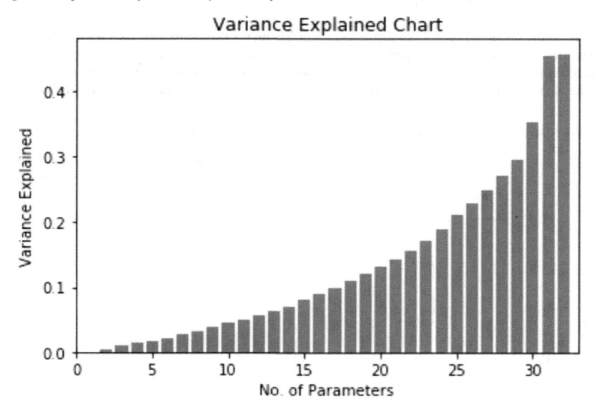

$$Accuracy = \frac{TP + TN}{TP + TN + FP + FN} \tag{3}$$

Precision is the probability that a negative sample is also negative as a result of estimation.

$$Precision = \frac{TP}{TP + FN} \tag{4}$$

The recall is the possibility of a positive sample in the real case to be positive as a result of the estimate.

$$Recall = \frac{TN}{TN + FP} \tag{5}$$

F1-score represents the harmonic average of precision and sensitivity values.

$$F_1 = 2 \times \frac{Precision \times Recall}{Precision + Recall} \tag{6}$$

Model Training and Tuning

In this study, Random Forest Classifier is used as it is with the default parameters. Gradient Boosting Classifier is a sophisticated algorithm with many more parameters. The first parameter to be decided is the learning rate. The algorithm is trained using a different number of estimators and the performance of the algorithm. **Figure 5** shows the model accuracy of the gradient boosting classifier algorithm.

Figure 5. Model accuracy of the gradient boosting classifier algorithm

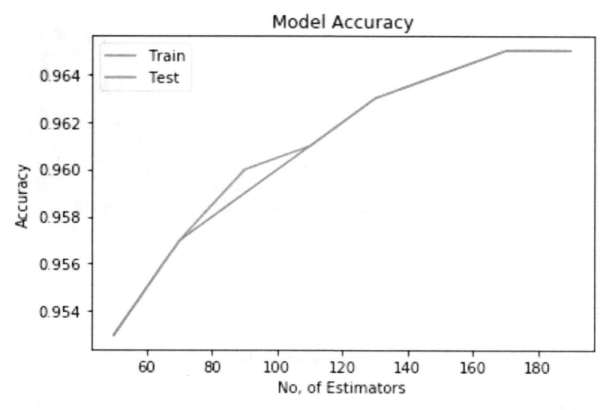

Findings from **Figure 5** indicates that Model Accuracy plateaus are 96.5% at 170 estimators with test accuracy. We applied 170 estimators for this study. **Figure 6** shows the model Processing graph of the Gradient Boosting Classifier Algorithm.

Model processing time increases linearly with the number of estimators.

Table 2 summarizes the execution time in seconds with different depths. Model accuracy increases marginally with the increase in the Maximum Depth, but the processing time increases 2n times as shown.

Table 3 provides the execution time in seconds with a different number of features. Whereas increasing the number of features, does not cause any improvement in the performance of the model as shown.

Figure 6. Model processing graph of the gradient boosting classifier algorithm

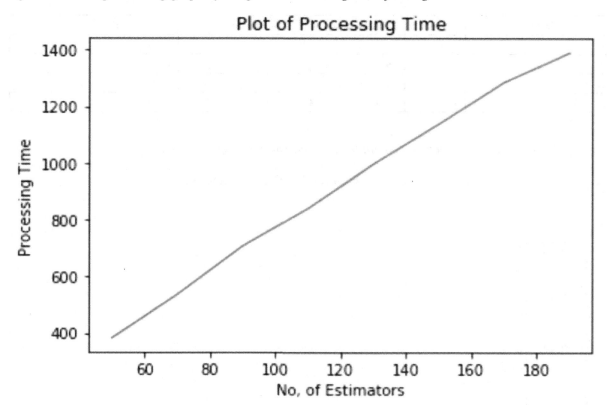

Table 2. The execution time in seconds with different depth

Features	Depth	Test Accuracy	Training Accuracy	Execution Time in Secs
4	4	0,945	0,945	147,0
4	5	0,954	0,954	263,0
4	6	0,958	0,959	488,0
4	7	0,963	0,963	754,0
4	8	0,967	0,967	1169,0

SOLUTIONS AND RECOMMENDATIONS

Figure 7 and **Figure 8** indicate the feature importance of the dataset for gradient boosting classifier and random forest, respectively.

Both models are mainly in agreement concerning feature importance as shown in the table below and thereby validates the correctness of the models. Here we have demonstrated 12 features out of 32. *Table 4* shows the feature rank of the dataset.

We have presented two models to identify malicious URLs before crawling the page. Table 5 illustrates the classification results. Findings in *Table 5* indicate that the Random Forest model provides the

Table 3. The execution time in seconds with the different number of features

Features	Depth	Test Accuracy	Training Accuracy	Execution Time in Secs
4	4	0,964	0,964	604,0
5	4	0,964	0,964	711,0
6	4	0,965	0,965	1286,0
7	4	0,964	0,965	940,0

Figure 7. Importance of features as computed by gradient boosting classifier

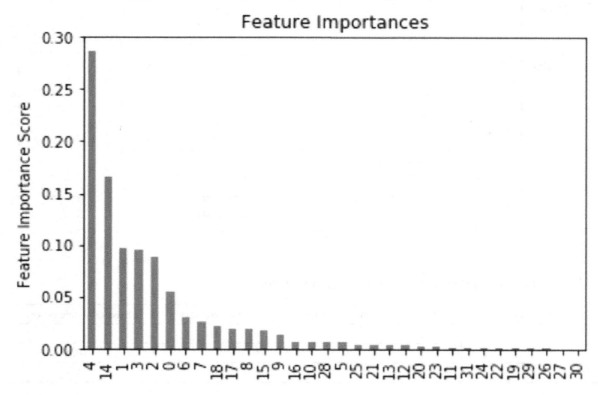

highest classification performance and performs the best out of the models tested, with 98.6% accuracy on the test data.

We used 64. bit python 3.5 environments in our development. *Table 6* indicates the processing environment.

FUTURE RESEARCH DIRECTIONS

With the development of new machine learning and AI-based models, new security services are expected which may change many aspects of our security issue through CPS.

Figure 8. Feature importance as per random forest

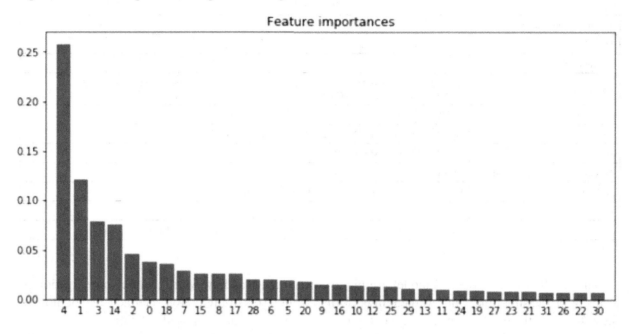

Table 4. Agreement of both models

Feature Rank	Random Forest	Gradient Boosting Classifier
1	4	4
2	1	14
3	3	1
4	14	3
5	2	2
6	0	0
7	18	6
8	7	7
9	15	18
10	8	17
11	17	8
12	28	15

Table 5. Test results of the models

Model	Precision	Recall	F1 Score	Accuracy	Execution Time in Secs
Random Forest	0,965	0,986	0,979	0,986	325,0
Gradient Boosting	0,965	0,965	0,947	0,965	825,0

Table 6. Processing environment

Machine Configuration	
System	HP Pavilion 14-ce1003tx
Operating System	Windows 10
Processor	Intel® Core™ i7-8565U (1.8 GHz base frequency, up to 4.6 GHz with Intel® Turbo Boost Technology, 8 MB cache, 4 Cores)
Memory	16 GB DDR4-2400 SDRAM (1 x 16 GB)
Graphics	NVIDIA® GeForce® MX150 (2 GB GDDR5 dedicated)
Hard Disk	512 GB PCIe® NVMe™ M.2 SSD
Machine Learning Software and Libraries	
Dataset	https://archive.ics.uci.edu/ml/datasets/URL+Reputation
Language	Python
Libraries	Pandas, Pandas_ml, SciPy, Numpy, Scikit Learn, os, Time, Matplotlib and Prettytable

The results of the proposed model are highly encouraging and are worth further investigation in terms of processing time, improvement in performance in terms of prediction accuracy, and deploying the solution in the production environment to test the efficacy of the proposed solution.

As future work, by use of J48, SVM, KNN, and NB machine learning algorithms can incorporate to compare the algorithms concerning processing time and performance of accuracy for malicious URL detection.

CONCLUSION

With the developing computer and system technologies, people exchange information over the Internet that attracts people due to the convenience of services they offer day by day and beyond that, they do many other things related to daily life. During these processes, users have intelligence and critical information such as descriptive usernames and passwords. Most network applications detect their users with them. The rapid increase of the web pages and applications caused them to become the primary target for the attackers. Today, the number of malicious websites has increased considerably. Malicious behavior of trusted or malicious users threatens network applications. Users who are unaware of anything become a victim only by visiting these harmful pages. Attackers can exploit the web environment more easily by uploading or embedding malicious code on the web page instead of spreading the malware. According to the Google Research Center, over 10% of web pages contain malicious code. Therefore, the detection of harmful web pages has become very important to protect the users of the web environment from these threats. In this respect, determining whether web pages directed to users are used for malicious behavior is of great importance for the institution and individual users to overcome the situation with minimum damage. Recent years have witnessed detecting Malicious URL has a significant role in cybersecurity applications. Malicious URL has been a severe threat to cybersecurity. Without any questions, CPS can be considered as a crucial step in the development of data-accessing and data-processing services available on the Internet.

Researchers have studied to gather effective solutions for Malicious URL Detection. Machine learning approaches have been widely applied in Malicious URL detection. In this study, the data of the web pages used for phishing shared in the UCI data warehouse are used. This research analyzed the performance of machine learning algorithms for malware detection. We applied Random Forest and Gradient Boosting machine learning algorithms for malicious URL detection. The experimental results of the proposed method indicate that the performance of the Machine Learning Model (Random Forest) in processing the large dataset and predicting the website as benign or malicious is significantly pretty impressive (98.6%). This indicates we can very quickly build deployable and reliable machine learning models for malicious URL detection.

REFERENCES

Alshboul, Y., Nepali, R. K., & Wang, Y. (2015). Detecting malicious short URLs on Twitter. *Twenty-first Americas Conference on Information Systems*, 1-7.

Bannur, S. N., Saul, L. K., & Savage, S. (2011). Judging a site by its content: learning the textual, structural, and visual features of malicious web pages. *Proceedings of the 4th ACM Workshop on Security and Artificial Intelligence*. 10.1145/2046684.2046686

Bazrafshan, Z., Hashemi, H., & Fard, S. (2013). A survey on heuristic malware detection techniques. *The 5th Conference on Information and Knowledge Technology*, 113-120.

Bengio, Y., Simard, P., & Frasconi, P. (1994). Learning long-term dependencies with gradient descent is difficult. *IEEE Transactions on Neural Networks*, *5*(2), 157–166. doi:10.1109/72.279181 PMID:18267787

Breiman, L. (2001). Random forests. *Machine Learning*, *45*(1), 5–32. doi:10.1023/A:1010933404324

Canali, D., Cova, M., Vigna, G., & Kruegel, C. (2011). Prophiler: a fast filter for the large-scale detection of malicious web pages. In *Proceedings of the 20th international conference on World wide web*. ACM. 10.1145/1963405.1963436

Cova, M., Kruegel, C., & Vigna, G. (2010). Detection and analysis of drive-by-download attacks and malicious JavaScript code. In *Proceedings of the 19th international conference on World wide web (WWW '10)* (pp. 281-290). Raleigh, NC: Association for Computing Machinery. 10.1145/1772690.1772720

Egele, M., Kolbitsch, C., & Platzer, C. (2009). Removing web spam links from search engine results. *Journal in Computer Virology*, *7*(1), 51–62. doi:10.100711416-009-0132-6

Firdausi, I., Lim, C., & Nugroho, A. (2010). Analysis of machine learning techniques used in behavior-based malware detection. In *2nd International Conference on Advances in Computing, Control and Telecommunication Technologies*. ACT. 10.1109/ACT.2010.33

Friedman, J. H. (2002). Stochastic gradient boosting. *Computational Statistics & Data Analysis*, *38*(4), 367–378. doi:10.1016/S0167-9473(01)00065-2

Garera, S., Provos, N., Chew, M., & Rubin, A. D. (2007). A framework for detection and measurement of phishing attacks. In *Proceedings of the 2007 ACM Workshop on Recurring Malcode* (S. 1-8). Alexandria, VA: Association for Computing Machinery. 10.1145/1314389.1314391

Gupta, S., & Singhal, A. (2018). *Dynamic Classification Mining Techniques for Predicting Phishing URL. In Soft Computing: Theories and Applications* (pp. 537–546). Singapore: Springer.

Gyongyi, Z., & Garcia-Molina, H. (2005). Web Spam Taxonomy. *First International Workshop on Adversarial Information Retrieval on the Web (AIRWeb 2005).*

Han, J., Kamber, M., & Pei, J. (2012). Data Mining Concepts and Techniques (3rd ed.). Morgan Kaufmann Publishers.

Heartfield, R., & Loukas, G. (2015). A Taxonomy of Attacks and a Survey of Defence Mechanisms for Semantic Social Engineering Attacks. *ACM Computing Surveys, 48*(3), 39.

Hou, Y. T., Chang, Y., Laih, C. S., & Chen, C. M. (2010). Malicious web content detection by machine learning. *Expert Systems with Applications, 37*(1), 55–60. doi:10.1016/j.eswa.2009.05.023

Jeong, S., Lee, J., Park, J., & Kim, C. (2017). The Social Relation Key: A new paradigm for security. *Information Systems, 71*, 68–77. doi:10.1016/j.is.2017.07.003

Kazemian, H. B., & Ahmed, S. (2015). Comparisons of machine learning techniques for detecting malicious webpages. Expert Systems with Applications. *Expert Systems with Applications, 42*(3), 1166–1177. doi:10.1016/j.eswa.2014.08.046

Kim, W., Jeong, O.-R., Kim, C., & So, J. (2011). The dark side of the Internet: Attacks, costs and responses. *Information Systems, 36*(3), 675–705. doi:10.1016/j.is.2010.11.003

Komiya, R., Paik, I., & Hisada, M. (2011). Classification of malicious web code by machine learning. *Awareness Science and Technology*, 406-411.

Kulkarni, V. Y., Sinha, P. K., & Petare, M. C. (2016). Weighted hybrid decision tree model for random forest classifier. *J. Inst. Eng*, 209-2017.

Kuyama, M., & Kakizaki, R. S. (2016). Method for Detecting a Malicious Domain by Using WHOIS and DNS Features. *The Third International Conference on Digital Security and Forensics (DigitalSec2016)*, 74-80.

Liu, H., Pan, X., & Qu, Z. (2009). Learning based Malicious Web Sites Detection using Suspicious URLs. *Software Engineering*, 1–3.

Ma, J., Lawrence, K., Saul, K., Stefan, S., & Geoffrey, M. (2009). Identifying Suspicious URLs: An Application of Large-Scale Online Learning. In *Proceedings of the International Conference on Machine Learning (ICML)* (pp. 681-688). Motreal: ICML. 10.1145/1553374.1553462

Ma, J., Saul, L. K., Savage, S., & Voelker, G. M. (2009). Beyond blacklists: learning to detect malicious web sites from suspicious URLs. *Proceedings of the 15th ACM SIGKDD International Conference on Knowledge Discovery and Data Mining*, 1245–1254. 10.1145/1557019.1557153

Ma, J., Saul, L. K., Savage, S., & Voelker, G. M. (2011). Learning to Detect Malicious URLs. *ACM Transactions on Intelligent Systems and Technology, 2*(3), 24. doi:10.1145/1961189.1961202

Makhoul, J., Kubala, F., Schwartz, R., & Weischedel, R. (1999). Performance measures for information extraction. *Proceedings of DARPA Broadcast News Workshop*, 249-252.

Manek, A. S., Shenoy, P. D., Mohan, M. C., & Patnaik, L. (2014). DeMalFier:Detection of Malicious Web Pages using an Effective ClassiFier. Data Science & Engineering, 83-88.

Ntoulas, A., Najork, M., Manasse, M., & Fetterly, D. (2006). Detecting spam web pages through content analysis. *Proceedings of the 15th International Conference on World Wide Web*, 83-92. 10.1145/1135777.1135794

Parekh, S., Parikh, D., & Sankhe, S. (2018). A New Method for Detection of Phishing Websites: URL Detection. *2018 Second International Conference on Inventive Communication and Computational Technologies (ICICCT)*, 949-952. 10.1109/ICICCT.2018.8473085

Patil, D. R., & Patil, J. B. (2015). Survey on Malicious Web Pages Detection Techniques. *International Journal of u- and e- Service. Science and Technology*, 8, 195–206.

Rieck, K., Holz, T., Wiiems, C., Dussel, P., & Laskov, P. (2008). Learning and classification of malware behavior. In *International Conference ¨ on Detection of Intrusions and Malware, and Vulnerability Assessment* (pp. 108-125). Springer. 10.1007/978-3-540-70542-0_6

Santos, I., Devesa, J., Brezo, F., Nieves, J., & Bringas, P. (2013). OPEM: A static-dynamic approach for machine-learning-based malware detection. *Advances in Intelligent Systems and Computing 189 AISC*, 271-280.

Shabtai, A., Moskovitch, R., Elovici, Y., & Glezer, C. (2009). Detection of malicious code by applying machine learning classifiers on static features: A state-of-the-art survey. *Information Security Technical Report*, *14*(1), 16–29. doi:10.1016/j.istr.2009.03.003

Singh, T., Troia, T., Carrado, V. A., Austin, T. H., & Stamp, M. (2016). Support vector machines and malware detection. *Journal of Computer Virology and Hacking Techniques*, 203-212.

Souri, A., & Hosseini, R. (2018). *A state-of-the-art survey of malware detection approaches using data mining techniques*. Human-centric Computing and Information Sciences. doi:10.118613673-018-0125-x

Statista. (2020). *Number of unique phishing sites detected worldwide from 3rd quarter 2013 to 1st quarter 2020*. https://www.statista.com/statistics/266155/number-of-phishing-domain-names-worldwide/

Symantec. (2020). *What is Malicious Website?* https:// us.norton.com/internetsecurity-malware-what-are-malicious-websites.html

Ucci, D., Aniello, L., & Baldoni, R. (2019). Survey of machine learning techniques for malware analysis. *Computers & Security*, *81*, 123–147. doi:10.1016/j.cose.2018.11.001

Verma, R., Crane, D., & Gnawali, O. (2018). *Phishing During and After Disaster: Hurricane Harvey. In Resilience Week (RWS)* (pp. 88–94). Denver, CO: IEEE.

Ye, Y., Chen, L., Wang, D., Li, T., & Jiang, Q. (2008). Sbmds: an interpretable string based malware detection system using svm ensemble with bagging. *J. Comput. Virol.*, 283.

Zhang, W., Jiang, Q., Chen, L., & Li, C. (2016). Two-stage ELM for phishing Web pages detection using hybrid features. *World Wide Web (Bussum)*.

Zhang, W., Ren, H., & Jiang, Q. (2016). Application of feature engineering for phishing detection. *IEICE Transactions on Information and Systems*, *E99-D*(D), 1062–1070. doi:10.1587/transinf.2015CYP0005

KEY TERMS AND DEFINITIONS

Lexical Features: It is the feature that distinguishes malicious URLs from benign URLs.

Malicious URLs: Compromised URLs that are used for cyber-attacks are termed as malicious URLs.

RF: Random forest creates a forest and somehow does it randomly. The "forest" that is established is a collection of decision trees that are mostly trained by the method of "bagging".

URLs: The abbreviation of uniform resource locator, which is the global address of documents and other resources on the World Wide Web.

WHOIS Information Feature: It includes domain name registration dates, registrars, and registrants. So if the same individual registers a set of malicious domains, we used such control as a malicious indicator.

Chapter 9
Video–Based Human Authentication System for Access Control

Chintan M. Bhatt
Charotar University of Science and Technology, India

Kevin R. Patel
https://orcid.org/0000-0002-5662-8222
Charotar University of Science and Technology, India

Yashvi Nileshbhai Raythatha
Charotar University of Science and Technology, India

Poojan S. Dharaiya
Charotar University of Science and Technology, India

Chirag Jethva
Charotar University of Science and Technology, India

Karan Mehul Kathiriya
Charotar University of Science and Technology, India

Vidhya Piyushbhai Kothadia
Charotar University of Science and Technology, India

Deep Kothadiya
Charotar University of Science and Technology, India

Vaishali Mewada
Charotar University of Science and Technology, India

Mayuri Jamanadas Popat
Charotar University of Science and Technology, India

ABSTRACT

The issue of security is paramount in any organisation. Therefore, the authors intend to aid in the security of such organisations by bringing a video based human authentication system for access control which is a type of cyber physical system (CPS). CPS is an integration of computation and physical processes; here the computation is provided by face detection and recognition algorithm and physical process is the input human face. This system aims to provide a platform that allows any authorized person to enter

DOI: 10.4018/978-1-7998-5101-1.ch009

or leave the premise automatically by using face detection and recognition technology. The system also provides the administrator with the access to the logs, wherein he/she would be able to access the details of the people entering or leaving the organisation along with the live video streaming so that there is no sneaking of any unauthorized person with any other authorized person. The administrator can also do registration on behalf of a new person who requires access to the premises for a restricted amount of time only as specified by the administrator.

INTRODUCTION

There are many methods available around us that grant access after authenticating the person. For example, many of the organizations use an RFID base id-card scanning system or password-based authentication system to grant access, but in these kinds of systems, flaws are always there because as we know ID-cards can be stolen or we can miss-place it. Passwords are not secure every time. So nowadays most popular and secure methods are used for this kind of application such as biometrics identification. Many biometric identification systems are used like eye-retina, fingerprints, voice, face, etc. but while designing the system we must consider many factors as all of these methods have some pros and cons. We must take care of measures like cost, accuracy, reliability of the system, etc. In this chapter, the authors have used a face-based authentication system because nowadays spoofing is something which is a prominent threat associated with a fingerprint-based authentication system. Also, a voice-based authentication system is not that secure as face-based as we are aware that there may be a possibility that the biometric may get confused between voices or anyone can mimic anyone's voice. So, amongst all the biometrics, the face-based authentication system seems more secure. Currently, various methods available are face detection and face recognition. Like face recognition can be classified based on appearance, feature, or a hybrid mixture of both. The authors have implemented face recognition using the DLIB library which uses convolutional neural networks (CNN), a feature-based classification for face recognition. Using Face detection algorithm human faces are detected from the surrounding environment (background). At the time of face detection, various features like eyes, nose, jaw, etc. are identified and encoded. The encodings are stored in a database for further comparisons. When a person is detected, to recognize the person the features are encoded, and the encodings are compared with those stored in the database. If the encodings are nearly the same then that person is said to be authorized and the door is unlocked for him/her else an alert is passed to the security guard whenever an unknown person is detected. The objective of making this kind of system is to protect the organization from an unauthorized person right from the entrance of the premise only. If an un-authorize person tries to break into the building the security guards are alerted by sending the notification through the system and a photo of the person is captured and stored in the database so that even if he/she breaks into the building forcefully than he/she could be traced easily through this system. This system can also manage visitors as well as the interns coming to the organization and require only temporary access to the premise. They are given permission for a specific period and after that, the system will automatically deny his/her request to enter. Though this time can also be extended or reduce as per the administrator's choice as the only administrator have the right to change the validity date. As here system automatically detects the faces from the surrounding, and identify those faces and take the decision whether to grant access or not based on the face recognition results, CPS can be useful in designing this system, as it is used to monitor the behavior of the physical process and take appropriate actuating actions.

Cyber-Physical System (CPS)

Cyber-Physical System (CPS) is used whenever we want to monitor the behavior of the physical process and want to take actuating action to change that behavior to increase the performance and to make the physical environment more secure. Cyber-Physical System consists of basic two components.

1.   Physical System
2.   Cyber System

The physical System is a natural man-made system which is primarily monitored or controlled by the Cyber System. Cyber System consists of networking components or has several communications, sensing, and computing devices. The problem with CPS is that whenever the interaction between these two systems increases then there are more chances of having security vulnerabilities in the system. Because as we know, the hackers can hack the system and that will be dangerous in many aspects. So, we must take care of the security vulnerabilities that can arise in the system. Research on the solution of removing the security vulnerability and how to check that interaction between two systems is safe or not is in demand.

Let's first understand the general workflow of the CPS along with its application in "Video-Based Human Authentication System for Access Control". It can be divided into 4 phases:

Figure 1. Cyber-physical system (CPS)

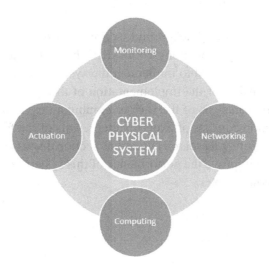

- **Monitoring**: This is one of the most fundamental processes in the system. This is to check if the given cyber-physical system is working well or not. And by doing so we can ensure that the system can achieve its goal for which it has been designed. And if we find that it's not performing well enough then we can change or modify the process to reach desired goals. In the face recognition-based system, video capturing through the camera is similar to that of the monitoring phase in CPS.
- **Networking**: The Cyber-Physical System is made up of many components so there's always a need to process the data which is generated by another component. So, for doing this first we have to aggregate the data and there should be some mechanism such that components can communicate with each other, so Networking is used for this. For example, we can say that system has many sensors. These sensors generate some data and according to application requirements, we need to process and analyze the data. This can't be done in the sensors. So, we have done it in another component. For that, we must transfer that data in that component for which networking is required. In the face recognition-based system, the camera stream is sent to computing servers where face detection and recognition algorithm is applied after pre-processing and video framing.
- **Computing**: Computing is done on the data collected during the monitoring. It is done for applying to reason and for analyzing the data. After doing computation we can check for the performance of the system or we can check if the system is satisfying some criteria or not. If it isn't then we can perform some modification or operation on the system such that it satisfies the criteria. For example, we can say that some sensors which are giving the data about the temperature, we can analyze the data by doing some computation, and then we can change the system such that it works well in the future as temperature changes can affect the system. In the face recognition-based system, faces are detected from the frames and recognized based on data stored on the system and the results are sent to the next phase.
- **Actuation:** Actuation is used for executing the operation which was determined when we applied computing on the data generated in the monitoring step. These operations are nothing but the changes that are required to do on the system to achieve the goals of the system and to make it better. In the face recognition-based system, a decision is taken whether to grant the person access or not based on the results of the previous phase.

This chapter is structured as follows: Background section consisting of research and development in the field of face detection and recognition along with cyber-physical system done up till now, Methodology section consists of the method used to implement the system along with the system architecture. The implementation section consists of the implementation of the system shown by the images of the running system and comparative analysis of the various combinations of face detection and face recognition algorithms. Results section consists of experimental results of the face detection and recognition algorithms used in this system. Future Research Directions section discusses the future scope of research that can be done in the future to improve the performance of this system. At last, the Conclusion section concludes the study of the whole chapter.

BACKGROUND

In 2013, I. Yugashini et al. proposed architecture for an automated face recognition system for door access control application. Principle component analysis (PCA) is used which is an Eigen face-based face recognition algorithm. This results in variations in the set of faces rather than being specified to only one region like eye, nose, lips or eyebrows, etc. Testing the images by comparing them with the training images the door can be automatically be accessed, (Yugashini, Vidhyasri & Gayathri Devi, 2013).

In 2014, Song Han et al. proposed architecture for "Intrusion Detection in Cyber-Physical System: Techniques and Challenges". In the paper, the integration of intrusion detection and mechanism into the Cyber-Physical System (CPS) was discussed consequently. Song Han et al. discussed that CPS is the descendant of existing systems. CPS is also a combination of real-time embedded systems, DCS, and multiple types of communication devices. Thus, CPS inherits all the properties present in their antecedents, which mainly include real-time operation, heterogeneity, distributed control, and management. Also, if the system fails to reply to the events in real-time, it is going to are damaged irreparably during an unattended time. For example, in the industrial manufacturing process, the products may be thoroughly damaged or disqualified if the required water temperature cannot be accurately controlled and adjusted promptly. Hence, the expected intrusion detection mechanism must perform in real-time (an online manner), such that the system is protected consistently without any delay. To detect such problems the potentially suited detection techniques for CPS were discussed, (Song Han, Miao Xie, Hsiao-Hwa Chen, and Yun Ling, 2014).

In 2014, Shaxun Chen et al. have proposed a sensor-assisted face recognition system for the authentication system in smartphones. Their proposed system uses a motion sensor to infer the position and orientation of the face. Motion sensor readings are used to differentiate the shake of the smartphone with the shake of video that has been recorded in the authentication system. So, the system can eliminate virtual camera attacks. To spoof the system, attackers may use high-quality images so to counter it; the proposed system also uses the 'Nose Angle Detection Algorithm'. In this way, it will counter 2D media attacks also. The proposed system takes 2 seconds to authenticate a person which is very fast. This system also uses an ambient light sensor to improve authentication accuracy by adjusting screen brightness. This type of system must be accurate as well as fast. So, for faster detection, it uses OpenCV HAAR cascade, (Chen, Pande & Mohapatra, 2014).

In 2015, Hteik Htar Lwin et al. proposed architecture for automatic door access using face recognition. They proposed a 3-subsystem architecture- face detection, face recognition, and automatic door access. For face detection, they have implemented viola jones face detection technique and for face recognition, they have used Principle component analysis (PCA). The limitation in face detection was that it can only detect the frontal face, profile face was not detected, (Hteik Htar Lwin, Aung Soe Khaing & Hla Myo Tun, 2015).

In 2015, Ylber Januzaj et al. proposed architecture for real-time access control based on face recognition. Principle Component Analysis (PCA) algorithm is used for face recognition. They have used AT and T database from the 90s, for negative images. These images are used to train the system for higher accuracy. The system is embedded with Raspberry Pi 3B+ microcontroller. The pi camera is used to detect the faces and comparing them with the stored positive images, for the recognized face the magnetic lock opens, and the door can be accessed, (Ylber Januzaj, Artan Luma, Ymer Januzaj & Vehbi Ramaj, 2015).

In 2016, Ali Akbar shah et al. proposed a system that is used to identify the location of the face. For face detection, they have used HAAR cascades and extracted the Eigen features by the eigenfaces algorithm. Then they have gone for geometric transformation in which they have divided the width of the frame into 4 parts and have set a range and according to that LED are arranged. So that if the face is detected in their range than that LED is blown. This system can be further used for gestures for controlling devices, (Shah, Zaidi, Chowdhry, and Daudpoto, 2016).

In 2016, Kaipeng Zhang et al. proposed a framework for Joint Face Detection and Alignment Using Multi-task Cascaded Convolutional Networks. They proposed a new framework to integrate adaptive mining of hard samples using unified cascaded CNNs by multitasking learning. The proposed CNN consists of three stages. stages. In the first stage, it produces candidate windows quickly through a shallow CNN. Then, it refines the windows by rejecting a large number of non faces windows through a more complex CNN. Finally, it uses a more powerful CNN to refine the result again and output five facial landmarks positions. Experimental results demonstrated that their methods consistently outperform the state-of-the-art methods across several challenging benchmarks (including FDDB and WIDER FACE benchmarks for face detection, and AFLW benchmark for face alignment) while achieves real-time performance for 640×480 VGA images with 20×20 minimum face size, (Zhang, Zhang, Li and Qiao, 2016).

In 2016, Delina Beh Mei Yin et al. have proposed a system called "MyAccess" that uses TFA (Two-factor Authentication) instead of SFA (Single Factor Authentication). "MyAccess" has two steps for authentication in which the first step includes authentication of information like what you have such as Password, PIN, or private key (where they have used NFC (Near-Field Communication) sticker that is attached to your profile), etc. And the second step includes authentication of information like what you are such as your face, fingerprint, etc. They have introduced this system because the Single Factor Authentication system can be subjected to threats of breaching and the accuracy of this type of system can be increased by adding extra layers of Authentication. The accuracy of this type of system can be increased by improving face detection and face recognition accuracy, (Mei Yin et al., 2016).

In 2016, Z. Boulkenafet et al. proposed research work on "Face Spoofing Detection Using Color Texture Analysis". This research work introduces an approach for detecting face spoofing using color texture analysis. Earlier researches on face spoofing detection schemes were mainly focused on luminance information of the face images which means discarding the chroma component which is very useful for discriminating fake faces from the true ones. The architecture includes the exploitation of the joint color texture of the luminance and the chrominance channels by extracting the low-level feature descriptions from various color spaces. To be more specific, the feature histograms are computed over each band separately. During the research, the experiments were extensively performed on the 3 most challenging datasets. The 3 datasets are CASIA Face Anti-spoofing database, MSU Mobile Face Spoof database, and the Replay attack database, the outcomes were excellent compared to the state of art. On the CASIA FSD and the MSU MSFD, the proposed facial color texture representation supported the mixture of CoLBP and LPQ features computed over HSV and YCbCr color spaces outperformed the state of art, while very competitive results were achieved on Replay-Attack database. Finally, in inter-database evaluation, the facial color texture representation showed better generalization capabilities, and hence suggesting that color texture seems to be more stable in unknown conditions compared to its gray-scale counterparts, (Boulkenafet, Komulainen and Hadid, 2016).

In 2017, Umm-e-Laila et al. have provided a comparative analysis of real-time face recognition algorithms. The comparative analysis of algorithms like eigenfaces, fisher faces, and LBPH. In that, they have concluded that LBPH gives high accuracy but is slower compared to other algorithms while fisher faces are faster than every other algorithm but have less accuracy. So, it is better to have an algorithm slower but with high accuracy rather than less accuracy, (Umm-e-Laila et al., 2017).

In 2018, Shakir F. Kak et al. have presented in their paper about various models of face recognition like Appearance Based Techniques, Model-Based Techniques and the mixture of both the models that is Hybrid Based Techniques. Including the models, they have also presented different distance measurements and classification and shared some of the standard face databases like FERET database, Fcae94 database, etc. These databases were used to check the performance of any new algorithm, (F. Kak, Firas Mahmood Mustafa, and Valente, 2018).

In 2018, Peace Muyambo made the system to hunt out misplaced persons of Zimbabwe and returns information regarding their location. Rather than operating media to seek out the misplaced persons, the system will make live streaming feeds and details, which can help them to small down the search area instead of exploring the whole nation. Live streaming will come from the CCTV cameras placed in different areas in the country. He carried analysis of different face Recognition Techniques like Appearance Based Approaches, Eigenface Technique, Principal component analysis (PCA), Linear Discriminant Analysis (LDA), Independent Component Analysis (ICA), Hidden Markov Model (HMM), Local Binary Patterns Histograms (LBPH) and mentions their advantages and disadvantages and also discovers the efficiency and accuracy of the system for Local Binary Patterns Histograms (LBPH), (Muyambo, 2018).

In 2018, Ayman A. Wazwaz et al. have given a comparative analysis of different values of scale factor and minimum neighbors. They concluded that by increasing the scale factor it decreases the image quality and thus that increases the error percentage. They also concluded that the receiver with more nodes gives less congestion and latency rather than using the receiver with a single node. To speed up the processing time two or more servers are used, (Wazwaz, Herbawi, Teeti and Hmeed, 2018).

In 2018, Chathurika S. Wickramasinghe et al have surveyed different regulation techniques for deep learning. One of the deep learning techniques is CNN (convolutional neural network) which is used for processing grid-like topologies such as images and videos. The combination of CNN with CPS is used in many ways like intrusion detection, classification, and detection of malware variants, etc. The main aim of this paper was to reduce the generalization of error that is, the model should react correctly on non-trained data and for that, the regularization techniques are used. For CNN, Drop out, weight decay, drop connect, etc. are used. This technique reduces the over-fitting of data and drops some units (Drop Out method) or restricts the weight to grow into too large value until necessary (weight decay), (Wickramasinghe, Marino, Amarasinghe & Manic, 2018).

In 2019, Puja S. Prasad et al. presented a survey paper that was on deep learning-based face recognition. They proposed two approaches to remove the difficulties like Partial occlusion and Illuminations. The two approaches are: VGG-Face Network and another one is Lightened CNN. They concluded that deep learning models are more robust towards the misalignment of the face, (Prasad, Pathak, Gunjan, and Ramana Rao, 2019).

In 2019, Maheen Zulfiqar et al. proposed deep face recognition for biometric authentication. They represented a convolutional neural network (CNN) based face recognition system that detects faces in an input image using Viola-Jones face detector and automatically extracts facial features from detected faces using pre-trained CNN for recognition. The overall accuracy of 98.76% was achieved; this depicts the effectiveness of deep face recognition in automated biometric authentication systems, (Zulfiqar, Syed, Khan, and Khurshid, 2019).

In 2019, Guanjun Guo et al. proposed an algorithm which is useful in detecting the smaller sized images based on CNN. They showed that in the current state of the art the algorithms proposed for face detection are based on the quality of the image but what they have shown is the algorithm on fast face detection based on discriminative complete features. They have introduced a new feature that is sliding window strategy which is performed before the CNN layers and a nonlinear mapping which is indeed performed before the linear classification layer of CNN which reduces the complexity of computation. This helps in detecting the images of the smaller size irrespective of the quality of the image, (Guo et al., 2019).

In 2020, Shruti Ambre et al have proposed a simple architecture in which they made a face recognition system using Raspberry Pi. In this system, they have used RPI camera which will stream the live video and it will be forwarded to the Raspberry Pi which will then detect the faces from the captured frames and will compute the face encodings and then the encodings will be compared by the encodings stored in the known database and then the labels which are stored with the encodings will appear on the screen if the encodings are matched with any of the encodings using KNN classification. The connection of the Raspberry Pi and the devices is such that they are connected to the virtual network i.e. VNC and here the server is raspberry pi and its clients are the devices that are connected to it. Raspberry Pi relates to TCP/IP with Ethernet and Devices connected to Raspberry Pi. The algorithms used for face detection are HAAR cascade, HOG, and Linear SVM and for face recognition, the algorithms used are OpenCV, DLIB's library of python. It was diving into 3 subsystems which are dataset creation in which a dataset is created where the photos of the person are stored and the labels that are the name of the person will the file name of the respective photos. Next comes dataset training each image is extracted from the path where it is stored and is converted to RGB. Then the face is detected by HOG and Linear SVM algorithms while the face is recognized by using the DLIB's deep metric model which gives 99.38% accuracy. Then comes the dataset testing in which when the camera module live streams the video In real-time than the OpenCV's HAAR cascades are used for detecting and localizing the face in the frame. OpenCV is used to convert the image in a grey-scale for face detection and to RGB for face recognition. To calculate the distance between the embedding of the detected face and the face in the database KNN classification is used, which returns the True value if the distance is greater than tolerance 0.6 or false value for every label and the votes for each true value is calculated. The label with the maximum votes is selected and the name is used to label in output live video stream, (Ambre, Masurekar & Gaikwad, 2020).

Figure 2. Proposed system architecture derived from the architecture of CPS

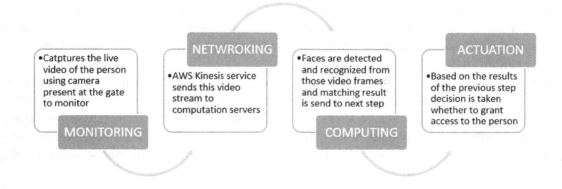

METHODOLOGY

The proposed system is designed to automatically grant access to authorized persons using live face recognition technology. This system can be easily implemented within any organization where security in terms of authenticity and authorization is a major concern. The proposed system architecture is derived from the architecture of CPS as shown in Figure 2.

The system consists of the hardware-software solution as shown in Figure 3, which requires two cameras connected with Raspberry Pi, one at the entrance side and one at the exit side, through which live video frame would be captured. Through Raspberry Pi 3 camera's live stream is loaded into a web portal and Google Coloboratory Platform using AWS Kinesis live video streaming service. This live video stream is processed, and frames are being generated at the rate of 27 FPS using Open-CV library on Google Coloboratory Platform using an API call, which would detect the human faces those from frames and then apply face recognition algorithm on the detected those faces to find the suitable match from the database. The face recognition algorithm provides face encoding that is compared with the face encodings stored on the database, the results of the comparison are returned to the web portal. If the person's match is found and is valid, then the signal is sent to Raspberry Pi to open the door, and access is granted to the person automatically. If a person's data match is not found onto the system, then alert is given to the security personnel. The security personnel would decide whether to grant the person access or not. If the security personnel permit, that person to enter, security personnel need to do a simple registration, so that the person's activity could be monitored and tracked through the system. Security personnel can also set the access expiration time limit for that granted temporary visitors to access the premises for the specific time, after that time the person would not be given access directly, he/she need to visit the security personnel for renewing his/her access ID again.

Logs along with the photos are maintained for the person trying to enter and leave the premise. Through the web portal, the security personnel would be able to see live video feeds from the cameras so that there is no sneaking of any unauthorized person along with any other authorized person. The web

Figure 3. Block diagram of the proposed system architecture

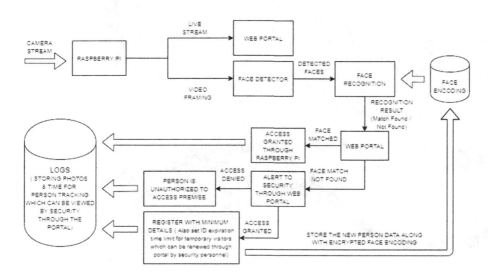

portal can also be used to access logs of any person who tries to enter/leave the premise on any date by applying various kind of filters (sorting according to in-time, out-time, name, etc.) on the data thus can also monitor any persons activity's for security reasons.

IMPLEMENTATION

The proposed system is developed in Python3 environment using the Django framework along with Boostrap4 and JavaScript for the web portal. This system uses Firebase's real-time database and Google cloud storage to store all the details of the person along with photos and to maintain logs. To avoid data theft, the face encodings are encrypted by using AES (Asymmetric Encryption Standard) and then stored into the Firebase real-time database. This system runs on Google Colaboratory with GPU to detect and recognize faces from the video frames.

Video Acquisition and Framing

This system has been tested with the help of the Pi camera module having a resolution of 2MP. The Pi camera is connected to the Raspberry Pi module as shown in Figure 4. The live video frames are captured using cv2.VideoCapture() and then uploaded to the web portal and Google Colaboratory using AWS Kinesis service API. The live frames coming to the portal would be streamed, and security personnel would be able to access the live video stream and monitor the activity of the person entering or leaving the premises.

Figure 4. 2MP Pi camera connected with Raspberry Pi 3

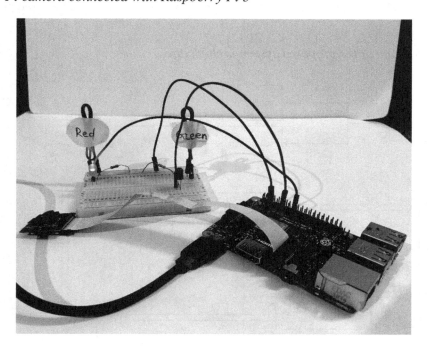

Face Detection

After receiving frames from Raspberry Pi through AWS Kinesis service, those frames are processed on Google Colaboratory where our face detection and recognition backed is hosted. The system detects and crops the faces from wild images using a face detection algorithm. Presently we can find a variety of efficient face detection algorithms that detect faces from wild images. The authors have used pre-trained models for detecting faces and cropping faces from wild image for this system. This system requires the algorithm which has characteristics like speed, accuracy, and robustness as in this chapter our focus is on processing live stream, and delay or latency in processing may also affect the overall performance of the system. Thus, the authors have tested our system with some popular algorithms like HAAR Cascading, LBP Cascading, CNN face detector, DLIB face detector, MTCNN face detector, and ResNet10 detector models on GPU using Google Colaboratory. For testing each model, authors have used custom test dataset containing 134 images with faces in wild and measured the time taken for each model to detect faces within those wild images and noted time taken for each model in seconds as shown in Figure 3 As we can observe that the MTCNN face detector is taking highest time around ~1873 seconds, LBP Cascading took around ~160 seconds, HAAR Cascading's frontal face detector took around ~83 seconds, CNN detector took around ~16 seconds, DLIB took ~16 seconds and that of ResNet10 took around ~12 seconds.

Figure 5. Time is taken for different models to detect faces from 134 images on GPU

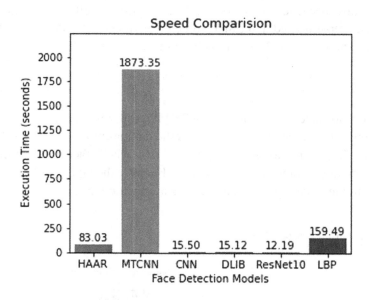

The authors have tested these models over 134 test images and problem is that HAAR, DLIB, LBP, and ResNet10 detect faces up to some orientation angle only (i.e. detecting side face was difficult with this models) on the other hand CNN and MTCNN can detect portal faces (i.e. side faces). Moreover, HAAR, LBP, and ResNet10 have larger FN (False Negative) & FP (False Positive) value than that of

Table 1. Performance results of various algorithms for 134 images on GPU

Model	Test Size	Actual No. of Faces	Detection Faces	False Detection	Accuracy (%)
HAAR CASCADE	134	139	105	34	75.53%
MTCNN	134	139	138	1	99.28%
CNN	134	139	128	11	92.08%
DLIB	134	139	130	9	93.52%
RESNET10	134	139	112	27	80.57%
LBP CASCADE	134	139	111	28	79.86%

other models used as seen in Table 1. Thus, this can increase the overhead of processing those non-faces detected using HAAR, ResNet10, and LBP during live streaming and affect the overall performance of the system. Moreover, MTCNN takes more computation time according to CNN for detecting faces from wild images as shown in Figure 5. Thus, to achieve a better performance we have used a CNN face detector to detect the faces from wild images in this system. This detected face location is passed to face recognition algorithm for recognizing them.

Face Recognition

As the system aims to authenticate a person and giving access through face-recognition, we must use the face-recognition algorithm which is fast (because it will work on live stream) as well as gives the most accurate results. So, the authors have implemented and tested some of the models for face recognition and have found results that aid us to decide which algorithm is best for this system.

OpenCV Face Recognition

Most of the times people use OpenCV for face recognition using SVM because it is easy to implement and gives average results when it comes to predicting the face from the database for similarities, but in this kind of application where identifying an unknown identity (the person whose face is not in the database) is very much important, this model is somewhat not accurate. Because the OpenCV recognition model predicts the detected face from the database faces and returns the confidence value which is the

Figure 6. Results of using OpenCV for face recognition

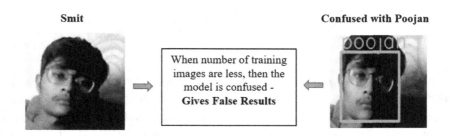

Smit   Confused with Poojan

When number of training images are less, then the model is confused - **Gives False Results**

value used for knowing how much the prediction is strong. Lesser the confidence value more accurate the prediction is. But this prediction is dependent on the number of training images you have given to the model as shown in Table 2. So OpenCV recognition can be used where we have a large number of faces for training the model (Though it has some limitations when it comes to dynamic recognition). In addition to that when an unknown face is given for test to OpenCV recognition model it will always predict that face with one of the faces in the database but with high confidence value as shown in Figure 6 and using this algorithm for our system can grant unknown person permission also to enter the premise which is theft to security. So, an alternative option is to recognize the unknown person by setting the threshold for the confidence value correctly. If the model predicts the face with a high confidence value, the threshold value then it is an unknown face. But this method also has a disadvantage because as described earlier if the training set has fewer training images of a person then also it will predict the person's face with high confidence value and it is more likely to be higher than the threshold value set for identifying unknown face. So even if the person is known it will be predicted as unknown. Moreover, our system must be flexible enough so that it can also recognize new people coming at runtime which increases the training sample size thus varying the confidence value for the same person each time a new person is registered.

Table 2. Confidence values of predictions of the model trained with the different number of training images for a person

Sr. No.	Training Images=15	Training Images=35	Training Images=65	Unknown Face
1	124.21	70.86	38.41	58.00
2	124.28	71.84	39.28	62.91
3	100.47	70.43	39.09	66.08
4	121.00	64.46	40.40	75.06
5	108.35	67.33	39.77	77.98
6	107.38	71.13	40.08	80.23
7	120.78	70.82	39.11	78.56

From Table 2 we can observe that OpenCV is predicting the unknown person as Poojan with lower confidence value than the values in column 3 (Test Image=15). Thus, due to these disadvantages and flaws, it won't be feasible to use OpenCV for face-recognition to implement this system as there are high chances of not identifying an unknown person.

Table 3. Results of the Eigenface recognition model with different face detectors

Detection Algorithm	Test Size	True Detection	True Recognition	Accuracy (%)
HAAR	634	613	596	94.01%
MTCNN	634	632	601	94.79%
CNN	634	634	582	91.79%

Figure 7. Results of Eigenface - HAAR cascading

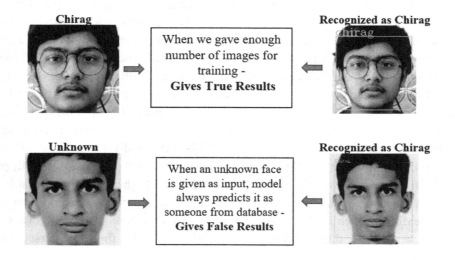

Eigen Face

Eigenface is a face recognition algorithm that uses the PCA (Principal Component Analysis) technique of dimensional reduction. Dimensional reduction of images is essential as all the images may contain some noise and it must be removed otherwise high error or misclassification may occur. In Eigenface, training images are converted to the image vector from the image matrix. After that, the mean face (average face vector) is constructed from training images. Then normalized faces of training images are constructed by subtracting mean face. From normalized faces, the covariance matrix is constructed. Eigenvalues and Eigenvectors are retrieved from this covariance matrix. As Eigenface uses PCA for reducing the dimensionality of the dataset thus, we need to choose k best eigenvectors (k<<<i) that is best for dimensional reduction. After that, we will create Eigenfaces by dot production of eigenvectors and compute the weight of each image. During face recognition, the computed weight of training images is compared to test images given and based on that prediction is made which has maximum confidence value. The authors have trained and tested Eigenface algorithm with different face detection algorithms such as HAAR cascade frontal face, MTCNN and CNN with total 4468 training labeled face images and

Table 4. Results of the LBPH face recognition model with different face detectors

Detection Algorithm	Test Size	True Detection	True Recognition	Accuracy (%)
HAAR	634	613	612	96.53%
CNN	634	634	627	98.90%
MTCNN	634	632	470	74.13%
DLIB	634	634	634	100.00%
RESNET10	634	632	617	97.32%
LBP	634	619	617	97.32%

Figure 8. Results after using DLIB library gives more accurate results and identify unknown person correctly

total 634 testing image and found results shown in Table 3, these results are taken in ideal conditions with proper lighting and consisting of the frontal face only.

Even though they got an accuracy of more than 90% but this is only over known person's faces, but if unknown face comes then the accuracy may also decrease as this algorithm fails to identify unknown faces. It also has some disadvantages like Eigenface is sensitive to scale, it only accepts fixed training image size (i.e. 28 x 28px). So pre-processing is required for scale normalization. Here, the accuracy of the algorithm depends on the orientation of the face and intensity of light focused on the face from the surrounding. It is not robust to changes in the facial expression or disguise of the person changes. Moreover, the problem with this algorithm is the same as that of using OpenCV for face recognition as shown in Figure 7. This algorithm fails to identify an unknown face and generate confidence value based on training class size which is not feasible for this system as we need to set different threshold values every time a new person is registered.

Local Binary Pattern Histogram (LBPH)

Local Binary Pattern Histogram (LBPH) is a face recognition algorithm which uses Local Binary Pattern (LBP) which is not only simple but also very efficient texture operator which does the work of labeling the pixels of an image by thresholding the adjacent of each pixel and takes the result as a binary number

Table 5. Results of the DLIB recognition model with different detectors

Detection Algorithm	Test Size	True Detection	True Recognition	Accuracy (%)
HAAR	634	613	599	94.48%
CNN	634	634	608	95.90%
MTCNN	634	632	589	92.90%
DLIB	634	634	586	92.43%
RESNET10	634	632	618	97.48%
LBP	634	618	617	97.32%

Figure 9. Live video stream from the Raspberry pi (on left), Logs are generated dynamically (on right)

and the local binary pattern (LBP) had been designed for texture description. LBPH firstly, it trains the model, to do so it uses a dataset with labeled facial images of the people. Then LBP operation is applied. Here the first computational step of the LBPH is to create an intermediate image that describes the original image in a better way, by taking the facial characteristics (Radius and neighbors). In the next step, the intermediate image is used to extract the histograms. The Grid X and Grid Y parameters are used here to divide an image into multiple grids which are the main purpose of the LBPH algorithm. Now when we pass the test input image, a histogram is created for the input image. The newly created histogram is compared with the present histograms of trained images and returns the image with the closest histogram. Various methods such as Euclidean distance, chi-square, absolute value, etc. can be used for comparing. This returns the predicted max confidence for the recognition. The authors have implemented and calculated results of LBPH face recognition as shown in Table 4, where the reading is taken in ideal conditions with proper lighting, consisting of the frontal face only also all the testing images are of known person only. But as other algorithms it has some problems like face identification becomes difficult when the pose of the face is different from that of the training image. Face recognition suffers when changes in extreme facial expressions. Due to other objects or accessories, (e.g., sunglass) performance of the LBPH face recognition algorithm also gets affected. Moreover, LBPH also fails to identify an unknown person's face and return false results. But for this system, we need to manage new person coming at dynamically at the run time also, which LBPH fails to serve. Thus, we cannot us LBPH for recognizing the faces in this system.

DLIB's Shape Predictor

DLIB is a deep learning cross-platform library which has face recognition algorithm implemented within it which can recognize the human face by comparing the face encodings. The advantage of using the DLIB model to recognize the face is that its recognition is more accurate than other models like OpenCV, Eigenface, LBPH in differentiating known persons from an unknown person. In addition to that we don't require a large number of images to be trained for getting accurate results because DLIB recognition model is based one-shot learning and works by calculating 128-dimensional feature vector of faces, so whenever a face is given to test it extracts the 128-dimensional feature vector and calculates

Figure 10. Logs monitoring through a web portal

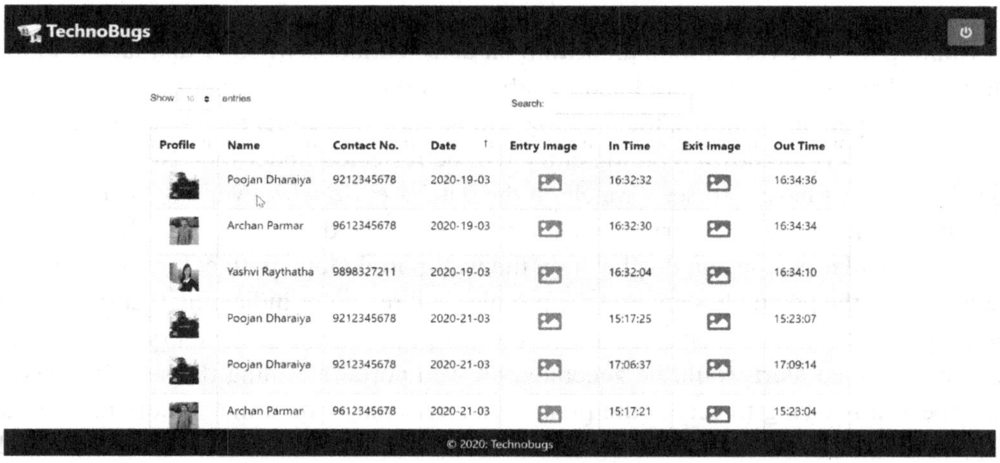

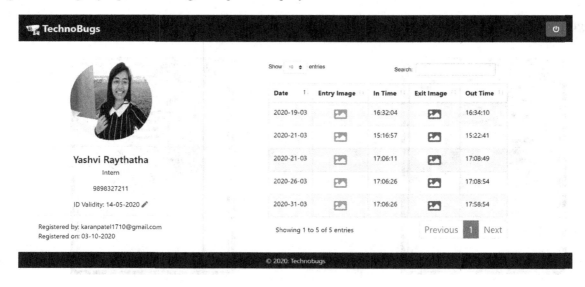

the Euclidian distance with the existing entries of faces' feature vectors in the database and finds the matches. The authors have implemented this algorithm and test the DLIB model with 634 images in ideal conditions and recorded the results as shown in Table 5. Although here are some of the flaws due to face-orientation and light effects, but these flaws are also there in the other face-recognition models. For these, we need to optimize the parameters according to our application to make it more accurate. Figure 8 shows some results of the same images given to OpenCV face recognition - when tested with the DLIB model with only one training image for each labeled face. As you can see DLIB identifies the unknown person very accurately than other algorithms.

Figure 11. Logs of a person along with person's profile details

Grant Access

Now after running the face recognition algorithm on detected faces, whether that face is known or not that result is sent back to the web portal and Raspberry PI through the database by creating its respective log entry. If the person is known, then the log will be reflected under the "Registered Person" child node but if the person is unknown then log entry will be reflected under the "Not Registered Person" child node. The authors have also set a watch on the database. So whenever any changes are made on to the database and if a new log entry is made under "Registered Person" node then it will fetch the details of that particular person and display it on the web-portal along with color-coding like the green color indicating that the person has entered the premise and red color indicating that the person has left the premise along with a live video stream as shown in Figure 9 and if the entry is made under "Not Registered Person" then alert would be generated on web portal alarming the security personnel that unregistered person is trying to access the premise. In addition to that, the authors have used LED in our prototype for indicating that access is granted or not to the person and whether the door should be open for him or not. If the person is recognized and his ID has not expired then the green LED will glow indicating that the door is opened for him/her and if the person is not recognized or is unknown then the red LED will glow indicating that the door wouldn't open for him/her. Security personnel can also monitor the logs that are generated along with photos whenever any person is trying to enter or leave through this system as shown in Figure 10 and can also monitor the activity of a specific person through a web portal as shown in Figure 11.

New Person Registration

Whenever a new person wants to access the premise of an organization he must be registered with the system. Security personnel can help the person with the registration process by entering minimal details along with the frontal face photo or that person along with other metadata like when was the person registered, which security personnel made that person registration on behalf of him, etc. The face is

Figure 12. Results of drawing a bounding box around the detected face from the wild image

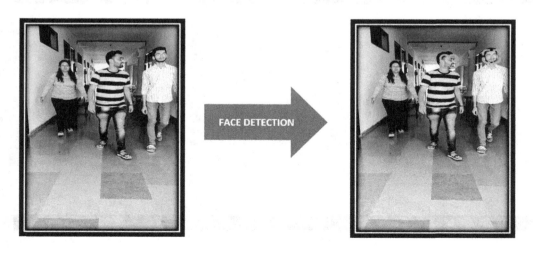

detected, and face encodings are generated for the face. Now as we know it is not secured to store the encoding directly on the system because an attacker can try to create a false ID by storing the face encoding directly in the database. Thus, the authors have encrypted those faces encoding using AES encryption as it is very hard to decipher and get the key used with this system and then storing the encrypted face encoding into the database. Now if an attacker manages to access the database and manages to create false ID directly on the database then the face ID created on the database would be considered as invalid and access would not be granted for that unauthorized person. Thus, provides extra security to the system.

RESULTS

After testing multiple algorithms and keeping in mind each model is having its disadvantages, the authors have chosen the most accurate models for detecting faces and recognizing those faces from a live video stream. Thus, for detection, the authors have chosen CNN face detector for this system which localizes human face from the scene and returns the left top coordinate and right bottom coordinate locations where the face is detected in the frame as shown in Figure 12. As you can see in Figure 12, the algorithm is only able to detect faces with good accuracy up to some threshold distance (i.e. how far the person is from the camera). This threshold distance can vary approximately between 10ft to 15ft according to the environmental condition like background contrast, brightness, and resolution of the camera. But if the face is within that threshold distance than the algorithm can even detect faces irrespective of its orientation as you can see in Figure 12, a portal face (side face) along with a frontal face is detected.

Now after detecting faces, we must recognize the faces thus the authors have chosen DLIB's face recognition model which is most accurate amongst other models in detecting unknown faces as shown in Figure 13. The landmarks of the face from the test image are compared to that of encrypted encoding stored into the database in search of the matching face from the database. As shown in Figure 13 the face encodings of the two detected faces are compared with encoding on the database and identified the person.

Figure 13. Results after performing face recognition

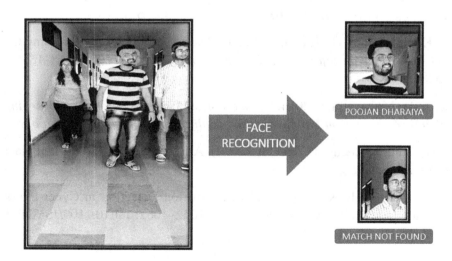

FUTURE RESEARCH DIRECTIONS

The following are some suggestions for future study.

- A variety of preprocessing techniques can be applied to reduce the unnecessary noise in from of brightness, contrast, etc. from the video frame before detecting faces.
- The latency of the system can further be reduced by using a more efficient video streaming technique or methodology.
- A more accurate and time-efficient model that is compatible with low system configurations like CPU and RAM can be used instead of the current face detection and recognition model.
- The proposed system can also be extended for use cases like Activity Monitoring, Pervasive Monitoring, and Attendance System.

CONCLUSION

The proposed system uses CNN based face detection model and DLIB's face recognition model that is used to grant access to authorized persons automatically. The current system is tested with a video stream of 21 seconds consisting of 634 frames and got accuracy around 95.70% in ideal conditions with proper lighting, brightness, and contrast levels on GPU. As in this chapter, we are using AWS Kinesis service for streaming live video stream to backend servers thus it creates latency of around ~5-10 seconds due to internet speed. Though there are some limiting factors like camera quality, the distance of the person from the camera, internet speed, and even the accuracy of the algorithms that are used in detecting and recognizing the person but still it can be more efficient and easy to manage system if the above-mentioned factors are taken care of in future.

REFERENCES

Ambre, S., Masurekar, M., & Gaikwad, S. (2020). Face Recognition Using Raspberry PI. *Studies In Computational Intelligence*, 1-11. Doi:10.1007/978-3-030-38445-6_1

Boulkenafet, Z., Komulainen, J., & Hadid, A. (2016). Face Spoofing Detection Using Colour Texture Analysis. *IEEE Transactions on Information Forensics and Security*, *11*(8), 1818–1830. doi:10.1109/TIFS.2016.2555286

Chen, S., Pande, A., & Mohapatra, P. 2014. Sensor-assisted facial recognition. *Proceedings of the 12th annual international conference on Mobile systems, applications, and services - MobiSys '14.*

Guo, G., Wang, H., Yan, Y., Zheng, J., & Li, B. (2019). A fast face detection method via convolutional neural network. *Neurocomputing*.

Han, S., Xie, M., Chen, H.-H., & Ling, Y. (2014). Intrusion Detection in Cyber-Physical Systems: Techniques and Challenges. *IEEE Systems Journal*, *8*(4), 1052–1062. doi:10.1109/JSYST.2013.2257594

Januzaj, Y., Luma, A., Januzaj, Y., & Ramaj, V. (2015). Real Time Access Control Based on Face Recognition. *International Academy Of Engineers (IA-E) June 10-11, 2015 Antalya (Turkey)*. DOI: 10.15242/iae.iae0615004

Kak, Mustafa, & Valente. (2018). A Review of Person Recognition Based on Face Model. *Eurasian Journal of Science and Engineering*, *4*(1).

Khan, M., Shaikh, M., bin Mazhar, S., & Mehboob, K., (2017). Comparative analysis for a real time face recognition system using raspberry Pi. *2017 IEEE 4th International Conference on Smart Instrumentation, Measurement and Application (ICSIMA)*.

Lwin, Khaing, & Tun. (2015). Automatic Door access system using face recognition. *International Journal of Scientific & Technology Research, 4*(6).

Muyambo, P. (2018). An Investigation on the Use of LBPH Algorithm for Face Recognition to Find Missing People in Zimbabwe. *International Journal of Engineering Research & Technology*, *7*(7).

Prasad, P., Pathak, R., Gunjan, V., & Ramana Rao, H. (2019). *Deep Learning Based Representation for Face Recognition*. Lecture Notes in Electrical Engineering.

Shah, A., Zaidi, Z., Chowdhry, B., & Daudpoto, J. (2016). Real time face detection/monitor using raspberry pi and MATLAB. *2016 IEEE 10th International Conference on Application of Information and Communication Technologies (AICT)*.

Wazwaz, A., Herbawi, A., Teeti, M., & Hmeed, S. (2018). Raspberry Pi and computers-based face detection and recognition system. *2018 4th International Conference on Computer and Technology Applications (ICCTA)*.

Wickramasinghe, C., Marino, D., Amarasinghe, K., & Manic, M. (2018). Generalization of Deep Learning for Cyber-Physical System Security: A Survey. *IECON 2018 - 44th Annual Conference of the IEEE Industrial Electronics Society*.

Yin, M. (2016). Electronic Door Access Control Using Myaccess Two-Factor Authentication Scheme Featuring Near-Field Communication and Eigenface-Based Face Recognition Using Principal Component Analysis. Academic Press.

Yugashini, I., Vidhyasri, S., & Gayathri Devi, K. (2013). Design And Implementation Of Automated Door Accessing System With Face Recognition. *International Journal Of Science And Modern Engineering (IJISME), 1*(12).

Zhang, K., Zhang, Z., Li, Z., & Qiao, Y. (2016). Joint Face Detection and Alignment Using Multitask Cascaded Convolutional Networks. *IEEE Signal Processing Letters*, *23*(10), 1499–1503. doi:10.1109/LSP.2016.2603342

Zulfiqar, M., Syed, F., Khan, M., & Khurshid, K. (2019). Deep Face Recognition for Biometric Authentication. *2019 International Conference on Electrical, Communication, and Computer Engineering (ICECCE)*. 10.1109/ICECCE47252.2019.8940725

ADDITIONAL READING

Akhtar, Z., & Rattani, A. (2017). A Face in any Form: New Challenges and Opportunities for Face Recognition Technology. *Computer*, *50*(4), 80–90. doi:10.1109/MC.2017.119

Beham, M. P., & Roomi, S. M. M. (2013). A REVIEW OF FACE RECOGNITION METHODS. *International Journal of Pattern Recognition and Artificial Intelligence*, *27*(04), 1356005. doi:10.1142/S0218001413560053

Gao, Z., Lu, G., & Yan, P. (2019). Recognizing Human Actions in Low-Resolution Videos: An Approach Based on the Dempster–Shafer Theory. *International Journal of Pattern Recognition and Artificial Intelligence*, *33*(04), 1956002. doi:10.1142/S0218001419560020

Jumahong, H., & Alimjan, G. (2018). Face Recognition Based on Rearranged Modular Two-Dimensional Locality Preserving Projection. *International Journal of Pattern Recognition and Artificial Intelligence*, *32*(12), 1856016. doi:10.1142/S0218001418560165

Li, Z., Huang, Z., & Li, W. (2019). Recognition of Colored Face, Based on an Improved Color Local Binary Pattern. *International Journal of Pattern Recognition and Artificial Intelligence*, *33*(04), 1956004. doi:10.1142/S0218001419560044

Zhao, H., Liang, X., & Yang, P. (2013). Research on Face Recognition Based on Embedded System. *Mathematical Problems in Engineering*, *2013*, 1–6.

KEY TERMS AND DEFINITIONS

Accuracy: Accuracy is defined as the ratio of the total number of correct predictions to the summation of the total number of correct predictions and the total number of incorrect predictions.

AWS Kinesis: Amazon Kinesis is a cloud service provided by Amazon Web Services that provides easy integration and access to live video streams along with fully managed capability using API like HTTP Live Streaming API.

Cyber-Physical System (CPS): Cyber-physical system is a computational system in which physical and software components are deeply intertwined and are monitored and controlled by different algorithms.

Face Detection: Face detection is a technology used for automatically localizing the human face from the given input scene in the form of a video or a digital image.

Face Recognition: Face recognition is the method that is used to extract features from the human face in form of encodings and compare it with previously stored encodings from the memory and returns the closest match if any, which is used for identifying or verifying the person through his face from a digital image or a video.

Section 3
Engineering Applications in CPS

Chapter 10
Optimizing WSNs for CPS Using Machine Learning Techniques

Mehmet Akif Cifci
https://orcid.org/0000-0002-6439-8826
Istanbul Aydin University, Turkey

ABSTRACT

Progress in wireless systems has enabled the creation of low-cost, ergonomic, multi-functional, miniature sensing devices. These devices come together in large numbers creating wireless sensor networks (WSNs), which serve for sensing, collecting, analyzing, and sending detected data to a base station. Problems arise, however, due to the limitations of sensor nodes (SNs), incorrect aggregation of data, redundant and similar data problems, data security and reliability, and some others related to WSN topology. This chapter proposes a novel method for solving WSNs problems to improve cyber-physical systems (CPS). As WSN is of increasing interest in CPSs, the authors put forward an approach for reconstructing WSNs. For traditional methods are not able to cope with such problems, this study takes up rendering WSNs more functional through artificial intelligence (AI) techniques which are considered to develop smart SNs through "intelligent computing," "deep learning," "self-learning," and "swarm learning" ability on the network to improve functionality, utility, and survivability of WSNs.

INTRODUCTION

Wireless Sensor Networks (WSNs) and Cyber-Physical Systems (CPSs) are currently two significant technical fields that are closely interlinked. There are various types of specific applications introduced for CPSs. For this reason, wireless communication and networking have been one of the fastest-growing fields over the last two decades. Significant progress has been achieved in the field of WSNs. More recently, the CPS has emerged as a promising tool to enhance human-to-human, human-to-object, and object-to-object interactions (Ahmadi & Bouallegue, 2017). CPSs will be more reliable and secure with the help of smart WSNs since more sensor inputs and richer network connectivity is required to minimize the burden optimization becomes necessary. It is, therefore, important to examine what has been learned in these fields to predict what can happen in the field of CPS and to determine what needs to be further

DOI: 10.4018/978-1-7998-5101-1.ch010

researched. Besides, recent technical advancements in CPS have verged computing to a wide variety of devices, including toys, home appliances, and tablets. In addition to increasing their computing capabilities, advancements are also allowing these devices to communicate with each other to accomplish individual or shared objectives via smart WSNs (Ahn et al., 2016). CPS is an intelligent system that includes both computational and physical components integrated seamlessly and interacting very closely to control and monitor the necessary area. Reliability and integrity of data is also an important attribute of CPS. For certain fields of application with high-reliability demands, it is particularly important to ensure the WSNs' reliability. Most researchers are currently searching WSNs' reliability for network topology, protocol reliability, and failure correction of the application layer while the latter being the traditional method. However, a new solution can be offered to WSNs' problems by using Artificial Intelligence (AI) methods (Kaur et al., 2018). The key CPS infrastructure that allows the device to get and distribute real-world data is the WSN. Today, most CPSs need a WSN infrastructure for sensing, communication, and actuation. However, studies show that the poor battery life of current WSNs is becoming a critical factor affecting the prospects of these emerging CPSs. The optimization of WSNs with AI methods is, therefore, necessary to prolong battery life and to cope with WSNs' emerging problems since they are generally known to be unreliable, stationary while mostly viewed as an extension of the existing network or the internet that collects data cost-effectively. Because of their resource limitations, WSNs do not have a pivotal role in common networks. While several examples demonstrate how sensor nodes can be deployed, it is aimed to solve coverage-related issues.

In contrast, others aim to solve network compatibility problems to prolong the overall network life-cycle. All in all, this study aims to solve most of these problems by using AI via which the WSNs will be optimized to be more secure and have a long battery life. In this study, the WSNs are aimed to be optimized by using AI algorithms for better CPSs. In particular, the smart WSNs in the integration of the physical and virtual environments of the CPS will be quite beneficial. Last but not least, another aim is to improve some insights about WSNs' optimization problem. The main objective of this study is to highlight the use of AI algorithms on WSNs for CPSs to demonstrate progress achieved so far by applying AI techniques to CPSs. Moreover, this study highlights concerns over future progress by examining the current conditions of AI on WSNs.

The remainder of this chapter is organized as follows: In the Background section, we present related work studied from the literature and the method underlying the research. The details about CPS is introduced in the Cyber-Physical Systems section. In the Wireless Sensor Network Issues section, we present an overview of the problems arising from WSNs. We present how AI approaches can be applied to WSNs in Using Artificial Intelligence Techniques in Wireless Sensor Networks section. Sensor Nodes System Architecture section introduces SNs system architecture while a new architectural enhancement is proposed. In the Proposed Architecture section, an overview of the SNs system with the AI techniques is offered as well as a model encapsulating the evolution pattern of AI solutions. The proposed model is reviewed in the Evaluation section, where finally, the study is finalized by the Conclusions section.

BACKGROUND

This section summarizes the existing studies on applied AI on WSNs optimization for CPSs. The comparison is provided by considering the studies in the literature. It is noted that a study by (Antonopoulos et al., 2016) benefit from AI techniques in which the WSNs aim to improve their abilities to adapt to the environment in which they are. We notice that many aspects of this work are missing because the study focuses solely on the adaptation of SNs to the environment. Energy efficiency issues, data problems, privacy breaches, real-time data, and irregularity of topology are not the basis of the study presented.

In contrast, these issues have to be taken into account. In other words, we present not only one specific but also focus on energy-efficient protocols, accurate collection of data, unnecessary and similar data problems. We also study the security and the reliability of the data as well as the autonomous arrangements in WSNs topology.

The study by (Melendez & McGarry, 2017) has focused on a routing algorithm that utilizes AI techniques to improve WSNs service quality. In this new protocol architecture of WSNs, service quality, reliability, fault tolerance, and energy requirements are proposed. Besides, data collection techniques and WSNS integration into more extensive networks are examined. For such reasons, different algorithms are emphasized. This study differs from the current studies in a sense to solve the problems of unnecessary and similar data problems by using intelligence to save energy and extend the life of the SNs. Another objective of this study is to provide both energy-saving solutions and long lifetime SNs by AI techniques. However, the researchers of "Classification and comparison of routing protocols for wireless sensor networks," and the authors focus only on energy efficiency (Han, Y., & Lee et al., 2016). They claim that the SNs are deployed in a selected zone with the minimum movement for SNs with high power consumption. Therefore, the crucial points to consider are how to intensify the power consumption of the nodes to increase the longevity of the network. However, the SNs with no intelligence yet cannot guarantee it. Any WSNs with shortening of intelligence when such intensive algorithms are applied will fail. Here, unlike this study, we propose various AI techniques to be able to cope with both unnecessary workloads of the algorithm and similar data problems together with battery life. The studies on smart WSNS placement on CPSs, however, remain limited while most works in this area considered being more about infrastructure.

Nevertheless, the key goal of these studies is mainly to prolong battery life. Propagation model evaluations and little effort were made in developing optimization algorithms to enhance WSNs placement (Toral-Cruz et al., 2015). Besides, a common solution to problem-wording is too discreet the coverage area into several finite candidate locations. This generally led to WSNs' issues with placement, which can be easily solved by the Off-The-Shelf integer programming addressing issues as a multi-integer linear programming problem. The researchers proposed two non-trivial reformulation approaches to turn the problem into a convex mixed-integer system and a linear mixed-integer, respectively, to allow an overall optimal solution by the use of a branch-and-bind method (Panerati et al., 2019). The authors provided a study on the reliability of current WSNs transportation protocols (Gaber et al., 2018). Researchers study various reliability schemes based on redundancy and retransmission methods using various packet or event reliability combinations in terms of recovery of missing data using hop-by-hop or end-to-end systems. Current WSNs reliability models, most of which are based on graph theory and probability theory has been widely studied. Connectivity reliability by (Tolk et al., 2019) investigates the probability of a network being connected for a certain period in the event of a node or link failure. Another study analyzes the end-to-end latency, packet transmission rate, and other network parameters to improve the reliability of CPS performance (Mihalache et al., 2019). Moreover, the optimization of WSNs for CPSs is influenced by various factors such as failure of the device, environmental influences, task changes, and network updates. These factors and network behavior are difficult to be described or calculated by mathematical models.

CYBER-PHYSICAL SYSTEMS

CPSs are engineered systems built from the integration of computation, networking, and physical processes. Scholars frequently simplify it as CPS, which are integrated systems where embedded computers and networks are used to compute, communicate, and control the physical processes (Gal & Ghahramani, 2016). CPS combines physical and technological skills, which can communicate with people through separate technology. CPSs are systems of control. Smart, real-time, adaptable, networked, and potentially connected CPSs in the loop are distributed. CPSs require the use of advanced techniques and methodologies in terms of cyber protection like privacy, resiliency, malicious attacking, and intrusion detection. They have various applications, such as robotics, military, connectivity, healthcare, transportation, development of technology, and infrastructure (Humayed et al., 2017). Typical CPS architecture features the network of physical input and output interacting parts. CPS connects the computer and physical components to enhance usability, performance, protection, reliability, adaptability, and functionality. The integration of internet and human experiences (communications, networking, sensing, storage, processing, and control) and physical environments (hardware, materials, and sensors) transforms the technological facilities of the future. The CPS comprises intelligence with visualization, which helps the individual with most of their day-to-day activities (using sensors and actuators) (Goumopoulos et al., 2020). CPS used in apps for features including flight control, aircraft electronic cabin windows, adaptive cruise controls, car theft controls, remote house safety simulation, cell-phone location, human pacemakers, robot vacuum sensors, robotic medical monitoring, and e-commerce. The future CPS capabilities include road traffic engine, medical emergencies, electricity, security, environmental, law enforcement, and construction (Yu et al., 2016).

The CPSs' goals are infinite, while the implications are far-reaching. Multidisciplinary approaches for the understanding of models, methods, approaches, abstractions, analysis, and design will create a better environment to improve the quality of living through new validation tools, timely checks, and post-facto certification. To meet this new CPSs climate, the current educational system will have to be updated as well. Moreover, CPSs demonstrate more efficiency, reliability, and protection in wireless networking. In future engineering systems with new capabilities, CPSs are expected to play an important role with the help of better smart WSNs (Arioua et al., 2016). The CPSs' architecture, set up, and automation with WNSs will surpass the autonomy, functions, usability, reliability, and cyber safety standards more than expected.

Furthermore, cost-efficient analysis, design, verification theory, and tools are also a matter of CPSs technology as it is completely implemented as WSNs interact with input and output. It dramatically improves adaptability, flexibility, performance, protection, security, functionality, and reliability. Today, CPS is one of the main areas in security and civil defense science. The importance of CPS due to network access and the cloud environment has been increased recently by the use of smartphones. The cloud environment offers complex computing tools and processing facilities, which would be impossible under local resource constraints.

Wireless Sensor Network Issues

WSNs consist of many small and low-cost sensor nodes (SNs) powered by small non-rechargeable batteries as equipped with various sensing devices (Delicato et al., 2020). Recently these devices have been used widely. Their popularity has been rapidly increased by the widespread use of WSN in military, civil, physical, and biological fields due to the desire to control these kinds of areas. Development in technological areas and the decline of SNs' prices, the growing interest in health, safety, monitoring of environment, and habitat have enabled the extensive use of WSNs (Grover et al., 2016) in such areas of agriculture, industry, traffic, education, etc., WSNs are being widely used and spread to almost all sectors. WSNs are both independent and cluster-like tools that use sensors to observe moisture, temperature, pressure, light, sound, vibration, noise level, pollution, environmental, or physical conditions on their own. In this study, we aim to introduce the optimization of WSNs' performance with the help of Artificial Intelligence (AI) techniques. As the SNs are battery-powered, their life is limited.

For this reason, the primary purpose of this chapter is to consider prolonging the life of SNs by using AI methods. There is the need for intelligent SNs that can think and act human-like to be able to cope with issues so that the SNs would learn and function. At the end of the study, some solutions will be presented in which SNs will learn to cope with battery problems.

For intelligence can be defined as humanly thinking, reasoning, perceiving objective facts, comprehending, judging, drawing conclusions, abstraction, learning abilities, and adapting to the environment and new situations, smart nodes are going to act intelligently as the study shows. When it comes to 'intelligence,' in the literature, however, it strikes a different connotation to humans at first. For some, the concept of AI stands for an electromechanical robot. Furthermore, these electromechanical robots try to take the place of its creator. Nevertheless, the general view suggests that there must be a clear distinction between man and machine. So, AI is a science that is concerned with mechanisms acting like people when facing complex problems and producing solutions human-like (Mohamed et al., 2020).

When betting on AI, it is anticipated that the machine takes the characteristic features of human intelligence, imitates them, and treats them as people do when confronted with problems. This feature is, of course, gained by applying advanced algorithms. According to the necessity of the proposed approach, which logical attitude is to be displayed against which effect, will utilize the appropriate algorithms that are exhibited. Besides, the ultimate goal of AI is to create autonomous systems that imitate a person's intelligence, pedagogy, and interaction capabilities (Chaâri et al., 2016). In this context, AI is a generic name given to the technology of the development of machines that can produce human behaviors, which are created entirely by artificial means and without the help of any living organism.

It is a fact that the frequency band allocated for the use of WSNs is limited. AI techniques are proposed for WSNs instead of the traditional methods so that it causes waste of energy in WSNs and leave SNs dead. Hackmann, Gregory, et al. claim that traditional methods are not useful for better results in WSNs so that they are to be replaced by new AI techniques (Kafi et al., 2017). As stated above, this study aims to apply AI techniques to WSNs to increase data security, data integrity, and better prolong battery life as well as the afford effective ways of sensing data, speed, and energy-saving solutions.

WSNs come forward in several independent, small, low-cost, and low-energy consumed SNs that collect data about their environment and work together collaboratively to send detected data to centralized endpoints (Kim et al., 2017). SNs compile and analyze the data they sense from the medium and transmit it to the base station via the Sink. A typical WSN consists of hundreds or even thousands of SNs that are interconnected and communicate with each other through a wireless medium (Li et al., 2017). Radio-linked distributed sensors cooperate to form a detection network system, which allows information to be accessed anytime, anywhere. It performs this function by collecting, processing, analyzing, and spreading data. Thus, the network plays a useful role in the formation of an intelligent data environment. The main research themes of WSN are coverage area, network communication, connection network lifetime, power, data reliability, and data safety. In recent years, there has been a growing interest in the use of AI methods and Distributed Artificial Intelligence (DAI) to develop new applications for WSNs usage (ÇİFÇİ & ELÇİ, 2017).

In WSNs, the ability to demonstrate intelligent behaviors through AI techniques has been gained. WSNs have a large number of tiny SNs as well as dense distribution features and a varying topology structure. It is the most cost-effective and energy-saving solution to gather data and send it for analysis. All of these applications and protocols are running on the WSNs most of the time without the need for human interaction. WSNs are efficient with low energy but scalable and robust. Also, it is adaptable to the changing environment, topology, and demonstration of intelligent behavior within the scope of application. It is easy to use WSNs as they are easy to set up since they do not require any infrastructure or human intervention. WSNs perform tasks by perceiving, calculating, and passing actions in the environment. They can also organize themselves (self-organizing) and can adapt to many applications and mediums. Table 1 shows a comparison between WSNs and other conventional monitoring technologies. As listed, WSNs can cover a large number of cheap sensors. Furthermore, they are naturally resistant to faults and node failures due to their distributed structure while they can be deployed in remote and hostile environments.

The presence of a large number of SNs in the WSNs increases the cost of these nodes in terms of total network cost. The important point is to extend the coverage of these nodes and reduce the cost by lowering the error margin (Girão, 2017). The situation in sensor networks can cause a high number of collisions and blockages in the network. In such a case, the lag time could be increased, and energy efficiency reduced. Moreover, if the number of samples reported by the sensors is large, then it can also cause the expected amount of data to be exceeded. Besides, the energy-saving and dynamically changing nature of WSNs extends the life of the WSNs as well as allowing them to learn the optimal routing path and transfer it to subsequent nodes (Ruan et al., 2017). Although there are different medium access control protocols (MAC) for them, it is thought that energy saving will be at the top level with AI methods. The complexity of typical routing problems is reduced by separating them into more straightforward sub-routing.

In each sub-routine, the nodes select the best topology by taking into account their local neighbors to provide low-cost, efficient battery, and real-time data. By using relatively simple calculation methods and classifiers, the routing problems will meet the requirements of the service quality. AI will be benefitted from such a basis as error prevention and power-saving so that there will be a jump in service quality.

Table 1. Differences between WSN technologies and other monitoring technologies

Sensor Networks	Conventional technologies
Low-cost SNs	Expensive, excessively complex structures
Effective in large areas	Effective in small spaces
Track remote, inaccessible, hostile environments	Monitoring supervised environments
Durability and robustness against node faults	No-fault tolerance
Irregularly sampled data sets	Regularly sampled data sets
Distributed structure	Built-in central structure
Low bandwidth connection	High bandwidth connection
Battery-powered SNs	

Designers of WSNs may think that they are doing great. However, it is not as what they believe, especially since the data collection and reliability of the data, the topology of SNs, battery problems, fault tolerance, and data security are taken into consideration. Because not all these issues can be done with just designing WSNs, besides, these problems need intelligence to be resolved (Sangaiah et al., 2017). However, AI experts must see machine learning (ML) as a rich field with a wide range of themes and models. Figure 1 shows the SNs field to prove this. The SNs connected clusters are used to collect the necessary data, while the collected data is analyzed and sent to the sink node. The sink node can be thought of as the top node to which other SNs are connected, receives the incoming data, and sends it to the base station.

Figure 1. Sensor node model

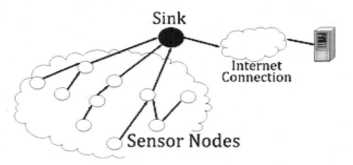

Understanding these kinds of AI techniques will be useful for those who want to apply AI techniques to WSNs. AI algorithms for a large number of WSNs applications provide extraordinary flexibility (Loureiro et al., 2017). The following section is reminiscent of some of the theoretical concepts and strategies used to adopt ML in the context of WSNs.

Using Artificial Intelligence Techniques in Wireless Sensor Networks

During human existence, the brain, eyes, ears, and other sense organs consistently receive, store, and send data in the form of electrical signals. In light of the obtained data, the brain achieves (process data) to comprehend and reach conclusions. This is what essentially to be done with AI. All AI techniques try to manage to solve the problems in the way humans do. As seen in Figure 2, AI observes its environment. Then it executes the data detected and transfers it to the decision stage where AI methods decide whether to put them into action or not. Finally, AI performs as it observes, and such a cycle continues throughout.

An intelligent sensor is a structure that changes its behaviors to optimize its ability to collect data and communicate with a sink node or base station through intermediaries that comply with the surrounding environment. So, the functionality of smart sensors can be described as self-measurement, self-verification, and self-compensation. Self-calibration indicates that the sensor can monitor the measurement conditions to determine if a new measurement is needed. Techniques for self-validation uses mathematical modeling to find a solution for error propagation. For information accuracy, it uses confirmation methods to provide high verification. Some of the AI techniques in the field of ML utilized in this study are

Figure 2. AI decision cycle

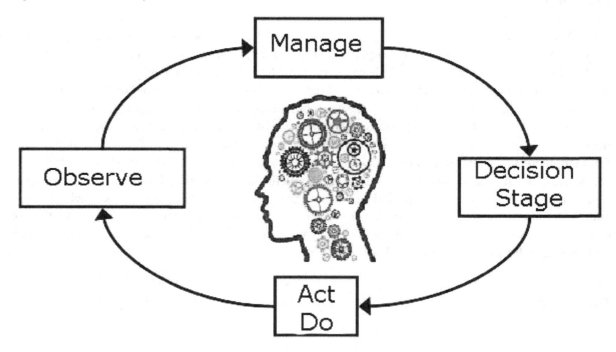

Artificial Neural Network, Fuzzy Logic, and Neuro-Fuzzy Logic, as well as herd Intelligence, etc. These learnings become possible with intelligent sensor structures and algorithms applied to the WSNs. The use of AI techniques plays a crucial role in the creation of intelligent sensor structures. Table 2 shows the benefits of AI techniques used in WSNs.

Table 2. The benefits of AI for WSNs

Step 1: As WSNs often monitor dynamic environments as they may change due to reasons such as the location of SNs, soil erosion, or sea turbulence. The intelligent sensors that can observe such climatic conditions need AI to act smart.

Step 2: WSNs may be required to collect information about difficult to reach and hazardous locations. In such cases, WSNs must have strong AI algorithms that can measure themselves to the unrest situations.

Step 3: Thanks to the cyber-physical system of WSNs, it will start to use the ML via which communication has made smarter decisions and increased support to the system. Here, AI aims to perform its tasks with limited human intervention.

Large-scale sensor networks collect and send data at very large sizes. This significantly affects the energy efficiency of the SNs. AI algorithms are presented as solutions to such issues. AI algorithms make the nodes smarter and eliminate unnecessary data because AI has algorithms that learn to clean out the duplicate or unnecessary data gathered. In general, the algorithm that is envisaged to be used in the optimization of WSNs is AI algorithms (Khan et al., 2016).

In the following sections, a new sensor model will be presented for the sensors based on the sensor system architecture.

Sensor Nodes System Architecture

Smart SNs vary in size and dimension. They can be assumed as extremely simple as miniature computers in terms of their interfaces and components. These devices make a substantial impact when they work collectively while having very little capacity on their own (Cao-hoang et al., 2017). They can be as much as a dust cloud or about the size of a shoebox. In Figure 3, the connected SNs are presented. These nodes that work in cooperation pass the data obtained through the gateway path to the base station. The sensing nodes can be placed in places where there is a life-threatening condition and are capable of trading four seasons. The sensing nodes have a flexible structure so that if any of the nodes in the same field fail, then WSNs continue to produce information at acceptable levels. The data being extracted is redundant and can be transmitted to the base station with the help of other nodes in the cluster as long as it has energy. The hardware to transmit data via the signal is also located in these nodes. Having limited energy, computing power, and communication resources is a disadvantage because it requires the use of a very large number of SNs in large fields. Here, nodes are aimed to be smarter and save energy with AI learning techniques (Hasan et al., 2017).

Figure 3. Sensor nodes

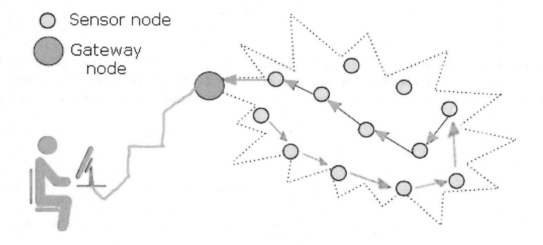

The intelligent SNs used in WSNs are nodes that can calculate, collect information, and communicate with others as connected nodes in the network.

The major components of the SNs are microcontroller, Transceiver, external memory, power supply, and sensors (Shimly et al., 2019). The components of the SNs are shown in Figure 4. A new battery (power supply) is added to the designed model to minimize the risk factor by taking precautions against the exhaustion of the existing power source during the flow of the rush critical data and deterioration. This will alleviate the burden resulting from both encoded codes, and the SNs will have a longer life. The microcontroller at the node also controls the functionality of other components and the node contents of the controllers' other components. The Transceiver uses the Industrial Scientific and Medical Band (SBT) of the SNs. In this way, free radio broadcasts are provided on broadband and global handhelds.

The power supply calculates energy consumption at the SNs. More and more energy is needed for data communication at the SNs.

Nevertheless, it requires less energy. The key energy to deliver one kilobyte to a distance of one hundred meters is energetic equivalent to achieving 3 million commands in a processor which processes one hundred million commands in the primary (Parulpreet et al., 2019). SNs are hardware devices that can produce measurable responses to physical changes such as temperature and pressure. Sensors measure or perceive the physical data of the area to be observed.

Figure 4. The proposed sensor node architecture

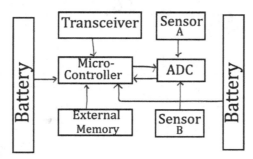

THE PROPOSED ARCHITECTURE

In this section, a new and different model is proposed for SNs. The new model will benefit from AI methods, and it will be presented with AI techniques together. The new model is aimed at the extent of the battery life of the SNs by resolving such issues such as data security, real-time data, similar data problems, and unnecessary data extraction.

In the proposed model, the 'node number 3' transfers data to the 'node number 2' instead of connecting to the Sink node directly because the smart 'node number 3' chooses the shortest path. It is understood that 'node number 6 and 7', which have previously communicated with each other, carry the same kind of data so that even 'node number 7' has all the data of 'node number 6' that is why 'node number 6' can go sleeping and save energy. In Figure 5, 'node number 10' is the far distance from the sink node.

When it comes to 'node number 10', it will take benefit of the 'node number 6' and will transfer its data to the 'node number 7' via the 'node number 6' instead of connecting sink node directly. All these scenarios take place with AI methods scaling, such as filtering out unnecessary data and prioritizing important data as it passes through the 'node number 5' will take place due to the nearest Neighbor and herd intelligence method of AI techniques.

While applying AI techniques on nodes, the physical conditions of the environment in which the node is present are taken into account, as well as which technique and environment are needed. The AI technique is automatically selected in case of danger (risk), urgency (emergency), and safety (security) (Paul et al., 2017).

Figure 5. An example of the proposed system

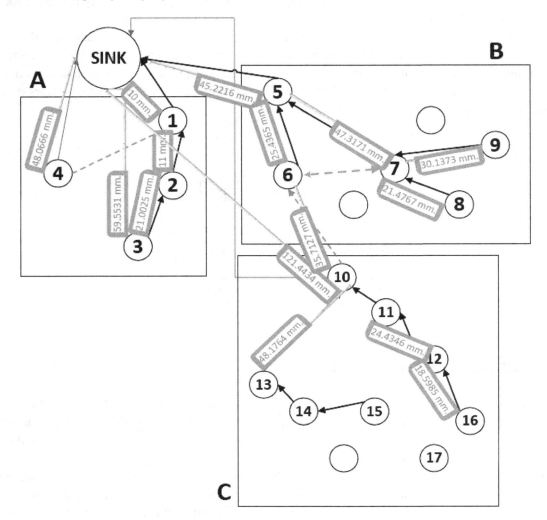

Supervised Learning

k- Nearest Neighbor

In k-Nearest Neighbor (k-NN), an SN chooses the nearest node to transfer the sensed data (Pearl et al., 2019). It classifies based on the tags of similar data samples (i.e., output values). For example, missing readings of SNs can be estimated using average measurements of neighboring sensors within a given diameter to ensure the integrity of the half-value (Diaz-Rozo et al., 2017). A few operations are performed to determine the closest set of nodes. For instance, Euclidean Distance is the simplest method of using inter-node distance (Rawat et al., 2014). The function does not need the high computing power of the nearest Neighbor to the local point. This factor makes a distributed learning algorithm appropriately for the k-Nearest Neighbor (k-NN) WSNs when combining neighboring nodes' associated readings. Since

Figure 6. The k-NN model and SNs

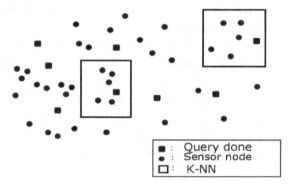

the distance to different data samples does not change, it has been shown that the k-NN algorithm can provide erroneous results when analyzing problems with high-dimensional gaps. In WSNs, the most important application of the k-NN algorithm is in the query processing subsystem. The k-NN is illustrated In Figure 6. Data are grouped differently since data sets of the same property are separated by the same group as it is also supervised.

Decision Tree

Decision Tree is a classification method that is used to estimate the labels of data by iterating input data through the learning tree. During the process, the data are classified according to their properties. There are various solutions in the literature about the decision tree algorithm to solve the design challenges of different WSNs. Decision tree in WSNs provides a simple but effective way to define connection reliability by defining several critical features such as loss rate, error tolerance, average time, and average restore time (Reichherzer et al., 2016). For example, an SN controlling the battery is about to run out of a critical threshold to continue to collect data or transfer it urgently, whether important or unimportant. At that point, decision tree algorithms will decide which action to take. The decision tree is the most utilized AI technique when the adaptive SNs is in the data transfer and chooses the nearest neighbors and sends the sensitive data to the neighbors (when there are problems such as energy, security) to the selected neighbors. However, the decision tree is only linearly divisible, given that it works.

Artificial Neural Network

Artificial Neural Networks (ANN) learning algorithm is built with decision unit chains used to identify nonlinear and complex functions (Rubin et al., 2014). It is a parallel-distributed knowledge-based structure. As is known, ANN is formed by taking the basic working principles of the human brain as an example. The primary function of the ANN is to teach the computer how to act when nodes face a problem. By examining and understanding the issues, it is ensured that similar problems are answered wisely. ANN itself is a data processing method. One of the important characteristics that distinguish ANN from other learning types is to follow the learning method with examples instead of programming. With this feature, most of the negativity that other programs have is not found in ANN. Due to the high computational requirements to learn network weights in WSNs, it is not as common and easy to use

ANN in distributed formats as expected. However, in centralized solutions, neural networks can learn more than one output and decision boundaries at the same time. This allows the same model to solve several problems in the network at the same time.

ANN can be used to analyze new incoming data via SNs. It is a great advantage that ANN can mimic the learning process of the human brain. Transmitted data may or may not work with ANN, whether it is linear or not. Even if it is complicated with noisy and sloppy problems, it will help detectors perform much work in a shorter time and save energy. ANN comes into play when artificial neural cells connect. ANN design consists of input, intermediate, and output layers (Figure 7). ANN is a complex and nonlinear processor that can collect information after compilation, compile, connect weights between cells, store information, and generalize in the resulting findings.

Figure 7. Artificial neural networks model for WSNs

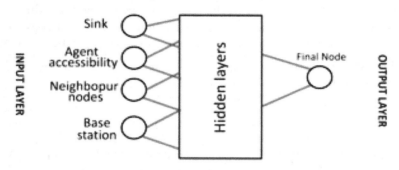

AS Al-Anbagi et al. stated in their study, the ANN approach has been proposed to find an efficient convergent route from the SNs and has shown that the convergence route is most effective at reducing power and network time delay (Say et al., 2016). This method is presented as a calculation tool for solving the problem of restricted neural networks. The proposed approach will facilitate the formation of a possible convergence routing algorithm for future high-speed nodal networks because the implemented hardware can achieve a very high response rate of the ANN. However, ANN has a negative side to the battery when used because a very high amount of processing power is required without learning the machine as well as small memory and low processing necessary for widespread use (Serpen & Gao, 2014). The design of the solution is not intuitive, as it requires a very high amount of training set. Although it has online versions, it cannot be applied without high resource requirements and the proper environment. Such as in ANN, hundreds of SNs can be seen as the logic works, assuming that consists of thousands of ANN.

WSNs are highly data-centric, so the collected data, while being transferred, should be effective and consume minimum power. Each SN consists of multiple sensors embedded in the same node. Each SN thus becomes a data source. These raw data streams cannot be transmitted immediately to the neighboring node or base station. A cluster of SNs forms a cluster so that each node transfers data to a cluster head and then sends cluster head data to the base station.

For this reason, clustering and classification techniques are essential. Thus, it can add a new dimension to the WSNs paradigm. Therefore, effective data clustering techniques should be used to reduce the data redundancy and ultimately reduce the overhead on the communication. This can be done very well

Figure 8. Support vector machine model for WSNs

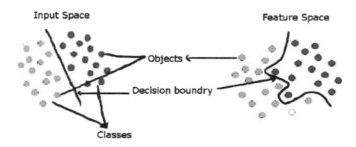

using some algorithms developed in the ANN paradigm, as it can be easily adapted to the WSNs. ANN consists of small computing units called neurons that are arranged in different layers while connected. Simple mathematical calculations are performed in each neuron. There are many advantages of using ANN in WSNs. Simple parallel-distributed estimates, such as distributed storage and data integrity, are provided by ANN for WSNs requirements. Thus, memory usage can be minimized. SNs can be clustered in different groups in terms of lowering network size. As a result, it also reduces the cost of communication and memory.

Support Vector Machines

Support Vector Machines (SVM) are the type of instructor learning. It is an ML algorithm, which learns to classify data by points use tagged training samples (Goumopoulos et al., 2014). For example, an approach used to detect the malicious behavior of a node makes use of SVM to investigate the temporal and spatial correlations of data since SVM divides space into pieces to provide the findings of the NAA as features in the visualization. As illustrated in Figure 8, the parts are separated by as wide a margin as possible and are classified according to the sides of the cavities, as shown by the entries.

An SVM algorithm that optimizes a square function with linear constraints provides an alternative to a multilayer neural network with convex and unconstrained optimization problems. In WSNs, the possible applications of SVM are security and location. For instance, an SN determines optimally via SVM in an environment that an approaching cistern or an object is a friend or foe.

Fuzzy Logic

In this study, Fuzzy Logic (FL) is used as the main application of sense. FL emulates the philosophy of human thinking, which is much more flexible than calculations made by computers in general and offers many unique features that provide a particularly good option for the problem of control (Sharma & Kumar, 2018). This programmable system is inherently robust, requiring no precise noiseless input that can fail. Output control is a smooth function despite a large number of input variations. Since the FL controller processes user-defined rules governing the target system, it can be easily enhanced to improve system performance or change it to a large extent.

Having a node with a high initial energy value requires that the remaining energy is at a relatively high value despite the high-energy consumption rate (Singh et al., 2017). Hence, nodes with higher rates of energy consumption have higher connection costs. The FL input variable 'network distance' allows the

Figure 9. K-Means clustering for WSNs

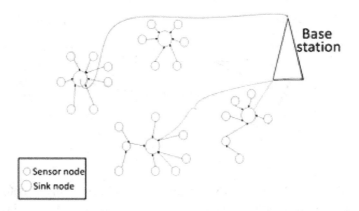

selection of minimum skip routes. Hence, lower node costs are assigned to nodes near the gate since they do not require high output power. Each SN is given a dynamic weight according to its current location. When neither detection nor an inactive node is assigned to the highest value, a node performing these two tasks is assigned a minimum weight. This modifier helps in the selection of nodes that are inactive or only in a detection state. Thus, a node with a high weight value becomes suitable for the next hop and results in a lower value of the link cost. The fuzzy routing aims to maximize the lifetime of the sensor network and reduce the cost of the link between the two SNs. WSNs lifetime is generally defined as the time when the energy level of the first SN drops to zero. The FL rule base is set to effectively balance not only the longevity of the sensor network but also the orientation-loaded SNs that have sufficient energy to continue to perform their sensing tasks at the maximum number of nodes.

The proposed fuzzy system estimates a quantitative value associated with the quality of each route to support the routing protocol in the selection of various feasible routes. For this reason, the routing protocol should define which route to use to send aggregated data to minimize the time required sending a certain number of messages depending on the route quality. The packet loss rate and the lifetime of the first SNs are defined as the first node death period due to battery depletion (Tomić et al., 2017).

Unsupervised Learning

Unsupervised learning is not tagged. In other words, there is no output vector. The purpose of an uncontrolled learning algorithm is to divide the set of samples into different groups by investigating the similarity between them.

K-Means Clustering

The K-means clustering uses patterns to separate data into different classes (Buscema et al., 2018). The algorithm works iteratively to assign each data point to one of the K groups based on the features that are provided (Xiao et al., 2015). This uncontrolled learning algorithm is widely used in SNs clustering problems with linear complexity and simple feasibility. K-means clustering is the grouping of similar objects (Figure 9), while the clustering of a data set is performed as partitioning the clusters according to their specific characteristics. As shown in Figure 9, the SNs are arranged side-by-side form clusters.

These clusters are bound to a leader node that is connected to the base station and provides data flow. K-means clustering algorithm is the most commonly used method in various fields such as visualization, pattern recognition, learning theory, computer graphics, neural networks, AI, and statistics. Practical applications of the WSN cluster include topics such as uncontrolled learning, proximity searching, time series analysis, model classification under navigation, and energy saving.

To solve problems such as scalability and energy wastage, WSNs commonly use K-Means clustering. The clustering algorithms limit the communication in the local area and only pass on the necessary information to the sink node through its existing nodes. A group of nodes come together to form a cluster and select a cluster head (leader) for local interactions between cluster members to control the selected group of nodes. Cluster members usually communicate with the cluster head, and aggregated data is transmitted per cluster to save energy. Cluster heads may form another cluster layer between themselves before reaching the parent node.

In their approach, Ramadan et al. have proven that SNs make independent decisions without any centralized control (Xing et al., 2020). Firstly, an SN decides to be the head of the Cluster (CH) with a probability p and reflects its choice. Each non-CH SN determines its cluster by selecting the CH as it may be reached by saving the most energy. Being a CH is rotated periodically among the SNs to create a balance. The rotation is performed by making each SN choose a random number "T" within a range of [0, 1]. An SN becomes a CH for the current rotation by supposing that the number is less than the threshold, as shown in Equation 1, where p is the desired percentage of CH and r is the current round number while G is the set of nodes been CHs in previous rounds. Besides, the CH is expected to have a long communication range so that the data can reach the base-station from the CH directly without wasting any energy.

$$T(i)= \begin{cases} \dfrac{p}{1-p*\left(r\,mod\,\dfrac{1}{p}\right)} & if\ I \in G \\ 0 & Otherwise \end{cases} \tag{1}$$

Swarm Intelligence

The definition of swarm intelligence (SI) is not clear yet. It is a hypothetical system that is self-regulating and collective behavior (Fei et al., 2019). Swarm management systems include simple agents, whereas they can usually communicate with the nearest neighbors and may show some intelligent behavior. The source of inspiration often comes from nature, especially from biological systems. WSNs work in a decentralized manner in many ways, such as social groups in the environment (e.g., bird flocks, ant colonies, etc.) that try to fulfill their tasks collectively with simple neighbor-neighbor interactions. One of the goals of this study is to investigate whether the behavioral tendencies of natural systems can benefit the WSNs performance or not. For example, SI is investigated to solve the problems and speed up data flow from failed nodes.

In the model of Figure 10, the problem-solving behavior of nodes that carry data packets is illustrated. Here, the depth density of packets arriving at a time interval of 1 second is shown as (a) the host node

Figure 10. Problem-solving behavior of SNs carrying data packets

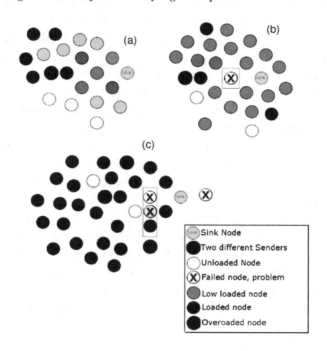

can move in much packet-free environment; (b) a failed node causes significant problems, and its nodes may have two or more group compartments; (c) after the activation of the second sender, the obstacle is intended to be supported by an overloaded node which causes the packet flow from behind the network to follow a less cramped path than the parent node. It is believed that energy savings can be achieved despite the density of codes and algorithms applied as the resulting collision probabilities are unnecessary and can eliminate similar data problems since collisions and unnecessary data flow can cause much more energy loss at the SNs.

Agent nodes follow straightforward rules. Although there is no centralized supervisory structure that determines how individual factors are to be guided (Gharehchopogh & Gholizadeh, 2019), the intermediaries must act locally randomly to some extent. Intermediaries lead to the emergence of "intelligent"

Figure 11. Swarm intelligence model for WSNs

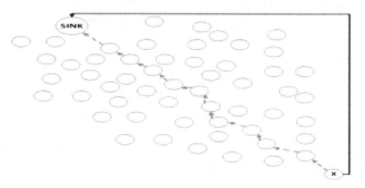

global behaviors unknown to the individual. Another proposed model for the WSNs is provided in Figure 11. It shows in this model that it is experiencing both time and energy loss when node X directly tries to reach the sink node. It implies that it does not reach its goal regularly at the time of the granted. Instead of transferring the sensed data directly to the sink node, the X-node uses SI that benefits handheld implementation. SI makes it possible via other nodes to reach the sink node in a concise time while the X-node will return to sleep again in low-energy mode.

There have been some experiments run on the same topic in the literature. Such as Fortier, Nathan, et al. designed an experiment in their study related to SI in which each particle's position has been defined by a 2-dimensional vector of real numbers xi ∈ R2 where $0 \leq x \leq M$ for each x ∈ xi. While Li et al. explained the position and velocity for each particle initialized randomly, it is updated as described in Table 3.

Table 3. Swarm intelligence algorithm

Step 1: repeat
Step 2: for each particle position $x_i \in P$ do
Step 3: Evaluate position fitness f(xi)
Step 4: If $f(x_i) > f(P_i)$ then
Step 5: $P_i = X_i$
Step 6: end if
Step 7: If $f(x_i) > f(P_g)$ then
Step 8: $P_i = X_i$
Step 9: end if
Step 10: $V_i = WV_i + U(0,\emptyset_1) \otimes (P_i - X_i) + U(0,\emptyset_2) \otimes (P_g - X_i)$
Step 11: $Xi = X_i + V_i$
Step 12: end for
Step 13: until finish criterion is met

The goal of this algorithm is to search for sensor network layouts that maximize the lifetime of the WSNs.

$$\text{Lifetime} = \text{mini} = 1 \ldots n \ (T_{failure}, i) / T_{max} \tag{2}$$

Each SI will search for optimal x and y positions for its associated SNs. A global network layout, consisting of the coordinates determined by the best particles, will be maintained by the algorithm. The lifetime of this comprehensive layout will be used to measure the quality of each particle's position (Lalropuia & Gupta, 2019).

EVALUATION

This section explains the parameters and presents the results that supervised and unsupervised learning algorithms explored in this article. We performed experiments with AI techniques on WSNs to improve CPSs in various separate scenarios. The proposed model was trained to optimize WSNs to have a better battery life to cope with its problems. WSNs are hybrids of SNs by means of imitating the distribution of software representatives over networks. It is essential to use tool-based models to assess different strategies. For a particular application, the agents are in communication to check network resources and to facilitate the use of AI. To achieve this, they use the MAC protocol model that includes all communication protocols. For WSNs to become more effective, it is inevitable to utilize existing deterministic models as well. Their functioning usually depends on the state of the platform in the physical model; Hardware and measuring devices are battery models responsible for checking whether the SN consumes its battery by calculating the consumption of the battery power. The media model connects the node to a 'real world' via a radio channel and one or more physical channels. Besides, a multi-agent hybrid model is proposed to mimic the Deployment of software representatives over any WSNs. It is targeted to use multi-agents to control network resources and facilitate intelligence, where the basic deterministic models determined, are used. These models define the node's platform, power consumption, radio channel, and media. Besides, topology and physical variables should be added according to the simulated application.

Finally, software agents are used to fulfilling all the tasks required by the applications' working example. The proposed system consists of detection nodes. These nodes emerge from the intelligent SNs in the physical environment. The goal of the smart nodes is to comprehend, understand, perform a business, and communicate. Practical Deployment may require more than one SN. Because of a particular node cannot use all sensors, there is a need for more than one sensor. In Figure 5, there are three different nodes connected to the sink node. Since 'node number 1' is the closest node, there is no need to spend too much energy while it has to consume too much energy if 'node number 3' is far away.

The efficiency of the proposed model is displayed in Figure 5,6,7, and 9 by using AI methods. The findings show that there is not a sharp increase in loss values at the beginning of the training. WSNs do not have many burdens because of the slightly optimized algorithms.

FUTURE RESEARCH DIRECTIONS

With the adoption of AI algorithms in WSNs, we must consider the limited resources as well as the variety of patterns and pattern learning that will fit the problem at hand. Moreover, countless issues are still open to future research. Thus, more research efforts are needed to develop lightweight and distributed messaging techniques, online learning algorithms, hierarchical clustering patterns, and learning ML in the resource management problem of WSNs. Compared with conventional SNs, this study shows that the code density in the nodes will not be a problem since it is thought that an ideal SN life can be prolonged for at least 3-4 years while more intelligent decisions can be taken and an energy-saving system can be created. This work is expected to shed light on future work and is an initiative for CPS from AI algorithms being applied to WSNs seems inevitable.

CONCLUSION

In this study, the concept of using AI algorithms in WSNs and CPSs was discussed. The main focus of this study was on the placement of AI techniques into WSNs integrated with CPS. To achieve this goal, we applied AI techniques for solving the WSNs' problems and proposed new efficient methods to cope with them. It was demonstrated that these new techniques improve WSNs' and solve its problems and make CPSs more efficient, as provided in the proposed architecture. Besides, an attempt was made to solve SNs' existing problems by applying AI algorithms instead of traditional methods. In this regard, the SNs proved to be smarter, ensuring data integrity and security as well as a major improvement in energy efficiency. Another purpose of this study is to provide data reliability and integrity together to stop energy waste in SNs. To this end, the node architecture (Figure 4) becomes robust as it can be self-organizing to obtain data before the collapse. It also alleviates the excessive code burden created by AI algorithms supplementing a spare battery and providing intelligent SNs with the ability to "think smart."

AI principles, algorithms, and applications are used to make WSNs more intelligent, optimizing, and efficient in various aspects, such as energy-saving. In addition to Herd intelligence, many types of learning algorithms have been benefited from supervised and unsupervised learning. The multi-agent system approach allows WSNs to use rational agents to achieve such success. To facilitate the use of AI in WSNs, an architectural structure is utilized in the layer with multilayer systems. Besides, a layered architecture of WSNs can provide a modular structure for the system in networks.

Moreover, the proposed models in this research emphasize how WSNs work and how to make them intelligent. In terms of multiple agents, artificial communities, and simulated organizations, which is a distributed sensor network, can be efficiently deployed while goals can be achieved to perform measurements of physical variables on their own along with different types of rational agents that can be rewritten. The most appropriate strategy should be selected to meet all the requirements and measures, as well as monitoring of the physical variables. WSNs embedded with an ANN must adapt to changes in the dynamic environment to overcome difficulties after Deployment and operation.

WSNs are different from traditional networks so that protocols and tools that address unique challenges and constraints are needed. Consequently, WSNs require innovative solutions for energy-aware and real-time routing, security, timing, localization, node clustering, data collection, fault detection, and data integrity. AI provides a set of techniques that increase the ability of the WSNs to adapt to the dynamic behavior of their surroundings. From the discussions up to now, it is clearly expressed that many design difficulties in WSNs are could be overcome by using various AI methods.

REFERENCES

Ahmadi, H., & Bouallegue, R. (2017). Exploiting machine learning strategies and RSSI for localization in wireless sensor networks: A survey. *2017 13th International Wireless Communications and Mobile Computing Conference, IWCMC 2017.* 10.1109/IWCMC.2017.7986447

Ahn, J., Paek, J., & Ko, J. (2016). Machine Learning-Based Image Classification for Wireless Camera Sensor Networks. *Proceedings - 2016 IEEE 22nd International Conference on Embedded and Real-Time Computing Systems and Applications, RTCSA 2016.* 10.1109/RTCSA.2016.29

Antonopoulos, C., Dima, S. M., & Koubias, S. (2016). Event identification in wireless sensor networks. In *Components and Services for IoT Platforms*. Paving the Way for IoT Standards. doi:10.1007/978-3-319-42304-3_10

Arioua, M., El Assari, Y., Ez-Zazi, I., & El Oualkadi, A. (2016). Multi-hop Cluster Based Routing Approach for Wireless Sensor Networks. *Procedia Computer Science*, *83*, 584–591. doi:10.1016/j.procs.2016.04.277

Buscema, P. M., Massini, G., Breda, M., Lodwick, W. A., Newman, F., & Asadi-Zeydabadi, M. (2018). Artificial neural networks. In *Studies in Systems*. Decision and Control; doi:10.1007/978-3-319-75049-1_2

Cao-hoang, T., & Duy, C. N. (2017, April). Environment monitoring system for agricultural application based on wireless sensor network. In *2017 Seventh International Conference on Information Science and Technology (ICIST)* (pp. 99-102). IEEE. 10.1109/ICIST.2017.7926499

Chaâri, R., Ellouze, F., Koubâa, A., Qureshi, B., Pereira, N., Youssef, H., & Tovar, E. (2016). Cyber-physical systems clouds: A survey. *Computer Networks*, *108*, 260–278. doi:10.1016/j.comnet.2016.08.017

Çifçi, M. A., & Elçi, A. (2017). Yapay Zekâ İle Kablosuz Algılayıcı Ağları Eniyileme. *Türkiye Bilişim Vakfı Bilgisayar Bilimleri ve Mühendisliği Dergisi, 10*(2), 64–76. https://dergipark.org.tr/en/pub/tbbmd/issue/33390/339255

Delicato, F. C., Al-Anbuky, A., Kevin, I., & Wang, K. (2020). *Smart Cyber–Physical Systems: Toward Pervasive Intelligence systems*. Academic Press.

Diaz-Rozo, J., Bielza, C., & Larrañaga, P. (2017). *Machine Learning-based CPS for Clustering High throughput Machining Cycle Conditions*. Procedia Manufacturing. doi:10.1016/j.promfg.2017.07.091

Fei, X., Shah, N., Verba, N., Chao, K. M., Sanchez-Anguix, V., Lewandowski, J., ... Usman, Z. (2019). CPS data streams analytics based on machine learning for Cloud and Fog Computing: A survey. *Future Generation Computer Systems*, *90*, 435–450. doi:10.1016/j.future.2018.06.042

Gaber, T., Abdelwahab, S., Elhoseny, M., & Hassanien, A. E. (2018). Trust-based secure clustering in WSN-based intelligent transportation systems. *Computer Networks*, *146*, 151–158. doi:10.1016/j.comnet.2018.09.015

Gal, Y., & Ghahramani, Z. (2016). Dropout as a Bayesian approximation: Representing model uncertainty in deep learning. *33rd International Conference on Machine Learning, ICML 2016*.

Gharehchopogh, F. S., & Gholizadeh, H. (2019). A comprehensive survey: Whale Optimization Algorithm and its applications. *Swarm and Evolutionary Computation*, *48*, 1–24. doi:10.1016/j.swevo.2019.03.004

Girão, P. S. (2017). Wireless sensor networks. *22nd IMEKO TC4 International Symposium and 20th International Workshop on ADC Modelling and Testing 2017: Supporting World Development Through Electrical and Electronic Measurements*. 10.4018/ijaec.2016100101

Goumopoulos, C., & Mavrommati, I. (2020). A framework for pervasive computing applications based on smart objects and end-user development. *Journal of Systems and Software*, *162*, 110496. doi:10.1016/j.jss.2019.110496

Goumopoulos, C., O'Flynn, B., & Kameas, A. (2014). Automated zone-specific irrigation with wireless sensor/actuator network and adaptable decision support. *Computers and Electronics in Agriculture, 105,* 20–33. doi:10.1016/j.compag.2014.03.012

Grover, J., & Sharma, S. (2016, September). Security issues in wireless sensor network—a review. In *2016 5th International Conference on Reliability, Infocom Technologies and Optimization (Trends and Future Directions) (ICRITO)* (pp. 397-404). IEEE.

Hasan, M. Z., Al-Rizzo, H., & Günay, M. (2017). Lifetime maximization by partitioning approach in wireless sensor networks. *EURASIP Journal on Wireless Communications and Networking, 2017*(1), 15. doi:10.118613638-016-0803-1

Humayed, A., Lin, J., Li, F., & Luo, B. (2017). Cyber-physical systems security—A survey. *IEEE Internet of Things Journal, 4*(6), 1802–1831. doi:10.1109/JIOT.2017.2703172

Kafi, M. A., Othman, J. B., & Badache, N. (2017). A survey on reliability protocols in wireless sensor networks. [*ACM Computing Surveys, 50*(2), 1–47. doi:10.1145/3064004

Kaur, S., Bala, E., Deng, T., Shah, K., Vanganuru, K. K., Pietraski, P. J., ... Pragada, R. V. (2018). *U.S. Patent No. 10,051,624.* Washington, DC: U.S. Patent and Trademark Office.

Khan, A., Abas, Z., Kim, H. S., & Oh, I. K. (2016). Piezoelectric thin films: An integrated review of transducers and energy harvesting. *Smart Materials and Structures, 25*(5), 053002. doi:10.1088/0964-1726/25/5/053002

Kim, S., & Park, S. (2017). CPS (cyber physical system) based manufacturing system optimization. *Procedia Computer Science, 122,* 518–524. doi:10.1016/j.procs.2017.11.401

Lalropuia, K. C., & Gupta, V. (2019). Modeling cyber-physical attacks based on stochastic game and Markov processes. *Reliability Engineering & System Safety, 181,* 28–37. doi:10.1016/j.ress.2018.08.014

Li, X., Li, D., Wan, J., Vasilakos, A. V., Lai, C. F., & Wang, S. (2017). A review of industrial wireless networks in the context of industry 4.0. *Wireless Networks, 23*(1), 23–41. doi:10.100711276-015-1133-7

Loureiro, J., Rangarajan, R., Nikolic, B., Indrusiak, L., & Tovar, E. (2017, August). Real-time dense wired sensor network based on traffic shaping. In *2017 IEEE 23rd International Conference on Embedded and Real-Time Computing Systems and Applications (RTCSA)* (pp. 1-10). IEEE. 10.1109/RTCSA.2017.8046307

Melendez, S., & McGarry, M. P. (2017, January). Computation offloading decisions for reducing completion time. In *2017 14th IEEE Annual Consumer Communications & Networking Conference (CCNC)* (pp. 160-164). IEEE.

Mihalache, S. F., Pricop, E., & Fattahi, J. (2019). Resilience enhancement of cyber-physical systems: A review. In *Power Systems Resilience* (pp. 269–287). Cham: Springer. doi:10.1007/978-3-319-94442-5_11

Mohamed, N., Al-Jaroodi, J., Jawhar, I., Idries, A., & Mohammed, F. (2020). Unmanned aerial vehicles applications in future smart cities. *Technological Forecasting and Social Change, 153,* 119293. doi:10.1016/j.techfore.2018.05.004

Panerati, J., Schnellmann, M. A., Patience, C., Beltrame, G., & Patience, G. S. (2019). Experimental methods in chemical engineering: Artificial neural networks–ANNs. *Canadian Journal of Chemical Engineering*, *97*(9), 2372–2382. doi:10.1002/cjce.23507

Parulpreet, S., Arun, K., Anil, K., & Mamta, K. (2019). Computational Intelligence Techniques for Localization in Static and Dynamic Wireless Sensor Networks—A Review. In *Computational Intelligence in Sensor Networks* (pp. 25–54). Berlin: Springer. doi:10.1007/978-3-662-57277-1_2

Paul, S., Guha, D., Chatterjee, A., Metha, S., & Shah, A. (2017). Comparison between Conventional Network and ANN with Case Study. *Int. Res. J. Eng. Technol*, *4*(8), 1795–1803.

Pearl, J. (2019). The seven tools of causal inference, with reflections on machine learning. *Communications of the ACM*, *62*(3), 54–60. doi:10.1145/3241036

Rawat, P., Singh, K. D., Chaouchi, H., & Bonnin, J. M. (2014). Wireless sensor networks: A survey on recent developments and potential synergies. *The Journal of Supercomputing*, *68*(1), 1–48. doi:10.100711227-013-1021-9

Reichherzer, T., Satterfield, S., Belitsos, J., Chudzynski, J., & Watson, L. (2016, May). An agent-based architecture for sensor data collection and reasoning in smart home environments for independent living. In *Canadian Conference on Artificial Intelligence* (pp. 15-20). Springer. 10.1007/978-3-319-34111-8_2

Ruan, T., Chew, Z. J., & Zhu, M. (2017). Energy-aware approaches for energy harvesting powered wireless sensor nodes. *IEEE Sensors Journal*, *17*(7), 2165–2173. doi:10.1109/JSEN.2017.2665680

Rubin, M. J. (2014). *Efficient and automatic wireless geohazard monitoring* (Doctoral dissertation). Colorado School of Mines. Arthur Lakes Library.

Sangaiah, A. K., Sadeghilalimi, M., Hosseinabadi, A. A. R., & Zhang, W. (2019). Energy consumption in point-coverage wireless sensor networks via bat algorithm. *IEEE Access: Practical Innovations, Open Solutions*, *7*, 180258–180269. doi:10.1109/ACCESS.2019.2952644

Say, S., Ernawan, M. E., & Shimamoto, S. (2016). Cooperative path selection framework for effective data gathering in UAV-aided wireless sensor networks. *IEICE Transactions on Communications*, *99*(10), 2156–2167. doi:10.1587/transcom.2016ATP0012

Serpen, G., & Gao, Z. (2014). Complexity analysis of multilayer perceptron neural network embedded into a wireless sensor network. *Procedia Computer Science*, *36*, 192–197. doi:10.1016/j.procs.2014.09.078

Sharma, G., & Kumar, A. (2018). Fuzzy logic based 3D localization in wireless sensor networks using invasive weed and bacterial foraging optimization. *Telecommunication Systems*, *67*(2), 149–162. doi:10.100711235-017-0333-0

Shimly, S. M., Smith, D. B., & Movassaghi, S. (2019). Experimental Analysis of Cross-layer Optimization for Distributed Wireless Body-to-Body Networks. *IEEE Sensors Journal*, *19*(24), 12494–12509. doi:10.1109/JSEN.2019.2937356

Singh, P., Khosla, A., Kumar, A., & Khosla, M. (2017). Wireless sensor networks localization and its location optimization using bio inspired localization algorithms: A survey. *International Journal of Current Engineering and Scientific Research*, *4*, 74–80.

Tolk, A., Barros, F. J., D'Ambrogio, A., Rajhans, A., Mosterman, P. J., Shetty, S. S., & Yilmaz, L. (2018, April). Hybrid simulation for cyber-physical systems: a panel on where we are going regarding complexity, intelligence, and adaptability of CPS using simulation. In *SpringSim* (pp. 3–1). MSCIAAS.

Tomić, I., & McCann, J. A. (2017). A survey of potential security issues in existing wireless sensor network protocols. *IEEE Internet of Things Journal, 4*(6), 1910–1923. doi:10.1109/JIOT.2017.2749883

Toral-Cruz, H., Hidoussi, F., Boubiche, D. E., Barbosa, R., Voznak, M., & Lakhtaria, K. I. (2015). A survey on wireless sensor networks. In *Next Generation Wireless Network Security and Privacy* (pp. 171-210). IGI Global.

Xiao, F., Sha, C., Chen, L., Sun, L., & Wang, R. (2015, April). Noise-tolerant localization from incomplete range measurements for wireless sensor networks. In *2015 IEEE Conference on Computer Communications (INFOCOM)* (pp. 2794-2802). IEEE. 10.1109/INFOCOM.2015.7218672

Xing, L. (2020). *Reliability in Internet of Things: Current Status and Future Perspectives*. IEEE Internet of Things Journal.

Yu, L., Blunsom, P., Dyer, C., Grefenstette, E., & Kocisky, T. (2016). *The neural noisy channel*. arXiv preprint arXiv:1611.02554

ADDITIONAL READING

Carrero, M. A., Musicante, M. A., dos Santos, A. L., & Hara, C. S. (2017, November). A reusable component-based model for WSN storage simulation. In *Proceedings of the 13th ACM Symposium on QoS and Security for Wireless and Mobile Networks* (pp. 31-38). 10.1145/3132114.3132118

Farivar, F., Haghighi, M. S., Jolfaei, A., & Alazab, M. (2019). Artificial Intelligence for Detection, Estimation, and Compensation of Malicious Attacks in Nonlinear Cyber-Physical Systems and Industrial IoT. *IEEE Transactions on Industrial Informatics, 16*(4), 2716–2725. doi:10.1109/TII.2019.2956474

Khosla, R. (2017). Time synchronization across multiple devices in network nodes (Master's thesis, NTNU).

Melicher, M., Šišmišová, D., Vachálek, J., & Belavý, C. (2019). A Cyber-Physical Systems Paper Survey About the Concept, Architecture and Challenges for the Deployment within the Concept of Industry 4.0. *Research Papers Faculty of Materials Science and Technology Slovak University of Technology, 27*(45), 49–54. doi:10.2478/rput-2019-0025

Mukherjee, M., Lu, Y. R., Matam, R., & Choudhury, N. (2018, January). Energy trading in sleep scheduling for wireless rechargeable WSNs. In 2018 10th International Conference on Communication Systems & Networks (COMSNETS) (pp. 429-431). IEEE. 10.1109/COMSNETS.2018.8328235

Trappey, A. J., Trappey, C. V., Govindarajan, U. H., Sun, J. J., & Chuang, A. C. (2016). A review of technology standards and patent portfolios for enabling cyber-physical systems in advanced manufacturing. *IEEE Access: Practical Innovations, Open Solutions, 4*, 7356–7382. doi:10.1109/ACCESS.2016.2619360

Zeadally, S., & Jabeur, N. (2016). Cyber-physical system design with sensor networking technologies. Institution of Engineering and Technology.

Zhang, J., Zhu, Y., & Xiao, F. (2019). Modelling and analysis of real-time and reliability for WSN-based CPS. *International Journal of Internet Protocol Technology*, *12*(2), 76–84. doi:10.1504/IJIPT.2019.099683

KEY TERMS AND DEFINITIONS

Artificial Intelligence: It is a set of software and hardware systems with many capabilities such as behaving human-like or numerical logic, motion, speech, and sound perception. In other words, AI makes machines think and percept like humans.

Artificial Neural Network: It is an information processing model inspired by the form of the brain in which biological nervous systems, such as the brain, process information.

Cluster Head: A cluster head is a node that gathers data from the cluster sensors and passes this data to the base stations.

Cyber-Physical Systems: It is an integration of computation, networking, and physical processes.

Deep Learning: It is an artificial intelligence technology that imitates the role of the human brain in data processing and the development of decision-making patterns.

Fuzzy Logic: Fuzzy logic is not the standard "true or false" approach; it is rather focused on "degrees of fact."

K-Nearest Neighbor: An algorithm that assumes similar things exists close to each other. Such similar things come together to become a group.

Swarm Intelligence: It is the discipline dealing with natural and artificial systems consisting of many individuals who coordinate through decentralized monitoring and self-organization.

Support Vector Machine: It is a supervised learning algorithm in ML used for problems in both classification and regression. This uses a technique called the kernel trick to transform the data and then determines an optimal limit between the possible outputs, based on those transformations.

Chapter 11
Multiplier for DSP Application in CPS System

Abhishek Kumar
Lovely Professional University, India

ABSTRACT

A cyber-physical system over field-programmable gate array with optimized artificial intelligence algorithm is beneficial for society. Multiply and accumulate (MAC) unit is an integral part of a DSP processor. This chapter is focused on improving its performance parameters MAC based on column bypass multiplier. It highlights DSP's design for intelligent applications and the architectural setup of the broadly useful neuro-PC, based on the economically available DSP artificial intelligence engine (AI-engine). Adaptive hold logic in the multipliers section determines whether another clock cycle is required to finish multiplication. Adjustment in algorithm reduced the aging impact over cell result in the processor last longer and has increased its life cycle.

INTRODUCTION

Artificial Neural Networks (ANN) depend on the simultaneous design and inclined by the human mind. ANN is a type of multi-processor program involving essential handling components known as neurons; The ANN has a complex network and versatile association between underlying components. The very first usage of ANN accompanied by the creation of the perceptron set out and related learning rule by Frank Rosen Blatt (Martin, 2002). Another critical advancement was incorporating the algorithm like back-propagation for training (Ajith Abraham, 2005). Image compression includes decreasing the measure of the memory expected to store a digital format. Aside from the current innovation for picture pressure, for example, JPEG, MPEG, and H.26x gauges, recent changes of neural systems are essence investigated. Fruitful utilizations of neural networks to vector quantization gotten settled. Different parts of neural system contributions around there are venturing up to assume significant jobs in helping with conventional compression methods (Venkata Rama Prasad Vaddella and Kurupati Rama, 2010).

The cyber-physical system (CPS) presented by (Ding 2019 and Kinsey, 2011); is a computational system organized of computational devices and physical conditions. Computational methods communi-

DOI: 10.4018/978-1-7998-5101-1.ch011

cate through a communication network and control physical situations through actuators and can receive feedback input about physical conditions employing sensors. The collaborator of a CPS should know about every device that impacts the functionality of the CPS.CPS framework models usually comprise of a large number of differential conditions. The synthesis of such complex equations using software on a programmable chip is moderate. A few past efforts to implement; models as equivalent circuits on Field-Programmable Gate Arrays (FPGAs), showing a massive increase in speed, because of the magnificent tie among fine-grained local communication, which is the prime focus in physical models and the fine-grained parallel computation component and connection network of FPGAs. A CPS system includes security in terms of software protocol. Hardware implementation of complex computation comes with the limitation of leakage issue, cyber-attack says during computational device leaks side information. Intruder utilizes this information to get access to the device. A conventional cybersecurity mechanism cannot detect or block such a category of attack (Greenword, 2005). Recently, Artificial Intelligent (AI) is a work in progress to protect the CPSs.

Concerning digital security, AI advancements are utilized to measure information that originates from various sources of data. Artificial neural system is a framework that accepts the input, processes according to an algorithm, and furnishes results. Two primary aspects of machine learning are preparing and deduction of the data. Deduce with numerous varieties of typically lower exactness multipliers, gives off an impression of being a decent counterpart for FPGA models. Current FPGAs (Langhammer, M., & Baeckler, G., 2018). now have over a million lookup tables (LUT) mixes, which proposes that they are appropriate for executing these sorts of exhibits. Training requires, requires higher precision arithmetic computations.

The chapter is organized as follows; background highlights the needs of the DSP multiplier for the Xilinx AI engine, the MAC unit with aging indicator provided in the implementation of MAC, and the application of MAC with different types Verilog HDL. Simulation result with the conclusion and future direction has been discussed in the consecutive section.

BACKGROUND

All advanced FPGAs contain implanted multipliers. The FPGA asset blend is categorized, with exact functionalities are assembled into one section. The associations allying the DSP Block and logic core expected to help the operator symbol and collects a notable number of routing. This decrease gadget adaptability, and expands the power utilization per activity. We can, in this manner, see that the logic core for arithmetic computation for learning inference is critical. Arithmetic computation in FPGA frequently utilizes the carry chain to implement a logic structure. New methods will all go used entirely of logic structure, which goes before the string of carrying, with the inclusion of the instance of incorporation of the created partial product. Contextually, any necessary logic structure which can't be entirely mapped on to the lookup tables (LUTs) holding up the carry chin will be determined out of band, and just the single bit after-effects of the out of band work routed to the logic structure of carrying. FPGAs are off the rack programmable gadgets that give an adaptable stage to actualizing custom equipment usefulness at a low improvement cost (Shawahna et al., 2018). They introduced chiefly plenty of programmable rationale structures, known as configurable rationale squares (CLBs), a programmable interconnection arranges, and a large number of reconfigurable input cells and output cells around the boundary. Moreover, they have a vibrant arrangement of installed segments, for example, advanced procession processing (DSP) squares utilized to execute complex computation viz multiply and accumulate (MAC) unit.

FPGA early adopters utilized LUTs and adders to actualize components (multipliers), construct DSP capacities, FIR channels, FFTs, etc. Since Xilinx gadgets are preferred to deal with requesting new computational applications, explicit components were made DSP slice advancement in the Virtex®-II FPGAs in 2001. Sit on Moore's Law, Xilinx has expanded the quantity of LUTs only 400 units in the XC4000 FPGA to over 3.7 million LUTs count and more than 12,200 DSP slices counts in recent FP-GAs (Corradi, G., 2018) An expansion inaccessible asset of more than multiple times. In response to the non-linear increment sought after by cutting edge remote and applying machine learning for higher register thickness and power requirement, Xilinx has started exploring adaptable design, prompting the improvement of the AI Engine. Alongside versatile engines (configurable rationale) and scalar engine structure, a firmly incorporated diversified computational stage. Computer-based intelligence Engines result in 5-times higher computer density in vector-based calculations (Li, Z., Zhang, Y., Wang, J., & Lai, J., 2019). Adaptable engines give adaptable custom processes and data processing. Scalar Engines provide complex programming support.

The goal of Artificial intelligence Engine gotten from severe computation-based applications utilizing DSP. The AI Engine was created to give four essential advantages:

1. Deliver 3 to 8 -times more computational capacity
2. Reduce computational power by half
3. Provide deterministic, real-time DSP capacities
4. Improve the design productivity

Multiply and accumulate operation are the most common operation performed by DSP block in FPGA. The MAC task is a simple step that processes the result of two multiplicands (B and multiplier (C) sum that item to the accumulator (A). MAC operation on A illustrated as

$$A \leftarrow A + (B \times C)$$

Modern PCs consist of a devoted MAC, comprising of a multiplier unit actualized with combinational logic blocks succeeded by adder stage and accumulator register, which holds up the outcome. The content of the register is given back to the adder's input such that on the individual clock cycle, the content of the multiplier is summed up with register. Multipliers implemented with Combinational units comprise a lot of logic block, yet process a product rapidly than the older technique of multiplication shifting and adding. The adders and multipliers are the significant segments in the plan of the MAC (Multiply and Accumulate) unit (Kawahito, S, 2008). Multiplier, adder, and accumulator together structure a MAC unit, which is broadly utilized in microchips and computerized signal processors for computationally escalated applications. The MAC unit supports the enormous number of advanced signal processing (DSP) applications. It accomplishes signal capacity to the microcontroller for distinct applications example are servo and sound control. The execution unit in the processor realizes a 3-phase pipelined arithmetic technique that streamlines more massive multipliers like 16×16. This algorithm supports both input size of 16-bit and 32-bits.

The primary role in DSP processor configuration is to upgrade the execution speed and throughput of the MAC system to accomplish high performance (Ganesh, 2017). There is a requirement of low

Figure 1. Block diagram of MAC

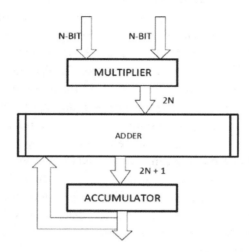

power utilization as a result of expanded portable electronic items, and in this manner, low power MACs are picking up significance. Macintosh, an execution unit in the processor, realizes a 3-stage pipelined architecture design that optimizes 16×16 multipliers, presented in figure 1 (Upadhyay, 2015; Baran, 2010). MAC comprises a multiplier understand with combinational logic succeeded by an adder and a collector(flip-flop) that holds up the outcome. The outcome of the register feedback to the adder's contribution such that on each clock cycle, the yield of the multiplier is summed to register again. Combinational multipliers needed a lot of hardware components; however, they perform computation quickly than shifting and adding the traditional multiplier method.

IMPLEMENTATION OF MAC

Because of the complexity of physical models, past methodologies were focused on utilizing exceptionally simplified models. Facilitate models must not showcase the genuine nature of physical frameworks of adequate accuracy with execution speed. Enhanced efficiency acquires increasingly commemorate models, and these need large numbers of computational cells.

In the Digital Signal Processing (DSP) applications, the necessary activities, for the most part, include Multiplication and summation. The processor requires to spent maximum time and hardware resources to complete a multiplication task compare to other arithmetic operations like addition and subtraction (Patil, 2018). To achieve the high-performance DSP application for real-time applications, effective Multiply Accumulate Unit (MAC) is continuously a backbone. Over the most recent couple of years, the principal focal point of MAC configuration is to upgrade its speed. The general block diagram of the project is shown below, which shows the main components to be used in doing the project. The ingredients used in this project demonstrated in figure 2(Ganesh, 2017).

1. Multiplier
2. Flip Flop

Figure 2. *MAC System*

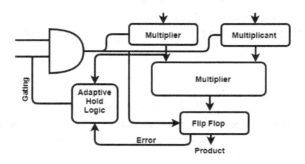

3. Adaptive Hold Logic

The MAC unit consists of a generation of partial products and addition. The performance of the presented systems relies upon the return of the multipliers. If the multiplier excessively slow, the exhibition of the whole system will get diminished. Subsequently, it is critically important to have elite multipliers. To enhance the MAC execution, we can delay associated with the critical path by embedding an additional pipeline register, either for partial product unit or associated with the partial product unit and the last full adder, but increasing the overhead, energy requirement, and delay. MAC operation is carried in two-step multiplication, which is slower than the second stage adder. In this work, the MAC unit with adaptive hold, logic, and razor flip flop are presented to provide feedback for result updates. The multiplier furnishes higher performance through the variable latency, modify the AHL unit to decrease power consumption and latency. The timing infringement is diminished dependent on razor flip flop, and the Adaptive Hold Logic variable-latency strategy separates the circuit in 2 sections, they are known as the shorter and the longer paths. Execution accomplished efficiently in one cycle for the shorter path. On account of longer paths, it requires one more (two) clock cycles to complete. If shorter paths are initiated every now again, the average of variable-latency designs is superior to the customary models.

Additionally, it is notable that multipliers consume majority power in calculations. Thus, low power column-bypass multipliers and row-bypass multipliers reduce the delays and power consumption. Implies if the input bit is zero, do not activate the corresponding row/column.

The general progression of MAC design is as per the following: when input arrives, the multiplier enables the column bypassing technique, and AHL operates all the while, as per the number of zeros in the multiplicand AHL chosen. Input requires one or two cycles. In the event two clock cycle requirement to finish execution, the AHL will yield '0' and disable the clock signal for the flip-flops, else, AHL will generate '1'. At the point when column -bypass multiplier complete the activity, the outcome passes to razor flip-flops. Razor flip-flops verify whether a path delay along with timing error. While timing infringement occurs implies the clock cycle isn't long sufficient for the present activity to finish, and the processed result of the multiplier must be wrong. In this way, the razor flip-flops yield an error to trigger the system, which indicates present activity should be re-executed utilizing two clock cycles to guarantee the event is right. The additional re-execution cycles brought about by timing infringement cause punishment to an overall average delay (Menon, 2006; Bañeres, 2009).

Notwithstanding, our presented AHL circuit can precisely foresee whether the input needed one or two cycles. Just a couple of information may result in a timing deviation. If AHL circuit judges incorrectly, additional re-execution cycles didn't deliver critical timing corrupt.

Aging Indicator

The aging indicator shows if the circuit has to be preserved through essential deprivation due to the aging impact. The aging indicator is executed as a sequential fashion that examines several mix-ups over a particular proportion of action and over a specific percentage of assignment to reset to low (zero) on the completion of these exercises. Since the clock cycle is unnecessarily short, the row or column bypassing can't complete this movement viably, causing timing encroachment. Due to the aggressive scaling of metal oxide semiconductor field-effect transistor MOSFET device dimensions and associated electric fields (Du, 2012), aging has brought up a profound issue. Estimations on the transistor's parameter were used to determine the circuit design margins to ensure reliability. The following aging effect observed in integrated-circuit sub-90nm CMOS technologies by (Ozcan 2019) (a) Hot Carrier Injection (HCI), (b) Time-Dependent Dielectric Breakdown (TDDB), (c) Bias Temperature Instability (BTI) and (d) Electro-migration (EM).

Adaptive Hold Logic

The adaptive hold logic (AHL) is the essential segment in the aging ware variable delay multiplier. The AHL unit comprises an aging indicator, two judging units, one multiplexer, and a D flip-flop. The specific activity of the AHL circuit as per the following; while the input pattern arrives, judging blocks decide whether input requires several clock cycles either one or two to finish up two outcomes to the multiplexer. The multiplexer picks up one of the results dependent on the yield of the aging indicator analyzed (Su, 2010; Karthikeyan, 2020). Then an OR activity is executed between and after effect of the multiplexer. The Q signal is utilized to decide the input of corresponding D flip-flop. If the input requires one clock cycle, the yield of the multiplexer is 'High.' Gating signals will receive 'High,' and the flip flops will latch up with new data to the flip flop in the following cycle. Then again, when the yield of the multiplexer is 'Low,' implies there is a requirement of two periods to finish, OR gate yield 'Low' to D flip-flop. In this way gating signal will be 'Low,' which disable the clock signal, flip-flops in the following cycle. The aging indicator exhibits if the circuit has endured a noteworthy fall down due to the aging effect. The indicator executed like an up counter that counts the number of errors in a specific measure and reset to zero towards the last step of this task. If the clock period is excessively short, the row or column bypass multiplier can't finish these activities effectively, resulting in timing infringement. Timing infringements would be gotten by razor flip-flops, which produces error signals. If errors occur often and cross the predefined threshold, it implies circuit endured noteworthy timing degradation as a result of the aging effect. The indicator will yield 'High' else 'Low' to demonstrate the aging impact is not notable, and no activities required.

Judging Blocks

There are two intermediate judging blocks in the AHL unit. The first unit deciding on the block will create an output 'High' if the number of zeros counts in the input sequence is larger than the predefined

Figure 3. Booth multiplication stages

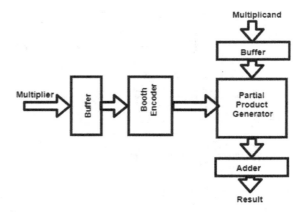

limit (n). When the counts of zeros in the input sequence are greater than (n+1), the second unit's yield is deciding on 'High.' The user sets the limit value of (n). The activity AHL (Jon, 2000) circuit is as per the following if the input is provided. Both judging units will decide the sequence requires one or two clock cycles to finish their activity and pass both outcomes to the multiplexer.

INTERNAL COMPONENT OF MAC UNIT

Three underlying blocks of MAC are multiplier, adder, and accumulator.

Multiplier Architecture

Low power consumption and decreased time delay have been a significant measure of VLSI design. Digital multipliers are vital sections of elite high-performance systems, for example, FIR filters, microprocessors and digital signal processors, microchips, and computerized signal processors. The quality of a DSP IC is verified by three parameters area, power, and delay. Minimizes area, smaller delay with low power consumption are the central goals to accomplish. The multiplier is the most repetitive unit in DSP's IC. The binary multiplier performs Multiplication with repeated addition. Different types of multipliers exist in literature; a standard method is shit and adds algorithm. Array multiplier, carry-save multiplier, row/column bypass multiplier, booth multiplier, etc. In parallel, the partial multiplier product to be added in parameter determines the multiplier performance. Each multiplier operates with a multiplication result of 100% accuracy, but precise computing comes with a significant drawback. It cannot optimize all parameters of the circuit. However, accurate computing is necessary for some applications, like pictures and multimedia processing, which can bear error and produce a result. Inexact computing admired us for reducing the difficulty in implementation and reducing the power dissipation.

Figure 4 Array Multiplier

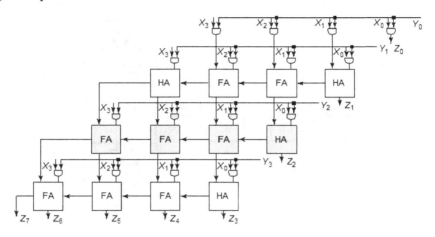

Booth Multipliers

Parallel executions in (Parhi, 2007) which result in a fast-parallel multiplier, will, in general, utilize more area and consumes extra power. While sequential multiplier implements with the minimized area and superseding low power, it brings about a slow multiplier. Booth multiplier implementation in (Lie, 2008) utilizes a 32-piece by 8-piece and requires four cycles to complete a 32 ×32-bit multiplication. This execution captures a balance among power, hold-up, and region and needs more cycles to execute. However, it sets aside much less effort for each period and needless area than a 32×32-bit equal multiplier. Traditional multiplication circuits utilize latency as the general circuit clock cycle so as execute precisely. Then again, the possibility of a critical path is activated in short. By and large, the way path delay is smaller than the critical path delay. The entire cycle time frame will bring about significant planning waste because of the critical path, utilizing the essential path delay. In this manner, the variable-inactivity configuration was anticipated to diminish the planning misuse of conventional circuits. Parallel MAC is widely used in computerized signal processing and video/design applications. Another architecture of multiplier and accumulator (MAC) for high-speed Multiplication and summing arithmetic.

The Booth multiplier decreases the number of iteration steps to perform Multiplication as a contrast with conventional multipliers. The booth algorithm examines the operands of multipliers and trips. The carry chains of this calculation can diminish the counts of addition required to deliver the product outcome contrasted with ordinary duplication calculation, where an individual bit of the operand is multiplied with the corresponding bit of multiplicand.

The booth multiplier presented in figure 3; can be partitioned into two phases. In the main stage, the Partial Products are shaped by the Booth encoder and Partial Product Generator (PPG). In the second stage, the fractional items got in the above are converged to frame the outcomes. Rather than adders here, the 5:2,4:2,3:2 compressor can be utilized to decrease the carry propagation. Booth algorithm is implemented as booth encoding and booth selection. Before Multiplication, we require the two operands, a Multiplier, and a Multiplicand, which are to be put in a buffer. In binary multipliers, the partial products are generated by performing AND operation(multiplying) the bits of multipliers with multiplicand bits. Thus, the variety of AND gates are utilized in typical binary multipliers for the partial product. When

Figure 5. Row bypassing methodology

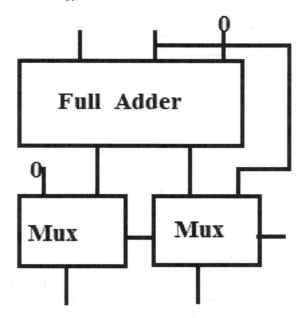

the multiplier bit is zero, then a line of zeros is added to the past fractional item. When the multiplier bit is one, then the multiplicand is added once to the past halfway items with a position move towards left.

The advantage of booth multiplier is a reduction in partial product generation, preferably with more than 16-bit input. The disadvantage of booth multiplier is a complexity to circuit and generation of partial product in booth encoding.

Figure 6. Column bypass multiplier

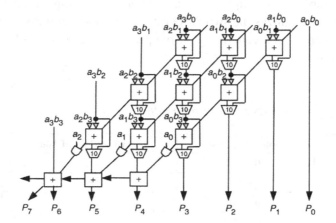

Table 1. Comparisons of delay of 8×8 bypassing multiplier

Delay (ns)	Ripple Carry Adder	Carry Look Ahead Adder	Carry Select Adder
Row Bypassing	28.369	24.365	21.369
Column Bypassing	23.345	21.365	18.267
Row-Column Bypassing	30.253	26.38	23.645

Array Multiplier

The array multiplier (AM) presented in figure 4 is a fast multiplier. An array of multiplier multiplies 4-bit inputs and gives the product an 8-bit output. The array contains (n-1) number of rows in the carry-save adder (CSA). A particular row of CSA contains (n-1) number of the full adder (FA) cell. A full adder in carry-save adder possesses two outputs signal; the sum and carry discussed in (Parhi, 2007). The sum output tends to downward, and the carry tends to flow lower-left full adder. The ending row consists of a ripple carry adder (RCA) for carrying propagation, and it adds up the delay. Full adders of array multiplier remain active irrespective of input, maximize the power consumption. Each phase of the parallel adder receives some partial product and carry spread to the next line. In a nonpipelined multiplier, all fractional part is created simultaneously. For an n×n bits multiple, the vertical and level postponement both equivalents to the deferral of an n bit full adder.

The advantages of an array multiplier are its regular structure, more straightforward in implementation. Lower design time compares to tree multiplier. Array multiplier has eased to implement pipelining and follow the proper shape.

The limitation of array multiplier is a worst-case delay, require high power and increased area overhead.

Row / Column Bypass Multiplier

Multiplier consumes the maximum power in the DSP block, and it is required to develop a low power multiplier. A complimentary metal-oxide field-effect transistor (MOSFET) based integrated circuit is default choice to have small power circuits over FPGA. Power consumption classifies as static and dynamic power, in which active power comes with the major components. Dynamic power strongly depends on data to be processed and increases with switching activity. Here switching activity presents the probability of the number of bits flips between two consecutive input data. Gray coding is adopted to re-arranges the input to minimizes the switching rate. In bypass multiplier, particular row or column in bypass to activate, which are not generating partial product. If coefficient bit zero, that row/column would not require to activate.

Table 2. Comparisons of power of 8×8 bypassing multiplier

Delay (nW)	Ripple Carry Adder	Carry Look Ahead Adder	Carry Select Adder
Row Bypassing	0.8235	0.9364	0.9824
Column Bypassing	0.8356	0.9875	1.002
Row-Column Bypassing	0.7526	0.9925	0.9753

In row bypassing in multiplier bit coefficient, if any bit of the multiplier bits comprises '0,' i.e., relating row containing all '0'. With the goal that the previous sum need not given to this row, it tends to be bypassed to the following row for counts. Thus, eliminating the row of '0,' the calculation is decreased, and power utilization diminished. The Row bypassing multiplier keeps down the switching rate by bypassing the particular row whose multiplicand bis are zero. It implies that if the multiplier bit is zero, that particular row of adders would be disabled. A special circuitry implemented with a multiplexer to detect if the row is zero.

Figure 7. Wallace tree Multiplier

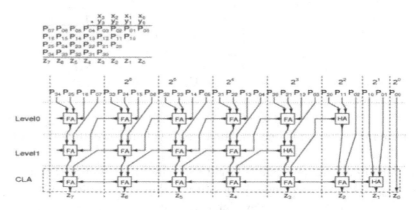

It comprises a three-stage gate, full adder, and multiplexers. The input data be summed inputted to the full adder through three-stage gates. The enable input to the multiplexer is the corresponding multiplier's bit. If the multiplier bit that is applied to the multiplexer is zero, the three stages go into high impedance state, and along these inputs are not inputted to the full viper. The prior sum is selected as

Figure 8. 3:2 Compressor schematic

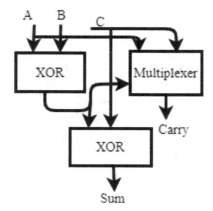

Figure 9. 5:3 compressor architecture

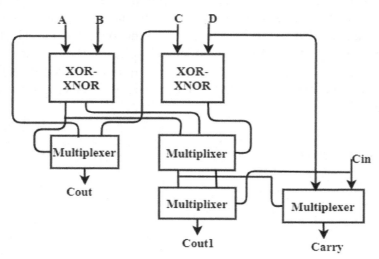

the current sum. If the multiplier bit is one, the three-stage get empowered at that point, and the inputs are applied to the full adder.

A column-bypassing multiplier presented in figure 6, is improved multiplier than the array multiplier (AM). The column bypass multiplier underlying cell is a dull adder followed by a multiplier. Unlike array multipliers, when an input state is not available, the full adder will be disabled, minimizing power consumption. Hence, the FA is restructured to add two units of tristate gates and one unit of a multiplexer (Calimera, 2012; Anuskha, 2019). The multiplicand's bit 'a_i' is utilized as the select input to the multiplexer to choose the FA's outcome.

Similarly, 'a_i' likewise utilized as a select input of the tristate primitive to leave the input path of the FA. When a bit is 'Low,' the contribution of FA is impaired, and the sum output of the present FA is equivalent to the sum output from upper FA. Among these lines decline the power consumption of the multiplier. When 'a_i' is 'High,' the typical sum result is selected.

Figure 10. 7:3 Compressor architecture

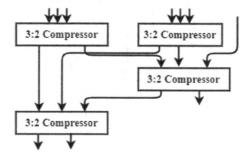

Figure 11. Accumulator architecture

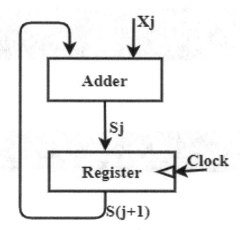

The partial product adder is adjusted in a tree-like design, to decrease both the critical path delay and the requirement of adder cell counts—the discussed structure in figure 7 for the Wallace tree multiplier. The tree multiplier acknowledges significant equipment investment funds for bigger multipliers. The propagation delay is diminished too. Indeed, it tends to be demonstrated that the propagation delay of the tree is equivalent to O (log3/2 (N)). While generously quicker than the carry-save the structure of considerable multiplier word lengths, the Wallace multiplier possesses the burden of being shift unpredictable, which complexes the assignment of an efficient design.

Row bypassing strategy executes bypassing the multiplicand bit makes the partial product zero; it is better regarding power. The column bypassing method introduces the utilization of the additional hardware, to keep a tactical distance from the beginning point of carrying propagation. This method reduces area and minimizes power consumption as the section bypassing multiplier uses just a single multiplexer, while the row bypassing procedure utilizes two multiplexers. Along these, there is an improvement in the

Figure 12. Razor D flip flop

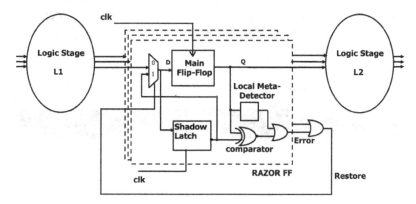

Figure 13. Simulation result of the MAC unit

Figure 14. Simulation result waveform of AHL

column bypassing multiplier by reducing the multiplexer counts. Row and column bypassing strategies are executed to improve the multiplier productivity by diminishing the switching activity. If the multiplicand or multiplier bit is zero, full adder doesn't perform, results in low power consumption regarding one dimensional bypassing. On comparing, the outcomes with Barun multiplier and bypass multiplier show the most significant speed. On account of dynamic power and area, a 2-dimensional bypassing technique requires minimal force and area when contrasted with row and column bypassing. Hence, it can wind up that column bypassing offers minimal delay, and 2-dimensional bypassing procedures consume the least power. The utilization of various adders like carrying look-ahead adder (CLA), carry select adder (CSA) separated from ripple carry adder (RCA) in the last stage assisted with improving as far as delay discussed by (Fowers, 2014) in table 1 and 2.

Wallace Tree Multiplier

A 16-bit multiplier is developed by utilizing Wallace tree architecture presented in Figure 7. Partial product is included four phases. Adders and various compressor blowers are being used to limit the work on each stage. The compressor is the combinational block requires to implement the more multiple are logical AND, OR, XOR. To perform addition half adder and full adder in preferred (Swati, 2016). The compressor can perform the addition of the higher number of inputs, the compressor focused. The compressor made up of an adder block. The compressor maps a piece of higher information to lower the number of outputs with summation operation (Gahlan, 2012). A full adder is basic 3:2 compressor units of 3:2. It accepts three numbers of input and map as a sum and carries at the output terminal.

Figure 15. Simulation result of column bypass multiplier

Compressor and adders are utilized carefully to achieve the minimum number of results at the output created, regarding segment number 10, where ten bits are inputted at the first stage. Ten bits mentioned above could be included by utilizing two counts of 5-3 compressor; however, it will accept ten) five of each compressor) and produce six (three of every compressor) outputs.

Compressors

Rather than it, we experimented with one 7-3 compressor, and a full adder cell produces five output in particular (3 of the compressors and two from full adders) that, in the long-run, decline the counts of bits of the following stage. Regarding column number 16 in which sixteen partial products are included along the primary stage. Sixteen partial product items included utilizing a 7-3 compressor, a 6-3 compressor, and a full adder cell, these three compressor models would result in 8 output. Alternatively, two 7-3 compressors can furnish this task, produce six outputs, and the other 2 bits are advanced to the second stage. At last, eight bits remain for the 2nd stage expansion without including an additional adder (Mandaloi, 2017). In this manner, by utilizing the least number of adders and compressors, partial products can be included out with bargaining. The count of bits is left for the following stage activity.

3:2 Compressor

3:2 compressor presented in figure 8 are utilized instead of full adder cells because of multiplexer designs and the XOR gates delays, henceforth increasingly reasonable for the ternary addition capacity. Regarding complex preparing, the two 3 LUT usages can be blended without any problem with encompassing logic.

$$Sum = A \oplus B \oplus C$$
$$Carry = (A \oplus B)C + (\overline{A \oplus B})A$$

5:3 Compressor

The 5-3 Compressor presented in figure 9 has five numbers of inputs (A, B, C, D, and C_{in}) to produce three outputs, namely (Sum, Carry, and C_{out}). The four inputs A to D and the Sum output possess a similar weight. The information C_{in} is the outcome from a previous compressor and the C_{out}, Carry yield holds the following critical bits after Sum bit. Carry and Cout hold the next bit's weight after sum. Carry, and C_{out} bit are inputted to the half-adder cell to generate Cout1 of the slimmer weight corresponding to

Table 3. Comparisons of different multiplier

	Array Multiplier	*Booth Multiplier*	*Wallace tree Multiplier*
Area (Total CLB's)	3280.50	2800	3321.50
Delay (ns)	37.23	25.33	18.93
Power (W)	7.57	6.66	7.32

Carrying in, and C_{out2} possesses the following significant bit weight after carrying. This design of 5:3 compressor utilizes the XOR-XNOR module and the MUX module, introduced in Figure 9.

$$Sum = (A \oplus B \oplus C \oplus D \oplus Cin)$$

$$Carry = (A \oplus B \oplus C \oplus D)Cin + ((\overline{A \oplus B \oplus C \oplus D})D)$$

$$Cout = (A \oplus B)C + (\overline{A \oplus B})A$$

7:3 Compressor

The 7:3 compressor presented in figure 10 utilizes four 3:2 blowers associated with the goal that accepts seven input and results in 3 output bits, namely (Sum, $Cout_1$, and $Cout_2$). The seven input and the Sum outcome has a similar weight while $Cout_1$ and $Cout_2$ prescribed the continuous two significant bit weight after sum.

ACCUMULATOR

Accumulator functions are similar to the counter. The major difference rather increases the counter an incentive by steady, accumulator includes the input value with the present values. It contains a register a D flip-flop and Full Adder (FA) cell. Accumulator cell drives the circuit under test (CUT) data sources, S[j+1] = 1, If X[j] = 1 and S[j] =0 and consequently X[j] = 0 and S[j] = 1. For output 1, either X[j] and S[j] should be the same.

Razor Flip Flop

The D flip-flop imprints the input, keeping changes with coordinated those of input D. Here, D stands for "data input"; flip flop gathers the value corresponding that is on the Q output. (Das, 2006) Razor D-flop flop is a flip flop with detection and correction of timing error. It monitors the error rate through the circuit activity and tunes supply voltage. Razor flip flop minimizes the latency and power requirement overhead of the circuit.

Figure 12 presented one input bit size of razor flip flop, which consists of the center flip-flop, a shadow latch, XOR gate, and a multiplexer. The center flip flop gets the outcome of the combinational block utilizing a clock signal, and a shadow latch gets the result using a deferred clock, which is obtuse than standard clock signal. Razor flop has in-built metastability hardened comparator. It validates the data sampled to latch at the fast clock rate. In the event of the latched bit to shadow, a latch is not quite the same from a corresponding main flip flop; it implies the path delay of present activity surpasses the clock period. The main flip-flop produces an unexpected result. On the off chance that abnormalities arise, the razor flip flop will produce error signal 'High' to advise the system to re-execute the activity and inform the adaptive hold logic (AHL) circuit.

An error occurred. Razor flip flops distinguish if the activity is viewed as one clock else activity is re-executed with two clock cycles. Even though the re-execution would appear expensive, the total cost is small due to the minimal re-execution recurrence. Error monitoring of the circuit observes both the global delay and local delay variation and doesn't experience the effect of voltage scaling. Accordingly, it does not require the voltage margin that considers as consistently right for circuit operation in traditional design. Another feature of razor flip flop is tuning of supply voltage, present a trade-off between penalty from error correction with power saving. Critical flop is implemented with razor flop based on dynamic voltage scaling (DVS). The error detection and error correction lead to power overhead. Power in razor flop reduces in the most cycle. The input to flip flop would not switches and power excess from switching and delayed clock gathered. Power saving feature included in the design by operating the at lower supply voltage dynamically. It further minimizes the additional power consumption due to the clock signal.

RESULT AND DISCUSSION

The recent development in programming and hardware implementation technologies and embedded systems are progressively being used. In the area extending from aviation and cutting-edge transportation technologies to smart grid and brilliant healthcare services—information processing system onto which the end-user is not informed about a physical computing device. There exists a secure link between the physical system and computing resources. Embedded system run is smaller in size and runs slower because there is no dedicated computational engine, like a general-purpose system like DSP unit or FPGA. The Cyber-physical system is an embedded system that emphasizes the secure link between the physical and cyber world. A CPS system should temporal and logically correct. The continuous interaction of physical, electrical, and cyber network systems worsens the occurrence of communication delays. CPS system analyzes their interrelationship across interconnected modules continuously. Adaptability is another feature of the CPS system based on feedback. Reconfigurability of FPGA attracts attention to implement the prototype of the AI-enabled cyber-physical system for DSP application. The selection of an efficient multiplier in the multiplicative unit improves the particular module's performance and complete system. Multiply and accumulate unit is implemented with the Xilinx ISE tool with the Verilog HDL programming language. An efficient column bypass multiplier has been used to implement the MAC unit. Figures 12, 13, and 14 present the MAC unit's simulation waveform, adaptive hold logic, and column bypass multiplier, respectively.

These maturing impacts are caused because of the scaling of transistors in VLSI chips, causes misfortune on circuit execution and lifetime, which are the primary factors in the VLSI circuit's dependability debasement. Hence, to decrease this maturing impact on CMOS, and Adaptive Hold Logic (AHL) circuit is established to be more productive than different techniques.

Obtained synthesis report from XST synthesis claims the device utilization consumes 53% of IOB and 4% of LUT from an available number of components on the Spartan3E FPGA family. Table 3 presents the comparison of the discussed multiplier in terms of the total number of configurable logic blocks (CLB), power, and delay. Array multiplier is conventional requires maximum are, high power consumption and highest propagation delay. The Booth multiplier is economical in area and power requirements. Wallace tree multiplier is considered the fastest multiplier but requires a large quantity of CLB's.

FUTURE RESEARCH DIRECTIONS

The future research direction are inclusion to security at the hardware root of trust. Limitations of hardware limitations are leaks side information, which an attacker can use to get access over the system unauthentically, known as a side-channel attack. Leakage cannot be avoided but can be altered. CPS system with AI technology hardware does not leak information along with leakage. Wireless and mobile health care system is another focus of the CPS system since the complexities involved in the implementation can go beyond the principle involved in physical and natural science. CPS system can enhance the security level of the digital authentication process in banking transactions and digital platforms. A CPS based alarm system can be revolutionized in a telemetry-based patient monitoring system where a vast setup is needed.

CONCLUSION

In this work, different varieties of the multiplier are implemented with Verilog hardware description language (HDL). Integration of intelligent computing with the DSP algorithm for the cyber-physical system complexed the implementation, which results in slower execution and large area requirement. An efficient multiplier must integrate into DSP computation to enhance computation speed. The multiplier is the accessible unit in the Xilinx AI engine, improving the DSP subsystem's performance like the MAC unit. The consideration of adaptive hold logic into the DSP multiplier exhibits aging informed variable latency. The multiplier is enabled to adjust the AHL to alleviate performance downsizing due to delay. Simulation waveform shows that the MAC unit with column bypass multiplier achieves a 20% reduction in LUT requirement and a 50% reduction in delay than the booth multiplier. MAC unit with AHL unit stands to reduce the aging impact and improve overall efficiency and performance. Multiplier integration with DSP slice enhances the communication speed, which ensures the robustness of the methodology against the communication delays dynamically.

REFERENCES

Abraham, A. (2005). Artificial neural networks. In Handbook for Measurement Systems Design. John Wiley & Sons. doi:10.1002/0471497398.mm421

Bañeres, D., Cortadella, J., & Kishinevsky, M. (2009, April). Variable-latency design by function speculation. In 2009 Design, Automation & Test in Europe Conference & Exhibition (pp. 1704-1709). IEEE. doi:10.1109/DATE.2009.5090937

Baran, D., Aktan, M., & Oklobdzija, V. G. (2010, August). Energy-efficient implementation of parallel CMOS multipliers with improved compressors. In *Proceedings of the 16th ACM/IEEE international symposium on Low power electronics and design* (pp. 147-152). 10.1145/1840845.1840876

Calimera, A., Macii, E., & Poncino, M. (2012). Design techniques for NBTI-tolerant power-gating architectures. *IEEE Transactions on Circuits and Wystems. II, Express Briefs*, 59(4), 249–253. doi:10.1109/TCSII.2012.2188457

Corradi, G. (2018). *The Value of Python Productivity: Extreme Edge Analytics on Xilinx Zynq Portfolio.* Xilinx, White Paper, WP502 (v1. 0).

Das, S., Roberts, D., Lee, S., Pant, S., Blaauw, D., Austin, T., & Mudge, T. (2006). A self-tuning DVS processor using delay-error detection and correction. *IEEE Journal of Solid-State Circuits, 41*(4), 792–804. doi:10.1109/JSSC.2006.870912

Ding, D., Han, Q. L., Wang, Z., & Ge, X. (2019). A survey on model-based distributed control and filtering for industrial cyber physical systems. *IEEE Transactions on Industrial Informatics, 15*(5), 2483–2499. doi:10.1109/TII.2019.2905295

Du, K., Varman, P., & Mohanram, K. (2012, March). High-performance, reliable variable latency carries select addition. In 2012 Design, Automation & Test in Europe Conference & Exhibition (DATE) (pp. 1257-1262). IEEE.

Fowers, J., Ovtcharov, K., Strauss, K., Chung, E. S., & Stitt, G. (2014, May). A high memory bandwidth FPGA accelerator for sparse matrix-vector Multiplication. *2014 IEEE 22nd Annual International Symposium on Field-Programmable Custom Computing Machines,* 36-43. 10.1109/FCCM.2014.23

Gahlan, N. K., Shukla, P., & Kaur, J. (2012). Implementation of wallace tree multiplier using compressor. *International Journal on Computer Technology & Applications, 3*(3), 1194-1199.

Ganesh, G. V., Kumar, D. P., Ram, J. S., Reddy, A. D., & Teja, M. P. (2017). Design of reliable multiplier using the bypassing technique. *International Journal of Pure and Applied Mathematics, 115*(8), 407–412.

Greenwood, G., Gallagher, J., & Matson, E. (2015). Cyber physical systems: The next generation of evolvable hardware research and applications. In *Proceedings of the 18th Asia Pacific Symposium on Intelligent and Evolutionary Systems* (pp. 285-296). Springer. 10.1007/978-3-319-13359-1_23

Hagan, M. T., Demuth, H. B., & Beale, M. (2002). *Neural Network Design.* China Machine Press.

Jon, S. J., & Wang, H. H. (2000, September). Fixed-width multiplier for DSP application. In *Proceedings 2000 International Conference on Computer Design* (pp. 318-322). IEEE.

Karthikeyan, S., & Jagadeeswari, M. (2020). Performance improvement of elliptic curve cryptography system using low power, high speed 16× 16 Vedic multipliers based on reversible logic. *Journal of Ambient Intelligence and Humanized Computing,* 1–10. doi:10.100712652-020-01795-5

Kawahito, S., Kameyama, M., Higuchi, T., & Yamada, H. (1988). A 32* 32-bit multiplier using multiple-valued MOS current-mode circuits. *IEEE Journal of Solid-State Circuits, 23*(1), 124–132. doi:10.1109/4.268

Kinsy, M., Khan, O., Celanovic, I., Majstorovic, D., Celanovic, N., & Devadas, S. (2011, November). Time-predictable computer architecture for cyber physical systems: Digital emulation of power electronics systems. In *2011 IEEE 32nd Real-Time Systems Symposium* (pp. 305-316). IEEE.

Langhammer, M., & Baeckler, G. (2018, June). High density and performance multiplication for FPGA. In *2018 IEEE 25th Symposium on Computer Arithmetic (ARITH)* (pp. 5-12). IEEE. 10.1109/ARITH.2018.8464695

Li, Z., Zhang, Y., Wang, J., & Lai, J. (2020). A survey of FPGA design for AI era. *Journal of Semiconductors*, *41*(2), 021402. doi:10.1088/1674-4926/41/2/021402

Liu, D. (2008). *Embedded DSP processor design: Application-specific instruction set processors*. Elsevier.

Mandloi, A., Agrawal, S., Sharma, S., & Shrivastava, S. (2017, August). High-speed, area efficient VLSI architecture of wallace-tree multiplier for DSP-applications. In *2017 International Conference on Information, Communication, Instrumentation and Control (ICICIC)* (pp. 1-5). IEEE. 10.1109/ICOMICON.2017.8279072

Menon, R., & Radhakrishnan, D. (2006). High performance 5: 2 compressor architectures. *IEE Proceedings. Circuits, Devices and Systems*, *153*(5), 447–452. doi:10.1049/ip-cds:20050152

Ozcan, E., & Erdem, S. S. (2019, July). A High-Performance Full-Word Barrett Multiplier Designed for FPGAs with DSP Resources. In *2019 15th Conference on Ph. D Research in Microelectronics and Electronics (PRIME)* (pp. 73-76). IEEE. 10.1109/PRIME.2019.8787740

Parhi, K. K. (2007). *VLSI digital signal processing systems: design and implementation*. John Wiley & Sons.

Patil, P. A., & Kulkarni, C. (2018, August). A Survey on Multiply Accumulate Unit. In *Fourth International Conference on Computing Communication Control and Automation (ICCUBEA)* (pp. 1-5). IEEE.

Prakash Nandi, Marimuthu, Balamurugan & Duraivel. (2019). Low-Power and Area-Efficient Approximate Parallel Design Using Bypassing. *Proceedings of International Conference on Recent Trends in Computing, Communication & Networking Technologies*. doi:10.2139srn.3428931

Shawahna, A., Sait, S. M., & El-Maleh, A. (2018). FPGA-based accelerators of deep learning networks for learning and classification: A review. *IEEE Access: Practical Innovations, Open Solutions*, *7*, 7823–7859. doi:10.1109/ACCESS.2018.2890150

Su, Y. S., Wang, D. C., Chang, S. C., & Marek-Sadowska, M. (2010). Performance optimization using variable-latency design style. *IEEE Transactions on Very Large-Scale Integration (VLSI) Systems*, *19*(10), 1874-1883.

Swathi, A. C., Yuvraj, T., Praveen, J., & Raghavendra Rao, A. (2016). A Proposed Wallace Tree Multiplier Using Full Adder and Half Adder. *International Journal of Innovative Research in Electrical, Electronics. Instrumentation and Control Engineering*, *4*(5), 472–474.

Upadhyay, H., & Chowdhury, S. R. (2015). A High Speed and Low Power 8 Bit× 8 Bit Multiplier Design Using Novel Two Transistor (2T) XOR Gates. *Journal of Low Power Electronics*, *11*(1), 37–48. doi:10.1166/jolpe.2015.1362

Venkata, R. P. V., & Rama, K. (2010). Artificial neural networks for compression of digital images: A review. *International Journal of Reviews in Computing*, *3*, 75–82.

ADDITIONAL READING

Alur, R. (2015). *Principles of cyber-physical systems*. MIT Press.

Giampa, P., & Dibitonto, M. (2020). MIP An AI Distributed Architectural Model to Introduce Cognitive computing capabilities in Cyber-Physical Systems (CPS). *arXiv preprint arXiv:2003.13174*.

Lai, J., Lu, X., Yu, X., Monti, A., & Zhou, H. (2019). Distributed voltage regulation for cyber-physical microgrids with coupling delays and slow switching topologies. *IEEE Transactions on Systems, Man, and Cybernetics. Systems*, *50*(1), 100–110. doi:10.1109/TSMC.2019.2924612

Lee, J., Bagheri, B., & Kao, H. A. (2015). A cyber-physical systems architecture for industry 4.0-based manufacturing systems. *Manufacturing Letters*, *3*, 18–23. doi:10.1016/j.mfglet.2014.12.001

Matas, K., La, T., Grunchevski, N., Pham, K., & Koch, D. (2020, February). Invited Tutorial: FPGA Hardware Security for Data centres and Beyond. In *The 2020 ACM/SIGDA International Symposium on Field-Programmable Gate Arrays*, pp. 11-20.

Pathak, J., Kumar, A., & Tripathi, S. L. (2020). High Level Transformation Techniques for Designing Reliable and Secure DSP Architectures. In *AI Techniques for Reliability Prediction for Electronic Components* (pp. 164–174). IGI Global. doi:10.4018/978-1-7998-1464-1.ch009

Vincent, H., Wells, L., Tarazaga, P., & Camelio, J. (2015). Trojan detection and side-channel analyses for cyber-security in cyber-physical manufacturing systems. *Procedia Manufacturing*, *1*, 77–85. doi:10.1016/j.promfg.2015.09.065

Wang, H., & Chen, X. (2020). A Fast Alternating Direction Method of Multipliers Algorithm for Big Data Applications. *IEEE Access: Practical Innovations, Open Solutions*, *8*, 20607–20615. doi:10.1109/ACCESS.2020.2967843

KEY TERMS AND DEFINITIONS

Ageing: Effect of the hardware block represents the degradation into parameter in % concerning time. HCI and BTI effect on underlying transistors estimate the fall of reliability of the complete circuit.

AI Engine: Xilinx's AI engine provides higher computation density for neural network algorithm implementation. These AI engines include SIMD and VLIW dedicated RISC scaler processor. It can perform 512 b fixed and floating-point computation.

Compressors: Used in this chapter implement the large size of the multiplier. It maps maximum input to minimum output; the primary cell of the compressors is an adder.

DSP System: Is a dedicated processor to perform a wide variety of signal processing operations.

FPGA: A semiconductor device prototypes the digital system. It is based around with configurable logic block connected via programmable interconnect. FPGA is reconfigurable.

MAC: Majorly used block in DSP system, it computes the product of two number and adds that product to an accumulator

Multipliers: Is one of the key hardware blocks in most digital signal processing (DSP) systems. Power dissipation and delay are the primary design constraint which can be optimized by enhancing the performance of underlying multipliers.

Synthesis: Is a process of transforming HDL design into a gate-level netlist.

Chapter 12
IoT Applications in Smart Home Security:
Addressing Safety and Security Threats

Rohit Rastogi

https://orcid.org/0000-0002-6402-7638

Dayalbagh Educational Institute, India & ABES Engineering College, Ghaziabad, India

Rishabh Jain

ABES Engineering College, Ghaziabad, India

Puru Jain

ABES Engineering College, Ghaziabad, India

ABSTRACT

Robotization has changed into a fundamental piece of our lives. Everybody is completely subject to mechanization whether it is an extraordinary bundling or home robotization. So as to bring home automation into thought, everybody now needs a heterogeneous state security, and in our task on residential robotization, such high security highlights are completely on the best possible consumption. Piezoelectric sensors are compelling for sharpening appropriated wellbeing checking and structures. An intrusion detection system (IDS) is a structure that screens for suspicious movement and issues alarms when such advancement is found. Some obstruction divulgence structures are fit to take practice when poisonous improvement or peculiar action is perceived.

DOI: 10.4018/978-1-7998-5101-1.ch012

INTRODUCTION

The Manuscript presents a detailed study wherein the Introduction section, the basic concepts of Big data, and CPS and IoT are explained. In the Literature Survey, the recent work of a few researchers has been explained. In the next section, the structure and functioning of the components used in this experiment like Arduino Uno, Piezoelectric-Transducer Sensor, RFID, LCD, GSM, and fingerprint sensor have been presented. Their working procedure has been explained in detail. At last, the Application aspect for home security using these components is elaborated. Then the future research direction, novelty, limitations, and conclusion are reflected.

An Intrusion Detection System (IDS) is a structure working on the principle of the Cyber-Physical System principle that screen for suspicious movement and issues alarms when such advancement is found. While impossible to miss worthiness and presentation is as far as possible, some obstruction divulgence structures are fit to take practice when poisonous improvement or peculiar action is perceived.

Security is an important issue nowadays, as the possibilities of intrusion are increasing day by day. The Cyber-Physical System is a network of physical objects devices, vehicles, buildings, and other items embedded with electronics software sensors, and network connectivity that enables these objects to collect and exchange data.

Big Data Analysis

It is the technology that is used to handle big data. Data science and predictive analytics can help you to achieve your business goals. Learn the process and benefits of implementing big data into your business. Big data analytics is the often complex process of examining large and varied data sets, or big data, to uncover information -- such as hidden patterns, unknown correlations, market trends, and customer preferences -- that can help organizations make informed business decisions.

Cyber-Physical System

It is a system in which a mechanism is controlled or monitored by computer-based algorithms. It includes autonomous automobile systems, robotics, automatic pilot avionics, and many more. In light of the structure of the interruption zone and there are some fundamental interests in it. The cyber-physical system involves enhancing the network to proficiently collect and analyze the data from various sensors and actuators then sends the data to the mobile phone or a personal computer over a wireless connection. Cyber-Physical Systems have progressed essentially in the last couple of years since it has created a new era in the world of information and communication technologies.

The Cyber-Physical System allows objects to be sensed and controlled remotely across existing network infrastructure, creating opportunities for more direct integration of the physical world into computer-based systems, and resulting in improved efficiency, accuracy, and economic benefit; when it is augmented with sensors and actuators, the technology becomes an instance of the more general class of cyber-physical systems, which also encompasses technologies such as smart environment grids, smart homes, intelligent transportation, and smart cities.

IoT and Smart Automation

It is a technology that has made the non-connectivity appliance a connectivity appliance. The appliances that contain technology that helps us to communicate with human and technology. Smart Automation is a technology that is to automate or automatic something by giving a single command. This technology reduces human efforts in the completion of work [Li et al., 2017] and [Goel et al., 2016].

LITERATURE SURVEY

The important goal of the Cyber-Physical System is to build a human interactive system using an RF controlled remote. Now technology is accelerating so homes are also getting smarter. Modern homes are deliberately relocating from current l switches to the centralized control system, containing RF controlled switches. Today traditional wall switches situated in various parts of the home make it laborious t for the end-user to go near them to control and operate [Li et al., 2017].

Even further it turns into more problematic for the old persons or physically handicapped people to do so. Cyber-Physical Systems using remote implements an easier solution with Wireless sensor networks. To accomplish this, an RF remote is combined to the microcontroller on the transmitter side that sends ON/OFF signals to the receiver where devices are connected. By operating the stated remote switch on the transmitter, the loads can be turned ON/OFF globally using wireless technology [Asensio et al., 2019].

EXPERIMENTAL DESCRIPTION

Our project contains six major components which are as follows:

1. ARDUINO (UNO)
2. Piezoelectric-Transducer Sensor
3. RFID
4. LCD
5. GSM
6. Buzzer
7. Fingerprint Sensor

ARDUINO- UNO

The microcontroller board depends upon ATmega328P (datasheet). 14 are moved data/yield pins (6 of which can be used as PWM yields), 6 direct information sources, a 16 MHz quartz gem, a USB affiliation, a power jack, an ICSP header, and a reset gets. This consolidates everything expected to help the microcontroller; add it to a PC with a USB affiliation or power it with an AC-to-DC connector or battery to start it. Arduino is an open-source stage used to make Gadgets Ventures. Arduino uses a physical programmable circuit board (routinely perceived as a microcontroller) and uses a touch of programming, or IDE (fused improvement condition), which continues running on your PC, which is used to make and

Figure 1. ARDUINO UNO REV3 (ATmega328P)[Agarwal et al., 2018]

move PC code. The Arduino stage has still ended up being critical with individuals, which is just beginning with the hardware, and in light of the current conditions. Despite the most recent programmable circuit sheets, Arduino does not require a free (planner) contraption to stack the new code on the board - you can generally use a USB interface. Also, Arduino uses the streamlined kind of IDE C ++, which makes the program more straightforward to learn. For a long time, Arduino gives a standard structure factor that breaks the segments of the microcontroller into a progressively open gathering [Asensio et al., 2019] and [Arora et al., 2016](as per Figure 1).

Uno Board and Form 1.0 Arduino Software (IDE) were the reference groupings of Arduino, which are by and by made for a snappy release. Arduino is the most preferred microcontroller which is used in Cyber-Physical security systems. UNO is the best board in the first place rigging and coding. UNO is the most used and recording driving social event of the whole Arduino family [Li et al., 2017) and [Goel et al., 2016].

The above-stated Table gives the whole specifications about ARDUINO UNO and which is retrieved from its Datasheet (as per Table 1).

Table 1. Technical speculations of ARDUINO UNO

Component	Specifications
Microcontroller	ATMEGA328P
Voltage	5V
Input	7-12V
Digital pins	14
PWM pins	6
Analog pins	6
DC per i/o pins	20 mA
Dc current	50 mA
Flash memory	32 KB
Sram	2 KB
Eeprom	1 KB (ATmega328P)
Clock speed	16 MHz
Led_builtin	13
Length	68.6 mm
Width	53.4 mm
Weight	25 gm

Arduino Functionality

Power USB: Arduino board is powered by using USB 2.0 which is connected from the computer or power bank for providing program and power.

Barrel Jack: Arduino can also be powered directly from the AC mains power by connecting this jack.

Voltage Regulator: It controls the voltage given by the USB port and Barrel Jack and distributes it into the processor and other elements.

Crystal Oscillator: It deals with time calculation. It has a frequency of 16 MHz.

Reset: This button is used to reset or refresh the Arduino board. By doing this the functioning starts from the first line of the program written in the board

Microcontroller: Arduino has many microcontroller series but in this project, we are using AT-MEGA328P.

Led Indicator: It glows up when the power is provided to the Arduino. If it does not turn on there is something wrong with the connection of power.

Digital I/O: It has digital I/O pins that are used to read the logic or in providing the output to the different modules such as LEDs, Relays, Bluetooth, etc.[Karpinskya et al., 2018] and [Agarwal et al., 2018].

PIEZOELECTRIC TRANSDUCER SENSOR

A device that uses the piezoelectric effect, to measure changes in pressure, acceleration, temperature, strain, or force by converting them to an electrical charge. A piezoelectric sensor is generally used in Cyber-Physical security. Piezoelectric sensors are versatile tools for the measurement of various processes like:-

1.   Sensing Touch
2.   The aroma in the Air
3.   Measuring Pressure/ Force
4.   Measuring Speed
5.   Measuring the impact
6.   Realizing Direction & position [Goel et al., 2016] and [Hofmann et al., 2019].

Working of a Piezoelectric Sensor

The physical sums normally evaluated by the piezoelectric sensor are accelerating and weight. Both weight and accelerating sensors manage a comparable rule of piezoelectricity, yet the crucial qualification between them is that the way wherein the power is associated with their recognizing part.

In this sensor, a wobbly film is put on an enormous scale to move the power associated with the piezoelectric part. It is generally a Cyber-Physical technology that works on change with pressure in the surrounding physical surfaces. On weight on this slight film, the piezoelectric material loads and starts making electric voltages. The yield voltage is concerning the proportion of associated weight (as per Figure 2).

Representation of a simple Piezoelectric Transducer is displayed in Figure 3.

Figure 2. Piezoelectric Sensor[Agarwal et al., 2018]

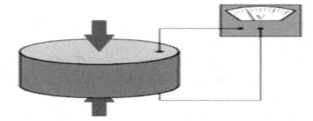

Working Principle

The force applied with a neutral axis (y) displaces the charge with direction, is perpendicular to the line of force [Niua et al., 2018] and [Aggarwal et al., 2015].

Piezoelectric Coefficient

A piezoelectric transducer has a great deal of DC yield impedance and it is displayed as a relative voltage source and channel organ. The voltage at the source is valid relative to the power, weight, or stress associated. The yield signal is then identified with this mechanical strength as if it has passed a similar circuit (as per Figures 4 and 5).

For use in the form of sensors, the repetition reaction area of the level of the plot is generally used

Figure 3. Connection of the piezoelectric sensor [Gupta and Rastogi, 2015]

between the high reaction pass-plot and the magnificent corpuscle. Burden and Spitz protest must be bigger for the fact that it does not need to lose less frequent intrigue. A disorderly similar circuit model can be used in the form, in which Cs speaks to the surface capacitance of the plane, which is guided by a standard recipe for the capacitance of parallel plates. Similarly, it can be added as an active source parallel to the source capacitance, the accent is connected to the direct charge [Kaul et al., 2015] and [Zheng et al., 2011] (as per Figures 6 and 7).

RADIO FREQUENCY IDENTIFICATION (RFID)

Figure 4. Piezoelectric sensors a voltage source in series with the sensor's capacitance [Nigam et al., 2015]

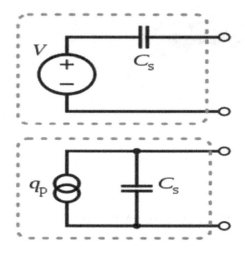

Figure 5. A piezo sensor outer specifications[Nigam et al., 2015]

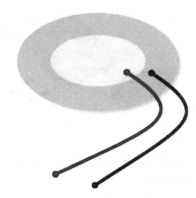

Figure 6. Piezoplate description for a piezoelectric sensor [Gupta et al., 2015]

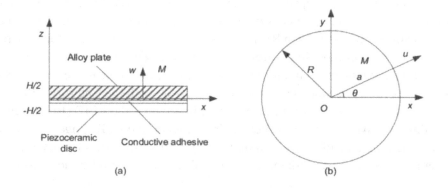

Figure 7. The dimension of a piezoelectric sensor [Gupta et al., 2015]

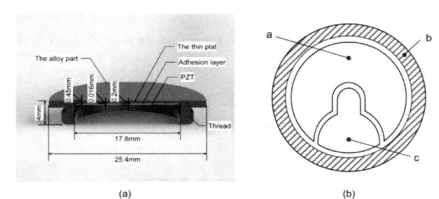

Figure 8. RFID module used in our experimental work [Gupta et al., 2015]

RFID uses electromagnetic fields to typically recognize and seek after the name that is fused into the things. Names have electronic-remote difficult to reach data. In Cyber-Physical System, wireless network protocols are used in communication between the microcontroller and the human. In this project, we are using the Radio Frequency-Identification technology is being used so that communication can become easy and also safe. It unconstrained imprints assemble essentialness from bordering RFIDs to customer's grilling radio waves. There is a region control source (battery) in the dynamic name and a couple of meters for every customer can work from RFID. Industry 4.0 brought new age benchmarks and among them, splendid preparing plant thought is surely the most huge [Zheng et al., 2011].

The Smart Factory thought relies upon the blend of the Manufacturing Execution System (MES) with the shop-floor level on one side, and on the contrary side with the Enterprise Resource Planning (ERP) level. The outstanding response for assembling things data is the RFID (Radio-repeat Identification) and Cyber-Physical Systems (CPS) structure. In this letter, the RFID-engaged Smart Factory has been arranged and facilitated inside the Learning Factory, and its show has been attempted. As for the plan of the system, it was made as fundamental as possible to enable understudies to manage it in the creation line condition to fathom and learn it. Dissimilar for an organized tag, the imprint should not be inside the customer's recognizable way, so it will, in general, be presented in the going with article. RFID is an advancement for customized ID and data get (AIDC) [Gluhak et al., 2011] (as per Figure 8).

These stresses accomplished the standard delineation of progress for prosperity and security issues. Use ISO/IEC 18000 and ISO/IEC 29167 on-chip cryptography methods to perceive the United Nations character, tag, and per customer confirmation and over-the-air protection.

Specification of RFID MFRC522

Module MFRC-522 fuses; RC-522 RFID RF-IC Card Sensor module for sending the S50 Fudan card and keychain for RC50. According to the MFRC522 client 13.56MHz contactless correspondence is related to "excellent three-table" of an excellent schematic chip card, a low voltage, unimportant effort, non-contact according to the customer chip, and "instrumentation" NXP convenient "handicraft contraception. The Mutual Fund uses RC522 Propelled Twik and Demodulation Idea to a wide extent of 13.56MHz in exceptional systems and shows without contact. 14443 A Strong Transponder Signal. The computerized part is surrounded and handles ISO14443A and Blonder affirmation. Also, for the support of Bolster QUICK CRYPTO-1 encryption probe, MIFARE cheese [Gluhak et al., 2011].

MFRC522 Bolster Mifare Game Plan Quickly form non-contact correspondence, formed in Table 2.2, as 424kbit or two-way information change standard. Customers of chips have been shown by the new assembling, MF RC522 MF RC500, and MF RC530 as an extraordinarily sorted 13.56 MHz card, and have different comparable properties, yet there are various highlights and irregularities are high. It is between host correspondence using SPI mode, reduces the connection, reduces the size and cost of the PCB board. MF522-A module receives exceptional Philips MFRC522 according to the client's circuit chip plot, easy to use, unimportant effort, sensible for gear changes, according to customer customers, the progress of edge applications, RF card terminal structure or customer's need to produce.

This module can be stacked in the illustration according to the client's position. The module uses 3.3V voltage through the SPI interface, the pair of straight lines can be exceptionally united with the

Table 2. Specifications and components of RFID

Component	Specifications
CURRENT	13-26mA
INPUT VOLTAGE	DC 3.3V
SLEEP CURRENT	<80uA
PEAK CURRENT	<30mA
FREQUENCY	13.56MHz
SUPPORTED CARDS	MIFARE1 S50,MIFARE1 S70, MIFARE ULTRALIGHT,MIFARE PRO, MIFARE DESFIRE PRODUCT
DIMENSIONS	40mm - 60mm
ENVIRONMENTAL TEMP	-20 to 80 C
RELATIVE HUMIDITY	5-95%
DATA TRANSFER RATE	10MBPS

client. Any CPU board correspondence module can ensure reliability and reliable work. Specifications of RFID are displayed in Table 2 [Sharma et al., 2015] and [Sharma et al., 2014].

Specification of RFID

Figure 9. Piezoelectric Buzzer (5v)[Sharma et al., 2013]

BUZZER

For a chime or beeper, for example, a sound hilling connotation, which can be mechanical, electromechanical, or snoozes electric, as shown in Figure 2.5, signature and beepers include the usual work-ready device, timekeeper, and confirmation of customer data, for example. A mouse snap or keystroke.

A Piezoelectric component is a gem or artistic that turns to some extent when connected to the voltage. Many types of Buzzers of different voice frequencies are being used in Cyber-Physical Systems (CPS) so that it can give the red signal before any tragedy happens. So if you supply the AC voltage on a two kHz, then at that point it turns further and reverses with the same speed as the AC signal, and gives a melodious voice. A similar effect works backward.

The most productive piece of the sound transducer is a metering plate of the piezoelectric, which is attached to the small metal stomach. When a voltage is connected to the plate of dirt, the cycle is connected incorrectly, causing the metal stomach to bend. At the point when a discontinuous voltage is connected to the point, the wired / metal-tilted section vibrates on the recurrence of the related voltage, and it fits to enable the hearing sound. In this occasion there is the mechanism of the mechanical resurgence of dirt/metal segment and the redistribution of related power banner, the vibration will be the most accurate, and sound construction will be the largest (Reverse redundancy of the lamp oil segment alone is exceptionally high, the option to listen to the sound is quite high, later it is a requirement for the metal stomach)(as per Figure 9) [Aggarwal et al., 2015] and [Shaquib et al., 2013].

Several characteristics need to be taken a mind of are:-

1. Dimensions (not including pins): 12mm diameter, 9.7mm tall.
2. Pins Length: 6mm long and 0.3" apart.
3. Crystal oscillation: 2 kHz
4. Input Voltage: 5v to 9v
5. Weight: 18.1gm
6. Principle Operation: Reverse Piezoelectric Effect
7. Material Used: Piezoceramic [Saquib et al., 2013] and [Shekhar et al.,2015]

Working of Piezoelectric Buzzer

Pizzeria buzzers use inverted piezoelectric theory to create ceramic disks for producing sound waves. A built-in oscillation circuit is included in the buzzer. Piezabuzer works on a wide temperature range and creates noise from soft and gentle to loud and aggressive [Marie et al., 2015].

When piezoelectric material is under pressure, the pressure causes the change in the surface of the material, as a result of these pressure differences, there are a surface and tension with the other. As a result, the positive charge collects on one side of the material, and the negative charge collects on the opposite side. This generator effect changes mechanical energy into electricity. In reverse piezoelectric effect, it is used in buzzer, by applying an electric field, the length of the surface changes and transforms electrical energy into mechanical energy, which creates sound waves, capable of detecting human ears. is.

Jacques and Pierre Curie discovered the piezoelectric theory in 1880, which was kept under a fixed crystal when they were under pressure, they used to produce electricity. When he continued to research this theory, he found that by applying electric fields in the piezoelectric crystal, he got accelerated. The discovery of ceramic materials made with barium titanate displays similar changes, which allow the use of both piezoelectric and inverse piezoelectric principles, including the development of Piezo buzzer [Saquib et al., 2013].

Figure 10. GSM 900A kit and its components [Agarwal et al., 2018]

Figure 11. The graph between frequency and magnitude [Gupta et al., 2015]

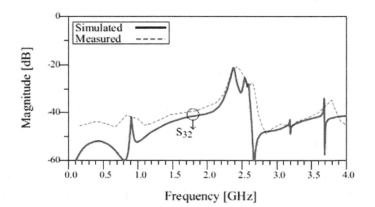

GSM 900A GSM / GPRS Modem

RS232 is working with dual-band GSM / GPRS engine - SIM900A, it works on repeat 900/1800 MHz. The modem is going with the RS232 interface, which gives you the right to stay connected with the microcontroller with the PC in the form of an RS232 chip (MAX232). BOD Rate is configurable from 9600-115200 through the AT Course. GSM is one of the most commonly used electronic devices in Cyber-Physical Systems so that communication can be possible between owner and machine. GSM is used for communication purposes as it provides the feature of calling, SMS, and also works at a different frequency. It just needs a SIM of any company so that it can communicate as instructed by the user. This is a GSM / GPRS-error-free quad-band remote, which works on the repetition of 850/900/1800/1900MHz and can be used not only on the Internet but also for oral correspondence.

In this case that it is related to the increase and a small derogatory speaker and for SMS. Remotely, undoubtedly a tremendous group (0.94-inch x 0.94-inch x 0.12 inch) with four L-shaped contacts on both sides so that they can be secured on different sides and floors. Inside, the module is guided by the AMR926EJ-S processor, which controls phone correspondence, Cyber Security, data correspondence (methods for an organized TCP / IP stack), and circuit correspondence (via UART and TTL interference interfaces) [Saquib et al., 2013] and [Qun et al., 2018].

The processor is also in charge of a SIM card (3 or 1,8 V) that should be related to the external mass of the module. Also, the GSM900 device integrates a basic interface, A / D converter, an RTC, an SPI transport, an IOC, and a PWM module. Radio part GSM phase 2/2 + is great and Class 4 (2W) is 850/900 MHz or Class 1 (1W) at 1800/1900 MHz. GSM / GPRS modem has an inward TCP / IP stack that enables you to communicate with the internet through GPRS. This M2M interface is suitable for SMS, the voice is similar to data-driven applications. Given the wide range of power supply, it gives the right to interfere with the supply of unregistered power. Using this modem, you can call and send via the voice call, SMS, read SMS, original AT course, and visit the web [Rungta et al., 2014].

Features
   ◦ Dual-Band 900/1800MHz.
   ◦ Configured baud rate.

Figure 12. LCD (16x2 alphanumeric display) [Kaul et al., 2015]

- ○ Holds SIM Card.
- ○ Network Status LED.
- ○ Inbuilt powerful TCP/IP protocol stack for internet data transfer over GPRS.

Applications
- ○ Access control devices
- ○ Cyber-Physical System technology using devices
- ○ Supply chain management

Working

In contrast to cell phones, a GSM modem does not have a keypad and show. It just acknowledges a few directions through a sequential interface and acknowledges those. These directions are called AT directions. The modem is a rundown of AT directions to teach you to do your errands. Each direction begins with "AT". That is the reason they are called AT directions. AT represents reflection (as per Figure 10).

In our straightforward venture, the program trusts that the portable PIN will be entered through the console. At the point when a ten-digit portable PIN is given, the program teaches the modem to send an instant message utilizing the succession of ATM directions (as per Figure 11).

Figure 13. Fingerprint module[Kaul et al.,2015]

Table 3. Specifications of the fingerprint sensor

Component	Specifications
Model	R307
Type	Optical Fingerprint Module
Interface	USB, UART(RS232 TTL)
Resolution	508 DPI
Voltage	DC 4.2-6V
Fingerprint Capacity	1000
Sensing array	300000 pixel
Fingerprint module size	52*20*22 (mm)
Effective collection area	11 * 15 (mm)
Scanning Speed	< 0.2 second
Verifying Speed	< 0.3 second
Matching Method	1:1; 1:N
FR	£0.1%
FAR	£0.001%
Temperature	-20C ---50C
Humidity	10-85%
Anti-static capacity	15KV
Abrasive resistance intensity	1 million times
Communications baud rate (UART):	(9600 × N) bps where N = 1 ~ 12(default N = 6, ie 57600bps)

LCD (LIQUID CRYSTAL DISPLAY)

A dimension board is visible or another electronically bent optical device that uses light-directed properties of liquid valued stones. Liquid pearls typically do not emit light, although they use foundation knowledge or reflector to create images in cinematography or monochrome. Cyber-Physical Systems uses LCD so that messages can be displayed on the screen and can be shown to the owner of the machine so that works get completed early. LCDs are open to indicate intangible images, (for example, usually in a valuable PC show) or fixed images with twisted objects that can be seen safe, for example, similar to a mechanical clock, presets Displays the words, digits, and seven-section. The LCD (liquid precious stone presentation) screen is an electronic showcase module and identifies a wide scope of usage. A 16x2 LCD show is an extraordinary fundamental module and it is usually used in various gadgets and circuits. These modules are favored by more than seven pieces and other multi-part LEDs. Due to being: LCDs are appropriate; easily programmable; There is no restriction for showing extraordinary and even custom characters (instead of seven pieces), movements, etc.

TheCyber-Physical System also uses 16x2 LCD so that message of long length can be displayed and also it features 2 line display. It implies that it can show 16 characters for each line and there are 2 lines of this type. In this LCD, each character is shown in a 5x7 pixel lattice. There are two registers in this LCD, for example, instructions and information [Sharma et al., 2013].

Figure 14. Fingerprint sensor circuit

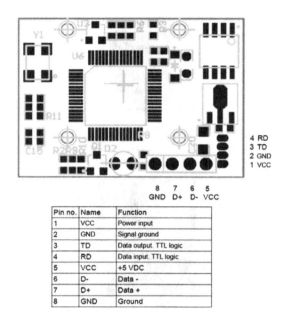

Pin no.	Name	Function
1	VCC	Power input
2	GND	Signal ground
3	TD	Data output. TTL logic
4	RD	Data input. TTL logic
5	VCC	+5 VDC
6	D-	Data -
7	D+	Data +
8	GND	Ground

The order register stores the guidelines given to the LCD. A guide is given to the LCD that it is used to run a predefined assignment, for example, it's beginning, its screen cleaned, controlling the cursor, controlling the showcase, and so on. The information store stores information shown on the LCD. The information is the ASCII estimate of the character shown on the LCD. Snap to know about the incoming structure of an LCD (as per Figure 12).

They use the same fundamental progress, at that point, to be told the truth, there are innumerable pixels in alternative images, whereas different grandstands have huge sections.

As shown in Figure 2.6, the use of LCD is a 16x2 alphanumeric display with a yellow monochromatic backlight. It is commonly used on 8051, AVR, Arduino, PIC, ARM, and so on.

There are certain Specifications in regards to these LCD's:-

Figure 15. Parallel connection of piezoelectric sensor [Shekhar et al., 2015]

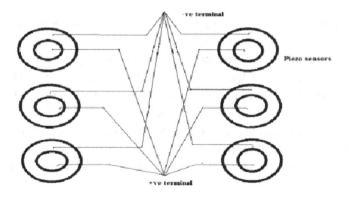

Figure 16. Arduino To RFID connection [Shekhar et al., 2015]

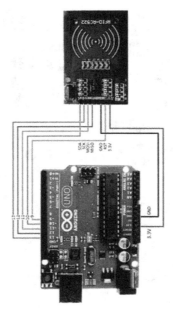

1. LCD Type: 16x2 Alphanumeric Displays
2. Size: 20x4 (2 Rows and 16 characters per Row)
3. Built-in industry standard HD44780 equivalent LCD controller
4. Operating Voltage: 5v to 9v DC
5. Backlight color: Yellow
6. Weight: 41gm
7. Chipset: HD44780 parallel interface chipset.
8. I/O pins: 16 pins
9. Mode of operation: 8-bit Mode and 4-bit Mode.
10. Pixel: Each character is built by a 5×8 pixel box [Agarwal, S. et al.,2014].

FINGERPRINT SENSOR

A fingerprint is the unique identification of a person who cannot be the same as the two people. Cyber-Physical System uses this technology so that security in terms of Data, personal information, files and many more can be secure. Also, fingerprint can be used in starting or stopping, authentication of the identity so that a false Id cannot disturb the physical system. The fingerprint is recovered from the crime through which the guilt person is found and punished. The impression of the fingerprint can be taken or copied by using moisture, grease, ink, and other substance on surfaces such as glass, plastic sheet, paper, and glass. Fingerprint through unique but keeps on changing due to age factor.

In India, Aadhaar Card is in trending these days due to its uniqueness as it has stored our two unique print which is Fingerprint and Retina which cannot be copied and is used in security checks whether the person is genuine or not. Data recorded in Cyber-Physical Systems so that it can be checked at the time of the function. It has recorded our all fingers including thumbs (as per Figure 13].

Yes, we can use this unique Biometric identification in making a security system so that there is a minimum number of loopholes present in it. In this project, we are using a biometric fingerprint reader R305 module which can be easily interfaced with a microcontroller. The user can store around 1000 number of fingerprint data in this module and can configure it in 1:1 or 1: N mode for identifying the person [Nigam et al., 2015].

Working Principle

Fingerprint processing includes two parts, fingerprint enrollment and fingerprint matching (the matching can be 1:1 or 1:N). When enrolling, the user needs to enter the finger two times. The system will process the two-time finger images, generate a template of the finger based on processing results, and store the template. When matching, the user enters the finger through the optical sensor, and the system will generate a template of the finger and compare it with templates of the finger library.

Table 4. RFID pin connections specifications

Components	Specifications
SDA	Digital 10
SCK	Digital 13
MOSI	Digital 11
MISO	Digital 12
IRQ	Unconnected
GND	GND
RST	Digital 9
3.3V	3.3V

Table 5. LCD to ARDUINO connection

LCD PIN	ARDUINO PIN
RS	PIN 2
ENABLE	PIN 3
D4	PIN 4
D5	PIN 5
D6	PIN 6
D7	PIN 7
R/W	GROUND

Table 6. LCD to peripherals and power system

Specifications	Components
VSS PIN	GROUND
PIN 16	GROUND
VCC	5V
PIN 15	5V0
10K RESISTOR	+5V
10K RESISTOR	GROUND
PIN 3	WIPER

Figure 17. Arduino To LCD connection [Gupta et al., 2015]

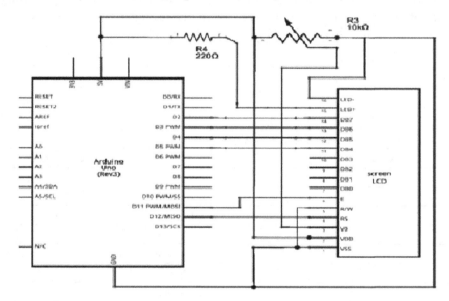

The system will compare the live finger with a specific template designated in the Module; for 1: N matching, or searching, the system will search the whole finger library for the matching finger. In both circumstances, the system will return the matching result, success, or failure [Zheng et al., 2011).

Security with biometrics can be done with the help of the R305 Fingerprint Module. This fingerprint sensor module will make adding fingerprint detection and verification super simple. These modules are

Table 7. GSM vs ARDUINO module

GSM MODULE	ARDUINO UNO
TX PIN	RX PIN
RX PIN	TX PIN
GROUND PIN	GROUND PIN

Figure 18. Arduino to GSM [Aggarwal et al., 2015]

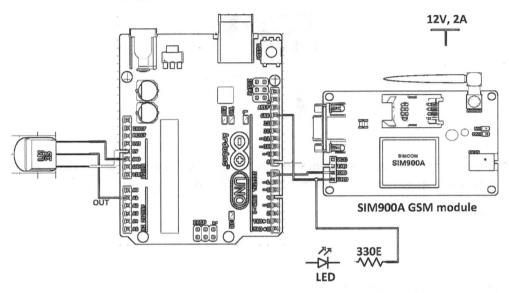

typically used in safes – there's a high powered DSP chip that does the image rendering, calculation, feature-finding, and searching. Connect to any microcontroller or system with TTL serial, and send packets of data to take photos, detect prints, hash, and search. You can also enroll new fingers directly- up to 162 fingerprints can be stored in the onboard FLASH memory. There's a red LED in the lens that lights up during a photo so you know it's working (as per Figure 14 and Table 3).

Fingerprint processing includes two parts: fingerprint enrolment and fingerprint matching (the matching can be 1:1 or 1: N). When enrolling, a user needs to enter the finger two times. The system will process the two -time finger images, generate a template of the finger based on processing results, and store the template [Zhang et al., 2019]. When matching, the user enters the finger through an optical sensor, and the system will generate a template of the finger and compare it with templates of the finger library. For 1:1 matching, the system will compare the live finger with a specific template designated in the Module;

Table 8. Fingerprint vs ARDUINO module

FINGERPRINT MODULE	ARDUINO
VCC	5V
GND	GND
CS	PIN 10
RST	PIN 9
A0	PIN 8
SDA	PIN 11
SCK	PIN 13
LED	3.3V

Figure 19. Applications of RFID using Arduino to GSM [Srivastava et al., 2014]

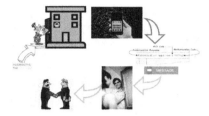

for 1: N matching, or searching, the system will search the whole finger library for the matching finger. In both circumstances, the system will return the matching result, success, or failure [Arora et al., 2016].

Specification

PROJECT IMPLEMENTATION

The Project Implementation of IDS can be explored in basic two sections:

- Hardware Design and Circuitry.
- Software Design and Programming

HARDWARE DESIGN AND CIRCUITRY

The IDS Module in our Project can be divided into 4main Circuit Connections:

1. Arduino To Piezoelectric Sensor Array
2. Arduino To RFID
3. Arduino To LCD
4. Arduino To GSM
5. Arduino To Fingerprint Sensor [Gluhak et al., 2011] and [Aggarwal et al., 2015]

Arduino to Piezoelectric Sensor Array

As per our requirement to get the input of intrusion from the piezoelectric sensor, by sensing the pressure-induced from the foot of the intruder, we have connected the Piezo sensors in a calculated fashion as shown in Figure and thus making an array of Sensors.

Parallel Connection Of Piezoelectric Sensor (as per Figure 15)

Thus 6-8 piezoelectric sensors are connected in parallel to increase the current.

Voltage of 1 sensor = 2.14v (normal pressure)
Voltage of Array = 2.14v
Current of 1 sensor = 0.5 mA
The current of Array = 4mA (All Pressed Properly)

Arduino RFID

As we needed to tackle the problem of false triggering of buzzer due to foot pressure induced by the authorized person, we deployed an RFID for the same purpose as in Figure 16.

Circuit Connection of Arduino with RFID

The Connection made in above Figure 15 is as follows tabulated in Table 4;

Pin Connections For RFID

ARDUINO to LCD

As in any research experiment or any device, the most important thing which is needed to be there is its User interfacing and its user-friendly nature. Thus LCD is doing the same purpose here as shown in Figure 3.3; it is not only giving directions to the user but also making it easy for the user to use the IDS more efficiently. On the programmers end it makes it easy to debug and check the proper functioning of the Module. Pin Connections are as follows in Table 5;

LCD to ARDUINO

LCD to Peripherals and Power System

ARDUINO to GSM

Connections of GSM to Arduino (as per Figure 18, Table 7)

ARDUINO to Fingerprint Sensor

SOFTWARE DESIGN AND PROGRAMMING

For accomplishing the need to integrate LCD, RFID, Buzzer &Arduino through Software, we required 4 different libraries.

1. RFID Read Library
2. RFID Function Library
3. Piezo Knock Sensor Library
4. LCD Read/Write Library [Sharma et al., 2014].

Applications of RFID using Arduino to GSM can be understood by several appliances which can be designed by a simple integration of components. Refer Figure 19 to understand the application of this module in different day to day perspectives.

PROCESS

- The Piezo-Electric Transducer-sensor detects intrusion and triggers an alarm as soon as a person applies pressure on the piezo – plate.
- Here the pressure energy gets changed into voltage needed to trigger the Arduino and thus making the alarm go on.
- To avoid a false Alarm due to intrusion of a legal person we will be using RF-ID security to stop any of the false triggerings so that our ID system will produce alarm only at intrusions.
- A message will be sent to the owner about the authorization access.

FUTURE RESEARCH DIRECTIONS

From the time immemorial it has been our prime rationale to improve the manners in which that can facilitate human endeavors, and make security a genuine cakewalk. Out of numerous methods for giving continuous security through the sensor, control, and Cyber-Physical Systems used around us, we conveyed the most appropriate Intrusion Detection System and the most ideal method for Cyber-Physical security system in a few viewpoints.

Research work utilizes two of the spearheading advances in their fields and guarantees an enormous prospect of IDS. Consolidating RFID with the current Piezo-based IDS ended up being another involvement in the field of Cyber-Physical Security Systems. The module planned by us was another idea in itself as the extent of this kind of framework can be interminable. The future viewpoints which can be seen rising through this module are excesses of extending from

1. RFID controlled GSM
2. Security for deaf and blind
3. Watt-less Security system or self-powered IDS
4. Automatic car parking system
5. Child safety and parental control systems.
6. Piezo-triggered security camera and other features.
7. Security for small children and women living at home alone.

In the entire procedure of making such a security framework we have found out about RFID, Piezo sensors, LCD, Zero PCB associations, Arduino, and its programming which helped us to comprehend the domain of IDS and its segments. The working of Intrusion Detection System (IDS) which is also an example of a Cyber-Physical System is made according to the human interactive product as it would be easy to interact with this Cyber-Physical System and can complete all the necessities required by the home alone people by using hardware and software in such a way that it will become an example for another product in the coming future. Henceforth it tends to be in all respects gladly finished up by us that the undertaking on Cyber-Physical System (CPS) worked precisely according to the decision and in this way denoting the heavenly end of this venture session.

CONCLUSION

The Advantage of this Cyber-Physical System over other systems is that it requires low or almost negligible external supply, précised, Clean System of Intrusion Detection. It can be made more convenient using a GSM module for remote Alarming. It is very easy to install and most important it is cost-efficient also.

Because of business plans, our security system serves at an affordable price with better security features as compared to other expensive Cyber-Physical systems. It has two checks at the doorstep. It targets women and children living in flats and apartments. Our key competitor is GODREJ whose security systems are quite expensive but are the most reliable ones in Cyber-Physical Systems. This system also features access control services and Theft and fire detection alarm. Also being cost-efficient will over a huge market as people always buy that costs less.

ACKNOWLEDGMENT

Our Sincere thanks to all direct and indirect supporters and well-wishers. Esteem gratitude to the Management of ABESEC, Ghaziabad India to provide excellent infrastructure to complete this work. The sincere guidance of Director sir, Prof. Shailesh Tiwari, and HoD-ECE, Prof. Sanjay Singh is also recognized. The ABESEC provided the infrastructure, staff support, and students' feedback, and fund to complete this. We especially thank for their time contribution to be part of this study. We also convey gratitude to Prof. D.K. Chaturvedi Sir, professor of DayalBagh Educational Institute, Agra for his mentorship and timely valuable suggestions.

REFERENCES

Agarwal, A., Goel, D., Tyagi, A., Aggarwal, A., & Rastogi, R. (2018). A Smarter Approach for Better Lifestyle in Indian Societies, In Progress in Advanced Computing and Intelligent Engineering. Advances in Intelligent Systems and Computing, (vol 563, pp. 355-362). Springer. DOI doi:10.1007/978-981-10-6872-0_33

Agarwal, S., Sharma, P., Rastogi, R., Kaul, U., & Jain, S. (2014) Unsupervised Classification of Mixed Data Type of Attributes Using Genetic Algorithm (Numeric, Categorical, Ordinal, Binary, Ratio-Scaled). In *Proceedings of the Third International Conference on Soft Computing for Problem Solving. Advances in Intelligent Systems and Computing,* (vol. 258, pp. 121-131). Springer. DOI 10.1007/978-81-322-1771-8_11

Aggarwal, K., Rastogi, R., & Mondal, P. (2015). An exhaustive review for infix to postfix conversion with applications and benefits. *Proceedings of 09th INDIACom;2nd International Conference on Computing for Sustainable Global Development,* 95-100. https://ieeexplore.ieee.org/document/7100228

Aggarwal, S., Rastogi, R., & Mittal, S. (2015). A Novel Approach for Communication Among Blind Deaf and Dumb People. *Proceedings of 09th INDIACom; 2015 2nd International Conference on Computing for Sustainable Global Development.* https://ieeexplore.ieee.org/abstract/document/7100321

Arora, S. R., Goel, P., Maini, J., & Mallick, P. (2016). Increasing Efficiency in Online Studies through Web Socket. *Proceedings of 3rd International Conference on Computing for Sustainable Global Development.* https://ieeexplore.ieee.org/document/7724316

Asensio, J. A., Criado, J., Padilla, N., & Iribarne, L. (2019). *Emulating home automation installations through component-based web technology.* Communication Magazine. doi:10.1016/j.future.2017.09.062

Gluhak, A., Krco, S., Nati, M., Pfisterer, D., Mitton, N., & Razafindralambo, T. (2011). A survey on facilities for experimental internet of things research. *IEEE Communications Magazine, 49*(11), 58–67. doi:10.1109/MCOM.2011.6069710

Goel, D., Agarwal, A., & Rastogi, R. (2016). A Novel Approach for Residential Society Maintenance Problem for Better Human Life. In R. Rajesh & B. Mathivanan (Eds.), *Communication and Power Engineering* (pp. 177–185). doi:10.1515/9783110469608-017

Goel, D., Agarwal, A., & Rastogi, R. (2016). A Novel Approach for Residential Society Maintenance Problem for Better Human Life. *International Journal of Urban Design for Ubiquitous Computing, 4,* 1–8. doi:10.21742/ijuduc.2016.4.2.01

Gupta, R., Rastogi, R., Mondal, P., & Aggarwal, K. (2015). GA Based Clustering of Mixed Data Type of Attributes (Numeric, Categorical, Ordinal, Binary, Ratio-Scaled). *BIJIT, 7*(2), 861-866. http://bvicam.ac.in/bjit/issues.asp?issue=14

Gupta, R., Rastogi, R., & Singh, A. (2015). A novel approach for vehicle tracking system for traffic jam problem. *Proceedings of 09th INDIACom; 2015 2nd International Conference on Computing for Sustainable Global Development.* https://ieeexplore.ieee.org/document/7100240

Hofmanna, P., Walchb, A., Dinkelmanna, A., Selvarayan, S. K., & Gressera, G. T. (2019). Woven piezoelectric sensors as part of the textile reinforcement of fiber-reinforced plastic. *Composites. Part A, Applied Science and Manufacturing, 116,* 79–86. doi:10.1016/j.compositesa.2018.10.019

Karpinskya, N. D., Chanceyb, E. T., Palmera, D. B., & Yamania, Y. (2018). *Automation trust and attention allocation in multitasking workspace. Communication Magazine.* doi:10.1016/j.apergo.2018.03.008

Kaul, U., Rastogi, R., Agarwal, S., Sharma, P., & Jain, S. (2015). A Novel D&C Approach for Efficient Fuzzy Unsupervised Classification for Mixed Variety of Data. In *Emerging ICT for Bridging the Future - Proceedings of the 49th Annual Convention of the Computer Society of India, CSI Volume 2. Advances in Intelligent Systems and Computing,* (vol. 338, pp. 553-563). Springer. https://link.springer.com/chapter/10.1007/978-3-319-13731-5_60

Li, H., Zhang, X., & Tzou, H. (2017). Diagonal piezoelectric sensors on cylindrical shells. *Journal of Sound and Vibration*, *400*, 201–212. doi:10.1016/j.jsv.2017.03.039

Marie, A., Celebre, D., Benedict, I., Medina, A., Zandrae, A., Dubouzet, D., Neil, A., Surposa, M., & Gustilo, E. R. C. (2015). Home automation using Raspberry Pi through Siri enabled mobile devices. *Proc. 8th IEEE International Conference Humanoid, Nanotechnology, Information Technology Communication and Control, Environment and Management (HNICEM)*.

Nigam, A., Rastogi, R., Mishra, R., Arya, P., & Sharma, S. (2015). Security of Data Transmission Using Logic Gates and Crypt Analysis. *CSI Communication*, 17. http://www.csi-india.org/communications/CSI%20June15%20Combine.pdf

Nigam, A., Rastogi, R., Mishra, R., Arya, P., & Sharma, S. (2015).Security of data transmission using logic gates and crypt analysis. *Proceedings of 09th INDIACom; 2015 2nd International Conference on Computing for Sustainable Global Development*, 101-105. https://ieeexplore.ieee.org/document/7100229

Niua, J., Ganga, H., Zhangb, Y., & Duc, X. (2018). Relationship between automation trust and operator performance for the novice and expert in spacecraft rendezvous and docking (RVD). *Applied Ergonomics*, *35*(4), 1–8. doi:10.1016/j.apergo.2018.03.014 PMID:29764609

Qun, C., Mei, L., & Xinyu, L. (2018). Bike Fleet Allocation Models for Repositioning in Bike-Sharing Systems. *IEEE Intelligent Transportation Systems Magazine*, *10*(1), 19–29. doi:10.1109/MITS.2017.2776129

Rungta, S., Srivastava, S., Yadav, U. S., & Rastogi, R. (2014) A Comparative Analysis of New Approach with an Existing Algorithm to Detect Cycles in a Directed Graph. In *ICT and Critical Infrastructure: Proceedings of the 48th Annual Convention of Computer Society of India*. Springer. 10.1007/978-3-319-03095-1_5

Saquib, S. T., & Hameed, S. (2013). Wireless Control of Miniaturized Mobile Vehicle for Indoor Surveillance. *IOP Conference Series Material Science and Engineering*, *51*(3), 452-465. 10.1088/1757-899X/51/1/012025

Sharma, P., Rastogi, R., Aggarwal, S., Kaul, U., & Jain, S. (2014). Business Analysis and Decision Making Through Unsupervised Classification of Mixed Data Type of Attributes Through Genetic Algorithm. *BIJIT, 6*(1). http://bvicam.ac.in/bjit/issues.asp?issue=11

Sharma, R., Jain, A., & Rastogi, R. (2013). A New Face To Photo Security Of Facebook. *Proceedings of the Sixth International Conference on Contemporary Computing (IC3-2013)*. https://ieeexplore.ieee.org/document/6612231

Sharma, S., Rastogi, R., & Kumar, S. (2015). A revolutionary technology to help the differently abled person, *Proceedings of 09th INDIACom; 2015 2nd International Conference on Computing for Sustainable Global Development*. https://ieeexplore.ieee.org/document/7100324

Shekhar, S., Rastogi, R., & Mittal, S. (2015). Linear algorithm for Imbricate Cryptography using Pseudo Random Number Generator. *Proceedings of 09th INDIACom, pp. 89-94; 2015 2nd International Conference on Computing for Sustainable Global Development*. https://ieeexplore.ieee.org/document/7100227

Srivatava, S., Rastogi, R., Rungta, S., & Yadav, U. (2014). A Methodology to Find the Cycle in a Directed Graph Using Linked List. *BIJIT, 6*(2), 743-749. http://bvicam.ac.in/bjit/issues.asp?issue=12

Suresh, S., Yuthika, S., & Adityavardhini, G. (2016). *Home Based Fire Monitoring and Warning System*. Academic Press.

Zhang, L., & Wang, G. (2019). Design and Implementation of Automatic Fire Alarm System Based on Wireless Sensor Networks. *Proceedings of the International Symposium on Information Processing (ISIP'09)*, 410-413.

Zheng, S. R. (2011). The Internet of Things. *IEEE Communications Magazine, 11*, 30–31. doi:10.1109/MCOM.2011.6069706

ADDITIONAL READING

Lee, E. A., & Seshia, S. A. (2010). An Introductory Textbook on Cyber-Physical Systems, ACM. https://people.eecs.berkeley.edu/~sseshia/pubdir/IntroducingCPS.pdf

Sedigh, S., & Hurson, A. (2012)., CPS, Introduction and Preface, Advances in Computers. https://www.sciencedirect.com/topics/engineering/cyber-physical-systems

KEY TERMS AND DEFINITIONS

Artificial Intelligence: In computer science, artificial intelligence (AI), sometimes called machine intelligence, is intelligence demonstrated by machines, in contrast to the natural intelligence displayed by humans and animals. Leading AI textbooks define the field as the study of "intelligent agents": any device that perceives its environment and takes actions that maximize its chance of successfully achieving its goals.

Automated Security Systems: The smart home promises a futuristic home experience where everything you need is just a simple voice command away, even when you're far from home. Some very cool gadgets let you do a lot with home automation, many of which are incorporated into home security systems. These include smart doorbells, smart locks, smart cameras, smart thermostats, smart lights, and smart smoke alarms.

Big Data Analysis: Extremely large data sets that may be analyzed computationally to reveal patterns, trends, and associations, especially relating to human behavior and interactions.

Cyber-Physical System: It is a system in which a mechanism is controlled or monitored by computer-based algorithms. It includes autonomous automobile systems, robotics, automatic pilot avionics, and many more.

GSM Applications: The Global System for Mobile Communications (GSM) is a standard developed by the European Telecommunications Standards Institute (ETSI) to describe the protocols for second-generation (2G) digital cellular networks used by mobile devices such as mobile phones and tablets.

Home Automation: Home automation or domestics is building automation for a home, called a smart home or smart house. A home automation system will control lighting, climate, entertainment systems, and appliances. It may also include home security such as access control and alarm systems.

IoT-Automation: The Internet of things (IoT) is a system of interrelated computing devices, mechanical and digital machines provided with unique identifiers (UIDs) and the ability to transfer data over a network without requiring human-to-human or human-to-computer interaction.

Mobile Automation: Mobile automation, as the name suggests, refers to 'automation' that is done on mobile devices. Automation is the process whereby one automates the testing of an application - in this case, a mobile application - which can be a WAP site or an app. This can be done by using tools and helps in reducing the testing time cycle.

Piezoelectric Sensor: A piezoelectric sensor, also known as a piezoelectric transducer, is a device that uses the piezoelectric effect to measure changes in pressure, acceleration, temperature, strain, or force by converting these into an electrical charge. The prefix piezo is Greek for press or squeeze.

Smart Automation: Automation has never been more important than in today's business environment. The wave of digital transformation and evolution has created customer interactions that can happen at any time and in huge and unpredictable volumes. The rapid pace of market change means that agility is becoming an organizational survival skill, yet many organizations are suffering under a heavy load of legacy applications and associated manual processes.

Weighted Automata: Weighted finite automata (WFA) are finite automata whose transitions and states are augmented with some weights, elements of smearing.

Chapter 13
Applying a Methodology in Data Transmission of Discrete Events From the Perspective of Cyber–Physical Systems Environments

Reinaldo Padilha França
State University of Campinas (UNICAMP), Brazil

Yuzo Iano
State University of Campinas (UNICAMP), Brazil

Ana Carolina Borges Monteiro
State University of Campinas (UNICAMP), Brazil

Rangel Arthur
State University of Campinas (UNICAMP), Brazil

ABSTRACT

Most of the decisions taken in and around the world are based on data and information. Therefore, the chapter aims to develop a method of data transmission based on discrete event concepts, being such methodology named CBEDE, and using the MATLAB software, where the memory consumption of the proposal was evaluated, presenting great potential to intermediate users and computer systems, within an environment and scenario with cyber-physical systems ensuring more speed, transmission fluency, in the same way as low memory consumption, resulting in reliability. With the differential of this research, the results show better computational performance related to memory utilization with respect to the compression of the information, showing an improvement reaching 95.86%.

DOI: 10.4018/978-1-7998-5101-1.ch013

INTRODUCTION

Cyber-physical systems (CPS) are computer and collaborative systems, which consist of a combination of a software component with mechanical or electronic parts. Whose operations are monitored, coordinated, controlled, and integrated by communication and computing cores; such as control, monitoring, data transfer, and data exchange are generally performed via the internet in real-time. By analogy with the internet, which has transformed the way humans interact with each other. Cyber-physical systems transform how people interact with the physical world around them, in which it's possible to cite for example transportation, health, manufacturing, agriculture, livestock, energy, defense, buildings, and others. Bearing in mind that economically speaking, still, several challenges await overcomings (Shu et al, 2016, Chaâri et al, 2016, Xiong et al, 2015, Besselink et al, 2016, Shu et al, 2016, Chaâri et al, 2016, Liu et al, 2017).

Smart devices are making increasingly enhanced with expanded capabilities, and having as a positive factor that they are low-cost technologies. It is still considered that several of these smart devices rely on high-speed wireless networks, which can be used together with cellular networks 4G. Considering the advent of the Internet of Things (IoT), where each connected object can retrieve information from the environment, manage it, and share it with other devices or users. CPS creates an increasingly consistent synergistic environment (Tao et al, 2017, Jeschke et al, 2017).

Cyber-physical systems are a fundamental part of the 4.0 industry, just as they are important to robots, the Internet of Things, and networked machines, being clear and practical examples of cyber-physical systems. The IoT is a functional, distributed environment comprised of a variety of intelligent devices that detect the environment and can act on it, and with the assistance of the CPS. These devices have the efficiency of monitoring the external environment, collecting data and information about the real world, and generating an environment with ubiquitous computing allowing each connected device to communicate with other connected devices. IoT aims to make the Internet more comprehensive, resulting in the devices being interconnected and collaborating, working either as single sensors or as a set of sensors. Thereby creating intelligent macro term signals that can act as whole systems (Tao et al, 2017, Hermann et al, 2016, Lee et al, 2015).

CPSs are used wherever complex physical systems require communication with the digital world allowing optimization and efficiency in their performance, which play an important and growing role in the industrial process and in the production control (creating intelligent factory). In particular in the context of the IIoT (Industrial Internet of Things), and are also used in energy supply, traffic control, and transport assistance, assisting drivers and operators, as well as in the range of several other areas (Lee et al, 2015, Wang et al, 2015).

As already said, a cyber-physical system is a system composed of collaborative computational elements, integrations of computation, networking, and physical processes. Which includes sensors and components to move or control a mechanism or system, the actuators. Allowing the system to acquire and process the data to connect the CPS to the outside world to control physical entities with economic and societal potential impact. Where such data is made available to the network-based services that use these actuators to directly impact the measurements made in the real world. Leading to the merging of the physical and cyberspace worlds into the Internet of Things (Lee et al, 2015, Mosterman & Zander, 2016).

The computing elements articulate, chain, communicate, interconnect, and relate with digital sensors, interconnecting all the structures distributed intelligent in the environment to achieve deeper knowledge. Thus, allowing a more precise action, monitoring the actuators, and even the virtual and physical indicators, that modify the virtual environment and physical in which they are executed, within a CPS. The generation predecessor of the CPS is known as embedded systems. Where they have been applied in diverse areas such as energy, health, manufacturing, transportation, automotive, aerospace, chemical processes, entertainment, civil infrastructure, as well as client and consumer applications. However, in this phase of embedded systems, the focus was more on the computational elements, while CPS focuses and emphasizes the role of the connections between the computational elements and physical elements. Creating the link and the integration of the dynamics of the physical processes with those of the software and networking, through abstractions and modeling, design, and analysis techniques as a whole (Lee & Seshia, 2016, Hehenberger, et al, 2016).

CPS leverages advances in a customized way in health care, traffic flow management, emergency response, electric power generation, and even delivery services, as well as in several other areas. Making real the relationship and interaction by human components engineered for function through integrated physics and logic. Extending the Internet of Things (IoT), Industrial Internet, Smart Cities, Smart Grid, where the term "smart" can be Anything (ranging from cars, buildings, homes, hospitals, to manufacturing itself). In a physical scenario, digital actuators act, collect and modify the environment in which common users live. In the virtual scenario, CPS is employed to collect information and data from users' virtual activities, covering their iterations in social networks, virtual blogs, or even e-commerce sites, and may respond in some pre-configured manner to the data to make predictions about the actions or needs of digital users (Hermann et al, 2016, Lee et al, 2015, Zhang et al, 2015).

Viewing the historical context, the terminology "cyber-physical systems" emerged in mid-2006, by Helen Gill, through the NSF (National Science Foundation), the US government agency. However, its roots are older and deeper, coming from understanding through the correlation of terms "Cyberspace" and "cyber-physical systems". In the same way as "cybernetics" (coined by Norbert Wiener, an American mathematician, who had a huge interest in the development of control systems theory), rather than viewing one as being derived from the other (Nakajima et al, 2017, Zheng et al, 2016).

In simple terms, the cyber-physical system is the interconnection of cyber means virtual and physical means real systems. Combining digital and analog devices, interfaces, networks, computer systems, and the like, with the natural and man-made physical world, using three basics technologies which are Embedded Systems, Sensor and actuation, and Network and Communication System (IoT). Creating an inherent interconnected and heterogeneous combination of behaviors in these systems, which takes real-time data smartly from the physical system and its environment with the help of sensors, actuators, among others. And then gives a real-time signal command to the actuator of the desired work, result in Smart Home, Smart Grid, for example (Cintuglu et al, 2016, Song et al, 2017).

A couple of real applications of CPS include in a manufacturing scenario, they can refine processes by sharing real-time data and information across industry machines. Providing a greater degree of visibility and control over manufacturing supply chains, suppliers, business systems, and customers, improving the traceability and safety of goods. Already in a health scenario, they can be used to monitor in real-time and remotely the physical conditions of patients, improve treatments for invalid and elderly patients. Also used in neuroscience research to better comprehend human functions with therapeutic robotics and interfaces support brain-machine, for example (Tao et al, 2017, Jeschke et al, 2017, Lee et al, 2015, Wang et al, 2015).

In a renewable energy scenario, digital sensors and other intelligent devices monitor the network to handle it and manage greater reliability by improving energy effectiveness. In a scenario for cities, they can be applied to smart buildings, with intelligent devices and CPSs interacting to decrease energy consumption. Increasing security and environmental protection (being able to determine the extent of damages in possible suffering after unforeseen events and helping to avoid structural failures), affecting in increasing the comfort of the residents. An example of an application with a global scenario in Europe and North America, which has almost all critical infrastructure in cyber-physical systems electricity production and distribution, ventilation systems in tunnels, drinking water production, subways, house and sports arenas, trains, aircraft, and so on (Cintuglu et al, 2016, Arghandeh et al, 2016, Moness & Moustafa, 2015).

In the transportation scenario, there may be communication between individual vehicles and infrastructure, sharing real-time data and information on traffic, or even vehicle location, thereby preventing accidents or congestion, resulting in time and money savings. CPS also can be applied in an agricultural setting, collecting key information on climate, land, and other data types to create more precise systems of agricultural management, resulting in better use of resources, generating improvements in irrigation, soil moisture, plant health, among others. In a computational scenario, CPSs can interact with applications to optimize them to work with users' contexts and actions or to monitor available resources, driving virtual environments to better understand the system and user behaviors. In the same way, they can be applied to the analysis of information stored on e-commerce websites and even popular social networks visited by users, trying to make predictions about interests and even make recommendations from links, digital friends, pages, posts, or even products (Xiong et al, 2015, Besselink et al, 2016).

The overcoming brought and surpassed by the cyber-physical systems, which allow a broad and modern vision for the new services of society, which is based on the exchange of information between the cyber world where information is exchanged and transformed. And the physical world in which people live and digital processes take place, possibly they are conducive to transcending the scales of time and space. Today's technology enables digital crowdsourcing, distributed computing, information sharing among digital users, and the development of collective intelligence, which is one of the factors to the achievement of CPSs and Smart Cities concept. Which utilizes digital crowdsensing for the cooperative supervision of the urban environment and the collective operation of the action in the accomplishment of tasks of common interest in an efficient manner, creating a sensing infrastructure with a dynamic capacity of topology, self-adjusting. That allows the functioning of a system with an efficiency of performance, that has an acquisition of data accurate and reliable processes, machines, and components (Cintuglu et al, 2016, Song et al, 2017, Ahmad et al, 2016).

Based on all the cited aspects, this research promotes the objective to implement the DES (Discrete Event Simulation) based model, designate CBEDE (Coding of Bits for Entities employing Discrete Events) to refine the transmission of data and information in digital communication systems. Using modulation format DQPSK (Differential Quadrature Phase Shift Keying) employing Rician Fading, which can be employed in environments with Cloud technology and Big Data in environments and scenarios with CPS application. Improving the digital transmission of data, athwart a pre-coding process of bits employing discrete events in the digital signal before the modulation step. It is DES an effective tool with capacity for a broad variety of communication problems since discrete event relates with the modeling of the system as a sequence of operations performed on entities (transactions) such as data packets, bits, that is, the very exchange of data and information. So, will be discussed the conception of methodologies that collaborate with the deployment of the CBEDE methodology.

The present chapter is organized as follows: Section Big data in Cyber-Physical Systems argue about data volume technology within the CPS topic, Section Cloud Computing in Cyber-Physical Systems addresses the mobile technology within the CPS topic. Following the flow of the chapter in Section Big data and Cloud Computing, highlights the technologies for joint operation and harmony, Section Discrete Events and Entities discusses the technology employed in the research. Section AWGN Channel and Rician Fading discuss the behavior of Fading in digital transmission, Section Differential Quadrature Phase Shift Keying (DQPSK) examines the modulation format employed. Following the text, in Section Methodology it is argued concerning the framework, showing the modeling of transmission channel AWGN, describing the proposed structure based on the discrete event. Thus, in Section Results, it explains the outcome and profit and benefit of research, and in Section Future Research Directions it deals with the continuing search for research and, finally, in Section Conclusions, the observations and findings are explored as also the potential of the research addressed.

Big Data in Cyber-Physical Systems

In the current and modern days, CPS exists and is present everywhere contextualizing in distinguished sizes, with distinctive functionalities, characteristics, and properties, as witnessing the growth of CPS technology. Where along with the Internet of Things (IoT) is rapidly developing technologies that are transforming our society, through Big Data technology, which is foreseen to revolutionize our world, creating new services and applications in a variety of sectors as seen previously. Data is incredibly important for most modern factories in the world. Thus the analysis of these data will measure every step of a factory flow and determine the potential theoretical bottlenecks at any step of the process, allowing them to optimally determine what they need to solve, expand and improve (Lee et al, 2015, Babiceanu, & Seker, 2016, Xu & Duan, 2019).

A diversity of sensors and actuators inspect the actions and interactions in the physical world, which results in data, where they are directed to the cyber world, are examined to the state of the physical world. And generating the respective digital portrayal of the physical entities, such digital representation is employed to derive knowledge respective the state of the physical world from the perspective of analysis. The Big Data domain refers to how intelligently and efficiently, to mine such data to filter them and infer trends, patterns, and projections as accurate as possible (Babiceanu, & Seker, 2016, Xu & Duan, 2019, Ochoa et al, 2017).

Advances in wireless communication, in computing and sensing devices, along with the cost reduction of these technologies, had a vast and positive effect. Which is a certain accelerated aspect of the evolution of CPS that embracing the IoT digital paradigm providing sundry types of services as weather monitoring, digital surveillance, vehicular traffic management, control of production activities, among others. Thus, the employment of these technologies results in a volume of fine-grained data, which needs to be processed, correlated, and interrelated. Generally demanding large data analytics for the extraction of useful knowledge that can be used by the software services which control these systems (Watteyne et al, 2016, Burg et al, 2017, Lu et al 2015).

The data produced in CPS related to the observations obtained by digital sensor devices that are associated with the environmental environment, i.e. those able to be handled by computational processes of the digital cyber world. In the same sense, relating the crescent utilization of social networks offering near real-time digital users sensing properties as a complementary, where CPS can be used to help understand the real world, and provide proactive digital services to those users. Thus, there is a growing trend in CPS along with a need to integrate with Big-Data applications in the form of data gathering or data analysis (Negri et al, 2017, Mourtzis et al, 2016).

CPS today is more and more present applied in our daily life and business process management, and tomorrow's CPS needs to far exceed the systems of today's capability, adaptability, resiliency, safety, usability, and security, where their data volume needs to have such characteristics. The world where human beings live and do business relies mostly on how to intelligently and correctly use Big Data and how to retrieve useful information from the massive data. Where Big Data comes in being used in large, complex, or rapidly generated, is because of the multitude of constantly flowing data streams coming from many sources every day. To understand that volume of big data requires cutting-edge tools and techniques that can analyze and extract useful knowledge (Lee, 2015, Biffl et al, 2017).

A large volume of data related to several challenges which include effective data collection, cleaning and storage, data latency, and real-time analytics. So, Big Data Analytics has become an essential component for extracting value from data. The own nature of CPPS (Cyber-Physical Social System) data introduces new commitments and challenges to distinct stages of data manipulation, comprising its processing of data sources, identification of data sources, and even fusion of distinct types and scales of data. Smart cities are an obvious example of CPSS technology, related to low-cost digital sensors, citizens sharing, government initiatives, and even interchange and exchange city-related digital messages on social networks. Still considering the wide volume of data by the digitally sensing of physical events due to spread sensor networks along with those collaborated by sensor-enabled smartphones, offering near real-time data large-scale sensing. Big Data enters into intelligence mining to assist intelligent and responsive services in urban settings, extracting knowledge and information out of the data. Through technology and analytics techniques, forming the digital picture of urban dynamics, relating and having properties to guide the decision-making of both city inhabitants and city authorities (Xue & Yu, 2017, Cassandras, 2016).

It is true and knows that today a huge volume of industrial data for CPS exists, in this way Big Data analytics and information processing in CPS, can realize the knowledge and information extraction from the large sensing data in CPS. And other aspects as fundamental security and privacy, producing in urban big data system endowed the potential of creating more tenable, sustainable, and digitally environment-friendly related future cities, for example (Negri et al, 2017, Biffl et al, 2017).

Cloud Computing in Cyber-Physical Systems

CPS depicts digital systems relating computations tightly related and coupled to the physical world in which people live, together with the physical data that form the core component that propels and fuels that computation. Even so, CPS has a limited aspect, concerning computation and storage properties, concerning their tiny size and the use embedded into larger systems. However, with the emergence of cloud computing, there are opportunities to extend their capabilities by utilizing the advantages of cloud resources concerning the remote brain, big data manipulation, and virtualization. Where cloud computing has brought a major revolution with tremendous cost reductions related to the domain of non-real-time software development and therefore its execution (Shu et al, 2016, Chaâri et al, 2016).

There are cloud computing tools available that analyze, generate, and extract actionable intelligence from your data set. In the same way that to store and process the data, using cloud computing technology in CPS becomes a natural choice, where CPS joined Cloud, are considered the core technology of industry 4.0. Due to the main characteristic of cloud computing is the isolation of the application software from the underlying hardware infrastructure. Where software components can be executed flexibly on different hardware configurations, and in a scalable way (Lee et al, 2015, Wang et al, 2015, Shu et al, 2016, Chaâri et al, 2016).

Monitoring the traffic flow or power consumption in a large housing society, or monitoring the air quality of a large city, requires a strong IT infrastructure. Where the properties Cloud computing offers the opportunity of rapidly build, modify and provision CPS is composed of a set of cloud computing-based sensors, processing, control, and data services that allow the creation of such desired infrastructure. Cloud has abundant resources, essentially resource scarcity of physical worlds, allowing to store and to process data, where have been quite successful in integrating several applications areas comprise resource virtualization, on-demand data centers, storage, remote processing, and even big data analytics. As well as offering different categories of services to end-users, making both Cloud computing and CPS technologies complement each other with synergy and Harmony (Xiong et al, 2015, Besselink et al, 2016, Shu et al, 2016, Chaâri et al, 2016).

Thus, as previously elucidated, there has been an increasing interest in aggregating the Cloud properties into CPS technology. What has led to the emergence of new research areas such as cloud robotics, sensor clouds, and even vehicular clouds. Bringing benefits of CPS with Cloud Computing in the efficient use of resources, rapid development, and scalability as well as smart adaptation to the environment at every scale (Yue et al, 2015).

Big Data and Cloud Computing

Big Data is composed of 3 Vs being Volume, Speed, and Variety, due to the need to work with an infrastructure that allows the storage and retrieval of data of various formats at a high scale. Being a technology that uses solutions based on algorithms that capture and cross-data organized, regardless of systems such as ERP (Enterprise Resource Planning) that deal with business management, CRM (Customer Relationship Management) that do customer relationship management, BI (Business Intelligence) relating business intelligence. That is, reaching data not structured as content in various formats, such as videos, images, photos, which are produced mainly by social networks (Shoro & Soomro, 2015, Bajaj & Johari, 2016).

Cloud Computing consists of being the model that provides a set of computing resources conveniently, with on-demand access to the network and that can be quickly provisioned and released with management or interaction of the service provider. In simple terms is the offer of "computing as a service", it is not necessary to have a computer to be able to process and store data, this is the basis of the concept of Cloud Computing. If it is a technology that allows the creation and storage of data, online applications (in the cloud), being more advantageous for the user insofar as it is a scalable service, which is provided on demand, ie, is used as it does require (Rittinghouse & Ransome, 2016).

The relationship between Cloud Computing and Big Data is narrow, where the first is the infrastructure that, in a corporate environment, supports the second, which has enough capacity to process data in large numbers. The connection between these concepts is because to deal with Big Data, an infrastructure is needed that allows the storage, processing, and retrieval of the most varied types of data on a large scale, that is, it has a constant growth. As is well known, there are significant advantages in adopting Cloud Computing concerning traditional physical deployments. However, cloud platforms have several structures and sometimes need to be integrated with traditional architectures, because depending on the provider, its services computing works differently (Rittinghouse & Ransome, 2016, Assunção et al, 2015).

The processing and storage of a considerable amount of data require a good infrastructure, which is also capable of converting this data into valuable information for the company, where much of the Big Data applications interact with the data that is generated and stored online. The more Cloud Computing improves, the more it is a precursor and facilitator for the advent of Big Data, where although technology provides efficient data storage, collection, sharing, research, analysis, and even visualization (Assunção et al, 2015, You et al, 2015).

So the advantage of applying the two concepts simultaneously in business operations is that they help to reduce costs since cloud platforms are growing at an accelerated pace. Also, see an explosion in data generation where humanity has never generated so much data as in modern and current days, and the growth of data volume is exponential and constant. And so Big Data is the intelligence to search in that deep and extensive sea of information that is present in the cloud (Internet), being that the Cloud Computing is the cloud itself, having its devices dispersed throughout the planet for persistence and storage of the data being able to host information in various digital formats. Finally, Cloud Computing and Big Data are an ideal combination because together they provide a solution that is scalable and adaptable to large data sets and business analysis. In this sense, provided the advantage of the analysis brings a great benefit to the company, climbing as the needs of the business itself, avoiding unnecessary costs (Akter et al, 2016).

Discrete Events and Entities

The discrete simulation is characterized by events where the changes occur in a discontinuous way, that is, they undergo sudden changes. In this way, discrete events fit into a large diversity of communication cases, employed to model and represent the system as a digital sequence of operations through entities (transactions) of particular types such as data frame, data packets, or even bits. Being these are related to the consequence of actions taken in a system, which can be categorized as an occurrence accountable for the transition in the state of the digital system in which they act. In this sense, generating state changes at aleatory intervals of time, producing data, and therefore the digital knowledge and information (Cassandras & Lafortune, 2009, Artuso & Christiansen, 2014, Dammasch & Horton, 2008).

System state changes occur as events occur, events, in turn, occur at discrete points in time, presenting the same dynamic and stochastic behavior that a real system represents. Thus, the scope of actions that the technique of discrete events encompasses is subjective and is directly linked to the scenario in which the digital system is being modeled, where it has been utilized, and is used to model concepts with a high level of abstraction. That is doctors and patients in a healthcare context, the exchange of emails on a server to transmission, data packets between devices connected in a network. A notorious fact is that the technique is very robust in its abstraction, which can be applied in the broad context of a communication system, in more specific character in the transmission of data in a digital channel (Cassandras & Lafortune, 2009, Artuso & Christiansen, 2014, Dammasch & Horton, 2008).

These entities are discrete in discrete event simulation, are the consequence of actions that occur in the digital system, and can be intentional, of controlled spontaneous occurrence or with the verification of a condition. Where they usually produce state changes at random time intervals, being defined as discrete items of interest in a discrete event simulation, being its meaning depends on what is being modeled and the type of system used. It is important to emphasize a difference between the concepts of entities (is an instantaneous or discrete occurrence that can modify the state variable (output). In the same sense, that an incidence from another event, relatively) and events (is someway subordinate on what is modeled and the type of digital system, a conceptual idea that denotes a state alteration in a digital system) (Cassandras & Lafortune, 2009, Artuso & Christiansen, 2014, Dammasch & Horton, 2008).

AWGN Channel and Rician Fading

The communication digital channel is the medium accountable in which it supplies the physical link between receivers and transmitters, whether the wire or even due to a logical connection in a multiplexed medium. However, there is noise, which is to be a change in some of the characteristics of the signal transmitted by another signal external to the transmission system, or generated by the transmission systems themselves. Often due to the existence of disturbances in own channel of free space/atmosphere, where for many of the cases, the noise can be produced by the own equipment used to implement the systems of transmission, like amplifiers used in receivers and repeaters, the which produces noise, of thermal origin. It can also be by multiple causes, such as fading, related to the oscillation of the attenuation of the digital signal with several variables, including geographical position, time, and even radiofrequency. Where, unlike interference, these unwanted signals are random, it is not possible to predict their value at a future time instant. And since this noise is the result of a random process, it must be described and treated with statistical methodology. Thus, there must be modeling that is authentic and faithful to what exists in the real world, where the widely employed model to a wide set of physical channels is the Additive White Gaussian Noise (AWGN) channel. With the characteristic of modeling and representing statistically these types of noise, into the transmitted digital signals (Bossert, 1999, Lakshmanan & Nikookar, 2006, Barnela & Kumar, 2014).

The fading of a digital channel can be apportioned into large-scale fading, where the attenuation of the average power occurs or the loss in the digital signal path related to the displacement of the receiver upon large areas. As well as small-scale fading where it occurs related to a significant alteration in phase, amplitude, and angle of arrival of the digital signal due to minor changes in receptor position. The multiple replicas of the transmitted digital signal can succeed with distinct attenuations and consequently distinct delays to the receiver, which are summed in its antenna. Where fading by multipath affects the signal by scattering (time scattering or frequency selectivity) as well as by time-varying acting. So, Rician Fading is used when the dominant component of the received signal is stationary, i.e., when there is a normally found in channels with a line of sight, having a predominance of it, or the dominant route (Bossert, 1999, Lakshmanan & Nikookar, 2006, Barnela & Kumar, 2014).

Differential Quadrature Phase Shift Keying Modulation Format (DQPSK)

Determined by 4 feasible states 0, π, $+ \pi/2$, $-\pi/2$, relating that each symbol depicts two bits of information and shifted to about $\pi/4$ or $\pi/2$, totaling 8 status positions. The DQPSK (Differential Quadrature Phase Shift Keying) modulation format is a specific form of QPSK (Quadrature Phase Shift Keying). Whereas an alternative of being a symbol matching to a genuine phase parameter, this one depicts a phase variation. In this case, the set of bits depicted by a symbol generates a particular phase variation in the carrier signal, being that in the carrier, the corresponding bits related to data (symbols) are established associated on the phase alteration of the previous symbol (Venghaus & Grote, 2017, Zhou & Xie, 2016, Padilha et al, 2018).

Thus, as explained later, the DQPSK constellation (Figure 6), for the displaced version $\pi/4$, as well as its constellation rotated by 45° from the previous point, is also largely utilized in several airborne digital systems in association with other modulation technologies. Being also utilized for long-distance wireless digital communication, in cellular communication the WLAN 11a, 11b, 11g, 11n, CDMA, WiMAX (16d, 16e), satellite, DVB, among others. Which resists the crusty number of channel fading or even the most diverse channel conditions, employed by most of the cell phone towers for long-distance digital communication and also a digital transmission of the data (Venghaus & Grote, 2017, Zhou & Xie, 2016, Padilha et al, 2018).

METHODOLOGY DEVELOPED

Through a simulation environment comprising in a hardware platform with a configuration consisting of the Intel Core i3 processor with 4GB RAM, the methodology was developed. This tool was designed to imitate cloud environments and at the same time proposing improvements. Research also employed the DQPSK modulation format applied to the model modeling the digital communication system, improving the digital transmission of data, through a pre-coding process of bits applying discrete events in the digital signal before the modulation procedure. In the same step as in this simulated environment, Simulink of the MATLAB software (2014a) was employed.

Due to the consolidation of this platform simulation in the scientific medium, it was the reason for his choice. Still considering your libraries for development to be validated. Similarly, due to being assessed as a robust of modulation schemes concerning issues of noise immunity, immunity to interference, the DQPSK format was used in this study.

Still describing the development, 4 libraries were used:

[1] Communications System to model dynamic communication systems, to simulate, design, and analyze digital systems.
[2] DSP System is related to designing and simulating digital systems with digital signal processing.
[3] Simulink containing block diagrams related to multi-domain simulation for modeling of telecommunication digital systems.
[4] SimEvents related to discrete event simulation mechanism while containing the components to develop digital systems oriented to particular events.

Demonstrating the viability of bit 0 treatment, previous research (Padilha et al, 2018, França et al, 2018, Padilha et al, 2018) and (Padilha, 2018), showed significant achievements in the compression of the transmitted digital information. At the same time that jointly achieved a decrease in processing time, according to simulation. In this scenario, the proposal (CBEDE) grounded on the promotion of an AWGN hybrid digital channel, determined by the employment of the discrete event technique in the bit (focusing on both bits) generation process.

In the proposal (CBEDE) (Figure 1) the digital signals concerning bits will be generated and modulated in DQPSK. It will then follow an AWGN channel by the defined parameters (Table 01). The digital signal will then be demodulated and the Bit Error Rate (BER) calculus of the digital channel will be calculated. These values related to BER will be transmitted to the Matlab workspace, for equality verification and production of the BER graph.

The proposal-related modeling is similar to the model presented in Figure 1, differentiating that in the proposal (CBEDE), discrete events modeling in the pre-coding step is increased. The bits precoding

Figure 1. Traditional model of a telecommunication system

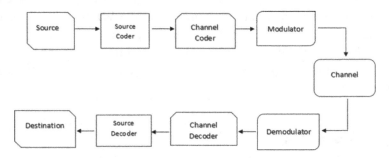

is understood as the discrete event methodology (proposed) in the step of generating signal bits (digital information) making it more suitable for a specific application.

The event-based digital signal is susceptible to manipulation by the SimEvents, which submits the conversion to the particular format for handling by the Simulink. Taking into account that both time-based digital signals and after event-based digital signals were in the time domain. Due treatment on emphasis on both bits, by generating as a discrete entity according to the parameters (Table 1). And so, Entity Sink demonstrates the conclusion respective to the modeling of discrete events by SimEvents.

Entity Sink is accountable by mark a certain point in the modeling, which ends the performance of discrete events. Which this signal (event-based signal) after is converted to a format according to the time-based digital signal. This conversion (employing the Real-World Value (RWV) function, and after rounding as per floor function) is derived from the need to obtain a particular type, an integer (bit). Also applying to a Zero-Order Hold (ZOH) suitable for discrete samples at regular intervals, which portray the effect of converting a digital signal to the time domain, requiring its reconstruction and maintaining each sample value respective for a specific time interval (Figure 2).

Figure 2. Proposed bit precoding

Posteriorly, the digital signal is modulated with the DQPSK and is introduced into the AWGN channel, and then demodulated to calculate the BER of the signal. which these values relative to BER, will then be calculated in the Matlab workspace, to equality validation and production of the BER graph, as illustrated in Figure 3.

Figure 3. Modeling of a digital telecommunication system employing the proposal (CBEDE))

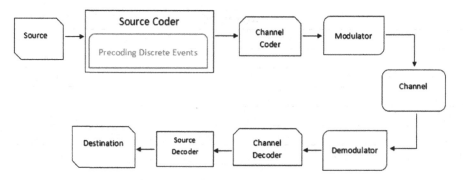

In the proposal (CBEDE) illustrated by Figures 1 and 3, the digital signals related to bits will be produced, taking into account the rule and mathematical logic illustrated in Figure 4.

Figure 4. Mathematical logic for generation M-ary numbers for bits

$$[0, M - 1] > [0, 2 - 1] > 0, 1$$

This rule and mathematical logic concerning PSK M-ary numbers generate randomly distributed integers in the interval [0, M-1], where M is the definition for bit representation, following the nomenclature of the MATLAB software. Figure 5 shows the respective generation of the bits utilizing this logic.

Figure 5. Traditional model of a telecommunication system

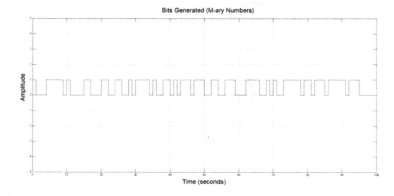

The related model's Figures 1 and 3 are executed according to 10000 seconds of simulation, still considering configuration defined according to parameters (Table 1).

Table 1. Parameters digital channel DQPSK rician

AWGN DQPSK		
Sample Time		1 sec
Simulation time		10000 sec
Eb/N0		0 a 12 dB
Symbol period		1 sec
Input signal power		1 watt
Initial seed in the generator	37	
The initial seed on the channel	67	

The validation of equality of the digital signals is attainable through the "size" and "isequal" functions of the Matlab, which are accountable for the mathematically proving that the digital signals have the same length and the size, also by BER, stating that the same amount of digital information will be transmitted (bits) in both the proposal (CBEDE) and the conventional methodology (AWGN channel). Thus, this verification will show that the proposal (CBEDE) does not add or even delete information to the originally transmitted digital signal.

The constellation aggregates as a function that performs analysis on both digital signals transmitted by the systems modeling. Given the DQPSK constellation, the signal can shift between + 45° or -45° related in phase during transmission. And still, retain the correct encoded information when demodulated at the receiver, the input signal alters its state, the constellation of the digital signal will have 8 points separated by 45°. This validation methodology has as function to affirm that the proposal (CBEDE) will not modify the number of bits transmitted by the signal. Since both signals transmitted in the conventional channel and the channel containing the proposal of this study (CBEDE), will be of the same size. In Figure 6 the DBPSK constellation diagram.

Figure 6. Theoretical DQPSK constellation

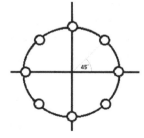

RESULTS AND DISCUSS

The Figure 7 incorporates the traditional modeling (left) and the proposal (CBEDE) of this research (right), showing digital signal transmission flow (relating to bits), produced and modulated in DQPSK by the AWGN channel. Regarding Figure 8, both constellations are shown according to 22 dB for the proposal (CBEDE) (left) and the traditional modeling (right).

Figure 7. Transmission flow DQPSK rician

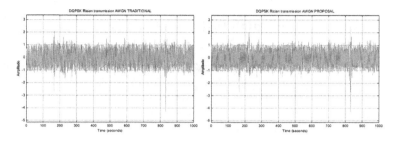

Figure 8. DQPSK Rician constellations according to simulation

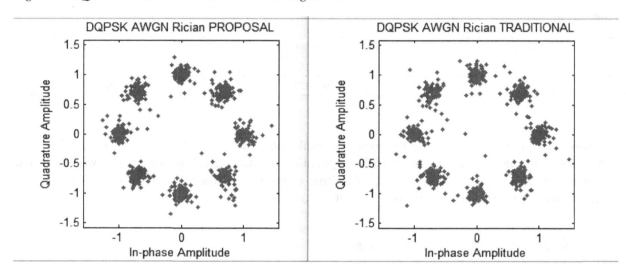

Both implemented models were examined according to the perspective of memory consumption. This assessment was made according to the analysis of the first simulation, as this is where the construction of the model in a virtual environment is performed from scratch occurs. Or even the portion of memory for the operating system is reserved for the execution, while the allocation of all the variables of the model occurs. Emphasizing the imitation of a real environment according to evaluation parameters.

Thus, the experiments considered concerning the memory calculation, calculating the total in MB (megabyte), the "sldiagnostics" function, discriminating the "TotalMemory" variable, which receives the sum of all the memory consumption processes used through the "ProcessMemUsage "parameter. The platform (Intel Core i3 and other features) chosen for the simulation is consistent with the dynamics of the real world, affirming efficiency, viability, and even applicability of the proposal (CBEDE). Two simulations of each model were then carried out, as displayed in Figure 9.

As fundamental as elaborating the methodology is an improvement of the transmission of a digital signal that demonstrates better performance, is to make the know-how available to the academic community. As well as to contribute to the area of study of the proposal (CBEDE) as well as the theme that this chapter deals with.

The respective amounts of memory consumption shown in Figure 9 are found previously are in Table 2:

Figure 9. Analysis of the first simulations concerning memory consumed by DQPSK Rician models

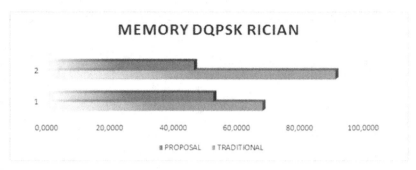

Table 2. Memory consumption

Simulation	TRADITIONAL	CBEDE
1	68,0781	52,5508
2	91,0820	46,5039

Still evaluating the relationship between the simulation of both models (proposal (CBEDE) x conventional), and analyzing their impact on the physical layer of the digital channel, scripts were prepared for treatment and exposition of the graph for BER (Figure 10) showing performance during digital transmission with noise varying from 0 to 12 dB.

Figure 10. BER related to models DQPSK Rician

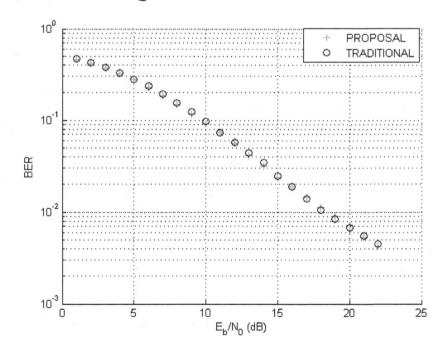

Cloud Computing (organizes all the data storage, making it possible and at the same step simplifying the routine) and Big Data are two technologies that are modifying the form businesses perform its functions. In this respect, this facilitates the use of Big Data technology which provides the capacity to deal with a huge volume of data. Both technologies act as a form of dematerialization, being accessible to any digital user with access to the internet. Thus, countless benefits are realized for any digital user who makes use of these two technological concepts, which are distinct from each other but relate (or connect) to one another.

Much of the information that is generated and searched currently is in the network. At all times that the people search for something that interests in the search engines, they perform different tasks through electronic devices, and purchase products online, and many other activities that somehow involve the use of the internet. Most of the decisions taken in and around the world are based on data and information. All these data, when in the hands of a company, become a valuable insight into the behavior of your target audience. All of this information can bring valuable insights and are eventually used to bring improvements and guide new decisions, so Big Data represents this ability to access the information and use it in favor of the business.

This proposal (CBEDE) brings a new approach for digital transmission carried out in the discrete domain through the employment of discrete entities in the step bit generation. Given the above context, discrete events can be employed in this way due to its conversion property in discrete entities. It is also worth mentioning that this approach resulted in a methodology employed in a lower level of application, acting on the physical layer of a digital transmission channel. Since commonly discrete events are used in the transport layer of systems. Still highlighting that the proposal (CBEDE) was able to cause a reduction in consumption of computational resources, i.e., memory, consisting of is an essential parameter that meets the current needs of the modern technological world.

Evaluating that that velocity is a factor when choosing a methodology, whether it is in use by companies, or universities, or even end-user, the proposal of this chapter (CBEDE) can be evaluated as the important allied to systems that employ Cloud technology. Considering that it is fundamental to endorse systems to perform intermediation between the cloud platform and end-users. Reflecting on this approach, the outcomes achieved by the proposal was 95.86% in the improvement of memory consumption.

Another essential issue is linked to data digital transmission for the memory consumption of the device. Since nowadays the cloud platforms are linked to mobile devices and mobile phones, said that they are related to the mobility that it provides to users. And the proposal (CBEDE) is used on these platforms, for improving the performance of ordinary tasks such as uploading or even sharing files, or even save their files in their "personal cloud".

Thus, to propose improvements and generate greater reliability, for slowness in communication-related to the velocity of Cloud platforms employed in the structure of a digital system, the proposal (CBEDE) demonstrate a lower memory consumption (95.86%) in digital data transmission, which obtained better results than the traditional methodologies that do not require the use of discrete events.

As discussed earlier, in cyber-physical system (CPS) environments, the elements of computation are coordinated and communicated employing sensors, which perform monitoring virtual and physical indicators, and even actuators, modifying the physical and virtual environment in which they are executed. These digital sensors associate all distributed intelligence in the digital environment to acquire a deeper understanding of the context in which they are appointed. In a physical scenario, actuators act, operate and transform the environment in which users are present. In this way, CPSs act on the data collected, to predict the actions or even needs of the digital users.

However, connecting a large number of devices simultaneously and in real-time can generate overloads in the system, generate crashes, and possible decreases in system accuracy. When a system crashes, it causes great annoyances to its users. This action removes the users from the systems since the speed and usability are primordial criteria for the use of any type of system. In this context the CBEDE methodology can be used in conjunction with CPS and IoT systems, aiming for a faster connection, accurate and secure data in real-time, because the proposed model presents low memory consumption. It is important to note that many times, the locking is due to the total or almost total occupation of the system during connection, transmission, and/or data analysis.

Employing the CBEDE to CPS may be a greater attraction of users who deal with the analysis of large daily data flow, such as e-commerce, application-based services, and social media marketing. In any of these scenarios, many people connect simultaneously and in real-time to the same system and want to get results quickly and accurately, such as finding the best price and the best product according to your need. At the same time, these platforms often capture data that is capable of profiling customers, aiming to optimize the experience in a certain platform. Therefore, when a large part of the server memory is guaranteed through the CBEDE methodology, the platform can meet both the needs of the entrepreneur and the client in a brief time.

FUTURE RESEARCH DIRECTIONS

Future research related to the proposal of this chapter comprise simulations on a bigger variety of hardware platform, that is, test the methodology in other architectures like Intel i5 and i7 Processors. Since these physical platforms are popular in the market nowadays. In the same way as performing digital data transmission tests via mobile devices, related to its increasingly mobile technological popularization, this mode of communication will be more present even more in recent years.

CONCLUSION

The technological evolution that the Internet of Things, Big Data, Cloud, and CPSs in particular, brings to the daily life of people, which increases the quality of services, is increasingly adopted. Improving efficiency, effectiveness, and safety in offices and homes, due to monitoring, inspect and controlling heat, cold, and humidity, for example. Also, supporting elderly people living alone, using non-intrusive wearable sensors or detectors installed in the house, to detect illness or accidents, and playing an alarm automatically. In the same sense, monitoring safety and movements of passengers in a public transport system, or of vehicles on a road. In agriculture optimizing crop yield and reducing pesticide and fertilizer use, identifying and delivering them only where they are needed; implementing intelligent, efficient production systems and manufacturing lines in the industry.

In the same way as monitoring and tracking shipments intelligently for optimal logistics and stock control. As well as collecting environmental data to support decision-making and public policy-setting, generating warnings of environmental threats such as wildfires, earthquakes, and volcanic eruptions. All of which are joint uses with CPS, where is seen and noticed their enormous extent of action in society. Where CPSs have great competence to change and refine every characteristic of people's lives more and more over time. And outperforming nowaday's distributed systems in terms of efficiency, security, usability, performance, reliability, breaking the critical challenges facing society.

Thus, this chapter has demonstrated that proposal (CBEDE) has broad competence in the improvement of digital communication services. Since the differential is in the employment of discrete events implemented in the physical layer of a transmission medium (channel), that is bit itself, assessing a low-level of abstraction. Which demonstrated better computational performance associated with memory utilization for the compression of the information of 95.86%. Directly connected cloud computing services and Big Data, due to the flow of data will consume fewer computational resources. And, thereby, it is possible to improve the operations between the connected devices, being connected to the CPS, with effects in the most varied types of businesses that use this type of technology in the most varied personalized schemes. Where companies will enjoy fast connections, reflecting on more efficient and productive processes, transforming business through modern communications-enabled work experiences aimed at efficiency in the transmission of data and information.

REFERENCES

Ahmad, A., Paul, A., Rathore, M. M., & Chang, H. (2016). Smart cyber society: Integration of capillary devices with high usability based on Cyber-Physical System. *Future Generation Computer Systems*, *56*, 493–503. doi:10.1016/j.future.2015.08.004

Akter, S., Wamba, S. F., Gunasekaran, A., Dubey, R., & Childe, S. J. (2016). How to improve firm performance using big data analytics capability and business strategy alignment? *International Journal of Production Economics*, *182*, 113–131. doi:10.1016/j.ijpe.2016.08.018

Arghandeh, R., Von Meier, A., Mehrmanesh, L., & Mili, L. (2016). On the definition of cyber-physical resilience in power systems. *Renewable & Sustainable Energy Reviews*, *58*, 1060–1069. doi:10.1016/j.rser.2015.12.193

Artuso, M., & Christiansen, H. L. (2014). Discrete-event simulation of coordinated multi-point joint transmission in LTE-Advanced with constrained backhaul. In *Proceedings of IEEE Eleventh International Symposium on Wireless Communication Systems* (pp. 106-110). 10.1109/ISWCS.2014.6933329

Assunção, M. D., Calheiros, R. N., Bianchi, S., Netto, M. A., & Buyya, R. (2015). Big Data computing and clouds: Trends and future directions. *Journal of Parallel and Distributed Computing*, *79*, 3–15. doi:10.1016/j.jpdc.2014.08.003

Babiceanu, R. F., & Seker, R. (2016). Big Data and virtualization for manufacturing cyber-physical systems: A survey of the current status and future outlook. *Computers in Industry*, *81*, 128–137. doi:10.1016/j.compind.2016.02.004

Bajaj, S., & Johari, R. (2016, February). Big data: a boon or bane-the big question. In *2016 Second International Conference on Computational Intelligence & Communication Technology (CICT)* (pp. 106-110). IEEE. 10.1109/CICT.2016.29

Barnela, M., & Kumar, D. S. (2014). Digital modulation schemes employed in wireless communication: A literature review. *International Journal of Wired and Wireless Communications*, *2*(2), 15–21.

Besselink, B., Turri, V., Van De Hoef, S. H., Liang, K. Y., Alam, A., Mårtensson, J., & Johansson, K. H. (2016). Cyber-physical control of road freight transport. *Proceedings of the IEEE, 104*(5), 1128–1141. doi:10.1109/JPROC.2015.2511446

Biffl, S., Lüder, A., & Gerhard, D. (Eds.). (2017). *Multi-Disciplinary Engineering for Cyber-Physical Production Systems: Data Models and Software Solutions for Handling Complex Engineering Projects.* Springer. doi:10.1007/978-3-319-56345-9

Bossert, M. (1999). *Channel coding for telecommunications.* John Wiley & Sons, Inc.

Burg, A., Chattopadhyay, A., & Lam, K. Y. (2017). Wireless communication and security issues for cyber-physical systems and the Internet-of-Things. *Proceedings of the IEEE, 106*(1), 38–60. doi:10.1109/JPROC.2017.2780172

Cassandras, C. G. (2016). Smart cities as cyber-physical social systems. *Engineering, 2*(2), 156–158. doi:10.1016/J.ENG.2016.02.012

Cassandras, C. G., & Lafortune, S. (2009). *Introduction to discrete event systems.* Springer Science & Business Media.

Chaâri, R., Ellouze, F., Koubâa, A., Qureshi, B., Pereira, N., Youssef, H., & Tovar, E. (2016). Cyber-physical systems clouds: A survey. *Computer Networks, 108,* 260–278. doi:10.1016/j.comnet.2016.08.017

Cintuglu, M. H., Mohammed, O. A., Akkaya, K., & Uluagac, A. S. (2016). A survey on smart grid cyber-physical system testbeds. *IEEE Communications Surveys and Tutorials, 19*(1), 446–464. doi:10.1109/COMST.2016.2627399

Dammasch, K., & Horton, G. (2008). *Entities with combined discrete-continuous attributes in discrete-event-driven systems.* Academic Press.

França, R. P., Iano, Y., Monteiro, A. C. B., Arthur, R., Estrela, V. V., Assumpção, S. L. D. L., & Razmjooy, N. (2019). *Potential Proposal to Improvement of the Data Transmission in Healthcare Systems.* Academic Press.

Hehenberger, P., Vogel-Heuser, B., Bradley, D., Eynard, B., Tomiyama, T., & Achiche, S. (2016). Design, modelling, simulation and integration of cyber-physical systems: Methods and applications. *Computers in Industry, 82,* 273–289. doi:10.1016/j.compind.2016.05.006

Hermann, M., Pentek, T., & Otto, B. (2016, January). Design principles for Industrie 4.0 scenarios. In *2016 49th Hawaii international conference on system sciences (HICSS)* (pp. 3928-3937). IEEE.

Jeschke, S., Brecher, C., Meisen, T., Özdemir, D., & Eschert, T. (2017). Industrial internet of things and cyber manufacturing systems. In *Industrial Internet of Things* (pp. 3–19). Springer. doi:10.1007/978-3-319-42559-7_1

Lakshmanan, M. K., & Nikookar, H. (2006). A review of wavelets for digital wireless communication. *Wireless Personal Communications, 37*(3-4), 387–420. doi:10.100711277-006-9077-y

Lee, E. (2015). The past, present and future of cyber-physical systems: A focus on models. *Sensors (Basel), 15*(3), 4837–4869. doi:10.3390150304837 PMID:25730486

Lee, E. A., & Seshia, S. A. (2016). *Introduction to embedded systems: A cyber-physical systems approach*. MIT Press.

Lee, J., Bagheri, B., & Kao, H. A. (2015). A cyber-physical systems architecture for industry 4.0-based manufacturing systems. *Manufacturing Letters, 3*, 18–23. doi:10.1016/j.mfglet.2014.12.001

Liu, Y., Peng, Y., Wang, B., Yao, S., & Liu, Z. (2017). Review on cyber-physical systems. *IEEE/CAA Journal of Automatica Sinica, 4*(1), 27-40.

Lu, C., Saifullah, A., Li, B., Sha, M., Gonzalez, H., Gunatilaka, D., Wu, C., Nie, L., & Chen, Y. (2015). Real-time wireless sensor-actuator networks for industrial cyber-physical systems. *Proceedings of the IEEE, 104*(5), 1013–1024. doi:10.1109/JPROC.2015.2497161

Moness, M., & Moustafa, A. M. (2015). A survey of cyber-physical advances and challenges of wind energy conversion systems: Prospects for internet of energy. *IEEE Internet of Things Journal, 3*(2), 134–145. doi:10.1109/JIOT.2015.2478381

Mosterman, P. J., & Zander, J. (2016). Industry 4.0 as a cyber-physical system study. *Software & Systems Modeling, 15*(1), 17–29. doi:10.100710270-015-0493-x

Mourtzis, D., Vlachou, E., & Milas, N. (2016). Industrial Big Data as a result of IoT adoption in manufacturing. *Procedia CIRP, 55*, 290–295. doi:10.1016/j.procir.2016.07.038

Nakajima, S., Talpin, J. P., Toyoshima, M., & Yu, H. (2017, January). Cyber-Physical System Design from an Architecture Analysis Viewpoint. In *Communications of the NII Shonan Meetings*. Springer. 10.1007/978-981-10-4436-6

Negri, E., Fumagalli, L., & Macchi, M. (2017). A review of the roles of digital twin in cps-based production systems. *Procedia Manufacturing, 11*, 939–948. doi:10.1016/j.promfg.2017.07.198

Ochoa, S. F., Fortino, G., & Di Fatta, G. (2017). *Cyber-physical systems, internet of things and big data*. Academic Press.

Padilha, R. (2018). *Proposta de Um Método Complementar de Compressão de Dados Por Meio da Metodologia de Eventos Discretos Aplicada Em Um Baixo Nível de Abstração* (Mestrado em Engenharia Elétrica). Faculdade de Engenharia Elétrica e de Computação, Universidade Estadual de Campinas.

Padilha, R., Iano, Y., Monteiro, A. C. B., Arthur, R., & Estrela, V. V. (2018, October). Betterment Proposal to Multipath Fading Channels Potential to MIMO Systems. In *Brazilian Technology Symposium* (pp. 115-130). Springer.

Rittinghouse, J. W., & Ransome, J. F. (2016). *Cloud computing: implementation, management, and security*. CRC Press.

Shoro, A. G., & Soomro, T. R. (2015). *Big data analysis: Apache spark perspective*. Global Journal of Computer Science and Technology.

Shu, Z., Wan, J., Zhang, D., & Li, D. (2016). Cloud-integrated cyber-physical systems for complex industrial applications. *Mobile Networks and Applications, 21*(5), 865–878. doi:10.100711036-015-0664-6

Song, H., Srinivasan, R., Sookoor, T., & Jeschke, S. (Eds.). (2017). *Smart cities: foundations, principles, and applications*. John Wiley & Sons. doi:10.1002/9781119226444

Tao, F., Cheng, J., & Qi, Q. (2017). IIHub: An industrial Internet-of-Things hub toward smart manufacturing based on cyber-physical system. *IEEE Transactions on Industrial Informatics*, *14*(5), 2271–2280. doi:10.1109/TII.2017.2759178

Venghaus, H., & Grote, N. (Eds.). (2017). *Fibre optic communication: key devices* (Vol. 161). Springer. doi:10.1007/978-3-319-42367-8_9

Wang, L., Törngren, M., & Onori, M. (2015). Current status and advancement of cyber-physical systems in manufacturing. *Journal of Manufacturing Systems*, *37*, 517–527. doi:10.1016/j.jmsy.2015.04.008

Watteyne, T., Handziski, V., Vilajosana, X., Duquennoy, S., Hahm, O., Baccelli, E., & Wolisz, A. (2016). Industrial wireless IP-based cyber-physical systems. *Proceedings of the IEEE*, *104*(5), 1025–1038. doi:10.1109/JPROC.2015.2509186

Xiong, G., Zhu, F., Liu, X., Dong, X., Huang, W., Chen, S., & Zhao, K. (2015). Cyber-physical-social system in intelligent transportation. *IEEE/CAA Journal of Automatica Sinica, 2*(3), 320-333.

Xu, L. D., & Duan, L. (2019). Big data for cyber-physical systems in industry 4.0: A survey. *Enterprise Information Systems*, *13*(2), 148–169. doi:10.1080/17517575.2018.1442934

Xu, T. (2017). *Digital signal processing for optical communications and networks*. InTech. doi:10.5772/intechopen.68323

Xue, Y., & Yu, X. (2017). Beyond smart grid—Cyber-physical–social system in energy future. *Proceedings of the IEEE*, *105*(12), 2290–2292. doi:10.1109/JPROC.2017.2768698

You, S., Zhang, J., & Gruenwald, L. (2015, April). Large-scale spatial join query processing in cloud. In *2015 31st IEEE International Conference on Data Engineering Workshops* (pp. 34-41). IEEE. 10.1109/ICDEW.2015.7129541

Yue, X., Cai, H., Yan, H., Zou, C., & Zhou, K. (2015). Cloud-assisted industrial cyber-physical systems: An insight. *Microprocessors and Microsystems*, *39*(8), 1262–1270. doi:10.1016/j.micpro.2015.08.013

Zhang, Y., Qiu, M., Tsai, C. W., Hassan, M. M., & Alamri, A. (2015). Health-CPS: Healthcare cyber-physical system assisted by cloud and big data. *IEEE Systems Journal*, *11*(1), 88–95. doi:10.1109/JSYST.2015.2460747

Zheng, C., Le Duigou, J., Hehenberger, P., Bricogne, M., & Eynard, B. (2016). Multidisciplinary integration during conceptual design process: A survey on design methods of cyber-physical systems. In *DS 84: Proceedings of the DESIGN 2016 14th International Design Conference* (pp. 1625-1634). Academic Press.

Zhou, X., & Xie, C. (2016). *Enabling technologies for high spectral-efficiency coherent optical communication networks*. John Wiley & Sons. doi:10.1002/9781119078289

ADDITIONAL READING

Alcaraz, C., & Lopez, J. (2020). Secure interoperability in cyber-physical systems. In Cyber Warfare and Terrorism: Concepts, Methodologies, Tools, and Applications (pp. 521-542). IGI Global. doi:10.4018/978-1-7998-2466-4.ch032

Amin, S., Salahuddin, T., & Bouras, A. (2020, February). Cyber-Physical Systems and Smart Homes in Healthcare: Current State and Challenges. In 2020 IEEE International Conference on Informatics, IoT, and Enabling Technologies (ICIoT) (pp. 302-309). IEEE.

Delicato, F. C., Al-Anbuky, A., Kevin, I., & Wang, K. (2020). Smart Cyber-Physical Systems: Toward Pervasive Intelligence systems.

Fantini, P., Pinzone, M., & Taisch, M. (2020). Placing the operator at the centre of Industry 4.0 design: Modelling and assessing human activities within cyber-physical systems. *Computers & Industrial Engineering*, *139*, 105058. doi:10.1016/j.cie.2018.01.025

Ge, X., Han, Q. L., Zhang, X. M., Ding, D., & Yang, F. (2020). Resilient and secure remote monitoring for a class of cyber-physical systems against attacks. *Information Sciences*, *512*, 1592–1605. doi:10.1016/j.ins.2019.10.057

Griffioen, P., Weerakkody, S., & Sinopoli, B. (2020). A moving target defense for securing cyber-physical systems. *IEEE Transactions on Automatic Control*, 1. doi:10.1109/TAC.2020.3005686

Han, S., Tang, L., & Chen, H. (2020). U.S. Patent Application No. 16/508,512.

Spensky, C., Machiry, A., Busch, M., Leach, K., Housley, R., Kruegel, C., & Vigna, G. (2020). TRUST. IO: Protecting Physical Interfaces on Cyber-physical Systems. In *Proc. IEEE Conference on Communications and Network Security (CNS 2020)*. IEEE. To appear. 10.1109/CNS48642.2020.9162246

Tan, S., Guerrero, J. M., Xie, P., Han, R., & Vasquez, J. C. (2020). Brief Survey on Attack Detection Methods for Cyber-Physical Systems. *IEEE Systems Journal*, 1–11. doi:10.1109/JSYST.2020.2991258

Waschull, S., Bokhorst, J. A., Molleman, E., & Wortmann, J. C. (2020). Work design in future industrial production: Transforming towards cyber-physical systems. *Computers & Industrial Engineering*, *139*, 105679. doi:10.1016/j.cie.2019.01.053

Xu, Z., He, D., Vijayakumar, P., Choo, K. K. R., & Li, L. (2020). Efficient NTRU Lattice-Based Certificateless Signature Scheme for Medical Cyber-Physical Systems. *Journal of Medical Systems*, *44*(5), 1–8. doi:10.100710916-020-1527-7 PMID:32189085

Zhu, T., Xiong, P., Li, G., Zhou, W., & Philip, S. Y. (2020). Differentially private model publishing in cyber-physical systems. *Future Generation Computer Systems*, *108*, 1297–1306. doi:10.1016/j.future.2018.04.016

KEY TERMS AND DEFINITIONS

Big Data: It is the technology that uses solutions based on algorithms that capture and cross-data organized, which allows the storage and retrieval of data of various formats at a high scale.

Cyber-Physical Systems: They are the elements of computation coordinated and communicated employing sensors, which associate all distributed intelligence in the digital environment to acquire a deeper understanding of the context in which they are appointed. Which monitor virtual and physical indicators, and actuators, which modify the virtual and physical environment in which they are executed. CPS act on the data collected, to predict the actions or even needs of the digital users as a whole.

Discrete Events: The discrete simulation is characterized by events where the changes occur in a discontinuous way, that is, fit into a wide variety of communication issues, derived from the results of actions taken in a system, which can be classified as an occurrence responsible for the change in the state of the system in which they act. system state changes occur as events occur, events, in turn, occur at discrete points in time, presenting the same dynamic and stochastic behavior that a real system represents, to represent the system as a sequence of operations entities (transactions) of specific types such as data packets, or even bits.

Fading: This related to the variation of the attenuation of the signal with several variables, unlike interference, these unwanted signals are random, including time, geographical position, and even radio-frequency. So, it is not possible to predict their value at a future time instant.

IoT: Refers to groups of digital devices (it consists only of sensors and other smart devices), that collect and transmit data over the Internet, low-cost network technology devices that can connect to all types of objects. This evokes a vision of a fully connected world, in which data and sensors transform everything from transport to energy management. Allowing different objects, to share data and information with certain tasks.

Rician: Rician is a type of Fading employed when the dominant component of the received signal is stationary, i.e., when there is a normally found in channels with a line of sight, having a predominance of it, or the dominant route.

Chapter 14
Cyber–Physical System for Smart Grid

Nagi Faroug M. Osman
Higher Colleges of Technology (HCT), UAE

Ali Ahmed A. Elamin
Jazan University, Saudi Arabia

Elmustafa Sayed Ali Ahmed
Sudan University of Science and Technology, Sudan

Rashid A. Saeed
iD https://orcid.org/0000-0002-9872-081X
Taif University, Saudi Arabia

ABSTRACT

A smart grid is an advanced utility, stations, meters, and energy systems that comprises a diversity of power processes of smart meters, and various power resources. The cyber-physical systems (CPSs) can play a vital role boosting the realization of the smart power grid. Applied CPS techniques that comprise soft computing methods, communication network, management, and control into a smart physical power grid can greatly boost to realize this industry. The cyber-physical smart power systems (CPSPS) are an effective model system architecture for smart grids. Topics as control policies, resiliency methods for secure utility meters, system stability, and secure end-to-end communications between various sensors/ controllers would be quite interested in CPSPS. One of the essential categories in CPSPS applications is the energy management system (EMS). The chapter will spotlight the model and design the relationship between the grid and EMS networks with standardization. The chapter also highlights some necessary standards in the context of CPSPS for the grid infrastructure.

DOI: 10.4018/978-1-7998-5101-1.ch014

INTRODUCTION

Energy and electricity are considered one of the most important sources entering in all areas of life at present. The revolutionary progress in our society and our economy depends entirely on how energy and electricity are managed. Energy transfer over long distances to meet the need for social and economic activities requires much effort. It needs electrical networks, which are substantial interconnected material networks that are the infrastructure and backbone of energy supply and use today (Yu et al., 2011). Recently, there is an increasing demand for green power generation and more energy-efficient use due to environmental concerns as well as limited non-renewable energy sources.

A report presented by (International Energy Agency,2014) defined as the world energy outlook report, indicates that the global energy demand is expected to grow by 37% by the year 2040, so, that energy efficiency is critical to relieving pressure on energy supplies while meeting increasing demands without shortage or interruption. Although renewable energy sources i.e. hydro, biomass, solar, geothermal, and wind are available, their harvesting is one of the most difficult challenges, so advanced technologies are needed to make this energy supply more reliable and safer. Internationally, several governments in many countries have adopted new energy policies and incentives using smart and modern technology, some of which have been widely disseminated. In the United States, the all-of-the-above energy strategy has been launched by President Obama. RE generation from wind, solar, and geothermal sources have doubled since 2008, and a 20% RE target by 2020 has been set (McCrone et al., 2020). In Europe, a 20% RE target by 2020 has also been set by the European Commission (Amin,2018). In China, a 15% RE target was set to achieve by 2020, and an even more ambitious target of 86% RE by 2050 has recently been set by the Chinese Government (Hove, 2020) (Amin, 2014).

According to what was previously mentioned, there is a need for a revolutionary rethinking of how to supply and use electrical energy efficiently and effectively. Smart Grids (SGs) are a new paradigm for energy supply and use efficiently, and intelligently integrating stakeholder behaviors and actions into the energy supply chain provides sustainable and safe electrical energy with high efficiency (Ali and Choi,2020). One of the most important elements of the success smart energy networks is the integration and smooth interaction of the infrastructure of the energy grid as physical systems, information sensing, processing, intelligence, and control as electronic systems. Besides, the use of cyber-physical systems (CPSs) enables us to address special integration and interaction issues in energy systems.

In Smart Grids that use information technologies in communications, computing, and control, a mechanism is needed to ensure the stability and security of the electrical networks. The process of integrating both advanced communications and control mechanisms into a physical network may be affected by some vulnerabilities and make it vulnerable to threats and breaches of network privacy. The security of these networks is often breached by manipulating data and adding other fake data to the smart grid control system (Gavriluta et al.,2020). CPS mechanisms play an important role in improving network defenses and detecting and mitigating attacks. AI technologies also aid in analysis processes and improve network reliability. The use of screening and assessment of contingencies strategies in the power system is contributed by a degree of protection to physical security. The use of contingency analysis (CA) helps to evaluate the security of the power system and covers faults, disturbances, and planned outages. the power systems steady-state and transient security analysis serves as a base of cyber-physical security for the smart grid. The cybersecurity system is one of the most important key elements in ensuring the confidentiality and security of the smart grid(Sun et al., 2016). In these systems, intrusion detection systems are used (IDS) firewalls to defend control centers and field devices against any external interventions. When using an IDS, it must be configured to adapt to the emerging and diverse patterns in the smart grid to effectively identify any malicious attempts.

In Smart Grids, different types of attacks may occur, in different Grid sections, i.e. in the generation, transmission, and distribution. In the generation department, cyber-physical attacks in the power control unit can affect the frequency stability in the power system. It can also mislead the load frequency control (LFC) and cause load interruption due to the fake frequency response. In the transmission section, analysis of data for monitoring circuit breakers and transmission controllers is one of the most important issues of the transmission system under large-scale malicious attacks. Most of the attack methods rely on manipulating in the control commands and changes the measurement data, which can disrupt lines, transformers, generators, buses, and substations in the transmission network (Haibo et al.,2016). Also, this kind of attack can damage the transmission substations hosting multiple measurements, control, and communication facilities. In a distribution system, one of the main threats to the AMI system is information privacy leakage. Attacks can occur by exploiting bi-directional communication to inundate the AMI system with malicious packets that may effectively paralyze measurement networks.

In this chapter, a brief concept about CPSs architectures for smart grid applications is presented. The Chapter reviews the CPSPS reference architecture and the concept of the energy management system (EMS), heterogeneous smart grid network, and distributed energy resources. Also, the chapter provides a brief idea about the smart grid security vulnerability, and considerations related to attack mechanism and security measurements, intrusion detection and prevention system (IDPS), hardware security, and critical infrastructure protection aspect. The Chapter also reviews a reliable and scalable communication for the smart grid and discusses several related issues i.e. big data analytics and applications for smart grid, Internet of things in the context of smart grid, and M2M communications. Data standardizations for electrical infrastructure are also reviews. Moreover, CPS Testbeds are discussed and focusing on different aspects i.e. smart power grids, cybersecurity, network, and communication issue.

BACKGROUND

In recent years, there are many studies presented by academia and industry in the field of smart energy network technologies. Most of them discussed the different workings of smart grid fundamentals, such as their structure, application, and potential impact (Yu et al., 2011). Others cover established and recently developed technical standards (Amin, 2018). In the field of electrical meters, the European Union plans to replace conventional electricity meters with smart meters until 2020. This leads to the main attention and detailed investigation of the privacy and security threats of this technology (McCrone et al., 2020). It is well known that maximum benefit and access to valuable employment is through interactions between people, companies, and entities in general. To create this interactive model, energy grids that operate on their infrastructure bases must be formed and linked to other sources and entities. The current energy networks are characterized by a typical central approach, as they transmit a few powerful power stations to various consumers (Ma and Li,2020). Moreover, renewable energy resources pave their way, it was expected that future users will not be simply consumers of energy but also producers.

The concept of the smart grid targets the provision of the next generation smart grid, which promises advanced configuration, interaction, and self-management (Assante, 2016). The smart grid is also known as a complex infrastructure that depicts system properties such as the multidisciplinary nature, operational and administrative independence of its components, geographical distribution, heterogeneity of network systems as well as emerging behavior and evolutionary development (McCrone et al., 2020). It is expected to be the key part of a global ecosystem of interacting entities, whose cooperation will give birth to innovative cross-industry services. One of the key driving forces behind these efforts is energy efficiency and better management of the available resources locally and globally. To achieve this, fine-grained monitoring and management are needed.

Many studies have been conducted in the cyber-security systems and their use in smart grids. (Sun et al., 2016) presented an advanced survey of the latest cyber-security in energy systems and presented cyber-security risks and appropriate solutions that further enhance the security of the electricity network. Also, this study provided a comprehensive overview of smart grid technologies, energy industry standards, and solutions that deal with cyber-security. (Gavriluta et al.,2020) presents a study of a cyber-physical framework for distributed control systems operating in the context of smart grid applications. The study also introduces the concept of distributed intelligence theories in the smart grid, and methods of verification testing in physical system applications, distributed computing platform, and Communication system. (George et al., 2020) presented a framework model that investigates cyber-physical architecture for modern electricity grids and captures the integration and interaction of complex layers for the cyber and physical types. The analysis of levels of the CPS-based architecture is explained, highlighting the model assumptions that were made to make this analysis possible.

Some other studies present a configurable framework at the system level for identifying compromised smart grid devices. As in the study by (Babun.,2019), the framework combines techniques for tracking system and function calls with signal processing and statistical analysis to discover vulnerable devices based on their behavioral characteristics. The effectiveness of this framework is measured by testing a smart grid substation that includes resource devices. The study also presented the outputs of analyzing six different types of scenarios for the hacking device with different resources and offensive payloads. The study proved that the proposed framework has an effective ability to discover CPS smart network devices penetrated with the system and call tracking technologies at the function level.

One of the physical-cyber infrastructure parts in smart grids, is the battery energy storage systems, as it is an important part that helps in achieving a sustainable and flexible smart grid system. Researchers in (Mhaisen et al.,2019), present an intelligent distribution model based on controlling energy storage systems and enabling cooperative and safe operations between them. The study explains how to implement control strategies as smart contracts and deploy them to a distributed network of battery energy storage systems nodes to operate them safely.

Recently, the concept of Energy Internet (EI) appeared, which aims to develop smart grids by integrating many forms of energy into a flexible and highly efficient network. (Kabalci el al.,2019) presented an analysis of IoT applications that are enabled in smart grids and smart environments, such as smart cities, smart homes, smart meters, and energy. It also provided a model for developing AI-based IoT applications. Additionally, the researchers discussed future challenges and issues for the concept of emotional intelligence based on Internet of Things applications and their use in smart grids. Moreover, the study provided a review of the IoT technologies and systems and infrastructure communications such as LPWAN and their use in smart grids based on CPS infrastructure.

CPSPS REFERENCE ARCHITECTURE

Cyber-Physical Systems (CPS) represent an amalgamation of computational and physical properties and can be found extensively in multiple domains including the electricity grid (Wadhawan et al., 2018). In previous years, technology innovations provided smart grid models capable of integrating the real world and virtual reality using built-in networked devices that provide a real-time exchange of information between them. The significant development in the field of communications and computing capabilities made it possible for the embedded devices to be available and deployed everywhere to monitor and control realistic operations on an unprecedented scale. Modern businesses rely on CPS to accurately sync the real-world status of backend systems and processes (Humayed et al.,2017). The cyber-physical smart power system (CPSPS) provides smart operations and processes for a smart grid system related to energy management, distributed resources, and systems heterogeneity.

Energy Management System (EMS)

EMS manages energy use by providing data to monitor and analyze the flow of electricity services (Ramalingam et al., 2015). It also analyzes data for other services such as steam, water, and compressed air. Electricity is not only generated but also different types of utility services through the consumption of energy sources, such as the use of electricity supplies (Rathor and Saxena,2020). Consequently, reducing the use of these services reduces energy consumption, and ultimately reduces energy costs.

Intelligent Electronic Devices (IEDs)

An Intelligent Electronic Device is a term used in the electric power industry to describe microprocessor-based controllers of power system equipment, such as circuit breakers, transformers, and capacitor banks. IDS devices are known to have the ability to connect to the LAN and communicate with other devices and have good processing capabilities (Wang and Shi, 2018). Many IDS devices are widely used for automation purposes. Automation of the home electricity meter can be done by using an IDS and programmable logic controller (PLC). Recently, smart electronic devices (IEDs) have been widely deployed in energy automation systems, because they have the advantages of integration and interoperability.

Heterogeneous Systems

The Smart Grid (SG) intelligently enhances the traditional power grid, allowing smarter management. To implement the smart power grid, SG needs to rely on a network that connects different node types and implement SG services, with various communication and power requirements. Het-Net solutions are unique as they benefit from allocating different radio access technologies (RATs) to different SG node types, but improving wireless resource efficiency and energy management is a complicated task. By exploiting the major KPIs of SG node types and critical features of RATs, joint communication functionality and energy cost are determined (Rengaraju et al., 2012).

Distributed Energy Resources (DER)

Any resource in the power distribution system is one of the crucial parts that work to produce electricity and is related to distributed energy resources (DER). It is vital to understand how these resources work to determine how the DER interacts with the power grid (Nanda et al.,2015). The DER operation characteristics are determined by the generation technology used. Concurrent machines act as traditional generators from a performance perspective. Asynchronous generation technologies, such as solar PV cells or fuel cell resources, also rely on their direct current (DC) for AC inverter technology to deliver energy to the AC system. DC to AC electrical performance requirements are designed to protect the user (general) and inverter equipment from electrical hazards as well as to provide the capabilities needed for reliable operation of the power grid to which asynchronous generators are connected.

SMART GRID CPS SECURITY VULNERABILITIES

Smart grids are vulnerable to a multitude of attacks, due to their cyber-physical nature. Such attacks can occur at their communication, networking, and physical entry points and can seriously affect the operation of a grid. Thus, the security factor of a smart grid is of the utmost importance. To properly secure a smart grid, we should be able to understand its underlying vulnerabilities and associated threats, as well as quantify their effects, and devise appropriate security solutions. More technologies are being developed as part of smart grid development and deployment to enhance system reliability (Sideris et al.,2019). The continuous development process is taking place in the smart grid to increase the capacity of the remote control and computer-based automation significantly, which helps to raise the level of communication and ensure the cybersecurity of the cyber-physical systems (CPSs). The cybersecurity of the power grid concerning issues of, CPSs structure in a smart grid, cyber vulnerability assessment, cyber protection systems, and testbeds of a CPS (Assante, 2016).

Attack Mechanisms and Security Measures

A smart grid is a primary CPS system whose security is a big concern. An agent-based smart grid is emerging as a next-generation smart grid infrastructure where complexity and scale-ability are creating a tremendous challenging environment for security. There are many attacks of various classes that can occur on SG or against one of its components. For the requirements of protection and defense against these attacks, the identity and appropriate disclosure mechanism must be defined. There are several different methods for the types of attacks and countermeasures that exist against them. The attacks are generally categorized based on the service of the victims or their device, as well as the type of attack (Mo et al.,2012). Table1 shows many categories of cyber-attacks that can occur on the smart grid and countermeasures as follows.

- Physical Layer Attacks.
- Network-based Attacks.
- Data Injection and Replay Attacks.
- SCADA attacks.
- Smart Meter Attacks.

Table 1. Descriptions of attack types

Attack Type	Security Affection	Location of Victim
Physical Layer	Data integrity, confidentiality, denial of service	Home area networks Neighborhood area networks Wide area networks
Network-Based	Confidentiality, availability	Home area networks Neighborhood area networks Wide area networks
Data Injection & Reply Attack	Confidentiality	Home area networks Neighborhood area networks Wide area networks
SCADA	Confidentiality, denial of service, integrity	Home area networks
Smart Meter	Confidentiality, integrity, availability, non-repudiation	Home area networks Neighborhood area networks

Intrusion Detection and Prevention System (IDPS)

In smart energy grids, IDS monitoring systems must be appropriate with the ability to detect and prevent preferred malicious activities resulting from exploiting vulnerabilities. This is done in conjunction with setting up smart network security mechanisms to prevent security vulnerabilities and mitigate their consequences, such as cryptographic algorithms and security protocols. The process of monitoring events that occur in the computer system connected to the power grid or in the grid itself is done by analyzing the signs of possible incidents of intrusion detection (Siaterlis et al.,2013). Intrusion detection is related to the IDS Information that sensors collect and being managed. Besides, the intrusion detection deals with many IDS sections i.e. database server to store all the data produced by the IDS, and a console to provide an interface for users and administrators so that they can check the status of the monitored system, receive alerts, investigate events, and configure the system. In the context of AMI, the main challenges to security solutions must be robust and seamlessly integrate with system operations (Rao et al., 2014). For IDS, these challenges translate into barriers associated with very accurate security solutions in incident detection, including unknown attacks. Blacklists and whitelists are typical detection methods, as shown in table 2, with comparative advantages and disadvantages.

Table 2. Comparative detection methods

Detection Methods	Defects	Features
Whitelist	False-positive error Essential to update rules frequently	To pass known good packets
Blocklist	Low-security degree False-negative error Essential to update rules frequently	To block known bad packets

IDSs depend on the host or the network. We also find that Hybrid IDS has higher performance in CPS. ADS integrated use of cybersecurity at substations provides a unique mechanism for detecting host-based anomalies by examining time anomalies in the substation's facilities (Hong et al.,2014). Cyber-attacks can also be identified by linking information from the Anomaly Detection Systems (ADSs) segment.

Hardware Security (HS) and Critical Infrastructure Protection (CIP)

Smart grids rely on a secure communication mechanism between devices to ensure safety. In a future smart home environment, the communication between the various smart devices, devices, and energy management systems with each other is carried out across the home network, which requires mutual authentication processes between them so that each device has a private encryption key that must be protected from theft or any kinds of attacks. The critical infrastructure includes the assets, systems, and networks, whether physical or virtual, are so vital to any energy grids that their incapacitation or destruction would have a debilitating effect on security, national economic security, national public health or safety, or any combination thereof (Rajkumar et al., 2010).

Smart Grid Vulnerabilities, Challenges and Solutions

In general, the smart grid is a huge complex network consisting of millions of devices and entities connected. The smart grid network integrates the traditional electric power grid with information and communication technologies (ICT), which helps to improve the efficiency of the energy system, and consumption through monitoring and control. Due to smart grid swelling and its association with data and network systems, there are many security concerns related to smart grid security. These security concerns summered to the vulnerability of the smart grid to different types of attacks (Sanjab et al.,2016). The presence of the flaws enables strangers to access the network, breaks the confidentiality and integrity of the transmitted data, and makes the service unavailable.

The vulnerabilities of smart grids are located in the following issues, which are classified as the most dangerous. (A) Customer security: accessing information about smart meters and knowing consumer data. (B) Intelligent devices: Smart devices used to manage both electricity supply and grid demand may be compromised and used as an attack on network entry points. (C) Physical security related to the smart grid components is mostly outside the utility buildings. (D) The lifetime of power systems: There is some old equipment that can be used with smart grids and are not sufficiently robust or incompatible with the devices of the current power system, which is likely to become a hole for penetration and attack on the grid. (E) Implicit trust between traditional power devices: The Device-to-device communication control can be exposed by spoofing and knowing the data that may affect the stability of the grid when any communication state between devices changes or any misleading information is sent between them. (F) Internet Protocol (IP) and commercial hardware and software: Although, IP standards in smart networks provide a great advantage because they provide compatibility between different components. However, devices using IP are probable to vulnerable to IP based network attacks i.e. IP Spoofing, Tear Drop, Denial of Service, and others (Fadi et al.,2012).

There are different security threats and challenges related to the smart grid i.e. the attacking and violation of a large volume of sensitive customer information. In addition to attacks that make hardware damage, malware proliferation in cyber systems, immediate system failure. moreover, the lack of physical protection against natural or environmental disasters in distributed control devices and insufficient control mechanisms in traditional systems that failed to account for cyber threats are also considered as vital security threats and challenges in Smart grids (Otuoze et al.,2018). Cybersecurity in the smart grid is sensitive that needs to develop solutions to security problems to face the existing vulnerabilities. Solutions such using flow entropy, sensing time measurement, transmission failure count, and signatures will enable us to detect DoS attacks. Flow entropy is used to analyze traffic to detect a DoS attack. Sensing time measurement enables to detect the jamming attack and DoS attack. Transmission failure count can detect jamming attacks to keep track of transmission failure. signatures method compares any suspicious activity to the known attack patterns and characteristics to detect the DoS attack. Other solutions such as filtering, reconfiguration, physical layer mitigation are used to mitigate the DoS attack on the network layer.

When considering the use of CPS in smart grids, the concept of security becomes more important in terms of behavioral and analytical factors. One of the most important challenges facing CPS security is the complexity of testing and analysis, which includes developing several engineering fields in software, mechanics, and electricity, in addition to systems and network engineering. Also, the complexity of design, implementation, methods, and methods of analysis and control (Kim et al.,2018). the Security and privacy solutions to CPS in smart grids must consider device protection, network access detection, malicious code detection, and application issues.

RELIABLE AND SCALABLE COMMUNICATION FOR POWER GRID

Future smart power grids require continuous data to operate with control decisions. The task of ensuring timely data access falls on the network That connects these smart devices. This network must be fault-tolerant. In intelligent energy networks that depend on the commodity communication infrastructure, failures may be greatly affected and cause inefficiency. Decisions that affect the real world are made based on data that is passed within a smart grid network. This effect makes it necessary to improve communication within the smart grid to ensure that the right decisions are made promptly (Mo et al., 2012). The common design of today's power grids follows a centralized command and control structure, i.e. most notably Supervisory Control and Data Acquisition (SCADA) systems relying on human monitors for decision making. SCADA systems provide the mechanism for identifying faults.

Distributed Network Protocol (DNP) creates a communication mechanism that connects devices to part of an automated system. This protocol operates several other protocols in SCADA systems to link the base station with RTUs and IEDs to ensure reliability, but they are weak towards security measures. The protocols in the DNP make connections in data networks so that geographically dispersed devices can transfer information to each other while ensuring that the required information is efficiently transferred to achieve specific performance goals, such as minimum delays or maximum productivity.

Big Data Analytics and Applications for Smart Grid CPS

The concept of big data is related to the mechanism of large amounts of data collection and analysis. It is also characterized by several key features, namely size, speed, honesty, contrast, and value (Yin et al.,2015). Smart meters such as smart energy meters use the captured data and take advantage of these features, for example when moving from reading one meter per month to every 5 minutes, that will turn into 308 million readings per million consumers, which leads to a huge amount of data flows to manage it. The process of combining real-time and heterogeneous big data analytics with other information such as consumption data, weather, different network behavior, rule-based readings, will help convert large-size data into actionable insights that are critical to effective SGs operations. It is necessary to have an integrated presentation of utility data and alignment of data across disparate groups and operating lines, in proportion to the amount of large data collected in cases designated for the power grid such as power outages. Therefore, energy networks that rely on data integrity gain insight into their operations and assets, enabling them to take proactive measures instead of just responding to events after they happen (Wu et al.,2017). Also, other aspects such as speed and contrast must be considered in capturing consumption data and the effect of big data with smart meters on them.

Artificial Intelligent analytical algorithms can provide methods for processing massive amounts of data. Automated learning techniques can also complete data management-related activities in a period short enough to be of practical use in the SGs, which is associated with monitoring equipment reliability, interruption prevention, or security monitoring. In SG environments, data types are not necessarily from traditional sources such as industrial control systems only, but also security cameras and weather forecasting systems, maps, graphics, images, and the web. In recent years, the Internet of Things has demonstrated a superior ability to link social media and call center dialog boxes with sources of information about energy grids and pairing with smart meters and network-generated data for decision-making and planning processes (Alahakoon et al., 2016). This tremendous ability to link big data requires SG-related data analysis, efficient methods of designing energy networks with an effective design, and their ability to interact with computational platforms and smart algorithms (Wu et al.,2017).

Internet of Things in the Context of Smart Grid CPS

The Internet of Things (IoT) has great benefits to contribute to the smart energy grids. In general, IoT is expected to grow to 50 billion connected devices by 2020 (Singh et al.,2014)(Xu et al.,2014). IoT based SGs enable to integrate the communications network to connect all energy-related equipment in the future like transportation and distribution energy infrastructure and electricity resources. Also, to other resources such as water, gas, and heat meters, to home and building automation. IoT increases the efficient performance of SG by smart computing models in dynamic network infrastructure with self-configuration capabilities based on standard and interoperable communication protocols. The IoT connectivity and accessibility enhance customer experience and competencies allowing greater interaction and control for consumers. Besides, IoT provides a quantity of data to manufacturers and service providers to reduce costs through diagnostics and meter reading capabilities effectively and smarter.

In SG environments, the Internet of Things related to the power system is known as the Energy Internet (Karnouskos,2010). However, since the physical laws governing electrical flows are different from those for the flow of information, it found that electricity cannot be distinguished between sources, which needs kinds of a cyber energy system environment in the context of the broader energy ecosystem to capture the landscape of vast areas and aspects of information and covered physical layers. Real-time information security and responsiveness to SG may still require closed and specialized networks separate from public networks vulnerable to cyber-attacks and weak real-time response. the full integration of the IoT and secure communication networks will meet the need for security and reliability of SG, in addition to the need for effective architecture and design to enable interaction and communication between stakeholders across social, economic and environmental fields to achieve optimal collective goals.

Machine to Machine Communication

One of the most important requirements in smart energy networks is the complete integration of a flexible and secure communications network with new energy management technologies in the smart grid (SG), as it requires a very large number of sensor nodes and operating devices. Also, smart energy networks must be able to broaden participation in generation, transmission, marketing, and service delivery to new stakeholders, and the ability to control and monitor applicants (Tan et al.,2011). The use of machine-to-machine communication (M2M) provides unique solutions to achieve the smart electricity grid, operating as a core unit in SG to deploy a large-scale monitoring and control infrastructure, thus providing great opportunities for information and communication technology.

The M2M-based smart meters provide demand management with high flexibility as the Smart Meter (SM) is a two-way communication device that measures energy consumption and delivers this information via some means of communication to the local tool. With almost real-time information available for example based on the energy flow in the network, different levels of tariffs can be calculated and made available to the consumer, the consumer can make a smarter and more responsible choice. The M2M communication mechanism allows the various SG components to work together efficiently and exchange the information produced by smart energy meters. Also, many of the widespread wireless sensing networks and actuators (WSANs) deployed in SG (such as generating electrical power systems or home applications) perform the monitoring task (León et al.,2007). WSANs work cooperatively to fulfill some of the functions required in SGs.

DATA STANDARDIZATION FOR ELECTRICITY INFRASTRUCTURE

The following section is intended to describe and identify the existing standards. A smart grid is the combination of subsets of elements into an integrated solution meeting the business objectives of the major players (see figure 1). The main system parts in the conceptual model are customer/ prosumer, bulk generator, power grid (transmission and distribution), and communication.

Customer / Prosumer

The smart consumption mechanism enables the response to demand and the ability to interact between distribution management and building automation as well as in smart homes by using an automated system that automates and improves living. It also links the home automation system with a variety of lighting, heating, and ventilation control products, and other devices with common network infrastructure to enable efficient and reliable operation. Building automation and control systems are the building masters. These systems include measuring, control, and management devices for all building structures, factories, outdoor facilities, and other equipment capable of automation. It also works on automatic control including logical functions, controls, monitoring, optimization, operation, manual intervention, and management, for energy-efficient, economical and reliable operation of buildings.

Figure 1. Conceptual smart grid model

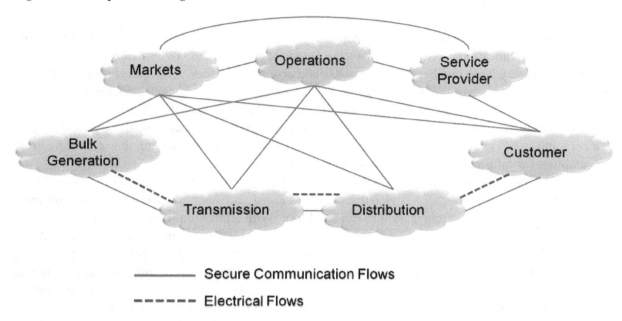

Bulk Generation

The smart generation includes the increased use of energy electronics for controlling harmonics, overcoming errors, and generating fluctuations from renewable energy sources in addition to the increased flexibility required for traditional fossil energy plants due to the increased volatility of feeding on renewable energy sources.

Power Grid (Transmission and Distribution)

The automation and protection of sub-power stations is a cornerstone of the secure transport network. This depends on the protection schemes, the efficiency of the energy quality control, energy control, and the quality management systems of the companies. The Energy Management System (EMS) provides an effective way to control the transport network. On the other hand, smart energy management systems work to support the decision and plan to protect the safety of the system and protect energy systems from instability and power outages better than traditional protection devices that protect basic equipment only.

System integrity protection schemes reinforce the goal of protective devices, to protect basic equipment such as transformers, from deadly fault streams so that uncontrollable chain reactions that begin with preventive actions are avoided. Protection systems like HVDC and FACTS provide effective control of energy flow and can help increase transmission capacity without increasing short circuit power. Mass deployment of distribution automation works on automation and remote control, and advanced distribution automation concepts further enhance the automatic self-configuration features of power grids (Kayastha et al.,2014). Also, using distributed energy resources to create separate cells known as Microgrids helps ensure energy supply in distribution networks even when there is a breakdown in the transmission network.

Communication

In the process of smart grid communication, only through the exchange of information at the grammatical level and indications can the benefits of the smart grid be realized. Smart Grid solutions will see a massive increase in data exchange for both monitoring and control capability. Therefore, the security of this data exchange and the hardware behind it will have an increasing impact.

Interoperability Standards

The reference structure IEC 62357 (see Figure 2), illustrates the communication requirements for applications requiring energy savings. Interoperability standards rely on the convergence of data models, services, and protocols to integrate an efficient and future system for all applications. This framework includes communication standards including semantic data models, services, and protocols for communications between the above systems and subsystems.

Figure 2. IEC 62357 reference architecture

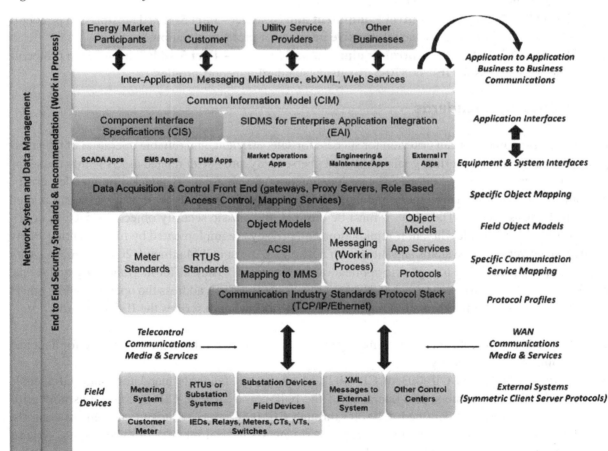

IEC 61850: Communication Networks and Systems in Substations

IEC 61850 communication standard appeared in the year 2004 to introduce the communication mechanism in the field of substation automation. This standard provides an effective response to the needs of the open and liberalized energy market, which requires reliable networks and highly flexible technology. It also provides a vision for leadership in communications technology for the office network sector, possible configurations for high functionality, and reliable data transmission. In this standard, industrial Ethernet, which is strengthened for sub-station purposes a speed 100 Mbps, provides sufficient bandwidth to ensure reliable information exchange between SG devices, as well as a reliable IED connection to the sub-station controller.

IEC 60870-5: Tele-Control Equipment and Systems

This standard appeared in the year 1994 as a standard specification for the use of information transfer in the field of the energy utility, as the standard became established worldwide in gas and water applications, especially remote control of electric energy. There are three parts to telecommunications:

- **IEC 60870-5-101, Tele-Control Equipment and Systems – Part 5-101:** Transmission protocols – Companion standard for basic telecontrol tasks
- **IEC 60870-5-103, Tele-Control Equipment and Systems – Part 5-103:** Transmission protocols – Companion standard for the informative interface of protection equipment
- **IEC 60870-5-104, Tele-Control Equipment and Systems – Part 5-104:** Transmission protocols – Network access for IEC 60870-5-101 using standard transport profiles.

Cyber Security Standards

Cybersecurity is an important criterion for success for safe, efficient, and reliable operation of the smart grid. Among the most important goals related to cybersecurity, protect all related assets within the scope of the smart grid from any kind of risks such as intentional cybersecurity attacks, unintended errors, equipment failure, information theft, and natural disasters. Most of the cybersecurity risks are related to the ICT infrastructure. Therefore, it must be ensured that classic security objectives such as confidentiality, integrity, availability, non-repudiation, and privacy are implemented by implementing safety controls in power supply systems and sub-power networks (Anwar and Mahmood, 2014). Cybersecurity requirements already exist for specific applications and domains. They differ in granularity and scope, ranking from process-oriented to technical standards. Some standards address the operator, while others contain very detailed implementation requirements. The following describes the IEC standards:

- IEC 62351-1 to 6, Power systems management and associated information exchange for data and communications security.
- NERC CIP-002 and CIP-003 to CIP-009 Cybersecurity standards mandatory and enforceable across all users, owners, and operators of the bulk-power system. CIP-002 specifies how critical cyber assets are identified. CIP-003 through CIP-009 covers security management controls, personnel and training, electronic security perimeters, physical security of cyber assets, systems security management, incident handling, and recovery planning.

- IEEE 1686-2007, IEEE standard for Substation Intelligent Electronic Devices (IEDs) Cyber Security Capabilities, specifies the functionality of intelligent electronic devices to address critical infrastructure protection programs.
- ANSI/ISA-99, Security for Industrial Automation and Control Systems, covers the process for establishing an industrial automation and control systems security program based on risk analysis, establishing awareness and countermeasures, and monitoring and Cyber Security management systems.

Standards Planning for the Smart Grid

Several criteria are providing favorable conditions for renewable energy or distributed generation connectivity to develop a smart grid:

- IEC 61727:2004, Photovoltaic (PV) systems are suitable for PV systems smaller than 10 kVA, connected with an LV distribution system.
- The IEEE 1547 series is a set of standards concerning interconnecting distributed resources with electric power systems. The IEEE 1547 Serial Standards are currently the most widely accepted in the field of distributed resources interconnection and have been formally affirmed as one of the first batches of the USA Smart Grid construction standards.
- IEEE 1547.1:2005, Standard for conformance test procedures for equipment interconnecting distributed resources with electric power systems. IEEE 1547.1:2005 was published in 2005, to describe the testing of the interconnection to determine whether or not it conforms to standards.
- IEEE 1547.2:2008, Application guide for IEEE 1547 Standard for interconnecting distributed resources with electric power systems to provide technical background on the standard.
- IEEE 1547.3:2007, Guide for monitoring, information exchange, and control of distributed resources interconnected with electric power systems. IEEE 1547.3:2007 published in 2007, to the monitoring of distributed systems.
- IEEE 1547.4: Draft guide for design, operation, and integration of distributed resource Island systems with electric power systems (draft). Its a guide for design, operation, and integration of conforming systems.
- IEEE P1547.5: Draft technical guidelines for interconnection of electric power sources greater than 10MVA to the power transmission grid, designed for distributed sources larger than 10 MVA
- IEEE P1547.6: Draft recommended practice for interconnecting distributed resources with electric power systems distribution secondary networks to describe practices for secondary network interconnections.

MULTI-DOMAIN CO-SIMULATION OF SMART GRID CPS

Computer algorithms enable monitoring and controlling the cyber-physical system (CPS) to be able to integrate with the physical world and networks (Rajkumar et al., 2010). In CPS, cyberspace components are controlled by algorithms usually implemented by computer-based software, while physical domain operations refer to physical behaviors in any other engineering field that may be controlled by cyber domain components. Physical processes and software components are interconnected in depth through mechanisms such as sensors, actuators, and networks (Derler et al., 2012). CPS includes smart grid, automotive systems, medical surveillance, process control systems, robotics systems, and automated avionics (Derler et al., 2012) (Lee, 2008).

Several studies are working on modeling communications networks to measure their ability to support next-generation energy system applications. These studies provide solutions using analytical models and aggregated traffic estimates based on smart grid use cases. However, event-driven simulation is required to model dynamic system behavior and to achieve network performance limitations at the utility level under difficult conditions. It would also be desirable to link communication system modeling with the simulation of smart grid applications emerging on actually deployed power systems. This shared simulation environment enables an assessment of the feasibility of using specific network technology to support communication-based smart grid control schemes on an existing part of the electrical network and vice versa, to define the range of control schemes that different communication technologies can support.

The common simulation platform can be designed by linking the Open DSS Simulator with the Network Simulator (NS-2) as presented by (Godfrey et al, 2010). The method is based on the input deployment of distributed energy resources on a model of the actual distribution circuit, and the base communication system is based on the IEEE 802.11 communication protocol. This study explains the possibility of introducing a wireless network to provide real-time sensing and control of power grids, a mechanism for examining the analytical model, the overall behavior of the wireless network, and the ability to perform detailed system analysis.

CPS TESTBEDS

Most CPS testing devices depend on the type of application you are running on. The testing mechanism may vary depending on the application as in the use of test devices to search in cyber-physical systems from UAV's to cooperative robots, from smart networks to vital infrastructure, and from industrial communications to cloud computing. Since CPS systems are a mixture of different subsystems consisting of sensors, networks, embedded systems, etc., their emergence has led to research and development of embedded systems, controls, networks, communications, and computing (Saeed et al.,2014). CPS testbeds from the findings are divided according to their application areas and presented below.

CPS Testbeds with Focus on Smart Power Grids

Electrical power system grids are a key area of cyber-physical systems and test research. Energy systems are going ahead side by side with revolutionary changes in engineering operating. Most of the work in the smart grid tested focuses on the structure of the system. Researchers develop and implement various types of system constructs on test spaces that consist of simulation, emulation, and hardware. The new generation of power grids requires a robust, flexible core shaft for communication to support changes to the system architecture that are provided through extensive use of information technology (Chakrabortty and Bose, 2017).

The information technology used in electrical networks has opened the way for attacks to the electrical grids. Recently, studies on smart grid tests are being done on a large scale to research energy security and control systems with modern communication systems. One such testbed is the use of power cyber at Iwo State University to test the system's vulnerability to cyber-attacks and to assess its impact (Ashok et al., 2016). These test surfaces are also used to test, verify, and validate various complex network models (Ashok et al., 2011). The Smart grid test survey provides detailed information on smart grid test lists and targeted search areas (Cintuglu et al., 2017).

CPS Testbeds with Focus on Cyber Security

Several studies have been carried out that rely on the use of test spaces for cybersecurity research which is a major concern due to the increasing use of the Internet and computers in the work of vital infrastructures such as smart energy networks, resource management, and transport infrastructure (Edgar et al.,2011) and (Kartakis et al.,2015). The studies concerned that as a result of the cyber-attack on the smart grid, it can identify problems of instability in these systems and increase malfunctions in the transmission lines. For such concerns and asses, the security of cyber-physical systems, EPIC is a European Union developed an experimental testbed platform that can contribute to cybersecurity testbed solutions (Siaterlis et al.,2013).

The study presented by (Soupionis and Benoist, 2015) clarifies several different attack scenarios on critical infrastructure as well as the involvement of the human factor. The test experiment was studied at South Dakota State University (SDSU) of the experiment to study the effects of cyber-attack and its effect on system effort. In this study, the change in real and interactive power generation due to the attack was explained. Also, in a study by (Poudel and Malla, 2017), mitigation of the attack using the optimum energy flow was reviewed. SCADA systems are also an important part of industrial communication networks and are widely used in critical infrastructures. Studies were also presented by (Miciolino et al., 2016) and (Pietro et al., 2013) discussing cyber-attacks on SCADA, communication systems, and industrial networks. Besides, a hybrid test study to assess cybersecurity based on cloud computing is presented by (Gao et al., 2015).

CPS Testbeds with Focus on Network and Communication

CPS research presented by (Marcus and Frey, 2014) reviews the communication concept focuses on the use of drones as M2M testing and demonstration basins. Drones-based experimental research focuses on various components of CPS such as network, sensor, and communications technology. In a study presented by (Jamshidi et al., 2011) and (Khan et al., 2016), UAV voids in the form of unmanned aerial vehicles are used to test and implement autonomous UAV tracking and navigation algorithms. Due to the development in CPS, it was found that there was an increase in the development of cloud manufacturing technologies (Liu et al., 2017).

A study submitted by (Liu et al., 2017) the CPS test is developed by linking two manufacturing sites to local area networks consisting of 7 devices equipped with the cloud via the Internet. The test uses the MT Connect method to obtain data on the state of manufacture and demonstrates 3D printing and monitoring of the printing process (Liu et al., 2017). The human in the ring is also an important aspect of cyber-physical systems. Test surfaces are used to verify and verify control algorithms for humanoid helper robots with an emphasis on caring for the elderly (Dimitrov et al.,2015). (Kumar et al., 2016) presented a test focusing on the connections between hardware and software components in a cyber-physical system.

FUTURE RESEARCH DIRECTIONS

The security of CPS systems against complex cyber-attacks is one of the most important challenges hindering the use of CPS in power networks. New attack tactics are constantly being discovered and current methods are also evolving making the security issue unpredictable and very dynamic. The differences between the security objectives of the smart grid and the IT networks require safer and more effective solutions (Aloul et al.,2012). Also, current types of attacks indicate that power systems may be vulnerable to potential security attacks. Therefore, studying security issues in CPS applications is an important engineering task. According to the general concept of CPS-based smart grid security, there are several future research directions as follows (Alcaraz and Lopez,2013) (Alcaraz et al.,2014).

- Improving smart meters, by developing a dynamic context-aware IDS/IPSs for detecting, preventing, and alerting unexpected changes according to system behavior.
- Improving the existing standardization frameworks for secure communication in smart grid applications.
- Developing wide-area situational awareness frameworks for cyber-defense solutions.
- Developing dynamic self-healing mechanisms such as cloud-based resilience.
- Developing new protocols for the requirements of smart grid applications.

CONCLUSION

The evolving technologies of communication and computing transform conventional power systems into cyber-physical, clever networks that have never before changed the scenery of electrical power systems and how humans interact with them. The interoperability of smart hyperphysical grids helps to build various intelligent CPS systems that face the big challenges of rising demand for loads and the ever-growing penetration of renewable energy sources. However, in most CPS implementations, the uncertainty and sophistication obstruct creation model analysis and thus involve the production of a general modeling system. The chapter gave an insight into clever CPS grids. it introduced the most effective technologies, i.e. AMI infrastructures based on different applications to improve system performance. The Chapter addressed the problems and opportunities that integration between power systems, communications systems, and computer systems has generated. In the heart of the emerging smart grid lies hyperphysical systems. They are indispensable because they can make the "glue" between the physique and the business side. However, several problems remain open and important efforts will be needed to understand how CPS can operate within a complex system such as the Smart Grid and how its interactions and collaboration in a CPS network can affect it.

REFERENCES

Abdulmalik, Lin, Li, & Luo. (2017). *Cyber-Physical Systems Security – A Survey*. arXiv.org

Abdulrahaman. (2018). Review Smart grids security challenges: Classification by sources of threats. *Journal of Electrical Systems and Information Technology*.

Adnan. (2014). *Renewable energy prospects: Chain*. IRENA International Renewable Energy Agency.

Adnan. (2018). *Renewable energy prospects for the European union*. IRENA International Renewable Energy Agency.

Alahakoon, D., & Yu, X. (2016). Smart electricity meter data intelligence for future energy systems: A survey. *IEEE Transactions on Industrial Informatics, 12*(1), 425–436. doi:10.1109/TII.2015.2414355

Alcaraz, C., Cazorla, L., & Fernandez, G. (2014). Context-awareness using anomaly- based detectors for smart grid domains. *International Conference on Risks and Security of Internet and Systems*, 17–34.

Alcaraz, C., & Lopez, J. (2013). Wide-area situational awareness for critical infrastructure protection. *Computer (Long Beach Calif), 46*(4), 30–37. doi:10.1109/MC.2013.72

Ali & Choi. (2020). State-of-the-Art Artificial Intelligence Techniques for Distributed Smart Grids: A Review. *MDPI Electronics Journal*, 1-35.

Aloul, F., Al-Ali, A. R., Al-Dalky, R., Al-Mardini, M., & El-Hajj, W. (2012). *Smart grid security: threats, vulnerabilities and solutions*. Int. J. Smart Grid Clean Energy.

Anders, H. (2020). *Current direction for renewable energy in China*. Oxford Institute for Energy Studies. Oxford University.

Anibal. (2016). *Smart Grid Security: Threats, Challenges, and Solutions*. arXiv

Anwar, A., & Mahmood, A. (2014). Cyber security of smart grid infrastructure. The State of the Art in Intrusion Prevention and Detection. CRC Press, Taylor & Francis Group.

Argyrios. (2019). *Smart Grid Hardware Security: Design Challenges and Paradigms*. IoT for Smart Grids.

Ashok, A., Hahn, A., & Govindarasu, M. (2011). A cyber-physical security testbed for smart grid. *Proceedings of the Seventh Annual Workshop on Cyber Security and Information Intelligence Research - CSIIRW '11*.

Ashok, A., Krishnaswamy, S., & Govindarasu, M. (2016). A remotely accessible testbed for Cyber Physical security of the Smart Grid. *IEEE Power and Energy Society Innovative Smart Grid Technologies Conference, ISGT*. 10.1109/ISGT.2016.7781277

Assante, M. J. (2016). Confirmation of a Coordinated Attack on the Ukrainian Power Grid. E-ISAC | Analysis of the Cyber Attack on the Ukrainian Power Grid.

Autenrieth & Frey. (2014). Pader MAC: Energy-efficient machine to machine communication for cyber-physical systems. *Peer-to-Peer Networking and Applications, 7*(3), 243–254.

Catalin. (2020). Cyber-physical framework for emulating distributed control systems in smart grids. In Electrical Power and Energy Systems. Elsevier.

Chakrabortty, A., & Bose, A. (2017). Smart Grid Simulations and Their Supporting Implementation Methods. *Proceedings of the IEEE, 105*(11), 2017. doi:10.1109/JPROC.2017.2737635

Cintuglu, M. H., Mohammed, O. A., Akkaya, K., & Uluagac, A. S. S. (2017). A Survey on Smart Grid Cyber-Physical System Testbeds. *IEEE Communications Surveys and Tutorials*, *19*(1), 446–464. doi:10.1109/COMST.2016.2627399

Derler, P., Lee, E. A., & Vincentelli, A. S. (2012). Modeling cyber - physical systems. *Proceedings of the IEEE*, 13-28.

Dimitrov, V., Jagtap, V., Wills, M., Skorinko, J., & Padir, T. (2015). A cyber physical system testbed for assistive robotics technologies in the home. *Proceedings of the 17th International Conference on Advanced Robotics*. 10.1109/ICAR.2015.7251475

Edgar, T., Manz, D., & Carroll, T. (2011). Towards an experimental testbed facility for cyber-physical security research. *CSIIRW '11: Proceedings of the Seventh Annual Workshop on Cyber Security and Information Intelligence Research*. 10.1145/2179298.2179357

Gao, H. (2015). Cyber-Physical Systems Testbed Based on Cloud Computing and Software Defined Network. *International conference on intelligent information hiding and multimedia signal processing (IIH-MSP)*, 337–340. 10.1109/IIH-MSP.2015.50

Godfrey, T., Mullen, S., Griffith, D. W., Golmie, N., Dugan, R. C., & Rodine, C. (2010). Modeling Smart Grid Applications with Co-Simulation. *First IEEE International Conference on Smart Grid Communications*, 291-296. 10.1109/SMARTGRID.2010.5622057

Govindarajan, R. (2015). Energy management techniques in smart grid. *International Journal of Applied Engineering Research*, *10*(15), 35720–35724.

He & Yan. (2016). Cyber-physical attacks and defenses in the smart grid: a survey. *IET Cyber-Physical Systems: Theory & Applications*.

Hodeghatta & Nayak. (2014). Intrusion Detection and Prevention Systems. In The InfoSec Handbook (pp. 225-243). Springer.

Hong, J., Liu, C.-C., & Govindarasu, M. (2014). Integrated Anomaly Detection for Cyber Security of the Substations. *IEEE Transactions on Smart Grid*, *5*(4), 1643–1653. doi:10.1109/TSG.2013.2294473

International Energy Agency. (2014). *World energy outlook 2014: Executive summary*. IEA Publications.

Jamshidi, Jaimes Betancourt, & Gomez. (2011). Cyber-physical control of unmanned aerial vehicles. *Sci. Iran. D, 18*(3), 663–668.

Karnouskos, S. (2010). The cooperative Internet of Things enabled smart grid. *Proc. 14th Int. Symp. Consumer Electron.*, 1-6.

Kartakis, S., Abraham, E., & McCann, J. A. J. A. (2015). A testbed for monitoring and controlling smart water networks. *CySWater'15 Proceedings of the 1st ACM International Workshop on Cyber-Physical Systems for Smart Water Networks*.

Khan, Alam, Mohamed, & Harras. (2016). Simulating drone-be-gone: Agile low-cost cyber-physical UAV Testbed (Demonstration). *Proc. Int. Jt. Conf. Auton. Agents Multiagent Syst. AAMAS*, 1491–1492.

Kheng, Sooriyabandara, & Fan. (2011). M2M Communications in the Smart Grid: Applications, Standards, Enabling Technologies, and Research Challenges. *International Journal of Digital Multimedia Broadcasting*.

Konstantopoulos, G. C. (2020). *Towards the Integration of Modern Power Systems into a Cyber–Physical Framework. Energies Journal.* doi:10.3390/en13092169

Kumar, P. S., Emfinger, W., & Karsai, G. (2016). A Testbed to Simulate and Analyze Resilient Cyber-Physical Systems. *International Symposium on rapid system prototyping (RSP), 2015*, 97–103.

Lee, E. (2008). Cyber physical systems: Design challenges. In Object Oriented Real-Time Distributed Computing. *11th IEEE International Symposium on*, 363-369.

León, R. A., Vittal, V., & Manimaran, G. (2007). Application of sensor network for secure electric energy infrastructure. *IEEE Transactions on Power Delivery*, *22*(2), 1021–1028. doi:10.1109/TPWRD.2006.886797

Leonardo. (2019). *System-level Behavioral Detection Framework for Compromised CPS Devices: Smart-Grid Case. ACM Transactions on Cyber-Physical Systems*.

Liu, X. F., Shahriar, M. R., Al Sunny, S. M. N., Leu, M. C., & Hu, L. (2017). Cyber-physical manufacturing cloud: Architecture, virtualization, communication, and testbed. *Journal of Manufacturing Systems*, *43*, 352–364. doi:10.1016/j.jmsy.2017.04.004

Ma & Li. (2020). Hybridized Intelligent Home Renewable Energy Management System for Smart Grids. *MDPI Sustainability Journal*, 1-14.

Miciolino, E. E., Bernieri, G., Pascucci, F., & Setola, R. (2016). Communications network analysis in a SCADA system testbed under cyber-attacks. *IEEE, 23rd Telecommunications Forum*.

Mo, Y. (2012). Cyber–Physical Security of a Smart Grid Infrastructure. *Proceedings of the IEEE*, *100*(1), 195–209. doi:10.1109/JPROC.2011.2161428

Naram, Fetais, & Massoud. (2019). Secure smart contract-enabled control of battery energy storage systems against cyber-attacks. *Alexandria Engineering Journal*.

Perumalraja. (2012). Communication requirements and analysis of distribution networks using WiMAX technology for smart grids. *Conference: Wireless Communications and Mobile Computing Conference (IWCMC), 2012 8th International*.

Pietro Di, A., Foglietta, C., Palmieri, S., & Panzieri, S. (2013). Assessing the impact of cyber-attacks on interdependent physical systems. *International Conference on Critical Infrastructure Protection*. 10.1007/978-3-642-45330-4_15

Poudel, S., Ni, Z., & Malla, N. (2017). Real-time cyber physical system testbed for power system security and control. *International Journal of Electrical Power & Energy Systems*, *90*, 124–133. doi:10.1016/j.ijepes.2017.01.016

Prabhash. (2015). Energy Management System in Smart Grid: An Overview. *IJRSI, 2*(12).

Rajkumar, R. R., Lee, I., Sha, L., & Stankovic, J. (2010). Cyber-physical systems: the next computing revolution. *Proceedings of the 47th Design Automation Conference, DAC'2010*, 731-736.

Rathore, Ryu, Park, & Park. (2018). A Survey on Cyber Physical System Security for IoT: Issues, Challenges, Threats, Solutions. *Journal of Information Process System*.

Saeed, A., Neishaboori, A., Mohamed, A., & Harras, K. A. (2014). Up and away: A visually-controlled easy-to-deploy wireless UAV Cyber- Physical testbed. *International Conference on Wireless and Mobile Computing, Networking and Communications*. 10.1109/WiMOB.2014.6962228

Siaterlis, C., Genge, B., & Hohenadel, M. (2013). EPIC: A testbed for scientifically rigorous cyber-physical security experimentation. *IEEE Transactions on Emerging Topics in Computing*, *1*(2), 319–330. doi:10.1109/TETC.2013.2287188

Singh, D., Tripathi, G., & Jara, A. J. (2014). *A survey of Internet-of-Things: Future vision architecture challenges and services*. IEEE World Forum on Internet of Things (WF-IoT), Seoul, South Korea. 10.1109/WF-IoT.2014.6803174

Soupionis, Y., & Benoist, T. (2015). Cyber-Physical Testbed - The Impact of Cyber Attacks and the Human Factor. *10th International conference for internet technology and secured transactions (ICITST)*, 326–331.

Sumit & Saxena. (2020). Energy management system for smart grid: An overview and key issues. *International Journal of Energy Research*.

Sun, Liu, & Xie. (2016). Cyber-Physical System Security of a Power Grid: State-of-the-Art. *Electronics Journal MDPI*.

Wang, J., & Shi, D. (2018). Cyber-Attacks Related to Intelligent Electronic Devices and Their Countermeasures: A Review. *53rd International Universities Power Engineering Conference (UPEC)*. 10.1109/UPEC.2018.8542059

Wu, X., Zhu, X., Wu, G.-Q., & Ding, W. (2017). Data mining with big data. *IEEE Transactions on Knowledge and Data Engineering*, *26*(1), 97–106.

Xu, L., He, W., & Li, S. (2014). Internet of Things in industries: A survey. *IEEE Transactions on Industrial Informatics*, *10*(4), 2233–2243. doi:10.1109/TII.2014.2300753

Yasin. (2019). Internet of Things Applications as Energy Internet in Smart Grids and Smart Environments. *Electronics Journal MPDI*.

Yatin, AlMajali, & Neuman. (2018). A Comprehensive Analysis of Smart Grid Systems against Cyber-Physical Attacks. *MDPI Electronics Journal*, 1-25.

Yin, S., & Kaynak, O. (2015). Big data for modern industry: Challenges and trends. *Proceedings of the IEEE*, *103*(2), 143–146. doi:10.1109/JPROC.2015.2388958

Yu, X., Cecati, C., Dillon, T., & Simoes, M. G. (2011). New frontier of smart grids. *IEEE Industrial Electronics Magazine*, *5*(3), 49–63. doi:10.1109/MIE.2011.942176

ADDITIONAL READING

Yuan, Y., Tang, X., Zhou, W., Pan, W., Li, X., Zhang, H.-T., Ding, H., & Goncalves, J. (2019). Data driven discovery of cyber physical systems. *Nature Communications*, *10*(1), 4894. doi:10.103841467-019-12490-1 PMID:31653832

KEY TERMS AND DEFINITIONS

Distributed Network Protocol (DNP): A protocol used between components of automation systems that are in process. It is used in resource systems like electricity and water companies. DNP developed for communication between different types of data acquisition and control equipment. It plays a crucial role in SCADA systems, as it is used by major SCADA stations, remote terminal units (RTUs), and smart electronic devices (IEDs).

Flexible Alternating Current Transmission System (FACTS): It is a system consisting of stationary equipment used to transfer alternating current (AC). It is intended to enhance control power and increase the power to transmit power to the grid. In general, it is a system based on power electronics.

High Voltage Direct Current (HVDC): A system use DC to transfer bulk energy over long distances. For long-distance power transmission, HVDC lines are less expensive, and losses are less compared to AC transmission. It connects networks that have different frequencies and characteristics.

Radio Access Technologies (RATs): Is a primary physical method of communication for a radio-based communications network. Many modern mobile phones support many RATs in one device such as Bluetooth, Wi-Fi, GSM, UMTS, LTE, or 5G NR.

Supervisory Control and Data Acquisition (SCADA): Is a control system architecture comprising computers, networked data communications, and graphical user interfaces (GUI) for high-level process supervisory management. SCADA enables monitoring and the issuing of process commands, like controller setpoint changes. It developed to be a universal means of remote access to a variety of local control modules, which could be from different manufacturers and allowing access through standard automation protocols.

Chapter 15
Bayesian Model for Evaluating Real-World Adaptation Progress of a Cyber-Physical System

Arif Sari

 https://orcid.org/0000-0003-0902-9988
Girne American University, Cyprus

Joshua Sopuru

 https://orcid.org/0000-0001-7049-0058
Girne American University, Cyprus

ABSTRACT

Cyber-physical systems, also known as CPS, have come to stay. There is no doubt, CPS would one day outnumber humans in industries. How do we evaluate the adaptation progress of these systems considering changing environmental conditions? A failed implementation of a CPS can result to a loss. Since CPSs are designed to automate industrial activities, which are centred on the use of several technologies, collaboration with humans may sometimes be inevitable. CPSs are needed to automate several processes and thus help firms compete favourably within an industry. This chapter focuses on the adaptation of CPS in diverse work environment. Considering the ecosystem of the CPS, the authors present a Bayesian model evaluating the progress of adaptation of a CPS given some known conditions.

INTRODUCTION

Cyber-physical systems (CPSs) focus on integrating computational applications with physical devices designed as linkages of collaborating cyber and physical components. Powered by data, these systems are considered intelligent and have the ability of automation. There is no doubt, CPS would one day outnumber humans in work environments. How do we evaluate the adaptation progress of these systems considering ever-changing environmental conditions?

DOI: 10.4018/978-1-7998-5101-1.ch015

As new technologies are introduced in an Organization, several practices change in other to adjust to the new work environment. CPS is designed to seamlessly fit into its environment in the shortest time possible and serve to reduce the cost of production, optimize production, and ensure efficiency in an organization. However, a failed implementation can result in a loss or a total closure of an organization. In addition to its implementation problem, interaction with humans may also pose a challenge. A general situation or condition of humans, activities including the facilities or equipment needed, and the environment of the activities are three fundamental factors influencing the adaptation of CPS (Chang. et.al, 2012).

Since CPSs are designed to automate industrial activities that are centered on the use of several technologies collaboration with humans may sometimes be inevitable. In such situations, CPSs may include features designed to support adaptation in a dynamic environment. According to research, challenges of adaptation increases in Industries with broadband structure (Panetto et.al, 2019).

The goal of this chapter is to provide a mathematical framework that will serve as a guide in developing Bayesian models to monitor the adaptation progress of CPS in industries.

In the past, automation was concentrated on some few business processes while the majority of processes are left unautomated. This however has changed due to the changing environment and the dire competition within industries. The need for optimization, which includes; production cost reduction, process efficiency, improved customer satisfaction/loyalty, reduction of waste, increased profitability (Niedermann and Schwarz, 2011), has led many industrial key players to opt for automation. Despite the importance, automation introduces, many industrial players are still skeptical about the idea of leaving the control of their business to CPSs. This, however, is about to change as the new industrial revolution (industry 4.0) powered by data and CPSs take over. Another driving technology of CPS is IoT. In time past the internet transformed communication and collaboration in many businesses, in these present times, the internet is not only influencing communication but also powering decisions in several industries. The IoT is a clear example of such usage of internet infrastructure to power Just-in-time production supporting a pull-based demand.

As businesses harness the power of data/information, CPSs are needed to automate several processes and thus help firms compete favorably within an industry. Considering the complexity in human behavior and the successful implementation of the Bayesian network in the prediction of human behavior, a Bayesian model can effectively be designed to predict the probability of an event given some known conditions (conditional probability). Considering known processes available within an industry, the progress of adaptation can be evaluated. This chapter follows are score-based approach in evaluating the rate of learning (adaptation) of a CPS given some known conditions. Evaluating the adaptation process of CPS will go a long way in achieving a wider adoption of CPS and the technologies they power. Some key challenges of adoption are, real-time control, real-time SOS, modularization of CPS, etc... These adoption challenges relate to adaptation problems and will be elaborated upon in this chapter. Another aspect to consider in adaption is the specific business process or sets of processes being automated. The more intertwine (cross-functional) a process is the more complex adaptation would appear. As processes move from one functional department to another, information is transferred from one CPS process to another and this calls for a control mechanism. The CPS ecosystem is designed to handle whatever complexity that may arise from communication between the CPS and its environment. In understanding adaptation, the ecosystem (Frame) is important and would be discussed briefly in this chapter.

The chapter is organized as follows. We started by reviewing some related literature, then we presented an overview of CPS and different terminologies needed in understanding its operations, next section presents of our research questions aimed to answer two questions, results of the experiment are then presented followed by relevant discussions on our findings, directions for further studies and finally the conclusion/summary of the chapter.

REVIEW OF RELATED STUDIES

It is no doubt that CPS systems managing different manufacturing lines will continue to emerge. Just as humans are expected to become professionals as they spend many years at work, CPS or intelligent machines are not excluded from such expectations.

Lee, Azamfar, and Singh (2019) investigated Blockchain technology and how it enables a better CPS architecture for Industry 4.0. In their work, they identified four key features a distributed ledger must have in other to be used for any CPS application. These features include energy consumption, the type of network access, the ability to execute orders automatically, and the type of network. It is important to note that one of the vital characteristics of blockchain technology is the immutability of data. For a CPC, the immutability of data can serve as a means of gaining experience in a distributed network.

Aste, Tasca, and Matteo (2017) in their work titled "Blockchain technologies: The foreseeable impact on society and industry" also mentioned immutability as one of the blockchains valued characteristics when it comes to data retention and event monitoring.

Lee, Azamfar, and Singh postulated that blockchain-enabled CPS will serve as a solution to several real-world implementation challenges facing CPS of which adaptation is one of such challenges. In their design, they believe addressing resilience, data integrity, interoperability, and security/privacy will create a better architecture to aid CPS interaction with the physical environment.

On the other hand, Zhou et.al, (2019) investigated ways to improve the dependability self-adapting of the CPS. In their work titled "Improving the Dependability of Self-Adaptive Cyber-Physical System with Formal Compositional Contract", they emphasize the importance of CPS to interact with the world in a decentralized way. To achieve this, they stated that achieving event observation and processing of decisions on time is key. To implement their requirements, they proposed a reliability contract-based consensus that ensures a large-scale implementation of their work.

To achieve a CPS having the ability to easily adapt to the changing environments and handle other real-world challenges, it will be proper to understand the modeling of CPS. Derler, Lee, and Vincentelli (2011) in their article titled "Modelling cyber-physical systems" discussed the challenges facing the modeling of CPS. Using the fuel management CPS of an aircraft as a case study, they discovered issues facing the modeling of CPS and proposed solutions that can be applied.

Some of the challenges they highlight are given below.

Models with Nondeterminate or Solver-Dependent

A CPS might be modeled as a crossbreed framework where physical procedures are referred to as constant time models of elements and calculations are depicted utilizing state machines, dataflow models, simultaneous/receptive models, as well as Discrete event (DE models).

Constant time models work with algorithms that numerically estimate the answers to differential conditions. The structure of such solvers is a built-up, yet a long way from-insignificant workmanship. Coordinating such solvers with discrete models is a more current issue, and issues endure in numerous accessible instruments. One of the issues that can emerge is that the output characterized by a model might be nondeterminate in any event when the fundamental framework being displayed is resolved. This implies that the model characterizes an assortment of practices, instead of solitary conduct. This can happen, for instance, when DEs are synchronous and the semantics of the demonstrating language neglects to indicate solitary conduct. Such non-determinism can astonish framework creators. Another difficulty that can emerge is that numerical solver regularly powerfully change the progression size that they use to increase time, and the conduct of the model can rely upon the chose step sizes. Once more, this will shock architects, who occasionally know the reason for the step-size choice.

Preventing Misconnected Model Components

The larger a model becomes, the harder it is to check for accuracy of associations between parts. Commonly model segments are profoundly interconnected, and the chance of mistakes increments. They identified three types of errors that can result from this. Transposition, semantic and unit errors. A Unit error happens when a port usurps information with unexpected units in comparison to those normal at the receiving port.

Modeling Interactions of Functionality and Implementation

These models certainly accept that information is registered and communicated in zero time, so the elements of the product and systems have no impact on framework conduct. Be that as it may, calculation and correspondence require some investment. They contended that to assess a CPS model, it is important to display the elements of programming and systems. Execution is to a great extent symmetrical to usefulness and ought to in this manner is not a fundamental piece of a model of usefulness. Rather, it should be conceivable to conjoin a practical model with a usage model. The last takes into consideration configuration space investigation, while the previous backings the structure of control methodologies. The conjoined models empower the assessment of communications over these spaces.

Modeling Distributed Behaviours

The distributed attribute of CPS requires techniques that encourage the creation of parts that are isolated in space. Demonstrating circulated frameworks adds to the intricacy of displaying CPS by presenting issues, for example, incongruities in estimations of time, organize delays, defective correspondence, consistency of perspectives on framework state, and appropriate agreement.

System Heterogeneity

A propensity all through the difficulties emerges from the characteristic heterogeneity and intricacy of CPSs. CPS coordinates differing subsystems. Regularly these subsystems have space explicit, and here and there very advanced demonstrating strategies. Incorporating the subsequent models to create all-encompassing perspectives on the framework turns out to be testing.

They concluded their studies by emphasizing the failure of most modeling techniques in addressing the issues they highlighted.

One of the challenges of modeling is incomplete data. In modeling the adaptation of CPS, the chosen algorithm or model needs to however in one way or the other handle missing data. Srivastava et. al (2013), in their work titled "Modelling Cyber-Physical Vulnerability of the Smart Grid with Incomplete Information," discussed modeling amidst incomplete data. According to them, reliable results can still be derived from models developed with insufficient data.

Lin, Sedigh, and Miller (2010) in their work titled "Modelling Cyber-Physical Systems with Semantic Agents" mentioned the difficulty in modeling a CPS. A major reason for this difficulty as highlighted by them is the complexity of CPS, interdependencies of components, and the differences in the operation of CPS.

It is of no doubt, modeling the behavior of the CPS is different from several other machines. Lin points out this difference and hinged them on the complexity of the CPS themselves. The Bayesian approach to complex system modeling has been proven by research to be effective in modeling behavior.

According to Stocker and Simoncelli (2008), researchers Alan and Eero proposed an extended Bayesian model of which they referred to an extended probabilistic model for solving human perception problems. They argued the importance of an unbiased evaluation in conducting behavioral experiments. According to them, a researcher's previous knowledge can affect his judgment regarding a person's behavior. The extended probabilistic model seeks to handle the previous perception problem of the researcher. To ascertain the ability of a Bayesian model in handling behavioral prediction, we discovered other interesting works done by renowned researchers. One such is the work done by Roshandel, Medvidovic, and Golubchik (2007). In their work titled "A Bayesian Model for Predicting Reliability of Software Systems at the Architectural Level" Complex software involving decision making and forecasting was modeled using the Bayesian network and the results were promising. In Bayesian modeling, however, there are important notes to have at the back of our minds. Hamilton, Pollino, and Jakeman (2015) highlight some important things to consider when modeling a real-world event.

There is an expanding inclination in data framework advancement to consider not just the usefulness which will be modeled, however, to give impressive thoughtfulness regarding the association around the framework. This expanded degree puts heavier prerequisites on the modeling language, which must be fitting for displaying any true movement, as opposed to simply the data preparing exercises to be modeled. True modeling can likewise be intriguing in situations where no new data framework is arranged, e.g. for the general investigation of the association's data, report, and additionally material asset streams regarding execution, accessibility, dependability, or security.

By and large, three parts of an item are significant while making a model

- The substance of an item relates to material nearness, for example, the nearness of a paper structure in a specialist's info container which triggers a specific action identified with that structure.
- The properties of an item are the information that can be separated from the item's substance, for example, the shade of the paper structure, its size, and thickness.
- The information conveyed by an item is the information' purposely coded onto the substance, for example, the letters composed on the above structure.

Bayesian networks can be utilized for grouping.

Backpropagation is a neural system calculation for grouping that utilizes a strategy for angle plummet. It looks for a lot of loads that can demonstrate the information to limit the mean-squared separation between the system's class forecast and the real class mark of information tuples. Rules might be extricated from prepared neural systems to help improve the interpretability of the scholarly system.

A support vector machine is a calculation for the characterization of both direct and nonlinear information. It changes the first information into a higher dimension, from where it can discover a hyperplane for information partition utilizing fundamental preparing tuples called support vectors.

The frequent pattern shows a strong relationship between characteristic worth sets (or things) in information and is utilized in characterization dependent on visit designs. Ways to deal with this strategy incorporate affiliated grouping and discriminant visit design-based arrangement. In acquainted grouping, a classifier is worked from affiliation rules created from visit designs. In discriminative successive example-based characterization, visit designs fill in as joined highlights, which are considered notwithstanding single highlights when constructing an older model.

Decision tree classifiers, Bayesian classifiers, arrangement by backpropagation, support vector machines, and classifying dependent on visit designs are on the whole instances of anxious students in that they use preparing tuples to develop a speculation model and along these lines are prepared for ordering new tuples. This diverges from lethargic students or occurrence-based strategies for grouping, for example, closest neighbor classifiers and case-based thinking classifiers, which store the entirety of the preparation tuples in design space and hold up until gave a test tuple before performing speculation. Subsequently, sluggish students require productive ordering methods.

In a genetic algorithm, populaces of rules "develop" utilizing activities of hybrid and transformation until all standards inside a populace fulfill a predetermined limit. Harsh set hypotheses can be utilized to around characterize classes that are not discernible dependent on the accessible traits. Fluffy set methodologies supplant "fragile" edge shorts for consistent esteemed qualities with participation degree capacities.

Binary classification scheme, for example, support vector machines, can be adjusted to deal with multiclass grouping. This includes developing a troupe of twofold classifiers. Blunder adjusting codes can be utilized to build the exactness of the group.

Semi-supervised characterization is helpful when a lot of Uncategorized information exists. It fabricates a classifier utilizing both marked and Uncategorized information. Instances of semi-unlabelled order incorporate self-preparing and training.

Dynamic learning is a type of supervised discovering that is likewise appropriate for circumstances where information is bountiful, yet the class marks are scant or costly to acquire. The learning calculation can effectively inquiry about a client (e.g., a human prophet) for names. To minimize expenses, the dynamic student means to accomplish high precision utilizing as hardly any named cases as could be expected under the circumstances.

Move learning plans to remove the information from at least one source assignments and apply the information to an objective undertaking. TrAdaBoost is a case of the example-based way to deal with move realizing, which reweights a portion of the information from the source assignment and utilizations it to get familiar with the objective errand, in this manner requiring less marked objective undertaking tuples.

A Bayesian classifier depends on the possibility that the job of a (characteristic) class is to anticipate the estimations of highlights for individuals from that class. Models are assembled in classes since they have normal qualities for the highlights. Such classes are frequently called normal sorts. The objective element might relate to a discrete class, which is not twofold.

The thought behind a Bayesian classifier is that, if an agent knows the class, it can foresee the estimations of different highlights. On the off chance that it does not have the least idea about the class,

Bayes' standard can be utilized to anticipate the class given (a portion of) the component esteems. In a Bayesian classifier, the learning specialist constructs a probabilistic model of the highlights and uses that model to anticipate the arrangement of another model.

A latent variable is a probabilistic variable that is not monitored. A Bayesian classifier is a probabilistic model where the characterization is an idle variable that is probabilistically identified with the watched factors. Grouping at that point become surmising in the probabilistic model.

UNCERTAINTIES

When structuring CPS the accessible information is frequently not sufficient to foresee all the run time conditions the system will experience (e.g., absent or erroneous information in regards to the accessibility of resources, concrete working conditions that the framework will look at run time, and the development of new necessities while the framework is working). With that in mind, Garlan (2010) contends that in today's programming, system vulnerability ought to be considered as a top-notch worry all through the entire life cycle of the CPS. With regards to versatile frameworks, Ramirez et al. (2012) give a scientific classification to a vulnerability that portrays regular wellsprings of vulnerability and their impact on adaptation, plan, and run-time periods of the CPS. Esfahani and Malek (2013) present a broad list of possible vulnerabilities associated with the adaptation of models. Also, these researchers explore vulnerability attributes, i.e., reducibility versus finality, changeability versus absence of information, and range of vulnerability. Perez-Palacin and Mirandola (2014) present another scientific categorization for vulnerability for adaptive systems dependent on three parameters: area of application, level, and nature of vulnerability. Mahdavi-Hezavehi et al. (2016) present a grouping structure for vulnerability in adaptive systems, which depends on an efficient audit of experiences coalited.

ADAPTATION

Adaptive CPSs can change their behavior at run time in other to accommodate changes in their environment. Eccentric conditions, for example, changes in the system condition, system deficiencies, new prerequisites, and changes in the need for certain requirements are a portion of the reason behind the adaptative requirements of CPS. To manage these vulnerabilities, an adaptive CPS should be able to evaluate itself, accumulate information, and break down choices in other to choose from the best options available to it. Various standards aimed at achieving adaptation have been proposed from previous studies. We sum up three standards and developed on these a framework for evaluating the adaptation of CPS. This chapter introduced: engineering-based adaptation, multi-specialist-based methodologies, and self-sorting-based methodologies.

Engineering-Based Adaptation

Engineering based adaptation (Oreizy et al., 1998) has been known over the years as very effective in handling adaptation uncertainties. The basic elements of engineering-based self-adaptation are characterized in the MAPE-K (i.e., Monitor, Analyse, Plan, Execute, and knowledge segment) reference model (Kephart and Chess, 2003). By consenting with the idea of the separation of adaptation needs based on different domains, the MAPE-K model has demonstrated to be a reasonable methodology for structuring input circles and creating self-adaptive CPS frameworks (Weyns et al., 2013a). One notable engineering-based self-adaptive architecture is Rainbow (Garlan et al., 2004). Rainbow utilizes a theoretical engineering model to evaluate programming framework run time determinations, asses model for imperative infringement, and when required, perform general or module level adjustments. Calinescu et al. (2011) present a model for evaluating the quality of self-adaptative based frameworks. This model expands on the MAPE-K design. In their structure, the high-level nature of administration necessities is converted into probabilistic fleeting rationale formulae that are utilized to recognize and uphold the ideal framework design while considering the quality conditions. Additionally, theory based on utility can be utilized (Cheng et al., 2006) to technically select the best quality proposed amidst clashing options, this allows for the choice of the best adaptation procedure for CPS in each domain.

Multi-Specialist-Based Methodologies

Multi-specialist-based methodologies are categorized as a decentralized framework where every part (specialist) is a self-ruling problem solver, regularly ready to work effectively in rapidly changing and unsure conditions (Wooldridge, 2001). These agents communicate to tackle problems that are above their capacities or information level. Multi-agent architecture has capabilities that are needed to build self-adaptive frameworks. agents are independent, objective coordinated substances. They get their versatility from objectives. When different agents are accessible, an objective can be accomplished by choosing among the agent at run time, for instance utilizing exchange (Fatima et al., 2006), as opposed to requiring a designed plan. An agent incorporates details of the situation or setting in which it operates or is expected to accomplish its objective. A calling agent can essentially post the objectives it wishes to accomplish and choose just those agents suitable to the objective and current preparing setting: the correct agent at the opportune time justified conditions. Also, an agent's internal procedures are normally connected with a setting condition portraying the environment/conditions in which the procedure can accomplish its determined objective.

Self-Sorting-Based Methodologies

Self-sorting is a dynamic and versatile procedure where a system obtains and keeps up the structure itself, without external control (De Wolf and Holvoet, 2004). Self-sorting aims to provide an adaptive framework that automatically retrieves order by itself. Self-sorting frameworks have the basic characteristics: increase in order, self-rule (no interference from external forces), versatility, and dynamicity. Self-sorting frameworks may uncover new behavior progressively as new environments emerge from the associations between parts at the neighborhood level. The development of self-sorting systems is regularly propelled by natural occurrences in the industry (Di Marzo Serugendo et al., 2006).

UNDERSTANDING THE LOGIC BEHIND CPS

In understanding CPS, we must in theory divide its components into two aspects of

- Cyber such as computer control/codes, data, communication, and potential networks, and

- Physical, involving movements within an environment

That is, a Cyber-physical system is the application of Cyber components or resources into the physical environment or space. For the sake of simplicity in understanding CPS, we will study them as multi-dynamical systems. Multi-dynamical study of systems ensures that complex systems are viewed as a combination of simple dynamic parts. This understanding helps in the understanding of the logic behind CPS.

Figure 1. CPS as a combination of several dynamic parts

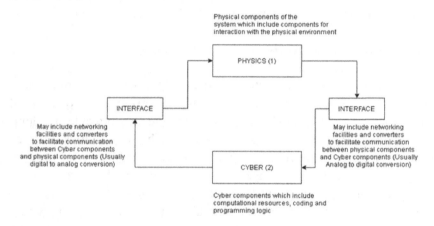

The Physics components identified as 1 or frame define the physical activities of a CPS which is necessary for adaptation and psychomotor skills.

ENVIRONMENT

A cyber-physical system interacts with two types of environments; cyberspace and a physical environment. The cyberspace makes it possible for communication while the physical environment is powered to enable interactions with physical components.

Cyber Space

A CPS needs to communicate or interact, the cyberspace employs a distributed style of information processing that allows messages to be passed within and between CPSs. Communication in CPS can be considered as direct or indirect. The internet via an IP address is an example of a channel of communication available for CPS. Proximity in this case or physical nearness of CPS systems is not significant when communication is done over the internet.

Direct channels transmit messages from one sending CPS to one or several receiving systems without any modification.

Indirect channels are implemented over a shared memory that is usually installed in the cyberspace. To send a message, a sending CPS modifies the state of the shared memory. In shared memory, the state can also be affected by changes in the cyber environment. This form of change is caused by Cyber dynamics.

Physical Environment

This environment consists of things (objects) and energy (Physical fields) whose characteristics are usually modeled as a dynamic network consisting of physical state variables. In the physical environment unlike the cyber environment proximity is important as interactions depend on the distance of CPS with objects or other CPS.

RESEARCH QUESTIONS

We plan to investigate the best approaches utilized in self-adjustment components and models to deal with vulnerability while developing CPS.

RQ1: How can previous knowledge of adaptation be applied to improve the adaptation of CPS:

Considering previous knowledge of existing adaptable techniques developed to address difficulties and concerns of adaptation of CPS, we look to intently inspect basic methodologies, contemplations, and advances to recognize effective models or strategies. The documentation of such previous knowledge should be used to support CPS developers. Furthermore, this previous knowledge can give a solid establishment to planning self-adjustment capacities in CPS design that can be additionally explored and improved by CPS analysts.

RQ2: How can previous knowledge help in understanding adaptation progress in CPS:

Documenting CPS performance within an industry can provide research data used to understand and predict CPS performance in different industries.

To answer these questions, we developed a Bayesian network based on available data.

Bayesian Adaptive Test

The procedure can be divided into two stages: model creation and testing. In the first, the understudy model is made while in the second one the model is utilized to test examinees.

Data Collection

To support the creation of a student model we have collected empirical data.

We created an implementation test for CPS in several industries. The test focused on the three fundamental factors influencing the adaptation of CPS as identified by Chang et al. (2012).

BAYESIAN MODELS FOR AN ADAPTIVE TEST

In this segment we go over the fundamental meanings of Bayesian networks, more information can be found in [Nielsen and Jensen, 2007, Kjærulff and Madsen, 2008].

The utilization of BNs in the evaluation of adaptation (learning) is examined in [Almond et al., 1999; Culbertson, 2014]. This section is centered around the creation of Bayesian systems models for adaptive learning. This is also discussed, for instance, in [Vomlel, 2004b; Vomlel, 2004a].

The Bayesian network is a graphical model representing conditional probabilities. It is made up of the following:

- Set of variables (nodes),
- Set of edges, and
- Set of conditional probabilities.

To develop a BN model for an adaptive model we must perform 3 stages:

1. characterize hubs of the BN,
2. characterize associations among hubs, and
3. determine beginning estimations of contingent likelihood tables.

During the adaptation test, we utilize standard BN deduction methods to update the system. This method measures the probabilities of known abilities to the probabilities of unknown experiences retrieved by data. One undertaking to explain during the test technique is the determination of the following unknown experience. This is repeated throughout the test experiment and it is represented below.

Let $s - 1$ represent the test steps. This means s unknown scenarios have been experienced by the CPS and form the evidence e: e = {Xi1 = xi1, . . ., Xin = xin |i1, . . ., in ∈ {1, . . ., m}}.

Leftover experiences possible is represented as Xs = X \ e

The objective is to choose an experience from Xs to be posed straightaway. We select experience with the highest probability. We process the total Shannon entropy overall expertise factors of S given proof e. This is gotten with the formula below:

$$H(e) = \sum_{i=1}^{n} \sum_{j=1}^{i_n} -P(S_i = s_{i,j}|e) \cdot \log P(S_i = s_{i,j}|e).$$

If for instance an experience X0 ∈ Xs with possible outcomes x 0 1, . . ., x0 p is selected. On adding the observed output, the state of the machine's overall experiences will change. The value of this new change increased by X0 = x 0 j, j ∈ {1, . . ., p} can be computed as follows:

$$H(e, X' = x'_j) = \sum_{i=1}^{n} \sum_{j=1}^{n_i} \frac{-P(S_i = s_{i,j}|e, X' = x'_j)}{\cdot \log P(S_i = s_{i,j}|e, X' = x'_j)} .$$

Figure 2. Scoring chart

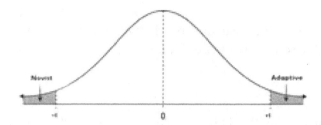

Obtaining the Total Score of New Experience Leading to Adaptation

BN models ordinarily produce scores of experiences gained in a model. Considering this study, this is not very helpful. Therefore, to obtain a score relating to the adaptation derived based on knowledge, we first convert the experience gotten by setting the score (SC) as a weighted aggregate of aptitudes (S1 = s1, . . ., Sn = sn):

$$SC \stackrel{\text{def}}{=} \sum_{i=1}^{n} s_i C_i$$

Since the various states or skilled levels, S is unknown during the experiment, we take an estimate of their sum as follows:

$$E(SC) = \sum_{i=1}^{n} \sum_{j=1}^{n_i} P(S_i = s_{i,j}) s_{i,j} C_i$$

From our design, the scoring values reflect the degree of expected adaptation for a feature. Figure 2 is a scoring chart explaining how scoring values are interpreted.

Table 1. List of features monitored

F1	Application domain
F2	Complexity of task
F3	Degree of human interference
F4	Duration of task
F5	Level of environmental Obstacle
F6	Machine/human-initiated
F7	Level of dynamism

Scored Features

Seven features we believe affect the adaptation of CPS was monitored and a scoring value assigned to them. Table 1 is a list and description of these features.

Probability Theory

The environmental conditions highlighted above are conditions that occur randomly with a different distribution. Observations are the outcome of the CPS behavior as these random variables play out.

To exacerbate the situation, the probability hypothesis is utilized to show an assortment of nuance various frameworks, which at that point troubles the effectively mistaken arithmetic for the unmistakable and frequently clashing philosophical implications of those applications.

The joint, or multivariate, a probability distribution over the set of random variables X, denoted by P(X). The probability of a conjunction of two sets of variables, $X \wedge Y$, is denoted as $P(X \wedge Y)$ and also as P(X, Y). The marginal distribution of $Y \subseteq X$ is then given by summing (or integrating) over all the remaining variables, i.e., P(Y) $= \Sigma Z = X \backslash Y P(Y, Z)$. A conditional probability distribution P(X|Y) is defined as P(X, Y)/P(Y). Two variables X and Y are said to be conditionally independent given a third variable, Z if P(X|Y, Z) =P(X|Z).In case a variable X is discrete, the variable is bounded by a finite set of possible values x, a probability is then denoted by P(X=x). In case the outcome space of a variable X is the set of real numbers R or a subset thereof, one uses the probability P(X£x).

METHODS

In a Bayesian model of adaptation, we will assume that the level of adaptation of the CPS cannot be directly observed only a corresponding change in behavior can be seen. If a scoring variable is maintained with values assigned to a previously observed change in behavior, these sets of observations would form prior knowledge for the Bayesian model. With Bayesian inference estimation of a change in behavior can be done by combining changes in scoring values with prior scoring values (prior knowledge). Let y represent all the previously observed score values while x changes in scoring values.

We derive a conditional probability function of *P(x|y)*, observation is made based on the posterior probability of x given y.

Based on Bayes' Theorem, this posterior probability is represented as

$$P(x|y) = \frac{P(y \mid x) P(x)}{P(y)}$$

Assuming a Gaussian distribution for the behavioral change and prior scoring values, we generate the equations:

$$P(y \mid x) = \frac{1}{\sqrt{2\pi\sigma_1}} \exp\left(-\frac{(y-x-\mu_1)^2}{\sqrt{2\sigma}}\right)$$

$$P(x) = \frac{1}{\sqrt{2\pi\sigma_p}} \exp\left(-\frac{(y-x-\mu_p)^2}{\sqrt{2\sigma_p}}\right)$$

where σ_1 and σ_p are standard deviations current score values and the prior scores, respectively, and μ_1 and μ_p are mean values of the distributions, respectively.

Based on these assumptions, we proposed the model in Figure 3

Figure 3. Bayesian model

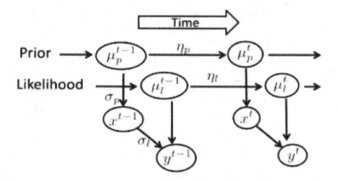

RESULTS

The results of our study are provided in this section. Results are gotten based on the F1-F7.

Score tests were performed for 23 CPS and results were documented as shown in table 2. Based on the scoring formula explained above, seven features were scored, and their averages were recorded. Mean and standard deviation errors resulting from the tests were computed for each CPS and each feature as shown in Table 3.

The probability distributions (scoring values) were determined by the model based on generated parameters. Only one feature was not fitted to the model, variance across feature was very small (<4%) and good to proceed with (Figures 4 & 5).

Test conducted on different CPS under dynamic scenarios. For example, CPS0021 shows F4 (27%) influences its adaptation better than any other feature tested. Other features with remarkable influence are F2 (23%) and F5 (22%). CPS022 and 027 also proved F4 as a major feature influencing adaptation with 27% and 25% respectively as shown in Figure 6 below.

Considering all CPS and features we observed that F6 achieved an overall percentage influence of 16%, F5 15%, while F4, F2, and F1 shared 14%, F3 and F7 appeared to be the least with 13%.

Table 2. Scored data collected

CPS Code Name	F1	F2	F3	F4	F5	F6	F7
CPS021	0.117611	0.823919	0.134078	0.98041	0.786873	0.662589	0.084569
CPS022	0.321076	0.612104	0.038703	0.692294	0.111805	0.667276	0.092005
CPS023	0.853125	0.035318	0.624768	0.77352	0.396986	0.800501	0.030685
CPS024	0.046791	0.943218	0.995086	0.10516	0.544703	0.169428	0.058993
CPS025	0.935993	0.234688	0.748217	0.086821	0.583321	0.97982	0.575294
CPS026	0.934503	0.348993	0.32435	0.912092	0.485991	0.05238	0.538299
CPS027	0.024247	0.68444	0.051342	0.849338	0.774809	0.320381	0.628672
CPS028	0.827841	0.898735	0.017481	0.099313	0.957317	0.512386	0.202273
CPS029	0.827531	0.596967	0.145938	0.584476	0.969428	0.313448	0.541642
CPS030	0.08856	0.788916	0.778531	0.531097	0.163927	0.981218	0.156801
CPS031	0.470692	0.447087	0.559851	0.033939	0.53277	0.137835	0.931143
CPS032	0.88882	0.118486	0.103906	0.295257	0.495065	0.462388	0.546519
CPS033	0.990656	0.337802	0.907895	0.524044	0.681886	0.541586	0.366616
CPS034	0.272216	0.30603	0.067514	0.779947	0.411913	0.161392	0.057377
CPS035	0.25045	0.248113	0.340173	0.276179	0.089959	0.226777	0.588902
CPS036	0.608669	0.132592	0.159343	0.887754	0.984835	0.063314	0.254584
CPS037	0.815396	0.104796	0.187749	0.114914	0.505083	0.823627	0.685152
CPS038	0.733367	0.770252	0.271322	0.680363	0.184445	0.943048	0.028096
CPS039	0.102007	0.029492	0.966244	0.152337	0.394657	0.702193	0.247361
CPS040	0.248508	0.476762	0.915876	0.010385	0.063326	0.222038	0.752881
CPS041	0.229487	0.051652	0.233772	0.129905	0.25876	0.636496	0.511042
CPS042	0.225551	0.628487	0.562303	0.134642	0.31919	0.920571	0.954445
CPS043	0.131301	0.575442	0.386254	0.925531	0.923227	0.270143	0.939489

Table 3. Mean and standard deviation of scores

	F1	F2	F3	F4	F5	F6	F7
Mean	0.475843	0.44323	0.413943	0.459118	0.505229	0.50308	0.424906
Standard deviation	0.347912	0.295411	0.333703	0.345276	0.292839	0.313701	0.309719

Further analysis was performed on the model concentrating on F6 (Machine/human initiated). Results show 89% accuracy in predicting adaptation based on F6, 88% based on F5, and 78% based on F4.

Figure 4. Standard deviation of observed features

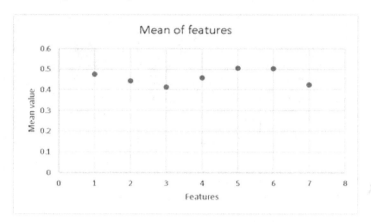

DISCUSSION

Based on Shannon's information entropy, we developed a scoring function to evaluate the level of experience a CPS acquires during operation. This scoring function increases as the level of experience of the CPS improves. Seven features were taken into consideration and a Bayesian model was developed based on the core values of these features. It was observed that out of the seven features experimented upon, F6 which tested for the mode of initialization of the CPS (Machine/human initiated) achieved a higher level of influence in evaluating adaptation. During this study, two important questions were asked (RQ1 and RQ2). The introduction of a scoring function shows that knowledge/skills can be progressively monitored and recorded in a variable $S_c = S_p + H_{(E)}$, in response to RQ2, μ_p^{t-1} referenced in figure 2 above is needed as prior knowledge in other to predict adaptation in CPSs.

Figure 5. Mean value of observed features

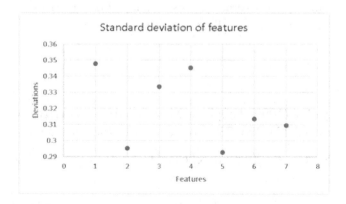

Figure 6. Results gotten from features tested

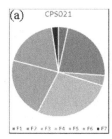 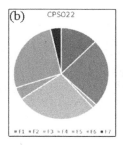 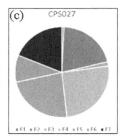

FUTURE WORK

So far in this chapter, we accessed a CPS quality dependent on its expectations to adapt to unknown situations. In doing this, we derived a scoring function to track the CPS experience over time. This method gives sensible results, yet with a few downsides. As a matter of first importance, the proposed scoring formula may not work in some conditions and as a result, cannot be used in all environments. For example, a major requirement of the derived equation is prior knowledge of the work environment. This may be considered a limitation to this research as some CPS is built to have no prior knowledge about their work environment. Further studies would involve researchers applying the same scoring formula to other machine learning algorithms that do not rely on previous knowledge.

CONCLUSION/SUMMARY

Adaptation in a CPS is progressive and should be evaluated continuously. We derived functions to evaluate previous and learned experiences of a CPS implemented in industry and calculated its learning and adaptive rate using a scoring function. It was observed that the summation of different experiences as the time of experiment increased drastically improved the CPS scoring value S. A BN was then implemented to understand the impact of several features on adaptation. In conclusion, one major feature of influencing adaptation is the mode of initialization of the CPS.

REFERENCES

Almond, R. G., & Mislevy, R. J. (1999). Graphical Models and Computerized Adaptive Testing. *Applied Psychological Measurement*, 23(3), 223–237. doi:10.1177/01466219922031347

Aste, T., Tasca, P., & Di Matteo, T. (2017). Blockchain technologies: The foreseeable impact on society and industry. *Computer, 50*(9), 18-28.

Calinescu, R., Grunske, L., Kwiatkowska, M., Mirandola, R., & Tamburrelli, G. (2011). Dynamic QoS Management and Optimization in Service-Based Systems. *IEEE Transactions on Software Engineering*, 37(3), 387–409. doi:10.1109/TSE.2010.92

Chang, J. H., Cho, Y. J., & Wu, T. L. A. (2012). *Human-Machine-Environment Interaction Analysis on the Washing and Changing of Toddlers' Caregivers*. National Taipei University of Technology.

Cheng, S. W., Garlan, D., & Schmerl, B. (2006) Architecture-based Self-adaptation. In *Conference on Performance Engineering (ICPE '14)*. ACM, pp 3–14

Culbertson, M. J. (2014). *Graphical Models for Student Knowledge: Networks, Parameters, and Item Selection* (Ph.D. thesis). The University of Illinois at Urbana.

De Wolf, T., & Holvoet, T. (2004). Emergence and Self-Organisation: a statement of similarities and differences. In *Proceedings of the International Workshop on Engineering Self-Organising Applications 2004* (pp. 96-110). Academic Press.

Derler, P., Lee, E. A., & Vincentelli, A. S. (2011). Modeling cyber-physical systems. *Proceedings of the IEEE, 100*(1), 13–28. doi:10.1109/JPROC.2011.2160929

Di Marzo Serugendo, G., Gleizes, M. P., & Karageorgos, A. (2006) Self-Organisation and Emergence in differences. *Proc. of the 2nd International Workshop on Engineering Self-Organising Applications.*

Esfahani, N., & Malek, S. (2013). Uncertainty in self-adaptive software systems. In *Software Engineering for Self-Adaptive Systems II* (pp. 214–238). Springer. doi:10.1007/978-3-642-35813-5_9

Fatima, S. S., Wooldridge, M. J., & Jennings, N. R. (2006). Multi-issue negotiation with deadlines. *Journal of Artificial Intelligence Research, 27*, 381–417. doi:10.1613/jair.2056

Garlan, D. (2010) Software Engineering in an uncertain world. *Proc. of the FSE/SDP workshop.* 10.1145/1882362.1882389

Garlan, D., Cheng, S.-W., Huang, A.-C., Schmerl, B., & Steenkiste, P. (2004). S-W. Cheng, A-C. Huang, Bradley Schmerl, and Peter Steenkiste. "Rainbow: Architecture-based self-adaptation with reusable infrastructure. *Computer, 37*(10), 46–54. doi:10.1109/MC.2004.175

Hamilton, S. H., Pollino, C. A., & Jakeman, A. J. (2015). Habitat suitability modeling of rare species using Bayesian networks: model evaluation under limited data. *Ecological Modeling, 299*, 64-78.

Hezavehi, E., & Ghafoori, K. (2016). Investigating the effect of relationship marketing aspects on customer satisfaction (Case Study: Boroujerd textile factory). *International Journal of Advanced Biotechnology and Research, 7*, 597–607.

Kephart, J. O., & Chess, D. M. (2003). The Vision of Autonomic Computing. *Computer, 36*(1), 41–50.

Lee, J., Azamfar, M., & Singh, J. (2019). A blockchain-enabled Cyber-Physical System architecture for Industry 4.0 manufacturing systems. *Manufacturing Letters, 20*, 34–39. doi:10.1016/j.mfglet.2019.05.003

Lin, J., Sedigh, S., & Miller, A. (2010, July). Modeling cyber-physical systems with semantic agents. In *2010 IEEE 34th Annual Computer Software and Applications Conference Workshops* (pp. 13-18). IEEE. 10.1109/COMPSACW.2010.13

Mahdavi-Hezavehi, S. (2016, November). Handling multiple quality attributes trade-off in architecture-based self-adaptive systems. In *Proceedings of the 10th European Conference on Software Architecture Workshops* (pp. 1-2). 10.1145/2993412.3010822

Niedermann, F., & Schwarz, H. (2011). Deep business optimization: Making business process optimization theory work in practice. In *Enterprise, business-process, and information systems modeling* (pp. 88–102). Springer. doi:10.1007/978-3-642-21759-3_7

Nielsen, T. D., & Jensen, F. V. (2007). Bayesian Networks and Decision Graphs (Information Science and Statistics). *Artificial Intelligence Research, 27*(1), 381–41.

Oreizy, P., Medvidovic, N., & Taylor, R. N. (1998, April). Architecture-based runtime software evolution. In *Proceedings of the 20th international conference on Software engineering* (pp. 177-186). IEEE. 10.1109/ICSE.1998.671114

Panetto, H., Iung, B., Ivanov, D., Weichhart, G., & Wang, X. (2019). Challenges for the Cyber-Physical Manufacturing Enterprises of the Future. *Annual Reviews in Control, 47*, 200–213. Advance online publication. doi:10.1016/j.arcontrol.2019.02.002

Perez-Palacin, D., & Mirandola, R. (2014) Uncertainties in the Modeling of Self-adaptive Systems. In *Proc. of the 20th International Conference on Software Engineering (ICSE '98)*. IEEE Computer.

Ramirez, A. J., Jensen, A. C., & Cheng, B. H. C. (2012) A Taxonomy of Uncertainty for Dynamically Adaptive Self-Adaptation with Reusable Infrastructure. *Computer, 37*(10), 46–54.

Roshandel, R., Medvidovic, N., & Golubchik, L. (2007, July). A Bayesian model for predicting the reliability of software systems at the architectural level. In *International Conference on the Quality of Software Architectures* (pp. 108-126). Springer. 10.1007/978-3-540-77619-2_7

Srivastava, A., Morris, T., Ernster, T., Vellaithurai, C., Pan, S., & Adhikari, U. (2013). Modeling cyber-physical vulnerability of the smart grid with incomplete information. *IEEE Transactions on Smart Grid, 4*(1), 235–244. doi:10.1109/TSG.2012.2232318

Stocker, A. A., & Simoncelli, E. P. (2008). A Bayesian model of conditioned perception. In Advances in neural information processing systems (pp. 1409-1416). Academic Press.

Vomlel, J. (2004a). Bayesian networks in educational testing. *International Journal of Uncertainty, Fuzziness and Knowledge-based Systems, 12*(supp01), 83–100. doi:10.1142/S021848850400259X

Weyns, D., & Ahmad, T. (2013, July). Claims and evidence for architecture-based self-adaptation: A systematic literature review. In *European Conference on Software Architecture* (pp. 249-265). Springer. 10.1007/978-3-642-39031-9_22

Wooldridge, M. (2001). *Multi-agent systems: an introduction*. Wiley.

Zhou, P., Zuo, D., Hou, K., Zhang, Z., & Dong, J. (2019). Improving the Dependability of Self-Adaptive Cyber-Physical System With Formal Compositional Contract. *IEEE Transactions on Reliability*. Advance online publication. doi:10.1109/TR.2019.2930009

KEY TERMS AND DEFINITIONS

Bayesian Networks: A probabilistic model representing sets of variables and their dependencies.

Cyber-Physical Systems: A computer system whose functions are monitored and managed by algorithms. Also known as CPS they comprise of physical and software components coexisting together and providing intelligence.

Self-Adaptation: The ability of a computer system to change parts or all it is working algorithm over time. Self-adaptation usually occurs over time as experience is acquired.

Compilation of References

Abadi, M., Budiu, M., Erlingsson, Ú., & Ligatti, J. (2009). Control-flow integrity principles, implementations, and applications. ACM Trans. Inf. Syst. Secur., 13. doi:10.1145/1609956.1609960

Abdulmalik, Lin, Li, & Luo. (2017). *Cyber-Physical Systems Security – A Survey.* arXiv.org

Abdulrahaman. (2018). Review Smart grids security challenges: Classification by sources of threats. *Journal of Electrical Systems and Information Technology.*

Abraham, A. (2005). Artificial neural networks. In Handbook for Measurement Systems Design. John Wiley & Sons. doi:10.1002/0471497398.mm421

Adadi, A., & Berrada, M. (2018). Peeking inside the black-box: A survey on Explainable Artificial Intelligence (XAI). *IEEE Access: Practical Innovations, Open Solutions, 6,* 52138–52160. doi:10.1109/ACCESS.2018.2870052

Adnan. (2014). *Renewable energy prospects: Chain.* IRENA International Renewable Energy Agency.

Adnan. (2018). *Renewable energy prospects for the European union.* IRENA International Renewable Energy Agency.

Agarwal, A., Goel, D., Tyagi, A., Aggarwal, A., & Rastogi, R. (2018). A Smarter Approach for Better Lifestyle in Indian Societies, In Progress in Advanced Computing and Intelligent Engineering. Advances in Intelligent Systems and Computing, (vol 563, pp. 355-362). Springer. DOI doi:10.1007/978-981-10-6872-0_33

Agarwal, S., Sharma, P., Rastogi, R., Kaul, U., & Jain, S. (2014) Unsupervised Classification of Mixed Data Type of Attributes Using Genetic Algorithm (Numeric, Categorical, Ordinal, Binary, Ratio-Scaled). In *Proceedings of the Third International Conference on Soft Computing for Problem Solving. Advances in Intelligent Systems and Computing,* (vol. 258, pp. 121-131). Springer. DOI 10.1007/978-81-322-1771-8_11

Aggarwal, K., Rastogi, R., & Mondal, P. (2015). An exhaustive review for infix to postfix conversion with applications and benefits. *Proceedings of 09th INDIACom;2nd International Conference on Computing for Sustainable Global Development,* 95-100. https://ieeexplore.ieee.org/document/7100228

Aggarwal, S., Rastogi, R., & Mittal, S. (2015). A Novel Approach for Communication Among Blind Deaf and Dumb People. *Proceedings of 09th INDIACom; 2015 2nd International Conference on Computing for Sustainable Global Development.* https://ieeexplore.ieee.org/abstract/document/7100321

Ahmad, A., Paul, A., Rathore, M. M., & Chang, H. (2016). Smart cyber society: Integration of capillary devices with high usability based on Cyber-Physical System. *Future Generation Computer Systems, 56,* 493–503. doi:10.1016/j.future.2015.08.004

Ahmadi, H., & Bouallegue, R. (2017). Exploiting machine learning strategies and RSSI for localization in wireless sensor networks: A survey. *2017 13th International Wireless Communications and Mobile Computing Conference, IWCMC 2017*. 10.1109/IWCMC.2017.7986447

Ahmad, I., Abdullah, A. B., & Alghamdi, A. S. (2009, October). Application of artificial neural network in detection of DOS attacks. In *Proceedings of the 2nd international conference on Security of information and networks* (pp. 229-234). 10.1145/1626195.1626252

Ahmadi, A., Sodhro, A., Cherifi, C., Cheutet, V., & Ouzrout, Y. (2018). Evolution of 3C Cyber-Physical Systems Architecture for Industry 4.0. *Proceedings of SOHOMA*, 448-459.

Ahmed & Elatif. (2015). Network Denial of Service Threat Security on Cloud Computing A Survey. International Journal of Scientific Research in Science, Engineering and Technology, 1(5).

Ahmed & Saeed. (2014). A Survey of Big Data Cloud Computing Security. *International Journal of Computer Science and Software Engineering*, 3(1).

Ahmed, Z. E., Saeed, R. A., Ghopade, S. N., & Mukherjee, A. (2020). Energy Optimization in LPWANs by using Heuristic Techniques. In B. S. Chaudhari & M. Zennaro (Eds.), *LPWAN Technologies for IoT and M2MApplications*. Elsevier., doi:10.1016/B978-0-12-818880-4.00011-9.

Ahn, J., Paek, J., & Ko, J. (2016). Machine Learning-Based Image Classification for Wireless Camera Sensor Networks. *Proceedings - 2016 IEEE 22nd International Conference on Embedded and Real-Time Computing Systems and Applications, RTCSA 2016*. 10.1109/RTCSA.2016.29

Ahuja, Jana, Swarnkar, & Halder. (2016). On Preventing SQL Injection Attacks. *IIT Panta Journal, 395*, 49-64.

Ahuja, R., Chug, A., Gupta, S., Ahuja, P., & Kohli, S. (2020). Classification and Clustering Algorithms of Machine Learning with their Applications. In *Nature-Inspired Computation in Data Mining and Machine Learning* (pp. 225–248). Cham: Springer. doi:10.1007/978-3-030-28553-1_11

Akter, S., Wamba, S. F., Gunasekaran, A., Dubey, R., & Childe, S. J. (2016). How to improve firm performance using big data analytics capability and business strategy alignment? *International Journal of Production Economics, 182*, 113–131. doi:10.1016/j.ijpe.2016.08.018

Alahakoon, D., & Yu, X. (2016). Smart electricity meter data intelligence for future energy systems: A survey. *IEEE Transactions on Industrial Informatics, 12*(1), 425–436. doi:10.1109/TII.2015.2414355

Alcaraz, C., Cazorla, L., & Fernandez, G. (2014). Context-awareness using anomaly- based detectors for smart grid domains. *International Conference on Risks and Security of Internet and Systems*, 17–34.

Alcaraz, C., & Lopez, J. (2013). Wide-area situational awareness for critical infrastructure protection. *Computer (Long Beach Calif), 46*(4), 30–37. doi:10.1109/MC.2013.72

Alcaraz, C., & Lopez, J. (2020). Secure interoperability in cyber-physical systems. In *Cyber Warfare and Terrorism: Concepts, Methodologies, Tools, and Applications* (pp. 521–542). IGI Global. doi:10.4018/978-1-7998-2466-4.ch032

Ali & Choi. (2020). State-of-the-Art Artificial Intelligence Techniques for Distributed Smart Grids: A Review. *MDPI Electronics Journal*, 1-35.

Almond, R. G., & Mislevy, R. J. (1999). Graphical Models and Computerized Adaptive Testing. *Applied Psychological Measurement, 23*(3), 223–237. doi:10.1177/01466219922031347

Alnakhalny, Almomani, Taha, Gupta, & Manickam. (2014). ICMPv6 flood attack detection using DENFIS algorithms. *Indian Journal of Science and Technology, 7*, 168-173.

Aloul, F., Al-Ali, A. R., Al-Dalky, R., Al-Mardini, M., & El-Hajj, W. (2012). *Smart grid security: threats, vulnerabilities and solutions. Int. J. Smart Grid Clean Energy.*

Al-Qatf, M., Lasheng, Y., Al-Habib, M., & Al-Sabahi, K. (2018). Deep Learning Approach Combining Sparse Autoencoder with SVM for Network Intrusion Detection. *IEEE Access: Practical Innovations, Open Solutions, 6*(c), 52843–52856. doi:10.1109/ACCESS.2018.2869577

Alshboul, Y., Nepali, R. K., & Wang, Y. (2015). Detecting malicious short URLs on Twitter. *Twenty-first Americas Conference on Information Systems*, 1-7.

Ambre, S., Masurekar, M., & Gaikwad, S. (2020). Face Recognition Using Raspberry PI. *Studies In Computational Intelligence*, 1-11. Doi:10.1007/978-3-030-38445-6_1

Amershi, S., Begel, A., Bird, C., DeLine, R., Gall, H., Kamar, E., . . . Zimmermann, T. (2019). Software engineering for machine learning: A case study. In *Proceedings IEEE/ACM 41st International Conference on Software Engineering: Software Engineering in Practice -ICSE-SEIP* (pp. 291–300). IEEE.

Amin, S., Cárdenas, A. A., & Sastry, S. S. (2019). Safe and Secure Networked Control Systems under Denial-of-Service Attacks. Hybrid Systems: Computation and Control, 31-45.

Amin, S., Litrico, X., Sastry, S., & Bayen, A. (2013). Cyber Security of Water SCADA Systems—Part I: Analysis and Experimentation of Stealthy Deception Attacks. *IEEE Transactions on Control Systems Technology, 21*(5), 1963–1970. doi:10.1109/TCST.2012.2211873

Amit, R., & Meir, R. (2017). *Meta-learning by adjusting priors based on extended PAC-Bayes theory.* arXiv preprint arXiv:1711.01244

Anders, H. (2020). *Current direction for renewable energy in China.* Oxford Institute for Energy Studies. Oxford University.

Anderson, D., Frivold, T., & Valdes, A. (1995). Next-generation intrusion detection expert system (NIDES). *The Summary (Indianapolis, Ind.).*

Anibal. (2016). *Smart Grid Security: Threats, Challenges, and Solutions.* arXiv

Antonopoulos, C., Dima, S. M., & Koubias, S. (2016). Event identification in wireless sensor networks. In *Components and Services for IoT Platforms.* Paving the Way for IoT Standards. doi:10.1007/978-3-319-42304-3_10

Anwar, A., & Mahmood, A. (2014). Cyber security of smart grid infrastructure. The State of the Art in Intrusion Prevention and Detection. CRC Press, Taylor & Francis Group.

Anwar, A., & Hassan, S. I. (2017). Applying Artificial Intelligence Techniques to Prevent Cyber Assaults. *International Journal of Computational Intelligence Research, 13*(5), 883–889.

Arash. (2015). A System Theoretic Approach to the Security Threats in Cyber Physical Systems Applied to Stuxnet. *IEEE Transactions on Dependable and Secure Computing.*

Arghandeh, R., Von Meier, A., Mehrmanesh, L., & Mili, L. (2016). On the definition of cyber-physical resilience in power systems. *Renewable & Sustainable Energy Reviews, 58*, 1060–1069. doi:10.1016/j.rser.2015.12.193

Argyrios. (2019). *Smart Grid Hardware Security: Design Challenges and Paradigms.* IoT for Smart Grids.

Arioua, M., El Assari, Y., Ez-Zazi, I., & El Oualkadi, A. (2016). Multi-hop Cluster Based Routing Approach for Wireless Sensor Networks. *Procedia Computer Science, 83*, 584–591. doi:10.1016/j.procs.2016.04.277

Arjovsky, M., Chintala, S., & Bottou, L. (2017). *Wasserstein GAN*. Retrieved from http://arxiv.org/abs/1701.07875

Arora, S. R., Goel, P., Maini, J., & Mallick, P. (2016). Increasing Efficiency in Online Studies through Web Socket. *Proceedings of 3rd International Conference on Computing for Sustainable Global Development*. https://ieeexplore.ieee.org/document/7724316

Arpteg, A., Brinne, B., Crnkovic-Friis, L., & Bosch, J. (2018). Software engineering challenges of deep learning. In *Proceedings 44th Euromicro Conference on Software Engineering and Advanced Applications -SEAA* (pp. 50–59). IEEE.

Artuso, M., & Christiansen, H. L. (2014). Discrete-event simulation of coordinated multi-point joint transmission in LTE-Advanced with constrained backhaul. In *Proceedings of IEEE Eleventh International Symposium on Wireless Communication Systems* (pp. 106-110). 10.1109/ISWCS.2014.6933329

Asensio, J. A., Criado, J., Padilla, N., & Iribarne, L. (2019). *Emulating home automation installations through component-based web technology*. Communication Magazine. doi:10.1016/j.future.2017.09.062

Ashok, A., Hahn, A., & Govindarasu, M. (2011). A cyber-physical security testbed for smart grid. *Proceedings of the Seventh Annual Workshop on Cyber Security and Information Intelligence Research - CSIIRW '11*.

Ashok, A., Krishnaswamy, S., & Govindarasu, M. (2016). A remotely accessible testbed for Cyber Physical security of the Smart Grid. *IEEE Power and Energy Society Innovative Smart Grid Technologies Conference, ISGT*. 10.1109/ISGT.2016.7781277

Assante, M. J. (2016). Confirmation of a Coordinated Attack on the Ukrainian Power Grid. E-ISAC | Analysis of the Cyber Attack on the Ukrainian Power Grid.

Assunção, M. D., Calheiros, R. N., Bianchi, S., Netto, M. A., & Buyya, R. (2015). Big Data computing and clouds: Trends and future directions. *Journal of Parallel and Distributed Computing, 79*, 3–15. doi:10.1016/j.jpdc.2014.08.003

Aste, T., Tasca, P., & Di Matteo, T. (2017). Blockchain technologies: The foreseeable impact on society and industry. *Computer, 50*(9), 18-28.

Autenrieth & Frey. (2014). Pader MAC: Energy-efficient machine to machine communication for cyber-physical systems. *Peer-to-Peer Networking and Applications, 7*(3), 243–254.

Avizienis, A., Laprie, J., Randell, B., & Landwehr, C. (2004). Basic concepts and taxonomy of dependable and secure computing. EEE Transactions on Dependable and Secure Computing, 1(1), 11–33. doi:10.1109/TDSC.2004.2

Awad, A. I. (2018). Introduction to information security foundations and applications. In *Information Security: Foundations, Technologies and Applications*. IET.

Babiceanu, R. F., & Seker, R. (2016). Big Data and virtualization for manufacturing cyber-physical systems: A survey of the current status and future outlook. *Computers in Industry, 81*, 128–137. doi:10.1016/j.compind.2016.02.004

Bagheri, B., Yang, S., Kao, H.-A., & Lee, J. (2015). Cyber-physical Systems Architecture for Self-Aware Machines in Industry 4.0 Environment. IFAC-PapersOnLine, 48(3), 1622–1627. doi:10.1016/j.ifacol.2015.06.318

Bahashwan, A., Anbar, M., & Hanshi, S. M. (2020). Overview of IPv6 Based DDoS and DoS Attacks Detection Mechanisms. *International Conference on Advances in Cyber Security*. 10.1007/978-981-15-2693-0_11

Bai, J., Wu, Y., Wang, G., Yang, S. X., & Qiu, W. (2006, May). A novel intrusion detection model based on multi-layer self-organizing maps and principal component analysis. In *International Symposium on Neural Networks* (pp. 255-260). Springer. 10.1007/11760191_37

Bajaj, S., & Johari, R. (2016, February). Big data: a boon or bane-the big question. In *2016 Second International Conference on Computational Intelligence & Communication Technology (CICT)* (pp. 106-110). IEEE. 10.1109/CICT.2016.29

Balasingham, K. (2016). Industry 4.0: Securing the Future for German Manufacturing Companies. University of Twente. School of Management and Governance Business Administration.

Bañeres, D., Cortadella, J., & Kishinevsky, M. (2009, April). Variable-latency design by function speculation. In 2009 Design, Automation & Test in Europe Conference & Exhibition (pp. 1704-1709). IEEE. doi:10.1109/DATE.2009.5090937

Banerjee, A., Venkatasubramanian, K. K., Mukherjee, T., & Gupta, S. K. S. (2012). Ensuring Safety, Security, and Sustainability of Mission-Critical Cyber–Physical Systems. *Proceedings of the IEEE, 100*(1), 283–299. doi:10.1109/JPROC.2011.2165689

Bannur, S. N., Saul, L. K., & Savage, S. (2011). Judging a site by its content: learning the textual, structural, and visual features of malicious web pages. *Proceedings of the 4th ACM Workshop on Security and Artificial Intelligence.* 10.1145/2046684.2046686

Baran, D., Aktan, M., & Oklobdzija, V. G. (2010, August). Energy-efficient implementation of parallel CMOS multipliers with improved compressors. In *Proceedings of the 16th ACM/IEEE international symposium on Low power electronics and design* (pp. 147-152). 10.1145/1840845.1840876

Barika, F., Hadjar, K., & El-Kadhi, N. (2009). Artificial neural network for mobile IDS solution. *Security Management*, 271–277.

Barnela, M., & Kumar, D. S. (2014). Digital modulation schemes employed in wireless communication: A literature review. *International Journal of Wired and Wireless Communications, 2*(2), 15–21.

Barreto, L., Amaral, A., & Pereira, T. (2017). Industry 4.0 implications in logistics: An overview. *Procedia Manufacturing, 13*, 1245–1252. doi:10.1016/j.promfg.2017.09.045

Bazrafshan, Z., Hashemi, H., & Fard, S. (2013). A survey on heuristic malware detection techniques. *The 5th Conference on Information and Knowledge Technology*, 113-120.

Bengio, Y., Lamblin, P., & Popovici, D. (2007). Greedy Layer-Wise Training of Deep Networks. *Proceedings of the Advances in Neural Information Processing Systems.* 10.7551/mitpress/7503.003.0024

Bengio, Y., Simard, P., & Frasconi, P. (1994). Learning long-term dependencies with gradient descent is difficult. *IEEE Transactions on Neural Networks, 5*(2), 157–166. doi:10.1109/72.279181 PMID:18267787

Bernardi, L., Mavridis, T., & Estevez, P. (2019), 150 successful machine learning models: 6 lessons learned at booking. Com. In *Proceedings of the 25th ACM SIGKDD International Conference on Knowledge Discovery & Data Mining* (pp. 1743–1751). ACM.

Berthier, R., & Sanders, W. (2011). Specification-Based Intrusion Detection for Advanced Metering Infrastructures. *IEEE 17th Pacific Rim International Symposium on Dependable Computing.* 10.1109/PRDC.2011.30

Besselink, B., Turri, V., Van De Hoef, S. H., Liang, K. Y., Alam, A., Mårtensson, J., & Johansson, K. H. (2016). Cyber-physical control of road freight transport. *Proceedings of the IEEE, 104*(5), 1128–1141. doi:10.1109/JPROC.2015.2511446

Bhamidipati, S., Kim, K. J., Sun, H., & Orlik, P. V. (2020). Artificial-Intelligence-Based Distributed Belief Propagation and Recurrent Neural Network Algorithm for Wide-Area Monitoring Systems. *IEEE Network*, *34*(3), 64–72. doi:10.1109/MNET.011.1900322

Biffl, S., Lüder, A., & Gerhard, D. (Eds.). (2017). *Multi-Disciplinary Engineering for Cyber-Physical Production Systems: Data Models and Software Solutions for Handling Complex Engineering Projects*. Springer. doi:10.1007/978-3-319-56345-9

Bitter, C., Elizondo, D. A., & Watson, T. (2010, July). Application of artificial neural networks and related techniques to intrusion detection. In *The 2010 International Joint Conference on Neural Networks (IJCNN)* (pp. 1-8). IEEE. 10.1109/IJCNN.2010.5596532

Bobba, R., Davis, K., Wang, Q., Khurana, H., Nahrstedt, K., & Overbye, T. (2014). *Detecting False Data Injection Attacks on DC State Estimation*. Retrieved from https://www.researchgate.net/publication/228373879

Bosch, J., Olsson, H. H., & Crnkovic, I. (2018). It takes three to tango: Requirement, outcome/data, and ai driven development. In *Proceedings SiBW* (pp. 177–192). Academic Press.

Bossert, M. (1999). *Channel coding for telecommunications*. John Wiley & Sons, Inc.

Botvinick, M., Ritter, S., Wang, J. X., Kurth-Nelson, Z., Blundell, C., & Hassabis, D. (2019). Reinforcement learning, fast and slow. *Trends in Cognitive Sciences*, *23*(5), 408–422. doi:10.1016/j.tics.2019.02.006 PMID:31003893

Boulkenafet, Z., Komulainen, J., & Hadid, A. (2016). Face Spoofing Detection Using Colour Texture Analysis. *IEEE Transactions on Information Forensics and Security*, *11*(8), 1818–1830. doi:10.1109/TIFS.2016.2555286

Bourlard, H., & Kamp, Y. (1988). Auto-association by multilayer perceptrons and singular value decomposition. *Biological Cybernetics*, *59*(4-5), 291–294. doi:10.1007/BF00332918 PMID:3196773

Breiman, L. (2001). Random forests. *Machine Learning*, *45*(1), 5–32. doi:10.1023/A:1010933404324

Briand, L. C. (2008). Novel applications of machine learning in software testing. In *Proceedings 8th International Conference on Quality Software* (pp. 3–10). IEEE. 10.1109/QSIC.2008.29

Bristol, U. o. (2020). *the Cyber Security Body of Knowledge*. Retrieved from https://www.cybok.org/

Brunelli, R., & Poggio, T. (1993, October). Face Recognition: Features versus Templates. *IEEE Transactions on Pattern Analysis and Machine Intelligence*, *15*(10), 1042–1052. doi:10.1109/34.254061

Bures, T., Weyns, D., Schmer, B., Tovar, E., Boden, E., Gabor, T., ... Tsigkanos, C. (2017). Software engineering for smart cyber-physical systems: Challenges and promising solutions. *Software Engineering Notes*, *42*(2), 19–24. doi:10.1145/3089649.3089656

Burg, A., Chattopadhyay, A., & Lam, K. Y. (2017). Wireless communication and security issues for cyber-physical systems and the Internet-of-Things. *Proceedings of the IEEE*, *106*(1), 38–60. doi:10.1109/JPROC.2017.2780172

Buscema, P. M., Massini, G., Breda, M., Lodwick, W. A., Newman, F., & Asadi-Zeydabadi, M. (2018). Artificial neural networks. In *Studies in Systems*. Decision and Control; doi:10.1007/978-3-319-75049-1_2

Caiza, G., Saeteros, M., Oñate, W., & Garcia, M. (2020). Fog computing at industrial level, architecture, latency, energy, and security: A review. *Heliyon (London)*, *6*(4), e03706. doi:10.1016/j.heliyon.2020.e03706 PubMed

Calimera, A., Macii, E., & Poncino, M. (2012). Design techniques for NBTI-tolerant power-gating architectures. *IEEE Transactions on Circuits and Wystems. II, Express Briefs*, *59*(4), 249–253. doi:10.1109/TCSII.2012.2188457

Calinescu, R., Grunske, L., Kwiatkowska, M., Mirandola, R., & Tamburrelli, G. (2011). Dynamic QoS Management and Optimization in Service-Based Systems. *IEEE Transactions on Software Engineering, 37*(3), 387–409. doi:10.1109/TSE.2010.92

Canali, D., Cova, M., Vigna, G., & Kruegel, C. (2011). Prophiler: a fast filter for the large-scale detection of malicious web pages. In *Proceedings of the 20th international conference on World wide web.* ACM. 10.1145/1963405.1963436

Cao-hoang, T., & Duy, C. N. (2017, April). Environment monitoring system for agricultural application based on wireless sensor network. In *2017 Seventh International Conference on Information Science and Technology (ICIST)* (pp. 99-102). IEEE. 10.1109/ICIST.2017.7926499

Cardenas, A. (2019). *Cyber-Physical Systems Security Knowledge area.* University of California.

Cardno, A. (2020). *6 Critical Ideas behind the Smart Factory and Internet of Things.* Retrieved from: https://blog.viz-explorer.com/6-critical-ideas-behindthe-smart-factory-and-internet-of-things-iot/)

Cassandras, C. G. (2016). Smart cities as cyber-physical social systems. *Engineering, 2*(2), 156–158. doi:10.1016/J.ENG.2016.02.012

Cassandras, C. G., & Lafortune, S. (2009). *Introduction to discrete event systems.* Springer Science & Business Media.

Cassell, J., Bickmore, T., Campbell, L., Vilhjalmsson, H., & Yan, H. (2000). Human Conversation As a System Framework: Designing Embodied Conversational Agents. In *Embodied conversational agents* (pp. 29–63). Cambridge, MA: MIT Press. doi:10.7551/mitpress/2697.003.0004

Catalin. (2020). Cyber-physical framework for emulating distributed control systems in smart grids. In Electrical Power and Energy Systems. Elsevier.

Čaušević. Hossein, & Lundqvist. (2017). Data Security and Privacy in Cyber-Physical Systems for Healthcare. Wiley Online Library.

Ceccarelli, A., Bondavalli, A., Froemel, B., Hoeftberger, O., & Kopetz, H. (2016). Basic Concepts on Systems of Systems. In *Cyber-Physical Systems of Systems: Foundations – A Conceptual Model and Some Derivations: The AMADEOS Legacy.* Springer International Publishing.

Chaâri, R., Ellouze, F., Koubâa, A., Qureshi, B., Pereira, N., Youssef, H., & Tovar, E. (2016). Cyber-physical systems clouds: A survey. *Computer Networks, 108,* 260–278. doi:10.1016/j.comnet.2016.08.017

Chakrabortty, A., & Bose, A. (2017). Smart Grid Simulations and Their Supporting Implementation Methods. *Proceedings of the IEEE, 105*(11), 2017. doi:10.1109/JPROC.2017.2737635

Chan, P. K., & Stolfo, S. J. (1993). Experiments on multistrategy learning by meta-learning. In *Proceedings of the second international conference on information and knowledge management* (pp. 314-323). Academic Press.

Chan, P. K., & Stolfo, S. J. (1993). Toward parallel and distributed learning by meta-learning. In AAAI workshop in Knowledge Discovery in Databases (pp. 227-240). Academic Press.

Chang, J. H., Cho, Y. J., & Wu, T. L. A. (2012). *Human-Machine-Environment Interaction Analysis on the Washing and Changing of Toddlers' Caregivers.* National Taipei University of Technology.

Chang, R. I., Lai, L. B., Su, W. D., Wang, J. C., & Kouh, J. S. (2007). Intrusion detection by backpropagation neural networks with sample-query and attribute-query. *International Journal of Computational Intelligence Research, 3*(1), 6–10. doi:10.5019/j.ijcir.2007.76

Chatila, R., Renaudo, E., Andries, M., & Chavez-Garcia, R.-O. (2018). Toward Self-Aware Robots. Frontiers in Robotics and AI, 5.

Chella, A., Pipitone, A., Morin, A., & Racy, F. (2020). Developing Self-Awareness in Robots via Inner Speech. Frontiers in Robotics and AI, 7.

Chen, X., Duan, Y., Houthooft, R., Schulman, J., Sutskever, I., & Abbeel, P. (2016). *InfoGAN: Interpretable Representation Learning by Information Maximizing Generative Adversarial Nets*. Retrieved from http://arxiv.org/abs/1606.03657

Chen, X., Kingma, D. P., Salimans, T., Duan, Y., Dhariwal, P., Schulman, J., ... Abbeel, P. (2016). *Variational Lossy Autoencoder*. Retrieved from http://arxiv.org/abs/1611.02731

Cheng, S. W., Garlan, D., & Schmerl, B. (2006) Architecture-based Self-adaptation. In *Conference on Performance Engineering (ICPE '14)*. ACM, pp 3–14

Chen, S., Pande, A., & Mohapatra, P. 2014. Sensor-assisted facial recognition. *Proceedings of the 12th annual international conference on Mobile systems, applications, and services - MobiSys '14*.

Chen, Y., Sun, E., & Zhang, Y. (2017). Joint optimization of transmission and processing delay in fog computing access networks. *9th International Conference on Advanced Infocomm Technology (ICAIT)*, 155-158.

Choudhary. (2012). CIDT: Detection of Malicious Code Injection Attacks on Web Application. International Journal of Computer Applications, 52(2), 19-26.

Choudhary, A., & Odubiyi, J. (2004). Context-based adaptive control in autonomous systems. *Proceedings from the Fifth Annual IEEE SMC Information Assurance Workshop*.

Chowanda, A., Blanchfield, P., Flintham, M., & Valstar, M. (2016). Computational models of emotion, personality, and social relationships for interactions in games. *Proceedings of the 2016 International Conference on Autonomous Agents & Multiagent Systems*, 1343–1344.

Çifçi, M. A., & Elçi, A. (2017). Yapay Zekâ İle Kablosuz Algılayıcı Ağları Eniyileme. *Türkiye Bilişim Vakfı Bilgisayar Bilimleri ve Mühendisliği Dergisi, 10*(2), 64–76. https://dergipark.org.tr/en/pub/tbbmd/issue/33390/339255

Cintuglu, M. H., Mohammed, O. A., Akkaya, K., & Uluagac, A. S. (2016). A survey on smart grid cyber-physical system testbeds. *IEEE Communications Surveys and Tutorials, 19*(1), 446–464. doi:10.1109/COMST.2016.2627399

Conner-Simons, A. (2016). *System predicts 85 percent of cyber-attacks using input from human experts*. Massachusetts Institute of Technology.

Core, M. G., Lane, H. C., Van Lent, M., Gomboc, D., Solomon, S., & Rosenberg, M. (2006). Building explainable artificial intelligence systems. In AAAI (pp. 1766-1773). Academic Press.

Corradi, G. (2018). *The Value of Python Productivity: Extreme Edge Analytics on Xilinx Zynq Portfolio*. Xilinx, White Paper, WP502 (v1. 0).

Cova, M., Kruegel, C., & Vigna, G. (2010). Detection and analysis of drive-by-download attacks and malicious JavaScript code. In *Proceedings of the 19th international conference on World wide web (WWW '10)* (pp. 281-290). Raleigh, NC: Association for Computing Machinery. 10.1145/1772690.1772720

Culbertson, M. J. (2014). *Graphical Models for Student Knowledge: Networks, Parameters, and Item Selection* (Ph.D. thesis). The University of Illinois at Urbana.

Dağlarli, E. (2020). *Explainable Artificial Intelligence (XAI) Approaches and Deep Meta-Learning Models. In Advances in Deep Learning*. IntechOpen.

Dahlmeier, D. (2017) On the challenges of translating NLP research into commercial products. In *Proceedings of the 55th Annual Meeting of the Association for Computational Linguistics* (vol. 2, pp. 92–96). 10.18653/v1/P17-2015

Dale, R. (1995). An introduction to natural language generation. *European Summer School in Logic, Language and Information, ESSLLI'95*.

Dam, H. K., Tran, T., & Ghose, A. (2018). Explainable software analytics. In *Proceedings of the 40th International Conference on Software Engineering: New Ideas and Emerging Results* (pp. 53-56). Academic Press.

Dammasch, K., & Horton, G. (2008). *Entities with combined discrete-continuous attributes in discrete-event-driven systems*. Academic Press.

Dao, N.-N., Kim, J., Park, M., & Cho, S. (2016). Adaptive Suspicious Prevention for Defending DoS Attacks in SDN-Based Convergent Networks. *PLoS One*, *11*(8), e0160375. doi:10.1371/journal.pone.0160375 PMID:27494411

Das, S., Roberts, D., Lee, S., Pant, S., Blaauw, D., Austin, T., & Mudge, T. (2006). A self-tuning DVS processor using delay-error detection and correction. *IEEE Journal of Solid-State Circuits*, *41*(4), 792–804. doi:10.1109/JSSC.2006.870912

De Wolf, T., & Holvoet, T. (2004). Emergence and Self-Organisation: a statement of similarities and differences. In *Proceedings of the International Workshop on Engineering Self-Organising Applications 2004* (pp. 96-110). Academic Press.

Dehaene, S., Lau, H., & Kouider, S. (2017). What is consciousness, and could machines have it? *Science*, *358*, 486–492.

Delicato, F. C., Al-Anbuky, A., Kevin, I., & Wang, K. (2020). *Smart Cyber–Physical Systems: Toward Pervasive Intelligence systems*. Academic Press.

Delicato, F. C., Al-Anbuky, A., Kevin, I., & Wang, K. (2020). *Smart Cyber-Physical Systems: Toward Pervasive Intelligence Systems*. Academic Press.

DeLooze, L. L. (2006, July). Attack characterization and intrusion detection using an ensemble of self-organizing maps. In *The 2006 IEEE International Joint Conference on Neural Network Proceedings* (pp. 2121-2128). IEEE.

Deng, C., Wang, Y., Wen, C., Xu, Y., & Lin, P. (2020). Distributed Resilient Control for Energy Storage Systems in Cyber-Physical Microgrids. *IEEE Transactions on Industrial Informatics*, 1. doi:10.1109/TII.2020.2981549

Derler, P., Lee, E. A., & Vincentelli, A. S. (2011). Modeling cyber-physical systems. *Proceedings of the IEEE*, *100*(1), 13–28. doi:10.1109/JPROC.2011.2160929

Derler, P., Lee, E. A., & Vincentelli, A. S. (2012). Modeling cyber - physical systems. *Proceedings of the IEEE*, 13-28.

Di Marzo Serugendo, G., Gleizes, M. P., & Karageorgos, A. (2006) Self-Organisation and Emergence in differences. *Proc. of the 2nd International Workshop on Engineering Self-Organising Applications*.

Diaz-Rozo, J., Bielza, C., & Larrañaga, P. (2017). *Machine Learning-based CPS for Clustering High throughput Machining Cycle Conditions*. Procedia Manufacturing. doi:10.1016/j.promfg.2017.07.091

Diez-Olivan, A., Del Ser, J., Galar, D., & Sierra, B. (2019). Data Fusion and Machine Learning for Industrial Prognosis: Trends and Perspectives towards Industry 4.0. *Information Fusion*, *50*, 92–111. doi:10.1016/j.inffus.2018.10.005

Dimitrov, V., Jagtap, V., Wills, M., Skorinko, J., & Padir, T. (2015). A cyber physical system testbed for assistive robotics technologies in the home. *Proceedings of the 17th International Conference on Advanced Robotics*. 10.1109/ICAR.2015.7251475

Ding, D., Han, Q. L., Wang, Z., & Ge, X. (2019). A survey on model-based distributed control and filtering for industrial cyber physical systems. *IEEE Transactions on Industrial Informatics*, *15*(5), 2483–2499. doi:10.1109/TII.2019.2905295

Ding, D., Han, Q. L., Wang, Z., & Ge, X. (2020). Recursive Filtering of Distributed Cyber-Physical Systems With Attack Detection. *IEEE Transactions on Systems, Man, and Cybernetics. Systems*, 1–11. doi:10.1109/TSMC.2019.2960541

Ding, J. (2015). *Intrusion Detection, Prevention, and Response System (IDPRS) for Cyber-Physical Systems (CPSs)*. In A.-S. K. Pathan (Ed.), *Securing Cyber-Physical Systems* (pp. 371–392). CRC Press.

Došilović, F. K., Brčić, M., & Hlupić, N. (2018). Explainable artificial intelligence: A survey. In *2018 41st International convention on information and communication technology, electronics and microelectronics (MIPRO)* (pp. 0210-0215). IEEE.

Du, K., Varman, P., & Mohanram, K. (2012, March). High-performance, reliable variable latency carries select addition. In 2012 Design, Automation & Test in Europe Conference & Exhibition (DATE) (pp. 1257-1262). IEEE.

Duraipandian, M., & Palanisamy, C. (2014, February). An intelligent agent based defense architecture for ddos attacks. In *2014 International Conference on Electronics and Communication Systems (ICECS)* (pp. 1-7). IEEE. 10.1109/ECS.2014.6892819

Durelli, V. H. S., Durelli, R. S., Borges, S. S., Endo, A. T., Eler, M. M., Dias, D. R. C., & Guimares, M. P. (2019). Machine learning applied to software testing: A systematic mapping study. *IEEE Transactions on Reliability*, *68*(3), 1189–1212. doi:10.1109/TR.2019.2892517

Edgar, T., Manz, D., & Carroll, T. (2011). Towards an experimental testbed facility for cyber-physical security research. *CSIIRW '11: Proceedings of the Seventh Annual Workshop on Cyber Security and Information Intelligence Research*. 10.1145/2179298.2179357

Egele, M., Kolbitsch, C., & Platzer, C. (2009). Removing web spam links from search engine results. *Journal in Computer Virology*, *7*(1), 51–62. doi:10.100711416-009-0132-6

Eisenhardt, K. M. (1989). Building theories from case study research. *Academy of Management Review*, *14*(4), 532–550.

Eleyan, A. (2017). Comparative Study on Facial Expression Recognition using Gabor and Dual-Tree Complex Wavelet Transforms. *International Journal of Engineering & Applied Sciences, 9*(1).

Elman, J. L. (1990). Finding structure in time. *Cognitive Science*, *14*(2), 179–211. doi:10.120715516709cog1402_1

Eltahir & Saeed. (2015). Performance Evaluation of an Enhanced Hybrid Wireless Mesh Protocol (E-HWMP) Protocol for VANET. *International Conference on Computing, Control, Networking, Electronics and Embedded Systems Engineering (ICCNEEE)*, 95 – 100.

Eltahir, Saeed, Mukherjee, & Hasan. (2016). Evaluation and Analysis of an Enhanced Hybrid Wireless Mesh Protocol for Vehicular Ad-hoc Network. *EURASIP Journal on Wireless Communications and Networking*.

Esfahani, N., & Malek, S. (2013). Uncertainty in self-adaptive software systems. In *Software Engineering for Self-Adaptive Systems II* (pp. 214–238). Springer. doi:10.1007/978-3-642-35813-5_9

Fang, C., Qi, Y., Cheng, P., & Zheng, W. X. (2020). Optimal periodic watermarking schedule for replay attack detection in cyber-physical systems. *Automatica*, *112*, 108698. doi:10.1016/j.automatica.2019.108698

Fang, H., Qi, A., & Wang, X. (2020). Fast Authentication and Progressive Authorization in Large-Scale IoT: How to Leverage AI for Security Enhancement. *IEEE Network*, *34*(3), 24–29. doi:10.1109/MNET.011.1900276

Farahnakian, F., & Heikkonen, J. (2018). A deep auto-encoder based approach for the intrusion detection system. *International Conference on Advanced Communication Technology, ICACT, 2018-February*, 178–183. 10.23919/ICACT.2018.8323688

Fatima, S. S., Wooldridge, M. J., & Jennings, N. R. (2006). Multi-issue negotiation with deadlines. *Journal of Artificial Intelligence Research, 27*, 381–417. doi:10.1613/jair.2056

Fei, B. K. L., Eloff, J. H. P., Olivier, M. S., Tillwick, H. M., & Venter, H. S. (2005). Using self-organising maps for anomalous behaviour detection in a computer forensic investigation. *Proceedings of the Fifth Annual Information Security South Africa Conference.*

Fei, X., Shah, N., Verba, N., Chao, K. M., Sanchez-Anguix, V., Lewandowski, J., ... Usman, Z. (2019). CPS data streams analytics based on machine learning for Cloud and Fog Computing: A survey. *Future Generation Computer Systems, 90*, 435–450. doi:10.1016/j.future.2018.06.042

Fernandez, A., Herrera, F., Cordon, O., del Jesus, M. J., & Marcelloni, F. (2019). Evolutionary fuzzy systems for explainable artificial intelligence: Why, when, what for, and where to? *IEEE Computational Intelligence Magazine, 14*(1), 69–81. doi:10.1109/MCI.2018.2881645

Ferrag, M. A., Babaghayou, M., & Yazici, M. A. (2020). Cyber security for fog-based smart grid SCADA systems: Solutions and challenges. Journal of Information Security and Applications, 52.

Ferrag, M. A., Maglaras, L., Moschoyiannis, S., & Janicke, H. (2020). Deep learning for cyber security intrusion detection: Approaches, datasets, and comparative study. Journal of Information Security and Applications, 50.

Finn, C., Abbeel, P., & Levine, S. (2017). Model-agnostic meta-learning for fast adaptation of deep networks. In *Proceedings of the 34th International Conference on Machine Learning-Volume* 70 (pp. 1126-1135). JMLR. org.

Firdausi, I., Lim, C., & Nugroho, A. (2010). Analysis of machine learning techniques used in behavior-based malware detection. In *2nd International Conference on Advances in Computing, Control and Telecommunication Technologies.* ACT. 10.1109/ACT.2010.33

Flick, U. (2018). Designing qualitative research. *Sage (Atlanta, Ga.).*

Fowers, J., Ovtcharov, K., Strauss, K., Chung, E. S., & Stitt, G. (2014, May). A high memory bandwidth FPGA accelerator for sparse matrix-vector Multiplication. *2014 IEEE 22nd Annual International Symposium on Field-Programmable Custom Computing Machines*, 36-43. 10.1109/FCCM.2014.23

França, R. P., Iano, Y., Monteiro, A. C. B., Arthur, R., Estrela, V. V., Assumpção, S. L. D. L., & Razmjooy, N. (2019). *Potential Proposal to Improvement of the Data Transmission in Healthcare Systems.* Academic Press.

Frans, K., Ho, J., Chen, X., Abbeel, P., & Schulman, J. (2017). *Meta-learning shared hierarchies.* arXiv preprint arXiv:1710.09767

Friedman, J. H. (2002). Stochastic gradient boosting. *Computational Statistics & Data Analysis, 38*(4), 367–378. doi:10.1016/S0167-9473(01)00065-2

Futia, G., & Vetrò, A. (2020). On the Integration of Knowledge Graphs into Deep Learning Models for a More Comprehensible AI—Three Challenges for Future Research. *Information, 11*(2), 122. doi:10.3390/info11020122

Gaber, T., Abdelwahab, S., Elhoseny, M., & Hassanien, A. E. (2018). Trust-based secure clustering in WSN-based intelligent transportation systems. *Computer Networks, 146*, 151–158. doi:10.1016/j.comnet.2018.09.015

Gahlan, N. K., Shukla, P., & Kaur, J. (2012). Implementation of wallace tree multiplier using compressor. *International Journal on Computer Technology & Applications, 3*(3), 1194-1199.

Gal, Y., & Ghahramani, Z. (2016). Dropout as a Bayesian approximation: Representing model uncertainty in deep learning. *33rd International Conference on Machine Learning, ICML 2016.*

Ganesh, G. V., Kumar, D. P., Ram, J. S., Reddy, A. D., & Teja, M. P. (2017). Design of reliable multiplier using the bypassing technique. *International Journal of Pure and Applied Mathematics*, *115*(8), 407–412.

Gao, H. (2015). Cyber-Physical Systems Testbed Based on Cloud Computing and Software Defined Network. *International conference on intelligent information hiding and multimedia signal processing (IIH-MSP)*, 337–340. 10.1109/IIH-MSP.2015.50

Gao, Y., Peng, Y., Xie, F., Zhao, W., Wang, D., & Han, X. (2013). Analysis of security threats and vulnerability for cyber-physical systems. *Proceedings of 3rd International Conference on Computer Science and Network Technology, ICCSNT*, 50-55. 10.1109/ICCSNT.2013.6967062

García, M. V., Irisarri, E., Pérez, F., Marcos, M., & Estevez, E. (2018). From ISA 88/95 meta-models to an OPC UA-based development tool for CPPS under IEC 61499. 2018 14th IEEE International Workshop on Factory Communication Systems (WFCS), 1-9.

Garera, S., Provos, N., Chew, M., & Rubin, A. D. (2007). A framework for detection and measurement of phishing attacks. In *Proceedings of the 2007 ACM Workshop on Recurring Malcode* (S. 1-8). Alexandria, VA: Association for Computing Machinery. 10.1145/1314389.1314391

Garlan, D. (2010) Software Engineering in an uncertain world. *Proc. of the FSE/SDP workshop*. 10.1145/1882362.1882389

Garlan, D., Cheng, S.-W., Huang, A.-C., Schmerl, B., & Steenkiste, P. (2004). S-W. Cheng, A-C. Huang, Bradley Schmerl, and Peter Steenkiste. "Rainbow: Architecture-based self-adaptation with reusable infrastructure. *Computer*, *37*(10), 46–54. doi:10.1109/MC.2004.175

Gharehchopogh, F. S., & Gholizadeh, H. (2019). A comprehensive survey: Whale Optimization Algorithm and its applications. *Swarm and Evolutionary Computation*, *48*, 1–24. doi:10.1016/j.swevo.2019.03.004

Giraldo, J., Sarkar, E., Cardenas, A. A., Maniatakos, M., & Kantarcioglu, M. (2017). Security and Privacy in Cyber-Physical Systems: A Survey of Surveys. *IEEE Design & Test*, *34*(4), 7–17. doi:10.1109/MDAT.2017.2709310

Girão, P. S. (2017). Wireless sensor networks. *22nd IMEKO TC4 International Symposium and 20th International Workshop on ADC Modelling and Testing 2017: Supporting World Development Through Electrical and Electronic Measurements*. 10.4018/ijaec.2016100101

Gluhak, A., Krco, S., Nati, M., Pfisterer, D., Mitton, N., & Razafindralambo, T. (2011). A survey on facilities for experimental internet of things research. *IEEE Communications Magazine*, *49*(11), 58–67. doi:10.1109/MCOM.2011.6069710

Godfrey, T., Mullen, S., Griffith, D. W., Golmie, N., Dugan, R. C., & Rodine, C. (2010). Modeling Smart Grid Applications with Co-Simulation. *First IEEE International Conference on Smart Grid Communications*, 291-296. 10.1109/SMARTGRID.2010.5622057

Goel, D., Agarwal, A., & Rastogi, R. (2016). A Novel Approach for Residential Society Maintenance Problem for Better Human Life. In R. Rajesh & B. Mathivanan (Eds.), *Communication and Power Engineering* (pp. 177–185). doi:10.1515/9783110469608-017

Goel, D., Agarwal, A., & Rastogi, R. (2016). A Novel Approach for Residential Society Maintenance Problem for Better Human Life. *International Journal of Urban Design for Ubiquitous Computing*, *4*, 1–8. doi:10.21742/ijuduc.2016.4.2.01

Goumopoulos, C., & Mavrommati, I. (2020). A framework for pervasive computing applications based on smart objects and end-user development. *Journal of Systems and Software*, *162*, 110496. doi:10.1016/j.jss.2019.110496

Goumopoulos, C., O'Flynn, B., & Kameas, A. (2014). Automated zone-specific irrigation with wireless sensor/actuator network and adaptable decision support. *Computers and Electronics in Agriculture*, *105*, 20–33. doi:10.1016/j.compag.2014.03.012

Govindarajan, R. (2015). Energy management techniques in smart grid. *International Journal of Applied Engineering Research*, *10*(15), 35720–35724.

Greenwood, G., Gallagher, J., & Matson, E. (2015). Cyber physical systems: The next generation of evolvable hardware research and applications. In *Proceedings of the 18th Asia Pacific Symposium on Intelligent and Evolutionary Systems* (pp. 285-296). Springer. 10.1007/978-3-319-13359-1_23

Grover, J., & Sharma, S. (2016, September). Security issues in wireless sensor network—a review. In *2016 5th International Conference on Reliability, Infocom Technologies and Optimization (Trends and Future Directions) (ICRITO)* (pp. 397-404). IEEE.

Gunning, D. (2017). *Explainable artificial intelligence (XAI)*. Defense Advanced Research Projects Agency (DARPA).

Gunning, D., & Aha, D. W. (2019). DARPA's Explainable Artificial Intelligence Program. *AI Magazine*, *40*(2), 44–58. doi:10.1609/aimag.v40i2.2850

Guo, G., Wang, H., Yan, Y., Zheng, J., & Li, B. (2019). A fast face detection method via convolutional neural network. *Neurocomputing*.

Gupta, R., Rastogi, R., & Singh, A. (2015). A novel approach for vehicle tracking system for traffic jam problem. *Proceedings of 09th INDIACom; 2015 2nd International Conference on Computing for Sustainable Global Development*. https://ieeexplore.ieee.org/document/7100240

Gupta, R., Rastogi, R., Mondal, P., & Aggarwal, K. (2015). GA Based Clustering of Mixed Data Type of Attributes (Numeric, Categorical, Ordinal, Binary, Ratio-Scaled). *BIJIT*, *7*(2), 861-866. http://bvicam.ac.in/bjit/issues.asp?issue=14

Gupta, S., & Singhal, A. (2018). *Dynamic Classification Mining Techniques for Predicting Phishing URL. In Soft Computing: Theories and Applications* (pp. 537–546). Singapore: Springer.

Gyongyi, Z., & Garcia-Molina, H. (2005). Web Spam Taxonomy. *First International Workshop on Adversarial Information Retrieval on the Web (AIRWeb 2005)*.

Ha, T., Lee, S., & Kim, S. (2018). Designing explainability of an artificial intelligence system. In *Proceedings of the Technology, Mind, and Society* (pp. 1-1). Academic Press.

Hadžiosmanović., Sommer, Zambon, & Hartel. (2014). Through the eye of the PLC: semantic security monitoring for industrial processes. *Proceedings of the 30th Annual Computer Security Applications Conference*.

Hagan, M. T., Demuth, H. B., & Beale, M. (2002). *Neural Network Design*. China Machine Press.

Hallenstein. (2018). *Review of Cyber and Physical Security Protection of Utility Substations and Control Centers*. Retrieved from http://www.psc.state.fl.us/Files/PDF/Publications/Reports/General/Electricgas/Cyber_Physical_Security.pdf

Halperin, D., Heydt-Benjamin, T. S., Ransford, B., Clark, S. S., Defend, B., & Morgan, W. (2008). Pacemakers and Implantable Cardiac Defibrillators: Software Radio Attacks and Zero-Power Defenses. *2008 IEEE Symposium on Security and Privacy*, 129-142. 10.1109/SP.2008.31

Hamilton, S. H., Pollino, C. A., & Jakeman, A. J. (2015). Habitat suitability modeling of rare species using Bayesian networks: model evaluation under limited data. *Ecological Modeling*, *299*, 64-78.

Han, J., Kamber, M., & Pei, J. (2012). Data Mining Concepts and Techniques (3rd ed.). Morgan Kaufmann Publishers.

Han, S., Xie, M., Chen, H.-H., & Ling, Y. (2014). Intrusion Detection in Cyber-Physical Systems: Techniques and Challenges. *IEEE Systems Journal*, *8*(4), 1052–1062. doi:10.1109/JSYST.2013.2257594

Hasan, M. Z., Al-Rizzo, H., & Günay, M. (2017). Lifetime maximization by partitioning approach in wireless sensor networks. *EURASIP Journal on Wireless Communications and Networking*, *2017*(1), 15. doi:10.118613638-016-0803-1

Hassan, M. B., Ali, E. S., Mokhtar, R. A., Saeed, R. A., & Chaudhari, B. S. (2020). NB-IoT: Concepts, Applications, and Deployment Challenges. In B. S. Chaudhari & M. Zennaro (Eds.), *LPWAN Technologies for IoT and M2MApplications*. Elsevier., doi:10.1016/B978-0-12-818880-4.00006-5.

Hassan, S. I. (2016). Extracting the sentiment score of customer review from unstructured big data using Map Reduce algorithm. *International Journal of Database Theory and Application*, *9*(12), 289–298. doi:10.14257/ijdta.2016.9.12.26

Hassan, S. I. (2017). Designing a flexible system for automatic detection of categorical student sentiment polarity using machine learning. *International Journal of u-and e-Service. Science and Technology*, *10*(3), 25–32.

Hatcher, W. G., & Yu, W. (2018). A survey of deep learning: Platforms, applications and emerging research trends. *IEEE Access: Practical Innovations, Open Solutions*, *6*, 24411–24432. doi:10.1109/ACCESS.2018.2830661

He & Yan. (2016). Cyber-physical attacks and defenses in the smart grid: a survey. *IET Cyber-Physical Systems: Theory & Applications*.

Heartfield, R., & Loukas, G. (2015). A Taxonomy of Attacks and a Survey of Defence Mechanisms for Semantic Social Engineering Attacks. *ACM Computing Surveys*, *48*(3), 39.

Hegde, Sridhar, & Shashank. (2017). Preservation of Sink-Node Location in WSN for SDN Paradigm. The National Institute of Engineering.

Hehenberger, P., Vogel-Heuser, B., Bradley, D., Eynard, B., Tomiyama, T., & Achiche, S. (2016). Design, modelling, simulation and integration of cyber-physical systems: Methods and applications. *Computers in Industry*, *82*, 273–289. doi:10.1016/j.compind.2016.05.006

He, K., Zhang, X., Ren, S., & Sun, J. (2016). *Identity Mappings in Deep Residual Networks Importance of Identity Skip Connections Usage of Activation Function Analysis of Pre-activation Structure*. doi:10.1007/978-3-319-46493-0_38

Hermann, M., Pentek, T., & Otto, B. (2016, January). Design principles for Industrie 4.0 scenarios. In *2016 49th Hawaii international conference on system sciences (HICSS)* (pp. 3928-3937). IEEE.

Herrero, Á., Corchado, E., Pellicer, M. A., & Abraham, A. (2007). Hybrid multi agent-neural network intrusion detection with mobile visualization. In *Innovations in Hybrid Intelligent Systems* (pp. 320–328). Springer. doi:10.1007/978-3-540-74972-1_42

Hezavehi, E., & Ghafoori, K. (2016). Investigating the effect of relationship marketing aspects on customer satisfaction (Case Study: Boroujerd textile factory). *International Journal of Advanced Biotechnology and Research*, *7*, 597–607.

Hinton, G. E., Osindero, S., & Teh, Y.-W. (2006). A fast learning algorithm for deep belief nets. *Neural Computation*, *18*(7), 1527–1554. doi:10.1162/neco.2006.18.7.1527 PMID:16764513

Hodeghatta & Nayak. (2014). Intrusion Detection and Prevention Systems. In The InfoSec Handbook (pp. 225-243). Springer.

Hofmanna, P., Walchb, A., Dinkelmanna, A., Selvarayan, S. K., & Gressera, G. T. (2019). Woven piezoelectric sensors as part of the textile reinforcement of fiber-reinforced plastic. *Composites. Part A, Applied Science and Manufacturing*, *116*, 79–86. doi:10.1016/j.compositesa.2018.10.019

Honegger, D., Oleynikova, H., & Pollefeys, M. (2014). Real-time and low latency embedded computer vision hardware based on a combination of FPGA and mobile CPU. IEEE/RSJ International Conference on Intelligent Robots and Systems, 4930-4935. doi:10.1109/IROS.2014.6943263

Hong, J., Liu, C.-C., & Govindarasu, M. (2014). Integrated Anomaly Detection for Cyber Security of the Substations. *IEEE Transactions on Smart Grid*, *5*(4), 1643–1653. doi:10.1109/TSG.2013.2294473

Hopfield, J. J. (1982). Neural networks and physical systems with emergent collective computational abilities (associative memory/parallel processing/categorization/content-addressable memory/fail-soft devices). *Proc. NatL Acad. Sci. USA*.

Hosseini, R., Dehmeshki, J., Barman, S., Mazinani, M., & Qanadli, S. (2010, July). A genetic type-2 fuzzy logic system for pattern recognition in computer aided detection systems. In *International Conference on Fuzzy Systems* (pp. 1-7). IEEE. 10.1109/FUZZY.2010.5584773

Houbing, Fink, & Jeschke. (2017). *Security and Privacy in Cyber-Physical Systems: Foundations, Principles and Applications*. Wiley-IEEE Press.

Houbing, S., Glenn, A. F., & Sabina, J. (2017). Key Management in CPSs. In *Security and Privacy in Cyber-Physical Systems: Foundations, Principles, and Applications* (pp. 117–136). IEEE.

Hou, Y. T., Chang, Y., Laih, C. S., & Chen, C. M. (2010). Malicious web content detection by machine learning. *Expert Systems with Applications*, *37*(1), 55–60. doi:10.1016/j.eswa.2009.05.023

Huang, X., Li, Y., Poursaeed, O., Hopcroft, J., & Belongie, S. (2017). Stacked generative adversarial networks. In *Proceedings - 30th IEEE Conference on Computer Vision and Pattern Recognition, CVPR 2017* (pp. 1866–1875). Institute of Electrical and Electronics Engineers Inc. 10.1109/CVPR.2017.202

Huang, F., Zhang, J., Zhou, C., Wang, Y., Huang, J., & Zhu, L. (2020). A deep learning algorithm using a fully connected sparse autoencoder neural network for landslide susceptibility prediction. *Landslides*, *17*(1), 217–229. doi:10.100710346-019-01274-9

Huang, Y.-L., Cárdenas, A. A., Amin, S., Lin, Z.-S., Tsai, H.-Y., & Sastry, S. (2009). Understanding the physical and economic consequences of attacks on control systems. *International Journal of Critical Infrastructure Protection*, *2*(3), 73–83. doi:10.1016/j.ijcip.2009.06.001

Humayed, A., Lin, J., Li, F., & Luo, B. (2017). Cyber-physical systems security—A survey. *IEEE Internet of Things Journal*, *4*(6), 1802–1831. doi:10.1109/JIOT.2017.2703172

International Energy Agency. (2014). *World energy outlook 2014: Executive summary*. IEA Publications.

Isola, P., Zhu, J. Y., Zhou, T., & Efros, A. A. (2017). Image-to-image translation with conditional adversarial networks. In *Proceedings - 30th IEEE Conference on Computer Vision and Pattern Recognition, CVPR 2017* (pp. 5967–5976). Institute of Electrical and Electronics Engineers Inc. 10.1109/CVPR.2017.632

Jabri, A., Hsu, K., Gupta, A., Eysenbach, B., Levine, S., & Finn, C. (2019). Unsupervised Curricula for Visual Meta-Reinforcement Learning. *Advances in Neural Information Processing Systems*, 10519–10530.

Jakaria, A. H. M., Yang, W., Rashidi, B., Fung, C., & Rahman, M. (2016). VFence: A Defense against Distributed Denial of Service Attacks Using Network Function Virtualization. *IEEE 40th Annual Computer Software and Applications Conference (COMPSAC)*. 10.1109/COMPSAC.2016.219

Jamshidi, Jaimes Betancourt, & Gomez. (2011). Cyber-physical control of unmanned aerial vehicles. *Sci. Iran. D, 18*(3), 663–668.

Jangir, R. (2016). *Apprenticeship learning using Inverse Reinforcement Learning.* Retrieved from: https://jangirrishabh. github.io/2016/07/09/virtual-car-IRL/

Januzaj, Y., Luma, A., Januzaj, Y., & Ramaj, V. (2015). Real Time Access Control Based on Face Recognition. *International Academy Of Engineers (IA-E) June 10-11, 2015 Antalya (Turkey).* DOI: 10.15242/iae.iae0615004

Jeong, S., Lee, J., Park, J., & Kim, C. (2017). The Social Relation Key: A new paradigm for security. *Information Systems, 71,* 68–77. doi:10.1016/j.is.2017.07.003

Jeschke, I. S., Brecher, C., Song, H., & Rawat, D. B. (2017). *Industrial Internet of Things and Cyber Manufacturing Systems.* Springer International Publishing. doi:10.1007/978-3-319-42559-7_1

Jia, D., Lu, K., Wang, J., Zhang, X., & Shen, X. (2016). A Survey on Platoon-Based Vehicular Cyber-Physical Systems. *IEEE Communications Surveys and Tutorials, 18*(1), 263–284. doi:10.1109/COMST.2015.2410831

Jiang, J. (2017). An improved Cyber-Physical Systems architecture for Industry 4.0 smart factories. International Conference on Applied System Innovation (ICASI), 918-920. doi:10.1109/ICASI.2017.7988589

John, R., Cherian, J. P., & Kizhakkethottam, J. J. (2015). A survey of techniques to prevent sybil attacks. *2015 International Conference on Soft-Computing and Networks Security (ICSNS),* 1-6. 10.1109/ICSNS.2015.7292385

John, M. M., Olsson, H. H., & Bosch, J. (2020). Developing ML/DL models: A design framework. *Proceedings of the International Conference on Software and Systems Process (ICSSP).* 10.1145/3379177.3388892

John, M. M., Olsson, H. H., & Bosch, J. (2020-1). AI on the Edge: Architectural Alternatives. *Proceedings of the Euromicro Conference on Software Engineering and Advanced Applications (SEAA).*

Jon, S. J., & Wang, H. H. (2000, September). Fixed-width multiplier for DSP application. In *Proceedings 2000 International Conference on Computer Design* (pp. 318-322). IEEE.

Jr, F. (2019). A comprehensive survey on network anomaly detection. In *Telecommunication Systems: Modelling, Analysis, Design and Management.* Springer.

Kaelbling, L. P., Littman, M. L., & Moore, A. W. (1996). Reinforcement learning: A survey. *Journal of Artificial Intelligence Research, 4,* 237–285. doi:10.1613/jair.301

Kafi, M. A., Othman, J. B., & Badache, N. (2017). A survey on reliability protocols in wireless sensor networks. [*ACM Computing Surveys, 50*(2), 1–47. doi:10.1145/3064004

Kak, Mustafa, & Valente. (2018). A Review of Person Recognition Based on Face Model. *Eurasian Journal of Science and Engineering, 4*(1).

Karimipour, H., & Leung, H. (2020). Relaxation-based anomaly detection in cyber-physical systems using an ensemble Kalman filter. *IET Cyber-Physical Systems: Theory & Applications, 5*(1), 49–58.

Karn, U. (2016). *Intuitive explanation convolutional-neural networks,* Retrieved from https://www.kdnuggets.com/2016/11/ intuitive-explanation-convolutional-neural-networks.html/3

Karnouskos, S. (2010). The cooperative Internet of Things enabled smart grid. *Proc. 14th Int. Symp. Consumer Electron.,* 1-6.

Karpinskya, N. D., Chanceyb, E. T., Palmera, D. B., & Yamania, Y. (2018). *Automation trust and attention allocation in multitasking workspace. Communication Magazine.* doi:10.1016/j.apergo.2018.03.008

Kartakis, S., Abraham, E., & McCann, J. A. J. A. (2015). A testbed for monitoring and controlling smart water networks. *CySWater'15 Proceedings of the 1st ACM International Workshop on Cyber-Physical Systems for Smart Water Networks.*

Karthikeyan, S., & Jagadeeswari, M. (2020). Performance improvement of elliptic curve cryptography system using low power, high speed 16× 16 Vedic multipliers based on reversible logic. *Journal of Ambient Intelligence and Humanized Computing*, 1–10. doi:10.100712652-020-01795-5

Kaspersky lab. (2018). *What is Cyber-Security?* AO Kaspersky Lab. Retrieved to 10.01.2020 https://www.kaspersky.com/resource-center/definitions/what-is-cyber-security

Kaul, U., Rastogi, R., Agarwal, S., Sharma, P., & Jain, S. (2015). A Novel D&C Approach for Efficient Fuzzy Unsupervised Classification for Mixed Variety of Data. In *Emerging ICT for Bridging the Future - Proceedings of the 49th Annual Convention of the Computer Society of India, CSI Volume 2. Advances in Intelligent Systems and Computing,* (vol. 338, pp. 553-563). Springer. https://link.springer.com/chapter/10.1007/978-3-319-13731-5_60

Kaur, Deepali, & Kalra. (2016). Improvement and analyst security of WSN from passive attack. *2016 5th International Conference on Reliability, Infocom Technologies and Optimization (Trends and Future Directions) (ICRITO),* 420-425.

Kaur, S., Bala, E., Deng, T., Shah, K., Vanganuru, K. K., Pietraski, P. J., ... Pragada, R. V. (2018). *U.S. Patent No. 10,051,624.* Washington, DC: U.S. Patent and Trademark Office.

Kaushik, S. (2018). *Enterprise explainable AI,* Retrieved from https://www.kdnuggets.com/2018/10/enterprise-explainable-ai.html

Kawahito, S., Kameyama, M., Higuchi, T., & Yamada, H. (1988). A 32* 32-bit multiplier using multiple-valued MOS current-mode circuits. *IEEE Journal of Solid-State Circuits, 23*(1), 124–132. doi:10.1109/4.268

Kazemian, H. B., & Ahmed, S. (2015). Comparisons of machine learning techniques for detecting malicious webpages. Expert Systems with Applications. *Expert Systems with Applications, 42*(3), 1166–1177. doi:10.1016/j.eswa.2014.08.046

Kelarestaghi, Foruhandeh, Heaslip, & Gerdes. (2018). *Vehicle Security: Risk Assessment in Transportation.* arXiv.org

Kelarestaghi, Heaslip, Fessmann, Khalilikhah, & Fuentes. (2018). Intelligent Transportation System Security: Hacked Message Signs. *SAE International Journal of Transportation Cybersecurity and Privacy, 1.*

Keneni, B. M., Kaur, D., Al Bataineh, A., Devabhaktuni, V. K., Javaid, A. Y., Zaientz, J. D., & Marinier, R. P. (2019). Evolving rule-based explainable artificial intelligence for unmanned aerial vehicles. *IEEE Access: Practical Innovations, Open Solutions, 7,* 17001–17016. doi:10.1109/ACCESS.2019.2893141

Kephart, J. O., & Chess, D. M. (2003). The Vision of Autonomic Computing. *Computer, 36*(1), 41–50.

Kettani, H., & Cannistra, R. M. (2018). Cyber Threats to Smart Digital Environments. In Icsde 18 (pp. 183–188). doi:10.1145/3289100.3289130

Khan, Alam, Mohamed, & Harras. (2016). Simulating drone-be-gone: Agile low-cost cyber-physical UAV Testbed (Demonstration). *Proc. Int. Jt. Conf. Auton. Agents Multiagent Syst. AAMAS,* 1491–1492.

Khan, M., Shaikh, M., bin Mazhar, S., & Mehboob, K., (2017). Comparative analysis for a real time face recognition system using raspberry Pi. *2017 IEEE 4th International Conference on Smart Instrumentation, Measurement and Application (ICSIMA).*

Khan, A., Abas, Z., Kim, H. S., & Oh, I. K. (2016). Piezoelectric thin films: An integrated review of transducers and energy harvesting. *Smart Materials and Structures, 25*(5), 053002. doi:10.1088/0964-1726/25/5/053002

Khatoun, R., & Zeadally, S. (2017). Cybersecurity and privacy solutions in smart cities. *IEEE Communications Magazine*, *55*(3), 51–59. doi:10.1109/MCOM.2017.1600297CM

Kheng, Sooriyabandara, & Fan. (2011). M2M Communications in the Smart Grid: Applications, Standards, Enabling Technologies, and Research Challenges. *International Journal of Digital Multimedia Broadcasting*.

Khodak, M., Balcan, M. F. F., & Talwalkar, A. S. (2019). Adaptive gradient-based meta-learning methods. *Advances in Neural Information Processing Systems*, 5915–5926.

Kim, T., Cha, M., Kim, H., Lee, J. K., & Kim, J. (2017). *Learning to Discover Cross-Domain Relations with Generative Adversarial Networks*. Retrieved from http://arxiv.org/abs/1703.05192

Kim, H., & Ben-Othman, J. (2020). Toward Integrated Virtual Emotion System with AI Applicability for Secure CPS-Enabled Smart Cities: AI-Based Research Challenges and Security Issues. *IEEE Network*, *34*(3), 30–36. doi:10.1109/MNET.011.1900299

Kim, S., & Park, S. (2017). CPS (cyber physical system) based manufacturing system optimization. *Procedia Computer Science*, *122*, 518–524. doi:10.1016/j.procs.2017.11.401

Kim, W., Jeong, O.-R., Kim, C., & So, J. (2011). The dark side of the Internet: Attacks, costs and responses. *Information Systems*, *36*(3), 675–705. doi:10.1016/j.is.2010.11.003

Kinsy, M., Khan, O., Celanovic, I., Majstorovic, D., Celanovic, N., & Devadas, S. (2011, November). Time-predictable computer architecture for cyber physical systems: Digital emulation of power electronics systems. In *2011 IEEE 32nd Real-Time Systems Symposium* (pp. 305-316). IEEE.

Klaine, P. V., Imran, M. A., Onireti, O., & Souza, R. D. (2017). A survey of machine learning techniques applied to self organizing cellular networks. *IEEE Communications Surveys and Tutorials*, *19*, 2392–2431.

Klein, G., Ojamaa, A., Grigorenko, P., Jahnke, M., & Tyugu, E. (2010, September). Enhancing response selection in impact estimation approaches. In *Military Communications and Information Systems Conference (MCC)*, Wroclaw, Poland.

Komiya, R., Paik, I., & Hisada, M. (2011). Classification of malicious web code by machine learning. *Awareness Science and Technology*, 406-411.

Konstantopoulos, G. C. (2020). *Towards the Integration of Modern Power Systems into a Cyber–Physical Framework*. *Energies Journal*. doi:10.3390/en13092169

Kornecki, A., & Zalewski, J. (2010). Safety and security in industrial control. *ACM International Conference Proceeding Series*.

Košťál, P., & Holubek, R. (2012). The Intelligent Manufacturing Systems. *Advanced Science Letters*, •••, 19.

Kravets, A., Bolshakov, A. A., & Shcherbakov, M. V. (2020). *Cyber-physical Systems: Industry 4.0 Challenges*. Springer. doi:10.1007/978-3-030-32648-7

Krizhevsky, A., Sutskever, I., & Hinton, G. E. (2012). ImageNet Classification with Deep Convolutional Neural Networks. Advances in Neural Information Processing Systems, 1097–1105.

Krizhevsky, A., Sutskever, I., & Hinton, G. E. (n.d.). *ImageNet Classification with Deep Convolutional Neural Networks*. Retrieved from http://code.google.com/p/cuda-convnet/

Krotofil, Cardenas, Larsen, & Gollmann. (2014). Vulnerabilities of cyber-physical systems to stale data determining the optimal time to launch attacks. *International Journal of Critical Infrastructure Protection*.

Kulkarni, V. Y., Sinha, P. K., & Petare, M. C. (2016). Weighted hybrid decision tree model for random forest classifier. *J. Inst. Eng*, 209-2017.

Kumar, P. S., Emfinger, W., & Karsai, G. (2016). A Testbed to Simulate and Analyze Resilient Cyber-Physical Systems. *International Symposium on rapid system prototyping (RSP), 2015*, 97–103.

Kuyama, M., & Kakizaki, R. S. (2016). Method for Detecting a Malicious Domain by Using WHOIS and DNS Features. *The Third International Conference on Digital Security and Forensics (DigitalSec2016)*, 74-80.

Lakshmanan, M. K., & Nikookar, H. (2006). A review of wavelets for digital wireless communication. *Wireless Personal Communications, 37*(3-4), 387–420. doi:10.100711277-006-9077-y

Lalropuia, K. C., & Gupta, V. (2019). Modeling cyber-physical attacks based on stochastic game and Markov processes. *Reliability Engineering & System Safety, 181*, 28–37. doi:10.1016/j.ress.2018.08.014

Langhammer, M., & Baeckler, G. (2018, June). High density and performance multiplication for FPGA. In *2018 IEEE 25th Symposium on Computer Arithmetic (ARITH)* (pp. 5-12). IEEE. 10.1109/ARITH.2018.8464695

LeCun, Y., & Fogelman-Soulié, F. (1987). Modèles connexionnistes de l'apprentissage. *Intellectica, 2*(1), 114–143. doi:10.3406/intel.1987.1804

Le, D. C., Zincir-Heywood, A. N., & Heywood, M. I. (2019). Unsupervised monitoring of network and service behaviour using self organizing maps. *Journal of Cyber Security and Mobility, 8*(1), 15–52. doi:10.13052/jcsm2245-1439.812

Lee, E. (2008). Cyber physical systems: Design challenges. In Object Oriented Real-Time Distributed Computing. *11th IEEE International Symposium on*, 363-369.

Lee, J., Bagheri, B., & Kao, H.-A. (2015). A Cyber-Physical Systems architecture for Industry 4.0-based manufacturing systems. Manufacturing Letters, 3, 18–23. doi:10.1016/j.mfglet.2014.12.001

Lee, J., Davari, H., Singh, J., & Pandhare, V. (2018). Industrial Artificial Intelligence for industry 4.0-based manufacturing systems. Manufacturing Letters, 18, 20–23. doi:10.1016/j.mfglet.2018.09.002

Lee, E. (2015). The past, present and future of cyber-physical systems: A focus on models. *Sensors (Basel), 15*(3), 4837–4869. doi:10.3390150304837 PMID:25730486

Lee, E. A., & Seshia, S. A. (2016). *Introduction to embedded systems: A cyber-physical systems approach*. MIT Press.

Lee, J., Azamfar, M., & Singh, J. (2019). A blockchain-enabled Cyber-Physical System architecture for Industry 4.0 manufacturing systems. *Manufacturing Letters, 20*, 34–39. doi:10.1016/j.mfglet.2019.05.003

Lee, J., Bagheri, B., & Kao, H. A. (2015). A cyber-physical systems architecture for industry 4.0-based manufacturing systems. *Manufacturing Letters, 3*, 18–23. doi:10.1016/j.mfglet.2014.12.001

Lehto, M. (2015). Phenomena in the cyber world. In *Cyber Security: Analytics, Technology and Automation* (pp. 3–29). Cham: Springer. doi:10.1007/978-3-319-18302-2_1

Leonardo. (2019). *System-level Behavioral Detection Framework for Compromised CPS Devices: Smart-Grid Case. ACM Transactions on Cyber-Physical Systems.*

Leong, A. S., Ramaswamy, A., Quevedo, D. E., Karl, H., & Shi, L. (2020). Deep reinforcement learning for wireless sensor scheduling in cyber-physical systems. *Automatica, 113*, 108759. doi:10.1016/j.automatica.2019.108759

León, R. A., Vittal, V., & Manimaran, G. (2007). Application of sensor network for secure electric energy infrastructure. *IEEE Transactions on Power Delivery, 22*(2), 1021–1028. doi:10.1109/TPWRD.2006.886797

Li, S., Li, W., Cook, C., Zhu, C., & Gao, Y. (2018). *Independently Recurrent Neural Network (IndRNN): Building {A} Longer and Deeper {RNN}*. Retrieved from http://arxiv.org/abs/1803.04831

Li. (2013). Security threats and measures for the cyber-physical systems. *Journal of China Universities of Posts and Telecommunications, 20*, 25–29. doi:10.1016/S1005-8885(13)60023-0

Liang, C., Wen, F., & Wang, Z. (2019). *Trust-Based Distributed Kalman Filtering for Target Tracking under Malicious Cyber Attacks*. Chalmers University of Technology.

Liang, F. (2019). *Machine Learning for Security and the Internet of Things: the Good, the Bad, and the Ugly. IEEE Access. Security and Privacy in Emerging Decentralized Communication Environments.*

Liang, M., & Hu, X. (2015). Recurrent convolutional neural network for object recognition. *The IEEE Conference on Computer Vision and Pattern Recognition*, 3367-3375. 10.1109/CVPR.2015.7298958

Li, H., Zhang, X., & Tzou, H. (2017). Diagonal piezoelectric sensors on cylindrical shells. *Journal of Sound and Vibration, 400*, 201–212. doi:10.1016/j.jsv.2017.03.039

Lin, J., Sedigh, S., & Miller, A. (2010, July). Modeling cyber-physical systems with semantic agents. In *2010 IEEE 34th Annual Computer Software and Applications Conference Workshops* (pp. 13-18). IEEE. 10.1109/COMPSACW.2010.13

Lin, J., & Kolcz, A. (2012) Large-scale machine learning at Twitter. In *Proceedings SIGMOD International Conference on Management of Data* (pp. 793–804). ACM.

Liu, Y., Hou, X., Chen, J., Yang, C., Su, G., & Dou, W. (2014). *Facial expression recognition and generation using sparse autoencoder.* doi:10.1109/SMARTCOMP.2014.7043849

Liu, Y., Peng, Y., Wang, B., Yao, S., & Liu, Z. (2017). Review on cyber-physical systems. *IEEE/CAA Journal of Automatica Sinica, 4*(1), 27-40.

Liu, D. (2008). *Embedded DSP processor design: Application-specific instruction set processors.* Elsevier.

Liu, H., Pan, X., & Qu, Z. (2009). Learning based Malicious Web Sites Detection using Suspicious URLs. *Software Engineering*, 1–3.

Liu, Q., Han, T., & Ansari, N. (2020). Learning-Assisted Secure End-to-End Network Slicing for Cyber-Physical Systems. *IEEE Network, 34*(3), 37–43. doi:10.1109/MNET.011.1900303

Liu, S., Xiao, F., Ou, W., & Si, L. (2017). Cascade ranking for operational e-commerce search. In *Proceedings International Conference on Knowledge Discovery and Data Mining* (pp. 1557–1565). ACM.

Liu, X. F., Shahriar, M. R., Al Sunny, S. M. N., Leu, M. C., & Hu, L. (2017). Cyber-physical manufacturing cloud: Architecture, virtualization, communication, and testbed. *Journal of Manufacturing Systems, 43*, 352–364. doi:10.1016/j.jmsy.2017.04.004

Li, X., Li, D., Wan, J., Vasilakos, A. V., Lai, C. F., & Wang, S. (2017). A review of industrial wireless networks in the context of industry 4.0. *Wireless Networks, 23*(1), 23–41. doi:10.100711276-015-1133-7

Li, Z., Zhang, Y., Wang, J., & Lai, J. (2020). A survey of FPGA design for AI era. *Journal of Semiconductors, 41*(2), 021402. doi:10.1088/1674-4926/41/2/021402

Lord, N. (2017). *What is Cyber Security? Data Insider.* Retrieved to 15.01.2020 https://digitalguardian.com/blog/what-cyber-security

Loskyll, M., & Schlick, J. (2013). Cyber physical production systems. *Automatisierungstechnik, 61*, 690–699.

Loureiro, J., Rangarajan, R., Nikolic, B., Indrusiak, L., & Tovar, E. (2017, August). Real-time dense wired sensor network based on traffic shaping. In *2017 IEEE 23rd International Conference on Embedded and Real-Time Computing Systems and Applications (RTCSA)* (pp. 1-10). IEEE. 10.1109/RTCSA.2017.8046307

Lu, C., Saifullah, A., Li, B., Sha, M., Gonzalez, H., Gunatilaka, D., Wu, C., Nie, L., & Chen, Y. (2015). Real-time wireless sensor-actuator networks for industrial cyber-physical systems. *Proceedings of the IEEE, 104*(5), 1013–1024. doi:10.1109/JPROC.2015.2497161

Luckow, A., Cook, M., Ashcraft, N., Weill, E., Djerekarov, E., & Vorster, B. (2016). Deep learning in the automotive industry: Applications and tools. In *Proceedings International Conference on Big Data* (pp. 3759–3768). 10.1109/BigData.2016.7841045

Lunt, T. F., & Jagannathan, R. (1988, April). A prototype real-time intrusion-detection expert system. In *IEEE Symposium on Security and Privacy* (Vol. 59). IEEE.

Lwakatare, L. E., Raj, A., Bosch, J., Olsson, H. H., & Crnkovic, I. (2019). A taxonomy of software engineering challenges for machine learning systems: An empirical investigation. In *Proceedings International Conference on Agile Software Development* (pp. 227–243). Springer. 10.1007/978-3-030-19034-7_14

Lwin, Khaing, & Tun. (2015). Automatic Door access system using face recognition. *International Journal of Scientific & Technology Research, 4*(6).

Ma & Li. (2020). Hybridized Intelligent Home Renewable Energy Management System for Smart Grids. *MDPI Sustainability Journal*, 1-14.

Ma, J., Lawrence, K., Saul, K., Stefan, S., & Geoffrey, M. (2009). Identifying Suspicious URLs: An Application of Large-Scale Online Learning. In *Proceedings of the International Conference on Machine Learning (ICML)* (pp. 681-688). Motreal: ICML. 10.1145/1553374.1553462

Maguire M., & Delahunt, B. (2017). Doing a thematic analysis: A practical, step-by-step guide for learning and teaching scholars. *AISHE-J: The All Ireland Journal of Teaching and Learning in Higher Education, 9*(3).

Mahdavi-Hezavehi, S. (2016, November). Handling multiple quality attributes trade-off in architecture-based self-adaptive systems. In *Proceedings of the 10th European Conference on Software Architecture Workshops* (pp. 1-2). 10.1145/2993412.3010822

Ma, J., Saul, L. K., Savage, S., & Voelker, G. M. (2009). Beyond blacklists: learning to detect malicious web sites from suspicious URLs. *Proceedings of the 15th ACM SIGKDD International Conference on Knowledge Discovery and Data Mining*, 1245–1254. 10.1145/1557019.1557153

Ma, J., Saul, L. K., Savage, S., & Voelker, G. M. (2011). Learning to Detect Malicious URLs. *ACM Transactions on Intelligent Systems and Technology, 2*(3), 24. doi:10.1145/1961189.1961202

Makhoul, J., Kubala, F., Schwartz, R., & Weischedel, R. (1999). Performance measures for information extraction. *Proceedings of DARPA Broadcast News Workshop*, 249-252.

Mäkitalo, N., Nocera, F., Mongiello, M., & Bistarelli, S. (2018). Architecting the Web of Things for the fog computing era. *IET Software, 12*(5), 381–389. doi:10.1049/iet-sen.2017.0350

Malik, M. M. (2020). *A Hierarchy of Limitations in Machine Learning*. arXiv preprint arXiv:2002.05193

Mandloi, A., Agrawal, S., Sharma, S., & Shrivastava, S. (2017, August). High-speed, area efficient VLSI architecture of wallace-tree multiplier for DSP-applications. In *2017 International Conference on Information, Communication, Instrumentation and Control (ICICIC)* (pp. 1-5). IEEE. 10.1109/ICOMICON.2017.8279072

Manek, A. S., Shenoy, P. D., Mohan, M. C., & Patnaik, L. (2014). DeMalFier:Detection of Malicious Web Pages using an Effective ClassiFier. Data Science & Engineering, 83-88.

Marie, A., Celebre, D., Benedict, I., Medina, A., Zandrae, A., Dubouzet, D., Neil, A., Surposa, M., & Gustilo, E. R. C. (2015). Home automation using Raspberry Pi through Siri enabled mobile devices. *Proc. 8th IEEE International Conference Humanoid, Nanotechnology, Information Technology Communication and Control, Environment and Management (HNICEM)*.

Masuda, S., Ono, K., Yasue, T., & Hosokawa, N. (2018). A survey of software quality for machine learning applications. In *Proceedings International Conference on Software Testing, Verification and Validation Workshops – ICSTW* (pp. 279–284). IEEE.

Maxwell, J. A. (2012). *Qualitative research design: An interactive approach* (Vol. 41). Sage publications.

McLaughlin, S. (2013). CPS: stateful policy enforcement for control system device usage. *Proceedings of the 29th Annual Computer Security Applications Conference*.

McLaughlin, S., Konstantinou, C., Wang, X., Davi, L., Sadeghi, A.-R., Maniatakos, M., & Karri, R. (2016). The Cybersecurity Landscape in Industrial Control Systems. *Proceedings of the IEEE, 104*(5), 1–19. doi:10.1109/JPROC.2015.2512235

McLaughlin, S., Zonouz, S., Pohly, D., & McDaniel, P. (2014). *A Trusted Safety Verifier for Process Controller Code*. San Diego, CA: NDSS. doi:10.14722/ndss.2014.23043

Meissner, H., & Aurich, J. C. (2019). Implications of Cyber-Physical Production Systems on Integrated Process Planning and Scheduling. Procedia Manufacturing, 28, 167–173. doi:10.1016/j.promfg.2018.12.027

Melendez, S., & McGarry, M. P. (2017, January). Computation offloading decisions for reducing completion time. In *2017 14th IEEE Annual Consumer Communications & Networking Conference (CCNC)* (pp. 160-164). IEEE.

Melis, D. A., & Jaakkola, T. (2018). Towards robust interpretability with self-explaining neural networks. *Advances in Neural Information Processing Systems*, 7775–7784.

Menon, R., & Radhakrishnan, D. (2006). High performance 5: 2 compressor architectures. *IEE Proceedings. Circuits, Devices and Systems, 153*(5), 447–452. doi:10.1049/ip-cds:20050152

Merwe, Zubizarreta, Lukcin, Rügamer, & Felber. (2018). Classification of Spoofing Attack Types. *Conference: European Navigation Conference (ENC)*. doi:10.1145/2523649.2523673

Michel, M., Beck, D., Block, N., Blumenfeld, H., Brown, R., Carmel, D., ... Yoshida, M. (2019). Opportunities and challenges for a maturing science of consciousness. *Nature Human Behaviour, 3*(2), 104–107. doi:10.1038/s41562-019-0531-8 PubMed

Miciolino, E. E., Bernieri, G., Pascucci, F., & Setola, R. (2016). Communications network analysis in a SCADA system testbed under cyber-attacks. *IEEE, 23rd Telecommunications Forum*.

Mihalache, S. F., Pricop, E., & Fattahi, J. (2019). Resilience enhancement of cyber-physical systems: A review. In *Power Systems Resilience* (pp. 269–287). Cham: Springer. doi:10.1007/978-3-319-94442-5_11

Miles, B. (2018). *The malicious use of artificial intelligence: Forecasting, prevention, and mitigation.* arXiv: 1802.07228

Miller, T. (2019). Explanation in artificial intelligence: *Insights from the social sciences. Artificial Intelligence, 267,* 1–38. doi:10.1016/j.artint.2018.07.007

Mitchell, R., & Chen, I.-R. (2014). A Survey of Intrusion Detection Techniques for Cyber-Physical Systems. *ACM Computing Surveys, 46*(4), 1–29. doi:10.1145/2542049

Mitchel, M. F. (1997). *Machine Learning*. McGraw Hill.

Mittal, S., & Tolk, A. (2020). *Complexity Challenges in Cyber-Physical Systems: Using Modeling and Simulation (M&S) to Support Intelligence, Adaptation, and Autonomy*. John Wiley & Sons.

Mohamed, N., Al-Jaroodi, J., Jawhar, I., Idries, A., & Mohammed, F. (2020). Unmanned aerial vehicles applications in future smart cities. *Technological Forecasting and Social Change, 153*, 119293. doi:10.1016/j.techfore.2018.05.004

Mohammed, M. (2018). *Requirements of the Smart Factory System: A Survey and Perspective*. MDPI Machines Journal.

Mohan, Bak, Betti, Yun, Sha, & Caccamo. (2012). *S3A: Secure System Simplex Architecture for Enhanced Security of Cyber-Physical Systems*. arXiv.org

Moness, M., & Moustafa, A. M. (2015). A survey of cyber-physical advances and challenges of wind energy conversion systems: Prospects for internet of energy. *IEEE Internet of Things Journal, 3*(2), 134–145. doi:10.1109/JIOT.2015.2478381

Monostori, L. (2014). Cyber-physical Production Systems: Roots, Expectations and R&D Challenges. Procedia CIRP, 17, 9–13. doi:10.1016/j.procir.2014.03.115

Morris & Gao. (2013). *Classifications of Industrial Control System Cyber Attacks*. First International Symposium for ICS & SCADA Cyber Security Research.

Mosterman, P. J., & Zander, J. (2016). Industry 4.0 as a cyber-physical system study. *Software & Systems Modeling, 15*(1), 17–29. doi:10.100710270-015-0493-x

Mourtzis, D., Vlachou, E., & Milas, N. (2016). Industrial Big Data as a result of IoT adoption in manufacturing. *Procedia CIRP, 55*, 290–295. doi:10.1016/j.procir.2016.07.038

Mousta, N., & Soukharev, F. (2018). *Crypto Agility is a Must -Have for Data Encryption Standards*. Retrieved from https://www.cigionline.org/articles/crypto-agility-must-have-data-encryption-standards

Mo, Y. (2012). Cyber–Physical Security of a Smart Grid Infrastructure. *Proceedings of the IEEE, 100*(1), 195–209. doi:10.1109/JPROC.2011.2161428

Munappy, A., Bosch, J., Olsson, H. H., Arpteg, A., & Brinne, B. (2019). Data management challenges for deep learning. In *Proceedings 45th Euromicro Conference on Software Engineering and Advanced Applications - SEAA* (pp. 140–147). IEEE.

Munappy, R.A., & Mattos, D.I., & Bosch, J. (2020). From Ad-hoc Data Analytics to DataOps. *Proceedings of the International Conference on Software and Systems Process (ICSSP)*.

Munappy, R. A., Bosch, J., Olsson, H. H., & Wang, T. J. (2020). Modeling Data Pipelines. *Proceedings of the Euromicro Conference on Software Engineering and Advanced Applications (SEAA)*.

Munirathinam, S. (2020). Industry 4.0: Industrial Internet of Things (IIOT). *Advances in Computers, 117*(1), 129–164.

Muyambo, P. (2018). An Investigation on the Use of LBPH Algorithm for Face Recognition to Find Missing People in Zimbabwe. *International Journal of Engineering Research & Technology, 7*(7).

Nakajima, S., Talpin, J. P., Toyoshima, M., & Yu, H. (2017, January). Cyber-Physical System Design from an Architecture Analysis Viewpoint. In *Communications of the NII Shonan Meetings*. Springer. 10.1007/978-981-10-4436-6

Naram, Fetais, & Massoud. (2019). Secure smart contract-enabled control of battery energy storage systems against cyber-attacks. *Alexandria Engineering Journal*.

Naseer, S., Saleem, Y., Khalid, S., Bashir, M. K., Han, J., Iqbal, M. M., & Han, K. (2018). Enhanced network anomaly detection based on deep neural networks. *IEEE Access: Practical Innovations, Open Solutions, 6*(8), 48231–48246. doi:10.1109/ACCESS.2018.2863036

Nazarenko, A., & Safdar, G. (2019). Survey on security and privacy issues in cyber physical systems. *AIMS Electronics and Electrical Engineering, 3*, 111–143. doi:10.3934/ElectrEng.2019.2.111

Negri, E., Fumagalli, L., & Macchi, M. (2017). A review of the roles of digital twin in cps-based production systems. *Procedia Manufacturing, 11*, 939–948. doi:10.1016/j.promfg.2017.07.198

Nguyen, G., Dlugolinsky, S., Bobák, M., Tran, V., López García, Á., Heredia, I., ... Hluchý, L. (2019). Machine Learning and Deep Learning frameworks and libraries for large-scale data mining: A survey. *Artificial Intelligence Review, 52*(1), 77–124. doi:10.1007/s10462-018-09679-z

Niedermann, F., & Schwarz, H. (2011). Deep business optimization: Making business process optimization theory work in practice. In *Enterprise, business-process, and information systems modeling* (pp. 88–102). Springer. doi:10.1007/978-3-642-21759-3_7

Nielsen, T. D., & Jensen, F. V. (2007). Bayesian Networks and Decision Graphs (Information Science and Statistics). *Artificial Intelligence Research, 27*(1), 381–41.

Nigam, A., Rastogi, R., Mishra, R., Arya, P., & Sharma, S. (2015). Security of Data Transmission Using Logic Gates and Crypt Analysis. *CSI Communication, 17*. http://www.csi-india.org/communications/CSI%20June15%20Combine.pdf

Nigam, A., Rastogi, R., Mishra, R., Arya, P., & Sharma, S. (2015).Security of data transmission using logic gates and crypt analysis. *Proceedings of 09th INDIACom; 2015 2nd International Conference on Computing for Sustainable Global Development*, 101-105. https://ieeexplore.ieee.org/document/7100229

Niggemann. (2015). Data-Driven Monitoring of Cyber-Physical Systems Leveraging on Big Data and the Internet-of-Things for Diagnosis and Control. *Proceedings of the 26th International Workshop on Principles of Diagnosis.*

Nikoloudakis, Y., Panagiotakis, S., Markakis, E., Mastorakis, G., Mavromoustakis, C. X., & Pallis, E. (2017). Towards a FOG-enabled navigation system with advanced cross-layer management features and IoT equipment. In Cloud and Fog Computing in 5G Mobile Networks: Emerging advances and applications. Institution of Engineering and Technology.

Niua, J., Ganga, H., Zhangb, Y., & Duc, X. (2018). Relationship between automation trust and operator performance for the novice and expert in spacecraft rendezvous and docking (RVD). *Applied Ergonomics, 35*(4), 1–8. doi:10.1016/j.apergo.2018.03.014 PMID:29764609

Ntoulas, A., Najork, M., Manasse, M., & Fetterly, D. (2006). Detecting spam web pages through content analysis. *Proceedings of the 15th International Conference on World Wide Web*, 83-92. 10.1145/1135777.1135794

Nugrahaeni, R.A., & Mutijarsa, K. (2017). Comparative analysis of machine learning KNN, SVM, and random forests algorithm for facial expression classification. *IEEE Xplore.*

O'Donovan, P., Gallagher, C., Bruton, K., & O'Sullivan, D. T. J. (2018). A fog computing industrial cyber-physical system for embedded low-latency machine learning Industry 4.0 applications. Manufacturing Letters, 15, 139–142. doi:10.1016/j.mfglet.2018.01.005

Ochoa, S. F., Fortino, G., & Di Fatta, G. (2017). *Cyber-physical systems, internet of things and big data.* Academic Press.

Ojamaa, A., Tyugu, E., & Kivimaa, J. (2008, November). Pareto-optimal situaton analysis for selection of security measures. In MILCOM 2008-2008 IEEE Military Communications Conference (pp. 1-7). IEEE. doi:10.1109/MILCOM.2008.4753520

Oreizy, P., Medvidovic, N., & Taylor, R. N. (1998, April). Architecture-based runtime software evolution. In *Proceedings of the 20th international conference on Software engineering* (pp. 177-186). IEEE. 10.1109/ICSE.1998.671114

Ozcan, E., & Erdem, S. S. (2019, July). A High-Performance Full-Word Barrett Multiplier Designed for FPGAs with DSP Resources. In *2019 15th Conference on Ph. D Research in Microelectronics and Electronics (PRIME)* (pp. 73-76). IEEE. 10.1109/PRIME.2019.8787740

Oztemel, E. (2010). Intelligent Manufacturing Systems. In *Artificial Intelligence Techniques for Networked Manufacturing Enterprises Management*. Springer London.

Oztemel, E. (2018). Literature review of Industry 4.0 and related technologies. *Journal of Intelligent Manufacturing*.

Pachghare, V. K., Kulkarni, P., & Nikam, D. M. (2009, July). Intrusion detection system using self organizing maps. In *2009 International Conference on Intelligent Agent & Multi-Agent Systems* (pp. 1-5). IEEE. 10.1109/IAMA.2009.5228074

Padilha, R. (2018). *Proposta de Um Método Complementar de Compressão de Dados Por Meio da Metodologia de Eventos Discretos Aplicada Em Um Baixo Nível de Abstração* (Mestrado em Engenharia Elétrica). Faculdade de Engenharia Elétrica e de Computação, Universidade Estadual de Campinas.

Padilha, R., Iano, Y., Monteiro, A. C. B., Arthur, R., & Estrela, V. V. (2018, October). Betterment Proposal to Multipath Fading Channels Potential to MIMO Systems. In *Brazilian Technology Symposium* (pp. 115-130). Springer.

Panerati, J., Schnellmann, M. A., Patience, C., Beltrame, G., & Patience, G. S. (2019). Experimental methods in chemical engineering: Artificial neural networks–ANNs. *Canadian Journal of Chemical Engineering*, *97*(9), 2372–2382. doi:10.1002/cjce.23507

Panetto, H., Iung, B., Ivanov, D., Weichhart, G., & Wang, X. (2019). Challenges for the Cyber-Physical Manufacturing Enterprises of the Future. *Annual Reviews in Control*, *47*, 200–213. Advance online publication. doi:10.1016/j.arcontrol.2019.02.002

Parekh, S., Parikh, D., & Sankhe, S. (2018). A New Method for Detection of Phishing Websites: URL Detection. *2018 Second International Conference on Inventive Communication and Computational Technologies (ICICCT)*, 949-952. 10.1109/ICICCT.2018.8473085

Parhi, K. K. (2007). *VLSI digital signal processing systems: design and implementation*. John Wiley & Sons.

Parisotto, E., Ghosh, S., Yalamanchi, S. B., Chinnaobireddy, V., Wu, Y., & Salakhutdinov, R. (2019). *Concurrent meta reinforcement learning*. arXiv preprint arXiv:1903.02710

Park, H. M., & Jeon, J. W. (2019). OPC UA based Universal Edge Gateway for Legacy Equipment. IEEE 17th International Conference on Industrial Informatics (INDIN), 1002-1007. doi:10.1109/INDIN41052.2019.8972187

Park, S., Kim, M., & Lee, S. (2018). Anomaly Detection for HTTP Using Convolutional Autoencoders. *IEEE Access*, 1. doi:10.1109/ACCESS.2018.2881003

Parrend, P., Navarro, J., Guigou, F., Deruyver, A., & Collet, P. (2018). Foundations and applications of artificial Intelligence for zero-day and multi-step attack detection. *EURASIP Journal on Information Security, 2018*(1), 1-21.

Parulpreet, S., Arun, K., Anil, K., & Mamta, K. (2019). Computational Intelligence Techniques for Localization in Static and Dynamic Wireless Sensor Networks—A Review. In *Computational Intelligence in Sensor Networks* (pp. 25–54). Berlin: Springer. doi:10.1007/978-3-662-57277-1_2

Patalas Maliszewska, J., & Schlueter, N. (2019). Model of a Knowledge Management for System Integrator(s) of Cyber-Physical Production Systems (CPPS). International Scientific-Technical Conference Manufacturing, 92-103. doi:10.1007/978-3-030-18715-6_8

Patil, D. R., & Patil, J. B. (2015). Survey on Malicious Web Pages Detection Techniques. *International Journal of u- and e- Service. Science and Technology, 8*, 195–206.

Patil, P. A., & Kulkarni, C. (2018, August). A Survey on Multiply Accumulate Unit. In *Fourth International Conference on Computing Communication Control and Automation (ICCUBEA)* (pp. 1-5). IEEE.

Paul, S., Guha, D., Chatterjee, A., Metha, S., & Shah, A. (2017). Comparison between Conventional Network and ANN with Case Study. *Int. Res. J. Eng. Technol, 4*(8), 1795–1803.

Pavic, I., & Dzapo, H. (2018). Virtualization in multicore real-time embedded systems for improvement of interrupt latency. 41st International Convention on Information and Communication Technology, Electronics and Microelectronics (MIPRO), 1405-1410. doi:10.23919/MIPRO.2018.8400253

Pearl, J. (2019). The seven tools of causal inference, with reflections on machine learning. *Communications of the ACM, 62*(3), 54–60. doi:10.1145/3241036

Pedireddy, T., & Vidal, J. M. (2003, July). A prototype multiagent network security system. In *Proceedings of the second international joint conference on Autonomous agents and multiagent systems* (pp. 1094-1095). 10.1145/860575.860812

Perez-Palacin, D., & Mirandola, R. (2014) Uncertainties in the Modeling of Self-adaptive Systems. In *Proc. of the 20th International Conference on Software Engineering (ICSE '98)*. IEEE Computer.

Perumalraja. (2012). Communication requirements and analysis of distribution networks using WiMAX technology for smart grids. *Conference: Wireless Communications and Mobile Computing Conference (IWCMC), 2012 8th International.*

Pfahringer, B., Bensusan, H., & Giraud-Carrier, C. G. (2000). Meta-Learning by Landmarking Various Learning Algorithms. In ICML (pp. 743-750). Academic Press.

Pietro Di, A., Foglietta, C., Palmieri, S., & Panzieri, S. (2013). Assessing the impact of cyber-attacks on interdependent physical systems. *International Conference on Critical Infrastructure Protection.* 10.1007/978-3-642-45330-4_15

Poudel, S., Ni, Z., & Malla, N. (2017). Real-time cyber physical system testbed for power system security and control. *International Journal of Electrical Power & Energy Systems, 90*, 124–133. doi:10.1016/j.ijepes.2017.01.016

Prabhash. (2015). Energy Management System in Smart Grid: An Overview. *IJRSI, 2*(12).

Pradhan, A. (2012). Support vector machine-A survey. *International Journal of Emerging Technology and Advanced Engineering, 2*(8), 82–85.

Prakash Nandi, Marimuthu, Balamurugan & Duraivel. (2019). Low-Power and Area-Efficient Approximate Parallel Design Using Bypassing. *Proceedings of International Conference on Recent Trends in Computing, Communication & Networking Technologies.* doi:10.2139srn.3428931

Prakash, P. K. S., & Rao, A. S. K. (2017). *R deep learning cookbook.* Packt Pub. Ltd.

Prasad, P., Pathak, R., Gunjan, V., & Ramana Rao, H. (2019). *Deep Learning Based Representation for Face Recognition.* Lecture Notes in Electrical Engineering.

Qun, C., Mei, L., & Xinyu, L. (2018). Bike Fleet Allocation Models for Repositioning in Bike-Sharing Systems. *IEEE Intelligent Transportation Systems Magazine, 10*(1), 19–29. doi:10.1109/MITS.2017.2776129

Radford, A., Metz, L., & Chintala, S. (2015). *Unsupervised Representation Learning with Deep Convolutional Generative Adversarial Networks*. Retrieved from http://arxiv.org/abs/1511.06434

Rajkumar, R. R., Lee, I., Sha, L., & Stankovic, J. (2010). Cyber-physical systems: the next computing revolution. *Proceedings of the 47th Design Automation Conference, DAC'2010*, 731-736.

Rakelly, K., Zhou, A., Quillen, D., Finn, C., & Levine, S. (2019). *Efficient off-policy meta-reinforcement learning via probabilistic context variables*. arXiv preprint arXiv:1903.08254

Ramirez, A. J., Jensen, A. C., & Cheng, B. H. C. (2012) A Taxonomy of Uncertainty for Dynamically Adaptive Self-Adaptation with Reusable Infrastructure. *Computer, 37*(10), 46–54.

Rao, C. S., Murthy, K. V. S., Appaji, S. V., & Shankar, R. S. (2020). Cyber-Physical Systems Security: Definitions, Methodologies, Metrics, and Tools. In *Smart Intelligent Computing and Applications* (pp. 477–488). Singapore: Springer.

Rastogi, Chaturvedi, Arora, Trivedi, & Chauhan. (2019). Framework for Use of Machine Intelligence on Clinical Psychology to Study the effects of Spiritual tools on Human Behavior and Psychic Challenges. *Journal of Image Processing and Artificial Intelligence, 4*(1).

Rastogi, Chaturvedi, Arora, Trivedi, & Mishra. (2018). Swarm Intelligent Optimized Method of Development of Noble Life in the perspective of Indian Scientific Philosophy and Psychology. *Journal of Image Processing and Artificial Intelligence, 4*(1). http://matjournals.in/index.php/JOIPAI/issue/view/463

Rastogi, Chaturvedi, Arora, Trivedi, & Singh. (2017). Role and efficacy of Positive Thinking on Stress Management and Creative Problem Solving for Adolescents. *International Journal of Computational Intelligence, Biotechnology and Biochemical Engineering, 2*(2).

Rastogi, Chaturvedi, Sharma, Bansal, & Agrawal. (2017). Understanding Human Behaviour and Psycho Somatic Disorders by Audio Visual EMG & GSR Biofeedback Analysis and Spiritual Methods. *International Journal of Computational Intelligence, Biotechnology and Biochemical Engineering, 2*(2).

Rastogi, R., Chaturvedi, D. K., Satya, S., Arora, N., Bansal, I., & Yadav, V. (2018). Intelligent Analysis for Detection of Complex Human Personality by Clinical Reliable Psychological Surveys on Various Indicators. *The National Conference on 3rd Multi-Disciplinary National Conference Pre-Doctoral Research.*

Rastogi, R., Chaturvedi, D. K., Satya, S., Arora, N., Saini, H., Verma, H., . . . Varshney, Y. (2018). Statistical Analysis of EMG and GSR Therapy on Visual Mode and SF-36 Scores for Chronic TTH. *Proceedings of International Conference on 5th IEEE Uttar Pradesh Section International Conference.* 10.1109/UPCON.2018.8596851

Rastogi, R., Chaturvedi, D. K., Satya, S., Arora, N., Singh, P., & Vyas, P. (2018). Statistical Analysis for Effect of Positive Thinking on Stress Management and Creative Problem Solving for Adolescents. *Proceedings of the 12th INDIACom; INDIACom-2018.*

Rastogi, R., Chaturvedi, D. K., Satya, S., Arora, N., Yadav, V., & Chauhan, S. (2018). An Optimized Biofeedback Therapy for Chronic TTH between Electromyography and Galvanic Skin Resistance Biofeedback on Audio, Visual and Audio Visual Modes on Various Medical Symptoms. *The National Conference on 3rd Multi-Disciplinary National Conference Pre-Doctoral Research.*

Rastogi, R., Chaturvedi, D., Sharma, S., Bansal, A., & Agrawal, A. (2017). Audio-Visual EMG & GSR Biofeedback Analysis for Effect of Spiritual Techniques on Human Behaviour and Psychic Challenges. *Journal of Applied Information Science, 5*(2), 37-46. Retrieved from http://www.i-scholar.in/index.php/jais/article/view/167372

Rastogi, R., Chaturvedi, D. K., Arora, N., Trivedi, P., & Mishra, V. (2017). Swarm Intelligent Optimized Method of Development of Noble Life in the perspective of Indian Scientific Philosophy and Psychology. *Proceedings of NSC-2017 (National system conference) IEEE Sponsored conf. of Dayalbagh Educational Institute, Agra.*

Ratasich, D., Khalid, F., Geißler, F., Grosu, R., Shafique, M., & Bartocci, E. (2019). A Roadmap Toward the Resilient Internet of Things for Cyber-Physical Systems. *IEEE Access : Practical Innovations, Open Solutions, 7*, 13260–13283. doi:10.1109/ACCESS.2019.2891969

Rathore, Ryu, Park, & Park. (2018). A Survey on Cyber Physical System Security for IoT: Issues, Challenges, Threats, Solutions. *Journal of Information Process System.*

Ravi. (2017). Embedded System and Its Real Time Applications. Available: https://www.electronicshub.org/embedded-system-real-time-applications/

Rawat, P., Singh, K. D., Chaouchi, H., & Bonnin, J. M. (2014). Wireless sensor networks: A survey on recent developments and potential synergies. *The Journal of Supercomputing, 68*(1), 1–48. doi:10.100711227-013-1021-9

Ray, L. (2020). Cyber-Physical Systems: An Overview of Design Process, Applications, and Security. In *Cyber Warfare and Terrorism: Concepts, Methodologies, Tools, and Applications* (pp. 128–150). IGI Global. doi:10.4018/978-1-7998-2466-4.ch008

Reichherzer, T., Satterfield, S., Belitsos, J., Chudzynski, J., & Watson, L. (2016, May). An agent-based architecture for sensor data collection and reasoning in smart home environments for independent living. In *Canadian Conference on Artificial Intelligence* (pp. 15-20). Springer. 10.1007/978-3-319-34111-8_2

Ren, S., He, K., Girshick, R., & Sun, J. (2017). Faster R-CNN: Towards Real-Time Object Detection with Region Proposal Networks. *IEEE Transactions on Pattern Analysis and Machine Intelligence, 39*(6), 1137–1149.

Rieck, K., Holz, T., Wiiems, C., Dussel, P., & Laskov, P. (2008). Learning and classification of malware behavior. In *International Conference ¨ on Detection of Intrusions and Malware, and Vulnerability Assessment* (pp. 108-125). Springer. 10.1007/978-3-540-70542-0_6

Rifai, S., Vincent, P., Muller, X., Glorot, X., & Bengio, Y. (2011). *Contractive Auto-Encoders: Explicit Invariance During Feature Extraction.* Academic Press.

Rittinghouse, J. W., & Ransome, J. F. (2016). *Cloud computing: implementation, management, and security.* CRC Press.

Roemer, R., Buchanan, E., Shacham, H., & Savage, S. (2012). Return-Oriented Programming: Systems, Languages, and Applications. ACM Trans. Inf. Syst. Secur., 15. doi:10.1145/2133375.2133377

Rosenblatt, F. (1957). *The perceptron, a perceiving and recognizing automaton Project Para.* Cornell Aeronautical Laboratory.

Roshandel, R., Medvidovic, N., & Golubchik, L. (2007, July). A Bayesian model for predicting the reliability of software systems at the architectural level. In *International Conference on the Quality of Software Architectures* (pp. 108-126). Springer. 10.1007/978-3-540-77619-2_7

Ruan, T., Chew, Z. J., & Zhu, M. (2017). Energy-aware approaches for energy harvesting powered wireless sensor nodes. *IEEE Sensors Journal, 17*(7), 2165–2173. doi:10.1109/JSEN.2017.2665680

Rubin, M. J. (2014). *Efficient and automatic wireless geohazard monitoring* (Doctoral dissertation). Colorado School of Mines. Arthur Lakes Library.

Rubio. (2018). Analysis of cyber security threats in Industry 4.0: the case of intrusion detection. *Lecture Notes in Computer Science, 10707*, 119-130.

Rubio, J. E. (2017). Analysis of Intrusion Detection Systems in Industrial Ecosystems. *14th International Conference on Security and Cryptography.* 10.5220/0006426301160128

Rungta, S., Srivastava, S., Yadav, U. S., & Rastogi, R. (2014) A Comparative Analysis of New Approach with an Existing Algorithm to Detect Cycles in a Directed Graph. In *ICT and Critical Infrastructure: Proceedings of the 48th Annual Convention of Computer Society of India.* Springer. 10.1007/978-3-319-03095-1_5

Saeed, A., Neishaboori, A., Mohamed, A., & Harras, K. A. (2014). Up and away: A visually-controlled easy-to-deploy wireless UAV Cyber- Physical testbed. *International Conference on Wireless and Mobile Computing, Networking and Communications.* 10.1109/WiMOB.2014.6962228

Saldaña, A., Vila, C., Rodríguez, C. A., Ahuett, H., & Siller, H. R. (2009). Cooperative Analysis of Production Systems with Simulation Techniques. In Cooperative Design (pp. 27–31). Berlin: Visualization, and Engineering. doi:10.1007/978-3-642-04265-2_4

Saldivar. (2015). Industry 4.0 with Cyber-Physical Integration: A Design and Manufacture Perspective. 21st International Conference on Automation & Computing, 11-12. doi:10.1016/j.jisa.2020.102500

Samek, W., Wiegand, T., & Müller, K. R. (2017). *Explainable artificial intelligence: Understanding, visualizing, and interpreting deep learning models.* arXiv preprint arXiv:1708.08296

Sandberg, H., Teixeira, A., & Johansson, K. (2010). *On Security Indices for State Estimators in Power Networks. First Workshop on Secure Control Systems (SCS)*, Stockholm, Sweden.

Sangaiah, A. K., Sadeghilalimi, M., Hosseinabadi, A. A. R., & Zhang, W. (2019). Energy consumption in point-coverage wireless sensor networks via bat algorithm. *IEEE Access: Practical Innovations, Open Solutions*, 7, 180258–180269. doi:10.1109/ACCESS.2019.2952644

Santoro, A., Bartunov, S., Botvinick, M., Wierstra, D., & Lillicrap, T. (2016). Meta-learning with memory-augmented neural networks. In *International conference on machine learning* (pp. 1842-1850). Academic Press.

Santos, I., Devesa, J., Brezo, F., Nieves, J., & Bringas, P. (2013). OPEM: A static-dynamic approach for machine-learning-based malware detection. *Advances in Intelligent Systems and Computing 189 AISC*, 271-280.

Saquib, S. T., & Hameed, S. (2013). Wireless Control of Miniaturized Mobile Vehicle for Indoor Surveillance. *IOP Conference Series Material Science and Engineering*, *51*(3), 452-465. 10.1088/1757-899X/51/1/012025

Sargolzaei, A., Crane, C. D., Abbaspour, A., & Noei, S. (2016). A Machine Learning Approach for Fault Detection in Vehicular Cyber-Physical Systems. 15th IEEE International Conference on Machine Learning and Applications (ICMLA), 636-640. doi:10.1109/ICMLA.2016.0112

Savran, A., & Sankur, B. (2017). Non-rigid registration based model-free 3D facial expression recognition Comput. *Vis. Image Underst.*, *162*, 146–165. doi:10.1016/j.cviu.2017.07.005

Say, S., Ernawan, M. E., & Shimamoto, S. (2016). Cooperative path selection framework for effective data gathering in UAV-aided wireless sensor networks. *IEICE Transactions on Communications*, *99*(10), 2156–2167. doi:10.1587/transcom.2016ATP0012

Scarfone, K., & Mell, P. (2007). Guide to Intrusion Detection and Prevention Systems (IDPS). NIST IR-7628 - SP 800-94.

Schmidt, R. M. (2019). *Recurrent Neural Networks (RNNs): A gentle Introduction and Overview.* arXiv preprint arXiv:1912.05911

Schnack, H. (2020). Bias, noise, and interpretability in machine learning: From measurements to features. *Machine Learning*, 307–328.

Schweighofer, N., & Doya, K. (2003). Meta-learning in reinforcement learning. *Neural Networks, 16*(1), 5–9. doi:10.1016/S0893-6080(02)00228-9 PMID:12576101

Sculley, D., Holt, D., Golovin, G., Davydov, E., Phillips, T., Ebner, D., . . . Dennison, D. (2015) Hidden technical debt in machine learning systems. In Proceedings Advances in neural information processing systems (NIPS) 28 (pp. 2503–2511). Curran Associates, Inc.

Serpen, G., & Gao, Z. (2014). Complexity analysis of multilayer perceptron neural network embedded into a wireless sensor network. *Procedia Computer Science, 36*, 192–197. doi:10.1016/j.procs.2014.09.078

Setoya. (2011). History and review of the IMS (Intelligent Manufacturing System). IEEE International Conference on Mechatronics and Automation.

Settanni, G., Skopik, F., Karaj, A., Wurzenberger, M., & Fiedler, R. (2018). Protecting cyber physical production systems using anomaly detection to enable self-adaptation. IEEE Industrial Cyber-Physical Systems (ICPS), 173-180.

Shabtai, A., Moskovitch, R., Elovici, Y., & Glezer, C. (2009). Detection of malicious code by applying machine learning classifiers on static features: A state-of-the-art survey. *Information Security Technical Report, 14*(1), 16–29. doi:10.1016/j.istr.2009.03.003

Shah, A., Zaidi, Z., Chowdhry, B., & Daudpoto, J. (2016). Real time face detection/monitor using raspberry pi and MATLAB. *2016 IEEE 10th International Conference on Application of Information and Communication Technologies (AICT)*.

Shanker, R., Luhach, A. K., & Sardar, A. (2016). To enhance the security in wireless nodes using centralized and synchronized IDS technique. *Indian Journal of Science and Technology, 9*(32), 1–5.

Sharma, P., Rastogi, R., Aggarwal, S., Kaul, U., & Jain, S. (2014). Business Analysis and Decision Making Through Unsupervised Classification of Mixed Data Type of Attributes Through Genetic Algorithm. *BIJIT, 6*(1). http://bvicam.ac.in/bjit/issues.asp?issue=11

Sharma, R., Jain, A., & Rastogi, R. (2013). A New Face To Photo Security Of Facebook. *Proceedings of the Sixth International Conference on Contemporary Computing (IC3-2013)*. https://ieeexplore.ieee.org/document/6612231

Sharma, S., Rastogi, R., & Kumar, S. (2015). A revolutionary technology to help the differently abled person, *Proceedings of 09th INDIACom; 2015 2nd International Conference on Computing for Sustainable Global Development.* https://ieeexplore.ieee.org/document/7100324

Sharma, G., & Kumar, A. (2018). Fuzzy logic based 3D localization in wireless sensor networks using invasive weed and bacterial foraging optimization. *Telecommunication Systems, 67*(2), 149–162. doi:10.100711235-017-0333-0

Sharma, K., & Rameshan, R. (2017). Dictionary Based Approach for Facial Expression Recognition from Static Images. *Int. Conf. Comput. Vision, Graph. Image Process*, 39–49. 10.1007/978-3-319-68124-5_4

Shawahna, A., Sait, S. M., & El-Maleh, A. (2018). FPGA-based accelerators of deep learning networks for learning and classification: A review. *IEEE Access: Practical Innovations, Open Solutions, 7*, 7823–7859. doi:10.1109/ACCESS.2018.2890150

Shekhar, S., Rastogi, R., & Mittal, S. (2015). Linear algorithm for Imbricate Cryptography using Pseudo Random Number Generator. *Proceedings of 09th INDIACom, pp. 89-94; 2015 2nd International Conference on Computing for Sustainable Global Development.* https://ieeexplore.ieee.org/document/7100227

Shimly, S. M., Smith, D. B., & Movassaghi, S. (2019). Experimental Analysis of Cross-layer Optimization for Distributed Wireless Body-to-Body Networks. *IEEE Sensors Journal, 19*(24), 12494–12509. doi:10.1109/JSEN.2019.2937356

Shishvan, O. R., Zois, D. S., & Soyata, T. (2020). Incorporating Artificial Intelligence into Medical Cyber-Physical Systems: A Survey. In *Connected Health in Smart Cities* (pp. 153–178). Cham: Springer. doi:10.1007/978-3-030-27844-1_8

Shone, N., Ngoc, T. N., Phai, V. D., & Shi, Q. (2018). A Deep Learning Approach to Network Intrusion Detection. *IEEE Transactions on Emerging Topics in Computational Intelligence, 2*(1), 41–50. doi:10.1109/TETCI.2017.2772792

Shoro, A. G., & Soomro, T. R. (2015). *Big data analysis: Apache spark perspective.* Global Journal of Computer Science and Technology.

Shu, H., Qi, P., Huang, Y., Chen, F., Xie, D., & Sun, L. (2020). An Efficient Certificateless Aggregate Signature Scheme for Blockchain-Based Medical Cyber-Physical Systems. *Sensors (Basel), 20*(5), 1521. doi:10.339020051521 PMID:32164220

Shu, Z., Wan, J., Zhang, D., & Li, D. (2016). Cloud-integrated cyber-physical systems for complex industrial applications. *Mobile Networks and Applications, 21*(5), 865–878. doi:10.100711036-015-0664-6

Siaterlis, C., Genge, B., & Hohenadel, M. (2013). EPIC: A testbed for scientifically rigorous cyber-physical security experimentation. *IEEE Transactions on Emerging Topics in Computing, 1*(2), 319–330. doi:10.1109/TETC.2013.2287188

Simonyan, K., & Zisserman, A. (2014). *Very Deep Convolutional Networks for Large-Scale Image Recognition.* ArXiv 1409.1556

Simonyan, K., & Zisserman, A. (2014). VGGNet. *ICLR.* doi:10.1016/j.infsof.2008.09.005

Singh, D., Tripathi, G., & Jara, A. J. (2014). *A survey of Internet-of-Things: Future vision architecture challenges and services.* IEEE World Forum on Internet of Things (WF-IoT), Seoul, South Korea. 10.1109/WF-IoT.2014.6803174

Singh, Sweta, & Jyoti. (2010). Hello Flood Attack and its Countermeasures in Wireless Sensor Networks. *International Journal of Computer Science Issues, 7.*

Singh, T., Troia, T., Carrado, V. A., Austin, T. H., & Stamp, M. (2016). Support vector machines and malware detection. *Journal of Computer Virology and Hacking Techniques*, 203-212.

Singh, D. P., Goudar, R. H., & Wazid, M. (2013). Hiding the Sink Location from the Passive Attack in WSN. *Procedia Engineering, 64*, 16–25. doi:10.1016/j.proeng.2013.09.072

Singh, P., Khosla, A., Kumar, A., & Khosla, M. (2017). Wireless sensor networks localization and its location optimization using bio inspired localization algorithms: A survey. *International Journal of Current Engineering and Scientific Research, 4*, 74–80.

Singh, P., Krishnamoorthy, S., Nayyar, A., Luhach, A. K., & Kaur, A. (2019). Soft-computing-based false alarm reduction for hierarchical data of intrusion detection system. *International Journal of Distributed Sensor Networks, 15*(10), 1550147719883132. doi:10.1177/1550147719883132

Singh, S., Kaur, A., & Taqdir, A. (2015). Face Recognition Technique using Local Binary Pattern Method. *International Journal of Advanced Research in Computer and Communication Engineering, 4*(3).

Skrop, A. (2018). Industry 4.0 - Challenges in Industrial Artificial Intelligence, International Scientific Conference on Tourism and Security. International Scientific Conference on Tourism and Security.

Someswararao, C., Reddy, S., & Murthy, K. (2020). Cyber-Physical System—An Overview. In Smart Intelligent Computing and Applications (pp. 489–497). Springer. doi:10.1007/978-981-32-9690-9_54

Song, H., Srinivasan, R., Sookoor, T., & Jeschke, S. (Eds.). (2017). *Smart cities: foundations, principles, and applications.* John Wiley & Sons. doi:10.1002/9781119226444

Soulié, F. F., Gallinari, P., Le Cun, Y., & Thiria, S. (1987). Automata Networks and Artificial Intelligence. In *Centre National De Recherche Scientifique on Automata Networks in Computer Science: Theory and Applications* (pp. 133–186). Princeton, NJ: Princeton University Press.

Soupionis, Y., & Benoist, T. (2015). Cyber-Physical Testbed - The Impact of Cyber Attacks and the Human Factor. *10th International conference for internet technology and secured transactions (ICITST),* 326–331.

Souppaya, M., & Scarfone, K. (2013). Guide to Malware Incident Prevention and Handling for Desktops and Laptops. NIST Special Publication 800-83 Revision 1.

Souri, A., & Hosseini, R. (2018). *A state-of-the-art survey of malware detection approaches using data mining techniques.* Human-centric Computing and Information Sciences. doi:10.118613673-018-0125-x

Sravanthi, K. (2019). Cyber Physical Systems: The Role of Machine Learning and Cyber Security in Present and Future. Computer Reviews Journal, 4.

Sridhar, S., Hahn, A., & Govindarasu, M. (2012). Cyber-Physical System Security for the Electric Power Grid. *Proceedings of the IEEE, 100*(1), 210–224. doi:10.1109/JPROC.2011.2165269

Srivastava, A., Morris, T., Ernster, T., Vellaithurai, C., Pan, S., & Adhikari, U. (2013). Modeling cyber-physical vulnerability of the smart grid with incomplete information. *IEEE Transactions on Smart Grid, 4*(1), 235–244. doi:10.1109/TSG.2012.2232318

Srivatava, S., Rastogi, R., Rungta, S., & Yadav, U. (2014). A Methodology to Find the Cycle in a Directed Graph Using Linked List. *BIJIT, 6*(2), 743-749. http://bvicam.ac.in/bjit/issues.asp?issue=12

Stakhanova, N., Basu, S., & Wong, J. (2007). A taxonomy of intrusion response system. *International Journal of Information and Computer Security, 1*(1/2), 169. doi:10.1504/IJICS.2007.012248

Statista. (2020). *Number of unique phishing sites detected worldwide from 3rd quarter 2013 to 1st quarter 2020.* https://www.statista.com/statistics/266155/number-of-phishing-domain-names-worldwide/

Stocker, A. A., & Simoncelli, E. P. (2008). A Bayesian model of conditioned perception. In Advances in neural information processing systems (pp. 1409-1416). Academic Press.

Stopel, D., Boger, Z., Moskovitch, R., Shahar, Y., & Elovici, Y. (2006, July). Application of artificial neural networks techniques to computer worm detection. In *The 2006 IEEE International Joint Conference on Neural Network Proceedings* (pp. 2362-2369). IEEE.

Stouffer. (2015). *Guide to Industrial Control Systems (ICS) Security.* NIST Special Publication 800-82.

Su, Y. S., Wang, D. C., Chang, S. C., & Marek-Sadowska, M. (2010). Performance optimization using variable-latency design style. *IEEE Transactions on Very Large-Scale Integration (VLSI) Systems, 19*(10), 1874-1883.

Sugiyama, T., Schweighofer, N., & Izawa, J. (2020). Reinforcement meta-learning optimizes visuomotor learning. *bioRxiv*

Su, J., Vargas, D. V., & Sakurai, K. (2019). One pixel attack for fooling deep neural networks. *IEEE Transactions on Evolutionary Computation, 23*(5), 828–841. doi:10.1109/TEVC.2019.2890858

Suman & Shubhangi. (2016). A Survey on Comparison of Secure Routing Protocols in Wireless Sensor Networks. *International Journal of Wireless Communications and Networking Technologies*, *5*, 16–20.

Sumit & Saxena. (2020). Energy management system for smart grid: An overview and key issues. *International Journal of Energy Research*.

Sun, Liu, & Xie. (2016). Cyber-Physical System Security of a Power Grid: State-of-the-Art. *Electronics Journal MDPI*.

Suresh, S., Yuthika, S., & Adityavardhini, G. (2016). *Home Based Fire Monitoring and Warning System*. Academic Press.

Swathi, A. C., Yuvraj, T., Praveen, J., & Raghavendra Rao, A. (2016). A Proposed Wallace Tree Multiplier Using Full Adder and Half Adder. *International Journal of Innovative Research in Electrical, Electronics. Instrumentation and Control Engineering*, *4*(5), 472–474.

Symantec. (2020). *What is Malicious Website?* https:// us.norton.com/internetsecurity-malware-what-are-malicious-websites.html

Tao, F., Cheng, J., & Qi, Q. (2017). IIHub: An industrial Internet-of-Things hub toward smart manufacturing based on cyber-physical system. *IEEE Transactions on Industrial Informatics*, *14*(5), 2271–2280. doi:10.1109/TII.2017.2759178

Tay. (2018). An Overview of Industry 4.0: Definition, Components, and Government Initiatives. Journal of Advanced Research in Dynamical and Control Systems.

Technology Trends. (2018). https://www.gartner.com/smarterwithgartner/gartner-top-10-strategic-technology-trends-for-2018

Teixeira, A., Sou, K. C., Sandberg, H., & Johansson, K. H. (2013). Quantifying Cyber-Security for Networked Control Systems in Control of Cyber-Physical Systems. In Workshop held at Johns Hopkins University. Springer International Publishing.

Teixeira, A., Shames, I., Sandberg, H., & Johansson, K. (2012). Revealing Stealthy Attacks in Control Systems. *50th Annual Allerton Conference on Communication, Control, and Computing (Allerton)*. 10.1109/Allerton.2012.6483441

Thomas, C. (2019, February 14). Artificial intelligence crime: An interdisciplinary analysis of foreseeable threats and solutions. *Science and Engineering Ethics*. PMID:30767109

Tolk, A., Barros, F. J., D'Ambrogio, A., Rajhans, A., Mosterman, P. J., Shetty, S. S., & Yilmaz, L. (2018, April). Hybrid simulation for cyber-physical systems: a panel on where we are going regarding complexity, intelligence, and adaptability of CPS using simulation. In *SpringSim* (pp. 3–1). MSCIAAS.

Tomić, I., & McCann, J. A. (2017). A survey of potential security issues in existing wireless sensor network protocols. *IEEE Internet of Things Journal*, *4*(6), 1910–1923. doi:10.1109/JIOT.2017.2749883

Toral-Cruz, H., Hidoussi, F., Boubiche, D. E., Barbosa, R., Voznak, M., & Lakhtaria, K. I. (2015). A survey on wireless sensor networks. In *Next Generation Wireless Network Security and Privacy* (pp. 171-210). IGI Global.

Tosun, A., Turhan, B., & Bener, A. (2009) Practical considerations in deploying ai for defect prediction: A case study within the Turkish telecommunication industry. In *Proceedings of the 5th International Conference on Predictor Models in Software Engineering* (pp. 11:1–11:9). ACM. 10.1145/1540438.1540453

Toygar, O., & Acan, A. (2003). Face Recognition Using PCA, LDA, and ICA Approach on Colored Images. *Journal of Electrical and Electronics Engineering (Oradea)*, *3*(1), 735–743.

Trifan, M. (2012). Cyber-Attacks (Viruses, Trojan Horses and Computer Worms) Analysis. *International Journal of Information Security and Cybercrime*, *1*, 46-54.

Tripathy, R., & Daschoudhary, R. N. (2014). Real-time face detection and Tracking using Haar Classifier on SoC. *International Journal of Electronics and Computer Science Engineering.*, *3*(2), 175–184.

Tsai, W. T., Heisler, K. G., Volovik, D., & Zualkernan, I. A. (1988). A critical look at the relationship between AI and software engineering. In *Proceedings Workshop on Languages for Automation Symbiotic and Intelligent Robotics* (pp. 2–18). IEEE. 10.1109/LFA.1988.24945

Tsang, E. (2014). *Foundations of constraint satisfaction: the classic text.* BoD–Books on Demand.

Turing, A. M. (1950). Computing machinery and intelligence. *Mind*, *59*(236), 433–460. doi:10.1093/mind/LIX.236.433

Ucci, D., Aniello, L., & Baldoni, R. (2019). Survey of machine learning techniques for malware analysis. *Computers & Security*, *81*, 123–147. doi:10.1016/j.cose.2018.11.001

Upadhyay, H., & Chowdhury, S. R. (2015). A High Speed and Low Power 8 Bit× 8 Bit Multiplier Design Using Novel Two Transistor (2T) XOR Gates. *Journal of Low Power Electronics*, *11*(1), 37–48. doi:10.1166/jolpe.2015.1362

Uřičář, M., Franc, V., & Hlaváč, V. (2012). The detector of facial landmarks learned by the structured output SVM. *VISAPP'12: Proceedings of the 7th International Conference on Computer Vision Theory and Applications*, 1, 547-556.

Vähäkainu, P., & Lehto, M. (2019, February). Artificial Intelligence in the Cyber Security Environment. In *ICCWS 2019 14th International Conference on Cyber Warfare and Security: ICCWS 2019* (p. 431). Academic Conferences and Publishing Limited.

Vaid, R., & Kumar, V. (2013). Security Issues and Remidies in Wireless Sensor Networks- A Survey. *International Journal of Computers and Applications*, *79*(4), 31–39. doi:10.5120/13731-1528

Vanschoren, J. (2019). Meta-learning. In *Automated Machine Learning* (pp. 35–61). Cham: Springer. doi:10.1007/978-3-030-05318-5_2

Varshney & Alemzadeh. (2016). On the Safety of Machine Learning:Cyber-Physical Systems, Decision Sciences, and Data Products. arXiv.org

Vats, P., & Saha, A. (2019). *An Overview of SQL Injection Attacks.* SSRN Electronic Journal.

Venghaus, H., & Grote, N. (Eds.). (2017). *Fibre optic communication: key devices* (Vol. 161). Springer. doi:10.1007/978-3-319-42367-8_9

Venkata, R. P. V., & Rama, K. (2010). Artificial neural networks for compression of digital images: A review. *International Journal of Reviews in Computing*, *3*, 75–82.

Verma, R., Crane, D., & Gnawali, O. (2018). *Phishing During and After Disaster: Hurricane Harvey. In Resilience Week (RWS)* (pp. 88–94). Denver, CO: IEEE.

Vilalta, R., & Drissi, Y. (2002). A perspective view and survey of meta-learning. *Artificial Intelligence Review*, *18*(2), 77–95. doi:10.1023/A:1019956318069

Vincent, P., Larochelle, H., Bengio, Y., & Manzagol, P.-A. (2008). Extracting and composing robust features with denoising autoencoders. *Proceedings of the 25th international conference on Machine learning - ICML '08.* 10.1145/1390156.1390294

Viola, P., & Jones, M. (2001). Rapid object detection using a boosted cascade of simple features. *Computer Vision and Pattern Recognition.*, *1*, 511–518.

Viola, P., & Jones, M. (2004, May). Robust Real-Time Face Detection. *International Journal of Computer Vision*, *57*(2), 137–154. doi:10.1023/B:VISI.0000013087.49260.fb

Vishnu Priya, T. S., Sanchez, G. V., & Raajan, N. R. (2018). Facial Recognition System Using Local Binary Patterns (LBP). *International Journal of Pure and Applied Mathematics*, *119*(15), 1895–1899.

Vomlel, J. (2004a). Bayesian networks in educational testing. *International Journal of Uncertainty, Fuzziness and Knowledge-based Systems*, *12*(supp01), 83–100. doi:10.1142/S021848850400259X

von Zengen. (2019). *A Communication Architecture for Cooperative Networked Cyber-Physical Systems. In 16th IEEE Annual Consumer Communications & Networking Conference*. CCNC.

Walsham, G. (1995). Interpretive case studies in IS research: Nature and method. *European Journal of Information Systems*, *4*(2), 74–81. doi:10.1057/ejis.1995.9

Wan. (2018). Physical Layer Key Generation: Securing Wireless Communication in Automotive Cyber-Physical Systems. *ACM Transactions on Cyber-Physical Systems*.

Wang, J., & Shi, D. (2018). Cyber-Attacks Related to Intelligent Electronic Devices and Their Countermeasures: A Review. *53rd International Universities Power Engineering Conference (UPEC)*. 10.1109/UPEC.2018.8542059

Wang, L., Törngren, M., & Onori, M. (2015). Current status and advancement of cyber-physical systems in manufacturing. *Journal of Manufacturing Systems*, *37*, 517–527. doi:10.1016/j.jmsy.2015.04.008

Wang, T., Liang, Y., Yang, Y., Xu, G., Peng, H., Liu, A., & Jia, W. (2020). An Intelligent Edge-Computing-Based Method to Counter Coupling Problems in Cyber-Physical Systems. *IEEE Network*, *34*(3), 16–22. doi:10.1109/MNET.011.1900251

Waschull, S., Bokhorst, J. A. C., Molleman, E., & Wortmann, J. C. (2020). Work design in future industrial production: Transforming towards cyber-physical systems. *Computers & Industrial Engineering*, *139*, 105679. doi:10.1016/j.cie.2019.01.053

Watteyne, T., Handziski, V., Vilajosana, X., Duquennoy, S., Hahm, O., Baccelli, E., & Wolisz, A. (2016). Industrial wireless IP-based cyber-physical systems. *Proceedings of the IEEE*, *104*(5), 1025–1038. doi:10.1109/JPROC.2015.2509186

Wazwaz, A., Herbawi, A., Teeti, M., & Hmeed, S. (2018). Raspberry Pi and computers-based face detection and recognition system. *2018 4th International Conference on Computer and Technology Applications (ICCTA)*.

Welinder, P., Branson, S., Mita, T., Wah, C., Schroff, F., Belongie, S., & Perona, P. (2010). *Caltech-UCSD Birds 200*. California Institute of Technology. CNS-TR-2010-001.

Weyns, D., & Ahmad, T. (2013, July). Claims and evidence for architecture-based self-adaptation: A systematic literature review. In *European Conference on Software Architecture* (pp. 249-265). Springer. 10.1007/978-3-642-39031-9_22

Wickramasinghe, C., Marino, D., Amarasinghe, K., & Manic, M. (2018). Generalization of Deep Learning for Cyber-Physical System Security: A Survey. *IECON 2018 - 44th Annual Conference of the IEEE Industrial Electronics Society*.

Wolf, M., & Serpanos, D. (2020). *Safe and Secure Cyber-Physical Systems and Internet-of-Things Systems*. Springer International Publishing. doi:10.1007/978-3-030-25808-5

Wooldridge, M. (2001). *Multi-agent systems: an introduction*. Wiley.

Wu, X., Zhu, X., Wu, G.-Q., & Ding, W. (2017). Data mining with big data. *IEEE Transactions on Knowledge and Data Engineering*, *26*(1), 97–106.

Xenonstack. (2019). *The Impact of Artificial Intelligence on Cyber Security*. Retrieved from https://www.xenonstack.com/artificial-intelligence-solutions/cyber-security/

Xiao, F., Sha, C., Chen, L., Sun, L., & Wang, R. (2015, April). Noise-tolerant localization from incomplete range measurements for wireless sensor networks. In *2015 IEEE Conference on Computer Communications (INFOCOM)* (pp. 2794-2802). IEEE. 10.1109/INFOCOM.2015.7218672

Xia, X., Liu, C., Wang, H., & Han, Z. (2019). *A Design of Cyber-Physical System Architecture for Smart City*. Recent Trends in Intelligent Computing, Communication and Devices.

Xing, L. (2020). *Reliability in Internet of Things: Current Status and Future Perspectives*. IEEE Internet of Things Journal.

Xiong, G., Zhu, F., Liu, X., Dong, X., Huang, W., Chen, S., & Zhao, K. (2015). Cyber-physical-social system in intelligent transportation. *IEEE/CAA Journal of Automatica Sinica, 2*(3), 320-333.

Xiong, M., Li, Y., Gu, L., Pan, S., Zeng, D., & Li, P. (2020). Reinforcement Learning Empowered IDPS for Vehicular Networks in Edge Computing. *IEEE Network, 34*(3), 57–63. doi:10.1109/MNET.011.1900321

Xue, Y., & Yu, X. (2017). Beyond smart grid—Cyber-physical–social system in energy future. *Proceedings of the IEEE, 105*(12), 2290–2292. doi:10.1109/JPROC.2017.2768698

Xu, L. D., & Duan, L. (2019). Big data for cyber-physical systems in industry 4.0: A survey. *Enterprise Information Systems, 13*(2), 148–169. doi:10.1080/17517575.2018.1442934

Xu, L., He, W., & Li, S. (2014). Internet of Things in industries: A survey. *IEEE Transactions on Industrial Informatics, 10*(4), 2233–2243. doi:10.1109/TII.2014.2300753

Xu, T. (2017). *Digital signal processing for optical communications and networks*. InTech. doi:10.5772/intechopen.68323

Yan, B., & Han, G. (2018). Effective Feature Extraction via Stacked Sparse Autoencoder to Improve Intrusion Detection System. *IEEE Access: Practical Innovations, Open Solutions, 6*(c), 41238–41248. doi:10.1109/ACCESS.2018.2858277

Yang, H., Zhan, K., Kadoch, M., Liang, Y., & Cheriet, M. (2020). *BLCS: Brain-like based distributed control security in cyber physical systems*. arXiv preprint arXiv:2002.06259

Yasin. (2019). Internet of Things Applications as Energy Internet in Smart Grids and Smart Environments. *Electronics Journal MPDI*.

Yatin, AlMajali, & Neuman. (2018). A Comprehensive Analysis of Smart Grid Systems against Cyber-Physical Attacks. *MDPI Electronics Journal*, 1-25.

Ye, Y., Chen, L., Wang, D., Li, T., & Jiang, Q. (2008). Sbmds: an interpretable string based malware detection system using svm ensemble with bagging. *J. Comput. Virol.*, 283.

Yin, M. (2016). Electronic Door Access Control Using Myaccess Two-Factor Authentication Scheme Featuring Near-Field Communication and Eigenface-Based Face Recognition Using Principal Component Analysis. Academic Press.

Yin, S., & Kaynak, O. (2015). Big data for modern industry: Challenges and trends. *Proceedings of the IEEE, 103*(2), 143–146. doi:10.1109/JPROC.2015.2388958

Yin, S., Kaynak, O., & Karimi, H. R. (2020). IEEE Access Special Section Editorial: Data-Driven Monitoring, Fault Diagnosis, and Control of Cyber-Physical Systems. *IEEE Access: Practical Innovations, Open Solutions, 8*, 54110–54114. doi:10.1109/ACCESS.2020.2980404

You, S., Zhang, J., & Gruenwald, L. (2015, April). Large-scale spatial join query processing in cloud. In *2015 31st IEEE International Conference on Data Engineering Workshops* (pp. 34-41). IEEE. 10.1109/ICDEW.2015.7129541

Yu, L., Blunsom, P., Dyer, C., Grefenstette, E., & Kocisky, T. (2016). *The neural noisy channel*. arXiv preprint arXiv:1611.02554

Yue, X., Cai, H., Yan, H., Zou, C., & Zhou, K. (2015). Cloud-assisted industrial cyber-physical systems: An insight. *Microprocessors and Microsystems, 39*(8), 1262–1270. doi:10.1016/j.micpro.2015.08.013

Yugashini, I., Vidhyasri, S., & Gayathri Devi, K. (2013). Design And Implementation Of Automated Door Accessing System With Face Recognition. *International Journal Of Science And Modern Engineering (IJISME), 1*(12).

Yu, X., Cecati, C., Dillon, T., & Simoes, M. G. (2011). New frontier of smart grids. *IEEE Industrial Electronics Magazine, 5*(3), 49–63. doi:10.1109/MIE.2011.942176

Zeiler, M. D., & Fergus, R. (2014). *LNCS 8689 - Visualizing and Understanding Convolutional Networks*. Academic Press.

Zeliadt, N. (2013). QnAs with Ann M. Graybiel. *Proceedings of the National Academy of Sciences*. 10.1073/pnas.1315012110

Zhang, K., Zhang, Z., Li, Z., & Qiao, Y. (2016). Joint Face Detection and Alignment Using Multitask Cascaded Convolutional Networks. *IEEE Signal Processing Letters, 23*(10), 1499–1503. doi:10.1109/LSP.2016.2603342

Zhang, L., Mu, D., Hu, W., & Tai, Y. (2020). Machine-Learning-Based Side-Channel Leakage Detection in Electronic System-Level Synthesis. *IEEE Network, 34*(3), 44–49. doi:10.1109/MNET.011.1900313

Zhang, L., & Wang, G. (2019). Design and Implementation of Automatic Fire Alarm System Based on Wireless Sensor Networks. *Proceedings of the International Symposium on Information Processing (ISIP'09)*, 410-413.

Zhang, W., Jiang, Q., Chen, L., & Li, C. (2016). Two-stage ELM for phishing Web pages detection using hybrid features. *World Wide Web (Bussum)*.

Zhang, W., Ren, H., & Jiang, Q. (2016). Application of feature engineering for phishing detection. *IEICE Transactions on Information and Systems, E99-D*(D), 1062–1070. doi:10.1587/transinf.2015CYP0005

Zhang, Y., Qiu, M., Tsai, C. W., Hassan, M. M., & Alamri, A. (2015). Health-CPS: Healthcare cyber-physical system assisted by cloud and big data. *IEEE Systems Journal, 11*(1), 88–95. doi:10.1109/JSYST.2015.2460747

Zhang, Z. H., Liu, D., Deng, C., & Fan, Q. Y. (2020). A dynamic event-triggered resilient control approach to cyber-physical systems under asynchronous DoS attacks. *Information Sciences, 519*, 260–272. doi:10.1016/j.ins.2020.01.047

Zheng, C., Le Duigou, J., Hehenberger, P., Bricogne, M., & Eynard, B. (2016). Multidisciplinary integration during conceptual design process: A survey on design methods of cyber-physical systems. In *DS 84: Proceedings of the DESIGN 2016 14th International Design Conference* (pp. 1625-1634). Academic Press.

Zheng, S. R. (2011). The Internet of Things. *IEEE Communications Magazine, 11*, 30–31. doi:10.1109/MCOM.2011.6069706

Zhou, P., Zuo, D., Hou, K., Zhang, Z., & Dong, J. (2019). Improving the Dependability of Self-Adaptive Cyber-Physical System With Formal Compositional Contract. *IEEE Transactions on Reliability*. Advance online publication. doi:10.1109/TR.2019.2930009

Zhou, X., & Xie, C. (2016). *Enabling technologies for high spectral-efficiency coherent optical communication networks*. John Wiley & Sons. doi:10.1002/9781119078289

Zhu & Sastry. (2010). *SCADA-specific Intrusion Detection / Prevention Systems: A Survey and Taxonomy*. University of California at Berkeley.

Zhu, L., Chen, L., Zhao, D., Zhou, J., & Zhang, W. (2017). Emotion Recognition from Chinese Speech for Smart Affective Services Using a Combination of SVM and DBN. *New Advances in Identification Information & Knowledge on the Internet of Things.* https://towardsdatascience.com/face-recognition-how-lbph-works-90ec258c3d6b

Ziegler, S., Crettaz, C., Kim, E., Skarmeta, A., Bernal Bernabe, J., & Trapero, R. (2019). *Privacy and Security Threats on the Internet of Things. In Internet of Things Security and Data Protection* (pp. 9–43). Springer. doi:10.1007/978-3-030-04984-3_2

Zulfiqar, M., Syed, F., Khan, M., & Khurshid, K. (2019). Deep Face Recognition for Biometric Authentication. *2019 International Conference on Electrical, Communication, and Computer Engineering (ICECCE).* 10.1109/ICEC-CE47252.2019.8940725

About the Contributors

Ashish Kumar Luhach received Ph.D degree in department of computer science from Banasthali University, India. Dr. Luhach is working as Senior lecturer at The Papua New Guinea University of Technology, Papua New Guinea. He has more than a decade of teaching and research experience. Dr. Luhach also worked with various reputed universities and also holds administrate experience as well. Dr. Luhach has published more 80 research paper in reputed journals and conferences, which are indexed in various international databases. He is also edited various special issues in reputed journals and he is Editor/Conference Co-chair for various conferences. Dr. Luhach is also editorial board members of various reputed journals. He is member of IEEE, CSI, ACM and IACSIT.

* * *

Sara Abdulrahman Mahboub is a PhD candidate, received her MSc Degree in Electronics Engineering (Telecommunication), 2015, and BSc in in Electrical and communication Engineering, Al Neelain University, 2011. She works in Jazan University. Her areas of research interest include, Wireless communication, smart system, sensing and Network Security.

Chintan Bhatt (Ph.D.) is currently working as an Assistant Professor in Computer Engineering department, Chandubhai S. Patel Institute of Technology, CHARUSAT. He is a member of IEEE, EAI, ACM, CSI, AIRCC and IAENG (International Association of Engineers). His areas of interest include Internet of Things, Data Mining, Web Mining, Networking, Security Mobile Computing, Big Data and Software Engineering. He has more than 5 years of teaching experience and research experience, having good teaching and research interests. He has chaired a track in CSNT 2015 and ICTCS 2014. He has been working as Reviewer in Wireless Communications, IEEE (Impact Factor-6.524) and Internet of Things Journal, IEEE, Knowledge-Based Systems, Elsevier (Impact Factor-2.9) Applied Computing and Informatics, Elsevier and Mobile Networks and Applications, Springer. He has delivered an expert talk on Internet of Things at Broadcast Engineering Society Doordarshan, Ahmedabad on 30/09/2015. He has been awarded Faculty with Maximum Publication in CSIC Award and Paper Presenter Award at International Conference in CSI-2015, held at New Delhi.

Jan Bosch is professor at Chalmers University Technology in Gothenburg, Sweden and director of the Software Center (www.software-center.se), a strategic partner-funded collaboration between 14 large European companies (including Ericsson, Volvo Cars, Volvo Trucks, Saab Defense, Scania, Siemens and Bosch) and five universities focused on digitalization. Earlier, he worked as Vice President Engineering

Process at Intuit Inc where he also led Intuit's Open Innovation efforts and headed the central mobile technologies team. Before Intuit, he was head of the Software and Application Technologies Laboratory at Nokia Research Center, Finland. Prior to joining Nokia, he headed the software engineering research group at the University of Groningen, The Netherlands. He received a MSc degree from the University of Twente, The Netherlands, and a PhD degree from Lund University, Sweden. His research activities include digitalisation, evidence-based development, business ecosystems, artificial intelligence and machine/deep learning, software architecture, software product families and software variability management. He is the author of several books including "Design and Use of Software Architectures: Adopting and Evolving a Product Line Approach" published by Pearson Education (Addison-Wesley & ACM Press) and "Speed, Data and Ecosystems: Excelling in a Software-Driven World" published by Taylor and Francis, editor of several books and volumes and author of hundreds of research articles. He is editor for Journal of Systems and Software as well as Science of Computer Programming, chaired several conferences as general and program chair, served on numerous program committees and organised countless workshops. Jan is a fellow member of the International Software Product Management Association (ISPMA) and a member of the Royal Swedish Academy of Engineering Science. In the startup space, Jan is an angel investor in several startup companies and serves on the board of Peltarion AB and on the advisory boards of Assia Inc. in Redwood City, CA, Pure Systems GmbH (Germany) and Burt AB (Sweden). Earlier he was chairman of the board of Auqtus AB, Fidesmo AB and Remente AB, in Gothenburg, Sweden. He also runs a boutique consulting firm, Boschonian AB, that offers its clients support around the implications of digitalization including the management of R&D and innovation. For more information see his website: www.janbosch.com.

Ferhat Ozgur Catak is an associate professor of Tubitak-Bilgem Cyber Security Insitute. His research interests are cyber security, machine learning.

Mehmet Cifci is a Computer Engineer and a Ph.D. in Artificial intelligence. As an artificial enthusiast, he is doing his Ph.D. On Deep Learning in 2019. His works focus on understanding the fundamental of Machine Learning. In his work, he basically focuses on understanding and defining the bits and pieces of what makes Artificial Intelligence. He loves trying innovation, implementing new architectures, and learning.

Ivica Crnkovic is a professor of software engineering at Chalmers University, Gothenburg. He is the director of ICT Area of Advance at Chalmers University, and director of Chalmers AI Research Centre (CHAIR). His research interests include component-based software engineering, software architecture, software development processes, software engineering for large complex systems, and recently AI Engineering - Software engineering for AI. Professor Crnkovic is the author of more than 200 refereed publications on software engineering topics, and guest editor of a number of special issues in different journals and magazines, such as IEEE Software, and Elsevier JSS . Professor Crnkovic was the general chair of 40th International Conference on Sofwtare Engineering (ICSE) 2018. He was also a general chair of several top-level software engineering conferences (such as ICSA 2017, ECSA 2015, ASE 2014, Comparch, WICSA 2011, ESEC/FSE 2007,) and PC Chair (COMPSAC 2015, ECSA 2012, Euromicro SEAA 2006, etc.). His teaching activities cover several courses in the area of Software Engineering undergraduate and graduate courses. From 1985 to 1998, Ivica Crnkovic worked at ABB, Sweden, where he was responsible for software development environments and tools. Professor Crnkovic received an M.Sc.

in electrical engineering, an M.Sc. in theoretical physics, and a Ph.D. in computer science in 1991, all from the University of Zagreb, Croatia. More information is available on http://www.ivica-crnkovic.net.

Evren Daglarli received a M.Sc. degree in Mechatronics Engineering with focus on Intelligent Systems and Robotics at ITU. He received a Ph.D. degree in Control and Automation Engineering with focus on Computational Cognitive-Neuroscience, Human-Robot Interaction at ITU. He worked as a research assistant at Atilim University, department of Electrical-Electronics engineering. He have many publications which are published in international journals, conferences/symposiums related with mechatronics, intelligent control systems and robotic areas. As a researcher, he took some duties and responsibilities in several national / international projects. He worked as a Project Engineer and also later department manager at a private sector technology and engineering company. He is a member of IEEE, ACM and ASME. Now he is working as a Faculty member, Lecturer/Instructor in Faculty of Computer and Informatics Engineering, Computer Engineering department at Istanbul Technical University.

Poojan Dharaiya is an undergraduate student in Computer Engineering at Charotar University of Science and Technology and will be graduating in 2021 with B.Tech in Computer Engineering. He is passionate about solving real world problems and eager to establish himself in research field of Data Science and Machine Learning.

Atilla Elçi is a full professor in the Software Engineering Department, Hasan Kalyoncu University, Turkey. He retired as full professor and chairman of the Department of Electrical-Electronics and Computer Engineering at Aksaray University (2012-7). He has served in Computer Engineering departments in various universities including METU, Turkey, and EMU, TRNC, since 1976. His professional practice includes the International Telecommunication Union (ITU), Switzerland, as chief technical advisor for field projects on computerization of telecommunication administrations of member countries (1985-97) and Information Technology & Telecommunications Pvt Ltd as founder/managing director, Turkey (1997-2003). He has organized IEEE ESAS since 2006, SIN Conferences since 2007; IJRCS Symposiums 2008-9, ICPCA_SWS 2012, LightSec 2016, ICAGNI 2018, and SSIC 2021. He has published over a hundred journal and conference papers and book chapters; co-authored a book titled The Composition of OWL-S based Atomic Processes (LAP Lambert, 2011); edited the Semantic Agent Systems (Springer, 2011), Theory and Practice of Cryptography Solutions for Secure Information Systems (IGI Global, 2013), The Handbook of Applied Learning Theory and Design in Modern Education (IGI Global, 2016), Metacognition and Successful Learning Strategies in Higher Education (IGI Global, 2017), Contemporary Perspectives on Web-Based Systems (IGI Global, May 2018), Handbook of Research on Faculty Development for Digital Teaching and Learning (IGI Global, June 2019), Artificial Intelligence Paradigms for Smart Cyber-Physical Systems and Challenges and Applications of Data Analytics in Social Perspectives (both in print by IGI Global, 2021), and the proceedings of SIN Conferences 2007-20 (ACM), ESAS 2006-20 (IEEE CS). He serves IEEE COMPSAC since 2005, track chair (2008-2015), Standing Committee Member since 2014. He is an associate editor of (Wiley) Expert Systems: The Journal of Knowledge Engineering and an editorial board member of MTAP, JSCI, IJAS, IJISS, and a guest editor for several other journals. He has delivered several keynote/invited talks and served as board member and reviewer for numerous conferences.

Reinaldo França, B.Sc. in Computer Engineering in 2014. Currently, he is an Ph.D. degree candidate by Department of Semiconductors, Instruments and Photonics, Faculty of Electrical and Computer Engineering at the LCV-UNICAMP working with technological and scientific research as well as in programming and development in C / C ++, Java and .NET languages. His main topics of interest are simulation, operating systems, software engineering, wireless networks, internet of things, broadcasting and telecommunications systems.

Rangel Arthur holds a degree in Electrical Engineering from the Paulista State University Júlio de Mesquita Filho (1999), a Master's degree in Electrical Engineering (2002) and a Ph.D. in Electrical Engineering (2007) from the State University of Campinas. Over the years from 2011 to 2014 he was Coordinator and Associate Coordinator of Technology Courses in Telecommunication Systems and Telecommunication Engineering of FT, which was created in its management. From 2015 to 2016 he was Associate Director of the Technology (FT) of Unicamp. He is currently a lecturer and advisor to the Innovation Agency (Inova) of Unicamp. He has experience in the area of Electrical Engineering, with emphasis on Telecommunications Systems, working mainly on the following topics: computer vision, embedded systems and control systems

Priyanshi Garg is a student of B. Tech (CSE) Third Year in ABESEC which is affiliated to AKTU. She is currently working on Yagyopathy where she is analyzing the data and translate them. She has a keen interest in coding and cyber security. Her hobbies are to watch movies. She wishes to do something for her society in coming future with her all resources.

Yuzo Iano, B.Sc. (1972), M.Sc. (1974) and Ph.D. degrees (1986) in Electrical Eng. at UNICAMP, Brazil. Since then he has been working in the technological production field, with 1 patent granted, 8 filed patent applications and 36 projects completed with research and development agencies. He has supervised 29 doctoral theses, 49 master's dissertations, 74 undergraduate and 48 scientific initiation works. He has participated in 100 master's examination boards, 50 doctoral degrees, author of 2 books and more than 250 published articles. He is currently Professor at UNICAMP, Editor-in-Chief of the SET International Journal of Broadcast Engineering and General Chair of the Brazilian Symposium on Technology (BTSym). He has experience in Electrical Engineering, with knowledge in Telecommunications, Electronics and Information Technology, mainly in the field of audio-visual communications and multimedia.

Chirag Jethva is currently pursuing his B. Tech degree in Computer Engineering from Charotar University of Science and Technology and will graduate in 2021. He is very passionate about Android application development and Artificial Intelligence.

Karan Kathiriya is an undergraduate student in Computer Engineering at Charotar University of Science and Technology and will be graduating in 2021 with B.Tech in Computer Engineering. He is passionate about solving real world problems, providing automated solutions and eager to establish himself in research field of Data Science Engineering.

Vidhya Kothadia is an undergraduate student in the Computer Engineering at Charotar University of Science and Technology and will be graduating in 2021 with B.Tech in Computer Engineering. she is an innovative software engineer with managing all aspects of the development process.

Ana Carolina Monteiro is a Ph.D. candidate at the Faculty of Electrical and Computer Engineering (FEEC) at the State University of Campinas - UNICAMP, where she develops research projects regarding health software with emphasis on the development of algorithms for the detection and counting of blood cells through processing techniques. digital images. These projects led in 2019 to a computer program registration issued by the INPI (National Institute of Industrial Property). She holds a Master's degree in Electrical Engineering from the State University of Campinas - UNICAMP (2019) and graduated in Biomedicine from the University Center Amparense - UNIFIA with a degree in Clinical Pathology - Clinical Analysis (2015). In 2019, he acquired a degree in Health Informatics. Has to experience in the areas of Molecular Biology and management with research animals. Since 2017, she has been a researcher at the FEEC/UNICAMP Visual Communications Laboratory (LCV) and has worked at the Brazilian Technology Symposium (BTSym) as a member of the Organizational and Executive Committee and as a member of the Technical Reviewers Committee. In addition, she works as a reviewer at the Health magazines of the Federal University of Santa Maria (UFSM - Brazil), Medical Technology Journal MTJ (Algeria), and Production Planning & Control (Taylor & Francis). Interested in: digital image processing, hematology, clinical analysis, cell biology, medical informatics, Matlab, and teaching.

Helena Holmström Olsson is a Professor in Computer Science at the Department of Computer Science and Media Technology at Malmö University, Sweden and a senior researcher in Software Center (https://www.software-center.se/). She received her Ph.D. from Gothenburg University in 2004 after which she joined LERO ('The Irish Software Research Centre') for a Post doc position at the University of Limerick, Ireland. Her research is conducted in close collaboration with industry and primarily with software-intensive companies in the embedded systems domain. Her research focuses on the digital transformation of industry and the opportunities and challenges digitalization brings. In particular, her research covers topics such as data-driven development, AI engineering and software and business ecosystems. As part of Software Center, she works closely with fifteen companies in the embedded systems domain on topics such as data monetization, new business models and strategies for partnering with new ecosystem entrants. In her most recent research, the introduction and integration of ML/DL technologies in large-scale embedded systems is a primary interest. Her research has been published in top-level information systems and software engineering journals and conferences (https://scholar. google.se/citations?user=bjGw_5QAAAAJ&hl=en&oi=ao). Helena is frequent reviewer for software engineering journals and conferences as well as actively engaged as program and track chair at several of the main software engineering conferences. Helena is a member of ISPMA (International Software Product Management Association) as well as a member of the Malmö University Board.

Kevin Patel is a diligent student pursuing his undergraduate degree in Computer Engineering from Chandubhai S Patel Institute of Technology, CHARUSAT. He has avid interest in areas such as Computer Vision, Automation Control & Intelligent Systems and Robotics.

Mayuri J. Popat is working as an Assistant Professor in U & P.U. Patel Department of Computer Engineering, at CSPIT-CHARUSAT. She Secured First Rank in XXVII Gujarat Science Congress in

Poster presentation of Proposed Idea jointly organized by Charotar University of Science and Technology and Gujarat Science Academy (G.S.A). She is currently perusing her PhD from Charusat University. Her Research area includes Sentiment Analysis in Machine Learning and Computer Vision.

Kalpana Ramanujam is currently working as Professor in Dept. of CSE at Pondicherry Engineering College. She completed Bachelor of Technology in Computer Science from Pondicherry Engineering College, during 1992-96. She completed Master of Technology in Computer Science from Pondicherry University in 1998. She obtained her Ph.D from Pondicherry University. Her area of interest includes Parallel and Distributed Systems &Computing, Algorithm design and Optimization. She has a teaching experience of 21 years. She has also received CMI (Charted management Institute) award in First line management and Technical leadership from Charted management Institute, London, UK. She has published more than 80 research papers in International Journals / Conferences. She is also a member of ISTE.

Rohit Rastogi received his B.E. degree in Computer Science and Engineering from C.C.S.Univ. Meerut in 2003, the M.E. degree in Computer Science from NITTTR-Chandigarh (National Institute of Technical Teachers Training and Research-affiliated to MHRD, Govt. of India), Punjab Univ. Chandigarh in 2010. Currently he is pursuing his Ph.D. In computer science from Dayalbagh Educational Institute, Agra under renowned professor of Electrical Engineering Dr. D.K. Chaturvedi in area of spiritual consciousness. Dr. Santosh Satya of IIT-Delhi and dr. Navneet Arora of IIT-Roorkee have happily consented him to co supervise. He is also working presently with Dr. Piyush Trivedi of DSVV Hardwar, India in center of Scientific spirituality. He is a Associate Professor of CSE Dept. in ABES Engineering. College, Ghaziabad (U.P.-India), affiliated to Dr. A.P. J. Abdul Kalam Technical Univ. Lucknow (earlier Uttar Pradesh Tech. University).Also, He is preparing some interesting algorithms on Swarm Intelligence approaches like PSO, ACO and BCO etc. Rohit Rastogi is involved actively with Vichaar Krnati Abhiyaan and strongly believe that transformation starts within self.

Yashvi Raythatha is an undergraduate student of computer engineering at Charotar University of Science and Technology and will be graduating in 2021 in Computer Engineering. She is passionate about doing the research work in Machine Learning and Data Science field.

Rashid A. Saeed received his PhD in Communications and Network Engineering, Universiti Putra Malaysia (UPM). Currently he is a professor in Computer Engineering Department, Taif University. He is also working in Electronics Department, Sudan University of Science and Technology (SUST). He was senior researcher in Telekom Malaysia™ Research and Development (TMRND) and MIMOS. Rashid published more than 150 research papers, books and book chapters on wireless communications and networking in peer-reviewed academic journals and conferences. His areas of research interest include computer network, cognitive computing, computer engineering, wireless broadband, WiMAX Femtocell. He is successfully awarded 3 U.S patents in these areas. He supervised more 50 MSc/PhD students. Rashid is a Senior member IEEE, Member in IEM (I.E.M), SigmaXi, and SEC.

Kevser Sahinbas is an Asst. prof at Istanbul Medipol University.

Rania Salih Abdalla Ahamed is a PhD candidate, received her MSc Degree in Electronics Engineering (Telecommunication), Sudan University of Science and technology, 2015. And, BSc in Electronics

&Telecommunication Systems, Al Zaiem Al Azhari University, 2004. She works in Jazan University. Her areas of research interest include, computer networking, IoT, and Network security.

Arif Sari is a full time Associate Professor and Chairman of the department of Management Information Systems at the Girne American University, North Cyprus. He received his BS degree - in Computer Information Systems and MBA degree - (2008 and 2010) at European University of Lefke, and Ph.D. degree (2013) in Management Information Systems at The Girne American University. He has been granted as Visiting Scholar of Sapienza University of Rome in Italy (2012). He is an IEEE, ACM, and IEICE Member since Sept. 2012 and has published various papers, book chapters, participated in variety of conferences in the fields of Network Security, Cyber Security, Network Simulation, Mobile Networks, Information Communication Technologies, Mobile Network Security and Mobile Security Systems. After investigation of national firewall systems in different countries such as China, Russia, United Kingdom, USA/NSA and Israel, Dr. Sari is currently working on national cyber-security firewall project named "SeddülBahir", which presented at Yıldız Technic University, Istanbul in December 2015. He is co-author of additional three textbooks in field of network, cryptography and cyber security.

Elmustafa Sayed Ali Ahmed received his MSc in Electronics & Communication Engineering, Sudan University of Science & technology in 2012. Worked (former) as a senior engineer in Sudan Sea Port Corporation (5 years) as a team leader of new projects in wireless networks includes (Tetra system, Wi-Fi, Wi-Max, and CCTV). Currently he is a head of marine systems department in Sudan marine industries. He is also working in Electrical and Electronics Engineering Department in the Red Sea University as a senior lecturer. Elmustafa published papers, and book chapters in wireless communications, computer and networking in peer reviewed academic international journals. His areas of research interest include, routing protocols, computer and wireless networks, and IoT. He is a member of IEEE, IEEE Communication Society (ComSoc), International Association of Engineers (IAENG), Six Sigma Yellow Belt (SSYB), and Scrum Fundamentals certified (SFC).

Joshua Sopuru is a Lecturer in the Department of Information Systems and focuses on the design and implementation of machine models for predictive analysis. He works with a wide variety of information systems to achieve technology-aided transformations for organizational growth and profit. He is an experienced Data Scientist and a system developer.

Srikanth Yadav was born in India on June 10, 1980. He received the Bachelor of Technology degree and Master of Technology degree in Information Technology from the "JNTUH" university, Hyderabad, Telangana, India, in 2003 and 2010 respectively. He is currently pursuing Ph.D in the Department of Computer Science and Engineering, Pondicherry Engineering College, Puducherry, India. His research interests include machine learning, deep learning, and intrusion detection systems.

Index

Ensure Quality Research is Introduced to the Academic Community

Become an IGI Global Reviewer for Authored Book Projects

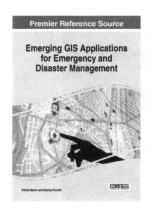

Premier Reference Source

Emerging GIS Applications for Emergency and Disaster Management

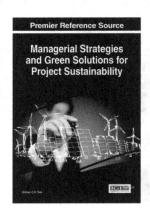

Premier Reference Source

Managerial Strategies and Green Solutions for Project Sustainability

Premier Reference Source

Comparative Approaches to Using R and Python for Statistical Data Analysis

Premier Reference Source

Solutions for High-Touch Communications in a High-Tech World

The overall success of an authored book project is dependent on quality and timely reviews.

In this competitive age of scholarly publishing, constructive and timely feedback significantly expedites the turnaround time of manuscripts from submission to acceptance, allowing the publication and discovery of forward-thinking research at a much more expeditious rate. Several IGI Global authored book projects are currently seeking highly-qualified experts in the field to fill vacancies on their respective editorial review boards:

Applications and Inquiries may be sent to:
development@igi-global.com

Applicants must have a doctorate (or an equivalent degree) as well as publishing and reviewing experience. Reviewers are asked to complete the open-ended evaluation questions with as much detail as possible in a timely, collegial, and constructive manner. All reviewers' tenures run for one-year terms on the editorial review boards and are expected to complete at least three reviews per term. Upon successful completion of this term, reviewers can be considered for an additional term.

If you have a colleague that may be interested in this opportunity, we encourage you to share this information with them.

IGI Global Proudly Partners With eContent Pro International

Receive a 25% Discount on all Editorial Services

Editorial Services

IGI Global expects all final manuscripts submitted for publication to be in their final form. This means they must be reviewed, revised, and professionally copy edited prior to their final submission. Not only does this support with accelerating the publication process, but it also ensures that the highest quality scholarly work can be disseminated.

English Language Copy Editing

Let eContent Pro International's expert copy editors perform edits on your manuscript to resolve spelling, punctuaion, grammar, syntax, flow, formatting issues and more.

Scientific and Scholarly Editing

Allow colleagues in your research area to examine the content of your manuscript and provide you with valuable feedback and suggestions before submission.

Figure, Table, Chart & Equation Conversions

Do you have poor quality figures? Do you need visual elements in your manuscript created or converted? A design expert can help!

Translation

Need your documjent translated into English? eContent Pro International's expert translators are fluent in English and more than 40 different languages.

Email: customerservice@econtentpro.com   **www.igi-global.com/editorial-service-partners**

www.igi-global.com

Publisher of Peer-Reviewed, Timely, and
Innovative Academic Research Since 1988

IGI Global's Transformative Open Access (OA) Model:
How to Turn Your University Library's Database Acquisitions Into a Source of OA Funding

In response to the OA movement and well in advance of Plan S, IGI Global, early last year, unveiled their OA Fee Waiver (Read & Publish) Initiative.

Under this initiative, librarians who invest in IGI Global's InfoSci-Books (5,300+ reference books) and/or InfoSci-Journals (185+ scholarly journals) databases will be able to subsidize their patron's OA article processing charges (APC) when their work is submitted and accepted (after the peer review process) into an IGI Global journal. *See website for details.

How Does it Work?

1. When a library subscribes or perpetually purchases IGI Global's InfoSci-Databases and/or their discipline/subject-focused subsets, IGI Global will match the library's investment with a fund of equal value to go toward subsidizing the OA article processing charges (APCs) for their patrons.

   Researchers: **Be sure to recommend the InfoSci-Books and InfoSci-Journals to take advantage of this initiative.**

2. When a student, faculty, or staff member submits a paper and it is accepted (following the peer review) into one of IGI Global's 185+ scholarly journals, the author will have the option to have their paper published under a traditional publishing model or as OA.

3. When the author chooses to have their paper published under OA, IGI Global will notify them of the OA Fee Waiver (Read and Publish) Initiative. If the author decides they would like to take advantage of this initiative, IGI Global will deduct the US$ 2,000 APC from the created fund.

4. This fund will be offered on an annual basis and will renew as the subscription is renewed for each year thereafter. IGI Global will manage the fund and award the APC waivers unless the librarian has a preference as to how the funds should be managed.

Hear From the Experts on This Initiative:

"I'm very happy to have been able to make one of my recent research contributions, "Visualizing the Social Media Conversations of a National Information Technology Professional Association" featured in the *International Journal of Human Capital and Information Technology Professionals*, freely available along with having access to the valuable resources found within IGI Global's InfoSci-Journals database."

– **Prof. Stuart Palmer,**
Deakin University, Australia

For More Information, Visit: www.igi-global.com/publish/contributor-resources/open-access/read-publish-model
or contact IGI Global's Database Team at eresources@igi-global.com

Printed in the United States
By Bookmasters